The Boston Globe STORY OF THE
CELTICS

Other Books by *The Boston Globe*

The Boston Globe Story of the Red Sox, edited by Chad Finn

The Boston Globe STORY OF THE
CELTICS

1946-PRESENT: The Inside Stories and
Acclaimed Reporting on the NBA's Banner Franchise

The Boston Globe

Edited by Chad Finn

Foreword by Isaiah Thomas

BLACK DOG
& LEVENTHAL
PUBLISHERS
NEW YORK

Black Dog & Leventhal Publishers
Hachette Book Group
1290 Avenue of the Americas
New York, NY 10104
www.blackdogandleventhal.com
 BlackDogandLeventhal   @BDLev

First Edition: October 2024

Published by Black Dog & Leventhal Publishers, an imprint of Hachette Book Group, Inc.
The Black Dog & Leventhal Publishers name and logo are trademarks of Hachette Book Group, Inc.

The publisher is not responsible for websites (or their content) that are not owned by the publisher.

The Hachette Speakers Bureau provides a wide range of authors for speaking events.
To find out more, go to hachettespeakersbureau.com or email HachetteSpeakers@hbgusa.com.

Additional copyright/credits information is on page 452.

Print book cover and interior design by Katie Benezra

Library of Congress Cataloging-in-Publication Data
Names: Finn, Chad (Sports columnist) editor.
Title: The Boston Globe story of the Celtics 1946-present : legendary players and performances from the NBA's banner franchise / The Boston Globe, edited by Chad Finn.
Other titles: Legendary players and performances from the National Basketball Association's banner franchise | Boston globe.
Description: First edition. | New York, N.Y. : Black Dog & Leventhal, 2024. | Includes index. | Summary: "From the nationally recognized Boston Globe (350K+ digital and print subscribers) comes the unique and fully authorized history of the Boston Celtics, told through their hometown newspaper"—Provided by publisher.
Identifiers: LCCN 2023059765 (print) | LCCN 2023059766 (ebook) | ISBN 9780762487530 (hardcover) | ISBN 9780762487547 (ebook)
Subjects: LCSH: Boston Celtics (Basketball team)—History. | Boston Celtics (Basketball team)—Press coverage. | Basketball—Massachusetts—Boston—History.
Classification: LCC GV885.52.B67 B685 2024 (print) | LCC GV885.52.B67 (ebook) | DDC 796.323/640974461—dc23/eng/20240401
LC record available at https://lccn.loc.gov/2023059765
LC ebook record available at https://lccn.loc.gov/2023059766

ISBNs: 978-0-7624-8753-0 (hardcover); 978-0-7624-8754-7 (ebook)

Printed in the USA

LSC-C

Printing 1, 2024

CONTENTS

FOREWORD

I was in Boston only two and a half years, but let me tell you, I learned something that I will carry with me for a lifetime: If you give Celtics fans your heart, they'll give you theirs right back.

I am so grateful for that, and I always will be. Even now, when I go to other cities, states, or countries, someone will come up and go, "I.T.! I'm a huge Celtics fan. Thank you." It's an amazing feeling to know that we have a bond that will last forever.

I always tell people, the way I am treated by Celtics fans, you would think I won a championship in Boston or played ten years for the team, when it wasn't close to that. But I think I know why fans feel a connection to me. I look like the guy you hoop with at the rec center on Saturday morning. I'm five foot nine. I'm normal. I look like your friends. People probably felt that they could do what I was doing because I was relatable.

But I believe there were other factors why we connected, too. My story—being the sixtieth and last pick in the 2011 NBA draft, how I was able to take advantage of any opportunities I had, how I was never satisfied, my fearless style of play—it resonated with people who put their hard hat on every day and go to work and get the job done, because that was my mentality, too.

When you're a player like that in a city like Boston, no matter what sport it is, fans will gravitate toward you. They know—*you* know—whether you're genuine or not, too. Celtics fans see right through insincerity and false hustle and all of that. You guys know what's real.

I think that applies to the media, too. The reporters are tough but fair. I don't remember one time that I had a bad experience with a reporter, from the *Globe* or elsewhere. You go through rough stretches throughout the season and people will write that, because it's their job. I was treated with respect and I tried to give that back.

It also helps to open yourself up, to show that you're a real person with actual emotions and not just some basketball machine, and to give a little bit of access to the work necessary to succeed in this league. I think Adam Himmelsbach captured that really well with an article that's in this book, when he came along for one of my late-night shootarounds on the road.

And then on top of all that, I mean, we were pretty fun, weren't we? When I came over from the Suns in the trade deadline in February 2015, the perception was that the Celtics were in a rebuild, after trading away Kevin Garnett and Paul Pierce after the 2013 season. But our roster was made up of guys who had been doubted or counted out before, and that became our identity. We brought the effort and energy every night, and we did not back down.

We were way more competitive and successful than I think people expected. It brought a different energy to the city. We didn't win a championship, but we got to the conference finals in 2017, and we *fought*, man. If I hadn't injured my hip, who knows what might have happened.

It's so funny, thinking back now to when I got traded to Boston, and how I had no clue at first that it would be the best experience of my NBA career. I mean, I grew up in Tacoma, Washington, as a true Lakers fan! Sure, I knew Celtics history, but basically all I knew about actually playing in Boston was that the Garden was *freezing* whenever I was there as a visiting player. I didn't get warmed up until people got in their seats.

I remember one conversation I had with the older Isiah Thomas. Right, the Hall of Famer, and rival of the Celtics in the eighties. You might not think he'd be the one talking up the Celtics, but he sure did. He called me after I got traded and told me, "This is going to be the best situation for your career." At that point, I could not see it. I didn't know anyone on the team.

And then when I sat down with Danny Ainge, who was the president of basketball operations then, I remember the first thing he said was, "You have the potential to be one of the best sixth men to ever play here." And I'm thinking, "You really have nobody on the roster for me to be coming off the bench." But he saw something that I didn't see. And I did eventually become a starter, so maybe I exceeded his expectations in a way.

You know how I really knew that this wasn't going to be a rebuild? When I got to Boston and set foot in the Garden for the first time as a Celtic. You realize that no matter what anybody else was saying on the outside, the energy is just about championships, about greatness. You see the retired numbers, you see all the pictures of the legendary players that are Celtics forever. That flipped the switch for me. Rebuilding? Nope. No way. Not here.

I looked up at the banners and the retired numbers all the time. All the time. You'll probably notice me doing it in old footage. And the vibe you Celtics fans brought to the building, well, that was unique. At this writing, I've played for ten different teams, and I know this to be the truth: That Garden energy every time you set foot on the court—whether it was a regular season game, a playoff, a game against the worst team in the league or against the best team in the league—was something you couldn't experience anywhere else.

The team memories were the best ones, but of course some individual moments have stayed with me. There were times when I'd be at the free throw line and having a good night with the whole crowd chanting "M-V-P! M-V-P!" That's something I dreamed of as a kid. I think about that now: That happened to me in a Boston Celtics jersey. I will remember it for the rest of my life. You guys don't do that for everybody.

As you probably know, there's more to this than just basketball to me. When my sister Chyna died in a car accident in April 2017, it left me in a dark, dark place in my life. To have the city gravitate toward me and treat me with love and respect and show support meant more than I can express. That's what brought us even closer. The city, organization, and fans went through a real situation with me. I saw all your signs in the arena. I felt the support. It was the most difficult time in my life, and you truly cared about me.

I come back to Boston now and get the same love as players who were there longer, or who put a couple banners in the rafters, or won MVPs. They did things that I didn't come close to doing, and yet the respect is there from the organization, and from all of you. I think that says a lot about Boston and my time there.

Yes, it was just two and a half years. But it was everything. My bond with Boston, the Celtics, and you, will last a lifetime.

—Isaiah Thomas, January 2024

INTRODUCTION

Basketball aficionados instantly recognized Red Auerbach's stroke of genius on June 9, 1978, when the Celtics president selected Larry Bird with the No. 6 overall pick out of Indiana State in the NBA Draft. Bird, who had begun his college career at Indiana University in 1974 before dropping out a few weeks into his freshman year and eventually matriculating to Indiana State, still had a year of school at the time of the selection. The relentlessly wily Auerbach had exploited a loophole that allowed a player to be selected if his original college class had graduated.

Perhaps being an aficionado was not even a requirement to appreciate the maneuver. Casual fans might have recognized Auerbach's coup, too. Bird was an acknowledged basketball marvel even before he put on a No. 33 Boston Celtics jersey for the first time. During that senior year in 1979, he led Indiana State—a program of modest success until his arrival—to 33 consecutive victories before it fell to once and future rival Earvin "Magic" Johnson's more potent Michigan State team in an NCAA men's final that remains the most watched college basketball game of all time.

Still, there's something special about greatness recognizing greatness. It enhances the anticipation of an athlete's arrival and further confirms what we—the aficionados and the casuals—believe we see. It must have been a thrill for readers to turn to the *Globe* sports section on May 1, 1956, and read that Auerbach had declared new draft choice Bill Russell—in his time a University of San Francisco and Olympic marvel—as "the greatest defensive center I've ever seen."

Any cynic that suspected hyperbole would soon recognize that Auerbach's assessment of Russell—who would lead the Celtics to 11 championships in his 13 seasons while staking an undeniable claim as the most reliable winner in American team sports—might have leaned toward understatement. And so it must have felt special again, 22 years later, when the *Globe*'s Bob Ryan—a basketball writer so knowledgeable and revered that he was referred to by fans, media peers, and even NBA players and personnel as "The Commish"—offered these prescient and clever words for the June 10, 1978, editions of the newspaper while assessing the selection of Bird.

Red Auerbach did not look as if he had swallowed the canary. He looked as if he had just consumed the entire aviary.

"I feel," he cooed, "that we did as good a job as we possibly could."

What Red did in yesterday's NBA Draft was acquire the rights to the best college player in the country. "How often," Red inquired, "do the Celtics get a chance to draft the best player in the country?" The answer, apparently, is once every 22 years.

That morning, over their Cheerios and coffee, *Globe* readers got to enjoy the best basketball writer of all time writing with grace, color, and foresight on the arrival of the player who would become the most beloved Celtic of all time and, like Russell, one of the finest players in the sport's history. The Cheerios could have been stale and the coffee bitter, but Ryan's insight and writing were a fresh treat, and all these years later, it stands as documentation of Bird's selection as excellent as the player himself.

This is no revelation to anyone diving into this book, but the Celtics are one of the marquee franchises in American professional sports—and depending on your rooting interests, perhaps "one of" is unnecessary.

The accolades and accomplishments are staggering. In June 2024, the Celtics won their 18th championship, breaking a tie with the Lakers—who won five in Minneapolis before moving to Los Angeles in 1960—for most in NBA history. The franchise won its first title in 1957, Russell and Tommy Heinsohn's rookie season, then eight consecutively from 1959 to 1966. The Celtics added banners to their collection again in 1968 and 1969—Russell's final season as a player and his last of three seasons pulling double duty as the coach after succeeding Auerbach.

With versatile John Havlicek, indefatigable center Dave Cowens, and elegant guard Jo Jo White leading the way in the 1970s, the Celtics secured two more championships in the decade, in 1974 over Kareem Abdul-Jabbar and the Milwaukee Bucks, and in 1976 over the Phoenix Suns, with the Celtics' triple-overtime victory in Game 5 topping most rankings as the greatest game in league history.

The "Big Three" era Celtics of Bird, Kevin McHale, and Robert Parish emerged as champions in 1981, 1984, and again in 1986, the latter being a veritable dream team with Bill Walton coming off the bench. The 17th banner came courtesy of a new Big Three—Paul Pierce, Kevin Garnett, and Ray Allen—in 2008, a team that was assembled in the clever Auerbach tradition by President of Basketball Operations Danny Ainge, a Celtics star in his own right in the '80s.

The Celtics' guiding principles, instituted by Auerbach upon his hiring in 1950 and buttressed permanently by Russell's unselfish, defense-oriented approach, is that the team comes before the individual, and winning comes above all. But winning players win games, and during their first four decades, the Celtics had the greatest continuous run of superstars any team has had in the sport's annals. It began with Bob Cousy, the ballhandling whiz from Holy Cross who was the franchise's first gate attraction. Then came the magnificent Russell, the foil to perceived Goliath Wilt Chamberlain, who won more and *did more to help his teams win* than any player before or since while also emerging as a champion of social justice away from the court. Tommy Heinsohn was a franchise institution as a player, coach, and beloved broadcaster, while bank shot-shooting Sam Jones may be the most underrated superstar in Celtics lore.

Havlicek began his career as a continuation of the franchise's sixth-man tradition that started with Frank Ramsey and ended it as the Celtics' all-time leading scorer. Bird's arrival came a gap year after Havlicek's retirement, and in his 13 seasons—and

we say this with apologies to Air Jordan in Chicago and Magic and Kobe in Los Angeles—he became as beloved and revered as any player has been in any single market. After some bleak times brought on by tragedy—the deaths of Len Bias in 1986 and captain Reggie Lewis in 1993—the Celtics found their next cornerstone a half-decade after Bird's retirement when Paul Pierce slipped inexplicably to No. 10 in the 1998 draft. Not even Rick Pitino could mess that up. All in all, the Celtics have retired 24 numbers—well, 23, since Jim Loscutoff, a sharp-elbowed role player on seven championship teams, asked that his nickname, "Loscy," hang from the rafters rather than his uniform digits.

What sweetened the success even more were the rivalries, both individual and team. Chamberlain, who played for the Philadelphia Warriors, Sixers, and then Los Angeles Lakers, was the most physically dominating player the league had seen, particularly in comparison with his peers, scoring 100 points in a game in 1962 and averaging an astounding 50.1 that season. But Chamberlain's teams beat Russell's just once in eight playoff encounters.

While the Celtics engaged in a stirring rivalry with the Philadelphia 76ers, particularly in the early '80s, their history is intertwined with that of the Lakers. The Celtics and Lakers met in the Finals eight times in the Russell era, and Boston won all eight meetings. The '80s brought more balance, when Bird and Magic, on opposite coasts with two different but spectacular teams, carried over their rivalry from their college days, elevating and perhaps even saving the NBA in the process. The Lakers won five titles in the '80s to the Celtics' three, Los Angeles winning two of three head-to-head Finals showdowns. The franchises met again in 2008, when the Celtics won their first title in 22 years, and in 2010, when the Lakers prevailed.

The Lakers-Celtics rivalry, particularly the Bird-Magic years, was the aesthetic pinnacle of professional basketball: as good as it got and as good as it could ever be.

To know what the Celtics became is to marvel at how it all began with such uncertainty. In the 1920s, the Celtics name was initially attached to a dominating barnstorming team, led by Joe Lapchick, considered a giant at 6 feet 5 inches. The incarnation of the Boston Celtics franchise that we know today was born on June 6, 1946, as one of 10 teams in the

Basketball Association of America. After competing for three seasons, the Eastern-based BAA and the National Basketball League, which originated in the Midwest, merged in 1949.

In a de facto Celtics history lesson on the closing of the Boston Garden, the Celtics' hallowed home (they packed up their iconic parquet floor and moved to the FleetCenter, now TD Garden, the following season), Ryan wrote in 1991: "The BAA came into being for one basic reason: the men who operated arenas housing National Hockey League teams were looking for an attraction to put fannies in their building when the hockey team was on the road. [Celtics founder] Walter A. Brown was one such hockey man. The president of the Bruins knew less than nothing about basketball, and no one in Boston was clamoring for a professional team. When speaking of winter sports, Boston in 1946 was what it would remain for the next 33 years—a steadfast hockey town. Then came Larry, and, well, you know the rest."

The *Globe*, in its 75th year of publishing when the Celtics were born, was there from the beginning in July, 1946, when reporter Harold Kaese's story laid out the fundamental logistics of the fledgling league: "The Boston team will play three home games against each Eastern rival, two home games against each Western rival, totaling 27 home games, and 54 games in all. There will be playoffs. Players will not be loaned, as they sometimes are in hockey . . . " From Cousy's arrival and the Russell dynasty, "Hondo" Havlicek's pair of '70s champs, the Larry Legend/Big Three era, then Pierce, Garnett, Allen, and the new Big Three, and now to the Jayson Tatum and Jaylen Brown-led championship contenders of today, the *Globe* has covered it all.

Globe writers' bylines topped stories on many of the most memorable games in not just Celtics history but league history. A short list: the four-overtime 1953 triumph over Syracuse; the 1957 double-overtime seventh game with St. Louis, when rookie Heinsohn's 37 points and 23 rebounds lifted the team after fellow rookie Russell fouled out; the memorable night versus Philadelphia in 1965 when Havlicek stole the ball; the 1976 triple-overtime victory over Phoenix; the ferocious 1981 comeback-clinching seventh game over archrival Philadelphia; the 1986 double-overtime victory over Chicago and 63-point-scorer Michael Jordan; Bird swiping Isiah Thomas's sleepy pass and

feeding Dennis Johnson for a layup when all looked lost in 1987; Pierce outdueling LeBron James in a seventh game in 2008; the clinching, cathartic 131-92 rout of the Lakers in Game 6 that same year, ending that 22-year championship drought.

Those early bylines, chronicling the rise of Cousy, Russell, and an almost unfathomable level of dominance, belonged to writers such as Kaese, good-natured Jack Barry, and Clif Keane, all of whom were associated with reporting on the Red Sox. (Keane, it must be acknowledged, was a problematic personality at best. Wrote Leigh Montville in the 2021 gem *Tall Men in Short Shorts*, his recollection of covering the 1969 Celtics as a young reporter, "There were a bunch of words [Keane] used but never said to the Black faces he might encounter," before detailing despicable specifics.) The quality of writing improved exponentially with the arrival of Montville and Bob Sales on the beat in the late '60s. The *Globe*'s depth chart only grew more impressive.

Bob Ryan and Peter Gammons—the definitive baseball writer of his generation and perhaps all others—started at the *Globe* on the same day, June 10, 1968. It was the sports journalism equivalent of getting Russell and Bird in the same draft. Ryan took over the basketball beat in the 1970 season and, with a passionate, opinionated writing style that made readers feel like he was talking directly to them, covered the sport with a flair unprecedented and still unmatched. Bryan Curtis, writing for *Grantland* in 2014, captured the essence of "The Commish" perfectly: "No one's game stories glowed with more opinion, more enthusiasm, more—call it what it is—fandom. No one was quite as likely, after Paul Silas would grab a rebound and throw it to Havlicek to start the break, to turn to a fellow Globie and give them a hug."

Ryan was so respected by those he covered that when Dave Cowens decided to retire early in the 1980 season, he told Ryan before he told Auerbach. Ryan helped him craft a piece for the *Globe* explaining his decision.

Ryan briefly shifted to the Red Sox beat, but the quality of the *Globe*'s Celtics coverage remained elite through the '70s, with stylist John Powers, columnists Montville and Ray Fitzgerald, and writers and reporters such as Larry Whiteside tracking the happenings on and off the parquet. If the Larry

Bird Celtics of the '80s were the franchise's most cherished teams—and there is no *if* about it—it ran parallel with the heyday of the *Globe*'s sports section. The most challenging aspect of assembling this compilation was deciding which stories to keep from among Ryan, Montville, Jackie MacMullan, Dan Shaughnessy, Ian Thomsen, and Michael Madden during the '80s glory days, when they often wrote brilliantly on the same games (often Celtics-Lakers) and topics (Bird-Magic).

Ryan and MacMullan—a lyrical writer whose reporting chops are so respected that Paul Pierce said with a laugh to Kevin Garnett during their introduction as teammates in 2007, "She'll get you to talk about things you never thought you would!"—have been honored by the Basketball Hall of Fame with the Curt Gowdy Media Award, given annually to one writer and one broadcaster for outstanding contributions to the sport.

So, too, has 2023 recipient Marc Spears, who covered the 2008 champions for the *Globe*, and more recent and current Celtics writers will warrant great accolades of their own as years pass. Baxter Holmes was the master of richly detailed feature stories, and Peter May, Shira Springer, and Michael Holley are among those who covered the beat with distinction.

Julian Benbow's byline on Celtics stories is always a welcome sight, while current beat writer Adam Himmelsbach—who has seemingly written a compelling feature on every significant member of the organization—and plugged-in national basketball columnist Gary Washburn form a tandem as complementary as a Rajon Rondo-Ray Allen backcourt. Shaughnessy, Tara Sullivan, Christopher L. Gasper, and occasionally yours truly offer insights and a wide range of opinions on the present-day Celtics.

Or Bob Cousy-Bill Sharman, if that's your preferred backcourt metaphor. Or K. C. Jones-Sam Jones . . . or Jo Jo White-Charlie Scott . . . or Ainge-DJ . . . or Marcus Smart-Jaylen Brown . . . or even the newest pairing, Jrue Holiday and Derrick White. Whatever your choice, the point remains the same. The Boston Celtics have had an abundance of wonderful, accomplished players in their rich history. The *Globe*, with style, accuracy, and insight, has documented all of it with our roster of writing All-Stars. We've been here from before Banner No. 1 through Banner 18, and you can count on us to be there for all the banners to come.

—Chad Finn

1 THE EARLY YEARS

(1946-1956)

I n his 57 years with the Celtics, Red Auerbach pulled off countless lop-sided trades and transactions, including perhaps the most astute move in professional sports history, when he maneuvered in the 1956 NBA Draft to select University of San Francisco center Bill Russell. But even savvy ol' Red required the intervention of basketball's version of a four-leaf clover from time to time.

Auerbach was hired by Celtics owner Walter A. Brown on a $10,000, one-year contract ahead of the 1950 draft, in which Boston held the first pick after winning just 22 games the previous season under coach Alvin "Doggie" Julian. Auerbach had oversight over all basketball decisions, but his feelings on a certain local hardwood hero did not jibe with those of New England sports fans who had clamored for the Celtics to select dazzling three-time Holy Cross All-America guard Bob Cousy.

"I don't give a darn for sentiment of names," said Auerbach, as quoted in the April 28, 1950, editions of the *Globe* upon his introduction as coach. "That goes for Cousy or anybody else. A local yokel doesn't bring more than a dozen extra fans into your building. But a winning team does and that's what I aim to have."

A fitting quote, for in the draft, held in Chicago two days before Auerbach's boisterous press conference, the Celtics had used that top pick on Bowling Green center Charlie Share, then selected Duquesne forward Chuck Cooper—the first Black player ever drafted in franchise history—with the No. 13 pick.

The Celtics, much to Auerbach and Brown's indifference, ended up with "the local yokel" anyway, receiving Cousy in a three-player dispersal draft after the Chicago Stags, who owned his rights, ceased operations. Cousy was the Celtics brain trust's third choice among the available players.

It turned out to be perhaps the most fortuitous break the franchise ever caught. Cousy, an innovative ballhandler and passer, proved to be the ideal floor leader of Auerbach's desired fast-break offense, quickly winning over his onetime skeptic. In his Celtics career, he would make 13 All-Star teams, star on six championship teams, and live up to the nickname "Houdini of the Hardwood," leading the league in assists for eight straight seasons.

Cousy's emergence as one of the fledgling NBA's great stars ushered in the first age of success for the Celtics while the league was desperate for stability.

‹ From left, Celtics point guard Bob Cousy, owner Walter A. Brown, and coach Red Auerbach in Boston, 1956.

The NBA, and the Celtics, too, were anything but an instant success. The Celtics were founded on June 6, 1946, by Brown as a franchise in the Basketball Association of America, which had hoped to benefit from the post-World War II economic boom and the steady popularity of college basketball.

The BAA merged with the National Basketball League in 1949, forming a 17-team league that would soon prove tenuous. By 1950, seven of the 17 teams folded, and only three of the remaining 10 (the Celtics, Knickerbockers, and Philadelphia Warriors) have endured since the inaugural 1946 season. The Celtics averaged roughly 2,500 in attendance in the first season, and through their first four years of existence, they had reportedly lost approximately $1 million while making just one playoff appearance. But Brown remained unbowed, selling most of his valuable Ice Capades stock to help keep the Celtics from going under.

At first, it wasn't much better on the court. The Celtics lost the first five games of their existence under coach John "Honey" Russell in the 1947 season. It could not have been a positive sign that their first home game at the Boston Garden was delayed an hour when a misguided warm-up shot by Celtic Chuck Connors damaged the backboard. (Connors would later find greater fame as an actor, most prominently starring in television's *The Rifleman*, where he appeared to be a better shot.) The Celtics lost that Garden opener to the Chicago Stags, 57-55.

Their first victory came in Game 6, a 53-49 defeat of the Toronto Huskies on November 16, 1946, in which Wyndol Gray paced the Celtics with 13 points. A few weeks later, in a December 1 loss to Chicago, Al Brightman became the first Celtic to score 20 points in a game. The Celtics might have lacked success in their earliest seasons, but they did not lack in admirable players, among them Ed Sadowski, their first All-NBA player honoree, who averaged 19.3 points per game in 1948; former Holy Cross star George Kaftan; and Arnie Risen, who in his later seasons would earn recognition from Russell for helping him acclimate to professional basketball.

The Celtics flourished with the mutual arrivals of Auerbach and Cousy, the acquisition of superb scorer Ed Macauley from St. Louis in the 1950 American Basketball League dispersal draft, and a trade with Fort Wayne in October, 1951, that brought smooth-shooting former Brooklyn Dodgers farmhand Bill Sharman. In 1953, the Celtics selected Kentucky star Frank Ramsey.

The NBA was a rough-and-tumble league when the Celtics first began finding success. In March, 1953, Cousy scored 50 points—making 30 of 32 free throws—in a brawl-filled four-overtime play-off victory over Syracuse, the franchise's first playoff series win. In a regular season matchup in November, 1953, a fight-plagued game between the Celtics and Philadelphia Warriors—with Cousy and Warriors star Neil Johnston the main card—required police intervention. That same season, in March, 1954, the Celtics were eliminated by the Nationals in the Eastern Division finals, with the deciding game marred by brawls. Only after the advent of the 24-second shot clock in October, 1954, did the foul-plagued sport take a welcome turn toward finesse, with the skill of the players finally on display.

For all their progress after Auerbach's arrival in 1950, the Celtics never finished higher than second in the Eastern Division through 1956, losing in the division finals three straight seasons from 1953 to 1955. In 1956, their record dipped to 39-33, and they were bounced in the division semifinals by Syracuse. It would be the last season until 1967 that they would not advance to the Finals. The Celtics were talented, but they needed a center. They were about to get one, and so much more.

Competition Looms as Brown Names Russell Coach, Gets 27 Home Dates for Pro Basket Ball

July 17, 1946 • by Harold Kaese

Walter Brown conceded the pennant to the Red Sox (even though Bob Feller was pitching for the Indians against them) and revealed his ambitious plans for Boston's new professional basket ball team. What brought basket ball to his mind was Lou Boudreau's zone defense against Ted Williams.

It was a strange sight to see Brown posing with a basket ball in his hands. If some of the Olympics, or amateurs with whom he toured Europe, had seen him, they would have wept, and said, "Alas, poor Walter."

Alas, poor Olympics! Alas, poor hockey! Here was the ice game's great champion saying, "This is the most important Garden step in the nine years I've been there. There are more basket ball players and fans around here than hockey players and fans. Hockey was the big game after the last war; basket ball game will be the big game after this one. And we won't have to sell basket ball."

With a coach like Honey Russell of the Original Celtics, membership in a closely-knit league, and 27 home games, basket ball is set to challenge hockey's Winter supremacy here. Details of Boston's new sports venture:

LEAGUE SETUP—Arenas own all teams in the new Basket Ball Association of America, except Buffalo, which will not compete this Winter. The Eastern Division: Boston, New York, Philadelphia, Providence, Toronto, Washington. The Western Division: St. Louis, Chicago, Cleveland, Detroit, Pittsburgh. A Pacific Coast Division will be ready in another year.

Maurice Podoloff of New Haven, a minor league hockey executive, is president of the association. He knows little about basket ball, a lot about sports promotion.

The Boston team will play three home games against each Eastern rival, two home games against each Western rival, totaling 27 home games, and 54 games in all. There will be playoffs. Players will not be loaned, as they sometimes are in hockey.

BOSTON SETUP—There'll be 10 players. They will play for no other team. Pay will be in proportion to attendances. "We won't bid fantastic prices against Western industrial teams," said Brown. Only players with outstanding records will be invited to try for the team. Practice starts late in October, the season in November.

HOME COURTS—As many games as possible will be played at the Garden, the rest at the Arena, which has a nifty new floor built by Tony DiNatale. With the Bruins having 30 home dates, the basket ball schedule may be a patched-up affair. Besides 27 pro games, there will be 14 college doubleheaders and one preseason game—a total of 42 basket ball nights.

PRO RULES—They will be like college rules, except where the pros think they can be improved. Brown said, "It will not be a case of everything goes."

NICKNAME—Brown is looking for one. He welcomes suggestions, may run a contest. The first nickname offered was Boston Yankees, an extremely bright suggestion.

THE COACH—Honey Russell had a year to go on his Manhattan College contract, but resigned for this chance. He has been in pro basket ball 28 years.

Russell is currently managing the Rutland baseball team in the Northern League, a semipro circuit made up chiefly of college athletes. His team is in third place.

A three-year contract brought him to the Boston pros. Brown thinks the game will be soundly established here by the end of three years. Russell hopes he is, too.

Providence Tops Celtics in Pro Opener, 59-53

November 3, 1946

PROVIDENCE—With Earl Shannon and Dino Martin leading in scoring, the Providence Steamrollers of the Basket Ball Association of America tonight defeated the Boston Celtics, 59 to 53, in the opening game of the season. Martin made 18 points and Shannon 15.

Stags Nose Out Celtics 57-55 in Hoop Opener

November 6, 1946 • by Jack Barry

Honey Russell's Boston Celtics dropped a heartbreaker, 57 to 55, to the Chicago Stags in their opening home game of the newly organized Basket Ball Association of America League last night at the Arena before 4,329 fans.

Despite a starting time delay of one hour when the glass backboard at the west end of the Arena was shattered during the Celtics' practice, the enthusiastic audience was presented with a thrilling exhibition, with spectacular shooting and fine floor play on tap.

ZASLOFSKY BRILLIANT

The individual brilliance of Max Zaslofsky, ex-Brooklyn St. John's crack forward, was the major difference in the winning of the ball game for Harold Olsen's Stags. This stellar one-handed and two-handed set-shot star dropped in 13 field goals and two fouls for a 28-point total, topping the Celtics' high man, Johnny Simmons, by 15 points.

However, the Celtics were far from disgraced, as the score indicated. Inability to stop Zaslofsky alone spelled defeat for Russell's courageous group, who played fine ball in spots and who came from behind after being in arrears, 10 to 4, to hold the lead until the seven-minute mark of the third period, when Zaslofsky ran wild.

The play of John Simmons, Red Wallace, Wyndol Gray for the major portion and Kevin "Chuck" Connors stood out for the Celtics, while the six-foot, nine-inch Charley Halbert, pivot man, deserved mention for the Stags. Connors' play defensively on the

Discouraging debut? Arena hands remove the glass backboard, shattered during pregame warm-ups before the home opener in their inaugural season.

giant Halbert was instrumental in keeping down the Stags score.

Kottman's Late Scores Give Celtics First Win in Pro Season, 53-49

November 17, 1946 • by Jack Barry

The Boston Celtics achieved their first Basket Ball Association of America victory in six starts last night when they downed the Toronto Huskies, 53 to 49, at the Garden before 5,176 fans.

A spectacular fourth period, which found the teams tied 38-all after its outset, thrilled the spectators as lanky Hal Kottman, scoreless in four previous games, tipped in six vital points, breaking a 46-46 tie with less than five minutes to play.

The Celtics were never headed thereafter, as they protected that margin, through heady stalling tactics.

As five minutes of play remained, and the score 46-all, Kottman took a smart pass from Johnny Simmons and flipped in a pivot shot for a Celtic 48-46 advantage. Then Kottman followed up his own shot and sank another vital two-pointer as the Celtics exerted continued pressure.

The big lad then converted two free tries and Boston was in with its initial victory as only George Nostrand's two foul shots represented the Huskies' final scoring.

Accuracy at the free throw lane decided the game in the Celtics' favor. They made 17 successful foul shots in 24 attempts. The visitors could cage only 15 in 30.

Connie Simmons, Kottman, Kevin Connors and Wyndol Gray were Boston's standouts, while player-Coach Ed Sadowski and George Nostrand, along with Roy Hurley and Mike McCarron, played well for Toronto. Sadowski was immense until forced to leave the game via the five-foul route.

They Can't Miss, If . . . Winning Team Sure to Make Pro Basket Ball Successful in Boston

December 5, 1946 • by Harold Kaese

There is no doubt whatsoever that the Celtics belong in Boston. Their record of three victories and 11 defeats qualifies them eminently for a place in our community. A poor record is the first requirement of any new professional team in Boston.

Boston pro teams always do it the hard way. The Bruins did it the hard way, the Redskins tried to do it the hard way, and the Yanks have been doing it the hard way. Who are the Celtics to let such predecessors show them up?

At that, the Celtics have made a more successful start than did the Bruins. Their record of 3-11 is good beside the 2-12 record of the 1925 Bruins—and look what the Bruins have grown into.

In their first game in Boston, played at the Arena 22 years ago last Sunday, the Bruins drew 1,340 fans. The Celtics in several games at the Garden have rivaled this trifling figure, which is another reason to believe that 22 years from now they, too, will be drawing 13,900 fans to the Garden 30 times or so a season.

NEED A WINNER

There is reason to believe, however, that pro basket ball will proceed to popularity as quickly as the Bruins—provided that the Celtics become a winner. Basket ball fans who have seen the Celtics in any one of five home games know that they, even with a 3-11 record, are as much superior to any college basket ball team in New England as the Yanks are to the Yale, Holy Cross, Boston College, or Harvard football teams.

The Celtics probably could beat the best college basket ball team in this section, if not in the entire country, and name the score. Unfortunately for their record, they are playing pro teams, not college rivals.

This new sports baby is like most infants. It took time to develop a little personality. Only now have players, teams, and coaching systems taken on an identity. Instead of a lot of anonymous Joes racing wildly over a polished floor, now the game has its Sadowskis, Baumholtzes, Riebes, Janisches, Fulkses, and Brightmans—names that mean something.

Basket ball dilettantes have learned that the St. Louis Bombers use a set attack with a weave; that the New York Knickerbockers use fast passes, set shots, and no pivot player; that the Detroit Falcons tonight will use a set offense, a lot of wild shots, and depend on tall players to get the ball off the backboard; and that the Providence Steamrollers use the throw-and-run Rhode Island style.

What style do the Celtics have—if they have any style?

WILL GET PLAYERS

Coach Honey Russell uses free play and set play. Free play is the best style for an experienced club. The Celtics are not an experienced club. They hired five experienced players to keep the club together, but these five so far have had trouble keeping themselves together.

Set play is better for an inexperienced team. It tells every man where he should be on every play. Some teams are so inexperienced that they can't find their way to the dressing room. Free play is not for them.

The Celtics have lost some heartbreakers. Examples: They had a one-point lead over Toronto with six seconds to play, and possession of the ball, yet lost. They led St. Louis by four points with 25 seconds to play, again had possession of the ball, and again lost.

"We need tough, hard-driving players," said Russell. And the Celtics are going out to get them. Not next season, but this season.

The Age-Old Question: Holy Cross vs. Celtics? Collegians Too Small, Says Pro Mariaschin

February 10, 1948 • by Harold Kaese

It's as unlikely as a Michigan-Notre Dame football game, a Dempsey-Wills fight, or an A. H. A.-A. A. U. hockey game, but a promotion that would pack the Garden and net at least $25,000 for some deserving charity would be a basket ball game between the Celtics and Holy Cross.

Pros vs. collegians. Which team would win? Sadowski vs. Kaftan. Who would score the more points? Riebe vs. Cousy. Who would display the better floormanship?

All through the Winter the swelling host of court fans have been arguing these questions. Surprising is the number of fans who think that Holy Cross could beat the Celtics. Experts lean the other way, but not unanimously.

As one said, "The Celtics should win, but I'm not so sure that they would. It's a game I'd want to see. There are times when Holy Cross makes you think they could beat anybody in any league."

Celtics followers say that the pros have too much class, too much savvy, too much height. Holy Cross rooters say that their favorites are too fast, too tricky, too inspirational.

Nothing but a game will settle the argument.

COLLEGES HAVE WEAK SPOTS

The question was put to Saul Mariaschin, Celtic who as a Harvard guard played against the Crusaders last season and has seen them play this Winter: Could the Celtics beat Holy Cross?

"That's like asking if a high school team could beat a college team," replied the dribbling musician. "Of course the Celtics would win.

"Pro teams are really all-star teams. They have a good man at every position at all times. But every college team has at least one weak spot, and it wouldn't take long for a pro team to take advantage of it. Pro teams are always looking for the weak man, and when they find him they hammer him.

"Holy Cross is a fine college team, but it has one weakness. It lacks height. Any good college team with height always gives Holy Cross trouble, because controlling the backboards is so important. Holy Cross is small compared to pro teams."

Doggie Julian isn't worried about the Celtics-Holy Cross argument, because he is too busy worrying about real and not hypothetical rivals. And he is logically worried about tonight's game with Temple at the Garden, because his Crusaders are meeting a good team, a taller team and a team that excels in getting the ball off the backboards. Temple is equipped to strike Holy Cross in its most vulnerable spot.

HOLY CROSS SUPERMEN?

Temple and Loyola of Chicago (Arena, Feb. 24) are regarded by Julian as the two toughest opponents left on the Holy Cross schedule. If neither can extend the Crusaders, then—bring on the Celtics!

Perhaps the pros could mutilate the fancy passing of the Crusaders; and Sadowski could run with Kaftan and cover him without fouling out before the half; and Riebe could make Cousy look like an amateur at handling the ball—but it's hard for Boston fans to think so.

In these parts, Holy Cross is a team of supermen, and the losses to Columbia, St. Louis and DePaul were inexplicable accidents, like the 'pick-off' pass used against Boston College last Fall.

Both sides may show a slight reluctance to join the venture, but what a worthy Boston charity needs right now is an exhibition game between the Crusaders and the Celtics. That is, unless Temple wins tonight, in which case, skip it.

Julian Quits as H. C. Coach to Take Post with Celtics

April 11, 1948

Alvin "Doggie" Julian, who in the past three years piloted Holy Cross basket ball to a record of 65 victories and only 10 losses, has resigned as court mentor of the Crusaders, he informed the Globe last night.

He will coach the professional Boston Celtics of the Basket Ball Association of America. Formal announcement will be made by Celtic officials tomorrow.

Rumors that Walter Brown, president of the Boston Garden and head man of the Celtics organization, would seek the services of Julian have been rampant for the past month, but they quieted down recently when the Boston quintet qualified for the playoffs.

The Celtics didn't draw any too well throughout the season and that evidently was what caused the Celtics to wean the former Muhlenberg coach away from the intercollegiate ranks. He succeeds Honey Russell, who still has a year to run on his contract.

It was impossible last night to get a definite confirmation from anyone directly connected with either the Celtics or Holy Cross. But at the same time, there was no denial.

Brown said, "I have no comment."

At Holy Cross, Gene Flynn, director of athletics, remarked, "As far as I know there has been no resignation and there is nothing I can say on the matter. Any statement will have to come from either Julian or Walter Brown, the parties chiefly concerned."

The Celtics, who brought professional basket ball into Boston for the first time on a high standard, haven't been a successful venture the past two seasons. There were rumors a couple of months ago that Brown would abandon the fort after the past season. In their debut, the Celtics were in the red $109,000, but the past season this total was cut about in half.

Brown, when he brought basket ball into the Garden and went along with the pros, said that he felt that it would take about five years to acclimate Boston sports fans to the game. And he has stuck by his guns, denying the recent rumor with the statement that the Celtic owners were ready to stick with the club for at least another two years.

There were reports of dissension among the players the past season and this, plus the acknowledged fact that Julian at the moment is the best known name in New England basket ball circles, decided the backers of the Celtics that the time was ripe to induce Julian to forsake the collegiates for the play for pay boys. And that inducement may see the H. C. coach nearly doubling the salary that he received at Mt. St. James.

Alvin "Doggie" Julian.

The Julian touch, which catapulted Holy Cross to a top rung among the nation's college quintets, is something that Brown and his cohorts hope will bring the much-needed growth in attendance at the pro games. There are many who would like to see the H. C. quintet of the past season step in to the pro ranks with Julian, but such a thing isn't probable as his two-time N. C. A. A. tourney five had only one senior among the regulars, Capt. Bob Curran. Bob Cousy, George Kaftan, Joe Mullaney, etc., are juniors.

Julian, during his three years at Holy Cross, saw his Crusaders annex the N. C. A. A. crown two years ago when it defeated Oklahoma in the East-West final at the New York Garden. This season it bowed to Kentucky in the Eastern final. That, incidentally, was the only time that the Worcester quintet had been defeated at Madison Square Garden in seven games.

The subject of Russell's status is open for speculation, if and when Brown has something to say on the matter. The former member of the Original Celtics, who is highly regarded in basket ball circles, has another year to go on his three-year contract. In addition to basket ball coach, Russell has also been serving as general manager of the Celtics, and it is possible that he will be retained in the latter position for the coming year. He left late yesterday for his New York home.

RUSSELL WANTED TO QUIT

Russell was reached at his New York home early this morning, and when the Globe informed him of Julian's resignation and his expected shift to the Celtics, he said, "Officially or otherwise, I don't know anything about it. All I do know is that in my last talk with Walter Brown, before I left for home, he told me that he would like me to be associated with the club.

"I knew that he was shopping around for a new coach, which was perfectly all right with me, for the truth is I wanted to quit the coaching game. I have been associated with the game, as a player and coach, for 30 years and am a little fed up with that end of it.

"My chief interest has been in seeing the sport go over in Boston and Doggie may be just the man to do it. His shift to the Celtics may be just the thing they need. I didn't have any luck with the club, but Doggie may be the salvation. He's so popular with everyone interested in the game that it may be the best thing for pro basket ball."

Walter Brown Has Been Licking Emergencies at Boston Garden Ever Since He Found a Way to Keep Snow on a Ski Jump

January 22, 1950 • by K. S. Bartlett

A big, ruddy-haired young man stood staring fixedly through a window at an array of fish, neatly nested on finely shaved ice.

A wide grin spread over his broad, pleasant face. He turned and hurried away.

Young Walter A. Brown, now president and general manager of the Boston Garden-Arena Corporation, had the solution of a first-grade problem which had been bothering himself, his father, the late George V. Brown, and other officials at the Garden.

The elder Brown, who had been for years manager of the Boston Arena—not then owned by the Boston Garden Corporation—had left the Arena to come to the Garden the year before. Ski jumps weren't so common around New England in 1935 and the new Garden management planned an indoor jump as a star feature of a sportsmen's show. The slope ran down from the second balcony. The snow-covered ice at the foot was no problem of course, being part of the surface on which hockey games had been played since the Garden opening in 1928.

But how to make snow or a reasonable facsimile thereof stick to the slope, especially with no refrigeration pipes underneath as there are just under the surface of the playing floor? Young Brown was in charge of the ski jump arrangements, and until the day when he happened to see the fish in the window, nobody had worked it out.

SHAVED ICE STARTED IT

Then, as now, Walter had an observant and inventive mind. That shaved ice pulled the trigger. Presently he was in the office of an ice company discussing the possibilities of a machine which would shave huge quantities of ice into snow-like fineness and spray it out as wanted. Also it must be a machine which could be mounted on a truck.

The machine was being made while the matter of making the "snow" stick on the slide was being discussed. Walter has always been a red-hot circus fan. He remembered the coco-matting the Ringling show uses in the East lobby to keep horses, elephants, and other animals from slipping. Laid down on the slope it held the snow sprayed on by the machine.

The ski jump, says Edward J. Powers, now vice president and assistant treasurer, was a huge success and was repeated in two successive years.

Today Brown is one of the biggest, big shot promoters of various sports, ice shows, and other events, which can be put on in the arena, there is in the country. Far and away the biggest in New

England, of course. He has innumerable other interests, and he'll tackle anything.

Only last week when the coach of the Boston Olympics resigned, Brown took on the job himself, saying he'd be a working bench coach, and make the trips with the team. It wouldn't take much provocation to make him a playing coach for he was something of a hockey star at Phillips Exeter in the middle 1920s and he did some coaching back in the 1930s.

He's up to his neck in many civic activities, with the Boys' Clubs a special interest.

GENUINELY KINDLY PERSON

He has a remarkable gift for spotting crowd-pleasing things. And he's a genuinely kindly person. Both traits have paid off for him often.

One day he was at the Arena. Three youngsters from Manchester, N. H., had come to skate at one of the public skating sessions. They wanted to have their skates sharpened but didn't know it would cost so much. They asked if they could have it done and mail the money after they went home.

"Sure," said Brown and went into a conference with his younger brother, Paul, now in charge at the Arena. Presently someone came running up to them exclaiming:

"Will you see what those kids are doing!"

Brown looked. The three New Hampshire youngsters were turning somersaults on skates and putting on a variety of other tricks. Later they starred for him for years in the Ice Capades, of which he is vice president as "The Hub Trio." They're with the Ice Cycles now.

There are innumerable stories of his ability to rearrange schedules on short notice.

There was the time when an important basket ball game was about to begin at the Arena. In pre-warm-up one player hit the protecting glass shield behind the basket so hard it fell and cracked—it's, of course, shatterproof—but it couldn't be used again. There were no spares at the Arena, but Brown sent to the Garden for a piece of the glass used for hockey games. It had been stored away because the rodeo was at the Garden. It took time to get it out.

A 360-pound section, big enough to use to replace the cracked Arena glass, was roped to the roof of a taxi. The taxi drove slowly across town.

Meanwhile, Brown kept the audience in their seats by announcing and personally handling a foul-shooting contest by members of the teams. The basket at the undamaged end was used.

Brown was born on his father's farm in Hopkinton, the eldest of a family of four boys and three girls. He did farm chores, went skating with neighborhood youngsters on the little rink his father built, and was bitten by the Marathon bug. He got over that. With his father, an official of the B. A. A., of which the younger Brown is now president, he watched the start in Hopkinton and sometimes was allowed to go partway along the course.

Some years ago Brown spotted Boston speed skater, named Lou White, at the Arena. He thought the young man had the makings of a long-distance runner. With Brown's encouragement he started training. He's done well. Last year he finished third in the B. A. A. Marathon.

Brown is married to the former Marjorie Hall of Arlington and lives in Newton Highlands. They have a six-year-old daughter, Marjorie, who's getting to be quite a skater.

Brown's schooling after grammar grades was varied, Hopkinton High School, Boston Latin and Phillips Exeter. He was graduated from the latter institution in 1926. He pitched and later at Exeter played first base on a good team.

Raymond Maguire, now with a Boston advertising firm, was a classmate of Brown's at Hopkinton. He recalls that when they were both 18, Brown and he started what was to be the first of Brown's promotions.

"It was a success, too," says Maguire. "For two Summers we rented the hall in the old Hayden Row Engine Hall, hired the Milford High School orchestra and had dances for young people, charging 25 cents admission. We cleared $200."

They also bought a piano out of the proceeds.

Howard Cahoon of Harwich, who was a dormitory mate of Brown's at Exeter and played on the baseball team with him, recalls him as a good man on the job. He's still a firm friend of Brown's, who isn't the sort that loses friends. They play a good deal of golf together on the Cape, Summers.

"He's the greatest guy that ever lived," says Cahoon. "Just the same fellow that he was as a boy in spite of all the success he's had."

That seems to be the general idea. In 1945, while Brown was in the service as a lieutenant colonel in G-2, Jerry Nason, Globe sports editor, wrote that although he was "temporarily out of the league" because of his war service, Brown remains "a sports phenomenon of the times—a big shot promoter who never has to my knowledge had type hurled at him with an underhand delivery."

Herb Ralby, one of the Globe's hockey experts who went to Europe with one of the A. H. A. teams Brown took on tour and sees him regularly at the Garden, is just as enthusiastic.

Globe photographer Charles F. McCormick, president of the Press Photographers Association of Boston, tells how Brown had a special three-deck platform built and mounted on a huge truck. This was for the photographers so that they would not have to ride, each in a single automobile sucking in smoke and exhaust fumes and often missing the best shots.

In fact, almost everyone seems to agree that Brown is a thoroughly good guy.

Recently the Press Photographers Association made it official by naming him as their "Good Guy of the Year" for 1949.

And almost everyone calls him "Walter," which he much prefers to "Mr. Brown."

Celts Pick Share Ahead of Cousy; Get Macauley

April 26, 1950

CHICAGO—The National Basket Ball Association, whittled down to a 12-team, two-division organization generally in major cities, today drafted 119 college cage stars to prepare for an all-out war for players with a new circuit formed by three expelled small-town members.

Charlie Share, lanky center from Bowling Green, O., was the No. 1 draft choice, selected by the Boston Celtics, who finished last in the N.B.A. Eastern division. Don Rehfeldt, Wisconsin center, who led the Big Ten in scoring, was second, picked by Baltimore.

It was expected that the N. B. A. teams, with negotiating rights established in their own organization, would make every effort to sign their top

selections before the new league could be ready to make concrete offers.

COUSY TO TRI-CITIES

Boston, reportedly in financial trouble midway through the 1950 campaign, came out with top luck in the draft. In addition to obtaining Share, the Celtics also nabbed center Ed Macauley, a former St. Louis University star who played last year with the St. Louis Bombers and finished fifth in league scoring.

The Celtics also drafted Charles Cooper, Duquesne; Bob Donham, Ohio State; Ken Reeves, Louisville; Jack Shelton, Oklahoma A. & M.; Frank Mahoney, Brown; Dale Barnstable, Kentucky; Frank Oftring, Holy Cross; Bob Cope, Montana State; Matt Forman, Holy Cross.

Bob Cousy, Holy Cross' great player who seemed a natural for Boston, was passed up by Pres. Walter Brown in favor of Share. Cousy was drafted by Tri-Cities.

Auerbach, New Coach, Says All Celts on Block

April 28, 1950 • by Herb Ralby

The Celtics' current manpower is the strongest and most talented in the four-year history of the pro hoop squad. Yet Arnold "Red" Auerbach, named yesterday as Doggie Julian's successor as coach, will trade anybody on the roster if he feels it will help the Celts.

"I don't give a darn for sentiment of names," declared the former Washington and Tri-Cities coach after he had been officially named the new Celts mentor by Walter Brown at a press luncheon. "That goes for Cousy or anybody else. A local yokel doesn't bring more than a dozen extra fans into your building. But a winning team does and that's what I aim to have."

WON TWICE AT WASHINGTON

Auerbach, who won two Eastern division titles with Washington and was beaten in the playoff finals by Minneapolis in 1949 and this past year lifted

Arnold "Red" Auerbach

[Ed] Leede. Remember, Leede has already made the grade and Cousy has to prove he can. Maybe he will but I think it was more important to us to get a big man like Share."

The new Celts coach, who was signed but not announced prior to the draft meeting, is high on Cooper because the ex-Duquesne star, who will become the first Negro to play in the N. B. A., is a crack rebound man.

"We are going to build a club, not to step up a notch or two just to make the playoffs," "Red" drove home, "but one to finish in first place if not next year, the year after. We want a team to compare with Syracuse and Minneapolis. We have height now. We need experience and balance."

Celtics Sign Cooper, 1st Negro in Majors

July 1, 1950

"I hope he'll be with us a long time," said Walter Brown, president of the Garden-Arena, nodding in the direction of a tall, good-looking Negro.

Charles Cooper, 23, an All-American basket ball player at Duquesne, said in a soft voice, "I'll do my best all the time."

FIRST TO SIGN CONTRACT

He had become the first member of his race to sign a contract to play for a major league basket ball team yesterday morning when he had been signed to a Celtics' contract by Brown.

"I don't think the pro game is too different from college ball," Cooper said. "I had a taste of the pro game playing with the Harlem Globetrotters against the College All-Stars this year on a tour of the country."

A great rebound man, he was the second draft choice of the Celtics this year. Charles Share, Bowling Green's 6-foot-10 ace, was the Celtics' first choice.

"I like to play a driving game," Cooper said. "My best shot is a two-hand overhead shot from the corners. I use very little arc on the shot."

Tri-Cities out of the doldrums when he took over during the season, is enthusiastic over his new post.

"I always had a hankering to come here," he related, "and I was on your Boston payroll as a scout while coaching at Duke last year before moving to Tri-Cities."

Auerbach was elated over the Celtics acquisition of Easy Ed Macauley, Ed Stanczak, Charlie Share and Chuck Cooper in the recent N. B. A. draft meetings at Chicago.

"I think we've got some real ballplayers now," he went on. "Macauley is the second-best center in the league to [George] Mikan now, and as time goes on, I feel he'll be the best. He is unselfish as a team player."

"Red" defended Walter Brown's choice of Share, 6 feet 11 inches, Bowling Green star, over local favorite Bob Cousy, in the college draft.

"Proof is that 11, at least, of the dozen league teams would have selected Share as their first draft choice," declared Auerbach. "I'm sure he will make the grade. Right now I don't regard Cousy as good as

SCOUTED TWO YEARS

Brown said Cooper had been scouted for more than two years. "Stan Noszka, Celtics' scout, was the first to recommend him. Doggie Julian, our former coach, wanted Cooper, too. Charlie will be a big help to the Celtics with his corner shots and with his ability to clear the backboards. He represents a big step in our efforts to add strength to our team."

Cooper is 6 feet 5 inches and weighs 215. His home is in Pittsburgh, where he was a letter carrier after his graduation from Westinghouse High School. In high school he was on the track and basket ball teams. He's fast; can run 440 yards in 52 seconds.

He played on the Boston Garden floor once, two years ago, but would rather not talk about it. "It was against Boston College," he said, "and I played the worst game of my career."

Cooper was in the Navy in 1945 and 1946 and played one year of service basket ball. His best season in college was two years ago, when he had an average of better than 14 points a game. His scoring potential was never realized at Duquesne because of the "hold-the-ball" style of play used by the Dukes.

Bob Cousy in his Holy Cross days, circa 1947.

Bob Cousy Assigned to Boston Celtics

October 6, 1950

The players of the Chicago Stags, the team which recently dropped out of the National Basket Ball Association, were allocated to other teams at a special meeting of the N.B.A.'s board of governors in New York yesterday.

This is how the players were distributed:

Bob Cousy to Boston.
Kleggie Hermsen to Tri-Cities.
Larry Foust to Fort Wayne.
Frank Kudelka and Joe Bradley
  to Washington.
Max Zaslofsky to New York.
Andy Phillip to Philadelphia.

Macauley Sets Celtic Scoring Mark in 100-90 Triumph

SCORES 33 POINTS AS KNICKS FALTER UNDER TORRID THIRD PERIOD BARRAGE

January 1, 1951 • by Jack Barry

Rallying behind the continued brilliance of Ed Macauley, the Celtics hurdled back into the N. B. A.'s Eastern sector first place as they overcame a one-time 15-point deficit to down the New York Knickerbockers, 100 to 90, at the Arena yesterday afternoon.

As 5,456 fans howled themselves hoarse, the Celtics fashioned a 30-point third period. This impetus carried them to a spectacular final stanza victory.

Macauley, who set a new Celtic individual game scoring mark for the season with 33 points, was aided immensely by Bob Cousy, who embellished his 21-point scoring total with another superlative ball handling exhibition.

MAHNKEN SHOT PROVIDES SPARK

Not to be overlooked in the tremendous second-half comeback, which marked the end of the Knicks' five-game winning streak and dropped them into third place, were the spirited performances of big John Mahnken and bustling Bob Donham.

Mahnken, taking a shooting dare from his personal opponent, the cagy Sweetwater Clifton, dropped a long two-hand set shot through the meshes to break an 85-all stalemate with five minutes to play in the final quarter. The Celtics were not headed after that.

Donham, whose customary late-game appearances seem to spur his mates to superior efforts, again sparked the third-period uprising with aggressive floor play, while scoring on the three shots he attempted. Donham was given a rousing ovation by the fans as he was relieved by Sonny Hertzberg for game-stalling purposes.

The Celtics spun ahead to a formidable late-game seven-point advantage, on three foul shots and a beautiful combination play between Cousy and Macauley.

In a delaying dribble, Cousy saw Macauley drift away from the covering Simmons and Bob sent a nifty lead pass to "Mac" under the hoop. Macauley scored, giving the Celtics a 90-86 advantage.

TAP-OFF TIPS

Macauley amazes even his teammates . . . the great center, perhaps the most valuable man in the league right now, including even George Mikan, did everything right. . . . Joe Lapchick, coach of the Knicks, sent in big man after big man to check Easy Ed and all they received for their troubles were personal fouls. . . . In addition to this tremendous offensive play, Macauley took care of Vince Boryla, fourth-leading scorer in the league, wrapping up that

worthy opponent in the second half. . . . Macauley has scored 590 points in 30 games for a 19.6 per-game mark.

This year's previous individual scoring high for one game was held by Cousy, who tallied 28 points at Baltimore. . . . Macauley's former high was 26.

Cousy Sets New Boston Records as Celtics Win, 93-83

39 POINTS, 16 BASKETS ECLIPSE FORMER MARKS

February 26, 1951 • by Clif Keane

Some people talk through their hats; and magicians are able to yank rabbits from theirs. But the person wearing the most talked about fedora yesterday was Walter A. Brown, owner of the Celtics basket ball team.

Out of it, Brown, last Fall, drew the name of Bob Cousy in a grab bag of names from the defunct Chicago Stags. Brown is still wearing the thing, and probably went to bed with it on his head last night after Cousy had broken a couple of local records in leading the Celtics to a 93-83 victory over the Philadelphia Warriors at the Arena.

The new records established by the ex-Holy Cross wonder were:

(1) Scoring 39 points to eliminate George Mikan's mark of 37, which the Minneapolis center established here Nov. 19, 1949, and

(2) Making 16 goals from the floor, to erase the previous total of 14 set by Ed Sadowski (Boston), Max Zaslofsky (Chicago), and Lazy Joe Fulks (Philadelphia).

Cousy also converted seven consecutive foul shots.

TALLIED ON 16 OF 25 SHOTS

Twenty-six of Cousy's points came in the first half. In the third period, with the crowd of 4,214 constantly imploring him to "keep on shooting," he was held to a single field goal.

But midway through the last quarter, when the Warriors still were battling the Celtics, and trailing only 81-73 despite Bob's great performance, Cousy scored the next 10 points for the Celtics while the Warriors were being held to a single field goal and foul.

In his collegiate career, Cousy's outstanding display came a year ago when he scored 36 points against Colgate. His all-time best, however, was 81 scored in a C. Y. O. game in St. Albans, N. Y.

Although a far cry from the league mark of 63 made by Fulks against Indianapolis, Feb. 10, '49, Cousy threw less than half the shots attempted by Lazy Joe in his record making. Fulks "hit" with 27 of 56 against Indianapolis; Cousy made good on 16 of 25 attempts.

Cousy had given a performance of almost equal stature earlier in the season against the Warriors. He scored 34 points against them. But when it was over, the Warriors, almost to a man, accused Cousy of being "a showboat."

With this display yesterday, however, the Warriors changed their tune considerably. "That was what we call a tremendous performance," said Ed Gottlieb, the team's coach. "Call it out of this world. It was real basketball playing right from the start."

The Warriors first assigned George Senesky to cover Cousy. But after the first period, in which Cousy scored 13 points, they changed their strategy and had Andy Phillip, all-star back-court man, work on him. They alternated both Senesky and Phillip in the second half.

'I Love Basket Ball,' but ... Celtics Seek Sharman, but He Says He'll Play Baseball in Cuba

September 26, 1951 • by Harold Kaese

What in the world is sports coming to?

When Bobby Doerr retired a few days ago, it was inferred that he would rather raise cattle than manage the Red Sox. And last night at Braves Field, Bill

Sharman indicated that he would rather play baseball in Cuba this Winter than basket ball in Boston.

Nobody condemned Doerr, and only a few hoop-wits will condemn Sharman, who is a rookie outfielder finishing the season with the Brooklyn Dodgers.

But Walter Brown and Red Auerbach of the Celtics will try hard to change Sharman's mind before the Dodgers leave town. Sharman was an outstanding first-year player for the Washington Capitols, until they went broke last Winter. An aggressive, punishing guard, Sharman won the respect of the Celtics for putting the noose on Bob Cousy.

"I love basket ball," admitted Sharman last evening, "but I've made up my mind to play baseball in Cuba. It will take a terrific financial deal to make me change my plans."

There is a clause in Sharman's contract with the Dodgers that permits him to play basket ball in the offseason if he chooses.

BASEBALL HAS MUCH MORE TO OFFER

"I saw the Celtics work out today," added Sharman, "and they sure have a big squad. Most of them are 6-6 or over. They look like a good team, all right."

Sharman, although only 6-2 and practically a pro basket ball midget, probably would rank as the No. 8 or 9 player on the Celtics squad this season. That's why Brown and Auerbach are working so hard on him.

But baseball—if he makes the grade as a big leaguer—offers so much more to Sharman than basket ball that he wants the experience Winter ball in Cuba will give him.

"I'm all set for Cuba," he said. "It's all arranged."

A righthand hitter who batted .285 for Fort Worth this season, Sharman obviously must improve his batting if he is to become a big leaguer. Last season he hit .288 for Pueblo, after signing with the Dodgers on leaving the University of Southern California, where he was an exceptional all-round athlete.

Until last evening, Sharman had never heard of Eddie Ehlers, the former Celtics player who quit basket ball to concentrate on baseball. He was an infielder in the Yankee farm system, and of course dreamed of wearing the New York uniform.

But Ehlers could not hit. The Yankees let him go. The Cubs grabbed him. He played at Springfield this summer, but now is reported as ready to give up baseball.

"It's a tough choice," said Sharman, "but baseball's the game if you can play up here. For one thing, you last longer."

Brown Threatens to Throw Basketball Out of Garden

SMALL ATTENDANCE HIT; 2,520 SEE CELTICS ROMP

December 3, 1951 • by Jack Barry

Boston Garden president Walter Brown, disgusted with the meager turnouts for recent Celtic games—only 2,520 saw yesterday's sixth win in seven home games—said last night, "I'll throw the whole works out of the Garden . . . and that means all basket

The Celtics' Bill Sharman (21) battles the Bullets' Frank Kudelka for a loose ball in front of a sparse Garden crowd.

ball if something doesn't happen soon in the way of improved attendances.

"It's a different reason every week," roared Brown. "We're no better off than when we started. I thought that when I gave them a good club they would come out. But I guess Boston fans just don't want basket ball!"

The Celts sent their scoring total over 100 for the third time this season as they trounced the Baltimore Bullets, 103 to 82, yesterday afternoon.

Basket Ball Comes Into Living Room.

TVIEWER SEES COUSY AS HERO, OFFICIALS VILLAINS

January 5, 1953 • by Harold Wade

Professional basket ball at its best came into the living room yesterday—but just how good is it?

The telecast over WNAC-TV of the Celtics-New York Knickerbockers game at the Arena was good. That is, the pictures were clear.

The entire court was shown. There was no trouble following the play, although it was impossible to see all the fouls. There were closeups of the basket as foul shots were taken. All in all it was a great success, pictorially.

The action was good—in spots.

The officials were good—good and prominent. They blew their horns like Little Boy Blue; they argued with the coaches, and even wound up arguing with each other.

COUSY GIVES GREAT SHOW

But armchair viewers want to take another look before they'll decide whether it is worth a Sunday afternoon of eye strain.

The first 20 minutes were terrible; the next few so-so. The last half was better; the last eight minutes great—because of the Celtics' comeback.

But basket ball on television was largely a one-man show. His name—Bob Cousy. The hardboard wizard was at his very best in some spots, and when he was passing, dribbling and shooting in his customary style, it became a good game to watch.

The plays Cousy set up for Bob Donham; Cousy's brilliant dribbling in, which he faked New York's Dick McGuire virtually out of his shoes; the underhand basket on which he tried to draw a foul—these were clearly depicted.

Ed Macauley scored 28 points—but watching him on television you didn't realize he was doing that well.

We don't know how it was on your set, but for some reason—and a mighty pleasant one at that—the sound of the referee's whistles didn't come into our living room too often. Maybe the kids were making too much noise with their Christmas toys.

Yet the officials made the first 20 minutes as uninteresting as some of the old flicker television shows you see late at night. The tempo picked up from then on, but the officials never let the boys go at it very long. A few quick baskets here and there livened the performance—but then it reverted to a foul-line parade.

The officials' arguments with coaches Red Auerbach of the Celtics and Joe Lapchick of New York were clearly pictured—although the reasons for the coaches making showboats of themselves are a little hazy.

And to top it all off, Lapchick got into an argument with the officials, and they concluded arguing with each other. It seems Lapchick wanted to know who called a foul against Macauley, and why two shots weren't awarded. Each official accused the other. It seemed to the guy in the easy chair the officials should have told Lapchick to stick to his coaching.

From a first impression, the televising of Celtics' basket ball games (they'll be on practically every Sunday for the next three months) will resolve itself into a duel between Cousy and the officials.

If the officials win—turn your sets off.

If Cousy wins—basket ball may be here to stay.

Celtics Win First Playoff Game, 87-81

22 STRAIGHT FREE TRIES IN LAST PERIOD DECIDE CONTEST AT SYRACUSE

March 20, 1953 • by Jack Barry

SYRACUSE—A superlative exhibition of pressure foul shooting in which they sank 51 free shots in 62 attempts—22 straight in the last period—gave the Celtics first blood in the best two-out-of-three series in the Eastern Sector N. B. A. playoffs, as they downed the favored Nationals 87 to 81 before 3,000 in the Coliseum.

Having lost 14 of 15 previous visits here, the Celtics won the one game they needed to keep themselves in contention and possibly prevent a return here Sunday.

GET EDGE IN THIRD

Boston managed to seize the advantage in the closing moments of the third period. This meant the ball game, as it decided the final period strategy of both clubs.

The Celtics were down, 47 to 44, with two minutes to play in the third period when the tide turned.

Bob Donham, spectacular in the early moments, batted home a rebound and Bob Cousy dropped in a one-hander from the side on Paul Seymour.

Donham and then Bob Harris sank free tries before Noble Jorgensen connected for a soft righthand push shot to bring the Nats back to a 50-49 deficit.

Harris converted another foul and after both Red Rocha and Bill Gabor missed free tosses, Cousy sent a spectacular long, one-hand push shot through from the side as the bell rang.

The Celtics took a 53-49 margin into the final period and it proved sufficient to dictate the strategy of the game.

Harris scored after Cousy took an offensive rebound to feed him for a 55-49 margin, and after Gabor sunk a foul, Donham, driving in after a Cousy assist, sank one to offset an Earl Lloyd conversion and a basket by Jorgensen.

Here, with eight minutes to play and the Celtics leading 57-53, the foul-swapping started.

25 STRAIGHT FOULS

Boston destroyed this strategy as it racked up 22 straight conversions. It got three in the third for a run of 25.

The Nats did not score a field goal until three minutes from the end, when Boston was ahead 79-66.

There were 96 fouls called.

Celts Nip Nats in 4 Overtimes, 111-105

COUSY GETS 50 POINTS; BOSTON SWEEPS SERIES. BRANNUM, SCHAYES SWAP PUNCHES, TOSSED OUT OF GAME IN SECOND PERIOD

March 22, 1953 • by Jack Barry

In an individual basket ball exhibition practically defying description, the Celtics' great Bob Cousy steered the Boston club to a four-overtime 111 to 105 victory over the rugged Syracuse Nationals before 11,058 frenzied Garden fans yesterday afternoon.

The Celtics' wizard thus placed Boston in a play-off with the New York Knicks in the National Basket Ball Association semifinals, starting Wednesday night in Madison Sq. Garden.

What Cousy did:

(1) Scored 50 points on 10 baskets and 30 free throws for a Garden-Arena record and season's individual scoring mark, after scoring only seven points in the first half.

(2) Scored 30 free tries in 32 "pressure" attempts.

(3) Tied the game at the end of regulation play at 77-all, with the third of his successive free tosses, to send the game into the first five-minute extra session.

(4) Scored six points in the first extra session, including the last free throw, which matched a Nats' conversion to bring about the second extra session.

(5) Scored two of four points in the second over-time to aid in bringing about a third extra session, which started 90-all.

(6) Scored eight of the Celtics' nine points in the third extra session, including two vital baskets. Here Cousy arose to the greatest heights, when with but 18 seconds left, he tied the game 97-all on two free throws, and after Syracuse went ahead, 99-97—WITH THREE SECONDS remaining, dropped in a beautiful one-hand push shot from 25 feet out to send the game into its fourth extra period, 99-apiece, as the crowd went wild.

(With this Cousy basket, Syracuse, which played half of the third overtime period and the entire fourth with Paul Seymour limping badly, trooped to its bench, practically a beaten club.)

(7) Scored nine of the 12 points in the final period, sparking the Celtics from a five-point, 104-99 deficit with three and one-half minutes left, as fans started leaving the building.

SCORES 18 STRAIGHT

Cousy sank 18 successive free tries and played the last two overtime periods despite the onus of five personal fouls. The great back-court ace was so exhausted that on two occasions, he all but "blew" the game for the Celtics with a bad shot and a weird pass, which lost possession in vital moments.

The marvelous machinations of Cousy overshad-owed a near-riot, instigated by fisticuffs between Bob Brannum and Dolph Schayes at the halfway mark of the second period.

Both players were ejected by referees Arnie Heft and Charley Eckman, who turned in nearly perfect officiating under the heaviest pressure.

Garden gendarmes presented a free-for-all, as Syracuse players, led by Paul Seymour and Bill Gabor, attempted to take on Boston's best-in-blue all by themselves.

Bob Cousy confounded the Nationals with his playmaking, scoring (50 points), and foul shooting (30 makes in 32 attempts).

SEYMOUR STAYS IN

Although Cousy alone kept Boston in N. B. A. contention and sent them into their semifinal series for the first time in seven years, the team as a whole contributed to this thriller.

After 63 minutes of pell-mell basket ball, the fourth extra session started with the teams 99-all. Fans with weak hearts had left the building before that.

The Celtics were down to a five of John Mahnken, Moe Mahoney, Ken Rollins, Chuck Cooper and Cousy, while the Nats played with player-coach Al Cervi, Wally Osterkorn, big Earl Lloyd, Red Rocha and Paul Seymour.

Seymour had twisted his right ankle with the score 93-apiece after two minutes of play in the third overtime. Rather than have an ineligible man replace him, which would have given Boston a technical foul shot (Syracuse having five men out of the game via six fouls and Schayes for fighting), Seymour remained in.

The Celtics, meanwhile, were handicapped with Brannum out for fighting and Ed Macauley, Bob Donham, Bill Sharman and Bob Harris out on fouls.

Here the Nats jumped ahead and seemed to have the game wrapped up as Cervi scored a free throw and then Cooper, on his sixth personal, fouled Rocha, with the Nats drawing the automatic extra throw as Chuck was forced to remain in the game, Boston being without eligible substitutes.

Rocha flipped in his shot and then Cervi, as the crowd booed, stepped up and tossed in the technical try. Syracuse got possession and the Celts were in a bad way.

It got worse. After Cervi muffed a free try, the alert Rocha drove to tip in the rebound for a 104-99 margin and the crowd moaned on their way to the exits.

But Cousy sank a free throw and batted home a Rollins rebound of a missed pop shot. Bob then stole a shallow Syracuse pass and went in alone for a soft left-hand backward two-pointer to knot the count as the crowd screamed.

With two minutes and 32 seconds left, freshman Mahoney grabbed the ball from Cervi. In the ensuing scramble, Mahnken was fouled and came through with a one-pointer. Earl Lloyd then fouled Rollins and Kenny dropped it in for a 106-104 margin.

The Celtics got a decided break moments later when the veteran Cervi went to the line for two tosses, and after flipping the first through, missed the second, with Cooper batting the rebound to Cousy, who drew a Rocha personal on his way down court.

The Cooz missed the first, his second miscue in 28 tries, but sank the second, with the Celtics still retaining possession, as Rocha had six personals on him.

With one minute and two seconds remaining, the Celts had a two-point margin, but Cervi, drawing his sixth personal, fouled Cousy and Bob sank both shots, with Boston regaining possession at 109-105.

Cooper scored on a free try and Cousy wound up the night flipping in a technical on the violation for a 111-105 victory.

Celts' Draft Choices Delight Auerbach

April 26, 1953 • by Jack Barry

With the conclusion of the National Basket Ball Association's seventh annual three-day meeting at the Hotel Statier yesterday, Coach Red Auerbach of the Celtics was pleased with his first two draft choices.

Auerbach plucked Frank Ramsey of the University of Kentucky and big Chester Noe of Oregon as his first two selections. "I like Ramsey," said the Celtics' coach. "He can bring that ball up the court like a [Jim] Pollard. He is big, tough and nasty and I know he can help us . . . he stands 6-4. He has a good outside set, can drive and can take care of his man on defense."

HEADED FOR SERVICE

Ramsey, who has a year of eligibility left (the Kentucky Wildcats were suspended from collegiate play this past year), may return for a fourth season of basket ball there . . . and again he may not. He is ticketed for Uncle Sam's service and Boston may have a two-year or possible three-year wait for this fellow. This does not disturb Auerbach, however, who said, "We drafted the best men we could get, whether we were to have him this year or three years from now."

Speaking of Cliff Hagan, Ramsey's running mate, third Celtic draft choice, who also has another year of playing left at Kentucky, if he prefers to return, Red said, "He is a good ball player . . . in fact was perhaps the best high school pivot man in the country.

"He may not be able to play there in the pro game, being only six-four. But I can say this for him. He can leap with men much taller than he is."

Cousy Injured as Celtics, Philly Players Battle

November 12, 1953 • by Clif Keane

It was Armistice Day and a packed crowd at the Garden was having such a pleasant time. The Harlem Globetrotters had been funny and the Celtics were creeping up on the Philadelphia Warriors in their N.B.A. game.

But at 9:57 of the second period a "war" broke out. Players piled into one another in a general melee, police leaped into the picture, and another armistice wasn't declared for almost 10 minutes. Bob Cousy was hurt, and so was everyone connected with the Celtics when the Warriors went on to win, 78-72, for their first victory here in two years.

There were many versions to who whacked whom, but it went about like this:

Both Cousy and Neil Johnston were chasing a loose ball headed out of bounds toward the press table. Johnston was a step ahead of Cousy, and as they reached the sideline, going full speed, Cousy elbowed Johnston and the big Philly center went careening to the work bench.

Johnston reached back and elbowed Cousy under the chin, sending the Celtic player reeling backwards—and flush into Chuck Cooper, who was trailing the pair just in case something happened. So Cousy wound up flat on his silks on the floor and watched this scene unfold.

Cooper piled into Johnston, draped over several writers, swinging his fists madly at the Warrior. Then both benches moved into the scene. Zeke Zawoluk leaped on Cooper; Bob Harris slashed into Zawoluk; then Ed Mikan went after Zawoluk.

All the while, Cooper kept pummeling Johnston. Big Bob Brannum decided he'd take a crack at Zawoluk. A half-dozen Warriors and Celtics were wrestling around in a little fracas, also. The police were pulling players apart and Danny Finn of the visitors got a little tough with one of them and almost got the business.

FOUL! WHO, ME?

Finally, order was restored. Amazingly, there were no broken jaws since there were enough punches thrown to hospitalize several people—and then came the *piece de resistance*.

"A foul on Joe Fulks," said the announcer. The officials probably thought the gaffer deserved one for not throwing any punches.

Cousy admitted making the first move. He had been held by Paul Walther and said he "was mad" as he twisted away from Walther and headed toward the ball.

"I pushed Johnston," he said, and it cost Cousy a badly bruised right side, which he had X-rayed at St. Vincent's Hospital in Worcester last night. He may be incapacitated for a couple of days, according to Dr. Thomas Kelley.

Maybe all the fight was taken out of the Celtics with their punch throwing since they couldn't do much right the rest of the game.

Boston did forge ahead, 31-29, at the half, but after Ed Macauley, high man in the game with 23 points, had dropped in a foul shot opening the third period, the Warriors chased the Celtics off the floor. They led once by 16 points, and only a brief spurt by Cousy in the last couple of minutes kept the score at all respectable.

This was the second defeat at home for the Celtics and leaves them with a 1-3 record—and when it was over coach Red Auerbach had this to say to the team:

"You fellows have something to think about the way you've been playing."

Game Syracuse Rallies to Eliminate Celtics, 83-76

FIGHT DELAYS GAME FOR 25 MINUTES. NATS' SCHAYES, SEYMOUR INJURED; BOSTON OUTPLAYED, OUTSMARTED

March 28, 1954 • by Jack Barry

The Celtics bowed out of National Basket Ball Association competition ingloriously at the Garden yesterday afternoon being given a triple lesson in basket ball playing, basket ball coaching and plain, ordinary courage by the Syracuse Nationals.

From the four-minute, six-second mark of the third period the beleaguered Nats, whose roster resembled a hospital ward, took the play away from the Celtics completely. Rallying from a 53 to 47 deficit, they won the Eastern Sector finals, 83 to 76, after a near-riot had delayed play for 25 minutes.

Thus, Al Cervi, who declared the victory was his "greatest personal thrill as player or coach," will send the Nats against the Western Sector winner for the 1954 title.

It well could be, however, that Cervi, who can still play if needed, will have to don a uniform himself, as the Nats' victory may have cost them the services of Dolph Schayes with a sprained left wrist and Paul Seymour with a possible broken right hand.

Owner Walter Brown, disturbed, disappointed and disgusted, calmly stated an hour after the game, "There's nothing wrong with the game, nor with Boston as a basket ball town . . . but I'll tell you this, if I have to lose, I'm certainly going to lose a lot cheaper than I am now."

Red Auerbach, a picture of despair in the dressing room and later when feeling up to the quoting mark, at least took the onus of the defeat on his own shoulders.

Said Auerbach, "I blew the ball game. I should have taken time outs when we had the lead in the third period when they only had one left and we had a couple, but I thought if I pressed 'em I'd force 'em to maybe take another, or we'd just run 'em off the court. I'll take the rap."

NATS CUT MARGIN

The Celtics and Nats were tied 21-all ending the first period and Boston sported a 50-40 margin at halftime on the springboard of a 29-point second period. Things looked very well.

The game Nats had cut the deficit to five, trailing 52-47, in three minutes of play, mainly because the Celtics played as a team 10 points down, running, heaving and passing wildly, taking poor judgment shots and playing right into Al Cervi's hands. Jack Nichols, Bob Cousy and Don Barksdale were the guilty parties setting up ball possession chances to the Nats here.

A hoop by Wally Osterkorn, after a ball steal and five foul conversions, overshadowed Barksdale's lone Celtic basket in this three-minute interval. A foul conversion by Gabby Harris, who had replaced

Barksdale, gave Boston a 53-47 advantage at the 4:05 mark of this period . . . and then it happened.

Schayes, taking the ball at the right of the center key-line, started a typical drive towards the hoop, when Harris, in a half-crouch defensive stance, hurtled big Dolph over his body.

Schayes was "out of action" for 10 minutes, retiring to the Nats dressing room, where Dr. Thomas Kelley sewed four stitches in the side of the player's head. In addition the big Nat center suffered what may be a badly sprained left wrist.

Harris' fouling of Schayes touched off a near-riotous scene, which was broken up by police, and the alert, aggressive referee Sid Borgia. Wally Osterkorn went after Harris here and hardly was some sort of peace restored when he attacked Ed Macauley after a conversational joust between the pair. Paul Seymour fractured his right thumb, hitting Macauley in the jam.

TAKE TIME OUT

Basketball rules state that a player must shoot his own foul shot or be barred from further participation. While Dr. Kelley was working on Schayes in the dressing room, the Syracuse club used up three more "time outs."

The rumpus delayed play about 25 minutes.

When Schayes finally returned, he missed both foul attempts. The Celtics led 53-47 here with seven minutes left.

To the end of the period the Celtics scored seven free throws with a pair of baskets by Cousy and a two-pointer by Bill Sharman. Meanwhile the Nats racked up five baskets, with the gangling rookie, Jim Neal, contributing a pair. These added to seven free throws left the Nats only two points down, 66-64, entering the final period.

In their surge, the plucky Nats stole the ball again from Cousy, grabbed rebounds and took advantage of the Celtics' insistence in stressing a fast-wild shooting weird passing offensive to put themselves right back in the ball game.

The Celtics still held the upper hand in the final quarter but their mental balance was out of kilter. They appeared to realize the tremendous battle they had on their hands in the face of the spirit and fight shown by the handicapped visitors, who had cut a 10-point deficit to a mere two, with Schayes,

Seymour and Earl Lloyd all on the bench, physically unable to play.

Barksdale dropped in a rush shot, when Cousy got the ball back to him from in deep. Here was one time the Boston club played basket ball the way it should be played.

The skinny Bob Lavoy managed to get in for an offensive rebound score to tie the ball game with eight minutes left and a triple pass found the aggressive Osterkorn under the hoop alone for a soft layup.

After a Sharman foul shot Nichols' pass attempt to Cousy was intercepted and George King seconds later backed Cousy in deep to turn and toss a soft one-hander from a foot in front.

Lavoy sank a foul, but Nichols kept the Celtics alive with a left-hand hook. Barksdale went out with six fouls and Lavoy again converted the foul shot. Bill Kenville likewise scored his shot after a Bob Donham foul.

NATS SLOW PACE

Cousy managed to score a basket despite bad position. But the clever King slowed the Nats' offensive deliberately, playing with time on their side. Lavoy tallied again from the charity stripe but Harris, still battling, stole from Osterkorn at mid-court to go all the way for a 76-75 reading, Syracuse ahead.

Here Stan Stutz called the first deliberate foul of the game on Harris, with Lavoy making one of two tries. The Celts lost a good chance at possession of the stray rebound on the Lavoy miss, when Ernie Barrett tapped the ball away instead of trying to catch it, with the alert Osterkorn cradling the ball.

This forced Cousy, playing close, to foul King, who made it. After Cousy and Donham missed basket tries, King picked up the rebound to flip to Lavoy alone under for a soft two-pointer and what was the ball game, 80-75 with two minutes left.

On a tap play between Osterkorn and Sharman, Nichols missed possession and Donham, fouling Kenville, saw Sid Borgia call another deliberate foul, but Kenville missed both tries.

Nichols took a weird left-hand hook shot as the harassed Celtics had no semblance of setting up team plays and Barrett fouled Kenville in the back court for an automatic two-shot penalty.

Kenville made one and after the Celtics again tried out-of-position desperation shots. The Nats rebounded to feed big Neal all alone for the game's last score.

The Syracuse bench was in bedlam, jumping around just before Neal's final score, hooting the Boston fans, shaking their fists in derision, showing their unbridled joy at coming from behind under the most difficult handicaps on an opponent's court.

'Celtics Quit'—Brown; Auerbach Status Vague

March 29, 1954 • by Jack Barry

Walter Brown, Celtics' owner, was still incensed over the collapse of his ball club when he was asked yesterday whether Red Auerbach will coach the team next season.

"I don't know," Brown snapped.

But although Brown is uncertain about his coach's status, there is little doubt how he feels about his players and their performance in the Syracuse series.

"THEY QUIT," he exploded.

Then, partially absolving Auerbach by implication, Brown asked, "What is a coach going to do when his team quits?"

"I want to win," Brown went on. "I'll do anything to win. I'll trade anyone on the ball club if necessary."

"Does that include Bob Cousy?" he was asked.

"I said anyone," Brown retorted.

SALARY CUTS THREATENED

Concerning Auerbach, Brown said, "Auerbach is the coach. We haven't talked yet about next year. He is not on a contract. In fact, he never had one. We just sign year to year. Up to now I've not thought of anyone else. And I don't know what plans he (Red) himself may have for the future.

"But I'll tell you this," Brown added vehemently, "if I have to lose, I'm certainly going to lose a lot cheaper than I am now. These guys will get what I think are honest salaries. And they can sign or refuse as they wish. I've been running this club with my heart for eight years, now I'm going to start running it with my head."

(Ed. Note—The Celtics organization lost about $30,000 this season).

"But we're staying in business. We've been knocked down for eight years, but we'll keep digging," concluded Brown, who is a charter member of the pro basket ball league along with Ned Irish of New York and Eddie Gottlieb of Philadelphia.

Cousy let it be known yesterday that he bore no ill feeling toward Coach Auerbach.

Said Cousy, "I think Red is a good coach. I've had no trouble with him. In my book there is not much a coach can do in pro ball. He makes the substitutions and tries to keep everyone happy. A coach can win or lose few games, I believe. I never care who is coaching. I'll play the same way all the time . . . to win."

Auerbach Stays as Celtics Coach; Takes Salary Cut

March 30, 1954 • by Jack Barry

Arnold (Red) Auerbach, whose status as coach of the Celtics was decidedly questionable Sunday night, was retained as bench leader of the Boston professional basket ball club for the 1955 season by owner Walter Brown yesterday.

While making no public announcement at last night's Celtics break-up dinner, Brown admitted later in the evening that Auerbach was rehired for next year.

"I rehired Red Auerbach," said the Celtics owner, "and I don't mind saying that he took a cut in salary. That was one of the conditions of his staying, which shows that I hold him partially responsible for the poor showing of our team this year."

"There were no conditions of any sort in his contract," said Brown, in answer to a query. "In fact, Red never has signed a contract with me. I have just been hiring him from year to year."

NINTH SEASON IN LEAGUE

Auerbach will be starting his ninth season in National Basketball Association ball, with owner coach Eddie Gottlieb of Philadelphia, the only other bench coach still in charge of an N. B. A. team since the loop's inception back in 1946.

The Celtics were picked by many preseason prognosticators to lead the Eastern Sector, but finished third to New York and Syracuse and were eliminated in semifinal round-robin play by the Nats.

Auerbach in his four-year regime in Boston won 166 regular-season games, dropping 112, while his playoff record over the same time has been six wins and 13 losses.

The Celtics coach came in for criticism when his charges were eliminated last year by New York, failing to hold a half-time 14-point lead, and this season, Saturday afternoon, when they lost to Syracuse after sporting a half-time 10-point margin.

The club received a blow yesterday when big Jack Nichols, late-season star of the team, announced his plans to retire from the pro game to enter either the University of Washington Dental School or Tufts Dental School here.

Should Nichols, however, be able to study at Tufts, he still would not play ball here as Walter Brown definitely stated last night, "I can't use any more players on a part-time basis. I had one, George Munroe, who attended Harvard Law School and played with the Celtics, but it doesn't work out."

Celtics Must Rebuild; Still Seeking 'Big Man'

March 29, 1955 • by Jack Barry

Next season looms as a rebuilding year for the Boston Celtics.

Owner Walter Brown has to be prepared for the possible loss of Ed Macauley (retirement) and Frank Ramsey (service) and to be handicapped again with a semi effective Jack Nichols, due to his Tufts Dental School work.

With Fred Scolari retiring after nine years in the N. B. A., Brown and Coach Red Auerbach can look forward to a nucleus of Bob Cousy, Bill Sharman, Bob Brannum and Togo Palazzi. Palazzi proved conclusively in the last two playoff games that he belongs.

CELTICS EYE SHARE

Red Morrison must show he has the stuff to be Boston's "big man," but Don Barksdale does not appear to be the answer to the rugged rebounding needed. Should there be a chance to buy Milwaukee's Chuck Share, Brown will toss his bankroll again at Ben Kerner.

The Celtics must come up with a big man, an able rebounder in the coming collegiate draft in April. Even then the chances of beating vastly improved Philadelphia with Tom Gola and others, Syracuse and New York for the three playoff berths loom as decidedly tough.

Brown and Auerbach can look ahead to 1957, which will see them picking up Lou Tsiropoulos, Cliff Hagan and either Holy Cross' Tom Heinsohn or one of the many brilliant seniors of next year leaving school. Ramsey feels he may be out of the Army by January, 1957.

The Boston Celtics' lineup in the winter of 1957 could well read: centers, Share and Morrison; forwards, Palazzi, Hagan, Wally Stokes (possible draft choice this spring) and either Jack Nichols or Bob Brannum. In the back court, Bob Cousy, Bill Sharman, Frank Ramsey and Tsiropoulos.

Brown, of course, is pleased with the improved attendance this year and feels that New England fans like what they saw.

CELTS WIN PLAYOFF OPENER

ONE OF 3 BEST COUSY EVER PLAYED

March 18, 1956 • by Clif Keane

Of all the basket ball games Bob Cousy has played, collegiate and professional, there are three that stand out.

> 1. A sensational display against Columbia in a losing cause when the Holy Cross whiz brought his club from far back late in the game with six baskets in slightly more than two minutes.

2. The 50-point display Cousy offered against the Syracuse Nats three years ago to bring the Celtics a four-overtime victory in the playoffs.

3. Yesterday against the same Nats.

There have been times when Cousy was more spectacular, but careless somewhere through the game. Many times he scored more than the 29 he poured through the basket yesterday. But never had he shown such mechanical perfection as against those Nats yesterday.

COUSY RELISHES VICTORY

The great player was quick to put the performance among his all-time best, especially since it came against the club he loves to whip. Those taunts from Al Cervi over the years have given Cousy a bitter hate for the Nats, and he sat licking his lips like a kid who was finishing off a double-decked ice-cream cone.

"Nice to beat those guys," he said in the Celtics' dressing room. "And I guess it was one of my best games, all right. I don't think I ever ran that much in two years on a court. But I wanted to win that game, so bad."

At the start, Cousy was a little fearful of just what was in store for him. At the other end of the court, Cervi had decided to use four big men, Dolph Schayes, Red Rocha, Ed Conlin and Earl Lloyd.

Who was going to cover the extra big man, who certainly would take either Cousy or Bill Sharman into the pivot with him?

As Cousy surveyed the huddled Nats' group, he offered to take the man who would move into the hole. Undoubtedly it was going to be Conlin, who had about three inches on Cousy and undoubtedly would be fed the ball consistently to. "I figured out that my longer reach would help more than Sharman could offer," said Cousy. "And I knew that with Sid Borgia refereeing under the basket, he wouldn't let Conlin get away with any backing in on me."

EVERYTHING OK AFTER CALL

"So I told Red [Auerbach] to let me handle him," said Cousy. "And sure enough, Conlin backed in on me early in the first quarter and Borgia called it on him. After that we were all right."

Cousy thought the Nats would hardly curl up and be easy bait for the second game at Syracuse Monday night. "But we can lick them up there," he said. "And if we don't, we'll beat them back here on Wednesday night."

Sharman, who had Rocha covering him until the Nats decided their strategy of four big men wasn't the answer, played another of his typically strong games, scoring 20 points.

Defensively, he stuffed George King inside his shirt, and the clever backcourt player, who usually gives the Celtics stretches of torment, wound up with only nine points.

RIVAL OWNER RAPS COUSY

"Why didn't they call some fouls on Cousy out there with Conlin?" asked Nats owner Danny Biasone. "Who is he that he can get away with pawing at everyone?"

"Aw, that wasn't it," said Cervi. "Cousy played a helluva ballgame."

"Yeah, you're right," said Biasone. "At his very best out there today. But I think we can still lick them, huh, Al?"

He didn't get too much consolation from Cervi, who half-smiled and said, "Well, let's hope we can. They're tough."

"The guy [Cousy] was marvelous," said captain Paul Seymour. "I never saw him better against us, anyway. A great show he put on out there."

'We Read the Papers'. Nats Were 'Up' and Fighting Mad at Story of Illegal Benches, Ball.

March 22, 1956 • by Herb Ralby

Bob Cousy, his head in his hands, and his eyes full of tears, sat stunned on one bench in the Celtics dressing room.

On another bench were Bill Sharman and coach Red Auerbach staring into space.

It just didn't seem possible to them that they had been eliminated from the N. B. A. playoffs by the underdog Syracuse Nationals.

"Nichols, Loscutoff, Hemric, Macauley," muttered Auerbach. "They just couldn't put the ball in the basket. Syracuse couldn't miss. It was one of those nights."

Bob Brannum, former Celt and now a prosperous candy salesman, was moving around consoling his ex-mates.

"That second-period stretch was the killer," he said. "They got seven straight baskets on seven shots. Man, that's real shooting. Schayes, Kenville, [Dick] Farley. They couldn't miss."

Arnie Risen, the eight-year veteran of N. B. A. competition, came over and put his arm around Auerbach.

"Sorry, coach," he consoled. "We just couldn't seem to get that big basket."

The 6-9 Risen, whose brilliant third-period play almost lifted the Celtics from a 12-point deficit into the lead, could offer no explanation.

"Some nights they drop for you," he said. "Other nights they don't. Everything they shot went right through the hoop tonight. We were bouncing them off the rim."

There was no denying that Syracuse was "up" for the deciding game and amid joyous war whoops and lifting their elated coach, Al Cervi, on their shoulders in the dressing, George King explained why.

INCENSED BY NEWS STORIES

"You guys (referring to the writers) won the game for us just as you have the past couple of years," King declared. "Two years ago we were just the garbage of the league. Last year we were something else.

"This time you claimed we used an over-inflated ball and had illegal benches. The boys were pretty mad at those accusations just as they were at the charges the past two years and we took it out on the Celtics."

Cervi admitted he didn't have to give his boys a pep talk before the game.

"We all read the papers," he said.

Auerbach Will Be Back in Fall; Brown Sees Hub Sold on Game

March 24, 1956 • by Jack Barry

Mid-season rumors that had Coach Red Auerbach of the Celtics accepting a college coaching offer were shattered last night at the Celtics breakup dinner.

He is definitely returning to coach Boston next year.

Auerbach told his player last night, "You had better be in condition when you report next year. If you're not, don't show up." He smiled: "That means I'll be back."

Owner Walter Brown expressed his disappointment that the Celtics were eliminated from the playoffs, but said, "After 48 hours to think it over I don't feel quite so badly.

"We had two jobs to do here in Boston. First, to sell basket ball, which I think we've done, and second, to try and win a championship.

"We haven't had the championship yet, but we can't get discouraged. This year's team, picked fourth before the season, gave it all they had. I'll always be proud of them," Brown continued.

Brown singled out his three old pros, Ed Macauley, Bob Cousy and Bill Sharman, for special mention, saying, "I'll never be able to do enough for them."

2 THE BILL RUSSELL DYNASTY

(1957-1969)

A full measure of Bill Russell's impact on the sport of basketball, culture, race, and American society as a whole requires not sentences, paragraphs, or chapters, but volumes. And yet his seismic and unmatchable effect on the Celtics can be found in seven neat words, tucked away in *Globe* writer Jack Barry's game story on the championship-clinching victory over the Philadelphia Warriors on April 27, 1964.

"Russell," he wrote, "*who does not know how to lose,* led the Celtics to their seventh world title in eight years . . . "

Who does not know how to lose. It was the perfect, matter-of-fact summation not just of Russell's tenure with the Celtics but also of his basketball life as a whole. During his time at the University of San Francisco and then as the fulcrum of the Celtics' dynasty, his teams played in 21 winner-take-all games. Russell's record in such games? 21-0.

No, Russell's Celtics did not win *every* year during his 13 with the franchise, including the last four (1966-69) as player/coach. They fell in the 1958 Finals, Russell's second year, to Bob Pettit and the St. Louis Hawks in six games, but there was a caveat. Russell missed Games 4, 5, and most of 6 after spraining his ankle in Game 3. And the Celtics did not win the title in 1967, falling to rival Wilt Chamberlain and the Philadelphia 76ers in six games in the East finals.

In all, the Celtics won 11 championships in Russell's 13 seasons, starting with his rookie year in 1957, when fellow freshman Tommy Heinsohn scored 37 points and grabbed 23 rebounds in a Game 7 double-overtime victory over the Hawks. The Celtics won in Russell's final year, 1969, when, despite finishing in fourth place in the East during the regular season, they found their form during the postseason, beating the Lakers of Chamberlain, Jerry West, and Elgin Baylor by 2 points in the seventh game of the Finals in Los Angeles.

In between those losses in 1958 and 1967, the Celtics won eight straight titles, with Russell's Celtics eliminating Chamberlain's team five times in that span. It was fitting, then, that when the Celtics prevailed in 1969—leaving balloons, prematurely placed for a Lakers celebration, suspended in the

‹ Bill Russell dunks with 2 seconds remaining and sends the matchup with the Sixers into overtime, February 9, 1969.

Forum rafters—Chamberlain, who habitually shrunk in big moments, pulled himself from the game, his disgusted coach Butch van Breda Kolff refusing to put him back in.

Chamberlain, who once scored 100 points in a game and averaged over 50 in a single season, is arguably the greatest individual player in basketball history. Russell is inarguably the greatest team player, his relentless rebounding and unprecedented shot-blocking prowess changing the sport from a horizontal to vertical game. Before or since, there is no more successful professional team athlete than Russell in American sports history. He lost, occasionally. He did not ever *know* how to lose.

Russell's reach and his fearlessness were not limited to the basketball court. "He is," Bob Ryan once wrote admiringly, "one of the most independent thinkers and magnetic personalities in the history of American athletics." Russell was a trailblazer among athletes using their platforms to take a stand on social and cultural issues. In 1963, he attended Martin Luther King Jr.'s "I Have a Dream" speech in front of the Lincoln Memorial during the march in Washington. In 1967, he joined other prominent Black athletes in speaking out in support of Muhammad Ali's refusal to serve in the Vietnam War.

When two of the Celtics' Black players were refused service at a hotel café in Kentucky in 1961, Russell helped organize a player boycott of a preseason game against the St. Louis Hawks. While race was never a factor in Red Auerbach's assemblage of his team—the Celtics featured the first all-Black starting lineup in league history during a game against St. Louis in 1964, and he tabbed Russell as his coaching successor, making him the first Black coach in the history of American team sports— Russell endured vile threats and behavior. While the Celtics were on a road trip in 1963, an intruder broke into Russell's home in Reading, defecated on his bed, and destroyed his trophy case. His relationship with Boston remained complicated for decades, though it softened in his later years.

The move that brought Russell to the Celtics was the preeminent example of Auerbach's uncanny abilities to identify talent and then maneuver to acquire the players he coveted. He persuaded two teams in 1956 not to draft Russell, getting one, the St. Louis Hawks, to trade its pick to him for two players, Ed Macauley and Cliff Hagan, then persuading the other, the Rochester Royals, to bypass Russell, offering some arena-filling Ice Capades dates as an enticement.

The acquisition of Russell, who would win five Most Valuable Player awards, was far from the only example of Auerbach's roster-building savvy. Bob Cousy and Bill Sharman were already established as the league's most dynamic back court when Russell arrived, and their fast-break style benefited enormously from Russell's shot-blocking, rebounding, and deft outlet passes. Heinsohn (a territorial pick from Holy Cross) and defensive stopper K. C. Jones, Russell's San Francisco teammate, were also selected in 1956, making it unquestionably the best single-team draft class in NBA history.

Each year, it seemed Auerbach added a new stalwart to the mix. Sharpshooting Sam Jones arrived in 1957 and would become a star in his own right, twice scoring 51 points in a game, including once in the playoffs. Steady Tom "Satch" Sanders arrived in 1960, then in 1962, the tireless and diversely talented John Havlicek came aboard after failing to make the Cleveland Browns as a wide receiver. Havlicek, who still ranks as the Celtics' all-time leading scorer, pulled off one of the most memorable feats in franchise history when his steal ("Havlicek stole the ball!" hollered play-by-play voice Johnny Most) saved Game 7 of the 1965 East finals against Philadelphia.

During the Russell dynasty, the Celtics featured the greatest winner the sport had ever seen and a trove of supporting talent so rich that eight members of the 1961 team, plus Auerbach, eventually made the basketball Hall of Fame—and that was before Havlicek arrived. There has never been anything like it, and never will be again.

CELTICS GET BIG GUY

BILL RUSSELL ACQUIRED FROM HAWKS. TEAMMATE JONES, HEINSOHN, HOUSTON OTHER SELECTIONS

May 1, 1956 • by Herb Ralby

The nation's most publicized basket ball player—Bill Russell of San Francisco—was acquired by the Boston Celtics at the annual draft of college players yesterday, but Celtics boss Walter Brown may have to vie with Abe Saperstein of the Globetrotters for his services.

The Celtics gained the rights to the 6-10 center through a deal with St. Louis. Ed Macauley was traded to the Hawks in return for the Hawks' No. 1 draft choice. Rochester had the first shot at the defensive star but passed over him in favor of Si Green of Duquesne.

St. Louis, the second-poorest team in the N. B. A., then had rights to Russell and surrendered him to Boston.

Les and Jack Harrison, owners of the Rochester club, are believed to have shied away from the high salary Russell will command. Besides, Celtics' Pres. Walter Brown, Fred Zollner of the Fort Wayne Pistons and Abe Saperstein of the Globetrotters are the only basket ball executives believed willing to pay the price for Russell.

In addition to Russell, the Celtics took K. C. Jones, Russell's play-making teammate at San Francisco who is credited with setting up the big center.

Tom Heinsohn of Holy Cross, the Celtics' territorial choice, was also drafted. No other team in either loop of the N. B. A. took advantage of its territorial choice.

Another local player, Jim Houston of Brandeis, was the ninth draft pick of the Celtics.

Neither Jones nor Russell will be available for the opening of the Celtics' 1957 season since the San Francisco stars have announced plans to play for the United States Olympic team. Olympic basket ball competition ends in mid-December.

Jones, in addition, is due to enter service but this will not upset Coach Red Auerbach's backcourt plans. "The other teams didn't want to wait for him," Red said, "but our back court is in good shape and we can afford to wait."

Obtaining Russell will give the Celtics the big rebounder and defensive man they have long sought and is the best thing that's ever happened at a draft meeting, according to Auerbach.

"He's the greatest defensive center I've ever seen," Auerbach said. "Sure he has weaknesses but they'll be remedied. He gives me a big man for the future."

Bill Sharman, Gentleman

May 9, 1956 • by Ted Ashby

CONDENSING IN ONE SENTENCE an appraisal of Bill Sharman, Boston Celtics back court torch, an observer could accurately describe him: "In nature, behavior and appearance, a gentleman." There are many other interesting notes about Sharman, however. One is that some of his 10 sports coats can be seen almost as far away as those new lights, most powerful in the world, on top of the Empire State Building.

—

THOSE JACKETS don't glow at night, so there have been no reports from airline pilots who might have sighted them flying over West Newton, where he lives with his wife and three children. There is an unusual thing about Mrs. Sharman, also. It's her name, which is Illeana. "Her mother," Bill explained, "named her after an English silver pattern."

—

WILLIAM WALTON SHARMAN got out of Texas just in time. He was only 2 when his father and mother, John and Olyamae, took him from Abilene to California. Another year or so of inoculation with the expansive Texas philosophy and he might have thought they were crossing the border into the United States. Maybe he'd have wanted Rhode Island as a field in which to play cops and robbers.

Celtics players Frank Ramsey, left, and Bill Sharman hold Christmas gifts for *Boston Globe* readers in December, 1957.

—

BILL ALWAYS has been a winner, always a money-maker. In high school he worked Summers sewing up sacks of wheat and barley at $8 and $10 a day. When he was graduated from the University of Southern California he was signed by the Brooklyn Dodgers. It meant an automatic $78 in the movies when, sitting at a desk, his only speaking part might be: "Good morning, Mr. Smith."

—

HE'S HAD 100 more-or-less minor movie parts, in 10 of which he had speaking lines. In "Athena," a story of health addicts, he doubled for Louis Calhern, executing some fancy gymnastics. He also was an alleged weight-lifter in that story. For $100 a day, he fled before a somewhat peaceful leopard which, nevertheless, had all its teeth.

—

"I DECIDED at one time to be a dentist," said Bill, "and took two years of pre-med at U. S. C. But I don't believe I ever would have been completely satisfied if I hadn't gone into professional sports. I gave up baseball because the Dodgers didn't seem to have any very definite plans for my future. Tennis, well, I once went to the National Junior championships. Golf? Played it, maybe, 15 times."

—

COURTEOUS, MANNERLY, well-spoken Bill, father of Jerry, 10; Nancy, 6; Janice, 2, can see a long way down the road. Of the 10 positions offered him when the Celtics closed their season this year, he took a public relations job with Cody Distributing Company here. It isn't a case of the firm hiring a "name." By the time he closes his basket ball career in three or four years he hopes to be a real wheel in the organization.

—

IF EVERYTHING else collapses, which is far from likely, Bill and his wife have 40 acres of land out in California. His present plans are to settle permanently in Greater Boston. But if ever he has to fall back on that acreage, there is enough cotton growing on it to stuff in the tops of 28,000,000,000 bottles of aspirin.

First-Year Players Seldom Praised

AUERBACH PULLS SWITCH, LAUDS FRESHMAN HEINSOHN

October 31, 1956 • by Jerry Nason

Standard dependables in our trade are:

1. Lloyd Jordan (Harvard) shuns sophomore football players as if they were pit vipers.

2. Red Auerbach (Celtics) won't lavish praise on N. B. A. first-year players . . . especially his own.

So it goes. Jordan is using sophomores this year, reluctantly or otherwise . . . and Auerbach is enthusiastically beating his gums about "freshman" Tom Heinsohn.

"Heinsohn," he promised, "is going to be a star.

"Not many first-year men do it . . . but I think he's going to give us double figures as a scorer. He has too many good moves for them to stop him."

Red was not one of Heinsohn's ardent admirers when the young gentleman was operating for Holy Cross. "Indifferent attitude," Red observed. "When a mistake is made he loafs back up the court." His change of heart is newsworthy.

"Not a change of heart," Red explained, "but a change in Heinsohn. He realizes that in the pros you go all out. He's watched the Cooz break his neck on defense.

"Heinsohn has the professional attitude. He'll be a star."

Auerbach is a candid guy who manages, often, to wedge his size 9 foot in his oral cavity.

The Heinsohn incident is a case in point. The big boy was in the Celtics' draft territory (100-mile radius). Naturally somebody asked Red, "What do you think of Heinsohn?"

And quite as naturally ol' honest-as-the-day-is-long Auerbach replied, "I don't like his attitude. He'll have to hustle to play N.B.A. ball."

Much was made of Auerbach's remark . . . calling back the days when he had suggested that another Holy Cross hero, Bob Cousy, was something less than a superman.

"Cousy," it was Auerbach's candid appraisal, "won't be great until he learns how to play defense."

A lot of feelings were hurt . . . but not Cousy's. His pride, maybe, took a jolt. But Auerbach was right. The N.B.A. picked Cousy's pocket on defense for a season . . . but when he learned defense he became the greatest player in the game.

Auerbach—"I know I have a bad habit of speaking out with the truth."

Bill Russell to Play for Celtics; Olympic Star Arrives in Boston

December 17, 1956 • by Clif Keane

Alas, Bill Russell is going to sign with the Celtics Wednesday, but he isn't the "big man" the Boston basket ball team has been looking for the past 10 years.

The San Franciscan checked into Boston yesterday with his bride of a week and brazenly admitted he lacked ⅜'s of an inch of being 6-10, a height that is given the official seal of a "big man" in professional basket ball. But he looks as though he'll do.

The Russells arrived by plane from Chicago, where the leading collegiate player of '56—and member of the winning Olympic team at Melbourne—had participated in a round-robin tournament over the weekend.

Celtics owner Walter Brown, who met the Russells at the airport, said that Russell hasn't definitely agreed to terms. "But I don't anticipate any trouble signing Bill," Brown said.

"I'm quite sure the announcement will come Wednesday," said Brown. "And I hope he will be able to play in the game against St. Louis here (nationwide TV) on Saturday afternoon."

Russell, well poised though he said it was his very first press conference, admitted he "had about agreed to terms with Mr. Brown."

Russell mentioned that he was born in Louisiana and moved to Oakland after attending the third grade. He said he is 22 and weighed around 215.

"And I'm 6-feet-nine and five-eighth's inches tall," he said. "Though I haven't measured myself for a couple of weeks. It could be I'm getting closer to six-ten at that.

"You know," he said, "there was a time in my life I was scared to go to sleep, afraid I'd be growing all night long."

By now he was warming up—and he answered the questions hurled at him thusly:

Q. "How about your shooting? Is it pretty good or as bad as some people say?"

A. "Haven't you heard? It's atrocious. I can't shoot at all. I shoot lefthanded but I like to think I'm ambidextrous. What was my average in college? In the second year it was 48 percent, the junior year 54 percent and the last year 51 percent. Yeah, I dropped all the way from 54 to 51 percent in a year. Isn't that awful?"

Q. "What is your favorite shot?"

A. "From directly above the hoop. That's a good percentage shot, believe me."

Q. "How do you think you'll make out in professional basket ball?"

A. "Life is a matter of adjustment. One adjustment after another. I'll do my very best to make that adjustment."

Q. "What was the Russian basket ball team like in the Olympics?"

A. "Very good fundamentally, but they put special emphasis on specialties. For instance, one man was a hooker and the next a jump shooter and the next a driver. That's not the way to do it. A man needs a lot of things to play, not a specialty."

How Russell Did

ROOKIE NERVOUS BUT PROMISING; TROUBLES PETTIT ON DEFENSE

December 23, 1956 • by Jack Barry

Bill Russell played 21 minutes in his Celtics debut yesterday, entering the game at the five-and-one-half-minute mark of the first period to tremendous cheering.

The big fellow gave a good account of himself defensively, and indicated that, with experience, he will pick up on offense.

Russell took 11 shots, the majority of the left-hand soft hook and push shot variety and scored on three. He had a bad day at the foul line, missing all four.

BLOCKS PETTIT SHOTS

He picked up early fouls, covering 7-foot Chuck Share and was tagged with three personals by half-time.

Late in the game, however, the 6-10 Celtic rookie blocked three successive shots from the league's leading scorer, Bob Pettit, which is no mean feat.

This gave indication he can do likewise against the league's lanky jump shooters, who have been raising havoc against the Celtics over the years.

After the game Russell admitted he was nervous even before the game started. . . . "And I was a lemon at the foul line . . . I guess I really choked on 'em out there," said the rookie.

Arnie Risen in particular had good things to say about Russell. . . . "He'll get better as he goes along," Risen said. "Right now, he'll block any shooter in the league who shoots straight over head and turns and shoots straight from the pivot, because he's so tall and can get up so . . . and he'll murder them on our defensive board."

Russell took quite a few rebounds off the defensive board late in the game and wound up with 16 in all.

Will Russell Revolutionize Pro Game?

December 24, 1956 • by Jack Barry

Bill Russell may revolutionize the game of basket ball.

Up until now great scorers like Pettit and Mikan or playmakers like Cousy have been the type of players to draw crowds for professional basket ball.

Yet Russell could be the first player to become a drawing card on his defensive ability.

More than 11,000 watched the new Celtic center Saturday at the Garden score only three baskets. And most of these people think Russell will do.

Right now, Russell is not a good shooter—at least not by pro standards. He had a .59 percent shooting average in his last year as a collegian, but he looked weak with his left hand from around the keyhole area Saturday . . .

Freddy Scolari, ex-Celtic, who has seen Russell two years on the Coast, says, "Bill is not a good shooter, not yet. And must learn to make himself a better foul shooter.

"He should get the Celtics about 12 points a game right now, I'd say," said Scolari.

But . . . the Celtics' need isn't for shooters.

The Celtics are paying Russell to rebound, block shots, play the high pivot, hand off and cover the jump shooters.

For years the Celtics have been losing the close ones because guys like jump-shooting Paul Arizin, George Yardley and Bob Pettit have been murdering them with high double-figure games.

Others include Neil Johnston with his hook shot. Dolph Schayes and center giants like Larry Foust, Chuck Share and Clyde Lovellette.

On two of the three occasions when Russell was inserted in the game Saturday, the Celtics gained points before he came out.

Says Matt Zunic, Boston University coach, who played in the old Basket Ball Association of America with Red Auerbach's Washington Caps: "I'll say Russell will help. He's even helping right now. Give him once around the loop then see.

"But watch him hand off and follow up. Why, he'll play that high pivot, block for Cousy and Sharman, set them up, hand off, and everything. And as he goes along he'll step and drive. They may never stop him from deep inside."

Behind all the comment on the "daring gamble" the Celtics took in risking the loss of established star Ed Macauley and tossing in a promising rookie such as Cliff Hagan to "chance" the procurement of Bill Russell . . . Red Auerbach just smiles.

ST. LOUIS WINNER, 100-98.

Auerbach, Celtics' Coach, Punches Owner of Hawks.

April 7, 1957 • by Jack Barry

ST. LOUIS—Fireworks were in order even before the Boston Celtics-Hawks game started at Kiel Auditorium tonight before 10,040, when Coach Red Auerbach of the Celts punched owner Ben Kerner of the Hawks. Kerner bled from the mouth after the blow which followed a wordy battle.

It was a fitting prelude to one of the year's most hectic basket ball games, which St. Louis won, 100 to 98, on Bob Pettit's 25-foot jump shot in the dying seconds of play.

Auerbach had complained about the weight of the basket balls to be used and then insisted that the height of the baskets be measured.

Ladders were brought out and Referees Arnie Heft and Sid Borgia observed the measuring, with the rims of the hoop being declared the necessary 10 feet from the floor.

Kerner, then, according to Auerbach, called the Celtics' coach a "bush leaguer," and Red let go with a left, clipping the Hawks' owner on the chin.

"I'm no Johnny Most," said Auerbach, "who does he think he is." (Most and Kerner had physical differences here a year ago with punches thrown.)

Police, ushers and players separated the pair.

Pettit's 25-foot jump shot, his 26th point, pulled out the thrilling victory for the underdog Hawks, who took a 2 to 1 lead in the best-of-seven for the N.B.A. title in Kiel Auditorium before excited customers.

Mostly Johnny

April 12, 1957 • by Ted Ashby

THE 13-YEAR-OLD BOY who sang "Wagon Wheels" over a New York radio station is today, 20 years later, the exciting voice of the Boston Celtics, Johnny Most. The microphone didn't frighten him then, and it obviously doesn't now. The live audience, however, scared him more or less rigid. Not so today, not even that chap at Fort Wayne who heckled him every game the Celtics played there for four years.

"HE HAD the same seat near me for each game," Most grinned. "Every time Fort Wayne got ahead, he'd give it to me good. We kept up a running gun-fight, so to speak. I didn't mind it, except that he tried to yell loud enough so that his remarks would carry over my microphone. Some of them did, too, and were obscene. What completely frustrated me was that he always left two minutes before the game ended."

BECAUSE of his highly emotional reactions to what is taking place before him, John probably is the most-talked-about sportscaster of the moment. Comments vary. "He's great." "He's crazy." "He should leave the rulings to the officials." "He knows basket ball, and he really gives you the ball game." "He entertains me. I don't know which I enjoy more, Most, himself, or the contest."

TO ALL THIS, the controversial Johnny remarks: "I get myself all worked up before a game so that

I CAN be excited. Furthermore, I think it's part of my job to convince the listeners that the games are worthwhile for them to come and see. And, traveling with, eating with, plus, as was the case last year, actually living with the Celtics makes it virtually impossible to be impartial."

"DO YOU," someone interrupted, "ever say anything you later regret?" He responded: "I know you don't mean anything such as profanity, for I never use it. I will say quite frankly, though, that at a pitch of great excitement I have said things which, after I calm down, I would just as soon wish I hadn't said. It takes me several hours after a game to come from the emotional level where I've been."

HIS first sports broadcast, after his voice cracked at 15 while singing for money, and a whirl at radio acting didn't work out, was as a pinch-hitter in 1947 at a small radio station in Pennsylvania. He has since broadcast for the New York football Giants, Brooklyn Dodgers, New York Knickerbockers, and on a sports show with the unforgettable Johnny Mize, among other pro jobs.

SAID MOST, who currently is doing an afternoon disc jockey show for WVDA (the station is considering giving him a five-hour stint): "I would say I'm fairly excitable, yes. And I completely and absolutely enjoy myself broadcasting a game. I like music, especially swing. I like to write serious poetry. And I have a secret ambition. Some day I'd like to be a sports columnist. I'd like to be one right now, for that matter."

JOHN'S athletic career would not get him into any Hall of Fame. He did, though weighing only 165, play high school and college (Alabama) baseball, basket ball and football. His father (a dentist) and mother, John and Rose Most of the Bronx, insisted he go to college. "Let's just say I was an unnatural athlete. I had to work awfully hard to make the teams. I like to put it this way—I was the only spectator with a number on his back."

(First panel) Arnie Risen splits the St. Louis defense of Jack McMahon, left, and Bob Pettit to score an important basket, while (second panel) Bob Cousy gets a shot up against Med Park during the 1957 Finals.

Finale Goes 2 Overtimes. Celtics Win NBA Title, Beat Hawks, 125-123

April 14, 1957 • by Jack Barry

The Celtics, after an 11-year wait, pushed the blood pressure of 13,909 rooters to the bursting point before edging the game St. Louis Hawks, 125 to 123, in a double-overtime thriller at the Garden yesterday afternoon to win their first National Basket Ball Association championship.

Although it was a team victory, owner Walter Brown had the firmest handshakes for Tommy Heinsohn, Frank Ramsey, Bill Russell and a grand ole' pro, Arnie Risen.

Heinsohn, banishing any doubt that he is the freshman of the year, totaled 37 points, took 23 rebounds and scored eight of the Celtics' 22 markers in the double overtime.

Russell scored the game-saving basket at the end of regulation play. Then he topped this with a tremendous block on Jack Coleman's shot which would have given the Hawks the victory.

In addition, the Celtics' second great freshman took 32 balls off the boards in a terrific defensive exhibition and counted three points in overtime.

Ramsey delivered seven of his club's eight points in the first overtime. Then he tossed in a 20-foot push shot to extend the Celtics second-overtime margin to 124 to 121, which practically meant the ball game.

Risen, playing his 12th year of professional basketball, left the game via the six-foul route to a tumultuous ovation. He played 20 minutes, hit six in 12 from the floor, took 10 rebounds and hustled all the way.

Oddly, the Celts won with the greatest backcourt in pro ball's history, Bill Sharman and Bob Cousy contributing only five floor baskets.

PHILLIP, NICHOLS SHARP

Andy Phillip and Jack Nichols added 13 points while playing a total of 19 minutes. And Phillip made fine defensive contributions. Bob Pettit, in 56 minutes of action, had 39 points, 19 rebounds and 11 of 13 at the line.

Players evicted on fouls were Jack Coleman, Hagan, Ed Macauley and Jack McMahon for the visitors, plus Heinsohn and Risen.

With the score in the second overtime tied at 121 and two and one-half minutes left, Ramsey calmly converted a free try when hit by Macauley. It was Easy Ed's sixth, so Hannum came off the bench for the first time in three weeks.

This move, a necessity, had a decided bearing on the outcome.

Here Russell went high to block Med Park's goal try and with possession the Celts saw the amazingly cool Ramsey hit a right-hand push shot from outside the key for a 124-121 lead as the house resounded with cheers.

[Slater] Martin sank a free throw, cutting the Celts' lead to one point. Then Slater stole from Ramsey at midcourt. Hannum missed a shot but the Hawks got the ball out-of-bounds.

The canny Phillip fouled Park, who made one, but missed the second. This was actually a break for the visitors, because they got the rebound and had a possible chance for a game-winning basket.

But with 17 seconds left and the Hawks trailing, 124-123, Hannum was called for "traveling" by Mendy Rudolph and that was all Boston needed.

Desperate, Hannum then was all over Jim Loscutoff for a personal foul. Loscutoff made the first of two, missing the second.

Then with one second left, Hannum hurled the ball the length of the court and both Bob Pettit and Park had shots, each missing.

The bell ending the game—which saw the lead change 38 times and the score tied 20—brought fans pouring onto the floor. They picked up the Celtics—especially Heinsohn—and paraded to the team's dressing rooms.

St. Louis Beats Celtics, Takes NBA Title

PETTIT GETS 50; HAWKS WIN, 110-109

April 13, 1958 • by Jack Barry

ST. LOUIS—The St. Louis Hawks defeated the Celtics, 110-109, to capture the final playoffs here tonight, with Bob Pettit scoring 50 points before a packed house at Kiel Auditorium.

The great Hawk forward had 19 points in the last quarter, during which the Celtics came from behind to lead by a point at the 4-minute mark.

But Pettit, with 11 straight points at one stage, and five more later on, pulled the Hawks ahead.

The last minute was a tug-of-war with the Celtics having two chances to pull ahead.

With the Hawks leading, 105-104 and the Celtics in possession of the ball, Bill Sharman was called for charging.

Again, the Celtics had a chance when Tommy Heinsohn missed a foul when the Celtics trailed by a point.

Pettit finished off his scoring spree in the last few seconds, scoring on a short jumper and a layup, while Sharman wound off the Celtics' scoring with 10 seconds left.

RUSSELL RAPS DIXIE INSULT

BROWN BACKS UP CELTICS STAR; 'I'LL NEVER EMBARRASS MY PLAYERS'

November 26, 1958 • by Jack Barry

Bill Russell of the Celtics lashed out yesterday at the segregation treatment he received at Charlotte, N.C., Monday night, and it appears that the Boston Celtics will not book any more games south of the Mason-Dixon line.

"I don't care if we ever go back down there," said owner Walter Brown last night. "I know one thing, I'll never do anything to embarrass my ballplayers."

Russell and teammates K. C. Jones and Ben Swain stayed at a Negro hotel in Charlotte, while other Celtics spent the night at a downtown hotel. Sam Jones, the Celtics' other Negro player, remained with his folks who live in the vicinity.

Minneapolis' Negro players, Elgin Baylor, Ed Fleming and Alex Ellis, also stayed at the Negro hotel.

Russell told the Charlotte News, "I don't believe in segregation. It's against my principles. I came down here with my team and had to eat and sleep apart from them. I was shocked and hurt. I don't think we'll ever come back."

Celtic coach Red Auerbach said it was Russell's first trip South with the Celtics, but he had trouble once before in St. Louis, where a restaurant refused to serve the players with Russell along.

The occasion was the final playoffs last Spring. Russell, along with Bob Cousy, Tommy Heinsohn, and a couple of newspapermen, dropped into an all-night cafeteria, and when the counter man refused to serve Russell, the group left without ordering.

The incident was repeated at a second eating place. Finally Russell went to his hotel room without a late-night snack.

Said Auerbach, "The State Department has asked Bill to make a special foreign tour as an official good will ambassador. He received all these honors, represented his country in the Olympics and has trouble getting a place to stay and eat in this country."

COUSY SAVES CELTS

CROWD CARRIES ACE OFF FLOOR. VETERAN STEERS BOSTON TO EASTERN CHAMPIONSHIP

April 2, 1959 • by Francis Rosa

The old master.

What else can you call Bob Cousy?

That's what coach Red Auerbach called him in the Celtics' dressing room as he gently tapped his left arm after Boston had beaten Syracuse, 130 to 125, to win the N.B.A.'s Eastern Division crown.

Cousy was stretched out on his back on a table in the middle of the floor. He looked too weary to get up and take off his uniform. For more than 10 minutes he stayed on the table.

"If the next series (vs. Minneapolis, starts Saturday) is any tougher than this," said Cousy, "I won't be around here for the seventh game."

He said it half jokingly. But there was no one to argue with him.

At game's end, joyous Boston fans carried Cousy off the floor—a tribute seldom paid a professional athlete.

Cousy, probably still weak from a virus attack, had played himself into the floor in the last two minutes.

The Celtics had a three-point lead when Cousy reverted to the dribbling act that had first made him Boston's Mr. Basketball. The obvious strategy for the Celtics (rebound ace Bill Russell had fouled out) was to wait out the 24-second clock before shooting. It had just the man to do it, Cousy.

He dribbled the ball around and through three Syracuse players. Then stopped and threw up a one-hander from the right edge of the keyhole. The ball hit the strings as the 24-second buzzer sounded. Boston had a 126 to 123 lead and that was the game.

Cousy had put on his show with his knees virtually buckling under him from exhaustion, his face almost distorted and with one eye on the clock.

He was hugged lovingly by Jim Loscutoff and Auerbach before the game was over. And later as Larry Costello fouled him in the backcourt, he patted his backcourt rival as if to say, "It's all right."

Then the fans were all over the court and Sam Jones, who played probably his best game of the season, was jumping up and down. The fans grabbed Cousy and carried him to the edge of the court. Then he was let down to grab the coattails of an usher and hurry to the dressing room.

How tired was he? "It isn't just being physically tired," he said. "It's the emotional drain of a pressure game like this. We felt helpless out there when we were 16 points down in the first half. We had good shots, but the ball wasn't going in. There's nothing you can do—just feel helpless."

Said Auerbach, "That's one of the toughest games and one of the best teams we've played."

"Bring on the Lakers," Loscutoff shouted through a cigar.

And Cousy didn't feel like moving off the table.

Somebody said to him, "Somebody slugged Arnie Heft (the referee)." "Slugged him?" asked Cousy, "They should have kissed him."

He meant the officials had done a good job with a tough game. According to the officials a Syracuse fan insulted Heft, and Norman Drucker, the alternate official who was sitting nearby, tried to restrain the fan. Heft was cocking his arm to throw a punch when coach Paul Seymour of Syracuse stopped him.

What about the Lakers? "Let's face it," said Cousy, "they can't be any tougher than Syracuse. Our biggest problem will be overconfidence."

Celtics Sweep Lakers Series

April 10, 1959 • by Jack Barry

MINNEAPOLIS—Overcoming the Lakers for the fourth straight time in final series play and for the 22d consecutive time over a two-year period, the Boston Celtics became the first club in National Basketball Assn. history to win the world professional championship in four straight games.

Red Auerbach, only coach still in the business after 13 years of league play, was carried from the floor by his players as the Celtics, pressed to the limit and with their owner, Walter Brown, making one of his rare road appearances on nd, defeated their favorite cousins, 118 to 113, in a real thriller-diller from start to finish.

Proving once more they could win a pressure game on a foreign court, the Celtics looked to their big five of Bill Russell, Bob Cousy, Bill Sharman, Frank Ramsey and Tommy Heinsohn for a great clutch fourth period.

And the greatest five players ever rostered on a single club really came through with Sharman, playing his third magnificent game in a row, the leader this time, followed as usual by "money-in-the-bank" Ramsey.

Giving them vital possession when it meant the game was Russell, who grabbed 30 rebounds in all, with five of them coming in the closing moments of the final period when the Celtics were really pressed to protect their slim margin.

Heinsohn, who paced the first-half scorers with 17, chipped in with four needed points here, while Cousy, a bit off in his general play, had enough left to steer the Boston attack to victory per custom.

The game was tied 34-all at the end of the opening stanza, with Boston sporting slim leads of 64-62 and 88-87 at the ends of the next two before the triumph was finally achieved in the last period.

Not to be forgotten was big Gene Conley, who really made Coach Auerbach look great by finishing his Celtic career (maybe) with 10 points and eight needed rebounds.

The Lakers, determined to win one before their enthusiastic home following and in what was coach Johnny Kundla's last pro game, before taking over the Univ. of Minnesota job, fought Boston to the end. They went ahead, 97 to 96, on Bobby Leonard's drive-in at the fourth-minute mark of the final period.

The Celtics, still thinking of a possible long plane ride back here, then went to work in earnest. They scored 12 points against the Lakers four for a 108 to 101 reading with six minutes left.

Sharman had six of these, hitting three one-handers, with Ramsey, Cousy and Heinsohn contributing the other two-pointers.

A Russell basket partially offset baskets by Ed Fleming and Boo Ellis, along with a Leonard foul conversion, and Boston was in front, 110 to 106, with 4:38 left.

Sharman made a foul try, but Elgin Baylor, who reverted to his usual style, scoring 30 for the night, connected on a short jumper to place the Lakers three down, 111 to 108.

Here Ramsey set a beautiful pick for a 15-foot Sharman jump shot at the key and Mr. Russell rebounded twice on Laker misses to keep Boston in possession until Minny committed its seventh personal of the period with 2:46 left.

Russell made one of two attempts and Boston, with only four personals, saw Ramsey foul Baylor. Elgin, getting two tries, made both and Minny was four down, 114 to 110.

Here, after both Heinsohn and the Lakers' Ellis missed floor shots, Cousy, taking the ball off the boards, led Heinsohn with a smart well-timed bouncing pass which Tommy took for a neat running layup and a 116 to 110 margin.

Then the Celtics took full advantage of the 24-second limit to run out the remaining time for the victory.

CELTS NIP WARRIORS ON HEINSOHN'S SHOT

CLINCH EASTERN CROWN ON REBOUND, 119 TO 117

March 25, 1960 • by Jack Barry

PHILADELPHIA—Tommy Heinsohn, greatest offensive rebounder in the National Basketball Association, came through tonight to tap in a rebound as the gong sounded to send the Celtics into their fourth straight championship play.

They downed the Warriors, 119 to 117, in a tension-packed sixth game to the dismay of 12,661 howling fans, the largest paid attendance in Philly's pro history.

Heinsohn bashed home a rebound of a Bill Sharman missed shot, with practically the entire Warrior club surrounding him at the baseline directly under the Celtics hoop.

One could hear a pin drop in Conventional Hall, as Sid Borgia, after a moment's hesitation, signaled

"good" for the basket. That ended the Warriors' hopes for the 1960 season.

After appearing in for another near rout as the crowd-encouraged Warriors sped to a 22 to 11 lead at the mid-way section of the opening period, the Celtics kept plugging away to tie, pass and then fall behind the home forces on the uncanny shooting of Woody Sauldsberry and Guy Rodgers.

Bob Cousy and Bill Sharman were off their game until Cousy shook the shackles of his lethargy and poor shooting to come through in the final moments of the clutch last period. Earlier it was Sam and K. C. Jones, along with the unheralded Gene Conley, who kept the Celtics apace of the favored Warriors.

Once again the Celtics had to fight themselves, as well as the home forces, for they gave up the ball 21 times, which the alert and grateful Warriors accepted for 30 big—and we mean big—points. Philly lost it 16 times for 15 Boston markers.

The ball game was won and lost from the 3:52 minute mark of the tension-packed final period with Philly in front 110 to 105. At this point both Wilt Chamberlain and Bill Russell had five personal fouls and each had to be extremely careful.

Heinsohn made two foul tosses and Conley bashed in a rebound moments later to cut the deficit to 110-109, with Philly calling time.

Arizin then connected on his specialty, a jumper from the key, but Russell equalized with a turn-around soft hook on the stilt.

Sauldsberry sent the fans into ecstasy as he drove on the foul-burdened Russell, something he seldom does, for a two-pointer.

After Rodgers missed, Cousy found the net with a soft right-hand push at the key on a break and Boston again was one point away, 113 to 114.

The Warriors then missed a pair of attempts including a rebound, and Sharman, fouled by Rodgers, made both attempts for a Celtics' 115 to 114 advantage with 1:28 showing on the clock.

Here, however, Heinsohn fouled Arizin, and Paul converted both tries for 116 to 115, Philly lead with 1:11 left.

Chamberlain blocked a Celtic try here and Russell did likewise at the other end, but the alert Arizin grabbed the rebound, missed and Chamberlain, grabbing the rebound, was fouled by Conley for a three-for-two situation.

With a one-point margin, the Stilt evicted groans when he missed the first but sank the second, and then missed the vital penalty try, permitting Boston an opportunity to tie with a basket with only 35 seconds left.

This they did do after a time out, which saw Sharman come through with his patented jumper to the left of the key. With 30 seconds showing and the clubs knotted, 117 apiece, Cousy fouled Rodgers. Guy, who hit amazing jumpers all night, could not convert either of two free tries, with Russell grabbing the rebound and Boston calling its last time out.

With nine seconds left the play was to get Sharman to pass the ball in, take a return pass for the push shot. But Bill, played closely, drove in and flipped the ball up. Heinsohn had daylight from Chamberlain, who had moved over to double-team Sharman. Heinsohn went up and put the ball in.

The Celtics, joyously, did not wait for any "official" goal signal from either referee, jumping and pounding each other on the backs with Coach Red Auerbach leading them racing to their dressing room.

DOUBLE DRIBBLES

Basketball's double axiom . . . weak foul shooting can kill you and a club can win with a strong bench was certainly proven tonight . . . Gene Conley, along with K. C. and Sam Jones, pulled the Celtics over the rough spots when Cousy and Sharman still found it difficult to hit their true stride . . . Conley, played loosely by the scornful Warriors, hit four push shots and two rebounds in the second half, had seven in eight from the floor and took 13 off the boards . . . Russell, going all the way, had 25 points, out-rebounding the Stilt 25 to 24 and five of his 11 baskets were soft turn hook shots over the defending Chamberlain . . . The Warriors, worst foul shooting team in the league, paid the penalty, dropping their chance for the big money, by muffing 15 in 42, while Boston made good on 30 in 35.

CELTS WORLD BEATERS

EARLY SPREE SINKS HAWKS, 122-103

April 10, 1960 • by Jack Barry

Clicking to near perfection, the Celtics saved one of their finest team performances for the finale yesterday to wallop the St. Louis Hawks, 122 to 103, and win their third world's championship in four years, before a roaring crowd of 13,909 spectators at the Garden and a national television audience.

Red Auerbach's lads proved their claim to one of the greatest teams ever. They were sparked by Bob Cousy, Frank Ramsey, Bill Russell and Sam Jones in winning the seventh and final game of the series.

Bob Cousy, who said earlier in the series he "was slipping," was the Cousy of old. He was carried off the floor at the hectic conclusion. Cousy played all but one minute, scoring 19 points and handing off 14 assists.

Frank Ramsey aided immensely in lifting the Celtics with a brilliant first-half. He scored 24 points in all, while allowing rugged Cliff Hagan 19 points.

Bill Russell, who set a new playoff series total rebound record, outplayed Clyde Lovellette. He scored 22 points and collected 35 rebounds.

Sam Jones ignited a second-period spree, scoring 12 points himself and running the harassed Hawks' back-liners into the boards to draw roars of applause from Garden followers.

Tommy Heinsohn scored 22 points, including two spectaculars early in the game-winning second stanza.

Gene Conley, who joins the Philadelphia Phillies tomorrow, added quite a bit, with a valuable three-pointer in the winning surge and seven needed rebounds.

Bob Pettit led the losers with 22 points while Cliff Hagan had 19 and Lovellette had 18. The back court tandem of Si Green and Johnny McCarthy had 17 and 16 points, respectively.

The sellout crowd saw the silken-smooth Celtics break open the game with a 41-point second period and thus become the first team to defend its N.B.A. title successfully since 1954 when the Minneapolis Lakers grabbed the crown for the third straight time.

The much speedier but smaller Boston club had forged leads three times in the series only to see the Hawks rebound on each occasion. But the Celtics poured on too much of everything in the payoff scrap.

The Celtics trailed by one point at the end of the opening period but outscored St. Louis, 14 to 2, in less than four minutes of the second quarter to grab a 43 to 32 advantage. Cousy and Heinsohn, Boston's two Holy Cross products, tallied nine of those 14 points and that about spelled defeat for St. Louis as the Celtics built the margin to 18 points at halftime.

The shooting of Hagan and rookie Dave Piontek kept the Hawks in the game in Boston's big second period, the two accounting for 15 of St. Louis' 23 points.

St. Louis was able to narrow the gap only to 15 points in the third period. The closest the Hawks could come in the final quarter was 14 points, with Boston sitting on a 20-point bulge most of the way throughout the second half.

The Celtics sported a 64 to 52 margin with better than a minute to play when Sam Jones put the clincher on their hopes with two fast baskets.

Russell rebounded on his own hook try to feed Sam at the key for a short jumper and the speedy Jones cleverly faked a pass on a three-one break. He jumped at the keyhole area for a basket and a 68 to 52 Celtics margin.

Seconds before the final bell Ramsey intercepted a pass intended for his ex-Kentucky mate, Hagan, fed Cousy, sped down court to take a return flip from Bob and slip in a running layup in a picture move.

THAT'S 4 IN 5 YEARS.
C'S RETAIN NBA TITLE

April 12, 1961 • by Jack Barry

Proving their class the Celtics won their fourth world championship in five years as they rode to a magnificent 121 to 112 victory over the St. Louis Hawks in the fifth of the best-in-seven title series before a roaring "announced" 13,909 in the Garden last night.

Boston won the series four games to one.

Red Auerbach's lads made their final appearance after 89 National Basketball Association games a rousing one, with a spectacular third period which presented the world champs at their greatest, offensively, defensively and in spirited team play, which had the fans out of their seats practically throughout the entire third 12-minute session.

The Hawks, giving their all early, had made it a real ball game, mainly on the merits of their shooting twins, Cliff Hagan and Bob Pettit, trailing 62 to 61 as the clubs left the floor at intermission.

Coming out for the third period, Red Auerbach started a quintet of Bill Russell, brilliant all night, Bob Cousy, Frank Ramsey, Sam Jones and rookie Tom Sanders.

Cracking out from the start the Celtics ran the amazed Hawks 8 to 0 to set the tempo for the entire 12-minute period, which saw Boston outscore the beleaguered visitors 37 to 23 to wrap up the contest.

Russell and Sanders dominated the boards here, with Cousy triggering the fast break, and finding time to score 13 points. Sam Jones had 10 in the session and Russell eight as Frank Ramsey checked the previously hot-handed Hagan, who had 17 in the first half.

Paul Seymour had to lift big Clyde Lovellette before three minutes of the frame, so speedy and effective was Russell's offensive assault, with two running layups.

Pettit then was sat down with Boston in front, 76 to 65, and Hagan culled but eight points in the entire third period.

St. Louis got but one shot throughout the period. Russell and Sanders saw to that and the Celtics wrote a gaudy .577 shooting mark on the merits of 15 hoops in 26 attempts, while the offensive-stilled visitors could cull but nine in 27, so leech-like and aggressive were the Celtics' entire quintet.

Sanders set the terrific tempo in the third period with a right-hand dunker after the tap with neat passing from Cousy to Sam Jones.

Cousy then bounced a nifty pass to Russell through the key for a running layup. Russell walked in on a pass from Sam Jones on a break. Sam went in a layup seconds later, as Boston continued to own its defensive board, for eight quick points. Coach Paul Seymour ordered time out and removed Clyde Lovellette.

Next to leave the premises a few plays later were the guards, Si Green and Johnny McCarthy for Lenny Wilkens and Al Ferrari as Boston's backcourt was playing havoc with the visitors' back-linesman.

Applause greeted a Celtic maneuver, which saw Sam Jones tap to Cousy, who hit Sanders on a break and Satch responded with a short assist to the speeding Sam underneath. It forced another St. Louis time out and the Celtics were in front, 70-63.

The Hawks didn't quit. They just didn't have neither the horses nor the bench to cope with the Celtics, who did not want a return trip to St. Louis.

And although Boston entered the final period sporting a 99 to 84 margin on the merits of the spectacular third period, with its defense taking as many bows as its offense, the game was not yet won.

Unable to keep up such a pace both ways, the Celtics fell into their old trouble of trying to do it individually and apparently felt a hit too snug with their fourth-period starting 99 to 84 margin.

Pecking away, while Boston fell off in its shooting, the Hawks suddenly found themselves back in contention, trailing 102 to 98 with fully seven minutes to go. Pettit got his second wind and Lenny Wilkens started to ball-steal and cash in on a tiring Cousy.

Here Heinsohn took over. Tommy, who has had an "in-and-out" series, sunk two foul shots against a single Hagan free throw and hit a jumper from scrimmage as the Celtics were standing around,

not moving. Pettit kept the Hawks alive with a like jumper and Heinie hit again.

Here Heinsohn took the ball from Pettit to feed Cousy, who passed to Sam Jones for a neat side jumper, and the Celtics took a stronger 110-101 lead with 6:30 gone.

The teams matched points and fouls here with the Celtics killing final chances of the Hawks pulling a garrison finish. With two minutes left, Sam Jones ran away from his defender for another two-pointer. Russell then intercepted a Hawks pass, Ramsey took Bill's feed to lock it up, 120-109.

Segregation Hits C's Negro Stars

DENIED SERVICE AT KENTUCKY HOTEL, THEY FLY HOME

October 18, 1961

The planned happy homecoming for N.B.A. basketball stars Frank Ramsey and Cliff Hagan at Lexington, Ky., last night exploded into an unpleasant racial incident when Negro players on the Boston Celtics and St. Louis Hawks were denied service at a hotel coffee shop.

Five Negro members of the Celtics, Bill Russell, Sam Jones, K. C. Jones, Tom Sanders and Al Butler flew home after the refusal. So did Woody Sauldsberry and Cleo Hill of the Hawks. All refused to play in the exhibition game between the Celtics and Hawks at Memorial Coliseum.

Celtics' team owner Walter Brown said that the team and players "will never be embarrassed like this again because the team will never enter into a situation such as this again."

He said the entire Celtics squad could not consider leaving Lexington immediately because the game was under contract.

Boston's division of the NAACP declined to comment immediately on the situation.

The players refused to play despite long discussions with their coaches.

Art Lang, manager of the Phoenix Hotel where the players were denied service at a coffee shop, said the hotel did not have discriminatory policies and that the refusal to serve the Negroes resulted from a misunderstanding.

C's Stick with Defense; Collect Draftee Jackpot

GET HAVLICEK, FOLEY, HADNOT, 2 B.C. PLAYERS

March 27, 1962 • by Jack Barry

"All I can say is I'm satisfied," said Coach Red Auerbach of the Celtics upon returning from the annual N.B.A. collegiate draft meeting in New York yesterday.

John Havlicek, the Ohio State star, was the Celtics' first selection in 1962.

"Sure, there may have been other fellows we liked, but I think we got real good players in our first three picks."

The Celtics risked losing Holy Cross' Jack Foley by not taking the Crusader as a territorial selection, but the luck of the draw saw the nation's second-leading scorer among major colleges land in Boston's lap the second time around.

"Make it?" queried Auerbach to a scribe's question on Foley's chances in pro ball. "He's got a great chance, a real great chance."

Boston's first choice, which was number nine in the listing, was talented 6-6 John Havlicek of Ohio State.

"He is a fine all-around ball player," said Red. "I've seen him a few times and he is sound on defense, handles himself well and has the tools to be a real pro," said the Boston coach.

One thing Havlicek already has in common with the Celtics is the winning habit. He played in but five losing games with the Buckeyes in three seasons.

Celtics Romp; That's How Brawl Bounces

SAM JONES, WILT CLASH; RODGERS FLEES LOSCUTOFF

April 2, 1962 • by Jack Barry

The hockey fans would have loved it. To the howling edification of 13,496 fans, the Celtics ran over the Philadelphia Warriors, 119 to 104, yesterday at the Garden in a game enlivened by a series of fourth-period brawls.

Main bout combatants were:

1. Wilt Chamberlain, Philadelphia, 7-1, 250 pounds, vs. Sam Jones, Boston, 6-4, 205.

2. Jim Loscutoff, Boston, 6-4, 225, vs. Guy Rodgers, Philadelphia, 6 ft., 186.

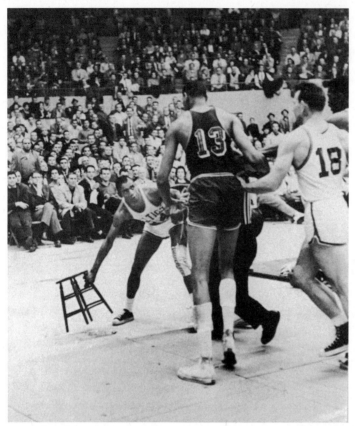

The Celtics' Sam Jones wields a photographer's stool during a fight with the Warriors' Wilt Chamberlain.

The Celtics had little trouble winning the game, taking a 72 to 49 halftime lead. Sam Jones out-rebounded, 12 to 9, and outscored, 15 to 11, Wilt Chamberlain.

The Celtics' team play is mirrored in their scoring spread with Tom Heinsohn 11, Bill Russell 12, Satch Sanders 10, Bob Cousy 9, K. C. Jones 7, and Carl "Remember Me" Braun, hitting all three set shots tried.

Chamberlain, per custom away from home, garnered but four hoops in 13 tries, getting but two points in the first period as the Celtics posted a quick 36 to 26 advantage.

Russell was perfection in timing Wilt's goal attempts on defense and Boston bossed the boards, 42 to 30.

With Boston in front, 94-70, Sam Jones, after being called on a brush foul against Chamberlain under the Philly basket, had words with the seven-footer and brushed Wilt's hand away. When Chamberlain indicated he was willing to mix, Sam picked up a handy stool, as David did his slingshot, to even the odds a little.

This brought every player to the floor with Loscutoff holding off the Wilt first and then Bill Russell using all his personal wiles and one arm to induce Chamberlain to "forget things."

Sam's description, "He was trying to break my hand."

Wilt, "He used obscene language and once he picked up that stool—he had better start running with it!"

Hardly had the police, referees and non-combatants settled things, when Rodgers punched Carl Braun, and another near riot started.

Apparently intending to match Sam Silverman's six-bout card, Rodgers, after being fouled by Loscutoff, with both under the Warriors' hoop, pulled Jim's leg.

The burly Celtic, wild with rage, headed for the Philly bench, and Rodgers, seeking Sam Jones' weapon, the "guiltless" stool, was saved from

In each case, the smaller man grabbed a stool, hastily vacated by a photographer, as an equalizing weapon.

There were several sideshow scraps, the most spectacular between Rodgers and Boston's Carl Braun wherein Rodgers belted the apparently unsuspecting Braun, then fled.

Peacemaking teammates, officials and police kept the flareups from becoming donnybrooks, and the only player thrown out of the game was Tom Heinsohn, who shoved Ted Luckenbill. Referee Sid Borgia felt it was deliberate aggression and chased Heinsohn.

Boston now leads the N.B.A. Eastern Sector play-offs three games to two with the teams returning to Philadelphia's Convention Hall for the sixth game tomorrow night. If a seventh game is necessary, it will take place at the Garden Thursday night.

possible decapitation when strong-armed Frank Radovich was able to hold Jim back.

Still burning at Meschery, Heinsohn, partly off balance, let himself go and crashed the unsuspecting Ted Luckenbill to the floor, and referee Sid Borgia sent him to the dressing room.

C's WIN WITH 2 SEC. LEFT

SAM JONES TIPS PHILLY, 109-107

April 6, 1962 • by Jack Barry

Dispelling once and for all the characteristic of timidity in the clutch, Silent Sam Jones came through with a $10,500 15-foot jump shot with two seconds remaining to give the Celtics a nerve-wracking 109 to 107 victory over the Philadelphia Warriors before a roaring, capacity 13,909 throng at the Garden last night . . . and the right to meet the Los Angeles Lakers for the world's basketball championship.

The Celtics and Lakers, who were present at the game last night, face each other Saturday afternoon at the Garden, 2:30, in a nationally televised affair.

The Celtics thus proved their world champion stature as they won their first close one of the seven-game series . . . when it was certainly obligatory . . . there was no tomorrow if this one was dropped and the Warriors, a most worthy foe, battled from a five-point deficit, trailing 107 to 102, to knot the game at 107-all with 25 seconds remaining.

Jones, without doubt the game's individual hero with 28 points, had considerable help, especially in the tough late stages when Boston battled from behind.

Bob Cousy's long bombs, K. C. Jones' defensive play and the ever courageous gunning of Tommy Heinsohn, along with Bill Russell's magnificent effort all night, finally pulled this one out for the locals, an emotional-wringer if there ever was one.

Russell battled Wilt Chamberlain all the way, scoring 19 to the Philly giant's 22, equaling him in rebounds with 22 and hitting all five pressure tries at the foul line.

In addition Bill blocked two Warrior would-be baskets in the vital pay-off last period leading to three of the Celtics' needed points.

The game's major drama was naturally wrapped up in the last period, which saw the Celtics down, 81 to 80. In this pressurized 12-minute period, Cousy hit for nine points, individual high, and ran the club to perfection like the master he is.

Even injury-ridden Frank Ramsey, hardly able to maneuver physically, came in to post a pair of fouls in two attempts and gain a two-pointer when Chamberlain was called for goal-tending, giving Boston an 86 to 84 margin at that juncture.

It was Ramsey's second effort at play but proved too much and coach Red Auerbach had to remove the plucky Kentucky Colonel, who got a stand-up ovation from the packed throng.

K. C. did a marvelous defensive job on the much bigger Tom Meschery, refusing to let the jump-shooter get his "spot" on the floor, giving him but one shot over the last six minutes.

Playing sound defensive and moving the ball better than in early periods, the locals spun from their 81 to 80 fourth-period starting deficit to what seemed like a fair 98 to 91 margin, with 5:20 gone.

Here is how the game was won.

With but 24 seconds left on the big Garden clock, the Warriors, setting up a play, naturally fed Chamberlain, who turned, dropped it in and was hit by Heinsohn in the act.

The big dipper dropped in the charity toss, Philly's 39th in 43 at the line, to tie things.

The Celtics called time and Sam Jones, with 11 seconds left, maneuvered to a position just past the foul stripe and as the clock showed but three seconds, let fly, the ball swishing through and the Warriors automatically calling time. Chamberlain was in no position to block Sam's attempt on this one.

About 500 fans rushed to the floor and had to be removed as the announcement from Weldon Haire echoed through the Garden . . . "There is one second of play remaining."

Ed Conlin took the ball out for the visitors and arced a high lobbing pass intended for Chamberlain, but Russell, positioning himself, batted it down, with Sam Jones, the game-winner, hugging it to his chest as the bell rang.

The fans stormed out on the floor vainly trying to carry Sam, Russell and Cousy to the dressing room.

HANDICAPPED CELTICS BEAT L.A. IN OVERTIME, 110 to 107

4 'REGULARS' FOUL OUT; BOSTON ROLLS IN CLUTCH. RUSSELL, SAM JONES, COUSY RUN SHOW IN EXTRA PERIOD

April 19, 1962 • by Jack Barry

Big Bill Russell, the man who does not know how to lose . . . still doesn't know how.

The great Celtics center, with consistent aid from fine-shooting silent Sam Jones, plus the spark provided by Col. Frank Ramsey, led the Boston club to its fifth world championship in six years and an unprecedented fourth title in succession. The Celtics defeated the plucky Los Angeles Lakers, 110 to 107, in a palpitating overtime session before an "announced" 13,909 followers at the Garden last night.

Thus, closing a terrific 14-game playoff pressurized pair of series against Philadelphia and Los Angeles, once again Boston rules the basketball world.

While Sam Jones provided the consistent scoring, getting 25 of his 27 points in the second half and five of Boston's 10 in the overtime period, it was Russell's dominance of the game that swung this one to Red Auerbach's never-say-die clan.

Big Bill, in a tremendous personal exhibition over the full 53 minutes of action, called on all his reserve, which was tested seven times by gigantic Wilt Chamberlain prior to the Lakers' seven-game setto, led the Celtics scorers with 30 points and tied an N.B.A. final playoff single game mark with 40 rebounds, 29 in each half. In addition Russell, who was once anemic at the foul line, calmly made 14 in 17, two big ones in overtime. He was finally carried off bodily by frenzied fans at the conclusion.

Ramsey, operating more freely than in any previous game, had a big hand in this one also. He totaled 17 points in the first 24 minutes to lead Celtic scorers. He was mainly instrumental, along with Russ, in posting Boston's slim 53 to 47 halftime margin.

Before a description of the hectic overtime session and a review of the final minutes of regulation play, when Boston literally "blew" the game, a word should be said for Elgin Baylor and Jerry West, particularly Baylor.

Going all but two minutes, the star Laker received a standing ovation when he fouled out of action with 2:20 left of the five-minute extra session and Boston in front, 107 to 102. Elgin had 41 points and took 22 off the boards as he was aided greatly by a sharp-shooting West, the other half of the Lakers one-two punch. West totaled 35 points.

In addition to his all-around effectiveness, Baylor fouled out a trio of Boston's corner strength— Tommy Heinsohn, Jim Loscutoff and Satch Sanders.

The teams played methodical, careful defensive ball in the main, with the contest not exhibiting the characteristics of previous Boston free-wheeling playoffs as they wound up knotted 75 apiece at the end of three stanzas.

The Celtics, despite their constantly depleted squad, managed to fashion a 96 to 91 margin and seemed ready to finish this in regulation time, but the combined losses of Baylor's three defensive rivals, plus under-par playing by the physically weakened Bob Cousy, granted a late-period reprieve to the visitors. They went from a 100 to 96 deficit to a tie with 18 seconds remaining.

The Celtics had the ball with a minute left and a four-point lead, 100-96, when Frank Selvy (ever a late-game terror to Boston) counted on a length-of-the-floor drive. Seconds later Selvy was on the spot in following a West miss, after the latter had stolen a telegraphed Cousy pass, and the teams were knotted at the century mark.

Ramsey missed an out-of-position keyhole try and with five seconds left the Lakers set up Selvy, whose lateral side shot missed. Russell grabbed the precious rebound and the clubs went into overtime.

Boston won its fifth world championship in overtime as follows: the Jones boys, Cousy, Ramsey and Russell opposed Baylor, Selvy, West, Krebs and LaRusso here.

After Baylor sank a pair of fouls, forcing Ramsey out on six personals, the seldom-used Gene Guarilia replaced the colonel. Guarilia did very well in the clutch sequence, grabbing a vital rebound on a Cousy hook miss to feed Russell for a two-hand dunker.

Guarilia had the unpleasant task of covering Baylor, but proved real effective. He forced Elgin to shoot off balance. The Laker star missed and Russell, per custom, took the rebound.

Sam Jones, handed a beautiful diagonal-cross-key pass by K.C. Jones, scored going under the hoop, and was hit by Rudy LaRusso, for the latter's sixth personal. Sam made the foul toss for three big points. Howard Joliff replaced LaRusso for the Lakers.

The tiring Baylor again missed by Guarilia and Russell, fouled by Krebs, made one in two. Boston got a break here as Coach Red Auerbach was frantically trying to get a time-out when big Bill got hit and Boston picked up a point it might not have had.

Guarilia fouled Baylor before the shot and Elgin missed, (he had 15 in 21 at the foul line) with the omnipresent Russell naturally taking the rebound, but Boston lost possession on a 24-second violation.

Here Baylor fouled Russell in a scrimmage under the Laker net and the Laker went out on six to a tremendous hand from the Boston fans. Russell made the foul toss for a 107-102 Boston advantage.

Tom Hawkins came in for Baylor and Selvy hit one in two free tries, with Russell again rebounding on the failure. Boston had a bit of luck here as K.C. Jones came up with a high rebound and fed Sam, who sank a jumper with 1:12 left. Sid Borgia then called an offensive foul on Selvy, which gave Boston possession again.

Jim Krebs fouled Cousy for his sixth personal and Bob, who missed six in seven in regulation, finally tossed in one of three attempts here and the Celtics appeared "home" 110-103, though Hawkins scored on a run-in.

With 25 seconds left, Sam Jones was called for an offensive foul and Hawkins hustled in a rebound, leaving the Lakers trailing, 110-107, with 20 seconds remaining and the game not over yet.

With 20 seconds left the visitors, with a man like Jerry West on the floor, still had a chance, albeit a slight one.

Cousy killed 13 seconds and then called a time out, with seven seconds left K. C. Jones took the ball in from out-of-bounds, fed Bob, who broke away from his defender and the Cooz dribbled a la Marques Haynes to the final bell . . . Which was drowned out by the mass of fans who all but crushed Bob at the scoring table, along with Russell and Sam Jones.

That was it . . . Five flags in six years, four in a row and as coach Red Auerbach said, leaving the Garden . . . "No practice tomorrow, fellows."

'So Many Things to Say': Cousy Falters For 1st Time

March 18, 1963 • by Gloria Negri

Bob Cousy, choking back tears, had come near the end of his speech. There wasn't a dry eye in the house.

His left hand gripped the lectern as he tried to tell fans and teammates how much they meant to him. "There are so many things to say . . . "

Cousy's voice faltered, faded, then gave out altogether. He buried his face in the towel around his neck. Still the tears came, and the house fell silent.

Then, a small girl by his side—12-year-old daughter, Marie Colette—held out her hand. In it was a white handkerchief. She hesitated a moment, then reached out and handed it to her dad.

Then, somewhere from among the 13,909 who jammed the Boston Garden Sunday to say goodbye to the Celtics' star, a voice yelled:

"We love you, Cooz!"

A torrent of applause and cheers rocked the Garden.

Marie (Ritterbusch) Cousy, called "Missy" by all, stood by her husband's side, pert and pretty in a green dress, fighting back tears.

"I'm too filled with emotion to say anything sensible," Missy confided. She did say she was "both glad and sad" her husband was retiring from pro basketball. Glad because he'll be able to spend more time at their Worcester home. Sad because of all the friends they'll leave.

Missy, Marie Collette, nicknamed "Rere," and their younger daughter, Mary Patricia, known as "Tiscia," stood by Cousy during the pregame ceremony.

Nearby sat his father, Joseph, and his mother, Juliette, once described by Cousy as "more French than Jeanne d'Arc." The elder Mrs. Cousy wore green, too, because it was also St. Patrick's Day.

There were kisses all around when the family joined dad in the center of the court. He got a big hug from a blond enchantress in a green dress, 12-year-old Martha Grady, daughter of Mr. and Mrs. John C. Grady, 21 Manning St., Needham.

Martha is the little cystic fibrosis girl who has often posed with Cousy for pictures taken on behalf of his favorite charity. Sunday, Martha presented Marie Collette and Mary Patricia with missals and silver prayer beads.

Brown-haired, brown-eyed Marie Collette, who wants to be a nun when she grows up, let loose a torrent of tears when her father entered the court.

"I want him to be home, but I still want him to play," she sobbed.

Out on the court, Missy fought a losing battle to keep a stiff upper lip. Her eyes filled when Rose Russell, wife of Bill Russell, presented her with two dozen roses from the other wives and kissed her on the cheek.

The wives last week gave Missy a charm with the inscription, "To Marie, love from all the girls on the row."

And they were in the same row Sunday—Section N, Row F—the row Missy has shared with them for the last 13 years.

And they wept as if it were their own husbands leaving the team.

But the women had no monopoly on the tears. There was a hint of them in coach Red Auerbach's eyes when he hugged his most famous player.

They appeared in the eyes of N.B.A. Pres. Maurice Podoloff, who squatted on a makeshift seat off center court. And there was deep regret on the face of Celtics co-owner Walter Brown when he said:

"I'm the guy who didn't want Bob Cousy. . . . What a genius!"

Missy cried again when Donna Marie Heinsohn, five-year-old daughter of Celtic Tommy Heinsohn, flounced out in a new pink dress and presented the elder Mrs. Cousy with a bouquet of green and white flowers.

Cousy's mother kept a handkerchief tucked under her bouquet. With a charming French accent, she explained: "I have spent my emotion last week in New York (where Cousy was honored at Madison Square Garden)."

Then she recalled how Cousy at age six had donned his uncle's top hat, brandished his cane and announced to her, "Mama, I will be a big man some day."

Mrs. Cousy laughed. "I knew he would come to a certain success, but this, never!"

His father, who used to drive a taxi in New York, watched the game with tears in his eyes, too. "I am glad he is quitting now," the elder Cousy observed. "He is almost 35 and still in good health. But this takes too much out of him. He will be a good coach."

Missy and her two daughters watched the game intently as if it were their first. The girls had banished their tears with boxes of Cracker Jacks.

Missy recalled that it was in this very spot that she spent her wedding day 13 years ago. The Cousys were married Dec. 9, 1950, but, then, because of a sudden change in game schedules, the Celtics had to meet the Syracuse Nats that night.

"We lost," Missy recalled ruefully. "And Dolph Schayes was here that day, too."

Schayes Sunday presented Cousy with a set of dishes from the Nats, "because now you're going to eat more meals at home."

SAM JONES' 47 PTS. PACE CELTS, 142-131

April 11, 1963 • by Jack Barry

Boston fans have yet to see the Celtics drop a seventh playoff game on the Garden floor.

Sam Jones, backcourt veteran, saw to that, coming up with 47 points to lead the world champions to a 142 to 131 victory [over Cincinnati] before 13,909 and then some, Wednesday night.

Outplaying the great Oscar Robertson in a personal man-to-man duel, Jones scored on 18 of 27 shots from the floor and missed only one in 12 at the foul stripe. His previous single-game high was 37 points made this year at Syracuse.

Jones was in action 41 minutes, hitting seven straight shots in the second period on his way to 19 for that session and came up with three steals of Royal offensive sorties for perhaps the finest single-game exhibition of his career.

Robertson scored 43 points, again going all but 15 seconds, but time and again permitted Sam room as the classy Royal captain was hounding the offensive area, rebound hunting.

Boston turned victory its way with a 40-point third session against the Royals' 29, as Sam scored 19 and Bill Russell owned the boards.

The victory, however, was far from a one-man job. Bob Cousy, determined not to go out with a loss, clicked for 21 points and handed out 16 assists, second high for the year for him, as he played 34 minutes.

Tommy Heinsohn, still consistent throughout, culminating a great series, belted home 31 points in 35 playing minutes with 11 in 20 from the floor including a daring hook that all but iced things late in the fourth period.

CELTICS WIN 5TH TITLE IN ROW

HEINSOHN'S KEY PLAYS NEAR END THROTTLE L.A. HOPES, 112 TO 109

April 25, 1963 • by Jack Barry

LOS ANGELES—Pressed to the very end, the champion Celtics nailed their fifth consecutive National Basketball championship to the mast-head Wednesday night with a pressure-packed 112-to-109 victory over the Lakers.

A packed Sports Arena watched enthralled as Tommy Heinsohn came through with some timely last-ditch plays that put this game beyond the reach of the Lakers, who blew both hot and cold during the night and missed narrowly of tying this game in the last few seconds.

Heinsohn, with the score 104 to 102 in Boston's favor, stole the ball to make the score 106 to 102 and put the Celtics in a strong position to clinch it.

Heinsohn's steal was a forerunner of further clutch efforts as the Lakers pressed and drew back to 106-104 position on Elgin Baylor's hoop.

After Sam Jones popped one for a lead of 108-104 with 48 seconds left, Dick Barnett hit for one basket (106-108) and followed with a free throw that made it 108 to 107 and the pressure really was on the Celtics.

Heinsohn then proceeded to hit four consecutive free throws and the score mounted to 112-107 and the game was beyond recall for the Lakers as only 13 seconds remained on the clock.

Baylor hit a hoop to make it 109 for the Lakers but Boston still had 112 on the scoreboard as time ran out.

Bob Cousy, playing his final game, threw the ball high into the air, signifying another Celtics championship. Bill Russell made a rebound of this ball.

It was a souvenir he didn't want to lose to the crowd.

And so the Celtics did it again. Cousy played his last game as a professional. He was injured in the fourth period, slipping on the wet floor, retired to the dressing room for a shot of novocaine and returned to provide the balance this Celtics team needed when matters became so tight.

Immediately after the game Coach Red Auerbach and Cousy were interviewed on national television and they raved about Heinsohn and Sanders and Russell and Ramsey.

Cousy was modest about his own performance and said about his ankle, "I turned it and it was painful at first. But Buddy LeRoux, our trainer, fixed it up with a shot of something and I was able to return."

Auerbach praised the Lakers and then said, "This is as great a thrill for us as any. All year long we've been hearing that we weren't going to win and that the Lakers would be the champions.

"All I would answer, and it's my answer tonight, was 'We're champs and we'll be champs until we're beaten.' We weren't beaten in this championship and we don't expect to lie down for anybody next year, either."

Heinsohn was the high scorer for the champions. He hit for 22 points and was followed closely by Tom

From left, Walter Brown, Bob Cousy, Bill Russell, and Red Auerbach at a postseason gathering on April 26, 1963.

Sanders, John Havlicek and Cousy, all of whom had 18 points.

The Celtics did not have an easy time of it. The Lakers were both hot and cold, but they were hot at the end and didn't quit. Elgin Baylor, one of the greatest in the league, plagued the Celtics all through the series and Wednesday night dropped in 28 points, getting most of them in the second half.

Jerry West, he with the floating set shot, was the individual high scorer for the night with 32 points.

So, it took the Celtics six games to polish off the Lakers, the same team they beat in the playoff final last season in the last few seconds.

It was an emotional scene at the end of the game. Cousy and Red Auerbach were on national television and the old buddies were seen together on the court for the final time.

Cousy, in enemy territory, still was accorded a tremendous hand from the Los Angelenos who recognize class like everybody else.

They say the finish of one of the greatest of all basketball careers, 13 years of brilliant play from a kid who came out of a New York high school just after the war with tremendous talent and a speech impediment.

He still has the talent, but not the impediment.

Cousy goes down in basketball annals as an all-time great and a Boston great who "made" the sport of basketball in this city and did much to mold the N.B.A.

That Cousy returned to the court for the last part of the final period was surprising. He was helped off the court and seemed to be hurt quite severely, but trainer Buddy LeRoux's ministrations were effective.

Cousy's mere presence on the court seemed to settle down this team as the Lakers started drawing closer and rushing to overtake a team that was determined to win this sixth game and put an end to one of the longest playoff series in the history of the league.

It is difficult to pinpoint the individual who contributed most to the fifth title in this final game. Maybe it was Heinsohn, the strong, muscular young man from Holy Cross. Bill Russell could have been it. Sam Jones and Tom Sanders were key men. And so was Frank Ramsey, who had his best playoff game and hit for 10 points.

As Auerbach said, they all played a part.

In the final analysis it was the alertness—and strength—of Gunner Heinsohn that provided the final margin of victory.

Heinsohn's accuracy from the foul line was the margin of difference after his steal of the ball with less than two minutes left.

It's questionable if Heinsohn ever before tied together four foul shots that meant so much.

So, it's all over. Cousy has retired. But he retired on a high note, backboning one of basketball's greatest teams to its greatest title.

Celts Clinch Sixth Straight Title

ELIMINATE WARRIORS, 105-99, ON RUSSELL'S CLUTCH DUNK SHOT

April 27, 1964 • by Jack Barry

Accomplishing a feat never before recorded in American pro sports, the Celtics drew down their sixth consecutive N.B.A. championship as they eked out a cliff-hanging 105-99 verdict over the scrappy San Francisco Warriors Sunday night before a howling 13,909 at the Garden and a nationwide television audience.

It was the league's perennial most valuable player, Bill Russell, who jammed home the vital 103d point on a two-hand rebound when he eluded the great Wilt Chamberlain to tally after Tommy Heinsohn missed a close-in shot.

Right here and now let it be said that Chamberlain was an immense ball player for the defeated Warriors. He scored 30 points, took 25 rebounds and, with speedy Guy Rodgers, provided the main opposition to the champions.

The Celtics were not to be denied, however, despite nearly blowing a 100-92 lead with 1:54 remaining in the final period.

A pair of baskets by Chamberlain and Al Attles around successful foul shooting sprung the still dangerous West Coast visitors to the lower end of the 101-99 count with 33 seconds left.

Here Russell came through with the big rebound.

Boston had but 10 seconds showing when it took the ball from out of bounds and Heinsohn missed on a left-hand hook, but then Russell eluded Chamberlain for the big hoop.

Here the still defiant Warriors broke down fast with Rodgers missing a hook attempt and the ball falling out of bounds for vital Celtic possession, and that was it.

With three seconds showing on the Garden clock and the fans already carrying Red Auerbach off the court, the officials had to cool off the overzealous patrons while John Havlicek went to the line to sink two of three foul shots.

The Celtics had to battle for this one, don't think they didn't. But Red Auerbach's lads did not relish a return trip to the West Coast and had what it took under pressure as they have now shown for six consecutive seasons.

There were plenty of individual heroes.

Frank Ramsey, forced into action against the huge Warrior front line because of foul trouble to Satch Sanders, came through with 18 points in 20 minutes, and both Walter Brown and Auerbach will definitely ask the colonel to come back for another year after this clutch exhibition.

There was Heinsohn, with 19 points and eight rebounds, including a spectacular 35-foot jumper to set up a 97-88 lead with 3:17 left.

Sam Jones hit 14 of his 18 markers in the second half, 10 in the third period.

John Havlicek had 14 points and four assists.

Sanders, with 11 points and 10 rebounds before fouling out with Boston in front, 97-92, received a standing ovation.

Russell, who does not know how to lose, led the Celtics to their seventh world title in eight years, cleverly avoiding serious foul trouble while going the distance, taking 26 off the boards, blocking seven shots and handing out six assists, one under the play-making Rodgers' total, which was high for the night.

The Warriors, down 100-92 and seemingly out of it at the 1:54 mark of the final chapter, really had the fans worried as they kept chipping away at Boston's margin.

The Celtics knew they were in for trouble at the outset when the Warriors, breaking fast, managed to post a period-ending 24-22 margin, with Wilt's nine points the pace-setter.

Boston shot .450, on 9 in 20 from the floor, but the visitors—with their burly front line rebounding—managed 26 floor shots, and hit only seven. But they picked up 10 points on fouls.

Over the second 12 minutes, Boston, paced by Ramsey's 11 points and the Colonel's three big assists, ran up a 45-41 margin at intermission.

Sam Jones came out of his slump in the third period, banging home 10 points, with Heinie adding six and Ramsey five as the Celtics matched the visitors point for point to enter the final period leading 74-71.

Wayne Hightower sank a pair at the line as did Attles, with the little back-court speedster then clicking on a 2-1 break with Rodgers to post a 100-97 reading.

Here Sam Jones made one in two at the line, where he had been very ineffective, missing five in nine all night, but Chamberlain turned in deep for a two-pointer and the visitors were still very much in contention, trailing 101-99, when Russ came through with a two-hand dunker.

More Than Anything Else, Walter Brown Was a Fan

September 9, 1964 • by Victor O. Jones

Back in the early 1930s, if you were looking for Walter A. Brown, the place to go was the lobby of the Boston Arena, then managed by his father, George V.

Brown. If it was during the Winter, you were almost certain to find Walter draped over one side of a radiator with Webster J. Morse, a sports writer from the nearby Christian Science Monitor, draped over the other side.

The topic of discussion was always the same—sports, and sport, but always sport. An indifferent athlete himself, Walter Brown, from his boyhood to his sudden death on the Cape on Labor Day, was essentially a fan, a rooter who lost himself in the joys and intricacies and excitement of athletic contests.

In this respect he was not very different from his father, but in the days I'm talking about, relations between George and his oldest son were strained. Lacking formal education himself, the father placed an inordinate value upon a college education. Walter, though far from dumb, was about as unacademic a man as you could hope to find. So, though he had graduated from Boston Latin and taken a year at Exeter, he didn't go to college. Instead he took to selling insurance in such time as he could spare from watching and talking sports.

So one Winter morning when Walter and Webbie Morse were draped over their favorite arena radiator, who should come bursting out of his office but the senior Brown, his always ruddy face ruddier than usual.

"Walter," he roared, "You'll never sell this guy any insurance if you haven't already. I'd go looking for other prospects elsewhere."

Well, old George V. lived to employ Walter as a highly useful assistant and the rest of us, not just in Boston, but as far away as Europe and Tokyo, got to admire him, not so much for his successful sports promotions, but as a rare human individual.

Sports, increasingly, is a field in which chicanery and double-dealing and corner-cutting are the measure of success. I know that, by definition, sports is supposed to be something else. And it was something else for Walter Brown. He had an almost childlike innocence in a field, which even at the amateur level, now is full of angles and in which wise guys and smart lawyers are at a premium.

Sports, nowadays, are based on contracts so full of fine print that even lawyers can't easily tread their way through the clauses. But Walter's contracts, even with the wrestling and boxing promoters, were largely a matter of a handshake. No employee of professional athletes ever had less trouble getting his players to sign contracts. His Celtics, for instance, the only professional team he ever exercised complete control over, were managed by a Red Auerbach who to this day holds no contract. A superstar like Frank Ramsey—every Spring before leaving for Kentucky—signed a blank contract, leaving it up to Brown to fill in the cash figures.

Of course Brown was a soft touch for every conceivable charity; he headed up dozens of drives of one kind or another. He had another attribute, rare in a day of status symbols—he was on a first-name basis with the lowliest ice-scraper, but also at ease with a polo-playing hockey player such as Stew Iglehart. He admired class, not in the social or money sense, but as a measure of individual quality.

He had a wonderful sense of humor, directed almost exclusively at himself. Freddie Corcoran, the golf promoter, is the only man who could rival Brown as a walking record book of sports, and as a story teller, Walter topped even Freddie. As an example of how he always turned his wry wit upon himself, consider his short talk on the occasion of Bob Cousy's retirement. Sentiment and oratory filled the Garden and tears were flowing freely.

Hardly a dozen of the thousands present ever knew or, if so, remembered that Brown had not wanted to sign Cousy for the Celtics. He confessed to this and, after a suitable pause, described himself with this phrase: "What a genius!"

Well, he was a genius as a human being—even if he temporarily disappointed his father by not getting himself a Yale degree. He was always uncorrupted by either success or failure. It never even occurred to him ever to take unfair advantage of anyone, or to deceive, or to obfuscate a situation. There was no guile, no trickery in him, but curiously perhaps, only the worst stinkers ever even tried to take advantage of him.

Walter Brown was the epitome of what a real fan or a real sportsman should be. He was a good man, and as the saying goes, "Good men are scarce." He will be greatly missed—and not just in the world of sports.

Celts Trounce Hawks

December 27, 1964

ST. LOUIS—The Celtics rebounded from a 10-point halftime deficit by holding St. Louis to 25 points in the last two quarters and won, 97 to 84, at Kiel Auditorium Saturday night.

The win, the Celtics' 28th against seven losses, kept them five games up on the Cincinnati Royals, who downed Philadelphia.

The Hawks led, 59-49, at intermission but, with Sam Jones hitting for 10 of his 32 points, the Celtics outscored St. Louis, 31-16, in the third period, to take a five-point advantage, 80-75, into the final quarter.

John Havlicek was the Celtic who broke the game open, though as he scored eight straight points without a St. Louis return to hike a 76-75 margin to 84-75, Boston was never in trouble after that.

[Ed. note. The Celtics featured the NBA's first all-Black starting five in this game: Bill Russell, Sam Jones, K. C. Jones, Tom Sanders, and Willie Naulls. It was not mentioned in the brief game story.]

Sam, the Celtics Man, Quiet Except in Clutch

April 4, 1965 • by Jack Barry

Five years ago, Carl Braun, then with the Knicks, remarked: "No wonder Boston keeps winning. If I had a guy like Sam Jones for a sub in my backcourt I wouldn't worry either."

A year later, Wilt Chamberlain said: "Sam Jones is the best ballplayer on the Celtics."

And he said this while Bob Cousy, Frank Ramsey, Bill Russell and Tommy Heinsohn were working as a unit.

Still later, 5-year-old William Felton Russell Jr., asked by his daddy to name the greatest basketball player, wowed 'em with "Sam Jones."

They know something, these people. But they weren't telling anything new to Mrs. Sam Jones or Mrs. Louis Jones of Durham, N.C., his mother, who have said all along that their "boy" is the greatest. His remarkable season with the Celtics only tends to bear out their sentiments.

Gladys Jones, a keen observer of basketball, is not one to speak softly of her husband's talents. "Sam is the greatest player in the game today," she proclaims. "And he will get even better."

Gladys Jones, enthusiastic and spirited, once stood up at a Celtics' wives' luncheon and took the writers to task for "giving up on the Celtics" under an early season assault by the Los Angeles Lakers.

She does admit, however, that she was surprised at Sam's high finish (fourth) in this year's most-valuable-player poll, behind Russell, Jerry West and Oscar Robertson.

"I honestly didn't think Sam would beat out Chamberlain in the voting," she said. "Or for that matter, Elgin (Baylor) or Jerry Lucas. I say that because I didn't think he'd get the votes he deserved—but I'm happy to see his value being appreciated more as he goes along."

Sam was pleased about his showing in the voting. "I could tell he was really excited the way he told me about it. He was inwardly emotional and couldn't wait to tell me," she smiled.

Sam admits Gladys knows her basketball. "We talk over games constantly. When Philly beat Cinci the other night we sat and talked about who would play me, who I would play—Greer, Costy or Bianchi, and things like that. She loves to talk basketball."

According to Gladys, Sam is not talkative after a Celtic loss. And neither is she.

"During the season Sam had his heart set on a few personal goals," said Mrs. Jones. "He wanted to play 80 games, which he had never done before, and he did. He wanted to break Tommy Heinsohn's Celtics' season's scoring mark without, of course, hurting his team value in any way. And he did.

"Then it was a real thrill to Sam, I know, when he went over the 2,000-point scoring mark for a Boston record. On top of this, to make the second N.B.A. All-Star team for the first time, and his fourth M.V.P.

finish, made it a wonderful year for him, and me, too," she said.

Sam modestly said, "I'm a Celtic because Frank Ramsey could play a corner!" Sam meant that Red Auerbach kept him after his first-year tryout (1958) as a back-court man, to take Ramsey's spot when Frank was switched to a forward.

"Not so," said Auerbach. "It might be partially true, but Sam was such a sound prospect, with rare, natural speed and shooting ability that I had to find a spot for him. Now he ranks with Robertson and Jerry West as the best back-court men in the N.B.A."

Mrs. Jones has kept a scrapbook of Sam's basketball feats since college days, including his service play and everything written about his Boston exploits.

His credentials are impressive. He has records by the handful such as his 2,000 points and his 25-point-a-game average, but among his major thrills is the 47-point game in the 1963 Eastern playoffs against Cincinnati.

Sam is pursuing his master's degree at Boston University. He needs one more year. He's also an up-and-coming insurance broker, intends to branch into real estate.

But right now everything is forgotten except the playoffs. Philadelphia openly fears him, for around the league Sam is called the deadliest shot from the backcourt.

Havlicek Tops All Hub Crooks

April 16, 1965 • by Bud Collins

Now I know who robbed the Plymouth mail truck—John Havlicek.

The only reason Havlicek isn't Summering at Walpole with the rest of the Brink's Club is that Specs O'Keefe didn't think he should blame an 11-year-old. But Johnny Havlicek must have been in on that job, too.

If your wallet is missing, if your piggy bank has been lifted, or if somebody has stolen your gal—put a tail on John Havlicek. Call DE 8-1212 and tell them you have the guy, the biggest thief the city has known.

He has been pretty clever at staying away from the law, but at 10:07 Thursday night Havlicek exposed himself in front of at least 17,000 people in the Boston Garden.

He was so quick and brazen and sure-handed in the great basketball robbery of 1965 that he made Willie Sutton seem like a pickpocket in a penny arcade.

Havlicek stole the ball with five seconds left in the 110-109 Boston victory. He stole the game, the Eastern Division pennant, and $51,000 that will go to the last-and-final-real-real champion of this nutball playoff madness. He stole Wilt (The Stilt) Chamberlain's chance finally to be a winner. It is reported he stole Wilt's lingerie as the Leaning Tower of Pituitary trudged to the shower while the hydrophobic crowd tossed Havlicek and Bill Russell and Arnold Auerbach around like ping pong balls.

Philadelphians would rather Havlicek had stolen the Liberty Bell, Betsy Ross' bungalow, the Main Line. But he decided on the ball and the ball game. The big pumpkin glittered before John like the Hope Diamond as it sped from Hal Greer's hands. He was an anti-missile as he shot at it, knocking the ball into the hands of accomplice Sam Jones.

"It looks," said Bill Russell, stroking the hair of his chinny-chin-chin, "like it went right to the wire."

The particular wire is an inch in diameter. It is a guy wire running from the backboard to the first balcony, just behind the baseline, helping support the basket. And from one of these four wires at the Garden Russell very nearly hanged himself and the Celtics.

They were a point ahead, at 110 to 109 with five seconds to play—about 100 heartbeats at Thursday night's rates. Russell took the ball out of bounds. The Celtics had merely to hold the thing, but he threw the ball too high. It struck the wire and the wire vibrated, boingggg, like Auerbach's vocal cords.

It was a rare thing to see, a violation that turned the ball—and seemingly the game   over to Philly.

Now they had it out of bounds, beneath the basket they were shooting for, and the five seconds loomed like a year in which to score the winning basket.

There was only one way for Boston to keep this game—to steal it. John Havlicek would steal a bone from Mother Hubbard's wolfhound if it would help win a ball game. So this one was easy. He went after Hal Greer's pass inbounds. With one hand he knocked it to Sam Jones. The other he put in the 76ers pockets and extracted their final-round playoff money.

Seventeen thousand people saw it, but do you think they'll holler "Cop"?

Even so, Police Comr. McNamara, your duty is clear. Arrest this man and put him in solitary until Sunday afternoon. Johnny the Dip needs peace and quiet and rest while he plots further crime against the tourists from Los Angeles.

Super-Celtics Do It Again

April 26, 1965 • by Will McDonough

The Celtics went on Summer vacation at 4:08 p.m. Sunday much richer, happier, and the basketball champions of the world for the seventh consecutive year.

They packed away their eighth N.B.A. crown by toasting 13,909 in the Garden to a 129 to 96 roasting of the Los Angeles Lakers.

And fittingly enough, the Celtics capped the season in style by putting on one of the most glittering displays of basketball the game has ever seen in the fourth quarter.

Already leading by a comfortable 16-point margin, the Celtics shut out the Lakers, 20 to 0, in the first five minutes of the fourth.

The crowd went wild, lobbing waves of applause off the Garden walls in a deafening response to the Celtics' artistry.

And Red Auerbach couldn't contain himself any longer either. When the Lakers finally called time in an attempt to halt the onslaught, Auerbach leaped off the bench, tossed a handful of his personalized cigars into the crowd, and then planted a kiss on the cheek of Mrs. Walter Brown, widow of the Celtics' former owner.

He then pulled the horses one by one—to get full acknowledgment on the applause meter.

Bill Russell grabs a rebound against the Lakers in the 1965 Finals.

an 87 to 71 margin starting the fourth quarter.

The 16-point spread was more than enough, but the Celtics didn't care. They wanted more and got it by running 20 straight points and building up a phenomenal 36-point lead.

Although Russell was fantastic with 30 rebounds, 22 points and 10 of 12 foul shots, he had plenty of help.

K.C. Jones, who teamed on championship teams with Russell at San Francisco U. and the U.S. Olympics, had perhaps his finest moment as a player.

K.C. scored 20 points for the first time in his playoff career, and wore the fabulous Jerry West in his vest pocket most of the contest.

West scored 33 points in all, but 11 of these came after K.C. left the game in the fourth quarter. And in the second quarter, when the Celtics started to pull away, West scored only one point—that coming after Auerbach was assessed with a technical foul.

Then there was Sam Jones, playing 43 minutes and firing in 22 points despite a virus and rash that have plagued him the last four days.

When it was over the Celtics had seven men in double figures. John Havlicek had 18, Tom Sanders 16, Larry Siegfried 11, and Willie Naulls 10.

Still there was more drama. When the blitz was on in the final quarter, the crowd called for Auerbach to put Tommy Heinsohn back in the game. But Red put in the scrubs instead, so Heinsohn ended his career as a Celtic on the bench.

This was a sad sight, but not as sad as watching the Lakers trying to cope with a Celtic team primed for the kill.

L.A. never had a chance. Russell saw to that. Under his tutelage, the Celtics outrebounded L.A., 77

First came Bill Russell, alias Auric Goldfinger in a basketball suit—the man with the Midas touch in the clutch.

Russell, who has never played on a loser when healthy, could almost have beaten the Lakers alone.

In the first period, for example, he personally outrebounded the entire Los Angeles team, 9 to 8.

This set the pattern. All afternoon Russell's left hand kept scratching the backboards for rebounds that would turn to offensive fast breaks in a matter of moments.

The Lakers made a match of it until the game reached the four-minute mark of the second period. Here the score was 36 to 36. Two minutes later the Celtics led by nine, a margin they held at the half.

Then they opened the third by outscoring the Lakers 7 to 1 in the first minute, and building up to to 51, and as a result took 115 floor shots, or 27 more than the Lakers.

With that kind of an edge there was no doubting the outcome. All that remained was to slice up a $51,500 playoff bonus money cake a dozen or so ways, and then go home to enjoy it.

Boston Romps to 120-112 Win

CELTICS CLINCH
EASTERN TITLE

April 13, 1966 • by Clif Keane

PHILADELPHIA—And now it's 10 straight times in the finals of the National Basketball Assn. championships for Bill Russell.

And once again Wilt Chamberlain has drawn a void.

Wilt wins all the individual titles.

Russell leads his club to championships.

The Celtics defeated the Philadelphia 76ers, 120 to 112, at Convention Hall Tuesday night, winning the best-of-seven series four games to one, and now they go into the championship round with either the St. Louis Hawks or the Los Angeles Lakers, the date of the first game being unsettled until the Western clubs finish their series.

The Celtics never had to fret, really, once they caught up with the 76ers in the first moments of the game. The 76ers went out ahead, 7 to 0, but then they sat back and watched the Celtics pour in eight straight points.

The game took on a weird picture when the two teams were introduced. The papers had played up a story before the game that Wilt had failed to report for a practice session Monday afternoon. The tall man, who won just about every record imaginable all season, said he was too tired to work out, and the fans at the hall gave him a slight bazoo when he walked onto the floor.

Now Wilt can rest while Russell goes on into the finals.

The tall man played fairly well, though he worked at the foul line as though it was something new to him, and the fire Wilt had in the game in Boston Sunday afternoon was missing all night.

The story broke like wildfire after the game that Coach Dolph Schayes was through. But once again it looks as though Mr. Chamberlain wants to run things just as he has all through his career.

Maybe he should be named coach of the club.

The Celtics played strongly up front in the game, with Don Nelson doing very well when things got a little sloppy with the Celtics. Sam Jones, especially, seemed to tire, but it was Nelson—and Russell— who pulled the team together the few times they were in any trouble at all.

The Celtics led by 10 points at halftime and when they went into the last quarter they were ahead by nine, but at the 8:22 mark they were all alone, 17 points ahead, with Johnny Havlicek and Nelson fairly wrecking the 76ers over the first few minutes.

But the Celtics had some trouble getting the ball in play over the final minutes, with the lads losing the ball twice on passes inbounds. But Auerbach fixed that quickly when he put back K. C. Jones, all taped up again, to kill off the final minutes.

With 1:50 left, the Celtics were ahead by only six, but Russell broke away from the pack for a stuff in, and when Havlicek scored with less than a minute in the game, and came back quickly for two foul conversions, the 76ers were gone for good.

At game's end, Russell chased after Wilt to shake his hand, and Wilt accepted it quite graciously. The tall man then patted a couple of other Celtic players and headed for his room while the 8,500 in the place walked out quite solemnly.

What happens to Wilt as a leader under conditions such as these is hard to explain. He had talked himself into feeling he was going to chase Russell off the court this year and he broke all records along the way. But this story about him getting tired was a sad one.

After all, he is quite a bit younger than Russell and had almost two weeks to sit by while Russell was having to work against the Cincinnati Royals.

When players saw that Wilt wasn't going to manhandle Russell as they hoped he would, the whole gang of them tailed off.

Wilt wound up with 46 points and had 34 rebounds. But the rebound story was a local one, just as it so often can be at home for Russell. Wilt didn't seem to be close to 34 rebounds, and maybe he was given a few during the practice session for the 76ers.

Russell had 18 points, as he did Sunday at home, and 31 rebounds, while Havlicek led the Boston scorers with 32 points and Sam Jones was only two behind.

The series was hardly as well played as several in the past between Wilt and Russell; there was a lot of scrambling all over the floor, but Nelson, a fine position player, seemed to pull together the Celtics a few times when they got too sloppy.

Well, things could go on and on, but the game hardly warrants any more gab about things. This man Russell just keeps going on and on and Wilt wilts. How a man can say he's tired and won't show up for practice—especially when he is paid over $100,000—is hard to explain.

He doesn't seem to be able to do a good job trying to tell his story when it matters.

Russell Expected to Coach Celtics

April 18, 1966 • by Clif Keane

William Felton Russell probably will be named the next coach of the Boston Celtics at a luncheon this noon at the Hotel Lenox.

If so, he will be the first Negro ever to coach a major professional team.

The press was told prior to the first playoff game between the Celtics and Lakers at the Garden Sunday that an important announcement would be made today. In all probability it will concern the replacement for Arnold (Red) Auerbach, who has announced his retirement as a coach.

The guessing game on who will replace Auerbach has been going on for over a year, and lately four names have been mentioned: Alex Hannum, recently deposed as coach of the San Francisco Warriors; Paul Seymour, who quit his post with the Baltimore Bullets; Bob Cousy and Bob Brannum, former Celtics players.

Cousy and Brannum have signed new contracts at Boston College and Norwich, respectively.

Why the sudden shift to Russell?

The Celtics approached Hannum at his West Coast home, but apparently nothing materialized from their talks. Hannum is also reported to be in line for the job at either Philadelphia or Baltimore, while Seymour, when he left the Bullets, didn't endear himself with the local powers.

The presence of Frank Ramsey at the game started rumors that he was around to be signed. But after the Celtics defeat, Ramsey said: "I couldn't take the job. I have too many commitments."

Possibly Russell hinted that he was thinking about taking the job following the team's victory over the 76ers in Philadelphia Tuesday night.

After the game, Auerbach said to Russell: "You can have tomorrow off, Bill."

Russell's answer was: "No, I'll be at practice, Red. And since you are going to Washington, I will coach the team in practice."

Russell has stepped in to coach the Celtics many times in his 10 years with the team, although no definite record has been kept since many of the nights he took charge were after Auerbach had been kicked out of games.

Russell has been asked many times if he would like to coach the team and his answers have always been negative. "I have enough butterflies in my stomach just playing," he has said.

He receives a salary of $100,001 as a player, and his contract has two years to run. Taking on the burden of coaching will probably give Russell another $25,000.

The players will accept the choice of Russell very willingly. They regard him as the greatest of all players. Possibly Cousy and some of the past Celtics players had mild disagreements with Russell, but nobody on this present team seems to be at odds with the great star.

Possibly Russell gave this reporter a hint in a recent cab ride in Philadelphia.

"Who do you think will coach the Celtics next year?" he asked.

"Either Hannum or Seymour," he said.

"You're probably wrong on both counts, Keane," said Russell.

Celtics Shatter Taboo...and Russell Faces Challenge

April 23, 1966 • by Carl T. Rowan

WASHINGTON—Professional athletics in America passed another great milestone this week when William Felton Russell was named to replace Arnold (Red) Auerbach as coach of the Boston Celtics.

Thoughtful, militant "Big Bill" thus becomes the first Negro to direct a major professional sports team, a development whose importance is being compared with Jackie Robinson's entry into organized baseball.

Racial drama, an air of tension, and myriad predictions of calamity attended Robinson's entry into baseball. They're absent with regard to Russell's appointment, and therefore, some may think the comparison overdrawn.

But the truth is that Russell's appointment may be even more important than Robinson's debut in terms of the long-range implications for American society.

Robinson had to prove that he could hit a curve ball, carry as much deodorant to the locker room as the white players, and remain silent in the face of abuse for a decent interval.

Russell's challenge now is to disprove anew the long-held notion, rarely spoken these enlightened days, that Negroes are long on muscle and short on brains.

Watch the baseball All-Star game this Summer. Chances are that half the starting players will be Negroes, and that a Willie Mays or Maury Wills or Frank Robinson will emerge as a hero.

But you will have to look long and hard to find a Negro in even a subordinate managerial capacity in baseball. And Negroes chuckle wryly at the thought of the men who own the teams explaining that there just aren't any Negro players around with the intellect of a, say, Yogi Berra.

Most Americans couldn't conceive of professional football without its Jimmy Browns and Bobby Mitchells and Gayle Sayerses. But pro football manages to get along very well without Negro coaches— or quarterbacks either, this too being a position of direction, of brains more than brawn.

The appointment of Russell would be meritorious simply for the fact that it indicates the Celtics' owners could look past Russell's dark, bearded face and see not only a super player but a man of "pride, intelligence, an active and appreciative sense of humor, a preoccupation with dignity" to use the words of a white writer who knows Russell, as I do not.

But the Celtics have done much more than point up the cowardliness, the backwardness of other operators of major sports teams. They have walked upon a tradition, a taboo as it were, that cuts across the whole spectrum of American life. That seldom-spoken tradition is simply that wherever an alternative is possible, Negroes are not to be put in positions of command over white people.

That was the "understanding" that caused the U.S. Navy to go through generations (up till the middle of World War II) without permitting a Negro to rise to officer rank.

That unspoken and sometimes not-even-consciously-acknowledged rule behind the fact that even today our military establishment is an operation in which you can find an abundance of Negro G.I.s at the front in Viet Nam but a handful of Negroes in command positions in the Pentagon.

The mere naming of Cmdr. Samuel L. Gravely to command a Navy destroyer or the appointment of Lt. Gen. Benjamin O. Davis Jr. to a top command post in Korea is big "news"—and that fact alone emphasizes what the common rule is.

The general taboo against giving a Negro the top spot is still largely unbroken in business and industry. In a few instances, soft drink, whisky and other firms conscious of potentially large Negro markets have named Negro vice presidents. But this is for the most part a public relations gesture.

Most firms are still hiring just enough high-level Negroes to acquire just enough visibility to keep the pickets away. The boards of directors and the executive suites stay lily-white.

The executive branch of the Federal government has, in recent years, dealt some harsh blows to the old taboo against placing Negroes in positions of command. But in most of American society people are still enslaved to a tradition that rests on old assumptions of the intellectual inferiority of the Negro.

The Celtics' owner has just said, "Away with that nonsense," and he put $125,000 where his mouth is.

Celtics Again!

EDGE LAKERS, 95-93, FOR 9TH TITLE

April 29, 1966 • by Bud Collins

With a team like the Celtics, who needs LSD?

There was the usual pandemonium and the usual outcome in the Old Asylum on Causeway Street Thursday night: Celtic madness, riots of ecstacy among the true believers, and at the end triumph, 95 to 93, for the beloved old giraffes who have hung so many pennant sheets in the Garden that it looks like a laundry.

Another one of those green and white sheets goes up on the line with 1966 World Champions printed on it.

"Everybody had a shot at me—Cincy, Philadelphia, and the Lakers—but the flag still goes up," cackled Arnold Auerbach. He laughed and he sounded demented. He had earned dementia, going through all this longest season of nutball.

"I feel drunk and I haven't had a drink," he screamed.

You could see why. Even though the Celtics led all the way, Red's ordeal was tougher on the stomach than a case of bourbon before breakfast.

The Celtics' new coach W. Felton Russell—also a rather consequential player—got the opening tap, knocked the ball to K. C. Jones, who moved it along to John Havlicek. Havlicek rolled it into the basket, and the 15,000-or-so worshippers gave out with a great hallelujah chorus, sounding as though voiced by lions.

Historians will want to know Auerbach's just-before-the battle-mother-speech to his troops prior to the seventh game. It was, as they say, a tremendous ear jerker. He pulled out all the stops because he had more hair to pull. He paced before his men and dropped three immortal words, over and over: "Defense and dollars. Defense and dollars."

There is nothing like defense to get dollars in professional basketball, and the Celtics were inspired by the thought of making an extra $800 per man.

Fred Schaus, the Los Angeles coach, had one consolation: he won't have to lose another title to Auerbach. This was the fourth time he went into the Auerbach meatgrinder—twice in the seventh game.

But he had to smile, even though it was a punched-out smile. "Who would ever have thought 95 points could win the championship game? Ninety-five points. If somebody said to me you're gonna hold them to 95, I would have known we were in.

"But," Schaus said, the gloom returning, "we couldn't hit. It was a combination of our being off and their defense rushing us into bad shots. When my two big men (Jerry West and Elgin Baylor) don't hit . . . well . . . "

The Celtics did play defense. So did the Lakers. Both teams' shooting was like the Groton-St. Mark's game—39 percent for the Lakers, 35 percent for the Celtics. But the local group, with W. Felton Russell guiding them, had the good sense to throw the ball in the direction of the hoop more times—105 to 88. Enough of these well-intentioned gestures fell in to keep them champions for an eighth straight year.

The best defense of the night was the entire court press staged by thousands of zealots who ran onto the floor, hoping to take home a piece of Auerbach for their living room shrines.

Bucking the wild mob was like going through a grape press. Youngsters were hanging from the baskets and from each other. They may have been showing affection for the Celtics, but it went too far. Incompetency by the police—too few of them at that—allowed the exuberance to become dangerous.

Chaos flowed into the Celtics' dressing room, but fewer of the celebrants were foaming.

Auerbach kissed the game ball. Then a photographer wanted Russell to kiss Auerbach.

It would have been a great picture for the Mississippi readers, but Russell wasn't feeling that delirious.

The king was dead, long live the king. That was the feeling as Auerbach stepped up on a bench to stand beside Russell. "You . . . are . . . the . . . grrrrrreatest."

Auerbach growled. He was right, just as he has been right through a decade of championship moves. Now he was buried as king after 1,037 victories, and the new king was beside him.

Russell gleamed with sweat, and with water from the final enactment of the annual ritual: immersing Auerbach in the shower. "This team was the shortest on ability, but the longest on heart of all the championship teams," he said.

"This is the last time I can get away with this," Auerbach said, dropping a cigar ash on Russell's head. "Russ probably won't let me in the dressing room next year. Well, I guess I did all right for a guy who never scored a basket."

Russell? He was Bill Russell. That's all you need to know. He was there, with 25 points and 32 rebounds, and playing Russellian defense, doing the things that impelled Gail Goodrich to name him the Big Flyswatter.

And the rest? How can you tell where one heart stops and the other begins—Sam . . . K.C. . . . Havlicek . . . Siegfried . . . Satch . . . Nelson . . . Naulls . . . Auerbach.

They made it a night of madness, of exultation and sadness, of goodbye Red and hello championship.

It took longer this time—97 games to bring the usual pandemonium and outcome. Now, Red, will you please order the champagne?

Russell Smiles: 'Well, Can't Lose 'Em All Now'

October 16, 1966 • by Bob Sales

Bill Russell settled onto the bench in front of his locker after the Celtics won their opener Saturday night, heaved a deep sigh and asked for the tapecutter. The coach doesn't blow smoke rings in the new era.

Otherwise, things are about the same. Russell controls the boards and K. C. Jones controls the ball game. Sam Jones provides the points and someone is always ready to come off the bench with a clutch performance.

"Well," Russell said, a smile crossing his face, "we can't lose 'em all now."

Russell was subdued as he inhaled a container of orange drink and talked about the ball game. He substituted Larry Siegfried for Sam Jones with 4:10

to go and the score tied, 107-107. Siegfried scored 14 points to pace the winning rally.

"I guess," Siegfried kidded afterward, "I made a genius out of him."

"There ain't no genius there," said Russell. "Sam had been digging and you could tell he was getting tired. You know you can always depend on Larry."

K.C. Jones, who played 46 minutes, sat across the room from Russell trying to catch his breath. He was bushed.

"I played too much," K.C. said, "but it's my fault. I should have told Russ. But he's got a million things to think about, playing and coaching. Winning the first one helps him."

Russell took a five-minute breather himself in the second quarter. He leaned on his knees, warmup jacket draped over his shoulders, peering intently at the action. "I didn't get a chance to enjoy it," he said.

Even though Russell was outwardly calm ("I'm too tired to get excited," he said), winning the first game was something special to him.

"Sure," he said, "I'm glad we got that first win. It will be altogether different now. I think we were all a little bit tight."

It was a night for standing ovations for Russell. He received one when he was introduced before the game and another as he led the Celtics back into the dressing room after the game.

Now the Celtics can get down to the game-to-game business of the N.B.A. season.

"Starting next game," K.C. Jones said, "I got to tell him when I'm tired."

Sam Gets 51; Celts Win, 118-109

March 29, 1967 • by Bob Sales

NEW YORK—Sam Jones set a Celtic record of 51 points Tuesday night, and they needed every one of them to reach the promised land of Philadelphia.

The Celtics pounded out a 118-109 victory over the Knicks at Madison Square Garden to win that playoff series, three games to one, and will play Philly at the Palestra Friday night.

Sam made 19 of 30 shots, running his defenders into so many screens they must have felt like they had green dye on their noses. He made 13 of 17 from the foul line.

The Knicks, urged on by a surprisingly partisan crowd of 17,173, refused to be buried, although the Celtics pushed them into the ground several times. Led by hustling Fred Crawford with 26 points, they kept coming back.

The Celtic bench did yeoman duty.

With Bailey Howell hobbled by a bad ankle and reluctant to shoot—he took no shots in the first half—Don Nelson bounded onto the floor to help out under the basket and chip in with some important baskets.

Russell gathered four personal fouls in the first half and sent Wayne Embry out to do the job in the second half. Embry did.

Willis Reed started the scoring in the third period with a jumper from the right corner that cut the Celtics' lead to 60-59.

Then Howell made his first shot of the day and the Celtics were off. With Embry boxing out underneath and setting up screens for Sam, Boston ground inexorably ahead.

Embry scored 15 points in 16 minutes. Nelson had 13 and 15 rebounds. That was all lovely supporting work. The star was Sam Jones.

Sam popped for 19 in the first period as Boston raced to a 31-22 lead. He had 29 at halftime, making 11 of 19 shots. And he just kept on grinding it out.

He hit a short jumper, following up his own shot, with 3:17 to go in the third quarter to break 40 and give the Celtics a nine-point lead.

He took a four-minute rest at the start of the last period and was in there popping at the end. He scored seven straight Celtic points, to match the Knick output through a three-minute stretch that led into the last two minutes.

76ers Dethrone Celtics, 140-116

April 12, 1967 • by Bob Sales

PHILADELPHIA—Brad Richman, 12, crinkled his face up in a smile at 10:50 Tuesday night and pulled a small cigar out of the inside pocket of his Philadelphia 76er blazer. He munched down on it and shrieked:

"Boston is dead."

Philadelphians of all sizes and shapes and gender and age were joining him as Convention Hall turned into a mass of shrieking and puffing humanity in the final seconds of the 76ers' 140-116 victory over the Boston Celtics. This one finally buried the Celtics.

It gave the 76ers the playoff series in five games and sent them into the final playoff series against the San Francisco-St. Louis winner for the N.B.A. title. It also ended Boston's streak of eight straight league titles.

It also ended seven years of frustration for Wilt Chamberlain and his normally placid Philadelphia brethren. That's what the histrionics were about.

The cigars were for former Boston coach Red Auerbach, who made a fetish of lighting a cigar as soon as he felt victory was his. These people had seen the act far too many times.

Philly coach Alex Hannum doesn't use cigars.

But you knew he felt safe when he removed Chamberlain with 1:14 to go and the 76ers leading, 133-114.

The roar would have made even Ringo Starr shudder.

Chamberlain played as if he were a man possessed, which he was. He swatted away shots, played volley ball with rebounds and raced up and back like a sprinter. He wound up with 36 rebounds, 13 assists and 29 points. That's a massive night's work.

The Celtics gave it their gamest shot. John Havlicek, who went 48 minutes for the third straight game, whipped in his last five shots and had 14 in the period as the Celtics raced to a 37-26 lead in the first quarter. Larry Siegfried had 12 points in the period.

The Celtics remained hot at the start of the second period. A three-point play by Havlicek with 7:37 to go gave them a 16-point lead and the press row partisans started mumbling about the greatest comeback in sports history.

The 76ers were having no part of that.

[Chet] Walker then came off the bench and turned the tables on Havlicek.

A driving layup by Walker, two free throws by Greer and consecutive baskets by Wilt gave Philly a run of eight and cut the Celtic lead to seven points. There were two minutes left in the half.

Walker made a three-point play and two free throws before Sam Jones retaliated with a foul shot for the Celtics. Greer and Howell matched baskets and the Celtics led by only five at the half.

The 76ers took charge after Havlicek started the second half with a jumper from the right corner.

Wally Jones popped from 20 feet on the left side. Wally Jones popped from the right corner. Hal Greer gathered in a flip from Chamberlain and made a short jumper. Wally Jones took a pretty pass from Walker and made a layup on a 2-on-1 break against Bill Russell. Luke Jackson blocked a shot by Howell, scrambled after the loose ball and jammed it in.

That all happened in less than two minutes. All of a sudden the 76ers had turned a 72-65 deficit into a 75-72 lead.

The Celtics made a run back at them, holding several more one-point leads as the teams exchanged baskets. The last Celtics' lead was 93-92 at 4:14.

The 76ers then went on an 8-1 tear—three by Wilt, three by Walker and a driving layup by Greer— to lead by six going into the final period.

The last quarter was for the sadists—who were out in force—as the Celtics scored only two field goals in the first four minutes and the 76ers rolled it up.

Two free throws by Walker gave them a 10-point lead at 7:51. It was 16 only 50 seconds later on a driving layup by Greer.

It was 20 with 5:54 to go as Matt Guokas dribbled in all alone for a layup. It was 25 as Greer cut around

Wilt for a layup with 4:15 on the clock. It never got to be 30.

That's when the people started to jeer the guys in Green and the cigars started to appear. The no smoking signs around this auditorium were ignored by both the patrons and the police.

Celtics Down 76ers for Eastern Title, 100-96

VICTORY MAKES BOSTON FIRST IN NBA HISTORY TO OVERCOME 3-1 SERIES DEFICIT—L.A. NEXT

April 20, 1968 • by Bob Sales

PHILADELPHIA—Bill Russell leaped up, both hands extended, grinning broadly, as the green uniforms surrounded him Friday night on the Spectrum's basketball floor. It was a sight to behold. He was a winner again—and it was delicious.

The Celtics had just topped the Philadelphia 76ers, 100 to 96, for the third straight time to win the playoff series, 4 games to 3, and enter the final round of the National Basketball Assn. playoffs.

"At this point," Russell said moments later, "it is my most satisfying victory." He has played for nine professional championship teams, two N.C.A.A. winners, and an Olympic champ. That covers a lot of victories.

"It's like the Peanuts cartoon," Philadelphia coach Alex Hannum said. He'd just lost another ball game and he said: "It's just like dropping an ice cream cone. There it is. But what can you do about it? You can't pick it up and eat it. It's gone."

The victory, which made the Celtics the first team in the league's history to come back from a 3-1 deficit, was mainly due to the Celtics' defense, led by Russell.

For the second consecutive game they did not allow the 76ers to score 30 points in a quarter, holding them to 40 in the first half on 16 of 55 shots, a horrible 29 percent.

"The breaks," said Wilt Chamberlain, who scored only 14 points for the 76ers, 12 in the first half, and took only two shots in the final 24 minutes.

"How do you explain the inability to hit the basket? Sometimes it's due to pressure. Sometimes it's due to defense. We just shot sub-par."

While the 76ers were shooting sub-par, the Celtics were grinding out a 12-point lead. A run of seven gave them a five-point edge in the first quarter, and they held it going into the second. Two baskets by Larry Siegfried and one by Sam Jones in succession extended their lead to 38-26 with 7½ minutes left in the half. They led by six at the intermission, 46-40.

Wally Jones bombed the 76ers back in the third period, scoring 12 of his 18 points, and the Celtic lead was down to 73-69 going into the final.

Hal Greer popped from 20 feet with 10:40 to go and the score was tied at 75-75. A 10-footer by Luke Jackson with 8½ minutes to go put the 76ers in front, 81-79, and the crowd of 15,202 roared. But the Celtics came back.

A hook shot by Russell and two free throws by John Havlicek put the Celtics back in front. Moments later Havlicek made a short jumper, fed Howell for a layup on a fast break and popped from the outside himself to give the Celtics a 93-88 lead. There was 3:44 to go.

The 76ers came with two points after that. With 32 seconds to go they trailed by three and had the ball. There was still time.

Wally Jones drove for the basket and missed. Don Nelson and Chamberlain came down with the rebound for a jump ball. Chamberlain controlled the tap and Chet Walker drove for the basket. Russell cut off his lane and blocked the shot, his 10th block of the game. The ball went to Hal Greer, who missed. Russell grabbed the rebound.

Two free throws by Sam Jones made it 100-95 with 10 seconds to go. With eight seconds left Walker missed the second of a two-shot foul and Wayne Embry grabbed the rebound for Boston. He dribbled into the corner and stopped.

"When I grabbed it," said Embry, "I said to myself, 'No one is going to take the ball away. They'll have to kill me first.'"

Then the game was over.

"Tear down those signs," shouted Embry, shaking a fist at the rafters, which were full of "Boston Is Dead" on bedsheets. Some kids were walking around with one that pleased Embry. It said: "Celtics Rule Once Again."

One sign was not torn down an hour after the game. It was the one on the 76ers' dressing room, announcing: "76ers—World Champion."

Chamberlain was sitting in front of his locker trying to explain why he did not go to the basket at all during the second half. He explained that the plays called for him to hit the hot man, which was Wally Jones, and that he was really only doing what he was told to do.

"As it turned out," he said wistfully, "I should have been more offense-minded. But that's the way the ball bounces. It's a corny phrase, I know. That's the way it was, though."

Greer and Walker led the 76ers with 22 and 19 points, respectively. Sam Jones had 22 for Boston, Havlicek 21 and Siegfried 18. Russell scored 12 and had 26 rebounds. Chamberlain led the 76ers rebounders with 34.

"It was a tough game, a physical game," said Chamberlain, "and they deserve it. They were tougher. We weren't as tough as we could be."

Celtics Champions Again

May 3, 1968 • by Bob Sales

LOS ANGELES—Weldon Haire, public address announcer at the Garden, hasn't used the line for a year. But he can ring the Celtics onto the Garden floor with it on opening night next season:

"Here come the world champion Boston Celtics."

The Celtics won the National Basketball Assn. title Thursday night with a 124 to 109 victory over the Los Angeles Lakers at the Forum, which wasn't nearly as close as the score would indicate.

And it was John Havlicek and Bailey Howell, with a total of 70 points between them, who sparked the Boston triumph and gave the Celtics—a team of "oldsters" many experts had classified as "washed up" earlier in the season—their 10th title in 12 years.

The victory, which gave the Celtics four victories in six games against the Lakers, was one the Celtics wanted badly. They did not want to go home to play a seventh game on Sunday.

"Don't be coming around here with that 'If we lose' talk," Sam Jones warned before the game. "We're gonna win it here tonight."

The purposefulness was carried onto the court.

With Havlicek scoring 16 of his 40 points and Larry Siegfried, 11, the Celtics held a 15-point lead halfway through the first period, which shrunk to seven at the end. It didn't take them long to stretch that lead to 20.

Sam Jones, guarded by Gail Goodrich, took him into the pivot and scored two turnaround jumpers that made the score 43-32 with 9:41 left in the half. Havlicek drove down the middle and Don Nelson hit a 20-footer to make it 47-32.

A basket by Jerry West stemmed the Celtics' rally for only a moment.

A free throw and a basket by Howell and two more baskets by Sam Jones extended the Celtic lead to 54-34 with 7½ minutes left in the half. The 15-to-2 spree took three minutes.

The Lakers' tremendous duo of Elgin Baylor and Jerry West both had subpar shooting nights. Baylor finished with 28 points and West had 22. Many of their points, however, came in the closing moments after the game was out of reach.

West, in fact, spent much of the final period on the bench, after playing under the strain of a sprained ankle.

West and Baylor scored only 10 and 11 points, respectively, in the first half and their reduced output was noticeable as Boston carried off a 20-point lead, 70-50.

Boston, however, continued to put the pressure on West, pressing and making the injured backcourt star strain his sore ankle by bringing the ball upcourt.

Coach Russell was hit with a technical in the last 30 seconds [of the third period] after he protested a foul called on player Russell on a move to the basket by Counts.

Havlicek came back in the last 15 seconds, though, with a foul shot and sneakaway basket to end the period with a Boston lead of 94-78. Havlicek had 30 by the end of the period.

Bill Russell was his indomitable self, controlling both boards and scoring 12 points while plugging the Lakers offensive lane. In an odd quirk Russ did not take a trip to the foul line until the last two minutes when he sank both ends of a two-shot foul.

Celts Draft All-America Jo Jo White

April 8, 1969 • by Bob Sales

The names were scrawled on the memo pad on Red Auerbach's desk: "Hill, Allen, White, Cannon, McCarter, Robertson, Smith, Beard."

These were the players the Celtics were interested in—and hoped would be available—when it was their time to choose in the National Basketball Assn. draft yesterday.

"Walk . . . Allen . . . Driscoll . . . Cannon . . . "

The teams picked as if a script had been written. Then San Diego asked for a moment. Auerbach glanced over at player-coach Bill Russell and John Havlicek, the Celtics' captain.

San Diego picked Bobby Smith of Tulsa. A collective sigh of relief was emitted.

"Portman . . . Gilliam . . . "

Now it was the Celtics' turn, Auerbach again glanced at Russell and Havlicek. He was grinning.

"Pick him," said Russell.

"Boston picks Jo Jo White of Kansas," Auerbach said. He was excited.

"He might go in the service," said Auerbach, as the draft choices droned on in the background. "But I don't care. He's the best player on that list."

Jo Jo White of Kansas, a 6-foot-3 backcourtman, was now Celtic property. Auerbach couldn't believe it.

"Warren . . . McCarter . . . Ogden . . . Davis . . . "

"I saw him play in New York," Auerbach continued. "He was something. He was really great. He's the only one I even drafted that I didn't ever expect to get. He has the greatest potential."

White, an Olympic star, the ninth man chosen in the draft, was the man Auerbach wanted.

He is a shooting backcourtman—who can take Sam Jones' place on the roster—and a playmaker. This is what the Celtics need most.

Havlicek got up to leave. The day's work was done. The Celtics' second-round choice was traded to Pheonix for Emmette Bryant—another Red Auerbach coup.

"Thank you for your kindness, your moral support, your tenacity and your fantastic judgment," Auerbach said.

Havlicek left. Auerbach continued to talk about White.

"He's a bona-fide All-America," said Auerbach. "He has the potential to become a fine, fine ball player. Maybe even a superstar."

How could eight teams pass a man that good? Part of it is that White is subject to the draft, meaning that the team that picks him may be without his services for several seasons.

"Part of it," said Auerbach, "is that a number of teams need big guys."

The Celtics could use a big man to back up Russell. But, said Auerbach, "[Lew] Alcindor has signed. [Neal] Walk (a 6-foot-10 center from Florida) has signed."

He paused.

"I always felt," said Auerbach, "that you pick the best player you can get. Then you worry."

Auerbach obviously thought he picked the best player available. So did Russell and Havlicek.

"He's really good, both on offense and defense," said Havlicek, who saw White play for the Olympic team against the Knicks.

Red did all the scouting, said Russell, "and he didn't think he'd be available."

White was. Now all the Celtics must do is sign him. It shouldn't be hard.

"Boston," said White by phone from Hawaii, where he will play in an All-Star game. "That's a good team to be with. I never even dreamed about being with them."

Celts Win on Last Second Jones Shot

OFF-BALANCE 17-FOOTER TOPS LAKERS, 89-88, TIES SERIES

April 30, 1969 • by Bob Sales

Sam Jones, off-balance and shooting awkwardly off the wrong foot, hit a 17-foot push shot with a second to go last night to give the Celtics an 89 to 88 victory over the Lakers at the Garden and tie the best-of-seven playoff series at two games apiece.

The deciding basket came on a play which the Celtics have practiced, but never used in a game. It started with seven seconds to go in the game.

Emmette Bryant, standing in front of the press table, passed the ball in to John Havlicek and scrambled to the foul line to set a screen. Bailey Howell and Don Nelson also were in the area setting screens.

Havlicek flipped the ball to Jones to the right of the key. Jones slipped as he received the pass. He recovered and tossed the ball softly toward the rim, on a high arc.

"All I wanted was to shoot the ball high with some backspin on it," said Jones later. "I thought it'd be short. But that way (Bill) Russell has a chance for a rebound."

Russell wasn't in the game. He was standing in front of the bench, rooting the ball in.

The ball hit the front rim, bounced high in the air and nestled on the back rim. Everyone on the floor—and in the Garden—was suspended, watching the ball.

Bryant started to pray silently. The ball nestled into the net. Howell leaped up, both fists over his head. Nelson started to scramble back on defense.

"Four-leaf clovers," said Bryant, touching his Celtic jersey, "were flying all over the place."

Balance Writes Happy Ending to Celtics' Cinderella Tale

SAM 'GLAD TO FINISH AS CHAMP'

May 6, 1969 • by Leigh Montville

LOS ANGELES—How many times had they done it? A million times? Maybe. It seemed like at least a million.

John Havlicek put his pale white arm around Sam Jones' brown shoulders. The green shirts on both men were wet and stuck to their bodies.

The Celtics arrive at Boston City Hall Plaza for the 1969 Championship celebration.

"Sam, old man, I just want to take one more picture with you," John Havlicek said, breaking into a grin. "Give them that Colgate smile."

Sam smiled. Havlicek continued to smile. Lights flashed. Cameras recorded.

This was the last time. This was the best time. It was Sam Jones' last locker room scene. It was the Boston Celtics' 11th National Basketball Association championship in 13 years.

It was the annual celebration. Another championship. Another flag for the top of Boston Garden. This was the toughest one. It was the best one.

The Celtics had won the title again with a 108-106 victory over the Los Angeles Lakers at the sold-out modern forum. The formula had been familiar—balanced scoring, defense, the fast break, work from center Bill Russell, but the situation had been alien.

The Celtics, since the playoffs had begun 18 games ago, had been underdogs. They had been the fourth-place finisher in the regular season, the ugly-sister invitation to the playoffs ball.

"Every year people used to talk about how we'd win the playoffs because of the home-court advantage," Jones said. "Well this year it was different. This year we didn't have the home-court advantage once.

"We had to win a game away from home in every series and we did it.

"On paper the Lakers had the greatest team, no doubt about it. But we had the greatest bench. Me? I'm glad to finish as a champion."

Jones, who scored 24 points to match his jersey number in the final-game win, started to take off the green uniform for the last time. The trunks, he said, would go back to Bailey Howell.

"They're his," Sam said, showing the label and Howell's stitched-in No. 18 for corroborating evidence. "We switched pants early in the season. Maybe it's superstition, but they do fit me better than my own."

Havlicek, standing next to Sam, backed against the wall, tried to undress his own emotions. He couldn't do it.

"Some day, when all this is over, I'm going to sit at home and try to figure all this out," he said rapidly. "The feeling now is something I just can't explain.

"I don't want to think about next season or anything like that. I want to sit down and enjoy what has just happened."

What had happened was what has happened over and over and over again in the N.B.A. The Celtics had done the big job at the big moment.

In the first five minutes of the game they had taken a 13-6 lead. They had nursed it, given away chunks of it, then nursed it again. When there were only nine minutes of basketball left, the lead had grown to 100-85.

"We wanted that early lead," Havlicek said. "In this series, it always seemed that the team that went ahead early was the team that won the game."

Then, as often happens, the Celtics hit a dry spell. A dry spell? The Gobi Desert was not nearly as barren as what the Celtics did in almost the next eight minutes.

They were outscored 19-3. Suddenly the margin was 103-102. The Celts' lead was down to one point.

Then, Don Nelson picked a basketball off the floor and took a jump shot from the foul line. The ball hit the back of the rim, the inside of the rim.

"A shot that hits the inside of the rim should never go in . . . but it did," Lakers coach Bill van Breda Kolff said.

The ball bounced up in the air. Swish. It came back down through the net.

"I was just hoping that shot would go in," Havlicek said.

"What can I say," Nelson said. "It was a lucky shot—the luckiest shot of my life."

Neither team took advantage of opportunities the rest of the way, until Larry Siegfried was intentionally fouled with 24 seconds left. He hit both shots, the score jumped to 107-102. The title stayed in Boston.

"We didn't have champagne in the dressing room," Havlicek said. "I never drank a glass of champagne in a Celtics locker room.

"We just don't have it—it's not superstition. We just don't have it."

Down the hall, at another, quieter dressing room there were five cases of unopened champagne. There were eight unopened bags of balloons at the top of the forum ceiling, and an unsliced victory cake in the Laker press room.

"That's the Celtics' strength—balance," Lakers coach Van Breda Kolff said. "Don't get me wrong, it's nice to have Jerry West to go to, but it would be nice to have four guys with him.

"You can't beat balance. The Celtics' balance was only getting old, that's why we stayed close.

"Four years ago? Sam Jones and those guys would have run away from us."

Van Breda Kolff gave a wistful smile at the thought, drank a soda. It was an old story.

Sam and John and Bill Russell and Bailey Howell and everyone in the other room were having their pictures taken. The Celtics were the World Champions once again.

Russell Reports:

'WE'RE CHAMPS, I HONESTLY DIDN'T THINK WE COULD DO IT, BUT WE'VE GOT ANOTHER FLAG . . . '

Bill Russell has led the Celtics to 11 National Basketball Assn. championships in 13 seasons. Here is his personal report on the toughest after last night's 108 to 106 triumph over Los Angeles. It concluded 18 playoff games most of which the Celtics were underdogs.

May 6, 1969 • by Bill Russell
(player-coach, Boston Celtics)

LOS ANGELES—Well, another chapter is over, I still can't believe it.

After 100 games we're champions again. I honestly didn't think it could be done but here we are with another flag.

It was awful hard getting here. Even when we had that big lead in the fourth quarter (98-81), I felt it was too early to count anything as won.

We had to keep it up and we did. We came up with the big plays and held on for a two-point victory.

Well, let's talk about my players, my friends who made this championship possible.

Guys like Bryant, you know this is his first championship. I guess he's the most thrilled guy of all. He's been in the league five years. He's really made a contribution, you know.

Bryant's sort of a story within itself. Last year he was expendable, put up for expansion and picked up by Phoenix. He said he wanted to retire. So they gave him to us for a Number 2 draft choice. And he ends up starting on the World's Championship team. That's pretty good traveling for one year.

This kind of thing has happened to guys before, but it's always nice to see.

I'm real happy for the guys, especially for the others on their first championship team.

Let me talk about Sam Jones for a minute. I think Sam finished a brilliant career in brilliant fashion. He had a great shooting night. He shot 10 for 16, which is good for anybody. He had 24 big points, he got seven rebounds, a couple of assists. I think he went out in great fashion. That's the way to end a career. He did a great job.

Siegfried—Larry had a hamstring pull, as we all know. But I don't know if everybody knows he pulled it again tonight. And in the last quarter it was really, really hurting him. He told me it was hurting him, but he wanted to play. He said he could do four or five minutes on one leg, and then cut it off. So I put him out there and I thought he did a good job. He brought the ball down well, and he had to guard West. I was just so proud of him, the way he conducted himself. Until you've tried to do something such as play basketball in real pain, you can't appreciate what it's like.

I've had the same injury, and it's like having a real bad toothache in your leg. I could appreciate what he was going through. It gave me a thrill to see the guy want to play.

And John Havlicek had his usual good game. He shot well, as usual, played good defense, and rebounded well. Made some clutch baskets.

Speaking of clutch baskets, let's talk about Don Nelson. He made the biggest basket of the night. It was a bouncer—the kind that gives you three heart attacks before it goes in. It hit the back rim, went straight up and looked like it would bounce out, but it bounced straight in. This was the key basket. It locked it up. I think that was the basket that broke their backs. And a difficult shot.

Now Bailey Howell didn't have what you'd call an outstanding series—for him. And Bailey is a worrier, which is something most people don't realize. You have no idea what agony he's been going through because his shooting was off. But it's hard to convince him—or anybody on the outside—that despite his shooting he played very well. Like I tell all the guys, shooting is only one part of the game. There are other phases of the game which are just as important. Playing defense, keeping your man off the boards, setting picks, giving a guy the ball when he's free and you're not, all these things.

He worried so much about the way he was shooting, though, that I really felt bad for him. And we did everything we could to get him up for it, but it was tough for him. When you win a championship anyway, all that goes out the window.

It's hard for me to believe that it's over. When I went into this game, I didn't know what was going to happen. And after it was over I kept saying, "It . . . it's really over." And finally it is over. We played 100 games and, like I told somebody before the game, I wouldn't trade this bunch of guys for any bunch of guys in the world.

Then again at halftime I told them, "You've got another 24 minutes out there. Whatever we're gonna do, win or lose, let's do it together." And I think this is one of the outstanding things about playing on a team like the Celtics. We play together, live together, take care of each other, worry about each other and I would feel the same way about these guys if we'd lost.

We see each other as men, and we judge a guy by his character, not by how well he shoots or how well he plays or anything like that. Strictly on character, because we are not awed by a man's reputation. We are a bunch of men that work together and we judge each other solely on character. Reputation has nothing to do with it. You can see the things we've achieved as a group and it's definitely thrilling.

In a sense it's strange to say, but we really identify with each other because we know each other. If one guy has a good night we're all happy because this guy's a friend of ours. We are proud of each other.

If Sam has a good night, we're proud of Sam and if John has a good night that's the way we feel about John, or Emmette or Bailey or Satch, or anyone. And so this is why it's always such a thrill for me because it's been that way on the Celtics since I've been with the team. And, as far as I know, it's always been that way.

If Russell Is Out, Will Heinsohn Be In?

July 31, 1969 • by Bob Sales

Tommy Heinsohn, former Celtics star, emerged last night as the prime candidate to succeed Bill Russell as coach.

It may not happen this season, if Red Auerbach can succeed in convincing Russell to return for one more year. Then it will happen next season, or the one after that.

"Right now," Auerbach said last night, "I'm not offering the job to anyone."

This was hours after Auerbach refused to bow to the power of Sports Illustrated and admit that Russell would retire. Russell announced his retirement in an article in the magazine.

Facing the glare of TV spotlights in his office at Boston Garden yesterday, Auerbach announced:

"The Celtics have a reputation for never quitting. Bill Russell has never quit. And I've certainly never quit. As far as I'm concerned, Bill Russell will be retired when he doesn't show up for the first day of training camp."

Training camp will open some time at the beginning of September. Auerbach hopes that he will be able to persuade Russell to return for another season by then.

"By golly," said Auerbach, "he means it 100 percent. I mean to change his mind."

Auerbach said that he and Russell's attorney, Morris Kirsner, had tried to convince Russell to change his mind. Russell has a year to go on a two-year contract worth more than $200,000.

"Money is not that important to him," said Auerbach. "You and I know that it should be. There's no question in my mind that the man must play another year for a variety of reasons. But I can't get to him."

Auerbach said he asked Russell for a logical reason to retire and received no answer. He is hoping that Russell will feel the itch to return as the season looms.

"I told him to hell with the exhibition games," said Auerbach. "I said I'd run the training camp for him. All I want is 82 games, five months."

Auerbach said that Russell would keep a commitment to appear at his basketball camp on Aug. 24. He said he'd talk to Russell again next week.

"It's strictly mental," said Auerbach, "That's what bugs me. He's in terrific shape. He's 15 pounds lighter than he was last year at this time. You can't do something for 13 years, at the emotional pitch he's been involved, and just give it up . . . I'm hoping time will be a factor. I'm hoping time will be a factor. I'm hoping time will heal this mental tension."

Auerbach said that Russell returned to Boston from the West Coast this week to talk to him about the Sports Illustrated article in person. He said that Russell had not talked retirement seriously to him before this.

"I don't care what he said," said Auerbach. "I'm not interested in that. I have no official document announcing his retirement."

Auerbach is banking on his personal power of persuasion, although he estimates his chances of talking Russell into changing his mind at about 10 percent.

"He's a stubborn, hard-headed guy when he makes up his mind," said Auerbach. "He's got certain principles and he sticks to them. But I'm stubborn and hard-headed, too, and I'll be banging away at him."

Auerbach said that he had talked to several former Celtics about taking over as coach—but "not this year." Heinsohn, he said, was among them.

"It's hard to offer a job to a guy if . . . " said Auerbach.

Bye, Bill, You Were Great

July 31, 1969 • by Harold Kaese

Goodby, Bill Russell, you were really something. Boston will remember you for a long, long time—your No. 6 soaring above the crowd for rebounds, your goatee wagging when you talked, your hands-on-the-hips slouch, your speed getting down the court when you opened up, your lefthanded foul shots, your generous setting of picks for teammates and, above all else, your quickness and timing blocking shots.

You had what Waite Hoyt said Babe Ruth had in abundance—destructive potential. You upset your rivals merely by being present. You made them hurry. You made them desperate. You awed them.

You dominated a team game as no other team game has been dominated by an individual. A pitcher often dominates a baseball game defensively, a quarterback often dominates a football game offensively, but when you were in the mood to play—which was most of the time, and always when the chips were down—the whole basketball game revolved around you.

You once said basketball players were the best all-round athletes of all, and were probably right. You were the best of the basketball players, although you never did and never will get the full share of credit you deserve.

Battle of the Giants: Wilt Chamberlain and Bill Russell.

You were too much the team player, the all-round player, the defensive player. You did not set the scoring records that inspire writers and make fans gape.

But you did everything else and you won. In your 13 seasons, the Celtics led their division nine consecutive times while you were in your prime.

And with you rising to one occasion after another, the Celtics won 11 out 13 championships, won 27 out of 29 playoff series and won 108 games while losing 59, for a .647 percentage.

Bill Russell, you were a revelation. You made basketball in Boston. You made Red Auerbach a

great coach, for he had never won a championship before you became a Celtic. You made champions, also, of such outstanding players as Bob Cousy, Bill Sharman, Frank Ramsey, Tom Heinsohn, Sam and K. C. Jones.

But nothing you did was more impressive than your intellectual and spiritual domination of Wilt Chamberlain, a man with even greater physical endowments than yours.

Yes, Bill Russell, you were really something, and we say goodby not in a magazine, but right here where we once said hello.

3 TWO MORE TITLES

(1970-1979)

With their 11 championships in 13 seasons, the Bill Russell-era Celtics of the late '50s and entire '60s stand as the premier dynasty in the history of American professional team sports, and such hallowed standing is unlikely to ever be relinquished.

Three more Celtics championships were captured in the NBA's glorious '80s heyday, when Boston vs. Los Angeles and Larry Bird vs. Magic Johnson kept fans enthralled with the most entertaining rivalry in league history.

Those two eras are and have remained the pillars of Celtic Pride. What came in between during the 1970s sometimes can be hidden in those tall shadows, but it was a time of remarkable success—the Celtics won championships in 1974 and again two seasons later, including a pivotal, exhausting 128-126 triple-overtime victory over the Phoenix Suns in Game 5 of the 1976 Finals that to this day is considered the greatest NBA game ever played.

Other NBA franchises cannot relate to losing a player of Bill Russell's magnitude for a simple reason. There has never been anyone else, rival Wilt Chamberlain included, to approach his magnitude. Yet his retirement as player and coach after the 1969 season did not leave the Celtics reeling or rebuilding. The Celtics went 34-48 in 1970, the first post-Russell season. But two savvy Red Auerbach draft choices—Kansas guard Jo Jo White, an Olympic hero chosen ninth overall in 1969 after teams selecting higher were scared off by a military commitment, and Florida State center Dave Cowens, the third overall choice in 1970, united with holdover superstar John Havlicek as cornerstones of a bright new era.

Havlicek remained the fulcrum of it all, an indefatigable, multifaceted, all-around player who could be counted on to deliver whatever coach Tommy Heinsohn—Russell's successor on the bench—required. *Globe* reporter Larry Whiteside captured the essence of Havlicek in a February, 1976, article, writing: "There is only one John Havlicek, the prototype of what is known as the 'small shooting forward.' There will be many imitators, and some of them will be pretty good at the things Havlicek does best. But to find a combination player who can run, shoot, play defense, and use his knowledge to extract every ounce of advantage out of a situation—well, that's tough to find."

‹ Dave Cowens was the leaping, hustling center for Celtics champions in 1974 and '76.

The term wasn't part of the basketball lexicon yet, but Havlicek, along with White and Cowens—both of whom would join him in the Basketball Hall of Fame someday—formed an authentic, diversely skilled Big Three. The stylish, smooth-shooting White made seven All-Star teams in his 10 Celtic seasons, earned MVP honors in the 1976 Finals after playing all 60 minutes and scoring 33 points in Game 5, and set the standard of durability by playing in a team-record 488 consecutive games.

Cowens, a 6-foot-9-inch, lefthanded redhead who played with boundless energy, was named the 1973 NBA Most Valuable Player after the Celtics won a franchise-record 68 games. (Their season ended versus the Knicks in the Eastern Conference finals after Havlicek suffered a shoulder injury; the Celtics avenged the loss en route to the title in 1974.) Wrote Bob Ryan in February, 1971: "To watch him soar gracefully to snatch a rebound, turning to start a fast break before his feet hit the ground, or to observe him executing a trick twisting layup is to see that rare, gifted individual who occasionally brightens our silly games and elevates them to new artistic heights."

Cowens was an unaffected character in admirable if sometimes bemusing ways. Early in what would be a disappointing 1977 season that led to a brief downturn in the Celtics' on-court fortunes, a burned-out Cowens took a leave of absence from the team, during which he passed his time by working as a Boston cabdriver.

After the Celtics defeated Kareem Abdul-Jabbar and the Milwaukee Bucks in seven games to win their first post-Russell championship in 1974—Cowens scored 28 points and frustrated the taller Abdul-Jabbar in the clincher—he was spotted the next morning curled up on a park bench in Boston Common, the sunrise ending his post-celebration outdoor slumber. "It was either very late or very early, depending on how you looked at it," he explained, "and I was dead tired from all the excitement."

If the Celtics' charge to the 1974 championship was exciting, then the victory in 1976 must have felt like the thrill of all thrills. Those Celtics—who featured rebounder extraordinaire Paul Silas and future Hall of Fame guard Charlie Scott, along with Havlicek, White, and Cowens in their starting five—found themselves facing an upstart Phoenix Suns team in the Finals.

Despite winning just 42 games in the regular season, Phoenix had knocked out defending champion Golden State in the Western Conference playoffs and was not intimidated by the Celtics, rebounding to win Games 3 and 4 of the Finals after the Celtics had won the first two at Boston Garden. That set up the epic, three-overtime Game 5, a game that included more plot twists than most entire playoff series.

The most memorable stretch occurred during the second overtime. Havlicek drove and hit a bank shot in the final seconds. The Celtics ran off the court rejoicing, believing they had a 111-110 win and a 3-2 lead in the series, only to be informed that two seconds remained on the clock. Referee Richie Powers, after announcing his decision, was punched by a fan.

The Suns' Paul Westphal then made a brilliant decision in the heat of the moment, calling a timeout that the Suns didn't have, thereby drawing a technical foul. That gave the Celtics one free throw, which White swished, but it allowed the Suns to inbound the ball at midcourt rather than under their own basket. On the ensuing inbounds, Phoenix's Gar Heard caught a pass and launched a banner-scraping turnaround jump shot, which swished at the buzzer to send the game to a third overtime.

In the third overtime, Heinsohn inserted a seldom-used, second-year player into the lineup. Glenn McDonald had played just 395 minutes all season, but the move proved genius. The only player on the court with fresh legs, he scored eight points, including six in a 63-second span, the unlikely hero in the Celtics' pivotal two-point win. Years later, McDonald recalled his heroics at a reunion of the 1976 team. "When I got home that night," he said, "I laid in bed and thought, 'What the hell did I just do?'" The Celtics clinched their 13th championship two nights later with an 87-80 win.

The rest of the decade wasn't as kind to the Celtics, at least on the court. Owner John Y. Brown's meddlesome ownership—among other transgressions against the sport, he traded three first-round picks to the Knicks for fading All-Star Bob McAdoo—nearly led Auerbach to leave for an offer in New York. The arrival of accomplished malcontents such as Marvin "Bad News" Barnes, Sidney Wicks, and Curtis Rowe tarnished the parquet.

Havlicek, 38 years old, retired at the conclusion of the 1978 season, scoring 29 points in his final game. The Celtics won just 32 games in his final season, but the future was bright thanks to some brilliant Auerbach foresight. He found one eventual stalwart, North Carolina-Charlotte forward Cedric Maxwell, with the 12th pick of the 1977 draft, and a year later boldly selected a certain junior eligible from Indiana State named Larry Joe Bird.

Years later, in his autobiography *Drive*, written with Bob Ryan, Bird shared one tantalizing what-if. "John said to me, 'If I knew that you were coming along and you were going to be as good as you are, I would have stayed.' He meant it. We missed each other by just one year."

Havlicek helped Celtics fans' basketball dreams come true for decades, and Bird—after that one-season hiatus—picked up where he left off. Still, who can resist imagining what it would have looked like if Havlicek had resisted saying goodbye until a season or two after Bird said hello.

Celtics Draft Cowens No. 1

March 24, 1970 • by Bob Ryan

There are two things every concerned Boston Celtic fan should do. Immediately.

The first is to wish for the continued good health of Dave Cowens, a 6-9, 225-pound senior from Florida State who was the club's first draft choice yesterday.

The second is to hope for the imminent collapse of two ABA franchises, the Washington Capitols and the Pittsburgh Pipers, since wily Red Auerbach acquired the NBA rights to the previously signed Charlie Scott (Washington) and Mike Maloy (Pittsburgh).

You never saw two happier men than Tom Heinsohn and Auerbach at the conclusion of the draft. In addition to Cowens ("We wanted him all the way"—Heinsohn) the Celtics got Jacksonville's "Reckless" Rex Morgan (6-5) in round two, and Florida State's Willie Williams, a 6-7 forward.

As expected, Detroit took Bob Lanier first, but San Diego passed up Pete Maravich (did they know something no one else did?) for Michigan forward Rudy Tomjanovich.

San Francisco had to forgo its spot as a result of the Zelmo Beaty deal (the Warriors got the NBA

rights to Big Z from Atlanta) and Atlanta went for Pistol Pete.

That was the setup when Red Auerbach announced that Boston would take Cowens, the key man in FSU's great season.

"This was exceptionally good for us," said Auerbach afterwards. "We were after Cowens for a month."

Heinsohn lauded the Newport, Ky., native as a kid "with good hands off being kind of a 'sneak-in' the boards," as well as rebounder.

"The most amazing thing," Heinie continued, "was his agility. He was the point man on their zone press."

The real cause for exultation in the Celtic camp was getting Morgan, the Jacksonville ace.

"I was hoping Jacksonville would get bounced quickly to keep him out of sight," explained Heinsohn. "He can do everything—go outside, drive and rebound, as well as pass. I just couldn't believe he'd last."

JOHN HAVLICEK

He's the idol of all other athletes in all sports. He is what an athlete should be.

February 28, 1971 • by Leigh Montville

Tom Heinsohn, the coach, is reciting the winners' litany.

It is Wednesday night and the Celtics have beaten the somewhat disinterested Los Angeles Lakers, 116-96, to keep their slim playoff hopes alive. The basketball saints, undressing in the carpeted Garden dressing room, are being thanked.

"[Hank] Finkel played a good game," Heinsohn says, "but he's played a lot of good games for us this year . . . "

"Uh-huh, uh-huh," the small chorus of reporters answered, not looking up from their notebooks.

"White got those fouls early because he was being aggressive, but he hung in there and did a great job . . . "

"Uh-huh, uh-huh . . . "

"And Artie Williams, I thought, came in and did the job. He played well against West . . . "

The praise continues and the response continues for five, maybe six minutes. Cowens and Kuberski, Nelson, Finkel again, get their lines. The referees get a few negative lines and then the litany ends. The chorus goes one way, the coach another.

At no time has John Havlicek's name been mentioned. He has collected 28 points (a game high), 11 rebounds (behind only the centers), seven assists (a game high), 47 minutes played (a game high) and he doesn't draw a word.

It is not an oversight. John Havlicek's performance never is mentioned this year. It is a fact of life. It is a constant. No one mentions that the uniforms are green and white, the basketballs round, the backboards glass, the rims orange, the popcorn cold, the Cokes warm. No one mentions John Havlicek's performance.

It is just something that is there, something that has been there every day of this long NBA season. He leads the team in scoring and assists and is second in rebounds. He has played an average of 45.5 minutes every time out on the court. He has guarded the hard guards, taken the hard forwards, brought the ball up court in times of stress. He hasn't fouled out once.

"He is having," Heinsohn says on another day, in answer to a direct question, "the best season any Celtic has ever had. And I include all the good years with Bill Russell. He has been truly amazing. The foundation of this team.

"Without him—and Don Nelson—we're just an expansion team . . . "

It is hard to realize that Havlicek is 30 years old now. It is hard to remember that he is in his ninth season, that he once was the sixth man (people said he couldn't shoot too well) and that once, six years ago, he stole a ball on an important play.

Even he, himself, finds it hard.

"I don't think about being 30 years old," he says in the locker room. "I don't figure I'm any older than any of these guys."

The guys now are mostly young. The average age on the starting five is 24.6. The center who dresses to Havlicek's right now is Finkel, not Bill Russell. The good-shooting guard to the left is White, not Sam Jones.

Home is now an apartment in Melrose (or in Columbus, Ohio, in the off-season) rather than in town. The roommates are a wife and a baby boy rather than Larry Siegfried and Clyde Lovellette. Life

is different. At home it is more quiet, more regular. On the road, it is more boring.

"When you're first here," Havlicek says, "there are certain things you want to see in every city. Like in San Francisco, you want to see Fisherman's Wharf.

"Well. Now I've seen Fisherman's Wharf. The last time we were in San Francisco a lot of these guys went down there, but I didn't. I stayed in the hotel. I'd seen Fisherman's Wharf."

For the spectator, the realization that Havlicek is 30 comes hard because the man does not look any different. Sure, the hair is different, longer and combed down in the front, but the weight is exactly the same it was the day Havlicek came off the Ohio State campus, 205 pounds. He still has that pale white complexion and his legs still have that lean, visible body look, almost models on which a professor would be able to point out each muscle, vein and artery.

"During the season," he says, "I have to watch myself, make sure I'm eating enough. It usually isn't a problem, though. I like to eat. After a game, that's my biggest pleasure, going out to eat."

Watching the way Havlicek eats is watching the way Havlicek lives. He does the right things. There is no extra motion. He is . . . tidy. He takes a steak and dissects it. Every extra piece of fat is trimmed neatly and put in a small pile. Never once does the lure of a crunchy, burned-out piece of solid calories get to him.

"You'd eat that?" he asks.

The over-30 world, pell-mell on the way to middle age, groans. . . .

The stories, by now, are legend.

"I guess everyone's heard them," Havlicek's mother, a visitor for the Laker game, says. "They're the same stories. Over and over."

They tell how Havlicek, the boy, always was running. How he ran to school. How he ran along the highway, trying to go from one one-mile highway marker to another. How he was always playing some kind of game, winding up at Bridgeport (Ohio) High School as a three-sport All-Stater. How he used to eat a quarter pound of butter—straight—like most kids eat a candy bar.

"He'd come home late some times," Mrs. Havlicek, a pleasant, gray-haired woman, says, "and I'd ask him 'John, where have you been?'

"He'd say he'd been down at the schoolyard playing. I'd say 'Who with?' and he'd say 'Oh, nobody, just by myself.'"

His mother, Havlicek says, is the one who has followed his basketball career closer than anyone. His father, an immigrant from Bohemia at the age of 12 who still works every day at 69, has enjoyed it, but. . . .

"He really isn't interested in sports like basketball," Havlicek says. "Oh, he's interested because of me and everything, but he likes European sports. Like the Olympics. He really gets interested in the Olympics. And soccer.

"Do you know what he really likes? Things like acrobats and jugglers. Gymnastics. Remember that show 'Super Circus'? He liked that show more than anything."

"I don't know how John got interested in sports," Mrs. Havlicek says. "I just knew he was always coming through the room, going to bed, throwing his balled-up underwear in the air and catching it, like it was some kind of game.

"Maybe it was his elder brother who got him interested . . . but then, no. His brother was always playing guns and cowboys and things like that, John always wanted to play some kind of ballgame . . . "

Ironically, the roles still hold. Havlicek still plays ballgames. His brother is employed by Olin-Matheson in Stamford, Conn.

Havlicek's development as a basketball player has been a rare thing to watch in Boston. The experience has been like watching a new car come down the production line in Detroit. Always, there has been movement, but accessories have been added continuously.

In the beginning, there was the defense and the running. There always was the running, a perpetual motion that would make a defender's brains fall out when he tried to keep up.

"Nah," general manager Red Auerbach says, "I never thought he'd turn out as good as he has. I hoped he'd be another Frank Ramsey."

He came in as the eighth draft selection in the country (there were only eight NBA teams then, remember?), fresh from an unsuccessful tryout with the Cleveland Browns (there were only 16 NFL teams then, remember?). He played forward and moved back to guard and developed his lefthanded

dribble. Other teams would sag off him on defense and he became a shooter.

He kept going and developing through the championship years, becoming a starter and 48-minute man for the first time in the 1966 playoffs, becoming the team's best playmaker after K.C. Jones left, forcing other teams to look for the 6-5 forward to combat what he did in the corner. His scoring jumped every year, his playing time increased and as parts of the championship teams retired to become coaches or college campus lecturers, Havlicek just seemed to take over their jobs.

Last year looked like the ultimate. With Russell finally gone, Havlicek seemed to take over everything. He led the club in every positive statistic, including rebounding.

But still there was one job left.

"Last year," Auerbach said, "Larry Siegfried was here, and John didn't have the ultimate responsibility for the way the game was run. Now, Siggie's gone and John has everything.

"I think it's helped him. I think it's helped us! He's having way-in-way his best season."

"He's just as cute now as Ramsey ever was," Heinsohn says. "Even when he makes a gamble, it's a good gamble. Cowens will make a gamble and if he loses, the guy will score. If John makes a gamble, he knows someone is going to be around to cover up. He's already checked that before he's moved."

About the running, still the flip-card association you get with Havlicek, he always has said he doesn't get tired. He always has said he doesn't let himself get tired. (Siegfried always used to say, "Oh yeah, look at his nostrils during a game, you could fit a half dollar in each one.")

Now, he amends that a little.

"I get tired," he says. "Everyone gets tired. But what good does it do to say you're tired?

"A guy comes home from work and says, 'Oh boy, am I tired.' Well, he IS tired, but saying it makes it worse. You have to have hobbies, an interest, something to look forward to.

"I'm interested in all sorts of things. I'll go to anything. Games. Car shows. Boat shows. Home shows. Movies. The theater. I just love to see things. There's so much I'd like to learn about . . . "

Havlicek, the person, is described in the same adjectives as Havlicek, the basketball player. Bob Woolf, his lawyer, is a typical friend.

"You couldn't write a nice enough article about John Havlicek," Woolf says. "No matter how well you write, you couldn't do it.

"John is my idol. He's conservative, realistic, a pleasure in every way. He's a perfect gentleman, humble, modest, a super athlete. What more can I say? I think the thing that proves all this is he's the idol of all other athletes in all sports.

"I couldn't think of any individual who's more like what an athlete should be."

Woolf's words, in the era of sports journalism most noted for the Howard Cosell sneer and the behind-the-scenes expose, probably sound old-fashioned and probably would draw a Cosellian grimace: But could the digger find dirt? Could he find an enemy?

As an interview, Havlicek is what a reporter wants. He is literate and truthful. He tells you what he thinks, what really is inside him, and laces it with anecdotes. Some guys mumble on their bad days, others will say anything the man with the micro-phone wants to hear. Havlicek just turns himself inside out.

He works on all the charities, and in public comes across with his wife, Beth, like Ryan O'Neal taking Ali McGraw for a walk along the Charles. His financial dealings, in a time of the big sports hold-up, have been quiet. He looked at the ABA two seasons ago, quietly listened to what was said, and signed a three-year Celtics contract without a whole lot of trouble.

"Let me put it this way," says Woolf, who delivers law school lectures titled "The Rare Human Being Called John Havlicek," "John Havlicek showed tre-mendous love and devotion for the Celtics and their organization two years ago. He exhibited it in an extraordinary way, turning down over a million dol-lars to stay with the Celtics."

Still, Havlicek is far from financial trouble. His contract, rumored to be $500,000 for the three years, is "the best in Boston," according to Woolf. He has his own sneakers, his own basketball and is a manufacturer's representative.

He even has that ultimate in success symbols, the Cadillac. The body is Kelly green. The convert-ible top is white. Significant?

"Not at all," Havlicek says. "Everyone says I picked the car because of the Celtics. I just liked the colors. If there'd been a nice brown I liked better, I'd have taken that."

Sure . . .

How long can it go on? How long can a machine run constantly before it burns itself out?

Heinsohn says at least five years, Auerbach says at least three. Havlicek says he will play next year, finishing his contract and 10 years in the league, and then he will evaluate.

For the moment, however, he will just keep rolling along, 29 points per game, 48 minutes, belt-buckle defense, seven-or-eight rebounds, six assists, playoffs or not.

It will be the same, day-to-day performance, the same, quietly efficient basketball.

It all will be so good, no one will ever mention it.

Russell's Number Retired, Privately

March 13, 1972 • by Bob Ryan

As usual, Bill Russell did things "my way." Oh, he consented to having his number raised to the raf-ters, all right. But he insisted it be done with no crowd present. And so it was.

Accordingly, at 12:55 p.m., five minutes before the Garden opened the doors for the crowd, Bill Russell's famed number 6 was hoisted aloft. The crowd consisted of a few writers, ushers, vendors, ABC personnel, players shooting baskets and the active Celtics who played with Russell, as well as Red Auerbach and Tom Heinsohn—and, of course, the lucky photographers who had come early.

That's why you missed the scene if you were a paying customer. "Red knows how I feel about this," Russell explained. "I'm not that type of guy."

Celts Deal off Scott for, Possibly, Silas

March 14, 1972 • by Neil Singelais

Back in 1970 Celtics Gen. Mgr. Red Auerbach figured he had nothing to lose by claiming 6-5 guard Charlie Scott in the seventh round of the NBA Draft.

Auerbach's reasoning at the time was that there wasn't any college talent left after the sixth round, so why not draft Scott on a hunch even though it was a foregone conclusion that Scott intended to sign a sizable contract with the ABA.

And Scott did just that. And in his first season with the Virginia Squires of the ABA, he led his team to the Eastern Division title. Scott has just set an ABA single-season scoring record (2,523) last week before jumping to the Squires to sign a contract with the Phoenix Suns of the NBA yesterday.

So Auerbach, who had gambled nothing, winds up considerably richer as a result of Scott's action.

The Celtics gave the Phoenix Suns the right to deal with Scott in return for an undisclosed amount of cash, and "a future consideration."

That "future consideration" is believed to be the Suns' 6-7 cornerman Paul Silas. But because court litigation is taking place between the two leagues over the Scott matter, the transaction will be finalized only if Scott legally winds up with the Suns.

Cowens: On the Court, Team Player—Off the Court, Individual

March 26, 1972 • by Bob Ryan

Poor Dave Cowens. How does he ever expect to make it? Doesn't he know that the path to Carson's Couch is not paved by mere basketball playing, that in order to be a "star" in 1972 it is necessary to report late to training camp, insult the owner, play only when you feel like it, thumb your nose at the fans and spend more time with your lawyer than with your team?

It's too bad. All Cowens has to offer is quality playing skill backed by a burning ambition to improve. He's popular with his teammates. His hustling style has made him popular with the diehard fans. He has proven that he was light-years better to have on a ball club than others (like Pete Maravich and Bob Lanier) who received far more publicity, and, sadly, far more money. But he is still not taken seriously by the national media.

If any of this bothers him, he has thus far managed to keep it a secret. The fact is that Dave Cowens marches not only to a different drummer, but to a completely different band. Of all the youthful phenoms in all sports, he may be the one most at peace with himself, most confident in the knowledge that he really is succeeding—his way.

Look at what he has accomplished in the last two years. He was a runaway choice as the Rookie of the Year in the players' vote last season. He was Co-Rookie of the Year in the writers' poll. He was the starting center for the East in this year's All-Star Game, and he played well enough to merit serious MVP consideration. He is one of only two (Hambone Williams is the other) major additions to a mediocre (34-48) Celtics' team of two seasons ago which now is a league power. Obviously, he had more to do with that turnaround than anybody.

He has done all this as a center, despite standing just 6-8½. A year ago, many "experts" pooh-poohed him, saying that, "He's too small to be a center, but he'd be a helluva forward." They were half right. He would now be a helluva forward, having improved his outside shooting the way he has. But, meanwhile, he has become no worse than the league's fourth (Abdul-Jabbar, Chamberlain, Thurmond) best center, and considering age, is the second best for the future.

That he became a Boston Celtic was half Red Auerbach's judgment, half luck. "Red went to see him play," relates coach Tommy Heinsohn, "and he made a big display of walking out after five minutes, hoping people would think he was disappointed. 'Tommy,' he told me when he got back, 'I found the kid we want.'"

The problem was getting him, however, and it wasn't until the day before the draft that the Celtics found out they had an excellent chance. The year was 1969. Detroit, picking first, was sure to take Bob Lanier. Atlanta, it was learned, was getting Pete Maravich, previously believed to be ABA bound. That left San Diego.

The Rockets, having a center in Elvin Hayes, went for Michigan forward Rudy Tomjanovich. Auerbach wasted approximately one half second before saying, "Boston takes Dave Cowens of Florida State." No one knew it yet, but from that moment the Celtics were on the road to recovery.

The rest, as they say, is history. There was the famed Stokes Game MVP appearance, the impressive rookie year, the early season sophomore play, the All-Star Game and, now, the drastic improvement in the second half of this season. And through it all, he's still the determined, dedicated individual he was when he arrived.

Home for Cowens was Newport, Ky., across the Ohio River from Cincinnati. The second oldest of six children, he gravitated naturally toward athletics, encouraged, but not pushed by his father, Jack, a strapping (6-5) man with a Lorne Greene shock of white hair.

Whatever natural propensities he had for playing hard were developed by his high school coach, Jim Connors. "Coach Connors had four priorities," Dave explains. "He always told us we were responsible to God, family, school and team—in that order. And he stuck by it."

Cowens admits that he may not always live up to that code, but that it doesn't make those values less meaningful. He in no way wishes to portray himself as a saint.

Newport Catholic was a running team, as was Florida State, and as are the Celtics. The latter, therefore, inherited a rebounding-oriented center

Coach Tom Heinsohn (left) has a word with Dave Cowens during a game against the Cavaliers in March 1972.

who had played fast-break basketball for seven years, a definite plus.

The hustle part of Cowens' game, of course, could not really be coached. "He's a 6-8 Havlicek," Heinsohn said after seeing him in the summer of '70.

As far as Cowens is concerned, greater praise than that hath no man.

"I'm proud to be compared to Havlicek," Cowens says. "He plays the game the right way, hustling all the time."

Playing the game the right way, in Cowens' terms, also extends to other areas. He respects rough, but clean competitors, players who give good, honest efforts, whether or not they're stars. He has a fond feeling, for instance, for both Chicago's Clifford Ray and Golden State's Nate Thurmond.

Though he has some great basketball instincts, there is no other way to describe him but calling him a "team" player. Statistics mean nothing to him. He doesn't need a writer telling him he's almost shooting 49 percent from the floor to know that he's a far better shooter than last year.

Off the court, however, he can only be described as being an "individual." He lives in a converted bathhouse on a Weston estate, not a high-rise at Kenmore Square or Charles River Park, the traditional havens for young bachelor athletes. Here he gets the privacy he seeks.

"I'm very happy out there," he says, "although I do wish I had a little more room, now."

He fits no stereotype images. What other local player ever filled in his idle hours off-court by attending an auto mechanic school in Everett, for instance? Or spend his first summer in Boston researching at Harvard for his degree in criminology?

He must surely be the first NBA center in history to wear braces. With his newly acquired wealth, he invested in some desired orthodontic work. The top braces were removed before the season, but the lower ones are still there. Imagine going back to the locker room after being humiliated by a redheaded kid wearing braces.

He has found Boston very much to his liking. "Everything is here if you want it," he contends. "No matter what you feel like doing, you can find it here."

He is not difficult to spot on the road. Generally wearing one of his "jock" caps (15 years ago they were called "Ivy League" caps), he walks with a shuffle and expression which has prompted Heinsohn to label him "Huck Finn," whom he certainly resembles, red hair and all. Movies and sleep comprise most of his daytime activity when the team travels.

An arrest and $36 fine in Florida last summer attest to his possession of a very human quality—a temper. There was a scuffle outside a gathering spot for young people in Tallahassee and a Cowens fist found its way onto a belligerent Floridian. "I don't think I need a judge to tell me if I was right or wrong," he explained, "but I am sorry for causing embarrassment to the club and the league. I learned my lesson, believe me."

His normal public demeanor is far more placid. You might never suspect that the tall, perhaps wide-eyed, young man standing next to you at the Sportsman's Show, or seated next to you at the Catholic Memorial-Lexington game, is the Boston Celtics' center. He's liable to turn up anyplace, since he's been known to show an interest, however temporary, in a wide range of subjects.

He can still move easily through his private life with a minimum of interference, even after his huge success. This, of course, is Boston, hardly a basketball Mecca which is half the story. But to the outside world, he still remains largely unknown. Even his All-Star performance hasn't increased the phone-ringing from syndicated columnists, and the like.

All of which suits him just fine. The only praise he seeks is from his peers. He puts a premium on high marks from but one fraternity, the basketball world. That writers and fans still underrate his impact and ability is of no concern to him.

His main concern now is getting ready for the playoffs. The Great Ankle Scare is over and he's eager to get started. "Winning the title," he says, "would be heaven."

In sum, the Celtics can consider themselves extremely fortunate to have stumbled across one of the few modern athletes of superstar ability whose hat size hasn't expanded, whose competitive zeal is increasing rather than decreasing and who always plays as if, well, as if he actually enjoys it. They also have the services of someone who finds it necessary neither to flaunt his lifestyle, a la Namath, nor to submerge it in an Orr-style shell.

He is that rarity—a totally honest, natural person who has no need for subterfuge of any kind.

But the best thing is this: as good as he is, he is bound to get better, and no one knows it better than the opponents, like Phoenix coach Cotton Fitzsimmons, who says, "The day that Cowens stops running out to the foul line when his name is introduced is the day I'll stop worrying about him."

No chance of that happening, Cotton, so why not do what the rest of us are already doing? Just relax and enjoy the show.

Knicks Win, 98-91—Hondo Hurt—All Is Woe!

April 21, 1973 • by Bob Ryan

Well, they did hold the Knicks to under 100 points.

Having thus dispensed with the positive development of last night's game with New York, let us analyze the Celtics' position after last night's dreadful 98-91 loss before 15,320 mourners (plus assorted Knick supporters):

- They blew the home-court advantage they worked so hard for.
- They trail 2-1 in the series going into New York's womb tomorrow.

- They ended the game with an injured John Havlicek, who hyperextended his right shoulder in the fourth quarter and was a one-armed ballplayer the rest of the way.

Suddenly, the series, which looked so promising after last Sunday's convincing triumph, looks suspiciously like last year's. New York can do no wrong, and it also keeps getting all the necessary breaks. There is no better winning combination.

When Don Nelson hit a long jumper with 11:24 remaining, the Celtics had closed the gap to 81-79 and were still riding the crest of a miniature wave, which had seen them erase a 15-point (69-54) third-quarter deficit. Everything looked great.

The euphoria was short-lived, however. In the next 1:47, Bill Bradley hit three straight jumpers and Walt Frazier contributed a sensational drive over Dave Cowens to get the lead back up to 10 points at 89-79. Boston would never again be in the ballgame.

It was immediately after this crucial stretch that Havlicek was noticed receiving attention on the bench for his shoulder. He had been playing a Havlicek game, and, in fact, entered the final period with 29 points. But in the fourth quarter—his quarter, ordinarily—he did nothing, and a tip-off that he was injured beyond instant repair came when he missed two free throws with 3:47 left, something he never does.

"I did it either late in the third period or early in the fourth," John explained. "I was fighting through a pick, something I've done a million times before. Only this time something happened."

That something might just cost the Celtics a legitimate shot at the title.

Celtics Try, Fail to Fill Havlicek's Sneakers

April 30, 1973 • by Leigh Montville

In the end, it hurt. You only can play without a total John Havlicek for so long.

"It took New York two games to find out what to do against John, but they did it today," coach Tom Heinsohn said late yesterday afternoon

after his Celtics finally had been sent home by the Knicks, 94-78, at the Garden. "They sagged off him on defense, then came up to challenge him on his dribble.

"But hey. He showed more guts in this series than any basketball player I've ever seen."

The loss of the NBA All-Star finally meant something. The Celts had hung on, winning those last two games to bring the best-of-seven series back to the Garden at a 3-3 tie, winning with big efforts from the bench and from the non-shooters like Don Chaney and Paul Silas.

Yesterday the efforts weren't there, and Havlicek wasn't either. His shoulder, injured in a collision with the Knicks' Dave DeBusschere in Game 4, was still too much of a problem.

"It felt better, better than at any time since it was injured," Havlicek said. "I even tried a righthanded layup early it felt so good. The ball just wouldn't go up there. There wasn't any strength. I was still bothered."

Havlicek stumbled to just four points, taking only six shots and making one. He couldn't make the big pass ("I couldn't get any force on the ball. I saw guys open."), couldn't make the big play.

And nobody was there this time to fill the hole.

Chaney and Silas, so good from the outside in Friday night's upset, were cold again. Nelson, the major replacement, couldn't slip free for those open shots. There wasn't any help—none at all—from the rest of the bench.

"We got by without John for those two games, but we couldn't today," Nelson said. "In the last game we needed John. We were playing without a 30-point man and today it hurt.

"I think all along we were playing with the thought that John is going to be John if we can just keep it going. Well, John wasn't John. You could see that right away today. He just wasn't any better."

The Celts locker room was not your typically sad closeout. Dave Cowens left quickly with the words "Gentlemen, it's been nice," but most of the players dressed slowly, talking with the various members of the Celtics organization and alumni who visited with their brief condolences.

There definitely was the general feeling that the best shot had been given, that the road had simply wound up with a bad-shooting dead end.

"Hey, I don't have any down feeling at all," Jo Jo White said. "We went out, we played as hard as we could. We did better than we did last year. This series could have been over without this game ever being played if a few things hadn't happened.

"I just wish this guy (nodding at Havlicek) hadn't gotten hurt."

"Awwwwwwwww, who knows what would have happened if he didn't get hurt," Tommy Heinsohn said. "But it would have been nice to find out. . . . "

Didn't Anyone Notice Jo Jo's Arrival?

January 6, 1974 • by Bob Ryan

In the beginning, there was pressure—far too much pressure—and that may have been the beginning of the problem. People thought it was easy to be Jo Jo White, and it really wasn't.

What he is now, it was believed he should have been four years ago. Erroneously cast as the prototype Celtic guard, and as an instant All Star, Jo Jo was, in fact, merely a talented player locked into a style completely antithetical to his new team's and with the further burden of a personality at once prideful, sensitive and hungering for proper direction.

It is, therefore, more than a little ironic that today, when he has achieved the professional stature long expected of him, that this success has been greeted with a loud public yawn. Jo Jo White has become the Celtic you never hear about.

"Jo Jo," says Tom Heinsohn, "has blended into our system. He isn't the star every night. He's almost like a wallflower. But he gets his 20 points and seven or eight assists, and people say, 'When did he do that?'"

While some people (Heinsohn included) prematurely labeled White a superstar in years past, the fact is that it wasn't until this season that he crashed through the barrier separating the very good players and the great. The reason is simple: He now does good things every night. Which is what being also called "superstar" is really all about.

And those good things involve more than just shooting the basketball, as White himself admits. "I've always pointed toward developing my overall game," he says. "There's still room for improvement, of course, but I felt more comfortable doing my job than in previous years. I feel I know what's going on while I'm out on the floor at all times."

The raps on Jo Jo in years past were numerous and justifiable in varying degrees. Only a year ago this week, for instance, his name quite literally exploded into the local papers and onto the airwaves following a television remark by then TV color man Guy Mainella to the effect that, "The Celtics are thinking about trading Jo Jo White."

The statement was completely off base, primarily because both Red Auerbach and Heinsohn have long professed, both publicly and privately, an admiration for White. But it was true that some of White's teammates were clearly unhappy with the way he had been playing (despite Boston's winning record), accusing him of un-Celtic like practices, ranging from failure to observe proper bench etiquette to the more serious charge of being unwilling to share the basketball with his mates.

White prefers not to dwell on the incident, but does admit that it had an impact on him. "I was playing my butt off," he says, "and the team was having a great year. I just wanted to know 'Why me?' Why were people on my back? But, at the same time, it made me want to play harder. It's not that I felt I had anything to prove, but it's just something I can't even put into words."

Whatever Jo Jo's innermost feelings on the matter, it was obvious to Celtics watchers that it had some effect. In fact, his elevation into his current stature as a first-class player seems to have dated from the incident. His total game improved in the second half of the year, and he enjoyed a truly sensational playoffs, peaking with a brilliant performance in the ballyhooed fourth game against the Knicks.

The seventh, and last, child of the Rev. George and Mrs. Elizabeth White ("You've heard of second hand?" he laughs. "I got seventh hand.") Jo Jo was born and grew up in what he calls the "front part" of the South Side Ghetto of St. Louis.

He remembers the neighborhood as "fun" to grow up in, although there were the normal number of tough times associated with that type of environment. Through the participation of an older brother

Jo Jo White, the Celtics' graceful guard on their 1974 and '76 championship teams.

and a cousin, he first immersed himself in football, until a hand injury scared his mother into warning him to give it up.

He first turned to basketball at age 11 in the Buder Recreation Center, and thus began an obsession that has lasted to this day. The good Rev. (Baptist) White, wary of past experience with the first six little Whites, was openly skeptical that young Jo Jo could really be spending all that time (like, until 12 midnight) shooting baskets at the rec center. "I just couldn't convince him that's what I was doing," recalls Jo Jo.

What convinced his father that Jo Jo had not spoken with a forked tongue was a visit to see his son play freshman ball at Vachon High. It was obvious to the older White that more than a little practice had gone into the making of that type of talent.

From that point, it was steady progression for White. He transferred to McKinley High after his sophomore year, becoming All-State and a household name to every national recruiter worth his Garfinkel Report.

More honors came—All-American, World University Games, Pan-Am Games, 1968 Olympic Games (no boycotter, he said, "I wasn't going to risk my pro career for something I didn't understand,") and, finally, first draft choice of the Celtics.

There were, however, a few problems. First of all, the Marine Corps Reserve had exercised its basic-training option, and instead of a training camp learning the Number One play, Jo Jo was slopping through the mud at Parris Island. This was no way for a rookie to get acclimated to the intricacies of a pro system.

Complicating matters was the fact that Jo Jo had just spent four years playing point guard for a possession team at Kansas. Like most Big Eight teams, Kansas featured a power game inside, running an occasional 4 on 1 every other Thursday.

"In college," Jo Jo points out, "I was taught that the ball was a gem." Now, he was with the Celtics, who were best symbolized by Cooz tossing a 70-foot hook pass to Heinie right after a rival basket.

Not that Jo Jo didn't ask for what he got. "It's one of the reasons I went to Kansas," he admits. "People said to me, 'Did you ever hear of a guard making All-American there? That's a big man's school.' Or, 'How do you expect to make All-American scoring 15 points a game?' I just told them I was going to be the first."

When Jo Jo was discharged from active duty, he joined the team, which was struggling through the painful first post-Russell year. When inserted into the lineup, he was given one basic instruction from the coach—SHOOT!

"That's what we counted on him for," Heinie says. "We wanted 20 points a game from him, because we weren't getting it from Siggy (Larry Siegfried) and the others back there. He helped Havlicek get us some consistent offense, and, when Cowens came, we had our three building blocks."

Critics argue that Heinie made one mistake. Having instructed White to concentrate on being a scorer at a point when it was necessary, he then neglected to tell him to stop pulling the trigger when it was obvious that he no longer had to do it himself. This was the crux of last year's little hassle, but it appears to be nothing but history now. "Jo Jo," says Paul Silas, "knows now he doesn't have to get 20 to help us win."

White has also been criticized for not being another Cowens or Havlicek, i.e., he doesn't go diving over press tables or into TV cameras for loose balls. White's reply: "Dave is always diving on the floor. That's the way he expresses himself out there, and he couldn't be as good as he is if he didn't. I try to make the game as simple and easy as possible. I think I can do my job without doing all that, and still be impressive."

Jo Jo feels, in other words, that he is playing as hard as he can within his style. It's the same with his general court demeanor. His facial expressions never convey his inner emotions, unlike those of, say, Cowens, which are a complete method actor's lesson during the course of a game.

White never complains about an adverse call ("I've seen games lost by guys having temper tantrums, and, with the exception of one ref overruling another, I've never seen anyone change a call"), his only concession to emotion being a Cheshire Cat grin he lights up with on the more hopelessly absurd decisions.

His approach to the game can be seen by the men he admires. Walt Frazier, for one. "I may not think much of him off the court," Jo Jo admits, "but Frazier is a great ballplayer. He may be overacting with that Mr. Cool routine, but he does handle himself well out there. He seems to know everything that's going on."

Jo Jo has long paid tribute to another smoothie, Oscar Robertson. "My idol always was Oscar," he says. "If you're going to be a good ballplayer, you must play a total game, the way he does."

Unfortunately, pizzazz has a lot to do with making a name for yourself, and Jo Jo is handicapped by a near-total absence of identifiable style. Oh, he does have a strange release on his jump shot (it almost looks like a screwball), and he is starting to develop a patent on two drives—a little running hook and a gorgeous underhand flip, especially from the base line—but you won't find many kids on the playgrounds throwing a move and yelling, "Jo Jo White!" the way they might for somebody else.

"When a guy plays like that," submits Heinsohn, "and makes it look so easy, then people forget how difficult it is."

For 12th time, Celtics Are Basketball's Best

HAVLICEK VOTED MVP; BUCKS BOTTLED, 102-87

May 13, 1974 • by Bob Ryan

MILWAUKEE—What could be more fitting in this Age of Nostalgia, when college students are discovering Fred and Ginger, everyone is dressing like Gatsby and the best thing a bar owner can do is have a jukebox playing Little Richard, than that the NBA title should return to the place where it seems it has always been—Boston!

There was nothing strange about it at all. Here were the Celtics in their grimy road greens, entering yet another road pit (remember Syracuse and Convention Hall?) meeting somebody for the ultimate prize, and then coming up with a Rembrandt of a defensive game to win their 12th league championship, and more importantly, the first in the "modern" (i.e., post-1969 Russell) era.

The 102-87 final score accurately reflects the difference between the Celtics and the Milwaukee Bucks in this game, and it points out the tremendous defensive job turned in by the determined Celtics, who saved a sagging, sniping, frustrating kind of defense for Kareem Abdul-Jabbar until the game which decided the series.

Through a combination of the usual full-court press (despite Don Chaney's early foul trouble) and an inordinate amount of sagging on Abdul-Jabbar, the Celtics were able to shut out the big man for a span of 17:58—from the waning seconds of the first period until 5:33 into the third.

In that time, Boston built up the 17-point lead (peaking at 63-46) which was to hold up in the face of a Milwaukee comeback that got the lead down as low as three on three occasions, the last at 71-68 with 11:30 remaining in the game.

That was a grim moment indeed for the Celtics, inasmuch as Dave Cowens, THE man in the most important game of his life, had picked up his fifth foul 17 seconds earlier by foolishly trying to go over the top to follow up his missed shot.

But that was as close as Milwaukee would ever come. For Cowens broke across the key for a running hook and John Havlicek hit Jo Jo White on a textbook two-on-one fast break to stifle Milwaukee's gathering momentum.

When Havlicek found Paul Westphal—brilliant, incidentally, in his biggest game—for a sneak-away and Paul Silas drove in for a Curtis Perry goaltended layup, the Celtics had come up with a run of eight straight to break open the game.

The Bucks' only remaining hope was Abdul-Jabbar, but, as in the second period, they simply

The 1974 Finals MVP John Havlicek greets fans at Boston's City Hall Plaza on May 14, 1974.

couldn't get him the ball. He scored but one field goal (in just four attempts) in the final period, and even that merely served as the prelude for the eventual back-breaking play, which would be submitted by Havlicek, the official series MVP.

"I called the play from the bench," said Tom Heinsohn, "because 85 percent of the time John Havlicek is going to deliver in the clutch." Now, Havlicek was not having much of a shooting afternoon (6 for 20), but that was of little concern to any Celtic.

Havlicek came off a double screen on the left, found himself confronted by Mt. Kareem, faked him into the rafters, and drove the lane for a three-point play. With 4:12 left, the play made the 90-79 score a death notice for the sickened 10,938 Milwaukee backers.

Havlicek's inconsistent shooting was not fatal because this was a day the Celtics did not lack for heroes. Begin with Cowens, the undersized center with the giant heart, who scored 28 points, pulled in 14 rebounds, hit from the men's room, jumped over buildings, and who played the last 10 minutes with five fouls. (Jabbar had 26 points, 13 rebounds.)

Big Red was a big man indeed when he popped in 10 points as the Celtics were turning a 22-20 one-quarter lead into a 53-40 halftime advantage. He got the team rolling with a 20-footer, which made it 33-28, and finished off the spurt later in the period with a trailer fast break jumper (White-to-Nelson-to-Cowens) and a bomb, which made it 53-38.

Nor could anyone possibly say enough about the truly spectacular clutch effort turned in by Silas, that intellectual and physical man among men who banged the boards, scored 14 points (even hitting from the outside), ran on the break and aided Cowens in harassing Abdul-Jabbar.

The final hero was Paul Westphal, a 31-minute man, and a killer on offense. It was Westphal who drove base line for a gorgeous lefthanded drive to answer the Bucks' first three-point incursion and handed out five assists and, in the words of Milwaukee assistant Hubie Brown, "created situations for everybody else."

With those three playing so well, with White continuing his tireless defensive digging and with Havlicek, despite only 16 points, providing stability and the needed one big play, the Celtics gradually pulled away from the tiring and psychologically crushed Bucks, until a three-point play by Havlicek (this one on a jumper) made it 98-79 with 1:34 left.

The Milwaukee concession came 23 seconds later when Costello pulled his elongated franchise, and it was left to the Finkels, Williamses, Hankinsons, Downings and Kuberskis to wrap it up, as the others started celebrating immediately with Heinsohn and assistant John Killilea on the sidelines.

The rebuilding job, therefore, is complete, and The Team That Red Built has won its own place in history, leaving but one question: How's the view from Everest, boys?

Auerbach's Five-Year Plan Puts Celtics at Top Again

May 14, 1974 • by Bob Ryan

If the best thing in the world today is being a Boston Celtic, then the second-best thing is having been present at their creation and seeing them work their way to the top.

Only somebody who was there five years ago, when the bottom fell out, could appreciate the impact of that sweet triumph on Sunday in Milwaukee.

What the Celtics did was to implement a Five-Year Plan and make it work. It would have worked in four had John Havlicek not gotten hurt in last year's New York series. It should now be perfectly obvious that the Celtics have been the best team for two years now and that only fate prevented them from winning a year ago.

The first step taken by Red Auerbach and Tom Heinsohn after the dismal (34-48) and boring 1970 campaign was to rid the team of the dissident and uncoachable veterans (Emmette Bryant and Larry Siegfried) who were trying to undermine Heinie's coaching authority, as well as a still classy, but fading Bailey Howell, and go with youth.

That meant that Jo Jo White and Don Chaney were going to be the back court of Boston's future, that Steve Kuberski was going to get a shot at being the power forward and that the team was going to turn its total attention to fast breaking, which the headstrong Siegfried had refused to do.

But all of this would have meant very little had Auerbach not decided that the collegian who could help him was Dave Cowens, an underpublicized 6-8½ kid from Florida State. To most, he was just a name from a magazine.

And so 1971 was the real beginning. "That was the key year," Heinsohn says. "I just threw them out there and showed them how we ran the fast break, and let them gain experience. We won 10 games in a row once by doing nothing other than run. I couldn't believe it."

Four-fifths of the starting five (Chaney, White, Kuberski and Cowens) were 24 years of age or younger. Fortunately, however, the fifth starter was a then 30-year-old veteran named John Havlicek, who was in the midst of what I still consider the greatest all-around year any basketball player has ever had. He and clever Don Nelson represented stability; the others youth and raw ability.

It was a fun year, even if they did invent numerous ways to lose games. I will never forget a home game in Detroit when they blew a four-point lead in the last 13 seconds and lost in overtime; or the night when Walt Bellamy stepped in front of Cowens to take an in-bound pass from midcourt and lay in the winning basket at the buzzer.

They were unable to beat either Milwaukee (0-5) or New York (0-6), and the constant cry from the snipers was, "You can't win with Cowens at center. Move him to forward."

They missed the playoffs by three games, a situation they rectified the following year when they won the Atlantic Division crown by eight games.

That 1972 year will always be Satch's season to me. They were stumbling along with a 14-10 record when Heinsohn replaced the inconsistent Kuberski with the rejuvenated Sanders in the lineup, and for the next three months Satch did the job in his old style until he gave out in March and faded completely in the playoffs. This was also the year Heinie installed the team defensive concept that culminated in this year's awesome playoff performance.

Boston simply was not ready for New York in the playoffs, and Cowens least of all. But he must have learned something, because he was consistently brilliant throughout the following season and went on to win the MVP award.

Last year was a personal trip. Considering the absence of an overpowering man in the middle, the performance of the Celtics had to be the greatest sustained team effort in NBA history. They played 82 games and were in 79 of them, failing to be in a position to win in the last six minutes but three times all year, an unprecedented achievement.

Auerbach had come up with his latest coup, the acquisition of Paul Silas from Phoenix as the needed power forward to help out Cowens underneath, and the subsequent increase of 12 victories was the happy result.

The playoffs will best be remembered for the injury to Havlicek in the third New York game, the infamous double over-time loss in New York on Easter Sunday, the fabulous fifth game triumph when Havlicek scored 18 points with one arm, and the bitter feeling of letdown when the party ended in Game 7.

Thus jolted, the Celtics entered the 1974 season with a rare sense of purpose. They viewed themselves as the uncrowned kings, as men against whom the fates had conspired.

There was, however, no way they were going to approach last year's maniacal effort. They jumped off to a 29-6 start (paralleling the previous year) before sliding into a win one, lose one, syndrome after Jan. 1.

Many fretted, wondering if they were good enough to simply step on the gas when the playoffs opened. Who knew? They had not been in this position before. Their previous calling card was a complete nightly effort. In the second half of this season they played like everyone else.

There were good signs, however. For one thing, they played their best ball in the second half against the best teams. Secondly, Heinsohn was using Havlicek perfectly, never overworking him. Finally, Cowens was sent home for a rest two weeks before the playoffs began. He returned with enough excess energy to light Spokane, Wash., for a year—as Kareem Abdul-Jabbar was later to find out.

Cowens was also busy being a minor prophet. Descending from the plane after the season-ending road trip to Washington and Philadelphia, he said,

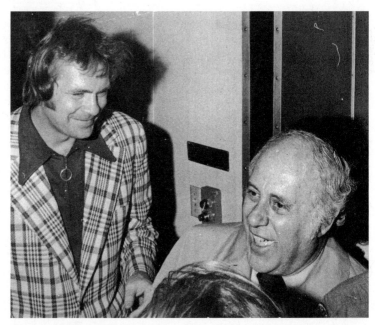

Tom Heinsohn and Red Auerbach, the masterminds behind the 1974 champions.

"In six weeks, there will be a thousand people waiting here for us."

"Will they be cheering or booing?" I asked.

"They don't come when you lose."

It was a strange statement, coming from Cowens, who is no jock, and who ordinarily is unable to understand fans and their motivation.

He also appeared to take it upon himself to ensure the accuracy of the prophecy. For openers, he battled Bob McAdoo through six harrowing games, turning in a superhuman fourth quarter (20 points, six rebounds) in Game 1 to set the tone for the playoffs.

Plagued with fouls, he wasn't much of a factor in the New York series, which only served to point out the team's depth. The three—forward front line of Kuberski, Nelson and Silas—bailed him out.

Havlicek, meanwhile, wasn't doing too badly himself, nor was White, who was steady defensively throughout. Starting with a 43-point showing in the third Buffalo game, Havlicek embarked on a playoff streak to rival anything ever done before. And, when he finally ran out of miracles in the seventh Milwaukee game, supporting actors like Silas and Paul Westphal came to the rescue.

Finally, it came down to a classic matchup of contrasting strengths and styles. The Bucks were a pattern, setup team relying on a 7-3 ⅝-inch center. The Celtics were a quick, small, aggressive and, as it turned out, determined team, which, in addition to everything else, were to get superb technical coaching from Heinsohn (offense) and John Killilea (defense).

Plus, they had one final edge. They had more competitors. They had a center diving on the floor to beat an Oscar Robertson to the ball, a forward (Silas) declaring the backboards off-limits while Cowens was bombing from long range, two guards hounding ballhandlers upcourt, and above all, players with enough mental discipline to stick to their offensive and defensive assignments for 48 minutes, and enough with intestinal fortitude to win three games on the road.

Credit belongs everywhere, but especially to Auerbach, who handpicked the coach and every player on the team, and who rebuilt a team from ashes in three years (remember, they could have won last year) without much money and without a No. 1 draft choice.

14 NBA Teams Say 'No,' but Auerbach Takes Scott

May 24, 1975 • by Bob Ryan

Charlie Scott, who once ranked with Arthur Fiedler, Gilles Gilbert and Patty Hearst as the unlikeliest inhabitants of the Western World ever to become Celtics, is now, believe it or not, a Celtic.

Red Auerbach did what 14 NBA teams refused to do yesterday when he accepted the noted penetrating guard and resident dissident of the Phoenix Suns in exchange for Paul Westphal and Boston's 1976 second-round draft choices.

Boston now owns both principals in the celebrated 1972 transaction with Phoenix. At that time the Celtics received Paul Silas as compensation for Scott's signing with the Suns upon his departure from the ABA Virginia Squires. "Knowing what we know now," says Suns general manager Jerry Colangelo, "I'd have to say we wouldn't have made the deal."

In the 6-foot-6 Scott, the Celtics have acquired one of the most physically gifted guards ever to play basketball. He has averaged 25 points per game during his stormy NBA career, but he has also disappointed his coaches (Butch van Breda Kolff, Colangelo and John MacLeod) with his lackadaisical approach to defense and his generally sour disposition. So disenchanted was he with both the Suns and the city of Phoenix, and they with him, that when Scott expressed a strong desire to be traded, Colangelo immediately contacted all 17 opponents. All but three said they were not interested in him, under any circumstances.

This trade, Auerbach's first body-for-body exchange since 1966 (Mel Counts for Bailey Howell), is sure to shock everyone who has read or heard about Boston's penchant for avoiding what are referred to in the trade as "head cases." Auerbach, however, usually knows what he is doing. "I'm not worried about Scott," he says. "He has always been a fine competitor. I've liked him since his college days."

Westphal, meanwhile, appears to be on the verge of an excellent career in his own right. There never were any questions about his head. What concerned the Celtics was his feet. He just didn't move them fast enough to suit the brass. "Westy should have a great career with them," contends Heinsohn.

The final analysis is simple: Phoenix gave up on a superstar-type talent ("His individual skills are exceptional," says Colangelo, "but we felt he didn't fit into our team concept."), one which Boston feels it can harness. Boston surrendered an exciting guard with star potential. With an old front court the Celtics are looking for back court firepower and now possess, along with the New York duo, the finest raw-talent guard package in basketball today.

Celtics Win, 128-126 in Triple OT

June 5, 1976 • by Bob Ryan

What do you say after you've seen the greatest game of professional basketball ever played? That there should have been two winners? That it would have been a bargain at $250 courtside? That no matter what happens in the final two games of the 1976 playoffs, two teams with heart are competing in the finals? That perhaps rarely in the history of any professional sport have so many incredible clutch plays been turned in during one game by so many people?

Yup, yup, yup and no doubt about it. A delirious mob of 15,320 fortunate patrons stayed at the Garden past midnight last evening to see the Celtics grab a 3-2 series advantage by virtue of a dramatic 128-126 triple-overtime victory over the valiant Phoenix Suns.

So much happened in the final 19 minutes of this memorable affair that the scintillating first half (in which the Celtics built up a 22-point lead, had it chopped to seven, and then mounted it back again to 16 at the half) seemed as if it had been played back on Easter Sunday.

By the time the team got around to settling the outcome, Dave Cowens, Charlie Scott, Paul Silas, Alvan Adams and Dennis Awtrey had all fouled out, and the game was being decided by the most improbable Celtic playoff hero since Gene Guarilia—Glenn McDonald.

It was McDonald, sent into the game when Silas fouled out at 3:23 of the third overtime, who came up with a minute and three seconds of big plays he and all those Celtic fans will long remember. His little spurt began with the score tied at 118, that deadlock having been provided by the next-to-last in an incredible string of Sam Jonesian baskets by Jo Jo White, who crammed 15 of his game high 33 points into the three overtime periods.

At 118-all, Jim Ard (another big hero) won a jump ball from Curtis Perry at the Suns' foul line. That turned into a Boston fast break on which McDonald deftly converted a pretty pass from White. Gar Heard—more on his astounding heroics later— missed a jumper and Don Nelson rebounded. On this transition John Havlicek spotted McDonald on a cross-over along the left base line and hit him with a crisp pass. McDonald hit a quick turnaround to make it 122-118.

Paul Westphal (an amazing fallaway) and White matched baskets, before Dick Van Arsdale missed— the Suns were tiring, at long last—and McDonald soared for the rebound. Curtis Perry (another hero in defeat) fouled him in the back court and McDonald calmly tossed in two free throws to give Boston a 126-120 advantage with 36 seconds remaining.

But these were the Phoenix Suns, a team which is becoming synonymous with such adjectives as gutsy, spunky, gritty and classy. The game was far from over, even when Ard, fouled intentionally off the ball, made two foul shots with 31 seconds left.

Those Ard foul shots were sandwiched between a pair of Phoenix baskets, a layup by Ricky Sobers— he's a rookie?—and a driving 360-degree banked spinner by Westphal. When McDonald lost the ball underneath the Boston basket, Westphal wound up with a sneak-away layup to close the gap to 128-126 with 12 seconds to play.

Again the Suns threatened, when Westphal actually got his fingertips on a looping pass intended for Ard. But Ard kept possession, and the Celtics were finally able to run out the clock, even as Heard and Van Arsdale were vainly trying to foul away from the ball in the hopes of regaining possession.

But if the ending was a battle of punched-out heavyweights, what set it up was worthy of Graziano-Zale at their peak. Take, for example, the second overtime, the final 19 seconds of which included: A White drive to give Boston a 109-106

Referee Richie Powers holds Dave Cowens back as he glares at the Suns' Curtis Perry during Game 5 of the 1976 Finals.

lead; a Van Arsdale 18-footer four seconds later; an immediate Westphal steal from Havlicek on the in-bounds pass; a Perry third try swisher from 15 feet to give the Suns their third lead of the entire ballgame; a Havlicek leaning banker with two seconds to play to give the Celtics, and their fans, what they thought was a 111-110 triumph; a crowd celebration on the court; a declaration by the officials that the Suns would still get a second to play; a technical foul on Phoenix for calling a timeout they didn't have in order to get the ball at midcourt; a White conversion of the technical to make it 112-110; and, finally, a perfect toss into the basket with no time remaining by Heard to send it into the third overtime.

Somewhere back around the start of the 6 o'clock news the Celtics had come blasting out of the locker room to annihilate Phoenix with great shooting (8 for 11 to start the game) and defense to move ahead by scores of 32-12 and 34-14.

The resilient, patient Suns were unmoved by the experience: they fought doggedly and implemented an increasingly sticky defense to pull within 16 (61-45) at the half and within five (77-72) after three quarters. Seemingly dead while trailing, 92-83 with 3:49 left, they rallied behind Westphal to go ahead,

95-94, on a Perry free throw which Havlicek matched with 19 seconds to play in regulation.

Towering figures abounded on both sides, but The Man with all the money on the table was White, who established his back court pre-eminence in this series with a great show. But any number of people could ask for a bow. To have seen this masterpiece was a privilege, and nothing less.

Fan Attacks Referee Powers

June 5, 1976 • by Tom Mulvoy

The picture needed no explanation. Referee Richie Powers was being attacked by a man at center court, Boston Garden.

Powers had been signaling that there was still time left (one second) in the second overtime of the Celtics-Suns game last night. This after John Havlicek had scored what was apparently the winning basket, and the Garden floor had been over-run by fans.

The CBS camera caught the action center stage. Powers and a man were grappling, and referee Don Murphy was moving in to help. In short order, police broke up the scuffle, and moved the fan off the court. Powers remained in the game.

A check with the Division 1 police station early this morning turned up no record of any arrest at the Garden regarding the Powers incident.

It's No. 13—Celtics bring it all back home

June 7, 1976 • by Bob Ryan

PHOENIX—It was a series triumph that should fix even more firmly in the minds and hearts of the American public the uniqueness of this country's most enduring sports legend, the Boston Celtics.

Barely 39 hours after winning the Greatest Game Ever Played, the Celtics acquired the official league imprimatur on their 13th championship by defeating the Phoenix Suns, 87-80, before a downhearted, emotionally spent crowd at Veterans Memorial Coliseum.

The road victory meant that this peculiarly resilient edition of the Celtics had won each play-off series in identical fashion. Against Buffalo, Cleveland and Phoenix, the Celtics won the first two games in relative ease at the Garden, lost a pair of games which were alternately frustrating and aggravating on the road, and then finished off a less experienced foe with a fifth-game home win and a solid sixth-game performance on the road.

The Celtics were not very sharp here yesterday, but they didn't have to be. It was evident from the start that each team had left its reflexes back on the Garden floor, the combination of the extreme expenditure of both physical and emotional energy on Friday, coupled with the adverse conditions of flying over 2,000 miles and playing at 12:30 the next day led to a sloppy first half. The teams committed 10 turnovers in the first quarter and Boston led by an embarrassing 38-33 halftime score.

The Celtics bus heads down Congress Street toward City Hall Plaza for the 1976 NBA Championship celebration.

Red Auerbach, Irving Levin, Johnny Most, Mayor Kevin White, and Tom Heinsohn at the podium during the Celtics' celebration.

The Celtics receive the championship trophy from Commissioner Larry O'Brien.

their three-piece suits, grabbed their briefcases and went to work. Starting with a pair of free throws by John Havlicek— he went to the basket to draw a dubious foul, strictly on experience—and climaxing with a pair of foul shots by series MVP Jo Jo White, Boston simply put the game away with an impressive run of 17-6. With 2:11 remaining in the game, the lead was 81-71.

The catalyst, appropriately enough, was the man whose spirit has made him synonymous with the entire concept of Boston Celticism. For it was Dave Cowens who really picked the team up, starting with the type of play that only he, among all centers, can be counted on to make. With the score 68-67 and with the burden of five fouls, which he carried for the last 10:09, Cowens stole Adams's dribble. Then came the added Cowens touch. Big Red barreled downcourt and finished the play with a backhand fast break drive on which he was fouled by Adams.

Even more than the fact that the three-point play put the Celtics up by four, the play represented his "what's-the-matter-with-the-rest-of-you-guys?" inspiration for the team. It was the one play most generally cited as a key event on both sides.

Still, there were the Suns, hanging tough at 73-71, with 4:23 left. Again the Celtics needed something to happen, and it came in the form of a 6-0 run in the next 1:25, Havlicek, a cold shooter all day ("My legs had no drive after playing 58 minutes on Friday"), swished a 22-footer after Paul Silas salvaged a broken pattern with a smart pick. Charlie Scott, once again a main man in a clinching sixth game, grabbed one of his 11 rebounds for a Boston possession.

Not too surprisingly, however, the teams did respond to the importance of the occasion by playing much better basketball in the second half. The Suns, in fact, rallied from an 11-point third-period deficit of 46-35 to tie the game at 54-all on an Alvan Adams follow-up of his own miss. And with 7:25 to play in the game, a Ricky Sobers foul shot gave them their first lead, 67-66, since 25-24. And the Coliseum was again in the process of transforming itself into the Madhouse on McDowell Street.

But the Celtics, as has been so often mentioned, have been there before. In the next 5:14, they donned

This forced the Suns into a timeout, but the momentum stayed with Boston. White, who finally scaled Backcourt Olympus in the playoffs, just blew by Paul Westphal for a drive to make it 79-71 with 2:58 left. By now, even the Suns' diehard fans knew it was over.

"We just kept our poise longer," explained Silas, which is true. But again there was the question of talent, which Boston most certainly possesses. Perhaps spurred on by a pep talk from White, Mr. Scott confined his energy to playing, and not complaining, and he came up with a classic Charlie Scott game, consisting of 25 points, 11 rebounds, 5 steals, 3 assists and several impetuous turnovers. With his added contributions, plus the clutch effort by Cowens (21 points, 17 rebounds, 10 points on the offensive boards), the Celtics were able to offset the combined White-Havlicek shooting of 9 for 30.

As for the Suns, their spunk was on display to the end, as they cut an 81-71 lead with 2:11 left down to 84-80 with 23 seconds to play before desperation fouls ceased to work. That flurry was the final punctuation mark to this series; if one were needed.

In other words, an excellent team was beaten by a great one. The 13th Boston Celtic championship will not carry an asterisk.

White—the Heart of the Celtics—Rolls with the Bad Bounces

January 16, 1977 • by Ernie Roberts

At first Jo Jo White thought that Charlie Scott merely had hit the floor hard and was stunned. Then he saw that left wrist bent backwards and the agony on Scott's face. Another crisis for the Celtics and more responsibility for White. Jo Jo's expression never changed. "Nothing surprises me anymore," he said later.

Maybe it is this placid exterior, this ultimate professional acceptance of life's vagaries, that deprives the great Celtics guard of his deserved public recognition.

On the court White's high-cheeked, wide-browed face resembles a wax mask. It is difficult to discern even at the blink of his eyes. His major emotional concession is a five-second stare at the referee after a palpably atrocious penalty.

In eight NBA seasons Jo Jo White has received two technical fouls. For the first he uncharacteristically was guilty of vocally protesting a call. Not against himself. Against teammate Dave Cowens. The other time White bounced the ball off the floor in disgust at a whistle. Typically, he then tried to catch it before it zoomed into the air and into the referee's view. But he missed.

The only occasion in Boston's memory on which Jo Jo White was unmasked was on a torrid Tuesday last June. The city was honoring the champion Celtics in a reception at City Hall Plaza.

Immaculately groomed as always with an eye-catching wide hat topping off his outfit, White was a dominant figure on City Hall balcony. He was effervescent, giggling, waving and shouting to the cheering thousands below.

Jo Jo, of course, was entitled. His Celtics had won the playoffs and White had been named the Most Valuable Player of that nationally televised championship. His long search for stature was ended.

Or was it? Here we are six months later. Jo Jo White is having probably his finest professional basketball season. He is leading the Celtics in scoring, assists and minutes played. He has been the floor general, the steadying influence on a squad beset by many personnel changes plus the defection of Cowens. "Jo Jo has held this team together, kept it in contention," says Asst. coach John Killilea.

So where does last June's MVP and the current heart of the Celtics stand in the public's balloting for the NBA All-Star squad?

First? Second? No, Jo Jo White at last count is sixth among the East guards.

People named Pete Maravich, Doug Collins, Nate Archibald, even Walt Frazier and Gail Goodrich, are ahead of Boston's less flamboyant star.

Under his calm exterior isn't White bothered by this putdown in All-Star ranking by the country's basketball fans? Or by a similar lack of respect from the NBA media, which has just once voted him to the All-League team and even on that occasion two years ago only accorded him second-team status?

"Sure it does," said White this week. "It bothers the hell out of me. But I can't let it affect my game, my attitude.

"It's been that way since I came into the league. Every year someone else is in there as an All-Star or All-League. People are going to do what they want and that's that.

"Y'know, I'm not looking for any special glory. I don't think I'm very egotistical. But it does help to get a pat on the back once in a while, some recognition for your work.

"I've never seen such a season for ups and downs as this one. That injury to poor Charlie, for example. We were just really getting used to one another in the back court. Now we've got to replace his 20 points a game, his pressure up front on defense, his help in the ballhandling.

"Cowens's return will help. We need him. We needed him when he left. I welcome him back with open arms."

Will Scott's absence for the next three months mean any difference in White's role in the backcourt?

"Not that I can see right now. I'll still keep bringing the ball up court, playing my game. That's what I get paid to do," said Jo Jo.

"I'm never really pleased with my game. I'm always trying to improve on things like turnovers and bad shots. I've been bothered with a bad foot along with all our other problems.

"But the thing that makes a champion is overcoming bad breaks like this. Playing as tough as you can. If you can do it night in, night out, that distinguishes the good player from the mediocre player."

There were 15 seconds left in Wednesday night's game at the Garden. The Indiana Pacers were leading by 11 points and their victory was assured. But Jo Jo White, who had been on the floor for 43 minutes and scored 30 points, was still racing around the floor, trying to intercept a pass.

The fans didn't notice. They were heading for the exits, talking about Dave Cowens and Charlie Scott. Maybe Jo Jo White should have been wearing his wide-brimmed hat and City Hall smile.

Celtics' Dave Cowens Fares Well on the Taxi Squad

April 14, 1977 • by Alan Richman

At 9:30 last night, I caught a cab on Tremont Street near the Boston Common. At 10 p.m., having followed a circuitous route of my own choosing, the cab arrived at The Globe.

"Twelve dollars even," said the hack driver.

"You want a tip?" asked the hack writer.

"Sure. Twenty percent," answered the driver.

Nothing out of the ordinary here, except that the cab driver happened to be a 6-foot-9 redhead with a second job that pays about $300,000 a year. My chauffeur was indeed Dave Cowens, the Boston Celtics' one-man taxi squad.

Why was he driving a taxi?

"I'm having a really nice time being something other than an athlete," Cowens said. "I'm just doin' something. I'm relaxed, having a good time."

My search for Cowens and his cab began at 7:30 p.m., about the time the Boston Bruins were starting their playoff game against the Los Angeles Kings. Up in the press room of the Garden, I heard whispers that Cowens was out cruising for fares.

Ordinarily, one would scoff at such a farfetched story, but with Cowens there is no such thing as a farfetched story. Remember the auto mechanics course? The Christmas tree farm? The saga of Foxboro? More than once he has said, almost wistfully, "I want to see what it's like to work every day . . . "

I called the sports department and told them I was going off to seek cab No. 352 of the Independent Taxi Operators Assn. Cowens picked up the cab in Roxbury late yesterday afternoon and was out on the street by 5 p.m. The ITOA denied any knowledge of his existence.

"If he was driving, this office would know," said the dispatcher at the main office. "I know 352. A kid from Southie drives it."

From 7:30 until 8:30, I hung around North Station, hoping Cowens would return to familiar haunts. Cab No. 353 cruised by, as did dozens of others, but no Cowens. For $2, one driver tried to raise cab 352 on his radio. He received word that car No. 352 wasn't answering any calls.

Another driver, Bill Raczkowski, reported seeing Cowens at the Hayes-Bickford cafeteria on Canal Street after the Tuesday night Celtics-Spurs playoff game. The cafeteria is a favorite of taxi drivers, but last night Cowens did not appear.

None of the ITOA drivers I questioned reported seeing Cowens at work. Obviously, the rookie driver was not out to get his meter retired.

From 8:30 until 9:30, I searched Chinatown and the Combat Zone. I was walking up Tremont Street towards the waterfront when cab No. 352 turned onto the street and went by at a rather abnormal rate of speed. By the time I could hail him he was two blocks away. I gave chase and caught him at a red light.

He did not know me. Despite his longshoreman's cap, I knew him.

"Hi, how you doin'," Cowens asked his customer. "What you been doin' this evening?"

For the moment, I decided not to tell him I had been looking for him. We chatted amiably about the lovely weather and the good feeling among the people on this warm spring night.

"Where to?" he asked.

"Newton," I said. "Take the turnpike."

"First or second Newton exit?" he replied professionally.

Halfway to Newton I confessed. Cowens, as I expected, was upset. "I haven't told anybody about this, not even the guys I play with," he said. "I think this is an abuse of my privacy. I can't do what I want without having it in the paper. Nobody ever asks how I feel about this. I can't do anything about it. I'm just here."

Cowens is by reputation a warm and unspoiled person. There are exceptions to this character analysis. He is not very friendly to reporters immediately after basketball games, and he is never friendly to reporters when they pry into his private life. He felt cab No. 352 was part of his private life.

"I'm a basketball player. Other than that, leave me alone," he said.

By the time we reached the Southeast Expressway he began to mellow. An old hometown Kentucky friend, Dave Guidugli, was riding in the front seat. He convinced Cowens that he had been caught fair and square.

Just before reaching The Globe Cowens offered a brief recap of his evening. I was his sixth customer and the only one to recognize him. "One guy thought he did, but I talked him out of it," Cowens said. He spent a little time hanging around South Station—so much for my North Station theory—took a fare to a Holiday Inn and then picked me up on Tremont Street.

One day behind the wheel cost Cowens approximately $50—$25 for rental of the cab, $17 for a hackney driver license, $8 for gasoline.

I did my part. I gave him a $3 tip.

Cornbread Gets His First Sample of Celtics' Pride

June 29, 1977 • by John Powers

The induction began at a Chinese restaurant in Brookline with lobster and the smoke from a long Auerbachian cigar. Later, down on Causeway Street, they had Cedric Maxwell take off his suitcoat, vest and shirt, and pull on a white team jersey.

"Take him upstairs," Red Auerbach was saying. "I want him to see the court and the dressing room and all that. And give him some shoes, socks, T-shirts . . . whatever he wants."

Yesterday, they gave Cornbread Maxwell everything a Celtic top draft choice is supposed to get . . . except a contract. That will presumably come later, once Auerbach, Maxwell and his representative, Cincinnati lawyer Ron Grinker, sit down again and discuss details.

It has all happened so quickly that a man needs time to get his bearings. Five years ago, Cedric Maxwell was worried about making his high school team. Three weeks ago, when Auerbach barked out his name over a conference call hookup on draft day, everybody in the country already knew him.

Maxwell was the gangly enthusiastic center/ forward/guard, bringing the ball upcourt against Michigan in the NCAAs. He was the sparkplug, the symbol, of one of the most sympathetic,

First-round pick Cedric Maxwell (wearing No. 42—he'd later switch to No. 31) with Tom Heinsohn (left) and Red Auerbach.

loosey-goosey, fun-running underdogs in college basketball history. The Cornbread Man.

He listens to all of this with an indulgent smile, tolerant of the myth but aware of the truth. The fact is the University of North Carolina at Charlotte played a disciplined game of basketball this year. They did run some patterns. They did have a respect for fundamentals. And it wasn't as though Maxwell thought up the nickname himself.

"That came from the movie, 'Cornbread, Earl and Me,'" Maxwell said. "Keith Wilkes played the basketball player, and everybody told me I looked like him and played like him. It was just a label that was applied."

The word was that Maxwell doesn't like the name, although he says now it doesn't really bother him. If the nickname is a fantasy, so are a lot of her things.

"Things have occurred so fast that it's kind of like being in a lucky dream world," he said. "We went from nowhere to national prominence, just like that,

and it's a big difference. Things happen so fast they make your head spin."

Disney used to love stories like this. So did the Brothers Grimm. Maxwell comes out of Kinston, N.C., a town of 2,000 with a big synthetic fiber plant on the Neuse River, near Camp LeJeune. "It's not a big river," he said. "Just a small stream that you might go bathing in. You might see Tom Sawyer coming down it in a boat."

He was cut from his high school varsity as a junior. None of the Tobacco Road people— Duke, North Carolina, Wake Forest or State— were interested.

East Carolina, a few miles away in Greenville, offered him a half scholarship. Only UNCC really wanted him among major colleges. "There was really no choice," he said.

So he went off to Charlotte, and slayed in the Sunbelt Conference against the likes of Jacksonville, Georgia State and New Orleans. If you follow New England college basketball, you saw him in

Springfield, at the Hall of Fame Tourney, two years ago, where UNCC pummeled UMass, 85-57, for the championship. Or at the NIT last year, where he led UNCC to the finals and was named MVP.

This year, he brought the 49ers to Fantasyland, the NCAA Final Four in Atlanta, where they came within a last-second dunk of upsetting Marquette and reaching the final against their high-rent cousins from Chapel Hill. That was Maxwell you saw, loping across the pages of Sports Illustrated.

And yesterday, with the cameras grinding inside Auerbach's office, they were handing him a Celtic Jersey to model. "Haven't changed colors much," said Grinker. "No-o-o," Maxwell replied, grinning. "Same green and white I was wearing in school."

He could smell the cigar smoke yesterday, and hear Tom Heinsohn's belly-laugh. And he could still sense the unfamiliar presence of lobster, Chinese-style, in his stomach.

"I'd been allergic to seafood," Maxwell was saying. "I'm worrying right now if I'm going to swell up."

Auerbach Takes a Positive Step, but Celtics Face a Long Trip Back

December 30, 1977 • by Bob Ryan

The Celtics are not just a messy living room after the kids have finished opening up the Christmas gifts; they are not merely an unmade bed which can be straightened out with 10 seconds of pulling and tugging. They are nothing less than downtown San Francisco after The Earthquake, so let us suffer from no delusions about the depth of the problem.

Having begun on that cheery note, I hereby submit that Step 1 in the rehabilitation process is fabulous. The acquisition of Don Chaney and Kermit Washington, combined with the removal of Charlie Scott, means that Red Auerbach has attacked the problem at its root cause by exchanging some Raw Talent for some Role Players.

It was, after all, by strategic blending of incomplete players that Auerbach fashioned the classiest empire in professional sports. Auerbach literally wrote the book on modern team play. The basketball world, at every level, is filled with Auerbach imitators, and why not? Red's style means fast breaks, aggressive defense, attention to detail, and a self-sacrificing attitude which inspires each man on the floor to ask the question, "What can I do to help us win this game?" If the current NBA champion Trail Blazers aren't a suitable replica of Red's vintage teams in basketball philosophy, then Rick Barry isn't a crybaby.

The only thing is, that somewhere along the line, Auerbach abandoned his own principles. Losing Chaney the first time could not be classified as anything but a mistake. Attempting to solve the team's apparent back court problems the following year by trading Paul Westphal for Scott was another mistake, even if it took a while for the full effects to take hold. Signing Sidney Wicks the first time was a reasonable gamble, but resigning him this season was an error, which made Neville Chamberlain's 1938 analysis of Hitler's intentions look like a minor misjudgment. And please don't ask me what all this John Johnson business was about. All I know is that Johnson starts for a team with a better record than Boston's and Curtis Rowe doesn't play anymore. Could more Auerbach arrogance have cost the Celtics the services of another potentially useful ballplayer?

The result of all these decisions was on display for West Coast fans to see a couple of weeks ago. The wretched performances of the Celtics revealed several members of the team to be quitters, utter frauds masquerading as professional athletes.

All it takes for a reasonably talented NBA team to win an occasional road game is a little heart, but this team not only doesn't win on the road, it doesn't even offer a mild threat to the spread. You want to know how bad the Celtics have been? Were they to play any team in the league on a neutral court, any bookie would make them the underdog. And that includes the Nets.

It will take more than one trade to turn this team around, but you've got to start somewhere, and Auerbach has made a fine beginning. Washington is not a great player, but he has the potential to be very good. In fact, I'll make the assumption that merely playing alongside Dave Cowens will enhance his effectiveness by about 20 percent. Washington is sort of an apprentice Paul Silas, a hard-nosed kid who knows exactly what he can contribute to a basketball team.

As for Chaney, he was formerly considered to be the prototype Celtic cog, a high-minded person who did only those things which he knew would benefit the team. Don Chaney has never put on a uniform for the betterment of Don Chaney, unlike a few others we've got on this team.

A word about the departed Mr. Scott. He means well; he really does. He did try to play it the Celtic way, in his own inimitable fashion, but he never really changed because he is constitutionally incapable of doing so. Charlie Scott plays hard, yes, but he does it not to win but to show you he's playing hard. The tragedy is that he doesn't understand this basic fact. No wonder Jo Jo White found that he could no longer live with him.

I think this trade was intended to have wide-reaching ramifications. More than merely bringing certain needed physical skills to the ball club, Chaney and Washington are being asked to bring a certain attitude. "We tried it a new way," Auerbach seems to be saying, "and it didn't work. We're going back to the old way." What had always distinguished the Celtics was unity on the court and professional respect off the court.

It's no secret that the 1977 Celtics are characterized by confusion on the court and a simple lack of common courtesy off the court. Or what else do you call Rowe's habitual lateness for buses and his buddy Wicks's frequent tardiness before games? They have taken Red's simple but dignified structure and stomped on it. Nobody can tell me these actions aren't reflected in their oft-mindless play.

I applaud Auerbach for doing something that must have been extremely difficult for him, which was to allow Chaney, a defector, back into the athletic family. I doubted that Red would ever do such a thing, but I'm certainly glad he has. He would show me even more by convincing his boss, Irv Levin, to do the ultimate and swallow the contract of Mr. Wicks, even if he must be placed on waivers to do it.

The subtraction would be a marvelous addition to team morale, and I'm amazed that neither Auerbach, Levin, nor Tom Heinsohn (the semi-heroic figure in this drama) appears to have grasped that reality. Once that chore is complete, then Cedric Maxwell should be inserted into the lineup and left there for a minimum of 35 minutes a night or six personal fouls, whichever comes first. He must be allowed to make

his mistakes, for I have looked into the front court future of the Celtics and it is Maxwell.

The important thing now is that spiritual help has arrived, and this is what the Celtics needed more than anything. Losing is one thing, but surrendering is another. If Don Chaney ever quits in a game, I swear to God I'll apply for the job as Wicks's agent.

Heinsohn Reaction: 'That's Life'

January 4, 1978 • by John Powers

He knew it was coming, even before he walked aboard the plane to Los Angeles last month. Even before the five West Coast losses made The Changes all but inevitable.

Tom Heinsohn had joked about it, with the ironic humor of a man who sees the gallows rope being prepared. "Well, at least they gave me a round-trip ticket," he had said, grinning, as he left Logan for five dismal evenings in Seattle, Phoenix, and points between.

He was philosophical about it yesterday, after he'd gone to practice and found Red Auerbach there waiting for him . . . after nine seasons of coaching the Celtics to five divisional titles and two NBA championships had ended with a brief chat and a handshake.

"That's life, man," Heinsohn was saying, an hour after Tom Sanders had replaced him. "I think the pressures were brought to bear even before the road trip. The last two games (a victory at Milwaukee and a last-minute loss at Chicago) probably didn't mean anything; I think Red just waited until after the holidays."

It seemed cold, the way he got the news, like a Madison Avenue executive finding his desk cleaned out and the locks changed. But Auerbach hadn't wanted to do it by telephone.

"I didn't want to call him," Auerbach would say. "I wanted to face Tommy, look him in the eye, and tell him just how I felt. As I said, in 32 years in the NBA, this was the most traumatic thing I've ever been through."

If it was traumatic for Heinsohn, he concealed it well. Through it all—the unrest from the veterans, the presence of owner Irv Levin in locker rooms from Causeway Street to Inglewood, the worst Celtic start ever, and public speculation about his future—Heinsohn performed his job with grace and wit. It wasn't easy.

"If, God forbid, we don't win any games out here," Levin stated after a loss in Los Angeles, "there are going to be a l-o-t of changes made."

The easiest ones were the trading of Charlie Scott and the dismissal of Heinsohn—and Heinsohn seemed resigned to his fate even before the Lakers game. He was coaching a team that had not won a road game in regulation time, and he saw 10 straight games away from the Garden lying ahead.

Auerbach knew about some veterans who didn't particularly care about winning, as long as the checks arrived on time. He also knew that an impasse had been reached, that communications had broken down between Heinsohn and the squad, and that something had to be done before a season went down the sewer.

And in an era of long-term, no-cut, lucrative contracts, it was simpler to dismiss a coach than trade away a ball club. Heinsohn wouldn't say that—but he knew it.

So after nine years, he will sit at home in Natick this morning and examine his options. "I have no plans right now," he said. "I have other careers I can pursue. I'm still in the insurance business, as I have been for 20 years. There's broadcasting, painting . . . a number of things.

"I'm not afraid of the world."

The Importance of Being Ernie . . .

February 3, 1978 • by Bob Ryan

I just hope it's not too late for Ernie DiGregorio to help the Celtics. Or for the Celtics to help him.

There was a time—and not too long ago, either—just when the thought of Ernie D leading a Boston fast break would have been sufficiently stimulating to carry any good Celtic fan through a boring

workday. Ernie D, perhaps the one legitimate Cousy heir yet produced, appeared born to play on the funny parquet floor.

But that was one damaged knee, two teams and many humiliations ago. There is absolutely nothing romantic about DiGregorio's presence in a Celtic uniform. He needed a job. The Celtics, saddled with injuries and age in the back court, were in the market for a guard who could bring the ball up and create some offense. Troubled player and troubled team got together, with the latter agreeing to take custody of the former for a 10-day free (practically) home trial. Strictly business, you see.

This is sadly ironic, because there has never been anything business-like about Ernie DiGregorio's approach to basketball. The sport has been his true romance from the age of 10. If there is one player in the NBA of whom it could truthfully be said, "This guy would play for nothing," it would have to be Ernie D.

This is not to say he hasn't been hardened. Very little has gone right for him since the night of Oct. 31, 1974, when most of his body went this-a-way while his knee went that-a-way. Ernie had been the 1974 NBA Rookie of the Year, and he had gotten off to a great start in his second year when he went down that fateful evening in Oakland. With few exceptions, his Wizard of Oz existence in the NBA has been more of a Last House on the Left disaster ever since.

Can he play? He says yes, but does anybody really know? Is he simply a victim of circumstance, or terminally slow feet, plus a not active enough pituitary gland? Perhaps we can rationalize his going from Buffalo to Los Angeles on the basis of salary, but what was the true story of his LA escapade? We can safely assume that Jerry West did not want DiGregorio around to begin with, but would the Laker coach be irrational enough to subdue him if he happened to demonstrate that he could help the team? I was told by someone I trust that Kareem Abdul-Jabbar had taken an immediate liking to Ernie and his method of delivering the ball. If so, why isn't he still a Laker? Sometimes I get the feeling DiGregorio has been lied to a lot these past three years, but I have no way of proving it.

I do know this: It's very easy to prove that Ernie D was one of the greatest college basketball players of all time. Surely, he was one of the most popular ever to play around here. If Bob Cousy started the fire that was college basketball in New England after WWII, Ernie DiGregorio was the one who rekindled the flame about 21 years later. In each case an average-sized, highly ethnic kid with abnormally developed peripheral vision delighted fans and dazzled teammates with unsurpassed ability to make a round leather ball sing athletic arias.

The public has an undying fascination with good small men in basketball, and DiGregorio at his best is one of the most lovable basketball players ever.

Moreover, Ernie D was not only a star, but he was also the star of the best college basketball team New England has seen in the past two decades. The 1973 Providence College team might very well have won the NCAA championship had Marvin Barnes not injured his knee during the semifinal game against Memphis State. No team was playing better basketball going into the tournament, and no player was in better form than Ernie D. He started off the Memphis State game with a display so fabulous that Sports Illustrated seer Curry Kirkpatrick still calls it "the finest 10 minutes of basketball I've ever seen in college."

This team, I submit, stimulated interest in college basketball in the Boston, as well as the Providence, area. And the player with the fan clubs was Ernie D, the little Italian kid from North Providence who fulfilled the fantasies of all those fans whose mothers, as Randy Newman might say, "had to pick 'em up to say hello."

The pros, meanwhile, were busy dismissing Ernie D. Too small, too slow, too fat, too white—you name the prospect's disease and they said he had it. Not until Ernie D embarrassed the Russians in that memorable Madison Square Garden affair did he become a hot item.

But he made it, didn't he? He was the league's best rookie and he damn near led the Braves past the Celtics in the playoffs. Sure, they talked about his deficiencies (Who can forget the scornful nickname, Ernie No-D?), but when they weighed the plus-minus factor, they noticed he was a big plus. This shouldn't have surprised anyone, because if they removed from the current NBA rosters all the players who were (a) "step slow" (b) "need more shooting range" or (c) "should be an inch-and-a-half taller" there wouldn't be enough guys left for one team's intrasquad scrimmage. Scouts spend 98 percent of their time looking for the All-Perfection team rather than a guy who can help their ball club.

Then came The Knee and DiGregorio's subsequent loss of basic respectability. Jack Ramsay buried him. Tates Locke buried him. Joe Mullaney buried him. Jerry West encased him in a three-piece cement suit and dropped him into the Pacific Ocean. You'd have to assume that if any of these men thought they could win more games with DiGregorio than without him that they'd play him. If anything, coaches might have been more inclined to play him than another guy they might not like, simply because of his salary. You've got to admit that none of this sounds particularly encouraging.

The best time for the Celtics to have gotten DiGregorio, says Red Auerbach, would have been when they had Bill Russell. He wouldn't have been too bad with Paul Silas, Don Nelson, a healthy Jo Jo White and a prime-of-life John Havlicek, either. But we all know the reality of the present situation. The Celtics are now staging "The Chorus Line" in real life, and Ernie D is just another budding starlet. A lot of grateful basketball fans will be rooting very hard for him to make it.

Guest Columnist | John Havlicek Says Goodbye

April 7, 1978 • by John Havlicek

If my birth had caused as much commotion as my retirement, I'm sure that it would have been the happening of at least the first half-century in one particular little town—Lansing, Ohio.

Although many small towns in the Ohio Valley claim me as their native son, my first 18 years were spent in that one town of a few hundred people. We were nurtured well there, for Lansing also produced the likes of Phil Niekro (Atlanta Braves), Joe Niekro (Houston Astros), Johnny Blatnik (St. Louis Cardinals and Philadelphia Phillies) and Bill Jobko (Los Angeles Rams and Minnesota Vikings).

For the first few days of my life, I had an identity crisis, because my parents, Frank and Mandy Havlicek, could not decide on a name for me. It wasn't until my mother's two brothers, John and

John Havlicek signs his first contract with the Celtics on August 1, 1962, with Walter Brown and Red Auerbach watching.

Joseph Turkal, visited the hospital that a decision was made. John Joseph Havlicek became official, sporting a genuine wrist bracelet with first, middle and last names included. April 8, 1940 . . . 8:45 a.m.

During the first years of my life, I've been told, I was not a very pleasant child. Crying and sickness were my trademarks. A combination of whooping cough and measles at the same time was almost my downfall. Lots of prayers, love and good care helped me survive the crisis, however, and I am often teased about how big I might have been if I had not been so sickly as a child.

From that point on, family, friends and good people supporting me have always been the backbone of my success.

Being a Midwesterner, my first year in Boston was a trial. I loved the team, but adjusting to city life was most difficult. The pace seemed to be about 100 times faster than I was used to, and although I was

a good driver in Ohio, I was terrified in Boston. My first decision was to send my car back home, feeling I was much safer on the MBTA than behind a wheel.

It didn't take long to change my mind, though. I grew to love Boston like a native. It is truly home to me now, and I plan to stay here. Since my first days here, the face of Boston has changed and blossomed like no other city that I have visited.

Your enthusiastic support has provided me with experiences and thrills I can never relive, but my memory will forever remind me of being hoisted on your shoulders, of thousands of faces at the airport, of miles of smiles in a parade, and warm handshakes wherever I go.

I can recall many instances in which you, the fans, through your support, helped produce victories for the Celtics. To a player, your loud, enthusiastic cheers say, "We're with you, we appreciate you, we know it isn't easy and we're doing what we can." It is a beautiful feeling.

I've experienced nights when your energy was transferred to me, and made me become better, made me dig deeper and come up with more, made me not as tired as my opponent, and made me perform better than I felt capable.

My career is ending now, and with it have come many ovations. I cherish them.

I see thousands of friends and smiling faces, and I say to you, "enjoy it as much as I, for you have helped my career be what it is."

I've been a lucky man in Boston. I had the opportunity to play my entire career in one city, with the people of that city behind me all the way.

When I first arrived, I joined a team of the best basketball players in the world. A championship team.

I arrived a youth and matured here. I arrived a bachelor and married here. My wife, Beth, to me, is like the song, "You Light Up My Life." We had precious children here. I have special true friends here. This city has made me a happy man.

It is my home. It is my city. I love you, Boston.

The Final Day of John Havlicek

April 10, 1978 • by John Powers

He'd rented the tuxedo—jacket, shirt, studs, cummerbund, black tie, all of it—because he thought that was how a man should go out after 18 years.

You should arrive at the office early on your last day, garbed in formal wear, drape each article on a separate hanger, and put on the uniform slowly, making sure the shoelaces were straight. You should have your speech written and rehearsed, and shake hands with everybody.

And then, you should take a deep breath and try to keep it all from crashing in on you. John Havlicek did all that yesterday, but the enormity of it was more than he bargained for, and on his final afternoon as a Celtic (Game No. 1,270), he twice wept openly, his face twisted, the lower lip trembling.

He also played 41 minutes, passed out nine assists, six of them in the first quarter of Boston's 131-114 victory over Buffalo, and scored 29 points, nine of them in a final two minutes that will stand for all time among the most dramatic in Boston sports history.

The game had been won by then, and Tom Sanders had replaced Dave Bing with Ernie DiGregorio, who'd vowed an hour earlier that he would get the ball to the Captain for a sneak-away and a dunk.

"Every time up the court," DiGregorio had murmured, grinning, "I'm going to be looking for him." As it happened, Havlicek was never able to get the opening he needed, although DiGregorio did feed him for a pair of breakaway reverse layins 11 seconds apart, as a capacity crowd of 15,276 (and more) rocked the building with an incredible ovation.

"I kept easin' away for the dunk," Havlicek would say, "but I just couldn't get it done. I would have tried it, though. You better believe it, after all that other stuff I was missing (11 for 33 on the afternoon, most of them jumpers off the rim). I figured, throw it all up. Bring out everything I've ever known."

So he did. And the last two minutes were magic—two free throws, two driving layins, a jumper in the lane off his own miss, and a final free throw (his 26,395th career point) with 29 seconds to play. Each one of them produced a tidal wave from the gallery . . . and then, with 15 seconds left, with play stopped and Scott Lloyd at the free throw line, Sanders sent Bing in for Havlicek, and ended an era on Causeway Street.

"Earlier, I'd said, 'John, I want to take you out,'" Sanders would say. "And he indicated he wanted to stay in. He said, 'I started my career running, and I want to end it running.' I wanted to go along with his wishes, but the time was too opportune."

Bing, who'd dressed next to Havlicek all year, came over and embraced him. So did Don Chaney, who'd spent nearly eight years on Boston teams with Havlicek and shared two championships with him. Then Havlicek walked to the bench, raised his hands to the crowd, sat down and sobbed, staring up at the clock.

He'd broken down at the beginning, after he'd made the two ritual layups as the clubs were whistled off, after he'd gone to midcourt, bowed twice, and let the noise wash over him. Shaken, he ran to the sidelines, waving his hand in a circle above his head. "Let's go, already," he told his mates, as the roar rose, crested, and rose again.

It lasted for eight minutes, laced with a rhythmic HON-do, HON-do, HON-do. And then Havlicek took his team onto the floor for the last time.

Halftime was easier on the emotions. He'd been prepared for that, for the Sportscoach camper (estimated at $50,000) the club would give him, for the remarks from Larry O'Brien, Dave Cowens, Red Auerbach and owner Irv Levin (who was roundly booed by the crowd).

And for his own speech, which he delivered "slowly and with a lot of deep breaths." He thanked Auerbach for drafting him, his family—Beth, Chris, Jill and his mother—for supporting him, and the fans for backing him. "You provided me with many thrills," he would tell them. "I'm going to remember most you people in the stands, and the flags hanging above me. What more can I say? Thank you, Boston. I love you."

After it was over, after the hurried exit, with police all around, and the all-comers mass press conference, he gave his final dressing room interview with bloody gauze stuffed in his mouth, courtesy of a wayward Larry McNeill limb in the second quarter.

Then he slowly put the tuxedo back on again, gathered up a copy of the final stats and a fourth-quarter running sheet and turned out the lights, as he'd promised clubhouse man Walter Randall he would. He walked toward the side door and stopped short, fishing through his pockets for his NBA championship ring.

"Knew I had one in here somewhere," John Havlicek said.

Celtics Draft Bird for Oh-What-a-Future

June 10, 1978 • by Bob Ryan

Red Auerbach did not look as if he had swallowed the canary. He looked as if he had just consumed the entire aviary.

"I feel," he cooed, "that we did as good a job as we possibly could."

What Red did in yesterday's NBA Draft was acquire the rights to the best college player in the country. "How often," Red inquired, "do the Celtics get a chance to draft the best player in the country?" The answer, apparently, is once every 22 years.

There are undoubtedly some unhappy Celtic fans this morning, since Larry Bird, the object of Red's affection, will not be available to the Celtics right away. Those who seek instant gratification cannot see the wisdom in drafting a player who won't sign for a year when this team needs so much help. Those people would not feel this way if they had ever seen Larry Bird play. Larry Bird is worth waiting for.

What is a Larry Bird? Larry Bird is a 6-foot-9, sturdy, blond-haired amalgam of Bob Pettit, Dan Issel, and Rick Barry. He has the shooting range and stick-it-in-your-face shooting style of Pettit, the all-around inside game and scoring savvy of Issel and the passing ability of Barry. Next to Earvin Johnson, he's probably the best passing big man around. He works hard on defense and has good instincts. He rebounds well and does not run away when the traffic gets heavy underneath. Just thinking of him playing with Dave Cowens makes me want to go out and buy seven basketball magazines.

He was available to the Celtics because none of the teams picking ahead of them were in a position to choose him without an assurance that he would play right away. Auerbach knew how much they all wanted him. "Portland, Kansas City and Indiana all would have taken him in preference to a Mychal Thompson or Rick Robey if they could have signed him. I'll tell you how badly Portland wanted him. They wanted to give me a player so they could move their second first-round pick from the seventh spot to sixth."

Ah, but Red had the luxury of two first-round picks, strategically located in the sixth and eighth spots. The sixth pick was the result of their dismal regular-season finish. The eighth spot was the result of a maneuver which has a chance to go directly into the Transactions Hall of Fame. In fact, if anything further is needed to cement the Auerbach legend, it will be the January deal with Los Angeles.

Consider the situation. The Celtics were losing ballgames. They had bad press. They had dwindling home crowds, and hostile ones, at that. They were, in a word, desperate. They could not possibly have been dealing from a position of less strength.

And so Auerbach (with help from owner Irv Levin) gave the Lakers Charlie Scott. Right away he pleased half the fans. In exchange he got a supposed LA problem, Kermit Washington. And Don Chaney. And a first-round draft pick. It would have been an equitable deal if he had just gotten Washington. Getting Chaney was nice. But extorting the draft pick on top of that was practically criminal. Especially when the draft gave them the luxury of picking Larry Bird, who everyone agrees is the best player in the country.

What makes Red's actions even more palatable is the fact that he has taken the high moral road in this matter. He is considering no strong-arm tactics. He has assured Indiana State coach Bob King that he will not pressure Bird to forsake his senior year, that he will wait until the 1979 college season is over before negotiating with Bird. I think that Bob King has nothing to worry about. For his part, Bird has issued a statement through the Sports Information Office at Indiana State expressing satisfaction over being drafted by Boston, reiterating that he wants to play another year of college ball and stating that he is looking forward to sitting down to negotiate with the Celtics "after completing my senior year."

Since hitting the absolute bottom of his career with the John Johnson fiasco, Auerbach has bounced back up off the canvas in his old aggressive style. He made the LA trade. He signed Ernie DiGregorio. He signed Kevin Kunnert as a free agent, thus making it possible for him to gamble on Bird. All that remains for him to do in order to restore full public support is to expunge Sidney Wicks and Curtis Rowe from our midst, no matter what the cost. By this time I am certain that Red realizes the depth of public feeling against these two players. Countless people have no intention of renewing season tickets unless these two are gone from the team. What he must understand is that people aren't asking for anything in exchange for these players. Fans just want them out of here so as not to poison, or otherwise impede, the others.

So let us acknowledge the continuing sagacity of the irrepressible cigar-smoking general manager. I just hope he doesn't choke on all those feathers.

NBA Allows Club Swap; Celtics, Braves Trade 6

July 8, 1978 • by Larry Whiteside

CHICAGO—The new era began with a half-dozen unanswered questions about the future. There was a trade that pleased both new owners but still has to be sold to Boston fans.

And, importantly, it begins with Red Auerbach, the main link between the Celtics' rich past and their new direction—sitting on a fence, wondering if there is still room in the brave new world for a 60-year-old living basketball legend.

"I'm becoming the owner of the Celtics because it's a challenge," said John Y. Brown, the 11th man to head the NBA's most prestigious club. "I know it's not going to be easy. But I'm not here to make a profit. I'm here to help build a winner. I mean for us to be competitive."

It all came to pass yesterday, just like clockwork. Ownership of the Celtics changed hands from Irv Levin to John Y. Brown in a complicated transfer that was approved by the NBA board of governors here by a 21-1 vote. It authorized Brown's purchase of the Celtics and the transfer of the Buffalo franchise to San Diego, under Levin's ownership.

There was a trade—a giant one considering the direction Boston had been going the last two years—as it sought to rebuild along the lines that brought it an NBA championship in 1976. Going to the new San Diego franchise are Kermit Washington, Kevin Kunnert and rookie Freeman Williams, who played at Portland State and is from the Los Angeles area.

San Diego also will get Sidney Wicks, providing "some problems not concerning his contract," said Brown, can be ironed out. "I certainly hope they can be," Brown said, adding that the issue may not be settled for a month.

Boston will get Nate (Tiny) Archibald, whippet former All-Pro guard at Kansas City who did not play last year because of an injury, former ABA scoring champion Billy Knight, and former Providence and ABA star Marvin Barnes. Additionally, Brown said he is working on a transaction that will soon bring a backup center to Boston to provide Dave Cowens with the help he might have gotten from Kunnert.

The deal was made possible when both Kunnert and Washington, both free agents represented by Donald Dell, signed contracts last week with the Celtics. Wicks has four years to go on a contract signed last winter.

"I'm not sure I would have made the exchange of franchises if we weren't able to complete these player transactions," said Brown. "I think an owner must have confidence in his players that they can do the job. Archibald's heel injury is healed and there's nothing wrong with Knight. Marvin just got married and is a changed man."

Former Celtics owner Irv Levin repeated his desire to own a club close to home. He added, "All these players we're getting are from California and we know what they can do. We know they are popular. Things have happened so fast that we've scarcely had time to iron out all the details. It is a very complicated transaction. I don't have a general manager, a coach or even a new name for the team. But all this will be worked out shortly."

One source indicated that Levin was anxious to leave Boston because, with Boston not making the playoffs this year, the club made only enough money to meet expenses, despite the fact it averaged more than 11,000 fans at home last season. Levin reportedly had to come up with around $250,000 out of his pocket to meet the team's interest payment on his estimated $3 million loan.

Brown said he felt it was necessary to leave Buffalo, where attendance averaged around 6,000 last year, because he had exhausted every possibility to make the club a venture that would support itself in future years.

"We were on the third rung of the ladder while I was there," said Brown, "behind the Sabres and the Bills. We made an effort to improve the team, but from an economic standpoint it just wasn't going to work out. I've got to think of that as an owner."

Brown added that when he was looking around for a new spot for his ownership, he didn't think of Boston until he met Levin last month in San Diego during the summer meetings.

"Irv and I started talking and the idea of swapping franchises just began to grow. The key was that we dealt in good faith and wouldn't let the lawyers or accountants change anything."

Brown said he is well aware that as a newcomer to NBA ranks, fans will be suspicious of him, particularly since he is not from New England. But he added he wants to maintain Boston's position and status nationally. To that end, he has offered Auerbach a new multiyear contract and said he is very happy with the Celtics' coaching staff of Tom Sanders and K. C. Jones, who now have three-year contracts.

"I'm a great believer in continuity," he said. "We had that for years with Adolph Rupp at the college level in Kentucky, and I can't see why we can't continue it here. I've made Red an offer which he calls attractive. He'll consider it and I hope he agrees to stay. It would be difficult without him."

Cowens Says Enough—Quits Coaching

April 9, 1979 • by Leigh Montville

He struggled with the cigar with the wooden fingers of a nonsmoker. Dave Cowens was not used to this.

He had the cigar, you see, and he had the matches and he was holding the cigar and was supposed to hold the matches and light one of them and puff at the same time and finally, he received some help. Assistant coach Bob MacKinnon came over and assistant K. C. Jones came over and together, forming a little circle in front of the Celtics bench, they got the damn thing going.

The smoke came out of the middle of them and for Cowens the end had arrived. Even with a minute and a half of basketball to be played in front of them, the absolute end had arrived.

The one-man-band experiment was history. He could take the cymbals from his knees, the saxophone from his chest and the weight from his back and concentrate only on what he does best. He was a player-coach no more. He was only a player.

"The cigar . . . the cigar was just a joke," Cowens said after his dual career and the Celtics' season had ended yesterday afternoon at the Garden with a 127-101 win over the coasting, playoff-bound New Jersey

Nets. "If we won, I just wanted to do it. Just like Red used to do."

He had announced his decision to quit to his team before the game. He had made the decision in the past weeks and months, gradually, as he had coached the final three quarters of the worst Celtics season in history.

His own voice had told him to quit, disappearing and hiding in the morning after being overworked at night. His head had told him to quit, aching in the morning as surely as the other physical parts of his body ached after playing the game. More than anything, though, his sense of perfection had told him to quit. He was doing two jobs, but he wasn't doing either of them as well as if he were doing one alone.

"Maybe you could do the job if you had a veteran team, like Bill Russell had when he did it," Cowens said he decided. "A team like that, you really don't have to coach. You have a lot of help.

"A young team like this, though, I just don't think anybody could do both jobs right. As a coach, you can work on things and practice and prepare all right, but when the most important time—the game—arrives, you have to hand the job to someone else. As a player, too, there are just too many distractions. There is just the feeling of doing an incomplete job. You're not doing justice to either job."

The gruesome qualities to the season are reflected by the numbers. The team finished at 29-53. The part of the season Cowens coached was 27 wins and 41 losses. The finishing stretch, the mind-boggling, sodden, injury-filled finishing stretch featured only six wins in the last 27 games.

"We just weren't tough enough," said Cowens. "You go through a season and you find out who's tough and who isn't. Some people came through for us, went out and played every night. Some didn't. They quit. It was just that kind of season, a season that I wouldn't wish anybody would have to go through."

Dave Cowens may not be the coach next year, but that does not mean that he will not remember those games when he was the coach.

"I've seen a lot of smirks and smiles from a lot of these hot dogs from around the league," he said with a bit of that old glare in his eyes. "There were some guys who worked their butts off on this team and they didn't deserve that. I remember who did it."

"Uh, Dave, could you give us a couple of examples of who those hot dog guys were?" he was asked.

"No need," the former coach and smoker of one cigar said. "They'll find out who they are. When they try to drive the lane next year . . . "

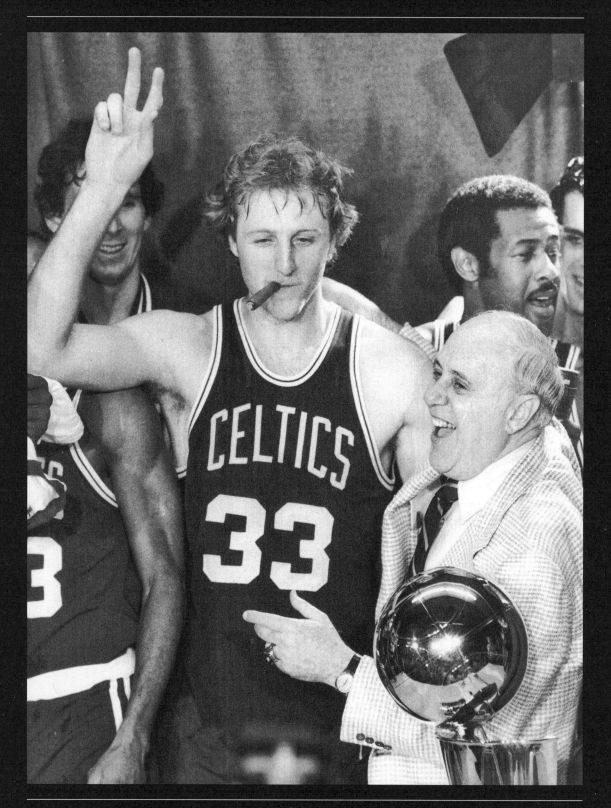

4 LARRY BIRD AND THE BIG THREE

(1980-1992)

During the course of his 13-year Celtics career, as Larry Bird became, if not the most revered athlete in the annals of Boston sports, one permanently deadlocked for the honor with Bruins icon Bobby Orr, countless writers, teammates, and colleagues alike searched for the right words to capture his magnitude.

And many did. After the 1986 Celtics—who must rank as the finest single-season NBA team in history for anyone lucky enough to have witnessed it in action—clinched the franchise's third and final championship of the '80s with a Game 6 throttling of the Houston Rockets, coach K. C. Jones said of his superstar forward's commanding 29-point, 12-assist, 11-rebound performance, "Larry Bird is where he wants to be. He has reached the pinnacle of basketball."

Bill Walton, who savored a renaissance season with the 1986 Celtics after his own extraordinary talents had been muted by injuries in previous seasons elsewhere, marveled at his teammate after those same Finals. "Nothing Larry Bird does surprises me," declared Walton, "and everything he does impresses me."

Five seasons later, Bird—battling through a chronic, painful back injury that would eventually abbreviate his career at age 35—returned from *banging his face on the court* in the second quarter of Game 5 of a first-round playoff series with the Indiana Pacers and provided a delightful Retro Larry performance with 30 points. The *Globe*'s Bob Ryan wrote, with elegance and expertise, that Bird was "the individual personification of all basketball has to offer."

But when his career played the cruel transition game of shifting from present to past tense following the 1992 season, it was his longtime rival, measuring stick, and foe-turned-friend-for-life that best summed up how we felt about Larry Bird.

On February 4, 1993, the Celtics held Larry Bird Night, an occasion to retire his number, share some laughs, reminisce one more time for all the old times, and make the retirement thing official. Magic Johnson, whose

‹ Larry Bird smokes Red Auerbach's cigar after the Celtics defeated the Rockets to win the 1981 NBA Championship.

similar selfless basketball sensibilities and symmetrical career on the opposite coast helped wind the Celtics-Lakers rivalry to its highest tension, was the guest of honor.

Magic, ever the entertainer, stole the show, at one point opening his Lakers warm-up jacket to reveal a Boston Celtics T-shirt underneath. When the festivities were complete and the lights turned down low, Johnson, upon departing the Garden, found the words that summed up the emotions of the night and the glorious era. "I didn't want it to end," he said. "I wanted it to go on forever."

Didn't we all, Magic. Those were the good old days, so special that we had the sense to know it while they were happening. The Celtics and Lakers combined to reach the Finals eight times in the '80s, with the Lakers winning five championships to the Celtics' three (1981, 1984, 1986). Three times they went head-to-head in the decade, with the Celtics prevailing in 1984 and the Lakers in 1985 and 1987.

For Bird, wrote Ryan, "the spectacular became totally routine. He would register triple-doubles, drill 3-pointers in traffic, make passes through openings that didn't exist and dominate ballgames because he possessed both skill and bravado." He won three straight Most Valuable Player awards from 1984 to 1986, a Rookie of the Year Award in 1980, an All-Star Game MVP, a playoff MVP, and was named first-team All-NBA during each of his first nine seasons while sharing top billing with Magic in the pre-Air Jordan NBA during their mutual heyday.

While Bird and Magic elevated their teammates with unselfish and relentless play, both were accompanied by extraordinary talent. Magic had the decorated likes of Kareem Abdul-Jabbar (who retired as the NBA's all-time leading scorer), Jamaal Wilkes, James Worthy, and Byron Scott on his side. Cedric Maxwell, who would win MVP of the 1981 Finals and put the Celtics on his back in Game 7 of the 1984 Finals, was already established as a building block at forward when Bird arrived in 1980, a year after Red Auerbach had the foresight to draft him as a junior eligible from Indiana State. ("I think people are going to like him," said agent Bob Woolf, in perhaps the biggest understatement in professional sports history, when Bird signed his rookie contract.)

A string of savvy decisions by Auerbach surrounded Bird with an array of talent. In June, 1980, he traded the No. 1 pick in the draft to the Warriors for center Robert Parish and a No. 3 pick, which was used on Minnesota forward Kevin McHale. It would quickly rank as one of the most lopsided trades in NBA history. The selfless Parish, one of the best running big men of all time, and McHale, who featured an endless array of defender-tormenting post moves, would join Bird on the best front line in NBA history, known as the Big Three.

The Celtics back court in the early Bird years featured veterans Tiny Archibald and Chris Ford (whose claim to fame is sinking the first 3-pointer in NBA history) and speedy Gerald Henderson. Auerbach's crafty dealmaking brought Brigham Young star Danny Ainge (who had committed to playing baseball for the Toronto Blue Jays) to the Celtics in November, 1981, and then in June, 1983, he acquired fearless defensive whiz Dennis Johnson— whom Bird would later call the best player he ever played with—from the Suns for plodding center Rick Robey. The Big Three plus DJ and Danny would form the starting five for the beloved 1986 powerhouse.

The highlights of the Big Three era could fill entire books rather than a mere chapter. In Bird's rookie season, the Celtics improved from 29-53 in 1979 to 61-21, the greatest turnaround in league history at the time. The first championship, with Parish and rookie McHale aboard, came the following season, with the six-game Finals victory over the Houston Rockets anticlimactic compared with the seven-game brawl with Julius Erving and the Philadelphia Sixers in the Eastern Conference finals. The Celtics fell behind 3-1 in the series, trailed by double digits in each of the final three games, and won them all. Bird's late bank shot in Game 7 was the only basket in the final three minutes of the Celtics' 91-90 win.

The Celtics won their second title of the decade in 1984, beating Magic and the Lakers in seven games. That series featured Henderson's game-saving steal in Game 2, a stunning McHale open-field tackle on the Lakers' Kurt Rambis in Game 4, and the infamous Heat Game (it was 97 degrees in the Garden at game time) in which Bird shot 15 for 20 for 34 points.

Bird was approaching the peak of his individual powers in 1985, hitting back-to-back game-winning buzzer-beaters in January, and dropping a Celtics-record 60 points on the Hawks in March, nine days after McHale had set a new standard with 56. "He should have gone for 60, and I told him that," laughed Bird after setting the new mark. But it was the

Lakers who would laugh last that season, beating the Celtics in six games in the Finals.

It was the first time in nine championship meetings with the Celtics that the Lakers had prevailed. But the Celtics did not retreat. They reloaded, swapping Maxwell for the oft-injured but gifted Walton, who savored a return to basketball relevance and good health. The Celtics won 67 games, went 40-1 at the Garden, dodged a 63-point performance by some kid named Michael Jordan in a first-round series with the Bulls, and crushed the Hawks and Bucks en route to a Finals matchup with . . . the Rockets, who had ousted the Lakers in the West finals. The Celtics defeated the Rockets in six games, with Bird putting up a 29-point, 11-rebound, 12-assist line in the clincher that Ryan called "a complete hostile takeover of the game."

Few basketball aficionados would have expected then that it would be the Big Three's last championship. Tragedy that changed the course of franchise history struck on June 19, 1986—just 11 days after Game 6 of the Finals—when Len Bias, an unfathomably athletic forward whom the Celtics had chosen out of the University of Maryland with the No. 2 overall pick, died of a cocaine overdose.

Bias would have eased the workload on Bird and McHale. Instead, injuries—to the feet and back for Bird, a foot for McHale—began taking a toll. The Celtics reached the Finals in 1987, with Bird's steal and feed to DJ to win Game 5 of the Eastern Conference finals versus the dastardly Pistons—another addition to the franchise's permanent lore. But the healthier and deeper Lakers took the title in six.

Bird and friends still delivered special moments on occasion—a Bird/Dominique Wilkins duel in Game 7 of the 1988 Eastern Conference semifinals, a 49-point performance against the Blazers in 1992—and 1987 first-rounder Reggie Lewis emerged as an All-Star in his own right. But an extraordinarily satisfying era in Celtics basketball came to an end too soon. Magic was so right. If only it could have gone on forever.

Bird Signs In—but Doesn't Dress for the Occasion

June 9, 1979 • by Leigh Montville

There was an appropriate touch of Billy Budd innocence to him. He was the young Bob Feller, played by the young Gary Cooper, everything filmed in black and white, a tractor still coughing in the background, the big-city folk just falling all over themselves, the whole scene seeming downright silly—all this money for playing basketball!—but as real as the shine on a new pair of shoes.

Larry Bird was just time-warp perfect.

You wanted the savior? You had the savior, direct from some B-movie idea about what and how the savior should be.

He sat in the midst of the three-piece suits and on top of all this sudden money and under all these heavy expectations with a fine, natural ease yesterday morning. What was all the fuss? No need to get all dressed up to celebrate becoming a millionaire. No need to slick down your hair and phony-up your act. What's the importance of a million dollars? Really?

"If everyone else was playing for $10,000 a year, I'd be happy playing for $10,000," Larry Bird said on the day he signed a contract with the Celtics to become the highest-paid rookie in the history of professional sports. "I'd be happy playing for nothing. To tell the truth, I'd be just as happy as I am now if I were going to be teaching school next year.

"I probably would live better if I didn't have the money. Now I've just got to worry about losing it."

He was real. No doubt about it. He obviously did not care about nothing. He was what he was. "Just a hick from French Lick." If he banged around the English language a bit, if he was casual in his red shirt and khaki pants while the big-timers were formal, then so be it. He was what he was. There weren't going to be any wrappers that had to be peeled away.

The Celtics drafted Larry Bird as a junior-eligible out of Indiana State in June 1978. Nearly a full year later, he joined Red Auerbach and Bill Fitch to officially announce that he had signed his contract.

He had gathered a long list of grumpy press notices on his way here, reports about being surly and uncommunicative as he and his Indiana State team rolled toward Cinderella happenings this year, but in the end he was easy. Not that anybody shouldn't be easy on the day he makes a million dollars or three, but he was down-home casual. He was easy, but not shiny and smooth.

"I think people are going to like him," his agent, Bob Woolf, said. "I walked in at the beginning and I really didn't know much about him. One of the first times I was with him, though, we were talking with all the people in Terre Haute about money. They brought up the name of Yankees pitcher Tommy John, who also is from Terre Haute. They said we should find out what Tommy John makes and go from there.

"Larry just stopped it all. He said he didn't want to know what Tommy John makes. He didn't want people bothering Tommy John. I said to myself, 'Well, OK, this kid's going to be all right . . .'"

"Sports is my life," Larry Bird said. He sounded as if he meant it.

"I was worried that I wasn't smart enough to graduate from college," Larry Bird said. He sounded as if he really had been worried.

"I told Mr. Woolf I would have been happier if he could just send the contract home for me to sign it," Larry Bird said. "I didn't want to leave the high school baseball team I was coaching in West Vigo, where I did my student teaching. We didn't have a good team at all, a bad team all season, but when we got into the tournament we started to play. We knocked off the 14th-ranked team in the state and tomorrow we're playing in the sectionals. I really wanted to be there."

He sounded as if he really was sorry. He said he was going to send a telegram.

There was a pleasant, unforced humility about him that somehow came through everything he said or did. He spoke about the virtues of teamwork as if it were a religion. He spoke about himself and his game with proper low-key confidence. Worries? How could he worry? He talked about worries as if they could not exist.

"All I worry about is being on practice on time and at the games on time," Larry Bird said. "Those are the only worries I have."

He was a Ring Lardner character, rolled through the typewriter and somehow made real. The buzz around him did not distract him, all the microphones and all the lights, the television stations actually recording this great moment live!!! He was the midwestern phenom, basketball in a dusty backyard, long days in the sunshine, shot after shot going through the hoop, a picture on the wall.

If he is to be the savior, then so be it. He would only say that he would try to do the best he could.

"Are you going to have to change your life any?" Larry Bird was asked.

"I can't play softball anymore," he said. "There's a lot of things I can't do with this contract. I don't think I can do anything, 'cept walk and ride in a wheelchair."

"Will that bother you?" he was asked.

"A little bit," he said. "It bothers me if I sit around and think about it. But I just grab a basketball and start playing and everything feels all right again."

His grand adventure has begun.

McAdoo Sent to Pistons

CELTICS GET TWO NO. 1S

September 7, 1979 • by Bob Ryan

The brief, unhappy Celtic career of Bob McAdoo ended yesterday when the three-time NBA scoring champion was sent to the Detroit Pistons as compensation for forward M. L. Carr.

The Pistons reciprocated by delivering two 1980 first-round draft picks—their own and a Washington choice acquired in the Kevin Porter compensation—to the Celtics.

Boston had been without a No. 1 draft pick for next season ever since John Y. Brown traded it to the Indiana Pacers for guard Earl Tatum last summer.

The teams had originally been unable to reach an agreement on the Carr compensation, and the

matter had been placed in the hands of commissioner Larry O'Brien. But late last week the Celtics initiated a renewal of the dialogue. "Red and I talked last Friday night," explained coach Bill Fitch. "We both agreed that if Detroit could somehow or other be given an opportunity to change their minds, they would. Red pursued it from there."

The Pistons had previously offered the Celtics two draft picks if Boston would give them McAdoo, but the picks were in 1980 and 1982. The Celtics weren't interested in a 1982 selection. "That," said Fitch, "requires too much of a crystal ball." But the 1980 draft is another matter.

"Let me stress," said Fitch, "that any Olympic year is a great talent year. If the 1980 draft were held right now, I'd bet that, of the first 14 players, seven would be centers—and I've never seen a draft like that."

By sending McAdoo to Detroit, the Celtics have cleared up several matters. First, they have increased the possibility of a smooth training camp. The thought of bringing a disgruntled McAdoo to training camp was anathema to all concerned. "It would not have been healthy," said Fitch, "to bring in a Bob McAdoo with a 'will move' label on him." The importance of a good training camp cannot be overstressed.

Secondly, the Celtics have erased any doubts or confusion that may have existed in the minds of Cedric Maxwell, Rick Robey and Jeff Judkins, the three most likely candidates to have been awarded to the Pistons if McAdoo had not been. All three of these players definitely fit into Boston's plans, whereas McAdoo never did.

Finally, the Celtics have relieved themselves of an annual salary burden of $500,000.

McAdoo was very pleased to leave Boston. "I wasn't a part of the Celtics team," he said. "The only reason I got to play was because Cowens was hurt. It's one of the best things that has happened to me. Detroit made a good deal. They're getting a proven player. The Celtics will be getting two unproven players."

In effect, the Celtics traded three 1979 No. 1 picks for M. L. Carr and two 1980 No. 1s. That's a deal anyone would have made, *n'est-ce pas*?

Celtics Break Fast with a Win, 114-106

October 13, 1979 • by Bob Ryan

They delivered. They had promised hustle. They had promised ball movement. They had promised excitement that had been missing here since the sixth game of the 1977 Philadelphia playoff series. What they had not promised was a victory, but to the delight of a rocking, roaring sellout crowd of 15,320, not to mention a television audience, the Celtics even came through with the ultimate reward for fan support, that being a season-opening 114-106 triumph over the Houston Rockets at the Garden last night.

This was a mutual fast-breaking, board-banging demonstration of the product, a display which would have sent the crowd home somewhat fulfilled even had the Celtics lost. "The crowd," said a hoarse Bill Fitch after his first game as Boston coach, "was fantastic. That's one of the big reasons I'm glad we didn't let this one get away, because the crowd did an even better job than we did."

There was little doubt that the fans had come to ogle Larry Bird, and let history record that he received his first Boston standing ovation with 3:22 remaining in the opening period after making a dazzling fast-break pass underneath to Cedric Maxwell. But they exited babbling about additional things, such as the coolheaded leadership of Nate (11 assists) Archibald, the unparalleled inside work of the rubbery Mr. Maxwell and, most of all, the combined great fourth-period efforts of Chris Ford and M. L. Carr, each of whom played his best ball of the night when they dumped the money on the table.

The showing had ramifications which may never accurately be measured. There had been much written and spoken about a "new" attitude, a "new" Cowens (13 rugged rebounds), a "new" Archibald, and a whole "new" passing attack built around Bird. Proof was needed.

The fans came. They saw. They screamed. It is difficult to believe that they won't be back.

Celtics Beat Out 76ers, Sign Maravich

January 1, 1980 • by Bob Ryan

Saying that "I've been trying to get here for 10 years," Pete Maravich signed a contract last night to finish out the season with the Boston Celtics.

The signing took place following the Celtics' 112-106 triumph over the Houston Rockets and capped an event-filled 28 hours since Maravich arrived in Philadelphia Monday night, ostensibly to sign a contract with the 76ers.

Instead, Maravich told the Sixers he was considering three other teams—Boston, Houston and Atlanta—and that he would be going to Boston the next day.

This came as news to the Celtics, who privately had conceded Maravich to their Atlantic Division rivals throughout Maravich's seven weeks of forced idlement with the Utah Jazz. That bizarre situation culminated with Maravich being placed on waivers late last week. Mindful of his large contract, no teams claimed him, and when the waiver period expired, Maravich flew to the East Coast to dicker with the two Eastern titans.

Red Auerbach, in fact, wasn't even in Boston when the day began. He was home in Washington, D.C., where he had been since Sunday and where he was planning to be until tomorrow. The only thing on his agenda was a trip to see Virginia play Duke in an important ACC battle tonight.

But before the day was over, Auerbach had returned to Boston, and Maravich—along with lawyers Art Herskovitz and Lee Zittrain, both out of Aliquippa, Pa.—was engaged in serious negotiations with the cigar smoker.

Maravich laid no raps on the 76ers. "Billy Cunningham is a good friend of mine and a fine coach, and the 76ers have a fine team," he said. "But when it came down to the end, I have always wanted to be here."

Maravich has known both Auerbach and Boston coach Bill Fitch for some time. Fitch is a close friend of Maravich's father, Press, who coached Pete at Louisiana State, where Maravich earned the nickname "Pistol Pete" while setting every NCAA career-scoring record of note. This tie didn't hurt the Celtics, either. But Maravich talked in the vein of so many people who fell in love with the parquet floor of the Boston Garden and grew up watching the Russells, Heinsohns, Havliceks and Joneses every Sunday on TV.

"A lot of people say nice things about the Celtics," Maravich explained, "but I think it's justified because they have 13 flags here. All I have in my house is one little United States of America flag. I would like to have been here before, but you can't always locate yourself geographically in this game. I have one goal, and that is something that eluded most players. I want to be on a championship team."

Things moved very quickly during this hectic day. Word was received out of Philadelphia last night that the negotiations with the 76ers, considered to be the only team in the running, had hit a snag. The Maravich camp contacted Auerbach, who returned to Boston, if for no other reason than Fitch had wanted Maravich all along. The Pistol arrived at the Garden at precisely 5:55 p.m., and his attorneys came in an hour later after a delayed flight from Pittsburgh. At 7:25, Auerbach emerged from his office to say that there would be no further announcements until after the game. Auerbach then watched the game with Houston in the company of Maravich while team counsel and business manager Jan Volk stayed downstairs in the Celtic offices, setting tongues wagging as people correctly surmised that a contract was being drawn up.

John Havlicek (consider him a recruiter) escorted Maravich to the Celtic offices at halftime, and, at 9 p.m., Celtic vice president Jeff Cohen announced that "There will be a press conference in the Blades and Boards Club after the game." Press conferences seldom are called to announce the absence of news.

Celtics Get Their Big Man: It's Parish

WARRIORS LAND TOP PICK; BOSTON WILL CHOOSE THIRD

June 10, 1980 • by Bob Ryan

The Celtics ended months of speculation about what they would do with their two first-round draft picks yesterday by trading both of them—the first and 13th selections in today's college draft—to the Golden State Warriors in exchange for 7-foot center and the third pick in the draft.

Barring an 11th-hour change of heart by the Utah Jazz, who own the second selection, this means that Minnesota forward-center Kevin McHale, a sturdy 6-11 banger out of the Mitch Kupchak-Jack Sikma-Rick Robey mold, will be Boston's choice with that third selection. The Jazz are expected to take Louisville's dynamic guard Darrell Griffith.

Golden State will kick off the draft using their first spot to select Purdue's 7-1 center, Joe Barry Carroll, whom Warrior executive Scotty Stirling labels "one of the top center prospects of the past 10 years." Utah will then take Griffith, as much for his box-office potential as for the actual level of his playing skill. The Celtics men will happily choose McHale, a hardworking kid from Hibbing, Minn., who began the college season as one of the top 10 prospects and who wound up as part of an elite triumvirate that included a classic low-post center (Carroll), a sensational off-the-ball guard (Griffith) and an industrious front court swingman (McHale).

What the Celtics did, in effect, was trade the 13th spot in the draft for Parish, a four-year veteran who is expected to provide defensive intimidation, rebounding and scoring (17 points per game the past two years) from the center position, while exchanging the first and third spots with a team coveting a player who, after much analysis, simply did not turn them on. "What it boils down to," opines Denver general manager Carl Scheer, who had lusted

Robert Parish (bracketed by Bill Fitch, left, and Red Auerbach) was all smiles after joining the Celtics in a trade with the Warriors.

for McHale in the days before he entered this final celestial realm, "is how much you like or dislike both Carroll and Parish. It's just your personal opinion. Obviously, Boston did not have a lot of confidence in Carroll."

It's interesting that the 22-year-old Carroll and the soon-to-be 27-year-old Parish (Aug. 30) should be involved in the same trade, for it is Parish with whom Carroll often has been compared as a prospect. "Their bodies and their playing skills are very much alike," said Bill Fitch. "If you handed each man a sheet this summer asking them to work on certain things in the offseason, it would contain the same things. However, we won't have to worry about how Parish reacts to NBA officials, NBA travel or NBA life in general. If Robert Parish were coming out with this year's crop of college players, there is no doubt he would go No. 1."

Parish was the 1976 first-round draft choice of the Warriors. He has compiled some impressive stats in his NBA career, but he has left too many people with the impression that he doesn't care. Nevertheless, he was fourth in the NBA in blocked shots two years ago, a season in which he also led the league in defensive rebounds per minutes played.

He finished seventh in rebounding this season (10.9 per game), but his blocked shots fell off by a whopping 102, a situation he attributes to a balky ankle.

The Celtics are of the opinion that he has things to learn, and that he will benefit greatly from his new surroundings. Says one rival coach: "I've never been a Parish fan. I've always wondered about his motivation. But guys have a way of turning around when they get into that Celtic green."

The swap of the Nos. 1 and 3 gives the Celtics a shot at McHale, a player who has grown on just about every scout, general manager and coach. And the Celtics were not subtle. It's McHale they're after, not Griffith. This is not to say that they don't value Griffith. "Should Utah change their mind and take McHale," says Fitch, "you won't hear any moaning and groaning from us. It's not bad when the worst that can happen to you is getting Darrell Griffith."

However, the addition of McHale does pose certain questions. Are the Celtics writing off Cedric (Free Agent) Maxwell? Both Red Auerbach and Fitch vehemently deny this is the case. Are the Celtics dissatisfied with Rick Robey? Again, there is a denial. In fact, Fitch issued an unsolicited Robey testimonial during yesterday's press conference, and made sure that a positive mention be included in the accompanying press release. Finally, can the Celtics possibly find room for Dave Cowens, Maxwell, Larry Bird, Robey, M. L. Carr, McHale and Parish in the course of the average 48-minute game?

As for McHale, the feeling around the league is that he is heading to the right place. "He's hardworking," lauds one rival. "A banger. He can play both positions. What else can I say? He's a Celtic."

Meanwhile, the Celtics are assembling a truly monstrous collection of physical players. The team that for 20 years was the league's smallest could now go 7-foot, 6-11, 6-11, 6-9, 6-8 and 6-8 up front. They're going to be a helluva sight at the airport.

CELTICS TAKE MCHALE, FEEL HE'S BEST

June 11, 1980 • by Bob Ryan

Like many other areas of life, the NBA Draft isn't exactly what it used to be.

Whereas it once was conducted quietly in a tiny team office, now the Celtics invite the public to a crowded eating room.

Whereas as recently as two years ago the entire affair was conducted in 2½ hours, yesterday's first round consumed 55 minutes all by itself.

Whereas once the first-round choice would remain a mystery figure until training camps, even to the minicult that comprised the local basketball community, Celtic fans yesterday had a chance to (a) see the selection perform by the magic of videotape and (b) meet him and hear him talk only three hours after he was first introduced to the press in New York, thanks to the magic of air travel.

And there is one other nuance that was certainly not an issue for two decades: For the second consecutive year, the Celtics are convinced they have come up with the best player in the draft. Last year his name was Larry Bird, and this year his name is Kevin McHale.

What was an assumption on Monday night became a reality yesterday shortly after noon, when the Utah Jazz chose Louisville guard Darrell Griffith as the second choice in the draft, thus freeing the

Celtics to take McHale, the man they really wanted. Jazz general manager Frank Leyden had left his office Monday night saying he was "99 percent sure" he was taking Griffith as the No. 2 pick in round one, but until the Utah club actually made the choice, the Celtics really couldn't be assured of getting the 6-foot-11 kid from Minnesota.

The Golden State Warriors initiated the draft by taking Purdue center Joe Barry Carroll with the No. 1 pick they had obtained from Boston the day before. Then came Griffith (but not before a long pause) and then McHale.

There wasn't much new the Celtics could say about McHale, who was praised for his aggressiveness, mobility and enthusiasm. The Celtics are simply in love with him, having rated him as the best forward, the second-best center and basically the best player in the draft.

The best description thus obtained of what he's all about actually comes from a neutral source, Phoenix general manager Jerry Colangelo. "He (McHale) has excellent hands and great timing," says Colangelo. "You can't say he's a great jumper, but he makes up for it with his timing, and he plays hard. Offensively, he has a variety of shots. He's just a great player."

That being the case, you can now understand the reason for the constant smiling and joking going on between Messrs. Fitch and Auerbach. But Fitch had said it the day before. "Red," said the coach, "has done it again."

Minnesota Mac Just Loves Being a Celtic

Celtics' No. 1 draft choice Kevin McHale has gone from a small town to a dynasty—and he's loving every second of it.

May 4, 1981 • by John Powers

HIBBING, Minn.—He left the Iron Range carrying an overnight Val-Pac, hooked up with his agent in Minneapolis and arrived in Manhattan pondering life in the Bay Area.

He'd been scouted, weighed, measured, graded, stamped prime and summoned to The City for drafting and media evaluation since the NBA was certain he'd go in the top three. Golden State, Kevin McHale was told by people who are supposed to know. Third pick overall. Boston will go for Joe Barry Carroll. Utah . . . they've gotta fill seats . . . will grab Darrell Griffith. Golden State will take you.

OK, McHale decided on Seventh Avenue Monday morning. Fine with me. And proceeded to muffle the cacophony 17 stories below with a map.

"Hear Boston made a trade?" agent Ron Simon informed him upon arising. "Holy cow," McHale thought. "A whole new perspective. Golden State'll take Joe Barry now." At 1 a.m., Utah GM Frank Leyden called. The Jazz were going to take Griffith. Had to.

McHale crossed two names from his mental mock list. "I wonder," he mused, falling asleep, "what it'd be like to play for Boston?"

The growth spurt, as Josephine McHale remembers it, began somewhere around 10th grade. Until then, her second son was a 5-8 hockey player with cold feet. "Thirty below," Kevin remembers. "An outdoor rink. It had to be warmer inside."

He began playing basketball at Hibbing High, making the Varsity when someone else left the squad. "He'd sprouted so fast that he was awkward," Paul McHale says, "with the legs and all. But you could see him progress in the 11th and 12th grades and get his coordination."

By senior year, McHale was 6-9 (the name was Irish, the genes Croatian) and the Hibbing Bluejackets were 25-2. They murdered people in the sub-regionals, literally doubling opponents' scores, and reached the state finals.

Where McHale's name was mentioned in the Daily Tribune, the accompanying adjective was usually "dominant." Four blocked shots in the first two minutes. One quarter, five shots, 10 points. Sixteen rebounds a game. Utah coach Jim Marsh began turning up at the McHale house. A lot.

"We got to really like him," Paul McHale says. "He'd drop by and we'd chew the fat. You might have found him here anytime."

Recruiting letters arrived by the boxful that winter, but most of them were left unopened. Utah, where Jeff Judkins showed him around, was the

only campus McHale visited—"Kevin felt he didn't want to waste anybody's money," says Josephine. And he went there mostly to be polite, because Marsh had been so earnest and persistent. McHale knew he was going to Minneapolis. And the U of M. "I wanted to be a Gopher," he says. "As simple as that. Home ties, home state."

He'd been told he probably wouldn't start there as a freshman: the six best Gophers were all returning. But by the third game, McHale had cracked the lineup, shooting 55 percent and grabbing a dozen rebounds a night.

His marksmanship remained reasonably constant for four years (1,704 points in all, second only to Mychal Thompson in U of M history), but that was gravy. McHale summoned up visions of Sikma, Cowens, Robey, a runner and banger who wasn't afraid to stick his nose and elbows in for a rebound.

His parents rarely missed a game, driving 180 miles each way. "Many nights it would be 30 below zero," Paul remembers, "and there's a lot of desolate country between here and Minneapolis. You're praying all the way back that the old car is going to keep going."

On the way, Josephine would tell her husband that Son No. 2 was going to be a pro. "She could see it. I'd tell her, 'Don't say that to other people. They'll think you're bragging.'"

McHale played in the World University Games and beat out Ralph Sampson for the starting job on the US team at the Pan American Games last summer. Bobby Knight, who does not love everybody, loved him.

He played in Madison Square Garden as Minnesota made the NIT final this winter. He was visible, highly visible, in the postseason draft showcases—the Coaches' All-America game in Indianapolis, the Pizza Hut and the Aloha Classic, where he was MVP. Carl Scheer, who wanted McHale badly at Denver, winced. Too many people who hadn't noticed before were drooling. He was no longer a masked man from the Range.

The day of the Guaranteed Public NBA auction is the day of the locust at 52d and 7th: the jammed lobby and staircase at the Sheraton Centre evoke the last days of the Saigon embassy. Everyone has to, *needs* to get upstairs.

Uptown dudes in high-cut Connies and clip-boards and stockbrokers stealing a few minutes at noon are pushed shoulder to shoulder and 20 across, surging vaguely toward the mezzanine as noon comes and goes and the first name filters down . . . Carroll . . . Carroll . . . Carroll. Yeah.

Upstairs, security guards block the doors to the Imperial Ballroom B, where the scene is somewhere between a Democratic state convention and the old Copacabana on a Saturday night. (Man, I got to get *in*. You don't *understand*. You *do* know who I am?)

Tables for each club are plunked in the middle like lily pads. The Public is stuffed at the rear, just inside the doors. Up front, the commissioner is talking into a microphone . . . 6-foot-4, 190 pounds, from Loueeville. Darrell Griffith. McHale nods. No surprise there.

"Boston," O'Brien continues, to a chorus of boos from Knickerbocker provincials, "selects 6-foot-11, 235 pounds . . . "

"That's me," McHale concludes, and the next four hours are a yo-yoing blur. McHale walks through the partition and moves across a dining room where place settings, luncheon rolls and full water glasses wait untouched to the press room.

Carroll is still being interviewed at the podium, two feet above a thicket of microphones held by eager Manhattan gnomes. "Give it my best shot," he murmurs repeatedly. "Do the best I can. Can't predict the future."

Within nine seconds, McHale is also surrounded by gnomes, who have managed to grasp the essentials. He is a big man labeled for Boston, which now has a number of big men. He is an Irish name joining the Celtics. For 30 seconds of quick tape, that is an encyclopedia.

For 10 minutes, McHale talks in four directions at once (fortunately, this is easy: no Celtic since Charlie Scott gets words out faster) as the gnomes scribble key phrases. "Elated . . . remember watching Red Auerbach on TV as a kid . . . my father's dancing a jig right now . . . fun to play with The Bird . . . help the team any way I can . . . like a dream come true."

The draftees are walking in one by one now, and the gnomes recede and regroup around them. North Carolina's Mike O'Koren, dazed, enters the room on tiptoe. "Michael can't come down," McHale proclaims, delighted. "He's flying. He's excited. Noo Jersee."

Left unattended for a moment, McHale scans the room for an unoccupied phone. "How do I dial?" he asks a bystander. "One and out?"

A receiver is lifted in the North Country, area code 218. "Lynn? . . . How you doing? . . . Isn't that super? . . . Mom there? . . . Yeah the line's busy at home."

"My mom's lost," McHale decides, hanging up the phone. "They can't find her. She's probably driving around aimlessly."

The next plane for Minneapolis leaves LaGuardia at 2:20, but Celtic VP Jan Volk says there has been a change of itinerary. "Red wants you to come up to Boston," he tells McHale and Simon. "Two o'clock shuttle."

It is now past 12:30, and the crosstown traffic is discouraging. "I sat in a cab for an hour this morning," Volk says. "We'd better get going."

"Ten minutes," McHale promises him. "I'll go pack." One Val-Pac, total? "Five minutes."

Outside a dozen refugee Boston fans, strangers in a strange land, rush toward him mumbling. "Autographs, gotta have autographs." McHale's eyes widen. "This is crazy," he tells himself. "Red Auerbach is waiting for me," he tells them, and slips up the back stairs to rendezvous in Simon's room.

"Thanks for the subway ride," he calls out to Simon's brother Howie.

"72d Street," Howie reminds him.

"I *love* 72d Street," McHale shouts, heading for the elevator. "My first time on a subway. And the lights go out for five minutes. Nobody even flinches. Nobody reacts. And I'm paranoid."

Well, semi-paranoid. McHale's line of play has taken him to Hawaii, Puerto Rico, Italy and every Gopher-eating pit in the Big Ten. New York, with its 7 a.m. jackhammers, disco skaters and scarcity of eye contact, amuses him as much as anything else.

The taxi careens out of 51st Street and points uptown at the bridges. "The Big Apple," McHale sighs, stretching his legs. "Crazy. A lot different than Hibbing, Minnesota."

The same man who rents the Hertz cars—roomy air-conditioned Oldsmobiles from Cluslau's across the street—also drives the limousine at Chisholm-Hibbing Airport. This is not exactly complicated work; four Republic airliners arrive every day and four depart, and all of them come through the Twin Cities at some point.

Actually, Hibbing considers itself a Twin City—Chisholm is only seven miles northeast on Rte. 169, seven miles of lakes and ore mines. Stay on 169 and you will cover the Range, its towns (Hibbing, Chisholm, Buhl, Virginia) like pellets on an iron necklace.

Lake Superior is 75 miles east, the Canadian border roughly 100 miles north; winters, which begin in November, are brutally cold. If you live here, you are probably a Slovenian, a Yugoslav, a Scandinavian or an Italian, your grandfather probably spoke broken English, and you work for a mining company for $16,000 a year. Your son probably plays hockey. Very well.

Bill Baker, whose last-minute goal tied the Swedes at Lake Placid and probably saved the gold medal, lives in Grand Rapids. The scrappiest, hungriest line on the US team—Buzz Schneider (Babbitt), Mark Pavelich (Eveleth), John Harrington (Virginia)—came off the Iron Range. So did Bob Dylan.

Hibbing, the largest town along the necklace (23,000) was named after Frans Dietrich Von Ahlen. Sort of. His mother's name was Hibbing. Von Ahlen, who had a nose of iron, unwittingly built his town atop the area's largest ore deposit in 1893.

Upon learning this two decades later, residents decided the iron was more important than the town and dismantled it piece by piece. The last building was finally resettled in 1958; the natural ores had all but run out by 1963.

"The steel companies weren't interested any longer," Paul McHale recalls. "There was an awful lot of unemployment here then. It drove home the point that mining was the lifeblood of the town. When miners weren't working, nobody else was either."

Fortunately, a lower-grade substance called taconite, in ready supply on the Range, produced tolerable iron if smashed to powder and sifted.

So people are employed and reasonably well off these days; Paul McHale, one of 11 children, will have worked for US Steel for 40 years this summer. His family lives in a comfortable one-story house on Outer Drive with a backboard on the garage, and they leave the doors open, as most folks do here.

All around town, huge stacks of firewood (which has jumped to $30 a cord) dry on front lawns, and nobody worries about theft. Crime is not a serious problem on the Range; beery teenagers

tearing around in cars seem to be the primary civic headache.

Pleasures are basic; half the homes are wired for cable TV, complete with Home Box Office and everything Ted Turner can put on the air. There is one movie house, the Lybba, a drive-in on the way to the airport and a fraternal row—Masons, Moose, Elks—on Howard Street.

There are also 10,000 lakes within driving distance (or so the license plates say) and more across the border. Paul McHale and his two sons have been known to find a fat walleye or two beneath the surface and have happened upon a partridge in the woods now and again.

Tomorrow morning after John McHale comes up from Wisconsin, Kevin and a mutual friend will fly across the border to Red Sand Lake and get lost for a while. When Kevin returns, he'll set up his weights in the garage. "And about a month before I go to Boston," he says, "I'll kick 'er down hard."

Once across the bridge, the traffic melts away; Boston by 3 p.m. will be no problem. "Like Chinese food?" McHale is asked.

"Yeah, once in a while, sure."

"Auerbach," he is informed, "loves Chinese food."

"Bahston," McHale says. "Hope I don't pick up that twang."

Before McHale boards the shuttle, he gets the full Chamber of Commerce briefing. Lots of Irish in Boston, great Italian food. Share the building with a train station. Nothing—the ocean, the mountains, the woods—more than an hour away. College town. If you like Minneapolis . . . Good fishing. Celtic Pride taken seriously.

At 3:20, McHale walks into the Blades and Boards Club at the Garden, sits down next to Bill Fitch and Auerbach and squints at a bank of spotlights and gnomes who speak with twangs.

"How does it feel?" one of them says.

"I'm elated," Kevin McHale begins anew.

The Kevin McHale story appears somewhere deep in the sporting pages of the Daily Tribune *Wednesday afternoon. More precisely, it is a UPI roundup story that mentions McHale, the best basketball player to come out of Hibbing since Dick Garmaker (who played for the Lakers when they were near a lake), in the final few paragraphs.*

The Tribune had not planned on covering the triumphant homecoming at the airport; Dan Anderson, who is both the sports editor and his entire staff, is busy punching in softball scores. "Didn't know when he was coming in," Anderson says. "He didn't call us."

Anyway, everybody already knows McHale was drafted by Boston. The news went up in magnetic letters at the Village Inn and the Security State Bank and was posted on the garage door of Lynn Spearman's house down the street.

Besides, the draft was shown live on cable here. Shirley Von Alman could hear the McHale clan cheering from her house several doors down.

Now, at 5:32, the clan—which is to say Paul, Josephine, Tricia, Mary, niece Jeannie, her husband, Michael, and Lynn Spearman, Kevin's fiancée—has gathered in the airport lobby to render appropriate homage to the nation's No. 3 pick overall. They appear to be the extent of the welcoming committee and are not surprised by this. Republic Flight 997 is on time, and through the terminal window a 6-foot-11, 235-pound center/forward from the University of Minnesota sees a green banner unrolling—Welcome Home Boston Celtic.

"Oh no," Kevin groans, horrified. "Get that thing down."

"He's embarrassed," Josephine whispers.

At home, two shamrocks have been taped to the front door, and Kevin's car, the 14-year-old Brown Bomber, is in the driveway. The odometer reads 140,000. McHale plans to drive it to Boston. Why not? Hasn't broken down yet.

"Well, what do you think, Paul A.?" says Kevin, heading instinctively for the back door.

"Come around this way," says Paul.

"Now I get drafted, I use the front door, huh?"

"No," Paul says, pointing to a visitor. "I meant him."

Josephine goes in to prepare dinner—garlic bread, a platter of steaks, fried potatoes, salad with two kinds of dressing, cake with whipped cream and pineapple. There has always been plenty of food in the McHale house of necessity. "For a snack," recalls Josephine, "Kevin would come home and eat several slices of toast and one of those large cans of fruit cocktail. He'd eat it right out of the can."

McHale changes into a green T-shirt and gold Gopher shorts and flops lengthwise on the floor next to the bookcase, which contains the World Book encyclopedia and the Bible. "Lonnng two days," he says. "Feel cooped up." Presently, he opens a leather shoulder bag and starts passing out Celtic souvenirs, courtesy of the management.

He unfolds a pennant—"Red told me to put it on my wall and think about Boston." He pulls out a T-shirt. "Extra-extra large." He tosses a lighter to Lynn and decides his father should have a key chain that reads "World Champions." The gold lettering around the rim is starting to fade.

Although McHale has decided he'll be buying his father a new truck and his mother a dining room set, money is never mentioned. It is assumed that since both Auerbach and Simon are reasonable men, they will decide on a reasonable salary for the first Celtic Gopher since Kleggie Hermsen.

It is also assumed that McHale will do whatever is asked of him to earn it. "My job is to play basketball," McHale says. "Ron's job is to talk."

When letters and calls came from agents this winter, they largely went unanswered. McHale had heard good things about Simon, a Minneapolis attorney who doubles as president of the U of M alumni association. "I chose him," McHale says, "because he didn't need it."

Simon will take it from here. Rookie camp begins in August. The flight to Red Sand Lake leaves Saturday morning. "My brother John's organized," McHale says. "I just go along."

Now he wants to drive plastic golf balls a grand total of 30 feet. His younger sister Mary, who confirms his nine-hole scores on the side (yes, he did shoot a 40), may shag. Then again, she may not.

"I pulled a muscle," she says. "Right here."

"Can't have a pulled muscle there," McHale says clinically. "Gotta be at the point of attachment."

"I do," Mary says. "Really."

So McHale takes an iron and starts chipping balls toward a neighbor's house and shagging them himself. "Take a few swings, mother dear," he advises Josephine. "Loosen up." Josephine declines.

McHale shrugs, bends, chips, peers off into the distance, 30 feet away. "Right on line," he decides.

"Just like being in New York," he is told.

McHale nods solemnly. "No horns. No hustle, no bustle," he says. Home on the Range.

His Talents Fading, Cowens Quits Celtics

October 2, 1980 • by Bob Ryan

EVANSVILLE, Ind.—It came to an end in a motel room in Terre Haute.

Dave Cowens just came to the conclusion he couldn't play basketball the way he wanted to anymore. Jumping had always been the foundation of his game and now he found his greatest asset had deserted him. He might have stayed around to play defense, come up with an occasional scoring burst and provided leadership, but it wasn't enough. And so Dave Cowens, one of the truly great Celtics and one of professional basketball's best advertisements, officially retired yesterday morning, 24 days before his 32d birthday.

The announcement came as a shock to his teammates. "I had no idea this was coming," said Rick Robey, who can now think more about winning the starting center's job on the ball club and less about being traded. "I didn't know anything about it," said Chris Ford. "The only person I know of who had any idea was Ron Perry. Dave told him while they were eating on Tuesday night that he might retire in a couple of days, but, naturally, Ronnie didn't take him seriously."

But Cowens wasn't kidding. As he explains in his rather unique farewell to the fans, he was playing on "weakened and worn-out feet and ankles." Though he was scoring well on some occasions and though he remained the best defensive player on the squad, he felt extremely frustrated over his inability to rebound with his old power. He had degenerated into being just another 6-foot-8 basketball player, and he was professional. He had managed only 32 rebounds in 151 minutes of playing time over the first six preseason games, and in the Indiana game played on Monday night he missed some rebounds he would have had last year, when he was far from

Dave Cowens is greeted at Logan Airport by throngs of Celtics fans after winning the 1976 NBA title.

his old rampaging self on the boards. "I went back a lot between this year and last," he said, sadly.

His departure means that a very special era of Celtic basketball is over. He was the heartbeat of the 1974 and 1976 championship teams. He was also the only survivor of the 1976 outfit. It is almost impossible to comprehend that Cedric Maxwell, who won't be 25 until Nov. 21, is now the ranking Celtic in seniority.

LA Agog over Bird vs. Magic

December 29, 1980 • by Bob Ryan

INGLEWOOD, Calif.—"Magic Johnson Tries To Cage Boston's Larry Bird" . . . "Larry Bird's LA Debut."

These lines are from an ad bought by the Lakers and placed on Page 2 of yesterday morning's Los Angeles Times sports section. In the righthand corner is the message, "Sold Out." The real purpose of the ad, therefore, is in the middle of the box: "Good seats available for Phoenix, 7 p.m. Sun., Dec. 30."

And so the Celtics were welcomed to sunny Los Angeles for the single most awaited regular-season game in Laker history. The Forum had been sold out for weeks, and everyone from Pacific Palisades to Pomona wanted to be on hand when Earvin Johnson and Larry Bird, accompanied by such satellite stars as Kareem Abdul-Jabbar, Dave Cowens, Jamaal Wilkes and Cedric Maxwell resumed their rivalry last night.

Though the Lakers began the evening as a second-place team in the NBA's Pacific Division by a half-game (26-13 to Seattle's 25-11), in the mind of the local populace this game was to be a clear confrontation between the best in the East and the best in the West.

Each team prepped the night before in fine style, the Celtics rolling over San Diego, 118-97, and the Lakers cruising by Utah, 124-116, in one of those it-wasn't-as-close-as-the-score-indicated games. Each team had filled an enemy arena which had not seen a capacity crowd this season. And each team rightfully tried to downplay the importance of this game.

In truth, the Bird-Magic showdown was a totally inaccurate representation of the game (they don't even play the same position). It does figure, however, that star-crazy LA would blow this game out of proportion.

Bird began his LA stay with a press conference at the Forum. It didn't last long and he had no trouble fielding the soft questions.

He came prepared to correct an impression of brashness caused by a statement he had made in front of an NBC camera during last Saturday's "Sports World" show. In that interview he had jokingly referred to Magic as "the second-best player in the world," the unspoken implication being that he was the best.

"I knew they'd ask me about that," Bird explained. "I was ready for them."

The Celtics likewise appeared to be ready for the game. Their display of ball movement and shooting had impressed the San Diego fans and press. The latter, in fact, was puzzled when the Celtics not only failed to gush over their showing, but also indulged in some heavy self-criticism.

"We'll have to play a lot better tomorrow if we want to beat LA," Bird had opined.

But to the Clippers and the San Diego media, the Celtics had looked every bit as powerful as advertised. At any rate, they arrived in LA with no rest problems and no injury woes beyond the mending process of M. L. Carr's sprained right wrist. Whatever the Laker fans and local press wanted to make of the game, the Celtics at least felt they were up to playing it.

It's Back to Philadelphia

CELTICS STAY ALIVE WITH 111-109 WIN

April 30, 1981 • by Bob Ryan

This was one of those nights when you save the ticket stub, when you want to make sure you can prove you were there 15 or 20 years later.

This was the night when the Celtics saved face, when they kept themselves from an embarrassing five-game dispatch for the second consecutive year.

From left, the Celtics' Chris Ford, Larry Bird, M. L. Carr, Gerald Henderson, and Cedric Maxwell bask in their Game 5 win over the rival Sixers during their epic 1981 Eastern Conference Finals showdown.

This was the night when the most lovable Celtic of them all enjoyed the spotlight he so well deserves.

This was the night when the 1981 Celtics touched spiritual bases with some of their ancestors as they erased a six-point deficit in the final minute and a half and defeated the Philadelphia 76ers, 111-109, to send their series back to Philadelphia tomorrow evening for Game 6 of what is turning into a fascinating confrontation.

Great—truly great—team defense and the individual heroics of an almost-forgotten hero named M. L. Carr provided the Celtics with this stirring comeback triumph. Carr re-entered the game with 39 seconds to play and the Celtics trailing by a point (109-108) and went into a hustling routine that would make Pete Rose look like George Hendrick. Carr knocked one Sixer inbounds pass out of bounds (thus making the visitors waste a precious timeout to regroup), came up with an offensive rebound and the two go-ahead free throws with 20 seconds left following another 76er turnover, rebounded a Bobby Jones miss with four seconds left and sank one additional free throw with a second to play.

His only error came when he failed to miss a free throw in the proper manner. Stepping to the line with the team ahead by a point (110-109) and one second left, he was asked to miss his second and third tries after swishing his first one. But the third one came off the rim too flat, enabling Darryl Dawkins to rebound the ball and call the final 76er timeout. This gave Philly the ball at midcourt one point behind, a circumstance that has yielded countless last-second victors in this league. But Robert Parish sent the crowd home in the proper mood by stealing the inbounds pass.

Things certainly looked bleak for Boston as the game entered the final two minutes. The home team had seen a five-point (82-77) third-quarter lead erased by the tenacious visitors, who six times in the final quarter responded positively when the Celtics sliced the lead to two points. At 107-103, Philly, Larry Bird couldn't knock in a jumper, and when Dawkins sank two foul shots with 1:51 to go, and then stole a sloppy Bird pivot feed to Parish eight seconds later, the Celtics were down six without the ball and the crowd was starting to head up the aisles.

But Bill Fitch is no quitter, nor is his team. "I never thought about going fishing, playing tennis or answering anybody in the stands about what happened this year," Fitch related.

The 76ers were one possession away from a date in the final when Parish, again foul-plagued, and again not even a rough facsimile of the Parish (10 points, 5 rebounds in 29 minutes) who sparkled all season, switched off to thwart an Andrew Toney layup try. Tiny Archibald blasted down court for a spinning continuation three-pointer and suddenly Boston was back in the game with 1:20 left. Parish immediately blocked another Toney penetration, the ball rolling out to Bobby Jones, who promptly lost the ball out of bounds.

Bird, who worked ceaselessly for 32 points on a night when he could hit but one jumper, drove the lane and now it was 109-108 with 47 seconds left.

The rest of the game was a Philadelphia nightmare, and nobody was more victimized than Jones. Philly called one timeout with 39 seconds left (15 on the all-important 24-second clock), and Carr knocked the Jones pass out of bounds. The Sixers called for another timeout, and they had trouble getting it in again under the intense Boston overplaying pressure.

Amazingly, at the 28-second mark an Erving-to-Dawkins-to-Jones exchange was knocked loose, and Bird picked up the ball at midcourt to start a fast break. His flying runner was no good, but Carr hauled in the rebound and drew two fouls on a follow-up attempt. He calmly made both shots, and Philly called a 20-second timeout with 20 seconds left, leading to the Jones lefty miss and the Carr rebound. After Carr's rebound, fans flooded the floor, a la the triple OT game, and it took a while to clear the floor and resume play.

Prior to that final push, all Boston had to offer was a 20-8 first-quarter run that gave them a short-lived lead; the continuing brilliance of Archibald, whose poosh-'em-up penetrations kept Boston in the game for three periods; and the all-around savvy of Bird, who was the basketball equivalent of a pitcher flinging a 10-hit shutout without any of his best stuff.

But somehow the Celtics live, and judging by their school-boy reaction at the end of the game, the fist-shaking, the smiling and the back-slapping, they appear ready to play that Spectrum game at noontime today.

Celtics Win the Battle

OVERCOME 76ERS, 100-98, TO EVEN SERIES

May 2, 1981 • by Ray Fitzgerald

PHILADELPHIA—What a night. What action. Bodies were flying everywhere. Nobody would give an inch. Elbows were banging into rib cages, shoulders were slamming into other shoulders. It was nose-to-nose NBA violence all the way.

And that was just in the dressing room.

What happened on the basketball court last night as the Celtics beat both the 76ers and the Spectrum jinx, 100-98, to even the series between these talented giants almost defies description, but let me try.

People have been handcuffed and led away for lesser violence than what these teams inflicted on each other in last night's game.

The 76ers were desperate. They didn't want to go back to Boston. The Celtics were even more desperate. They did not want the season to end in Philadelphia. Desperate men turn to desperate measures, and what resulted last night was an excitement level about 30,000 feet above sea level.

The irresistible collided head-on with the immovable and produced one of the wildest, roughest junkyard fights in some time between large men in short pants.

Fouls were often called when players politely reached out and slapped at a man with the basketball. Fouls were often ignored as Robert Parish and

Darryl Dawkins in the pivot practiced karate on each other while jousting for position.

The old "no harm, no foul" NBA rule of thumb was extended to "no bleeding, no foul."

One vignette in the last quarter will suffice as an example. Larry Bird got a rebound and by the time he forced the ball into the basket five bodies were stacked like cordwood on the floor under the Celtics basket. It looked like a pileup on the far turn at Suffolk.

The emotion was not confined to the court. A fan jabbed Cedric Maxwell with a pencil when the Celtic player fell into the crowd, and Maxwell leaped on his assailant, precipitating a rather untidy melee near the Celtics' bench.

When the action was at its peak, a full cup of Coke hurtled down from the stands and splashed against the backboard and floor. The game was held up while Kevin McHale swabbed the backboard and Steve Mix mopped the floor.

When it was over, of course, players on both teams shrugged off the mugging and slugging as typical playoff basketball.

Intensity is a word you hear 100 times a night in an NBA locker room, but you will seldom see games played with as much intensity as last night's. M. L. Carr called it the most intense basketball game he'd ever been part of.

And wonder of wonders, the Celtics won it despite going into their usual Spectrum swoon at the start of the game.

They'd promised us they wouldn't come out of the gate like a three-toed sloth again. They'd told one and all that this time would be different, that they wouldn't tumble into a deep hole the way they had the last two times here, and be forced to claw their way out, like somebody buried up to his neck on the Mojave Desert.

This time, we were assured, they would come out snarling and wouldn't be run over by the 76er steamroller.

And yet, there they were once again, down by 17 points before you could say, "Get the number of that truck."

But the Celtics are getting to be world class at coming back from the grave. They should be; they've had enough practice at it.

One envisions a sense of panic when the Sixers come down on the Celtics like a giant sledgehammer as soon as the referee tosses up the opening tap.

Chris Ford tried to explain why that feeling doesn't infiltrate the Celtics.

"It's just a team feeling and we won't quit. It may sound like a bunch of bull, and if you're not part of the organization maybe you won't understand, but we feel it."

So the Celtics fought back once more down here, and this time the ball bounced right for them and wrong for Philly, and they won the game they had to win.

Cedric Maxwell hung on to Julius Erving as though the doctor was a rich relative. Robert Parish played like . . . well . . . Robert Parish. Larry Bird struggled his way to 25 points and 16 rebounds. M. L. Carr played terrific defense. Gerald Henderson filled in admirably when Tiny Archibald twisted his ankle. Archibald was his usual marvelous self.

"The seventh game should be a classic," said Carr.

It'll have to go some to match last night's war.

The Improbable Dream

CELTICS' THIRD STRAIGHT MAKES IT COME TRUE, 91-90

May 4, 1981 • by Bob Ryan

The Ghosts of Celtics Past didn't win it. The fans didn't win it. Their own shooting—be it from the floor or the foul line—certainly didn't win it.

Defense won it. Inspired, determined—maniacal is not even too strong a word—defense won it. It was more than a clinic; it was an entire postgraduate course, and because of it the 1981 Celtics have become a major part of basketball history.

What seemed so totally improbable with 1:43 remaining in Wednesday's fifth game, when the 76ers were one intelligent possession away from dispatching the Celtics in five games, became a gratifying reality yesterday with a 91-90 victory that completed a three-game blitz of the Sixers and sent the Celtics into the championship final against the Houston Rockets tomorrow night at the Garden.

As has been written approximately 173,464 times in the past week, only three other teams in NBA history had successfully extricated themselves from a 3-1 hole in a seven-game series. But in none of the other cases did the comebacking team win the three games it needed by margins of two, two and one. In none of the other cases did the comebacking team continually rebound from serious deficits the way this Celtic team did in the past three games. It is neither a hyperbolic, nor an ethnocentric statement to contend that this was, without question, the gutsiest series comeback in the 35-year history of the world's foremost basketball league.

In order to win the game, the series and the everlasting devotion of a fanatical following that has become as intense as any this town has ever seen, in any sport, the Celtics held the 76ers to one point in the Philadelphians' last 10 possessions. Trailing by an 89-82 score with 5:24 remaining following a classically acrobatic Julius Erving reverse layup of his own miss, the Celtics limited the 76er offense to a lone foul shot by Maurice Cheeks with 29 seconds left, and Boston leading by that 91-90 score. In those final 324 seconds, the 76ers committed five turnovers (three being steals by the truly incomparable Larry Bird, of whom too much simply cannot be said), missed six shots (three on one possession) and came away with that one foul shot when two were needed.

Bird capped a series in which he averaged 27 points and 13 rebounds a game with what proved to be the game-winning basket, a Havlicekian stop-and-pop banker from 17 feet on the left following his own defensive rebound. The score was tied at 89 apiece with 1:07 left (on two Bird foul shots—he is shooting 91 percent from the line in the playoffs) when Darryl Dawkins powered in for a layup. Now it must be understood that during those final five-plus minutes only acts considered to be barbaric by Huns and Visigoths were to be considered worthy of Darrell Garretson's and Jake O'Donnell's whistles. Both Robert Parish and Cedric Maxwell hammered Double D who, not too surprisingly, missed the shot. Bird somehow emerged from the ensuing altitudinous convention of violent tall people with the rebound, whereupon he proceeded down the left sideline.

"I don't really know what happened," Bird later explained, "but I wanted the ball in my hands. That's the only place in the world I wanted it." He never

gave it up, dribbling into the forecourt and calmly banking in the tie-breaking basket with 1:03 left.

But this was hardly the end of the story. When M. L. Carr picked off an atrocious right-to-left Erving cross-court pass intended for Bobby Jones 14 seconds later, the fans were ready to light up their mental cigars. But Lionel Hollins poked the ball away from Gerald Henderson, and away went Cheeks, who would wind up being fouled by a retreating Henderson with 29 seconds left.

The Celtics had one thing in their favor; namely, that they were not in the bonus. This became a paramount issue when Cheeks' first attempt clanked off to the right. He sank his second shot, pulling the Sixers within one point.

The Celtics worked the ball down until Carr fired up a corner jumper with six seconds remaining in the game, and one on the 24-second clock. Parish, a major factor amidst some foul trouble, picked off his fifth offensive rebound of the day, only to lose it to Jones with one second to play.

One more second of good defense now separated the Celtics from their 14th trip to the championship final. Jones tried a lob pass underneath to Erving, but the ball hit the top of the backboard, and Maxwell came down with the rebound as the delirious patrons mobbed the floor.

Boston never really had any outside shooting, except an occasional Bird jumper. Archibald shot 3 for 14. Chris Ford was 3 for 10. Parish was a mediocre (for him) 7 for 17. The bench shot a combined 4 for 19. So what did the Celtics do for offense?

One thing they had was Maxwell, who submitted a 19-point, 6-rebound game on top of another outstanding defensive job on Erving. They also had control of the offensive boards, where they bagged 19 points on 18 offensive rebounds, to Philly's 8 and 14, respectively. Eight of Parish's 16 points were on the offensive boards. And, of course, they had Bird, whose 23 points included his second three-pointer of the playoffs.

Spurred by the crowd, the Celtics opened the fourth period with eight unanswered points in the first 2:12, the final two being a clock-beating bomb by Carr. What Boston did not know was a) that it would go 6:44 without a field goal and b) that Doctor J was preparing his final series assault.

Erving, only a peripheral offensive factor in the final four games of the series, threw his artillery at the Celtics over the next four and a half minutes, scoring 10 points on everything from a graceful fade away to the pretty follow-up that gave the Sixers the 89-82 lead with 5:24 to play.

But somewhere in here the Celtics decided that Erving just wasn't going to beat them, that somebody else would have to do it. "We began doubling Doc," recalled Bird. "It was almost helter-skelter. We started to go after everything."

Philly's demise began with an Andrew Toney (and whatever happened to *him?*) miss at 4:48, a shot leading to a Maxwell fast-break free throw. Bird promptly stole an Erving pass for what would prove to be the first of three consecutive Sixer turnovers. The momentum was all Boston's now, especially since the referees were, uh, letting 'em play underneath. Bird's theft of a Bobby-to-Caldwell dish-off at 4:02 became a Parish turnaround jumper with 3:44 to play (89-87). Bird tied the game at 89 with two foul shots (2:51) following a Hollins turnover. And that's where the scoreboard remained until the Bird banker, staying the same through three Philly misses (Erving twice and Hollins) and an Archibald missed jumper.

The defense had done it, all right, and what is defense but a product of determination and industriousness? "Philly is a better team physically," said Maxwell. "They have more natural talent than us. I'm not saying we don't have a lot of talent, but they can run faster and jump higher. The moral of this story is that a good team can beat a squad. They're a good team but we executed better in the end."

To defeat an outfit as strong as Philadelphia three straight times, however, a team needs something else. It needs luck, for sure, and it also needs heart. Even down six points on Wednesday with 1:43 left, the Celtics still thought they could win.

"Everybody believed," said Chris Ford. "We did because we never stopped believing." Think about this. In the past quarter century, has any other local institution, be it academic, financial, ecclesiastical, or athletic, given local citizens more to believe in than the Boston Celtics?

YES, THEY DID IT!

May 4, 1981 • by Leigh Montville

The kid made the trip for everyone else. He was 19 years old, maybe 20, wearing a blue shirt and a pair of blue jeans with a hole in one knee and he climbed to the top of the backboard at the east end of Boston Garden.

He stood first on the rim and then on top of the 24-second clock and he waved his arms and was part of the noise. Then he ripped off the net that was hanging from the rim.

A phalanx of Ogden security men in blue moved underneath him, but the kid just stuffed the net into the front of his pants and dove. He dove like a bird, dove into the people, dove from 15 feet above the old parquet basketball floor and somehow landed on his feet unhurt and free.

The Celtics had done it. As the kid ran from the court, ran out the door, the security men well behind, followed only by an ovation from the bulk of the sweaty sellout crowd that had remained, he was euphoria in full flight, exuberance on a tear, good times and a fat smile for the camera. He was basic Boston, just average, on this fine May afternoon, doing what just came naturally.

The Celtics had done it, indeed.

Dead a week ago, trailing, three games to one in a best-of-seven series to the accursed Philadelphia 76ers, they had clambered from the crypt in the most amazing ways. Three wins in a row . . . three come-from-behind wins in a row . . . the final one in this steam bath, this mixmaster of elbows and grunts and LOUD NOISE yesterday afternoon, 91-90, the result not certain until a final 76er pass bounced off the top of the backboard . . . the local professional basketball team had sent this town on its most emotional sports toot in a long, long time.

"How do you feel?" Celtic forward Cedric Maxwell was asked in the postgame locker-room crush.

"This is the highest high I've ever had," he said and he spoke for a lot of people.

This was a game, a series that assumed bigger and bigger proportions as it progressed. The game had become more than a game when it was played yesterday afternoon. The series had become more than a series. This was a front-page test to every word your drill sergeant ever uttered by any backyard coach. Don't quit? Try again? Pick yourself up? Brush yourself off? Make your own breaks? The Celtics somehow seemed to have been chosen to see if all this stuff works.

The way they did it became just bigger and bigger, better and better the longer the show progressed.

"Our lives became all basketball," effervescent forward M. L. Carr said. "You played basketball, talked basketball, answered basketball questions when you went to the grocery store. My kids were playing basketball in the driveway. I watched 'em. They were saying they were different players on the Sixers. Caldwell Jones, Doctor J. Andrew Toney. I heard my kid say that and I went out to guard him."

"We went to church this morning," M. L. Carr added. "Assembly of God Church in Needham. Pastor Jack got up there and in the sermon he said, 'This is the day Philadelphia goes on vacation.' All basketball."

The tension of the players became the tension of the fans. Vice versa. The games were so good, so close, so exciting, you almost didn't want to watch. Bigger and bigger. Better and better.

"What did you think they were going to do on that last play?" forward Maxwell was asked. "You were guarding Julius Erving. What did you think he was going to do?"

"I had no idea," Maxwell replied. "I was just guarding him, trying to react to what he did."

"Was he open if the pass had been better?"

"It would have been hard for him to get that pass and live," Maxwell said, only half joking.

The players tried to keep telling themselves to relax. That was their way of handling the emotion of the moment. Maxwell said he kept trying to think he was a kid, playing on a schoolyard, just a game, another game, nobody watching. Carr said he tried to focus the emotion, to feed off it without being carried away by it. The idea was to run through the emotion or run with it. Sitting somehow was worse than playing.

"A lot worse," said guard Chris Ford, up and down, from the bench, waving a towel, screaming and screaming some more. "I'd rather be playing than watching. That's for sure."

The bedlam at the end was just a natural reaction to all of this. The 9-1 Celtic run of points . . . the helter-skelter Celtic defense that just denied everything the Sixers tried . . . the go-ahead basket by Larry Bird . . . the one-second Sixer pass . . . the explosion of people and noise hitting the court in a burst, tables and chairs overturned, public relations assistant Francis O'Bryant scuffling with a spectator trying to steal away with the game ball, confusion, happiness, crowd joy and fear at the same time . . . everything just natural.

Four hours after the game had begun, two hours after it had ended, there still was a sizable crowd waiting on Causeway Street and in the parking lots surrounding the Garden. There still was the Garden. There still was drinking, still was yelling, still were people yelling "We Want Bird" as they waited for the Celtics leader to come out.

"Do you want to lie down in the back seat of my car?" television sportscaster Roger Twibell suggested. "Maybe we can get out of here that way."

"Four hours after the game," Bird said. "What the heck . . . "

He left the Garden in a hurry, down an elevator, through a door, into his gray Datsun that had pulled as close as possible. The people beat his back, beat on his car, yelled as he drove down the dark street underneath the screeching of the elevated trains. The people yelled as loud as they could.

There were no indications given that the day would ever end.

Celtics Dodge Rockets, 98-95

ANOTHER BOSTON COMEBACK DECIDES FIRST GAME OF FINAL

May 6, 1981 • by Bob Ryan

Some people have been saying that the Boston-Philadelphia series was the de facto NBA final round, so apparently the Celtics have decided to let Houston see what it missed.

In other words, it was business as usual at the Garden last night when the Celtics once again employed their new what-fun-is-a-lead-until-the-final-five-minutes? style of play to subdue the meandering Rockets by a 98-95 score and thus assume a 1-0 lead in the official championship finals.

The Celtics, now three victories away from their 14th NBA crown, teased the capacity crowd of 15,320 by again coming from behind, this time from deficits of 14 (22-8), 10 (55-45), 9 (64-55), and, finally, 7 (83-76 with 11:35 remaining). With Larry Bird leading them on in a dazzling display of all-around skill, they took control of the game with eight unanswered points that gave them a 96-91 lead with 2:54 left, only to go scoreless in the next 2:35, or until Bird capped an 18-point, 21-rebound, 9-assist game with a spectacular offensive rebound basket that created the final score with 19 seconds to play.

Bird was mildly awesome in the fourth period, when he just wouldn't allow the Celtics to blow this opening game. Six of his last eight points were on the offensive boards (where the aggressive Celts picked up an astounding 33 points). Included in that total was a breathtaking lefthanded flying follow-up of his own missed 22-footer that Red Auerbach—now pay attention, please—termed "the greatest play I've ever seen."

That particular basket had pulled the Celtics within one at 87-86, but it was his final basket that put away the game. Boston had come into possession of the ball with 1:29 left after a goaltended Tom Henderson drive had pulled the tenacious Rockets within one at 96-95. The Celtics retained possession for what must have been an agonizing 70 seconds for the visitors as Tiny Archibald missed one shot and Robert Parish missed two. But key offensive rebounds (one by Parish and one a hustling Chris Ford play) gave Boston ownership of the basketball.

It was after Parish's miss of a running hook that Bird came up with his killing play. He barreled in for rebound No. 20, having a shot blocked on the right side. He promptly picked off rebound No. 21 and reversed to the left side, where he put in the game-clincher. "Remember," joked Bill Fitch, "that Larry was voted Man of the Year by the Lefthander's Association of America."

Boston Again King of Basketball Hill

May 15, 1981 • by Leigh Montville

HOUSTON—The picture from this one came on the presentation stand. Larry Bird reached downward and plucked the cigar from the little balding man's mouth and put it in his own mouth.

Smile! Larry Bird smoked Red Auerbach's cigar and the cameras clicked and all was right with the world again, at least that part of it in the faraway New England corner. The Boston Celtics were champions once more.

"Fantastic!" Auerbach shouted.

The Celtics won the National Basketball Assn. title for a record 14th time at the noisy Summit last night and they won it with grand style. They outlasted the Houston Rockets, 102-91, to win the best-of-seven series, four games to two. They persevered. They hung on. They won with exuberance and they exploded in the end.

"Pow!" Most valuable player Cedric Maxwell shouted as he gave a gigantic high-five slap to forward M. L. Carr.

"Pow-pow," Carr shouted as he gave two slaps to guard Tiny Archibald.

"Give me some pow," guard Chris Ford asked and, pow, he received more than enough. Pow! Pow-pow. Pow!

"Do you ever get tired of this?" Gary Bender, the CBS television man, asked general manager Auerbach.

Fans surround Larry Bird at Logan Airport the day after the Celtics clinched the 1981 NBA title.

"Never . . . never . . . never," Auerbach said, a mist of champagne covering his sports coat. "We're off the number 13, we're on to 14. These guys all of 'em—they were just fantastic . . . "

They were different, these Celtics. They were a Celtics team that never had won. There was not one of them who owned a championship ring. They were a collection of veterans who never had taken the full ride and young talent that made everything fit together. Veterans and talent . . . and, of course, the estimable Bird. The bona fide star who made all of the rest of it work.

There was Archibald, who refined his game, who became a passer instead of a scorer. There was Robert Parish, who came from San Francisco just this year to stand tall where Dave Cowens and Bill Russell once stood. There was Chris Ford, the quintessential journeyman, working hard and landing at the far end of a rainbow at the end. There was the rubber-band Maxwell, arms and elbows and snake-charmer ease, the man who blossomed most of all at the end. There was Carr and rookie Kevin McHale and Rick Robey and his brakeless mayhem and Gerald Henderson and Eric Fernsten and of course, Terry Duerod, Due.

They were brought together by Auerbach, the sly old gambler from the Kenny Rogers song. They were worked together by Bill Fitch, the coaching workaholic, videotapes and extra practice and no loose ends. Ever. They played with a college enthusiasm, hand-claps and hoots, for 99 games and they were the best during the regular season and they were the one-point survivors against the accursed team from Philadelphia and they were victors over both ennui and the Rockets in this anticlimax of a final.

They were the new Celtics, doing things a new way and ending up where so many of the old Celtics had ended. They were the best. By all measurements possible.

"Just sweet," Parish said at the thought of the end of it all. "Ooooooh. Good God, how sweet it is."

"Bring it to the Bronx," Archibald said, touching the NBA trophy.

"Bring it to Minnesota," McHale said.

"We're bringing it back to Boston," Carr said. "That's where we're bringing it."

The final win was as good as any to show how these Celtics played. With the Rockets coming out fast, playing their best basketball of the series, the Celtics came out even faster. They stayed a step ahead, a step ahead and then blew away to a 17-point lead in the first two minutes of the fourth period.

When there was a bit of sloppiness, when the Rockets made a good run, cutting the lead to three points and making the modern arena start to tremble a bit . . . well, there were the Celtics at the end. They were a team that always was best at the end. Bird was always around and Bird and Bird and Bird, and there he was, stuffing in that three-pointer from the far corner with 1:37 left to just about end the game and send announcer Johnny Most into his dog-level high keen.

"If ever a team celebrated, this is the one," Fitch said. "This is their first night off all year."

The trophy presentation was held in a separate area in the Summit and for this one, all the Celtics came. They stood on the podium together, laughing, giving each other some pow, and looking very much like the US hockey team in its celebration at Lake Placid.

"Pass those cigars around, Red," McHale, the rookie, shouted and the general manager did just that, emptying his pockets.

"One for one," McHale shouted again and again, over and over. One championship in one try.

"There is no way to explain about how I feel or how I played or how I contributed," Maxwell said.

The trophy was presented by NBA commissioner Larry O'Brien to Celtic owner Harry Mangurian. O'Brien said, "Now for the 14th time . . . " and handed the gold trophy over, and as he did, Auerbach peeked from the other side.

"Hey," Auerbach said, examining the trophy. "It's a new one."

Only he would know.

Larry Bird is front and center during the Celtics' victory parade.

Bird sleeps next to Celtics trainer Ray Melchiorre and the NBA Championship trophy on the flight back to Boston, May 15, 1981.

Bird Star of Show

May 19, 1981 • by Michael Madden

During a sunny lunch hour with 50,000 citizens in City Hall Plaza straining forward to catch his every word, one man stood at a microphone on a fourth-floor balcony of City Hall, looked down on the masses, his masses, paused and then brought down the house, the Hall and the Plaza with one sentence.

Unity and joy had finally returned, if only for a day, to City Hall.

No. Mayor Kevin White was nowhere in sight on this low-profile day for him, and no, those weren't his people outside City Hall. But Larry Bird was in full sound, and the Celtic looked at his people spread out below him, spotted a huge cardboard sign being paraded through the mob, digested the sign's message—"Moses eats [expletive]"—and finally spoke.

"I look out in the crowd and I see one thing that typifies our whole season," said Bird with gusto. "Moses does eat [expletive]."

The 50,000 people went crazy. Absolutely bonkers. They cheered wildly for minutes, a huge crescendo of sound and feeling that had built up since the Celtics won the NBA title last week and Houston's Moses Malone called them "chumps." Yesterday was the day Boston said thanks to the Celtics, hundreds of thousands of its people did, and it was the day a man in City Hall gave 50,000 people of Boston and a local television audience exactly what they wanted.

Ainge Signs On

November 28, 1981 • by Neil Singelais

Danny Ainge, the 22-year-old retired Toronto Blue Jay baseball player, officially became a Boston Celtic basketball player last night.

The Celtics announced at a hastily arranged Garden press conference that they had signed Ainge to a multiyear contract after having reached a financial agreement earlier in the day with the Blue Jays.

Celtic coach Bill Fitch said that Ainge "will play when he's ready. We plan to have him join us for practice by next Thursday, and he could be in uniform for his first Garden appearance when we play the New Jersey Nets Wednesday, Dec. 9."

"I've always wanted to be a Celtics, and I'm anxious to get going," said Ainge, "but it's going to take me a couple of weeks to get in shape. It will be coach Fitch's decision on how I can help. I feel I can play defense and come off the bench."

Fitch said he has no desire to put any undue pressure on Ainge, and added that he won't be looking for Ainge to provide the Celtics with immediate help.

"I doubt if Chris [Ford] and Tiny [Archibald] will still be around by the time we go after our ninth championship in a row," quipped Fitch. "For him [Ainge], it's just a matter of going out and catching up. He's four weeks behind every other NBA rookie."

Tod Rosensweig, Celtics public relations director, produced a Celtic jersey with the numeral 44 for the benefit of photographers and TV cameras. The last Celtic to wear 44 was Pete Maravich.

The Ainge signing was treated as a big media event by the Celtics, as Ainge held center stage. With the 6-foot-5 former Brigham Young All-America guard were his father, Don, and his attorney, Robert Quinney. The Celtics were represented by owner Harry Mangurian; general manager Red Auerbach; Jan Volk, the team's legal counsel; and Rosensweig. Watching the proceedings intently were Pat Gillick, vice president of operations for the Blue Jays, and Herb Soloway, the Blue Jays' attorney.

The Celtics declined to disclose what they will have to pay Ainge or the Blue Jays. But the American League baseball team had demanded $1 million from Boston for permission to deal with Ainge.

Gillick said that the Blue Jays' financial arrangement is with the team: "Our agreement has absolutely nothing to do with Ainge; it's strictly with the Celtics. All I can say is that we're satisfied with the agreement with the Celtics.

"The amount? It could be less than $1 million, and then again it could be more. If Ainge hadn't come to terms with the Celtics, we would have been glad to take him back. We still feel he has the ability to be a good baseball player."

The controversy surrounding Ainge erupted after Peter Bavasi, then the Blue Jay president, accused Auerbach of tampering with Ainge while he was still property of the Blue Jays.

Bavasi, who earlier this week resigned as president of the Blue Jays, took the Celtics to court on the tampering charge, and a New York jury found in favor of Toronto. The Blue Jays recently gave the Celtics permission to negotiate with Ainge for two weeks. The deadline was Monday. Last night the Celtics beat that deadline.

He's the Celtics' Big Chief

April 24, 1982 • by Bob Ryan

The nickname is perfect.

His vantage point is 84 inches above sea level, and his face seldom reveals the inward passion that

Robert Parish, battling the Sixers' Julius Erving for a rebound, was the most unsung member of the Big Three.

He is, after all, The Chief. Basketball games can be controlled by a tall man in the middle, especially one who understands the true value of a center, which is to be the team defensive coordinator. What has made Robert Parish so valuable, a legitimate candidate for the Most Valuable Player Award, in fact, is that he is a multidimensional player. He would be a major Celtics asset even without his 19 points a game or his 54 percent shooting. Working in concert with Kevin McHale, he anchors Boston's defense with blocks, intimidations and shouted instructions to his mates. At times, it's as if Dave Cowens came back, younger and taller. And when the subject is defense, there is no greater compliment.

REVITALIZED ROBERT PARISH HAS BECOME AN MVP CENTER

Lucas is correct. Parish is now a better player than he was a year ago, and his development is a major reason the Celtics must be considered the favorites to win the championship. "I see two differences," Parish contends. "I'm not getting in early foul trouble anymore. And I've got more confidence. Things are generally smoother for me this year. I didn't struggle in training camp, the way I did last year. This time I knew what to expect."

Such oratory is rare for Parish, who cultivates privacy and who has generally made an art form of avoiding interviews, especially with out-of-town people. Combined with his normally aloof on-court behavior, this approach to the press has created an Ol' Man River-type mystique. Robert Parish must know somethin', but as a rule, he prefers to say nothin'.

One thing Robert Parish knows is the value of inner peace. Many NBA executives, coaches, players and fans were startled last spring when Parish, who would have been eligible for free agency at the conclusion of the playoffs, signed a long-term contract that made him the second-highest-paid Celtic, behind only Bird. The assumption among NBA cognoscenti had been that Parish would test the market and make the Celtics bleed at least a little, which is the normal NBA behavior in such matters.

But Parish knew what he wanted, and that was to remain in Boston. "Boston asked me what I wanted," relates Parish. "I told them and I got it. That saved me from being in another bad situation. I didn't want to be a free agent and wind up playing

has driven him to the top of his profession. There is no more regal bearing in the NBA than his. Nor, at this point, is there a center in possession of more athletic skill. The nickname, a Cedric Maxwell designation, fits. Robert Parish is, in every way, *The Chief.*

His value to the franchise has escalated dramatically this past season. Neither friends nor foes can limit their praise of Boston's stellar center. "He should be the MVP," agree Larry Bird and Chris Ford. And Knicks forward Maurice Lucas has this to say: "Robert is at least 40 percent better this year than last. He's so confident now. In my opinion, as the year went on, Boston only rolled when Parish rolled. Not that Larry isn't a great player, but when Parish rolled, Boston rolled."

"Houston may have Malone," adds the irrepressible M. L. Carr, "but we've got our own Moses in Robert Parish. He led us to the Promised Land."

for a Cleveland or a Utah. The money would have been nice, but I wouldn't have been happy. It would have been Golden State all over again. Money isn't everything. Once you make that deposit, you're still unhappy."

Parish has discovered that, all things considered, winning is preferable to losing as a way of life. "Being on a winner," Parish explains, "is like being on a natural high all the time. Winning means exposure and credit for everybody. I'm playing a lot of the same basketball I played for Golden State, but with more intensity, I am more consistently enthusiastic. Winning does that."

In addition to being downright efficient, Robert Parish is currently the most aesthetically pleasing center in the NBA. This is not the way he was viewed when he came here in the draft day trade back on June 9, 1980. The few looks Boston Garden fans had of him revealed naught but a turnaround jump shooter who blocked a few shots and who frowned a lot.

The Robert Parish on display every night is flat-out fun to watch play basketball. He is a constant threat to sprint downcourt for a sneak-away layup or dunk. He intersperses his basic jump shot with sweeping hooks and graceful drives that would have been the envy of any 6-footer two decades ago. He has become a tireless worker on the boards. He blocks shots with ferocity, and he has become so attuned to the fast break while playing for the running-conscious Celtics that he occasionally even flings lefthanded outlets to streaking mates. Even the way he sometimes receives a high-post pass, arms and knees flailing in a "get-the-hell-out-of-my-way" symbol of defiance, is a kick.

But his calling card on offense remains that awesome looping jumper, an unblockable, unstoppable weapon that accounts for the majority of his points. He can connect on the shot from any angle and from distances ranging to upwards of 20 feet.

Parish's journey to NBA greatness began in Shreveport, La., where he was a star both in high school (Woodlawn) and in college (Centenary). He was 6-7 entering high school, 6-10 when he left after finishing as good a career as any Louisiana high schooler ever had, and 7 feet (his present height) when he came into the pros. The one constant, he says, is that he's always had the jump shot.

It's been well documented how Centenary was slapped with a severe NCAA probation following his freshman year. The Gentlemen (yup, Gentlemen) were kept out of postseason play for his final three seasons in college, and Parish was never included among the statistical leaders in the weekly NCAA releases. Accordingly, he became something of a legendary figure. The Best Player Nobody (outside of the Bayous, anyway) Ever Saw.

Well, almost nobody. The NBA scouts and general managers were aware of him, and he was the eighth man chosen in the 1976 draft. But for many reasons, beginning with the somewhat suspect level of his collegiate competition and his often unfathomable disposition, a lot of NBA people just didn't know how to assess him.

Parish feels he could have been better prepared for NBA ball than he was. "The style of play at Centenary was something like we play here," Parish contends, "but my coach [Larry Little] wasn't able to teach that much to a big man. I progressed my first two years, and that was it. I think I was behind in my game when I came into the pros."

The artful 7-footer realizes how close he came to being a mediocrity. "I could have been James Edwards," Parish admits, "a big guy with a jump shot and little else. The guy who helped me the most was [former Golden State assistant coach] Joe Roberts. He's the one who told me I shouldn't be a one-dimensional offensive player, just relying on the jump shot. He said that as I got older and couldn't jump as high or run as fast, I'd need variety to my game. Joe taught me little moves and tricks and how to keep my man off balance."

But the potential still was not being realized on the Warriors. Parish was regarded as just another stat guy who wasn't a winning center, and there was no reason to think otherwise after watching him perform during the Celtics' 1980 training camp. Parish looked lost in a Boston uniform, the symbolic low occurring the very night Cowens retired. Parish picked up five fouls in the first period of a game against Chicago.

"I just wasn't used to the continual running," he recalls. "It never stopped. I know now you've got to be in regular-season shape when you first come in. And I think they were hard on me because they didn't know what to expect. They didn't know if I had a competitive edge or was tough enough mentally to play here."

We know differently now. Placed in a vibrant atmosphere surrounded by complementary teammates and directed by a coach who not only demands excellence but who knows how to extract it, Parish has become as good an all-around center as there is in the league.

Parish relishes his teammates, who, he claims, make his life very simple. "When Max, Tiny [Archibald] and Larry are in there together, it makes my game easier because the opponents can't afford to double-team me. Playing with Kevin has helped cut down my fouls since I don't have to try to block everything. Playing with Larry helps my rebounding. And Tiny, well, I can count on one hand the number of times in two years I've been open and didn't receive the ball when I should."

To Parish, the Celtics' aura is a very personal experience. "I don't think it's the Boston 'mystique' that's important now," he claims. "It's the players themselves. The players we have now make the Boston Celtics. We have pride and confidence in ourselves, no matter how much we're down at the time. We'll very seldom beat ourselves. When the game gets tough, we don't usually make the big turnover or the crucial mistake. We make the other club do what it doesn't like to do.

"The most interesting thing about this team," Parish asserts, "is how all the stars have toned down their game for the good of the club. Take Tiny. He could still go out and score 25 points any time he wanted, but he knows it's not his job."

Robert Parish has done his job well enough to be called the best at what he does. And while some of his fans claim he's been overshadowed by the incessant Bird ink, Parish disagrees. "I think I'm getting my fair share of the recognition and the publicity," he contends. "I think my peers and the good basketball fans are aware of Robert Parish and what he can do."

Through it all, he remains a semi-stranger in our midst. "I'm a private person, a very private person," Parish explains. "I guess 'loner' is the word. I'm home a lot. I don't go out much, only if I have something to do. If you see me out, I'm going somewhere definite. You won't see me out just hanging around, socializing."

No matter. When the bell rings he's ready to play. He is The Chief.

It Was Nothing to Choke About

THE 76ERS FINALLY GET THE CELTICS OFF THEIR BACKS, 120-106

May 24, 1982 • by Bob Ryan

What ultimately mattered was that the players settled the affair without chippiness and without rancor. The teams went at each other hard, and when it was over, the team that had played the better money game had won. It was that simple.

Yesterday afternoon, before a hopeful gathering of 15,320 at Boston Garden, that team was Philadelphia. The new NBA Eastern Conference champions are the 76ers, who earned the distinction via a no-argument 120-106 dispatch of the Celtics, thus shattering the dreams of another miracle extraction from a 3-1 series deficit.

What also mattered was that the Celtics' fans elevated themselves and indeed the series itself with an unprecedented display of fourth-period sportsmanship. With 21 seconds remaining and the Celtics hopelessly beaten, a marvelous chant came down from the stands. "Beat LA! Beat LA!" they roared.

The game truly belonged to Philadelphia, and above all, to Andrew Toney and Julius Erving.

The former, a 7-for-31 shooter during Philly's losses in Games 5 and 6, showed what a terrifying force he can be by dropping in 14 of 23 shots en route to a 34-point game. The latter slipped in a quiet but deadly 29, and he was immense in the decisive second half, when the visitors stretched a shaky 52-49 halftime lead to an advantage as big as 17 in the final period.

As for the Celtics, theirs was a curiously flat performance. They played hard enough, but they were damaged by poor open shooting and by unforgivable turnovers of every description. The final figures of 22 turnovers for 29 enemy points would have made it difficult for the Celtics to have defeated Utah or Cleveland.

One notable thing Fitch did try was Bird in the back court to start the fourth period. The result of the Bird-Toney matchup was Andrew 5, Larry 0. With Philly up by a 96-80 score, Ainge replaced Parish and the Bird-in-the-back-court experiment was over for this season.

With the crusading Sixers in complete command, the final story became the Boston fans, who first started a standing ovation for the Celtics with 1:06 left (112-97) and who then came up with the "Beat LA!" chant that gratified the Celtics and startled the 76er entourage, who had come to think that the Celtics' backers were just another group of partisan animals. The Sixers were surprised that their great achievement, their restoration of self-respect, had been so recognized.

It was left for an angry Billy Cunningham to punctuate the proceedings. Stung by some acid Philadelphia media criticism, he stated his feelings bluntly, as follows: "I just want to thank the Boston Celtics fans, the way they responded at the end of the game. That truly showed me a great deal of class. And as competitive as these two teams are, it surely made me feel good, and that's what it's all about— the competition. The only other thing I'm going to say is that I'm just ecstatic for the 12 guys in there because everyone else abandoned us, and I'm just proud of them. Period. Goodbye."

Goodbye, as well, to the Celtics, who went down fighting, as always.

See you next year.

Celtics Trade Tillis for Wedman

January 15, 1983 • by Larry Whiteside

At the time, it seemed so strange when the huge crowd at the Garden kept chanting, "We want Tillis." Coach Bill Fitch didn't crack a smile, and neither did he put the rookie into what was an obvious blowout.

But only a few minutes after the Celtics had posted a devastating 133-108 victory over the New Jersey Nets last night, everyone knew why. In a classic case of the rich getting just a little richer, Boston announced after the game that it had sent Darren

Tillis, a 6-foot-11 forward and its No. 1 draft choice last spring out of Cleveland State, an undetermined amount of cash and its No. 1 draft pick this June, to Cleveland in exchange for forward Scott Wedman.

Wedman, 30, an eight-year veteran, is a former All-Star who played seven seasons at Kansas City before signing a four-year contract with the lowly Cavaliers last year for $2.8 million. Wedman, at 6 feet 7, is expected to be a power forward. Because of his ability to shoot from the outside and move without the ball, Wedman is considered a John Havlicek-type player. He is expected to join the club tonight in Richfield, Ohio, where the Celtics begin a three-game trip.

Wait until the rest of the NBA wakes up and learns about this latest Celtic coup. Boston not only got a proven player to fill a spot handled by a rookie who rarely saw action, but Cleveland is also picking up a substantial portion of Wedman's salary.

Who Would've Believed It Could Happen Here?

April 25, 1983 • by Michael Madden

A Tree bit a man yesterday afternoon in the Garden; a Tree 7 feet high and a forest wide curled its trunks around a man in little white shorts and gouged out the man's middle finger. It happened right here in downtown Boston, too, and not up in the deep woods of Maine, where nobody would believe it and everybody could doubt it. Amazing, huh?

No doubt about it, either. The Tree chomped at the man's finger on a nice quiet Sunday afternoon right in front of 15,320 people and a national television audience, too. CBS even got it on tape: Tree biting man. Be wary, be careful on those quiet springtime walks through the forest or through the backyard; keep an eye on those trees. It can happen.

Danny Ainge, the man bitten by a Tree, needed a tetanus shot and five stitches to close the wound that dug deep down to the tendon of his finger. Ainge wasn't so surprised that Tree bit him; the Tree had been shaking and blowing and wavering in the winds of defeat "and I was expecting something to happen," said Ainge. "I was ready."

Those very same winds were whistling Dixie to Atlanta, 66-52, in favor of the Celtics with 6:15 left in the third quarter, when Tree Rollins thundered home a monster stuff. Ainge and Rollins had crashed together a few moments earlier when Ainge was crashing through a screen "and the guy punched me in the chest," said Rollins. "Darell [Garretson, the referee] saw what Ainge did; everybody saw him throw the punch."

"What punch?" asked Ainge. "I put a fist in his chest," admitted the Celtic, "but it wasn't hard enough to hurt my wife. He had pushed me to set that off, and he had said something to the officials about it and I told him, 'Tree, how can you get mad at me for pushing you for what you just did to me?'"

But now Rollins, all 7 feet of him, had just crunched his slam, turned upcourt, and waiting for him a few feet away at the foul line was Ainge, all 6-4 of him. Instinctively, Ainge raised his shoulder, and instinctively, Rollins raised his elbow—both knew this was the moment of truth and justice—and Rollins slammed a Grade A lethal flying elbow into Ainge's head just as Ainge was readying his shoulder.

Rollins turned to face Ainge and Ainge ("I just reacted") charged at Rollins, picked up the Tree by the stump and felled him with a low, swooping, crunching tackle at the knees. "I went to tackle him so I couldn't be punched," said Ainge. "I wasn't going to get into a punching match with Tree."

Suddenly, both benches erupted and Boston's Larry Bird and Kevin McHale charged onto the pile where Ainge still had Rollins locked, pinned and down. Two, three, four Hawks also charged into the pile, and chaos, confrontation and confusion brawled everywhere.

"I didn't want to see Danny get hurt," joked McHale. "He may be a wimp but he's also my friend."

Bird knew instantly what he had to do—swarm into the pile and help Ainge. Bird said Ainge "must be a tough guy, since it took three of their guys to hold him down so one of their guys could bite his finger. It's a sad thing when a guy 7-1½ has to bite a guy who's 6-2."

Ainge and Rollins were still locked in the bottom of the pile when the Tree bit. "We were down on the ground and he had me wrapped up and I had him wrapped up and people were on top of him," said Ainge. "Then he just stuck my finger in his mouth . . .

I thought he was going to bite it off. I was trying to pull my hand away but he just stuck it in his mouth and chomped on it really hard."

The fight finally broke up. Ainge was tossed out of the game for the first time in his life and the cut on his finger was repaired. Celtics trainer Ray Melchiorre said he was mystified when he first saw the injury, that he wasn't sure what had caused it.

"But Danny knew what it was," said the trainer. "What's going to cause a bite like that? One of those mice running around here?"

Or a bite from a Tree?

Robey Dealt for Johnson

June 28, 1983 • by Dan Shaughnessy

Maybe Dennis Johnson will show up with an attitude that'll make Sidney Wicks look like John Havlicek. Maybe Rick Robey will prove to be the greatest thing to hit Phoenix since air conditioning.

Then again, maybe the venerable Redhead has done it again. Maybe Celtic fans will be sipping green beer next June, saying, "We knew we were on the right track when Red swapped Rick Robey for Dennis Johnson and a first-round pick last June."

Dennis, one of 16 Johnsons in the 1983 NBA Register, is a 6-foot-4, 200-pound 28-year-old. He's a seven-year NBA veteran who was MVP of the 1979 playoffs when he played back court for the champion Seattle SuperSonics. The Sonics cited "attitude" problems when they sent him to Phoenix for Paul Westphal in June, 1980. DJ is a four-time All-Star who's been named to the NBA's first team All-Defensive team for five consecutive seasons. His best offensive season was 1982, when he shot 47 percent from the floor and averaged 19.5 points per game for the Suns. Last season he averaged 14.2 points and shot 46 percent while teaming with Walter Davis in the back court.

"I'm going to a very good team with no regrets about leaving," said DJ. "All the times I came to play in Boston, I heard about the Boston tradition and mystique. Now, I get to be a part of it."

The Celtics have a glut of guards. Danny Ainge, Gerald Henderson, Quinn Buckner. Tiny Archibald and Charles Bradley are still on the roster. The acquisition of Johnson makes it easier for the Celtics to dump Archibald, who wants his release.

"We had to get a good, big defensive guard," said Auerbach. "Now we got a guy that can play Magic (Johnson) and (George) Gervin and (Reggie) Theus and (Andrew) Toney. He can shut guys off, which is something we did not have last year and could not have gotten in the draft. We now feel our back court is as good as any in the league."

Asked if he could stop Andrew Toney, Johnson said, "We only play them twice a year. At times he's come out on top and at times I have come out on top, but when I'm on the court he knows I'll be right there giving it to him."

What about Johnson's attitude?

"We checked him out carefully and he's a good kid with no bad habits," said Auerbach. "He was emotionally unhappy for a short time in Seattle, but Lenny Wilkens [coach of the Sonics] said he's a helluva kid who works hard."

Johnson said, "People perceive you for what you do on the court. I'm gonna get on the court and play the way I should play. That's what I say about my reputation."

It's Celtics' Night to Remember

JOHNSON BRINGS FRESH ATTITUDE

"People seem to think this world is problem free. Hell, I'm just like everybody else. I have them, too."

—Dennis Johnson

November 2, 1983 • by Larry Whiteside

He has always carried a label of being a free spirit in the purest sense. In good years and bad. It is what made Dennis Johnson's approach to playing professional basketball different.

When Johnson came into the NBA in 1976, it was thought that the Seattle SuperSonics had goofed in making a 6-foot-4 shot-blocking guard from tiny Pepperdine (Calif.) College their second-round draft choice. But in seven seasons, that same Dennis

Johnson has developed into the prototype of the big defensive guard that almost every NBA club now feels it must have.

While playing in Seattle and then Phoenix, Johnson became known as the complete two-way player. His defense frequently overshadowed his offensive production. But he always seemed to have the ball when the big shot was needed, and usually he hit it.

It is hard to find fault with a man who has been named to the All-NBA defensive team a record-tying five seasons and has averaged over 15 points, 4.5 rebounds and 3.5 assists a game. Yet, one owner, Sam Shulman of Seattle, and two coaches, Len Wilkens of Seattle and John MacLeod of Phoenix, have either publicly or privately complained of Johnson's "attitude."

Such are the contradictions in the life of the man called DJ who does not deny there have been problems but quickly adds that people don't judge books solely by their reviews and the same should be true for an NBA player.

"Sure, I've had some personality problems," says Johnson, who will be making his home debut as a starter for the Celtics tonight. "But they didn't come from a coaching or player standpoint. It came from management.

"It can happen easily. Somebody is going to say that Dennis Johnson has been on three teams and that means he must have a problem. But how many teams has Tom Nissalke coached, or Bill Fitch? What's the deal there? They don't have a problem?"

It is still difficult to fathom how the Celtics, of all clubs, were able to land a player with the talents of Dennis Johnson. He was acquired in June for backup center Rick Robey in a deal that raised more eyebrows in Phoenix than in Boston. He had apparently won his three-year battle with Suns management and was at peace with the world.

Johnson played well enough in his three years in Phoenix, a club that has replaced Philadelphia as the perennial NBA bridesmaid. But the peace he thought existed was a mirage. It had been well known but never publicly acknowledged that for two years the Suns felt they had a man clearly cut from the wrong mold, and that they had made a mistake in trading Paul Westphal to Seattle for him.

"Attitude" is a catch-all phrase in the NBA and usually means a player is not well liked by his coach.

Johnson's record has been one of excellence on the court.

His "attitude" problems mean his relations with front offices over money and over basic philosophy, as in Seattle, where Wilkens once called him a "cancer" to the Sonics.

Johnson had been the MVP of the 1979 NBA playoff finals, won by Seattle. But even before Wilkens' "cancer" outburst, the Sonics were unhappy because Johnson had demanded and won a five-year contract, which still has two years to go. Wilkens and Johnson feuded, with Wilkens claiming DJ was uncoachable and uncooperative.

After Johnson was traded to Phoenix in 1981, that one quote haunted him. When he sought to renegotiate his contract in the summer of 1981—the year Magic Johnson was given a million-dollar contract—he found resistance from the front office and finally had to bury the hatchet publicly to quiet newspaper stories that he was holding out.

Johnson knew his actions didn't endear him to management, but he still felt that his performance in the last two years had redeemed him in the eyes of the fans and his peers. One source close to the Suns, however, indicated that while MacLeod publicly praised Johnson, he didn't like his off-court manner and training habits.

Johnson admits his "attitude problem" did exist at one point. He agrees that his run-in with Shulman was a classic example of how not to conduct player-owner relations, and things went downhill from there. When Johnson left Seattle in a huff, the whole experience left bad feelings on both sides.

But things were different after his trade to Boston, as the Suns were roasted by their media. Johnson had heard that the Suns were looking for a trade to beef up inside, but he said there was no hint that he would be the bait, particularly since the Suns are still minus a big defensive guard and have shifted Walter Davis to the back court.

"At Seattle," said Johnson, "I just wanted a raise and he (Shulman) didn't want to give it to me. At times it left me bitter and left him bitter. I admit that it affected me in a different way and did carry over into my playing. But not totally.

"When I got traded, everybody, I guess, took a cue from that. I may have given that impression, I may not have. To prejudge or not to prejudge is an individual right. But nobody really asked me anything at that particular time. People automatically made judgments about me, and I let them think they were right. I didn't say anything. I let it be whatever they wanted it to be. But in the last three years, I've proved them totally wrong."

The trade to Boston did catch Johnson by surprise.

"My wife and I were shopping for a new home," he said. "I was surprised and shocked. I was bitter for the minute. But I'd faced it once and thus it wasn't all that hard to deal with this time. I said it means go to Boston, find me a place and get settled."

Johnson feels he has already won a measure of acceptance in Boston, especially from his teammates. He reported to training camp with the rookies, and coach K. C. Jones rewarded his hard work by giving him a starting job opposite Gerry Henderson.

"I'm the type of player that can't have too bad a year. I'm not a pure shooter," said Johnson. "Nobody counts on my shot going in every time like a Larry Bird or a Robert Parish, but I can shoot. The thing I do best is play defense, and I can't afford to slack on that even a little bit. My game is flexible.

"The day that one guard can dominate on defense is probably over. But I plan to get back as close to it as I can this year. It's going to take a lot of hard work."

Celtics Decision Sixers

October 17, 1983 • by Dan Shaughnessy

This was right out of Syracuse or Fort Wayne, circa 1955: You had the Celtics and a hated rival in a barroom brawl with Red Auerbach in the middle, taunting the enemy's big man by taking off his glasses and saying, "Go ahead, hit me, you big SOB."

Instead of Bob Brannum, Jim Loscutoff and Co., this was Larry Bird, Cedric Maxwell and the 1984 Celtics exploding in a preseason free-for-all against the world champion Philadelphia 76ers.

It was a night when henchman Rick Robey would have come in handy and Dennis Johnson was asking himself what he's gotten into. The Celtics beat the 76ers, 99-86, but the lasting image will be that of Auerbach descending from Loge 1, Row 6, Seat 1, crossing the court and confronting scab referees

Ralph Lembo and Jesse Hall, not to mention Moses Malone and Billy Cunningham.

Auerbach interceded with 8:20 left in the first quarter. That may seem early, but it took less than four minutes of action to produce two fights, two ejections (including Larry Bird), three technical fouls and Cunningham's ripped jacket.

Looking like a vagrant who'd staggered upstairs from the train station, a tattered Cunningham collected his thoughts when it was over and said, "That's a classic. A man sitting in the 10th row, and he comes out and discusses it. Only one person in the world could do that. It was fantastic. I love him. I wish I could do something like that."

The first indication that this was going to be a memorable night came with 9:37 left in the first quarter when Maxwell and Malone got into a scuffle underneath the Sixers basket. Max came up with a loose ball and was pushed by Malone. Maxwell backed off and fired the ball off Malone's shoulder. Malone went for Maxwell, and the pair collapsed in a heap.

"Ain't nobody gonna hit me with a ball," reasoned Moses.

Predictably, the benches emptied, and when order was restored, Max was smiling and Malone was snarling. Malone was tagged with a personal foul and Max picked up a technical.

A minute later, Parish was fouled by Malone and went to the line. Bird and [Marc] Iavaroni started jawing at the foul line, and after Parish's second free throw went in, the Celtics' superstar and the Sixers' statue were toe-to-toe, slugging it out.

This time, it got out of hand. Bird had to be restrained by K. C. Jones and a couple of teammates. At one point, he lunged forward and hacked away at Cunningham, who got hot and also had to be restrained.

"No comment," said Bird, who scored four points before his early exit.

The announcement of Bird's ejection sparked Auerbach's intervention. The resident legend confronted Lembo and Hall and said, "If you're going to throw Bird out, why not toss Malone?"

Sensing that he might be losing to a higher god, Cunningham tried to stop Auerbach. The scene got sillier when Malone and Auerbach started screaming at each other. Red's challenge to Malone went unanswered.

Simply, He's Great

May 14, 1984 • by Leigh Montville

The good feeling descended, a pink and pleasant fog, settling early around Larry Bird on this important afternoon. There will be a lot of stories that will say that he called for it, that he willed it to happen, but they will be wrong.

He simply knew what to do when it arrived.

"Nobody can say he will have a good day before he has it," the star of the Boston Celtics said yesterday after he scored 39 points, collected 12 rebounds and passed out 10 assists to help throttle the New York Knicks, 121-104, in this seventh and final game of this NBA playoff series. "You know you'll always be able to get the ball up close to the basket. You just don't know if it will go in."

Play the game. Play hard. That was Larry Bird's one thought on this day he certainly was trying to have a good game. But wasn't everybody on the celebrated Boston Garden floor trying to have the same good game? All he could do was to put himself in a position to have a good game.

If the cloud arrived—the invincible feeling, the feeling that any shot can be made at any time—he wanted to be ready to benefit.

"People will talk a lot about how he looked before the game, what he said, what he did but I don't think any of that is important," said guard Danny Ainge, who dresses next to Larry Bird in the Celtics' locker room. "I think it's a lot more important what happens early in a game like this.

"If you hit a few shots, if you get your confidence and your rhythm, then you're on the way. And when Larry's on the way it becomes contagious. You can see it. It goes through everyone on our team."

He was tired on Saturday. OK, hard to believe, but even Larry Bird gets tired. His teammates said his left arm was killing him, bruised from a whack earlier in this slugfest of a series. He was tired and his left arm hurt, but he slept a lot of hours and felt as good as he could feel at this time of the year on Sunday morning.

"Did you have any special thoughts, coming here, getting ready?" he was asked.

"Not really," he said. "I'm not a big one for coming in and doing a lot of talking and slapping everyone on the back. I just wanted 1 o'clock to come and get going."

He wanted to be involved in the game as soon as possible and he wanted to shoot some shots from the outside. He hadn't shot a lot from the outside in this series and he thought there might be some free air out there. Some room to work.

The idea was to run some plays for him early. Get him working. See if the cloud was there.

"Do you like to play games like this?" a reporter asked, hoping to elicit some kind of "Yeah, it's a time when men are men and boys are boys" type of response.

"Not really," Larry Bird replied. "I'd rather be up, 3-1, than play a seventh game. But I really did think we had an edge by playing here. At home."

The crowd usually does not affect him one way or the other. His usual routine simply is to shut the crowd out of his mind, to play the game in a mental closet, no windows or doors. He couldn't do that this time.

"It's the first time here the crowd has gotten to me," he said about the opening ovation. "I've never heard it louder. Not in Boston. I didn't know whether to cry or laugh. The crowd got me going."

The crowd seemed to bring the cloud.

How to describe the first half that Larry Bird unfurled? Teammate Cedric Maxwell said all the adjectives already have been used up for the things the guy does, so they have to be recycled. Larry Bird was terrific. And all the rest.

The Celtics won the tap and he took the first shot—from the outside, on a play run for him—and the ball traveled 16 feet and went through the net as if it had been attracted by a magnet. He was on the way. On a roll. Working.

His eyes seemed to have that see-in-the-dark, laser-beam directness. Give him the ball. Let him have it. He could do anything that was possible to do with it. Knock a bumblebee off a branch at 100 yards. Shoot a six-gun from a cowboy's hand at the other side of a room. Anything. Anything goes.

There was a stretch, seven minutes into the first period, when he was fouled twice in succession by Bernard King. Both times the fouls were early, before Larry Bird had a chance to shoot. Each time, he simply kept moving, taking the shot anyway.

The first was a lefthanded hook that banked high off the backboard and went through the hoop. The second was a long jumper from the side. Swish. Anything goes.

"I knew I had it then, I knew I was rolling," he said. "I just wanted to keep going."

He had 28 of his points by the half, nine of 13 from the floor, 10 of 10 from the foul line. Four of his rebounds. Three of his assists. Halftime was almost an intrusion. He wanted to keep playing, keep going.

"That's the thing," Larry Bird said. "You have your rhythm going, but it can leave at any time. I came out in the second half and it wasn't the same. I made a couple of bad passes. I was mad at myself."

Ah, but with five minutes left in the third period he was standing 24 feet from the basket when he received a pass from Ainge. The normal Larry Bird attempt for a three-pointer usually involves a look at his feet, a second look at the basket, a conscious decision to take the shot.

There was no deciding here. He unloaded without hesitation, and the ball cut through the net and landed with a thump on the floor that matched the falling Knicks' hearts. The lead now was 21 points.

"It was the same type of shot I took in the final game in Houston when we won the title," Larry Bird said. "I knew if I made the shot the game would be over."

The aftermath was almost more harried than the game. For a half-hour, for 45 minutes, he stood in the middle of cameras and reporters while his teammates were allowed to dress and leave. He was man of the day, man of the hour, man of the moment. He was the story.

"When did you know you'd have a great game?" Larry Bird was asked.

"When there was one minute and 55 seconds left and I was on the bench," he said. "You can't say you'll have a great game before or during a game. You can only say it after the game."

Say it now. He had a great game.

Grand Theft Motto

June 1, 1984 • by Leigh Montville

The time is 12:04 in the morning, Cedric Maxwell has taken the final inbounds pass from Larry Bird, and there isn't a Los Angeles Laker in sight.

The time has gone down to zero seconds on the big cube in the middle of the Boston Garden. The noise is everywhere. Maxwell has thrown the ball backward over his left shoulder.

Take this one home, darling. Take it home and save it in a special place.

The Celtics are alive somehow, anyhow, tell me how. They have defeated the Lakers in a 124-121 overtime grinder last night that they lost a half-dozen times and won a half-dozen more.

No, make that seven more. They won it the final time, too, didn't they?

The play to remember was Gerald Henderson's steal and layup with 13 seconds left in regulation time. Play to remember? Tell me what Celtics broadcaster Johnny Most was saying. Was he still on his feet at the end of his description? Tell me now. Save me the money when the record is pressed— *Henderson Stole The Ball!*

This was a play to tack onto the wall with all the other storied plays in Celtics history. Havlicek stealing the ball. Sam Jones pounding home that strange shot. Don Nelson and the other strange shot in LA. Frank Selvy missing the layup that could have won the game.

The situation was as dire as could be for the Celtics. Dire? They were gone, dead, finito.

The Lakers had a 113-111 lead that looked as big as a 14-0 pounding at Fenway Park going into the ninth. Kevin McHale had missed two straight foul shots—both back-rim jobs—and Worthy had grabbed the rebound. The Lakers had the lead and the ball with 20 seconds left when they called the timeout.

What did they have to do? Prance a little? Dance a little? They didn't even have to shoot. They could wait for the inevitable foul shots and go home with the victory. People were leaving the Garden and a certain Academy Award winner in a black shirt and sunglasses was screaming terms of endearment from the loge seats at his favorite team from Los Angeles.

What kind of chance did the Celtics have? None, until . . .

The Lakers' Magic Johnson passed inbounds to James Worthy and James Worthy passed to . . . oops, Gerald Henderson.

There he was, a water sprite on the move, anticipating the pass as if it were ticked out in advance in Morse code. Here he came on the fly.

"A big part of the play was Cedric Maxwell," Henderson said. "He put good pressure on the inbounds pass, forcing Magic to throw it to Worthy. You always want to put the ball in the hands of the big guy in that situation.

"He threw the ball high. It was hung out there for me."

The pass was as good as any fast-break pass the Celtics had thrown all night. The little guard zipped to the basket and dropped in the layup with 13 seconds left. The spectators who were on their way out suddenly had to turn around and find a seat somewhere in the middle of bedlam.

The Lakers, of course, had a chance to win the game now. They had a timeout, a tie score and the ball. And 13 seconds of time to operate.

They never took a shot. They weren't able to throw the ball in to Kareem Abdul-Jabbar, the leading scorer of all time and all of that. They weren't able to shake anyone free as the Celtics pressed everywhere. Magic Johnson only had stopped his dribble as the horn sounded. His pass and Bob McAdoo's attempted shot were late.

The overtime? How many times can the Celtics climb out of the grave? Dead again, trailing by three points—118-115—with Kareem churning into his big hook shot. Down by five? Nope, Kareem misses, Larry Bird grabs the rebound and there is Henderson again, flying away.

He scores the basket, is fouled on the play, makes the shot. Tie game. The Celts are alive again.

Go from there to the finish. The finish! The Celtics are dead again. They are trailing, 121-120. There are 14 seconds left. Scott Wedman has the ball in the corner, 13 feet from the basket. Scott Wedman? He hits the jumper.

Tell me this. What did Johnny say about that shot? Was he still standing? How about Robert Parish's steal at the other end as Bob McAdoo tried to drive with eight seconds? Tell me about that, Johnny. Say the words. Robert Parish, bending down, a 7-foot man knocking away a dribble. *Robert Parish Stole The Ball!* Tell me again, so I don't have to buy the record.

There are finishes . . . and there are *finishes*. This was one to fold between the covers of the old Celtics annual. This was one to hang on the wall.

This was one to put on the ark when the nearby river comes by the house at any moment. This was a saver.

It Was a Heart Attack

June 7, 1984 • by Leigh Montville

INGLEWOOD, Calif.—Never underestimate the Boston Celtics.

Never pull the blanket over their closed eyes until you've checked their pulse a half-dozen times. Even more. Never say they're finished until you've made sure that every person in the building has gone home, the results have been printed in the newspaper and, say, summer has arrived and one last basketball isn't being dribbled in one last gym in the United States of America.

Never—absolutely never—say "never" when this organization is involved.

Calling down all the memories, lighting all the votive lights from the past, cutting out a nice little piece of tradition from those flags from the Garden ceiling, this Celtics team walked into its own spotlight of glory last night. How to describe it? One more overtime win. One 129-125 stunner over the Los Angeles Lakers to tie this best-of-seven NBA final series at 2-2.

"This may be the first team in the history of basketball to win the NBA title without leading a game during regulation!" a man exclaimed in the fabulous Forum pressroom last night.

Almost. How to describe it?

Unilaterally predicted to be on the way toward doom—or at least an early series goodbye—against a powerhouse outfit that was running them ragged, the Celtics put up a hand, curled it into a fist and stopped their own demise. Nothing pretty. Nothing tinged with magic. They went into the middle of the Forum asylum and hammered out this win, took it away by force.

They changed the game the same way someone looks in a mirror and changes his outlook on life,

giving up smoking and fast living. They did it with stronger willpower.

"Not so fast," they said to the hordes of Laker gazelles.

"Stop and pay the toll," they said again and again and again.

"Make the layup," they added. "But pay the damn price."

Trailing, 68-58, to open the second half—in a series in which the leader at the end of the half always has been the eventual winner—the Celtics brought the game back to hard-rock, small-town-gym basketball. They inserted a hard edge of nastiness into the proceedings. They made this an emotional, tough basketball game.

The picture that characterized the change best was Kevin McHale of the Celtics knocking the Lakers' Kurt Rambis from here to Orange County. Rambis was thumping down the court on one of those Lakers fast breaks that killed the Celtics in Sunday's 33-point loss. He was in the air. The Forum crowd was ready for a fine, genteel explosion.

McHale just leveled the Laker. He arrived with a forearm that would have made him a fine part of the Los Angeles Raiders' defensive backfield. Rambis went flying. McHale went flying. Everybody suddenly wanted to fight everybody else.

"It's a different ballgame now," was McHale's message. "You like to play the other way. Let's see if you like to play this way."

The Lakers didn't like it.

The Magic Man, Earvin Johnson, who had run around the court in the first quarter for 11 points and a star-quality opening, suddenly was slow and hesitant. Kareem Abdul-Jabbar, registering points with that old machine-like ease, suddenly was a human being. He was throwing elbows at Larry Bird. He was yelling at Bird, at the referees, at anyone within yelling range.

The big Lakers' break was gone. The Celtics were going to work.

"How did they win?" you ask. "How, exactly, did they win?"

They won with ugly second shots. They won with Larry Bird, troubled with his shooting all night, forcing his way inside for those rebound shots, then returning to form at the foul line and with that sweetheart 13-foot fallaway with 16 seconds left. They won with Dennis Johnson and Robert (The

Chief) Parish—damned so often at the end of the third game that it seemed as if their pictures were on post-office walls—throwing their hearts on the Forum floor and going to work.

What about the overtime? How about Gerald Henderson, missing two foul shots, then stepping to the line and drilling the next two? How about DJ, unconsciously drilling four foul shots in the stretch? How about M. L. Carr and that celebratory dunk? How about Larry?

Never underestimate the Celtics. Never underestimate Larry.

"Sissies," he called his teammates after Sunday's game.

"We have to go to the hospital for 12 heart transplants," he said.

"We're going to win the World Championship," he also said.

He was everywhere as usual at the end of the game. Taking every shot in his bag. Doing everything he could. He was a vision from the olden times. Russell. Sharman. Cousy. Havlicek. Sam Jones, off the glass.

It is repetitive, a cliche to talk about Pride and Tradition and all that other syrupy glop, but what are you going to do? Send home the ambulance. Call off the folks from Waterman's. The men in the green shirts are coming home and the series is tied.

Never—no, never—say "never." Not with these guys.

Bird Brings the Heat as LA Goes Cold

June 9, 1984 • by Dan Shaughnessy

It was like the Fourth of July on the Esplanade. Through the steamy heat and haze, the maestro worked his magic and a storied Boston institution thrilled the assembled masses with a traditional performance of harmony and brilliance.

The Boston Celtics have taken their great expectations to the edge of flag 15. On a night on which a Bermuda air mass transformed the Causeway Street

train station into a fountain of sweat and Laker sorrow, the Celtics defeated the Los Angeles Lakers, 121-103, to take a 3-2 lead in the NBA best-of-seven championship series.

The victory was orchestrated by Mr. White Heat, Larry Bird. Bird broke out of a four-game shooting slump with 34 points (15 of 20 from the floor). He added 17 rebounds and controlled the night. He was equal parts Arthur Fiedler, Bobby Orr, and Andrew Wyeth. His teammates, especially Dennis Johnson, were similarly inspired and creative.

It was a game marked by absence of malice and of Los Angeles running, plus a sudden surge of Celtic board strength and defense. The Celtics outrebounded the Lakers, 51-37, and held LA to an unthinkable shooting percentage of .428 (39-91). It was easily the Lakers' worst shooting night of the playoffs.

Lakers coach Pat Riley had portrayed the Celtics as nothing less than basketball's Hell's Angels after Game 4 in the Forum, but Bird and the oppressive heat (97 degrees) were the most physical forces last night. Referee Hugh Evans left at halftime due to dehydration, Robert Parish sat out a stretch of the second half due to a leg cramp, and Bird was wrapped in towels when he wasn't playing.

The Celtics led by only two at the half, but it seemed to be Boston's kind of game. The Lakers were held to nine fast-break points in the first two quarters, six in the third and none in the fourth. Kareem Abdul-Jabbar (7 of 25 overall) struggled badly, and Dennis Johnson took the Magic from Earvin Johnson (9 shots, 5 rebounds, 13 assists, 10 points).

It started to get away from the Lakers when the Celtics opened the third period with a 13-3 run. Cedric Maxwell scored eight of the 13 with six free throws and a conversion of a Gerald Henderson feed. The other five came from Bird, who hit a rainbow and capped the crunching drive with a preposterous three-pointer. That made it 68-56. The Lakers never got closer than three. Boston's lead was up to 21 when Bird scored on a pretty drive as he was fouled with four minutes left.

"The man who made the difference was Bird," said Riley. "He was just awesome. He made everything work. He was the catalyst, and that's what happens when great players come to the front."

IT'S ANOTHER BANNER YEAR

CELTICS HOIST FLAG NO. 15

June 13, 1984 • by Leigh Montville

The celebration began with 26 seconds left in the evening. Larry Bird came running toward Dennis Johnson at the top of the foul circle in front of the Boston Celtics' bench and the two players stretched their right arms into the air and jumped.

Hello, America. Take a look at the new, old and perpetual world champions of basketball.

The Celtics had done it again.

"Pow!" Larry Bird said to Dennis Johnson as they exchanged high fives.

"Pow!" Dennis Johnson replied.

There were a few finishing touches to be added to the 111-102 victory in the seventh, winner-take-all game with the Los Angeles Lakers last night at the Garden, but there was no more doubt about what would happen. The Celts had done what they had said they would do all along.

"We're going to win the world championship," Bird had predicted as far back as two weeks ago, minutes after the Celtics had lost by 33 points and trailed in the series, 2-1. "This was just a step on the way."

"It's over," reserve forward M. L. Carr had said as recently as Monday night. "If the Lakers want to win a championship, they're going to have to play in a summer rec league. We're going to win this one."

Call it self-confidence. Call it arrogance. Call it whatever you want, but the Celtics flapped and fumed and fueled their way to this championship with their own mouths.

They yelled at the Lakers. They yelled at the press. They even yelled at themselves. No team in recent memory in any sport—not the L.A.-Oakland Raiders, not the Oakland A's, not the Big Bad Bruins—ever talked a better game and then went out and played it.

Danny Ainge (44) and the Celtics bench get the celebration started in the final minutes of Game 7.

Larry Bird implores the giddy crowd to stay off the Garden floor in the final moments of Game 7.

No matter what happened, these Celtics believed in themselves. That was their strength.

Down 1-0 in the series, trailing by two at the close of regulation? No problem. Gerald Henderson will steal the ball and tie the game. We'll win in overtime.

Down 2-1 in the series, trailing by 11 in the second half? No problem. Kevin McHale will knock Kurt Rambis into South America with a diving forearm. The entire game will be changed again. We'll win again in overtime.

Heat in the fifth game? Lovely. The Lakers won't have a chance. They'll be spun dizzy and stupid. No celebration after the sixth game, the Lakers beginning to run again? Forget it. Winning at home will be a lot more fun.

"Too bad we didn't win in LA," Cedric Maxwell said. "I figured on playing a little blackjack in Las Vegas at night. I already had the reservations."

He and Carr somehow were the masters of ceremony to it all, Larry Bird was the star, doing the rallying around all green and white flags on the floor. Max and M. L. were the chatters, the disturbers.

"Choke," Maxwell said to James Worthy and the Lakers in that fourth game, putting his hand to his throat and never denying what the motion meant.

Who says and does things like that in professional sport? Who? He was treating the NBA Finals as if they were some sort of league playoffs between two high schools that hate each other. Is that something that any other player would do?

Probably one. M. L. Carr.

"This team was going to do what it had to do," M. L. Carr said. "If it meant out-shooting 'em, we'd out-shoot 'em. If it meant out-rebounding 'em, we'd out-rebound 'em. If it meant out-fighting 'em, we'd out-fight 'em.

"This team would do what it had to do."

Bird—the unanimous MVP—was a starting point of everything. When he was going badly, he still kept going. He kept fighting, rolling, coming up with more rebounds than a man his size possibly should grab. When he was going well, the Celtics were flying.

He brought all the parts of his game into focus. He shot, he was on the boards, he passed, he edged into the passing lanes for little, sneaky deflections. When there seemed to be trouble in the house, he screamed.

"Played like sissies," was his most memorable quote after the third game.

"My teammates have to get me the ball," was his second most memorable quote after the sixth game. "If they get me the ball, we'll win it."

They got him the ball. The Celtics won it.

The sum—as Celtics tradition always has said it should be—was larger than the major parts.

There was Robert Parish, silent and unsmiling, latched onto the goggles of Lakers' center Kareem Abdul-Jabbar for the second half of the series. Headaches? Maybe the biggest one Kareem had was the man called The Chief. There was Dennis Johnson, criticized for his shooting, for his defense, for his personality in the first half of the series. He was shooting well, defending Magic Johnson into a haze, smiling at the end.

Gerald Henderson—*Henderson stole the ball!* He also shot without fear. Whenever needed. There was Scott Wedman, off the bench, hitting jumpers until he was injured. There was Danny Ainge, hitting his stride in the second and seventh games. There was Quinn Buckner, rolling in for defensive minutes. There was Kevin McHale, hero at home, bumbler on the road.

There was Max.

After Bird and DJ did their sloppy high fives, Maxwell went to the middle of the court with M. L. They went into a routine as choreographed as a Solid Gold special. Maxwell leaped. M. L. leaped.

"Pow!" Max said.

"Pow," M. L. returned.

Hello, America. It all happened just the way these guys said it would.

He Gave a Max-imum Effort

CEDRIC ROSE TO THE OCCASION FOR CELTICS IN FINAL GAME

June 13, 1984 • by Bob Ryan

He was lurking deep in the offensive bulrushes for the entire series. The attention had been focused on just about everybody else.

Get Larry Bird shots, get Robert Parish shots, get something out of Kevin McHale, hope those guards deposit all those open jumpers . . . nobody ever mentioned the possibility of getting the ball in deep to Cedric Maxwell.

But when the call came, *ooohhh*, was he ready. Start thinking about game-ball citations and you start thinking about Maxwell, whose 24 points (17 in the first half), 8 rebounds and 8 assists were crucial as the Celtics won championship No. 15, 111-102, over the Lakers last night.

"Max was ready," related assistant coach Chris Ford. "Max said before the game—really, after the sixth game—'Just ride my shoulders, guys.' He was really determined. He wanted the ball."

Cedric Maxwell maneuvers around a towering Kareem Abdul-Jabbar during Game 7.

His first attempt to score was a negated basket on which Darell Garretson called an offensive foul. That might have been the last bad thing to happen to him. It was evident from the start that he would be an integral part of the Celtics' offense. It was almost like the early days of the Maxwell career, when he parlayed his tremendous inside agility into many big scoring nights.

By halftime, Max had sunk 11 of 13 free-throw attempts. The Lakers appeared confused, as if they had forgotten how dexterous Maxwell is inside.

It was a vintage Maxwell performance, in that, mixed in with his scoring, was some superb offensive rebounding (five of his eight on the offensive end) and some intelligent passing. Max long ago established himself as the master of the inside-out pass to the wing man, and this skill was shown in the third period when he kept feeding Gerald Henderson for open jump shots. Max even put a little whipped cream on his sundae by swishing his first and only set shot attempt of the series in the third period, when the Celtics were singeing the LA inside double-teams for eight perimeter jumpers.

So easily were the Celtics getting the ball inside to Maxwell during the first half that it was necessary to inquire if there had been some technical adjustments made prior to the game. The answer was "No." It was just Maxwell conducting a postgraduate course in pivot play.

Maxwell had taken home the 1981 Finals MVP prize with a number of displays like this one. But in this series he simply hadn't been called upon to do much more offensively than to hang around waiting for a second shot. The Celtics obviously realized he was still capable of more involvement.

"The Lakers were so worried about stopping Larry [Bird]," said Danny Ainge, "that Max had some great openings. We all know how great he can be, and tonight he rose to the occasion."

Henderson Dealt to SuperSonics

October 17, 1984 • by Dan Shaughnessy

HOUSTON—He was a Boston Celtic when he returned from a late-morning practice at The Summit. By dinnertime, he was a Seattle SuperSonic, sitting alone in his Westin Galleria hotel room as his former teammates boarded a bus for a preseason game with Houston.

Three days after signing a contract that will pay him $350,000 per season, Gerald Henderson was traded to the Sonics for a 1986 first-round draft pick late yesterday afternoon.

Henderson's agent, Scott Lang, was hot.

"We feel we have been deceived," said Lang. "They negotiated in bad faith and were totally unethical. There's no way you decide you're trading a guard on a championship team in a three-day period. I would say this represents a vast departure from the negotiating practices the Celtics are known for when dealing with their own players.

" . . . They can do what they want when it comes to trading a player, but don't impose their distorted and perverted sense of fairness on Henderson and then ship him off somewhere."

Celtics general manager Jan Volk, who handled most of the negotiating in the Henderson deal, responded by saying, "That sounds to me like someone feeling very badly about the job they did for their client."

Henderson, a career Celtic and starting guard for the 1984 champions, maintained that he'd settled for less money to stay in Boston.

"It's pretty hard," said Henderson, 28. "I was pretty much stunned and shook up. This was the last thing I felt would happen after going through all this negotiating. There was some positive reinforcement that nothing like this would happen. I honestly feel a little deceived. When I signed, I thought everything was settled as far as the fact that there wouldn't be a trade."

"That certainly was not part of the deal," countered Celtics president Red Auerbach from his home in Washington. "I was there. I've never broken my word, and I never will. Gerald's a fine basketball player, but he did make one mistake. He told K. C. he was in shape, and he came in horrible shape. Missing training camp really hurt him."

Henderson missed Boston's first four exhibition games. He signed Friday, then played six minutes against Utah in Las Vegas Sunday night, and struggled.

After the Celtics were approached by the Sonics, coach K. C. Jones and his staff reviewed Seattle's proposal and gave Volk the go-ahead to make the deal.

"It was my decision in the end," said Jones. "I had problems with it, but it made basketball sense to me. This alleviates a minutes problem and leaves an opening for our young people."

Henderson's departure also lops $350,000 off the payroll and gives the Celtics two No. 1 draft picks in 1986. The Celtics undoubtedly considered the fact that the Seattle franchise is on the way down and might not make the playoffs in 1986. If that happens, Boston's pick will have a 1-in-7 shot at becoming the top selection in the draft. A lottery system is now used to determine the order of selection for the seven non-playoff teams.

Bird-Erving Fight Mars Celtics' Win

November 10, 1984 • by Dan Shaughnessy

It started as a Celtics-Sixers Five-Star Special, developed into an impressive Boston blowout, then deteriorated into an ugly street fight featuring the improbable ejection of two of the game's most storied players.

On a night when the Celtics bolted to a 24-point third-quarter lead over the heretofore undefeated Sixers and Larry Joe Bird threatened to rewrite the Boston record book, the Garden floorboards suddenly looked like post World Series downtown Detroit.

As a result, Boston's impressive 130-119 victory will be nothing more than a forgettable footnote when Garden groupies and basketball bards speak of the night that Bird and His Highness Julius Erving were ejected for fighting.

Boston led by 20 and Bird had 42 points in only 30 minutes when the old train station became a backboard jungle.

The seeds for chaos had been planted when referee Jack Madden injured his right knee and left the game with 8½ minutes left in the third period. Dick Bavetta had to do a Charles Lindbergh the rest of the way and encountered more turbulence than he could handle. It was like leaving Barney Fife in charge of Hill Street Precinct.

Meanwhile, Bird and Erving were emerging as a combustible duo. Erving had been in Bird's torture chamber all night, as Bird hit 17 of 23 shots. In the first half, he canned 12 of 17, scored 29 points and held Doc to one basket on nine attempts. Erving (3 for 13) didn't get any better after intermission, and by the end of the third, the good doctor was looking for a quiet private practice in the Berkshires.

"I'm sure Doc was getting frustrated," said Cedric Maxwell. "When a guy's got 42 points on you in 30 minutes, you've got to do something at that point to try to get him out of his game."

After Bird was called for an offensive foul (charging into Erving, adding an elbow for good measure), he and the Doc exchanged words as they

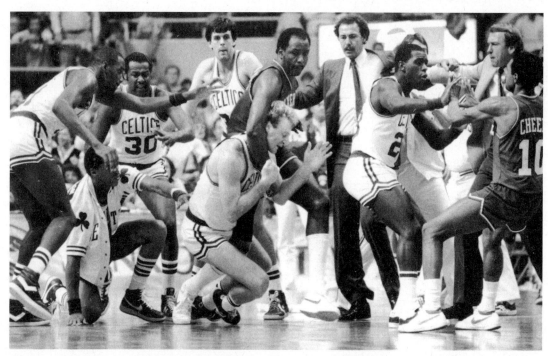

The Sixers' Moses Malone puts Larry Bird in a headlock (center) during a preseason fight between the rivals.

crossed midcourt. Bird gave the Doctor another elbow (as in, "Take two of these and call me in the morning") and all hell broke loose.

Bird was swinging as he was grabbed by Moses Malone (24 points, 15 rebounds and a poor attempt as peacemaker). Erving commenced jabbing, Malone got Bird into a headlock (with some help from Charles Barkley), and both benches emptied. Malone ended up tangling briefly with M. L. Carr, and Bird wanted a piece of just about everybody.

Bird and Erving refused comment after the game.

After the fracas, Bavetta gave Bird and Erving the obligatory heave. The ejection is the first of Erving's distinguished career and should do wonders for the sale of sneakers and a computer game that are jointly endorsed by Bird and Erving.

"Heck, it was no big deal," said Maxwell. "Neither one of 'em could bust a grapefruit."

Silence Is Golden

The unparalleled winning record of K. C. Jones speaks louder than his words.

November 26, 1984 • by Dan Shaughnessy

DALLAS—A soft-spoken man in a profession dominated by blowhards, K. C. Jones never has developed a knack for self-promotion. He's not particularly quotable, rarely gets thrown out of games, and doesn't make moves or comments that bring attention to himself or his coaching. He has, in fact, done little to publicly discourage the widespread notion that the multitalented Celtics could be adequately coached by your mailman.

Jones coaches the way he played—quietly, unselfishly, without headlines.

The results are the same. He wins.

An argument can be made that Jones is the winningest person in the history of basketball. He won two NCAA championships, an Olympic gold medal, eight NBA championships in a nine-year career, and directed the 1984 Celtics to a championship in his first year at the wheel. He has been a part of the second-longest winning streak in NCAA history (San Francisco won 56 straight), and the longest streak in

NBA history (Jones was an assistant coach when LA won 33 straight in 1972).

He has an extra pair of NBA championship rings from his years as an assistant coach, and in his three-year stint as head coach in Washington, the Bullets won more games than any NBA team. His only losing season in the last 20 years was when he was head coach of the ABA's San Diego Conquistadors, but he still took his team to the playoffs.

The 1985 Celtics are 11-1 as they prepare to meet the Dallas Mavericks in Reunion Arena tomorrow night. Boston's 135-124 victory over the Kansas City Kings Saturday raised Jones' Celtic coaching mark to 73-21 (.777) and put his lifetime NBA head coaching record at 228-112 (.671).

Despite all of the above, Jones is always overlooked when fans and media start throwing the credit around. He's noticed his lack of notice.

"It's always been a prevalent thought that when a team is very talented, you can just drop anybody in there and they can do the coaching," Jones says. "I just leave it alone. The people who want to think that way already have their answer. If I get into thinking about it, it takes my mind off the club . . . Does it bother me that I don't get the recognition? No, as long as these guys win games. That's my reward and that's what will keep me on the job."

Does Jones think any other coach could get as much out of these Celtics as he does?

"I doubt it," he answers.

There is evidence that Jones may be the perfect man for this Boston team. He's a communicator on a team with players that often face problems with playing time. He does not overreact and provides a light touch—important elements with a veteran team. He's also an ex-player (which players love), and an ex-Celtic (which Red Auerbach loves). He is not threatened by Celtic tradition because his fiber is woven into the flags he coaches under.

Bill Fitch could never cope with the flags and had trouble coping with his veteran Celtics in his final days. Fitch and Jones were never tight. Jones describes working under Fitch as "almost impossible" because "I was just being kept on the other side of the fence."

Shedding his vest of humility for a moment, Jones adds, "I'm awfully smart at the game of pro basketball. I've spent a lot of time in it as a player and a coach. My record is a combination of myself and my players. I could be a genius at the game and try to get that point across to the world, but I prefer having my players come across as geniuses."

Where the Heart Is

Even as his hoop legend grows, Larry Bird still fits in on the streets of French Lick.

February 3, 1985 • by Bob Ryan

FRENCH LICK, Ind.—They say it's really no big deal when Larry comes home. The townspeople are proud of him, all right, but as far as bugging him, or asking for autographs, uh-uh.

The problem is outsiders. "They come to the high school," says athletic director Larry Pritchett, "and they say, 'Do you have a bookstore? We need something that says Larry Bird on it? We need something to take home to the grandchildren.'" There is, of course, no bookstore, not in a high school with an enrollment of fewer than 300 students.

It's especially bad in the summertime. People are forever stopping in front of the Bird house (which isn't hard to find, given that it is the only residence in Orange County with a full-length basketball court, complete with glass backboards, in the front yard), snapping pictures and hoping to get a glimpse of the player. Says Larry's older brother Mark, "It's definitely the most traveled road in town."

The locals haven't exactly ignored Larry. Springs Valley High School's address is 101 Larry Bird Blvd., and the street sign is at least 15 feet high and is painted to resemble a basketball. They're very proud of Larry Bird, but when he's back they treat him as one of Georgia Bird's kids, not as the greatest basketball player who has ever lived. "He knows he'll always have his privacy here," says Pritchett.

There is one gratifying thing about paying a visit to French Lick. No one here has the audacity to claim that he or she somehow knew, somehow felt it in his or her bones, that Larry Bird, brother of Mike, Linda, Mark, Jeff and Eddie, would become the individual standard of excellence for future generations of basketball players.

They did know that Larry's primary interest in life was basketball, but that hardly distinguished him from hundreds of thousands of young Indianians who have gone before him, given that basketball is the mother's milk of Indiana sports life. Lots of young Hoosiers dream about playing for Indiana University and going on to the NBA, but Larry Bird wasn't one of them.

"Nope," admits Bird. "I never thought of anything like that. I just lived day to day. Playing basketball was just something I liked to do. Matter of fact, I still live day to day, although I have a little more security now."

Neither Georgia Bird nor brother Mark can recall young Larry ever mentioning being a college star, let alone playing in the NBA. "I do remember Larry liking Bill Walton, though," says his mother.

"Maybe," counters Mark Bird, "but the truth is that the only idol Larry ever had was Cher. That's right. Cher Bono. All he ever talked about was Cher when she and Sonny had that show on TV."

However strong Cher's appeal, basketball still came first. "I'd get up in the morning and the first thing on my mind would be playing ball," says Bird. "I'd go right to the gym after the first period in school. I couldn't wait to get back to the gym again. When school was out, it was no different. And it didn't hurt that at one time we lived right next door to some outdoor courts."

The Birds did a lot of moving mainly because Larry's father had an unstable work history due to a drinking problem. With constant family turmoil, basketball was an important outlet for a shy, skinny kid who was never encouraged by anyone to have any interest in matters intellectual. Basketball, it can truthfully be said, became Larry Bird's life.

It wasn't until the early fall of 1973 that Pritchett was made aware that life in French Lick was going to be more interesting than usual during that school year. Gary Holland had just taken over as head basketball coach at Springs Valley High after spending time as assistant to Jim Jones. "I hadn't talked a whole lot to Gary during the offseason," explains Pritchett, "but one day he walked up to me in the hall and said, 'We've got an All-State.' I said, 'Larry's that good, huh?' And he said, 'Do you realize he's up to 6-foot-6½ now?' and I had to admit I hadn't."

Bird had missed almost his entire sophomore year with a broken leg. (Typically, he refused to attend games if he couldn't participate. "Larry is not patient enough to sit down and watch," says Holland.) As a 6-2 junior he spent much of his time feeding senior star Steve Land. He was a decent high school player, nothing more. Then came the growth spurt. Unlike countless others, as he grew he lost none of his coordination.

TALENT EXPLODES
IN SENIOR YEAR

Larry Bird's senior year at Springs Valley will not soon be forgotten. He averaged 30 points and 17 rebounds a game. In one game he had 54 points and 38 rebounds. With Bird on his way to coach Holland's predicted All-State status, Springs Valley was able to pay back Patoka Lake Conference rivals such as Paoli, Orleans and Shoals for past indignities.

Were Larry Bird never to play a minute of college or professional ball, he would still be the object of adulation in French Lick solely because he had done so much for the town as a high school player. To paraphrase Jacques Barzun, "He who would understand the heart and mind of Indiana must understand Indiana high school basketball."

How important is it? Take the gymnasium at Springs Valley High. There are no rollaway bleachers. This is not a multipurpose school assembly hall. This is, by God, a house of basketball, intended for that purpose only. There are 2,700 bleacher-type seats firmly embedded in concrete. There is tremendous space in between the sidelines and the first row of seats. To play on this court is a privilege, not easily earned.

Color photos adorn the walls. Most of the pictures are of the better Springs Valley teams, such as the 1958 squad that actually went to the state finals, or Larry's senior squad, which went as far as the regionals. There is even a picture of a state championship cheerleading squad. And there is one individual photo, hovering above the doorway leading from the lobby to the arena itself. It's a tall, skinny kid wearing No. 33. Care to guess?

The games are carried on radio station WFLO-FM, with Springs Valley Herald sportswriter Kevin Smith on the play-by-play and Springs Valley high school teacher (and former head football coach) Chuck Akers as the color man. An astonishingly complete game program is available for a quarter and worth at least five times as much. It is very easy to conclude that nothing more important than a Springs Valley Black Hawks basketball game ever happens in town, and that's probably a correct assumption.

Basketball in this state is a religious experience. The state tournament dates from 1911, and to have a stickout team is a badge of tremendous honor. When a quiet unpretentious town such as French Lick comes up with a stickout team, the entire community is uplifted.

FRENCH LICK DRAWS
VACATIONERS

French Lick and neighboring West Baden, in reality, they are one corporate entity, are located in Orange County, in south-central Indiana. Bird has gotten many laughs by describing himself as "The hick from French Lick," but Midwesterners are quite aware of the town, because it has been a vacation haven for over a century and a half, or ever since the discovery of mineral springs there. A resort hotel was first built in the 1840s. When that first hotel burned down around 1900, a bigger, better hotel was built in 1901 and today the French Lick Springs Resort Hotel is a showplace encompassing some 2,000 acres of property.

From 1904 to 1949 gambling flourished, and locals tell the stories about the comingling of gangsters and politicians at the casino. Indeed, one of the favorite Bird family tales concerns the day that Larry's grandfather was given a $100 tip by Al Capone, an annual visitor, for carrying his bags. The hotel remains a major French Lick employer, exceeded in scope only by Kimball International, manufacturer of pianos and organs among other things.

But townspeople seldom have anything to do with the hotel that is not work-oriented. Says Georgia Bird, a lifelong resident of the Valley, "I had never set foot inside the hotel until they had a basketball banquet when Larry was a senior in high school."

The locals go their own way, pausing only to gaze longingly at some of the big cars that transport wealthy Midwesterners to their weekend of luxury inside the hotel. Daily life for the average resident of the Valley is not what an urban sophisticate would call exciting. "Bob Woolf couldn't wait to get out of here," recalls Georgia Bird. "I don't even think he lasted a day."

Orange County is among the poorer counties in the state, and the Birds were not overburdened with luxuries. But whereas Larry never had to worry about feeling out of place without fine clothes and other possessions in French Lick, he practically fell apart when he matriculated to Indiana University and discovered what other kids had. "I roomed with Jim Wiseman," Bird recalls, "and we shared a closet. I had a few pairs of pants, a few shirts and not much else. His stuff took over 95 percent of the closet, and it's not like he was all that rich. Everywhere I looked it was like that. I couldn't cope."

And Larry being Larry, he wouldn't ask for anything, either. As limited as her resources were, his mother would have helped him as much as she could, but he wouldn't ask.

"Larry never wanted anything from any of us," she says. "Even in high school, he wouldn't ask for a ring, a jacket or anything."

AN EXCUSE TO EXIT IU

Bird finally left IU after refusing to pay for a fee in a recreation course involving, of all things, bowling. He said that since he was on a basketball scholarship, he shouldn't have to pay, but the truth is that the fee was an excuse. Larry never wanted to go to Indiana in the first place.

"I believe," says Georgia Bird, "he was influenced by his father and his coach to go there."

Suffice it to say that the year and a half following graduation from high school in June 1974 was a tumultuous time in the life of Larry Bird. He went through the recruiting hassle (which, according to his mother, included then Purdue coach Fred Schaus crying over the phone when Larry told him he was going to IU), married and divorced a high school sweetheart and had to absorb the shocking news that his father had taken his own life. Throw in his culture shock at Indiana, and he was a psychological mess.

"I was 17½ when I got out of high school," Bird says, "and what I should have done was sit out a whole year right then, no matter where I went. I should have gone in with the idea of redshirting a year."

The rest is well-documented about how Larry dropped out of IU, briefly enrolled at tiny Northwood Institute in West Baden, left that school and then went to work for the French Lick Recreation Department. He went into AAU ball and was simply a monster. Tired of being bugged by people about his plans, he began telling everyone he wasn't sure what he was going to do. But he was. "I got so tired of people telling me what I should do," Larry explains, "but I always knew I'd go play for some college." Enter Indiana State assistant Bill Hodges. Terre Haute was more to Larry's liking than Bloomington, and so Bird became an Indiana State Sycamore.

GEORGIA BIRD AWAITS HER DISH

Georgia Bird is a legitimate basketball fan, so much so that she was unhappy about losing cable TV when she moved into her present house. "Larry promised me a dish," she sighs, "but he hasn't gotten around to it." She keeps close track of Larry's career, and she is the proud custodian of Larry Bird scrapbooks.

"Everything has worked out," she says. "I think Larry is better off not having gone to IU. Bobby Knight might have put him into a slot and not given him the freedom he needed on the court. And I think he was just born to be a Boston Celtic."

Whatever he was born to be, he decided to make himself a basketball player. Some say his first goal was to outdo brother Mark, a fine player for Springs Valley who played good small college ball and now donates time to coach the seventh-grade team. (Mark never tires of pointing out to Larry that he, Mark, is No. 5 on the one-season Springs Valley free throw percentage list at .792, while Larry is not even in the top 10.)

"I think he got some of his court awareness by playing with me and our brother Mike," contends Mark. "He'd do a lot of passing. He was always better than the other kids his age. He also took to coaching. Jim Jones would say that one man can't win or lose a game, and that got through to a lot of kids in this town."

Throughout high school, Bird's basketball playing time was not restricted to formal team practice. Says Holland, "It was not unusual for people around here to turn on the lights of the gym and play what we called 'get-up' games until midnight." Agrees Bird, "Coach Jones had us down there at 6 a.m. sometimes. He'd let us in the gym whenever school was out. He'd even give us haircuts there. He was a hell of a guy." (Jones is now the coach at Princeton,

Ind., which some may identify as the home town of Gil Hodges.)

ANOTHER BIRD ON THE COURT

Holland isn't quite as aggressive as Jones, and so today's Springs Valley Black Hawks need to be a bit more self-motivated. One of those kids is 6-5 junior forward Eddie Bird, the last of Georgia's six offspring. He is a 20-points-per-game scorer, a definite Division I prospect, and the unwilling heir to a frightening legacy. It's tough enough being 18 these days, without being Larry Bird's brother.

The constant refrain heard concerning Eddie is, "He doesn't work hard enough." Kids Mark, "At his age, Larry directed his energy toward basketball. Eddie directs his toward girls."

Maybe so, but his game does reveal the unmistakable influence of You Know Who. After all, they do play together during the summer even if Larry hasn't seen Eddie play an organized game since sixth grade. When Eddie gets the ball, he immediately looks inside to the post before thinking about shooting. He has excellent range with his jumper and is a scrappy rebounder. Like Larry, he also loves baseball and has indicated he would like to play both sports in college, if possible.

Eddie has been the recipient of Larry's largesse, and it concerns their mother. It seems that Larry bought Eddie a Trans-Am. "I don't know why he did that," she says. "Don't think we haven't heard about it." You know how small-town tongues can wag.

Well, Larry? "I just wanted him to have it," Bird explains. "He's a good kid, and I just wanted to do it. We didn't even have a family car when I was growing up."

It is the one bit of semiextravagance Bird has allowed himself back in French Lick. The house he built for the family is aptly described as "livable" by his mother. His major preoccupations when he comes back to French Lick are fishing, golfing and working in the yard. He is still Larry, hanging out with his old buddies. If you're looking for his MVP trophy, you'll find it perched on top of a refrigerator in the small studio apartment he uses as a bedroom adjacent to the downstairs family room.

So while he rakes in over $2 million a year, including endorsements, in a sense nothing has changed. There is a framed piece of embroidery on the wall of the family room with the following inscription: "A Bird Can Soar Because He Takes Himself Lightly." The worst thing that could happen to Larry Bird would be for an old French Lick buddy to say. "Geez, Larry, you've changed."

So no matter what heights Larry attains in his profession, no matter where he is forced to earn his living, they will never, ever succeed in taking the French Lick out of Larry Bird. He would not possibly allow it.

McHale's Day to Remember at the Garden

His 56 points set team record as Celtics beat Pistons, 138-129

March 4, 1985 • by Dan Shaughnessy

Imagine O. J. Simpson blocking for Eric Dickerson as the latter runs a sweep to break the NFL's single-season rushing record. Imagine Babe Ruth telling Roger Maris to look for a curveball before Maris steps into the box to hit home run No. 61.

Now close your eyes and imagine Larry Bird throwing one of his Y. A. Tittle bombs, which enabled Kevin McHale to break Bird's single-game, regular-season Celtic scoring mark. It happened yesterday at Boston Garden.

McHale shattered the team single-game (regular season and playoff) scoring mark with a 56-point performance in Boston's 138-129 victory over the Detroit Pistons.

This being a franchise built on team titles rather than personal bests, it seemed appropriate that the new boss was aided by the man who held the record prior to yesterday's game.

John Havlicek, holder of the Celtic single-game playoff high (54 vs. Atlanta in 1973) probably found out about it on the 11 o'clock news. Sam Jones (51 vs. Detroit in '65) might notice if he picks up USA Today this morning. Bob Cousy (46 vs. New York in '60) could have seen it watching cable TV in his Worcester home, listening to the praising phrases of SportsChannel colorman Tom Heinsohn (45 vs. Syracuse in 1961). But Bird was there in person, scoring 30 with 15 rebounds and 10 assists. He passed the ball to the white-hot McHale nine consecutive times down the stretch.

McHale etched his name into Celtic folklore by hitting 22 of 28 floor shots, 12 of 13 from the line. While torching a quartet of defenders (Kent Benson, Major Jones, Earl Cureton and Bill Laimbeer), the 6-foot-10 swingman from Hibbing, Minn., also managed to tie his career rebounding high (16) and find time to block three shots and hand out four assists.

"I'm going to frame the stat sheet and show it to my kid someday," said McHale. "I'll say, 'Look what your old man did one night.'"

McHale's 9-day-old son, Michael Kevin, made his first appearance at the Garden yesterday and was reportedly rendered speechless by his father's performance.

McHale scored 22 in the first quarter, one short of the Celtic record of Heinsohn. He had 31 at the half. Again one shy of the Celtic mark—Ed Macauley and Bill Sharman. Meanwhile, the Celtics had built a 70-60 lead over Isiah Thomas (33 points, 11 assists) & Co.

Benson was McHale's favorite target and got so frustrated in the third quarter that he picked up two technicals and was ejected.

"I think Kent wanted to take himself out to be honest with you," said Bird.

McHale had 43 after three, but didn't score in the first 5 minutes 12 seconds of the final quarter. With just over four minutes to play, he had only 47 points. That's when Bird took matters into his hands.

"In the last three or four minutes, when we had a 10- to 12-point lead, we knew we we're gonna win the game," said Bird. "Kevin had an opportunity to break the record, which is something not many people ever had. Most of his offense came within the flow of the game, but any time you only miss six shots and score 56 points you deserve to get the ball every time down the floor."

With four minutes left, Bird fed McHale for a jump hook (49 points). A few seconds later, both Bird and McHale were alone under the basket. Bird eschewed a layup, passing to McHale for two more (51). McHale went to the line after another Bird feed and missed the first of two. His second shot went in, giving him 52 with 3:05 left. The Celtics led, 134-118, and the Garden scoreboard was keeping everyone informed of McHale's flirtation with stat immortality.

Kevin McHale shoots a free throw for his 56th and final point, setting a Celtics record.

McHale missed a turnaround but beat the pack down the floor after a Piston turnover and caught Bird's touchdown bomb. A base line banker with 2:26 left pushed McHale (54) past Bird's 53-point effort vs. Indiana two years ago.

Havlicek's 54-point playoff mark was the final figure to fall. With 2:03 left, McHale was fouled by Terry Tyler. He made both and came out with 1:12 left.

"You can't explain it," said McHale. "You get warm and guys start looking for you . . . It's a snowball effect."

Does Bird think McHale's record will stand forever?

Bird laughed and said, "It might stand till the next game."

Bird Scores Team Record 60 as Celtics Top Hawks

MCHALE'S NINE-DAY-OLD MARK OF 56 TUMBLES IN 126-115 WIN

March 13, 1985 • by Dan Shaughnessy

NEW ORLEANS—Larry Joe Bird is on the cover of Time magazine this week—where all world figures ultimately land, and there is mounting evidence that he may be basketball's Roy Hobbs—the best there ever was.

It has been a season of epic achievement for Bird. He's won back-to-back games with "gimme the ball" buzzer-beaters, eschewed statistical immortality (a quadruple double) for the good of the team, and helped a teammate break his own scoring record.

Last night, Bird carved a new chapter in Celtic history and sports folklore. Nine days after graciously helping Kevin McHale break his own Celtic scoring record, the Hoosier hoopster went four up on McHale with a 60-point flashdance in a 126-115 victory over the Atlanta Hawks.

Like Babe Ruth, Bird called his shot. When McHale torched the Pistons for 56 on March 3 (breaking Bird's 53-point regular-season and John Havlicek's 54-point playoff record), Bird was asked if he thought McHale's franchise record would stand forever.

"It might stand until the next game," retorted Bird, who had spoon-fed McHale's final nine points, then chastised him for not going for 60.

Bird missed his prediction by one week, shattering the record just four games after McHale's performance. He made 22 of 36 floor shots, and 15 of 16 free throws, in 43 minutes.

"When I'm shooting the ball like that, nobody's going to stop me," said Bird.

You want perspective? Here's perspective. The Boston Celtics have been playing basketball since 1946, and now, in the starry season of 1985, team scoring records established in the first 3,308 (regular-season and playoff) contests have been smashed twice in the last five games.

"I thought 56 was pretty good," said McHale, who assisted Bird by fouling to stop the clock, then passed to him for points 59 and 60 at the buzzer. "But when you can't hold a record like that for 10 days, this must be a pretty tough team to play on."

"It's Kevin's own fault," joked Bird. "He should have gone for 60 that day, and I told him that."

Bird chose an unlikely site for his record, but again, it adds to the fable. Every hoop fan worth his sweatbands knows that Wilt Chamberlain went to the remote outpost of Hershey, Pa., for his storied 100-point game. Now we have Bird, breaking the Celtics record in Lakefront Arena on the campus of New Orleans University. Even Pete Maravich would have been impressed.

It had the feel of an exhibition game at the start. Atlanta had been averaging a pitiful 3,355 at Lakefront, but the Celtics attracted a sellout, and the green crowd cheered the Celts and booed the Hawks all night long. There was even a Carlos Clark banner (Old Miss Loves You Carlos).

"That's why their team is so good," said Atlanta general manager Stan Kasten. "They never have a road game."

Abusing a trio of Hawk defenders, Bird had 12 at the quarter and 23 at the half. The Celtics led by seven at intermission, but Dominique Wilkins (36 points) and Eddie Johnson (26) brought the Hawks back to a 69-69 tie early in the third.

Then Bird exploded, hitting fallaways, stepbacks, one-handed lofts, layups, and leaners. He scored 19 in the quarter, and 11 points in the final 3:10 of the third as the Celtics built a 100-89 lead. Bird was so destructive that defender Rickey Brown almost got into a fight with coach Mike Fratello when the period was over.

Scott Wedman preserved the lead with a couple of jumpers early in the fourth before Bird came back with 8:41 left. He scored 18 points in the final 5:11—which is exactly how many the Celtics scored in that stretch.

The record run started with a Bird layup with 5:11 left, which pushed the Celts to a 110-103 lead. It was only the beginning.

After a free throw and a couple of bombs, he was up to 49 and the Celtics led, 115-105 with 1:57 left. Victory was assured, and the Celts started thinking about the record.

With 1:26 left, Bird canned a 22-footer. With 43 seconds left he hit another 22-footer. Both shots were prayers for mere mortals. He was up to 54, then went to the line with 27 seconds left after being fouled by Kevin Willis. He made both for 55 and 56.

McHale immediately fouled Glenn Rivers, stopping the clock and giving Bird room for the record.

"Hell, I helped him out a little, too, so it works both ways," said Bird.

Then Bird made a preposterous three-pointer after a whistle ("My toughest shot of the night"— Bird). It didn't count, but his first free throw put him ahead of McHale. They high-fived, then Bird went back to the stripe for No. 58.

Rivers buried a three-pointer, then Bird missed a three-pointer. But McHale got the rebound and returned an old favor. Bird took the pass and canned a 17-footer at the buzzer to crack the 60 barrier. New York's Bernard King is the only NBA player with a 60-point game this season. He had 60 on Christmas Day against the Nets.

"I don't have anything to say," said a startled K. C. Jones. "I just sat and watched like everybody else."

First Blood

CELTICS CUT UP LAKERS IN GAME 1

May 28, 1985 • by Dan Shaughnessy

In baseball, it's 27 up and 27 down, no base runners. In bowling, it's 12 straight strikes and then Miller time. In college boards, it's 800 math, 800 verbal, hello, Harvard.

There are no perfect games in basketball, but the Boston Celtics came as close as anyone could ask yesterday, dismantling the Los Angeles Lakers, 148-114. In Game 1 of the 1985 NBA championship finals at the Garden.

If you have friends overseas, expect a call when they see this score in the International Herald Tribune. A glut of pre-series hype and analysis covered every possible outcome except a Celtic blowout, and those who failed to see yesterday's

Parquet Picasso will insist that the final score is a typographical error.

What a beating.

Perhaps still spooked by the horrors of 1984, the Lakers came out tentatively in the opening minutes yesterday. James Worthy, Byron Scott and Kareem Abdul-Jabbar missed shots they've been draining for six weeks, and LA failed to get back on defense. The Celtics scored 18 fast-break points in the first quarter and rode an 18-3 streak to a 38-24 lead at the end of one.

It was 79-49 by intermission and if this game had been played in Los Angeles, the Forum parking lot would have been a portrait of Mercedes gridlock at halftime. The Celtics held serve in the third and led, 108-79, at the end of three. The fourth quarter was played for the benefit of Mr. Greg Kite (seven points) and the rest of Boston's Pine Brothers, who drove it up to 138-101 before settling for a 34-point margin, the second-largest in the history of the NBA Finals.

The Celtics set other series records, including most points, most points in the first half (79), largest halftime lead (30), highest field goal percentage (.608), and most field goals (62). Boston's assist total (43) was within one of the record, and Scott Wedman (a/k/a Harvey Haddix) established a new mark by making 11 of 11 floor shots, including four three-pointers.

"I've never seen a team—with the exception of ours at times—shoot like that from the perimeter," said Lakers coach Pat Riley.

"I don't think there was no denying us today," added Larry Bird (19 points, 9 assists, 6 rebounds). "We did everything right."

Another Victory for the Archives

June 6, 1985 • by Leigh Montville

INGLEWOOD, Calif.—File this one away with all the rest. Open up the dusty books and run your finger down the index for "Big Games: Victorious" and insert the night of June 5, 1985.

Slide Dennis Johnson's name in there with all the rest, with all the other late-night heroes of the past.

Clip out a picture of the jump shot that left his hand with two seconds remaining in the game. Record his happy smile as the ball went through the hole with zero seconds on the fat scoreboard on the roof.

That's right. The Boston Celtics did it just one more time last night.

"All I could do was watch the spin of the ball," Celtics coach K. C. Jones said as he described Johnson's final shot that went through the climate-controlled air of the Fabulous Forum to give the Celtics a 107-105 win over the Los Angeles Lakers and stop just one more party in one more foreign port of call. "I watched the way he released the ball. I watched the spin. That's all I had a chance to do.

"Then I started cheering."

How does it figure? One more time this team was strung out, supposed to be stretched across the tracks and waiting for the train. One more time the entire City of Angels was ready to boogie, ready to go ahead, three games to one, in this best-of-seven series. One more time—gotcha—the Celtics found whatever they had to find in the fourth quarter.

What do these Celtics know? What water do they drink when they absolutely have to drink? How do they summon that concentration, blended with sure hands, that wins a basketball game in a confined number of minutes and seconds? How?

Here they were, dying, dead, gone with only nine minutes to go. The Lakers were ahead, 92-85, and the building was rocking to recorded music and a chant of "We're Not Going Back." How?

Kevin McHale was the one offensive force the Celtics had working. Kevin McHale and Dennis Johnson and that was it. Robert Parish was out of the offense by design and Danny Ainge was missing jumpers and Larry Bird, of course, still was troubled and...wait a minute.

That last basket was, in fact, by Larry Bird. It was a stand-up jumper, 15 feet, the exact type of shot he has been missing for a month. It was the shot the Celtics have been waiting to see for a long, long time. Wait a minute.

Larry Bird was back.

He was Charles Bronson walking onto the subway to see the transgressors who were making a lot of noise. He was Chuck Norris, himself. He was wearing a blue uniform and riding a painted horse and the sound of a trumpet was announcing his arrival.

He suddenly was here, there, and a familiar everywhere. One point on a technical foul as LA played a zone. A killer rebound on a Parish miss, a layup and foul shot. A stolen pass. A runner for two more points. Another stolen pass. Dennis Johnson, fouled by Magic Johnson.

Little more than a minute and a half had passed, but the team that was dead, going, gone, was ahead by a point, 93-92. Hold off on that poolside party. Cancel that order for extra dip. Maybe check that "We're Not Going Back" cheer for a while, too. The game was not only a game again. The specter of Larry Bird raced through this building as if he were Marley's Ghost.

"Seeing Larry shoot like that was like seeing an old friend return," Dennis Johnson said.

The edge now belonged to the Celtics. The score of the game may have fluctuated, back and forth one- and two-point leads, up and down, a ball of noise on the outside, but the edge now belonged to the Celtics. They were where they live. A close game. Closing minutes. They had hung long enough to create the situation they wanted.

"Welcome to my parlor," said the spider to the fly. That sort of stuff.

How many times could they have wilted? Trailing by three points after a familiar Kareem Abdul-Jabbar hook shot, a tough shot, a great shot, there was Ainge to hit a jumper to make the score 102-101 with 1:41 left. Trailing by two after a Kareem foul shot and miss, there was McHale hitting both of his foul shots with 1:12 left. Tie game.

There was Ainge again, after a Bob McAdoo miss, hitting another jumper with 33 seconds left. The Celtics led by two. There was Magic tying the game with a lovely rebound with 19 seconds left. There was...timeout, dribble, dribble pass to Bird. Pass back to Dennis Johnson. There was your next entry to the ledger. Bird was dancing up and down. M. L. Carr was waving that towel. Police were holding down some Celtics wacko who had run onto the floor. The crowd was walking out of the building with that dumbstruck feeling. Lightning bolts had landed on every LA head. Stones had been attached to every LA heart.

How do you figure it? One more time.

Bartender Says Bird Hit Him During Playoffs

CELTICS STAR MAY HAVE INJURED SHOOTING HAND

July 30, 1985 • by Dan Shaughnessy

It has been almost two months since the Celtics surrendered the NBA championship, and accounts over the past two days indicate that Larry Bird may have injured his right hand during a scuffle outside a downtown lounge on the night of May 16, in the middle of the Eastern Conference finals.

Bird's right index finger was badly swollen on the morning of May 19, following a Saturday game in Philadelphia, and his performance slumped markedly in most of the games following the alleged incident.

Mike Harlow, a 35-year-old bartender currently working at Little Rascals in the Quincy Market area, alleges that he was punched by Bird on that night after an altercation that began in Chelsea's, another area bar, and carried out to the corner of State Street and Merchant's Row.

"It happened," Harlow said Sunday night. "He sucker-punched me in the jaw."

Bird refused comment yesterday.

On the night of May 30, Bird was asked if he was involved in the alleged incident and answered, "No, and you can tell whoever made that up . . . "

Bird's attorney, Bob Woolf, said, "The reports I've heard have been totally uncharacteristic of any behavior Larry has had in the past. This is something they [Harlow's lawyers] have brought to my attention, and we're going to be looking into it. I will be speaking to them later in the week. Our options are to find out what the circumstances were and make a decision."

Bird isn't giving his side of the story now, but details of the night in question are beginning to surface.

The Celtics took a 2-0 Eastern Conference final series lead with a 106-98 victory over the Philadelphia 76ers on Tuesday, May 14. Two nights later, Bird was in Chelsea's with Celtic guard Quinn Buckner and a friend, Nick Harris. Bird is a regular customer at Chelsea's when the Celtics are in town.

Bird and Harlow, then Harris and Harlow allegedly got into a shouting match and a fight allegedly broke out between Harlow and Harris as the altercation moved outside. Massachusetts General Hospital has a record of a 39-year-old Nick Harris receiving emergency-room treatment on May 16.

An eyewitness who asked to remain unidentified said, "I don't know what happened inside over there, but there was noise and a scuffle as they came across the [State] street. Then Larry Bird went 'boom,' a nice swoop over the top with his right hand to the left side of the face."

Asked if he was certain it was Bird, the witness said, "I know what he looks like, and somebody that size you don't mistake. He was wearing a baseball cap with some insignia on it and a warm-up jacket. There's no doubt in my mind. He hit him and then a couple of guys from Chelsea's grabbed him and pulled him back inside."

A police car, with lights flashing, reportedly went down State Street (going the wrong way on a one-way street), but the Boston Police's Department of Informational Services shows no record of any arrests.

Chelsea's officials have been guarded about the alleged incident. Yesterday, Chelsea's manager Ray Malley said, "There was no situation. We've refrained from any kind of comment. You're way out of bounds if you believe Mike's story. It's not true."

Harlow has worked at several establishments as a bartender in the market area. He is 6 feet 2 and weighs over 200 pounds, and was an offensive lineman for Colgate University's football team in the early '70s.

Bird's right index finger was badly swollen before Sunday's Game 4 (May 19) of the Eastern Conference championship in Philadelphia, but Volk believes the injury occurred in Saturday's Game 3. Celtic trainer Ray Melchiorre said yesterday that Bird did not come to him for treatment of the hand before Game 3 or Game 4. Bird shot well (11 for 19) in the game immediately following the alleged incident, but he was 4 for 15 on Sunday and his numbers were unusually low for the remainder of the playoffs.

Walton Finally Gets a Foot in the Door

BILL OF SALE: MAXWELL TRADED

September 7, 1985 • by Dan Shaughnessy

He was a coveted coin-flip draft pick and a league MVP before broken bones broke his promise. Now he is a Celtic, and he has a chance to play in "the big games" for the first time since his major injury of 1978.

After two months of excruciating negotiations (stretching back to the days when the Red Sox were pennant contenders, if you can remember that far back), 6-foot-11-inch center Bill Walton officially joined the Boston Celtics yesterday. He was acquired from the Los Angeles Clippers in exchange for eight-year veteran Cedric Maxwell, plus the Celtics' 1986 No. 1 draft pick and cash.

While Boston's commuter crowd was gripped in rainy Friday afternoon gridlock, the Celtics presented Walton to the Boston media in the form of a tiny squawk box. Speaking from his home in San Diego, Walton said, "It feels really good to get it out of the way. I hope to be coming to Boston very soon."

He will wear No. 5 (last worn by John Thompson) and will be asked to play backup center and backup forward. He will move his wife and four sons to New England, but he will not transfer from Stanford to Harvard Law School.

"I'm halfway through law school, but I'm transferring to the Boston Celtics to play basketball," said Walton.

The oft-injured center-forward said that joining the Celtics should "certainly" prolong his career. With Messrs. Larry Bird, Robert Parish and Kevin McHale starting, Walton knows he won't be asked to contribute 35 minutes per game.

"Obviously my playing time will be dictated by the coach, K. C. Jones," said Walton. "By playing too much I develop stress in my lower leg. That's one of the nice things about coming to Boston. Most likely, the minutes will be kept down . . . The big problem is that I can't play 35-40 minutes a game.

"I think my skill level is still good."

Skill level, indeed. When talks about Walton's possible wearing of the green first came up, in June,

no one less than Bird said, "If we get Bill Walton, we're gonna be three times the team we were this year. He clogs up the middle, he's a great shot blocker and intimidator. And he can shoot and pass. He won't need to score with us, but he could give Robert some rest . . . When he's feeling good, there's nobody better than Bill Walton."

At the top of his game, in 1978, Walton was considered one of the most complete pivotmen in NBA history. During that MVP season, he averaged 18.9 points, 13.2 rebounds and 5 assists per game while leading the Portland Trail Blazers to a 50-10 record. It was then that he suffered a break of the tarsal navicular bone (below the left ankle). The Blazers would finish 58-24.

Walton played in only 14 games during the next four seasons. Since coming out of retirement in 1983, he has fractured a bone in his hand and had surgery for a bone spur of his right foot.

Walton was relatively injury-free last season and played in a career-high 67 games, averaging 10.1 points, 9 rebounds and 2.1 blocks for the lowly Clippers.

The former UCLA great reportedly made substantial financial concessions in order to join the Celtics. He will earn a guaranteed $450,000 per year for the next three seasons. He wouldn't comment on the interminable negotiations.

"I'm a different person than I was 12 years ago and a different basketball player, in some aspects I'm better and in some aspects I'm worse. Certainly when you're 33 there's some things you don't think you can do anymore."

The Celtics shed few tears over the departure of Maxwell. The Rubberband Man was MVP of the playoffs in 1981 and took over the seventh game of the 1984 title quest but hasn't been the same player since signing a long-term pact that pays him approximately $805,000 per season. He failed to recover from minor knee surgery last winter, then rejected a chance to participate in Boston's free agent/rookie camp. The Celtics have agreed to pay more than half of Maxwell's salary for the next four years.

Maxwell was introduced at a news conference in Los Angeles yesterday and joked, "I'm just taking up Bill Walton's spot. Don [coach Don Chaney] has already told me I don't have to practice."

Bird's Calling: Long Distance

NBA HAS FIRST '3-POINT KING'

February 2, 1986 • by Dan Shaughnessy

DALLAS—Larry Bird shredded the competition yesterday, hitting 11 consecutive three-pointers to beat Milwaukee's Craig Hodges, 24-12, in the final round of the first NBA Long Distance Shootout.

Bird was at his John Wayne/Muhammad Ali best when it was over. He walked into the pressroom, raised his arms and said, "I'm the new three-point king. And the ones that didn't think I could win can go to hell.

"My teammates got pumped up," he added. "Danny Ainge and Scott Wedman helped me, but the rest of my teammates didn't think I could win."

The grin never left Bird's face. He had never seemed happier. "I'd rather win the MVP," he admitted, "but this is more exciting. My teammates all told me Kyle Macy and Dale Ellis was going to beat me. And M. L. Carr—you remember him, he used to play for us?—he said he was still the best three-point shooter on our team. Hey, this is better than the slam dunk contest. Everybody can jump, but not everybody can shoot three-pointers.

"I'm on cloud nine now," Bird said. "I'm going to shoot threes all day tomorrow."

In addition to his bragging rights, Bird earned $10,000 for his efforts.

Bird made no attempt to hide the fact that prize money was a motivating factor. Despite his $1.8 million annual salary, he still looks at 10 grand with the eyes of a hungry French Lick garbage collector.

Asked if he were planning to donate the money to a charity, Bird said, "Yeah, the Larry Bird fund."

Bird Saves Celtics

February 15, 1986 • by Dan Shaughnessy

PORTLAND, Ore.—Celtics fans should take comfort in the knowledge that Larry Bird is all the way back to his MVP form of the past two seasons. He's been the scourge of the West thus far on this trip and last night he hit a 14-footer with three seconds left in overtime to give the Celtics a thrilling 120-119 victory over the Portland Trail Blazers.

While registering his second triple-double in as many nights, Bird scored a whopping 47 points in the Glass House. His arsenal included six lefty shots, a couple of payload three-pointers, one dunk and the usual assortment of stepbacks and sneak-aways. It was awe-inspiring, even when measured against his own lofty standards.

Bird won it with that 14-footer from out front while he was smothered by Jerome Kersey. Boston led, 120-119, and Portland called time. After the pause, Kersey took it into the lane and forced up a shot. The shot missed, no foul was called and the Celts were winners.

The Show Is Jordan's—but Celtics Steal It

BULLS FALL IN 2 OTS, 135-131

April 21, 1986 • by Bob Ryan

Only one man in the history of the NBA playoffs knows what it feels like to score 63 points at the highest level of competition and be denied the sweet smell of team success. But the hoop world knows that every other player and every other team is on borrowed time. The Celtics, Lakers, Hawks, Rockets and every other 1986 title aspirant had better seize whatever opportunity they can—Now!—because we are clearly at the dawn of the Age of Jordan.

"I would never have called him the greatest player I'd ever seen if I didn't mean it," said Larry Bird after yesterday's exhilarating, stimulating, emotional, exhausting and altogether brilliant contest. "It's just God disguised as Michael Jordan."

Bird's equation of Jordan to the Deity is understandable in light of Jordan's record-breaking 63-point effort in the Garden (a display that surpassed Elgin Baylor's 1962 playoff standard of 61), but let the record show that Bird was able to speak in the pleasant afterglow of victory. Despite all Jordan's virtuosity, the Celtics constructed a 2-0 series lead by walking (staggering would be a more apt description) off with a 135-131 double-overtime triumph in what could accurately be described as an epic contest.

They play 'em and we rate 'em, and there is no question that this game will make the Top 5, and maybe even the Top 3, of Greatest Celtic Playoff Games Ever among the Garden cognoscenti. This was pure athletic theater, and not until Orlando Woolridge airballed a desperation three-pointer with two seconds remaining in the second OT was there a legitimate chance for any Celtic owner, general manager, coach, player or fan to relax and light up that mental cigar. As long as Mr. Jordan is known to be present in this hemisphere, no rival lead is safe, no palm is dry, no throat swallows easily and no stomach is settled. A man who scores 63 points *out of the flow* is a man to fear, respect and idolize.

But justice, as we witnessed in Holmes-Spinks II, has nothing to do with winning and losing, for despite Jordan's 22 field goals and 63 points, he didn't make the biggest basket of the long, long afternoon. Jerry Sichting, a player whose game is to Jordan's as a 1955 Studebaker is to a 1986 Porsche, had that honor. For it was Sichting who took an inside-out pass from Kevin McHale and did what he has done faithfully all year—swished the foul line jumper. That basket broke the game's 13th tie and gave the Celtics a 133-131 lead with 57 seconds left in the second OT. And when Jordan missed a left base line jumper on the next Chicago possession, Robert Parish rebounded.

The ball went to Bird (36 points, 12 rebounds, 8 assists), who orchestrated a two-man game on the right wing with Parish. "As soon as he set the pick-and-roll, I gave it to him," said Bird, unconcerned that Parish had not scored a jumper all night and had established a bad case of the oopsies in his infrequent drives to the hoop. "When he goes, you've got to give him the ball. You don't worry about Robert Parish. I never do, because he's made a lot of big plays for this team."

That's no lie, and this time he took the pass and swished a 12-foot moon shot on the right base line to give Boston a four-point lead (135-131) with nine seconds remaining.

In any game such as this, there is invariably an individual of whom it can safely be said, "Without him, this would *definitely* have been an L." Yesterday afternoon, that man was the oft-maligned Danny Ainge.

You never would have pegged Ainge as a potential hero midway through the third quarter. He hadn't even scored a point by the time the aggressive young Bulls claimed their final 10-point lead (69-59). But before the period was over, he had erupted for 13, including 11 in the final 2:36, the last three of which came on a three-pointer that brought the struggling Celtics within one at 84-83.

Ainge would wind up with 24, and he would score two giant baskets, the first a lefthanded lane drive that would tie the score at 125-125 with 12 seconds left in the first OT, and the second an open 18-footer that would give Boston a brief 131-127 lead in the second OT, a lead that was quickly wiped out via two quick hoops by the irrepressible Jordan.

Chicago abandoned the first-game strategy of continual Jordan isolations, and he proved how brilliant he was by performing even better in the context of a normal offense than he did when 90 percent of the action was directed his way. The Bulls took the lead at 4-2 and clung to it stubbornly until a clock-beating 28-foot three-pointer by Bird gave Boston the lead at 93-92 and created the first of nine consecutive lead changes through 102-100 (an inside-out three-pointer by Bird from McHale).

Boston did everything but summon the ghost of Walter Brown in an attempt to knock out the Bulls, but the visitors would not succumb. A 108-104 fourth-quarter lead soon turned into a 111-110 Chicago advantage on the Jordan basket that gave him an even 50 points. A 116-113 lead with 45 seconds remaining in regulation (an Ainge-to-McHale alley-oop) evaporated when Charles Oakley hit a free throw with 34 seconds left, leading to the sequence (Bird miss, Parish momentary rebound, and Chicago steal/strip/maul/-who-knows-what-but-no-call) that set up the game's most controversial happening.

Leading, 116-114, with six seconds left, the Celtics had to dig in one last time to preserve the lead. With about a second left, Jordan up-faked Dennis Johnson and threw up a three-pointer that clanged off the rim as McHale arrived on the scene. Referee Ed Middleton called a foul on McHale after the shot. Did Jordan get hit? Did he spread-eagle smartly upon release and hit McHale? Do you ever make a call like this? Middleton did, and Jordan, naturally, sank both shots to create OT No. 1.

The Bulls surged ahead by four (123-119) on a Jordan three-point play with 1:39 left, but Sichting canned a corner jumper (missing the affixed free throw) and Ainge came through with that clutch drive. Jordan missed a left-side jumper and Bird rebounded with two seconds left. A Bird three-pointer was long and the weary troops entered the second OT.

Through the entire game, Jordan just kept scoring. And scoring. And scoring. This way. Horizontally. Vertically. Diagonally. In ways never conceived of by Hank Luisetti, Joe Fulks, Paul Arizin or even World B. Free. And, reminded Parish, "It's not like he was doing it in a summer league."

A question now arises: What is Michael Jordan capable of doing in his *own* building? Two-and-zero looks about 100 times better than 1-1 right now.

Celtics' Third Gear (36-6) Drives Out Hawks, 132-99

SPREE CAPPED BY 24-0 RUN

May 7, 1986 • by Bob Ryan

This ticket stub gets saved. This videotape gets put away. This program goes into the safe deposit box at the bank. This memory is tucked away forever in that special compartment of Celtics' fans' minds wherein reside only the golden moments, the ones where Johnny Most used to go into dog whistle and Emperor Arnold used to fire up the expensive stogies.

The Celtics outscored the Atlanta Hawks, 36-6, in the third period last night.

Atlanta had two field goals and two free throws in 12 minutes of play, and, yes, that is an NBA playoff low. The Celtics, who were already firmly in control of the game and had been since midway through the second quarter, finished the period with 24 unanswered points, sending the 265th consecutive Garden sellout crowd of 14,890 into delirium with a scintillating display of interior defense, transition basketball and Globetrotter-like passing, which transformed the game into something bordering on legitimate humiliation, but which never degenerated into farce, even if Danny Ainge got so excited he was reaching over writers to high-five fans, even as Kevin McHale was sinking two post-period free throws to conclude the historic run.

When the third period was over, the 66-55 Celtics halftime lead had ballooned to a scary 102-61 spread. The final score was 132-99, and when it was over, the fact that it also meant the end of this best-of-seven Eastern Conference semifinal series in five games was about the 134th thing on anyone's mind. Who doubted the Celtics would win the series? The question with this bunch for the last two months or so has been how much history it can make.

Is it possible to play better than the Celtics did in the final 5½ minutes of the third period last night? Danny Ainge and Dennis Johnson either forced exterior turnovers or directed people into traffic. Robert Parish, Kevin McHale and Larry Bird either blocked shots or made Atlanta's people change the ones they had in mind. The transition game was spectacular. The outside shooting was deadly. The passing was worthy of being shown 24 hours a day at the Hall of Fame. The Celtics were truly a beautiful basketball machine.

"It's hard for me to recollect any quarter like this in the 20 or 25 years I've been around," said K.C. Jones. "I'll have to see the films and see exactly what happened."

The Big Run started in the most innocent fashion possible when Bird, a killer from the opening tap (36 points, 10 rebounds and 14-for-24 shooting), sank a technical foul on an illegal defense violation. That made it 79-61 with 5:17 remaining in the quarter.

Dominique Wilkins, who ended a skyrocket year with a sad 4 for 14, then was trapped in a sideline double-team, losing the ball out of bounds. Bird got a quick pass and faked a couple of times before rifling a blind pass to McHale (25) for a layup. That was the play which blew the lid off the pressure cooker, inciting the crowd and setting in motion the forces that gave Celtics fans something to savor forever.

Before the period was over, the Hawks would have two shots blocked, commit two offensive fouls and make two other turnovers. The Celtics would respond with everything from a Parish layup on a superb looped-in Bird feed, to a Bird lefty overhead post-up banked jump hook (he was 7 for 7 with the left hand), to a great Ainge pass to a roaring McHale for a fast-break dunk, to an Ainge three-pointer which actually sent the normally unemotional Dennis Johnson into a war dance. All the while, the patrons were responding with a roar which forced people to turn up the volume of the TVs in Tewksbury.

Bird Has Most Value

May 29, 1986 • by Leigh Montville

The best time to watch him is before the doors open for business. Larry Bird is the only player on the Boston Garden floor and the games are being played in his head.

He will move around the outside of the foul circle and in back of the painted three-point line and he will keep shooting. Shot after shot. Television crews will be putting their cameras into place. The concession workers for the night will be arriving. Shot after shot.

A clubhouse guy for the Celtics named Joe Quatato will stand underneath the basket and catch the ball as it drops softly from the net. There will be little noise. Joe Quatato sometimes will throw a bounce pass with a thud off the wooden floor and sometimes he will throw a chest-high bullet, Larry Bird will go into that little rocker move and fire again. Shot after shot.

"Your imagination will be working at that time?" he was asked yesterday.

"Oh yes," Larry Bird said. "Definitely."

He will take the same shot 15 times and then, suddenly, his mind will conjure the picture of 7-foot-4-inch Ralph Sampson screaming out from underneath the basket to block the shot. "Oh-oh," Larry Bird will say to himself. "Here comes Ralph." He will change the arc of the shot. Higher, over those high arms and hands that only he can see.

"You have to use your imagination," Larry Bird said. "Say you're practicing a shot high off the backboard. Why would you ever practice that if you didn't see someone coming at you to block the shot? You're banking it high so the shot won't be blocked."

On the good days, which are most of the days, the ball will go through the basket with startling accuracy. There will be 10 in a row, 15, 20, 30, too many to count. The temptation is to say that the man will resemble a machine, oiled and perfect, but machines do not imagine. This is acoustic music, not something out of a synthesizer. This is invention as well as repetition, all this wrapped in the act of throwing a ball into the air, then throwing it into the air again.

On the bad days, there will be only mystery. Why isn't the ball doing what he wants it to do? Why?

"Everything is rhythm," Larry Bird said. "I'm not thinking about anything in the act of shooting— where my elbows are, any of that. Just rhythm. When I'm not shooting well, the shot will be short for some reason. It will feel good, the same, when I'm letting the ball go, but it will be short."

He will fight through one of these strange fluctuations as if it were a head cold. He will keep shooting and it will leave sometime. Never knew why it came. Never knew why it left. Keep shooting.

He has shot this way for as long as he can remember. Alone with a ball and a basket. The other parts of basketball are more spectacular—crowds and noise and friendship—but this is the foundation. This is where his game begins.

"Say you're playing basketball for an hour and a half, three-on-three," Larry Bird said. "You'll take maybe 100 shots during that time. Say you go out by yourself for an hour and a half. You can take 1,000 shots. Maybe more. Anywhere you want."

His brother Eddie, the kid who decided two days ago to go to Indiana State, will ask him to play full-court games during the summer, and Larry Bird will go, even though he is taller and far better than everyone else, but only for the running involved. The game will end and he will stay, alone, for the shooting.

He is not a weightlifter, never has been, except for those last three years in high school when he was trying to gain weight. He will run sometimes in the summer, five miles, no more, to stay in reasonable shape. He will eat what he wants to eat. There are no grand worries about the content of the cheeseburger or the water. He is a basketball player. He mostly prepares for playing basketball by working with a basketball.

"I never thought strength was real important for playing basketball," Larry Bird said. "The No. 1 thing is desire. The ability to do the things you have to do to become a basketball player. I don't think you can teach anyone desire. I think it's a gift. I don't know why I have it, but I do."

He finds people staring at him all the time when he leaves the house. He cannot go to a store or to a shopping mall because he will be followed and someone will tell someone else, "Look, he uses the same kind of soap I do." His attorney, Bob Woolf, says relatives of sick and dying people always are calling, asking for him to visit, just to spend a moment. It is as if people think he has learned a secret, something no one else knows, a secret that can heal and make better, a secret that has allowed him to go where no one else has been able to go.

Is there a secret?

"I know the secret to playing good basketball," Larry Bird, the best player on the planet, said yesterday after winning his third consecutive MVP award in the middle of his third championship series in three years, "but ain't telling what it is."

The secret is in Larry Bird's mind.

The Big Thrill

WALTON SEEKING HAPPY ANNIVERSARY

June 5, 1986 • by Michael Madden

HOUSTON—It has been nine years to this date since the Portland Trail Blazers and Bill Walton won the NBA championship. Walton, though, does not look back so much to then—June 5, 1977—than he does to a year ago in San Diego. A year ago, Walton was at home watching the Lakers and Celtics on television.

Walton remembers thinking, "'I wish I could get out there and play like that; I wish I could get out there and play in games like that.' I missed the intensity, the emotion, the skill level, the talent level . . . I just wanted to be involved again in those big games before those big, wild crowds."

Dreams can fade with the morning light. The dream had faded for Walton not so much because he no longer thought it possible ("I knew what I still could do"), but because he was waiting for the dream to come back to him. It is not subtle, this difference, this waiting for life to happen and its

opposite, the search and seizure of life. Did Walton make this new moment of June 5, 1986, happen?

"Oh, definitely," Walton replies. "I went after it. I was the one who initiated the trade talks with the Celtics and I was determined to get here. I was unyielding in my desire to get to Boston."

How many Bill Waltons have there been? Larry Bird says he remembers the Walton most of us recall, the Walton of UCLA destroying Memphis State in an NCAA tournament game of perfection 13 years ago. That is the image. Indelible.

"I remember seeing him play that one spectacular game in college," says Bird. "I think I was like most kids at the time; all I remember about him was that he had a ponytail and he was smoking bong."

Bong?

That's French Lick for you know what.

Walton, of course, was the basketball player of the bong-smoking counterculture, perfectly in tune with the counter times of the early to mid-'70s. Vestiges remain—Walton's T-shirt yesterday read "Dance for Disarmament"—but others have gone the way of the ponytail.

"We've got all kinds on this team," explains Robert Parish. "We've got Mormons, Danny Ainge and Greg Kite; we've got comedians, Kevin (McHale) and Larry (Bird), and we've got militants, me and (David) Thirdkill. We've also got a politician . . . Bill's the politician."

Walton says he would do nothing differently, that he regrets none of that so-long free fall from the pedestal of sports to his vague exile to that gray island where he landed—not on his feet, definitely not on his feet—that island of injuries, diagnoses, accusations and anonymity. What he says is, "I am what I am today because of what happened." That is true, although few of us accept that truth. Walton has perspective.

"Because of what's happened in my career," says Walton, "I think I have a much greater appreciation for what's happening right now. I have a need to get it done right now."

It?

A world championship.

"We're here now," explains Walton. "Let's get it done; let's win. What I mean is that it's very hard to get here . . . it may not seem too hard for Larry Bird, but it's hard for me . . . and once you're here, you want to take advantage of the chance you have."

Bill Walton stretches before practice at The Summit in Houston on May 31, 1986.

Walton had played terribly in the first half of Tuesday night's game, Houston's Ralph Sampson running amok on him in the second quarter but, in the end, it was Walton who won the game as much as any Celtic. His quick pass out to the perimeter set up Bird's three-point shot, and then Walton snatched an offensive rebound away from Hakeem Olajuwon with less than two minutes left and went up over Olajuwon for a reverse layup.

Walton will now sit back and enjoy such satisfying moments, such a difference from college when he was diffident with the media. Walton then was a man who did not enjoy who he was.

"In college, I was very shy, very self-conscious, but since then, I've grown up a lot and matured a lot," he says. "I just feel a lot more comfortable in this position than I was in college."

In the middle of all this, Walton is asked about a joking comment he made earlier in the week that he still doesn't feel accepted by the Celtics. From such a consummate Celtic player—even years before he became a Celtic—this was an interesting remark. Walton was asked if he still has the feeling he hasn't been accepted.

"No, I don't think I have," Walton says again.

Why do you feel that way?

"I don't know . . . I don't know," he replies. "These guys have been here a long time, these guys have been down this road many times before, and I'm just sort of new to this thing. It's a new experience for

me, a new feeling for me, and I've got to get what I came here for—that's to win the championship."

Other Celtics were asked about this and none agreed with Walton. They joked about him, they poked fun at him, they praised him, but none even hinted that Walton hasn't been accepted by the team. This seems more a feeling of Walton's, his own thought that he isn't a member of the Celtics until he is on a Boston team that wins an NBA title.

"If we win, that means I'm on the best team in the world, and that's what I want to be a part of," said Walton. "That's because basketball is the most fun thing in my life, it's the thing I enjoy doing the most, and when you're on the best team in the world, it's an unbelievable feeling of satisfaction and accomplishment and pride. I take a lot of pride in what we do."

Obviously.

A Celtic.

Houston Fights Back

IT WAS THE STRIFE OF THE PARTY

June 6, 1986 • by Leigh Montville

HOUSTON—The night did not unravel. The night exploded.

One minute, the Boston Celtics were thinking about champagne and parties and a 16th championship flag for the Boston Garden ceiling. The next minute, they simply were trying to survive on a dozen different fronts.

Blood was dripping down the left side of Celtics guard Dennis Johnson's face and onto his shirt. Houston forward Ralph Sampson was being led from the court, ejected for fighting. The sellout Summit crowd of 16,016 was howling, a cup was shattering on the floor, and the underdog Houston Rockets were on a furious emotional roll.

Championship? Everyone was on the way back to Boston—Houston Rockets 111, Celtics 96—in one furious, pulsating package.

"This was one of the most emotional games I've ever seen in this league outside of a championship Game 7," Rockets coach Bill Fitch said after his team's grand charge last night to climb within a game, 3-2, in this best-of-seven series for the NBA title. "I'm talking about a 15-minute, sustained period of time."

The time all of this emotion began was with 9 minutes, 40 seconds left in the second period. The Rockets were leading, 34-33, on this steamy Texas night, but what was one point? All signs were pointing toward the eventual coronation of the Celts.

What was one point?

The fight began. The emotion began. The one point stretched and stretched, grew and grew, and the Celtics never were that close again.

"That was the turning point," Celtics coach K. C. Jones said. "Things got so bad I didn't even have to coach in the second half. I could just sit and watch along with everyone else."

Seen on film a half-dozen times, the fight was a total Ralph Sampson production. He elbowed Celtics guard Jerry Sichting once. He punched Jerry Sichting once. He punched Jerry Sichting twice. The big man seemed to regard the smaller Celtics guard as a nettlesome fly, caught next to him underneath the basket on a switch of defensive men. He made the moves to remove the fly.

"I think Ralph was upset by the things that were said after the first two games, about how he didn't seem to be involved," Rockets reserve forward Jim Petersen said. "I think he showed here how involved he is."

"I thought a foul should have been called," Sampson said in a statement, refusing to answer questions. "I did what I had to do. It was an unfortunate accident, an unfortunate situation. I'm sorry, and we're going to Boston."

The fight expanded when Dennis Johnson came to Sichting's rescue, followed by Bill Walton. Johnson took a punch from Houston center Hakeem Olajuwon, opening the cut over his left eye. Walton took Sampson, dumping the big man to the floor with a headlock from behind.

There was a lot of milling. A lot of people were involved. Referees Jack Madden and Hugh Evans were left at the end to figure out a puzzling picture while the crowd stood and offered advice. Madden finally decided to eject Sampson, awarding a foul shot to Sichting.

"I will say this for Jack Madden," Bill Fitch said. "He said he had no other choice. He explained what he saw to me, and when I saw the replay, I saw exactly the same thing."

The statistical mind would have thought that this was the point the Celts would have been assured of No. 16. Here was a team losing its 7-foot-4-inch big man, its most ferocious player during the early going. The emotional mind said differently.

"When Sampson went out, we lost our intensity," K. C. Jones said. "The Rockets gained theirs. They ran all over us. We were organized chaos. Offensively. And defensively. We were there, but we were somewhere else."

The Celtics were the team that frayed and cracked, that couldn't keep up with the footrace. They looked tired, these Celtics did, against the Rockets' youth this time. They looked bothered and lost. They couldn't keep up.

Back to Boston on Sunday. Who would have guessed?

"Do you expect the Boston crowd will be excited by what has happened here?" K. C. Jones was asked.

"Oh, I'd suspect it probably will be a pretty docile crowd," the coach replied. "Sure."

So much for the coronation. This has become a basketball series for the championship of the world.

What many fans consider the best starting five in NBA history. From left: Danny Ainge, Larry Bird, Dennis Johnson, Kevin McHale, and Robert Parish.

CELTICS' CROWNING GLORY

BIRD BURIES ROCKETS

June 9, 1986 • by Bob Ryan

The Houston Rockets were like an unwary couple pulled over on the highway for going three miles over the speed limit by a burly Georgia cop with the mirrored sunglasses.

It wasn't their day. The cop's name was Bird. The bailiff's name was Bird. The court stenographer's name was Bird. The judge's name was Bird. And the executioner's name was—guess what?—Bird.

Welcome to Bird Country, boys, and while you're at it, why don't you congratulate the Boston Celtics on the occasion of their 16th NBA championship? He didn't make *every* shot, or grab *every* rebound, or account for *every* assist, or make *every* steal, or sell *every* hot dog, but he plugged himself into every conceivable aspect of the game to the extent that all the other players had to do was feed off his energy level. "Let's face it," said Kevin McHale, "when you play with a guy like Larry Bird, it gives you a lot of confidence."

Yesterday's final was Boston 114, Houston 97. The Celtics never trailed. There were no ties. The closest spread in the final 2½ periods was 11. With 7:20 remaining, it was up to 30 at 97-67. The suffocating Boston defense held Houston to 35 percent shooting in the first three periods.

The tone of the game was established in the first minute and a half. Ralph Sampson (who was to no-shows what Buddy Rich is to drummers) missed the first Houston shot and referee Jake O'Donnell called a loose-ball foul on Robert Reid. Whoa . . . there were no questionable loose-ball fouls called on the Rockets in Houston during Game 5.

Dennis Johnson drove to the basket, and McHale (29 points, 10 rebounds) shoved it back in with the underside of his left hand. Whoa . . . the Celtics weren't getting second shots in Houston. Houston set up, and Bird stole a Rodney McCray pass to start a fast break. McHale finished off with a silly-looking runner that bounced around a few times and fell in. Whoa . . . the rims in Houston would have kicked that baby all the way to Galveston, or so it seemed. Gee, it's great to be back home again.

Johnson, guarding Reid for the first time in the series (he simply asked K. C. Jones for the assignment), made him feel as if he were wearing a rain-soaked overcoat. The man who had 13 assists by halftime of Game 5 had 2 points and 2 assists by this intermission.

Down deep, McHale was swallowing the villain-ous Sampson (1-for-8 first half). Robert Parish was denying Hakeem Olajuwon and Bird was somehow or other playing McCray, Sampson, Olajuwon, Reid, Lewis Lloyd and every other Rocket this side of Zaid Abdul-Aziz.

"It was just tough defense from start to finish," said DJ. "Tenacious. They couldn't stand it."

By the first Houston timeout (14-6, Boston, at 8:32), the Rockets had more turnovers (5) than field goals attempted (4). At 20-9, the Rockets called for a 20-second timeout, as the Celtics had picked up 12 points via fast breaks and 4 more via second shots. It was pretty clear that the man in charge had put a whole new record on the turntable than the wall of noise he had on there the other night. This was a song the Celtics could dance to.

"The game just started totally different than the ones in Houston," reflected Jerry Sichting, who was a part of a big second-quarter unit. "We came out and picked up on defense. We should never have let it happen down there, but we knew how to correct the problem."

After Bird fed McHale for a dunk to make it 22-10, the Rockets made the first of two significant runs. Olajuwon brought them back with three consecutive steals on passes intended for Bill Walton, who at that point probably wished he could have traded places with Jerry Garcia's guitar pick.

"Here I was, just in the game, and I lose the ball three straight times," said Walton. "All I was thinking was that Larry was going over to K. C. and saying, 'Get that guy out of here!'" Walton would stick around to submit 10 points and 8 rebounds.

But Houston never could pull ahead. The Rockets got within one at 22-21 (McCray layup after Olajuwon steal No. 3) and 24-23 (McCray right-back fast-break layup). When McCray missed an attached free throw, Olajuwon grabbed the rebound and missed a turnaround. It would be Houston's last chance to go ahead.

By period's end, the Boston lead was up to 29-23. Houston crept back within three at 31-28, only to see the game get completely away from them in the next 5:28 as the unit of Bird, McHale, Parish, Sichting and the valuable Danny Ainge (19 points, 4 assists, 2 steals and 7-for-9 shooting) ran off a 16-4 spurt to make it 47-32.

By halftime, Bird was well on the way to his third triple-double of the playoffs and second of the Finals with 16 points, 8 rebounds, 8 assists, 3 steals and the wettest, dirtiest, grungiest-looking uniform since Pepper Martin's in the '31 World Series. He had involved himself in every conceivable operation during an emotional half of basketball, once bringing back John Havlicek memories with a fast-break leaner already from the foul line and another time even winning a first-period jump ball from Olajuwon.

It was 55-38 at the half, and the only reason it wasn't worse was Boston's atrocious foul shooting (11 for 21 in the first half). Seventeen is a nice margin, but the Celtics weren't merely interested in maintaining it. Embarrassed by the goings-on in Game 5, they wanted scalps.

And so did the fanatical crowd, which had gotten on Sampson from the beginning and wanted a game to place in the all-time memory bank. The fun really began at 59-45 when Parish hit Ainge for an inside-out, left-corner, buzzer-beating three-point swisher. Sampson (one field goal in the first 32 minutes) missed a hook and Ainge converted on a three-on-one fast break. Bird stuck in a three-pointer from the left with the arc of a Wade Boggs line drive (69-49). DJ made a power lefthanded right-to-left drive. Parish hit a moonshot. The Celtics led by 21 (82-61) after three.

Bird had one great crowd-pleasing move left in his repertoire. In his seven years, he has done a lot of outrageous things, but what he did at 84-61 ranks right near the top of anyone's list. He received a behind-the-back pass from Walton on the left base line, fumbled the ball, realized the 24-second clock was near expiration, and instead of dribbling toward the hoop for a potential foul, he started making his way through an obstacle course to the three-point line in the next corner. Arriving at his destination, he turned and swished a three-pointer. The sound that followed only remotely could be described as noise.

Bird finished with 29 points, 11 rebounds and 12 assists, and he was awarded the Sport magazine MVP award. He had promised the world beforehand that "everything's gonna be just fine," and, as usual, he had delivered. Marveled Houston's Jim Petersen, "I saw him take on five guys by himself. He's the best. At times, he doesn't seem to need teammates."

"Larry Bird," said K. C. Jones, "is where he wants to be. He has reached the pinnacle of basketball."

And so have the Celtics, whose victory yesterday was the 47th in 48 tries on the parquet, and who finished the season with 38 consecutive victories at home. "They weren't beating us here today," said McHale. "They hurt us the worst way they could in Game 5. They hurt our pride. It's not often that 12 guys together have on their game face, but that's what happened today."

And they'll all admit that one face was a little grimmer, a little meaner and a little more meaningful than all the others. "Nothing Larry Bird does surprises me," declared Bill Walton, "and everything he does impresses me."

Which is very similar to the way the NBA has viewed the Celtics as a whole for the past 29 years.

Magna Cum Laude Celtics Took the NBA to School

June 10, 1986 • by Bob Ryan

Do not forget that before the fall semester ever began, the Celtics' management had backed up the truck and carted away all the nonessential items in the attic. Gone from the team that lost the 1985 championship series in six games to the Lakers were Cedric Maxwell, Quinn Buckner, Ray Williams, Carlos Clark and M. L. Carr. What these players had in common was that none of them was

deemed athletically worthy of playing in the sixth and final game of the final series. K. C. Jones would entrust not one second of playing time beyond his first seven men in the most important game of the year. What the Celtics' school superintendent (Red Auerbach) and the principal (Jan Volk) did was add on, not destroy. Auerbach and Volk imported transfer students named Bill Walton, Jerry Sichting and Sly Williams. Walton and Sichting fit into their new environment, Walton making the high honor roll and Sichting earning solid B's and B-minuses. Sly Williams was expelled. Win some, lose some.

FALL SEMESTER— OCTOBER 25-DECEMBER 25; W-21, L-7

Is Larry healthy? Can Larry play if he isn't healthy? Will Larry *ever* be healthy? These were the questions hovering over the team when the season began.

Bird had been troubled by elbow and finger problems during the '85 finals, but an even bigger health issue arose over the summer. Larry Bird, the greatest basketball player in the solar system, had become one of the several million Americans plagued with a bad back. He struggled throughout the exhibition season, and when Opening Day arrived, there was some question about his availability.

Bird played in that game, but despite 21 points, 12 rebounds and 10 assists, he wasn't himself and everyone knew it. He shot 5 for 15, and such disturbing numbers would continue to creep into his box scores over the next two months. Blowing a 19-point, third-quarter lead, the Celtics were caught and beaten in overtime by New Jersey in the opener. Dennis Johnson missed two free throws with 10 seconds left that could have put the game away, but the evening's primary goat was the much-heralded Walton, who crammed five personal fouls and seven turnovers (of a team season-high 28) into 19 uninspired minutes. "I played a terrible game," sighed Walton. "It was a disgrace to my team and to the sport of basketball."

The first of 67 victories came the next evening, when the team silenced 20,900 revelers in the Richfield Coliseum with a 105-100 victory over the Cavaliers. Kevin McHale, who would continue a six-year pattern of improving every season, checked in with 21 points and 15 rebounds. But the first home game, though an impressive 117-106 victory over

Milwaukee (a team the Celtics would eventually defeat nine times in nine tries) was clouded by bad news on the medical front. Bird had to leave the game to have his back treated and missed the entire third quarter.

But McHale was off to a magnificent start, and Johnson and Robert Parish were still their All-Star selves, so the victories mounted. The first meeting with the hated 76ers was an easy 98-91 decision. Bird, though impaired, was still endlessly resourceful, as a 47-point performance accomplished with inside moves, trips to the line (13 for 13) and all-around moxie against Detroit (a 132-124 victory) demonstrated.

But Bird still wasn't right, and as December progressed, the Celtics offense began to stagnate. The team had lost four of eight when it arrived in New York for a Christmas Day date with the Knicks. After constructing a 25-point lead in the third period, the team went into a collective coma. Patrick Ewing led New York back, and the Knicks emerged with a 113-104 victory in double overtime. Bird shot 8 for 27, dragging his season's shooting percentage under 45 percent. Was Bird's back going to ruin the dreams of a championship?

Fall Semester grade: B+

WINTER SEMESTER— DECEMBER 28-FEBRUARY 20; W-21, L-4

Bird's cloud lifts. Walton asserts himself. Scott Wedman plays like the professional he is. The winter term is when the Celtics made people realize that calling them "great" would be an understatement.

The Madison Square Garden debacle embarrassed and angered the Celtics. They headed west and ran off quick victories over Utah and the LA Clippers to launch a spurt of 17 victories in 18 games, and it was in this stretch that Walton won over the basketball fans of Boston, Massachusetts.

There were three highlight games. The first occurred on Jan. 18, when the Celtics rallied from 23 points down in the second quarter to defeat the trash-talking Atlanta Hawks in overtime. Irked by some uncomplimentary on-court Atlanta patter, the Celtics came out in a maniacal manner in the third quarter, led by Bird, who scored 17 of his 41. Final: Boston 125, Atlanta 122. It was an oh-so-sweet ride home.

Highlight No. 2 came the following Wednesday, when the Lakers arrived in town. Walton was ready for business, scoring 11 points (5 for 6), grabbing 8 rebounds, handing out 4 assists and blocking 7 shots in what had to be the most productive 16 minutes any NBA center had all season. Johnson scored 22 and Bird 21, as the Celtics cruised (110-95) over the world champions despite a bad night (3 for 14) from McHale, who was experiencing serious difficulty with a sore Achilles' tendon.

The third part of the trifecta came four days later when the Celtics erased a 13-point, third-quarter deficit to Philadelphia behind a classic Bird long-distance shooting display (three three-pointers, including a 35-footer to end the period). Again, Walton had them hanging over the balcony railings with 19 points and 13 rebounds in 25 minutes.

By now they were operating without McHale, who would miss 14 games and four additional starting assignments. But Wedman stepped in to keep the machine chugging, averaging 15 points a game.

And now Bird was feeling better. Sessions with orthopedic physical therapist Dan Dyrek had helped his back, and by the time Larry hit the All-Star Game in Dallas Feb. 11, he was his old self. He walked off with the three-point shooting title (making 11 in a row at one point), and when the regular season resumed, he started assaulting the enemy beachheads as never before. When he destroyed Portland with 47 points, including the tying basket (to create an overtime) and the winning basket, he had accomplished back-to-back triple-doubles. He finished with three triple-doubles on one road trip and five in eight games.

Winter Semester grade: A

SPRING SEMESTER— FEBRUARY 23-APRIL 13; W-25, L-4

Life was now a gigantic *Ha-Ha*. The Atlantic Division race was over, and the only issue was going after the all-time league won-loss record. Bird, now completely cured of his physical problems, was deep into one of the great killer stretches of his career. Night after night, the issue of winning and losing was decided early. The only issues were such things as Bird's quest for a triple-double; Bird's phenomenal three-point shooting percentage (he went 25 for 34 at one point); Walton's astonishing rebounds-per-minutes-played ratio (he compiled such lines as 14 rebounds in 27 minutes vs. New York, 10 rebounds in 16 minutes against Chicago and 16 rebounds in 25 minutes in Houston); and Jerry Sichting's fairly amazing outside shooting (63.4 over his last 17 games).

Bird put a lock on his third consecutive MVP trophy by winning Player of the Month honors in February and March. He hit all 11 shots in the first half while scoring 33 points in San Antonio on March 13. He scored 34 in the first half of a blowout of Cleveland in Hartford on March 18. He scored 36, 35, 27 and 40 in consecutive games against Houston, Milwaukee, Washington and New Jersey.

Meanwhile, the team was breaking the NBA record for consecutive home victories in one season (29) with a 122-106 triumph over Detroit on April 2, and was finishing the year with a 37-1 record in the Garden and 40-1 home record overall. In one dominating display of power basketball, the Celtics compiled an average home-victory margin of 16 points a game for 13 games. The divisional title was clinched with 13 games left, the best record in the conference with 11 games left and the best overall record with six games left.

When it was over, the 67-15 record was the best in Celtics' history and the fourth best in league history. Only two of the 15 losses were not connected with outright giveaways, ejections or missing personnel. For sheer overpowering might, the NBA had seldom seen anything like it.

Spring Semester grade: A+
Season grade: A+
Teacher's comment: "Thanks"

CELTICS' NO. 1 PICK IS DEAD AT 22

MARYLAND'S BIAS COLLAPSES IN DORMITORY

June 20, 1986 •
by John Powers and Will McDonough

COLLEGE PARK, Md.—Len Bias, chosen by the Celtics as the No. 2 pick in Tuesday's NBA Draft, died yesterday morning of cardiorespiratory failure.

The 22-year-old University of Maryland basketball star may have used cocaine shortly before he died.

Celtics president Red Auerbach, reacting to reports that traces of cocaine had been found in Bias's urine, said he was told by Maryland basketball coach Lefty Driesell that the 6-foot-8-inch Bias probably used cocaine, perhaps for the first time, at a party early yesterday morning with college friends.

"Lefty called me in the afternoon and said there was further information," said Auerbach, interviewed by phone at his apartment in Boston. "He said he had been told by authorities that there were traces of cocaine in his urine. He understood that Bias was out someplace, had a couple of beers with his friends and came back to the dormitory.

"Some guy, another student, joined the party and allegedly said, 'Come on, let's have a real celebration.'" The student then allegedly produced the cocaine.

Robert Law, spokesman for the Prince George's County Police Department, denied last night that anyone in his department, which is investigating the incident, informed Driesell of any possible drug use by Bias.

"We have no evidence that drugs were used," said Law. "And we have no evidence that drugs contributed to his death."

University of Maryland officials said they could not confirm reports that Bias had used cocaine.

"I have no idea whether the report is accurate or not accurate," said Maryland athletic director Richard M. Dull. "I don't have the details of what may have occurred. But drugs weren't part of the lifestyle of the Lenny Bias that I knew."

Gordon Wangersheim, a member of the company that managed Bias, said that two of his company's representatives, Lee Fentress and Bill Shelton, took Bias to the Maryland campus around 10 p.m. Wednesday after his return from a whirlwind tour of Boston. According to Wangersheim, Fentress and Shelton said Bias was drug-free upon his return to campus.

Bias often joked, said Wangersheim, that the worst thing he did to his body was eat ice cream.

"As far as we know, Len was a clean young man," said Wangersheim, a marketing specialist for Advantage International. "He did not mess around. But I cannot say what went on in the dorm room. Who knows what happened there? He was with his buddies, he had just signed a big endorsement with Reebok . . . and hey, you're 22 years old. Who knows?"

Auerbach said he was "sick all over" upon watching national telecasts that constantly brought up the rumors of Bias's alleged cocaine use. "It's unbelievable that we tested him, and San Francisco [the Golden State Warriors] tested him, but there was never any trace of drugs."

According to Auerbach, Driesell said, "I swear on my life, I hope to die if this kid ever used drugs before."

Driesell, who had appeared at a news conference earlier yesterday,

Celtics coach K. C. Jones and No. 2 overall pick Len Bias on June 17, 1986.

could not be reached for comment last night.

Bias, who returned to campus Wednesday night after spending more than 24 hours in Boston, had passed much of the evening chatting with teammates.

"We were all sitting around talking," said Terrapin football player Bryant Covington. "We thought it would be one more day before he came back from Boston. He took us all by surprise. Everybody had been asking him questions, maybe for two hours. He said he'd gotten tired of that and told us, 'Look here, fellas, I'm trying to get away from this rut. I want to be alone.' He ran out to his car around 2, 2:15 (a.m.). He seemed perfectly well to me."

Bias was gone for about an hour, then returned to the dorm. He was reportedly talking with Maryland basketball teammates Terry Long and David Gregg at 6 a.m. in their dormitory room at Washington Hall, when he went into convulsions and fell to the floor. Long was said to have tried to revive Bias before he was taken to nearby Leland Memorial Hospital in Riverdale by emergency ambulance.

Doctors there tried drugs, electrical jolts and a pacemaker to resuscitate Bias, but he was

pronounced dead at 8:50 a.m., two hours after being admitted.

"There was no response," said Dr. Edward Wilson, attending physician at the hospital. "The heart was not pumping and the lungs were not working. As far as I know, it was a sudden collapse. Apparently, he had no idea it was coming, and there apparently were no chest pains preceding."

The state medical examiner's office in Baltimore performed an autopsy on Bias's body, but chief medical examiner Dr. John Smialek said that it would be 7-10 days before results would be complete. "Until all of the testing is complete, I will not be releasing any details of the examination," Smialek said.

Bias, an All-America forward who lived in nearby Landover, is the third Maryland basketball player to die in the last 12 years. Owen Brown died of heart failure in 1974 during a pickup basketball game one year after graduating. Chris Patton, a 6-9 sophomore, died in 1978, also during a pickup game on campus, of heart failure, caused by Marfan syndrome.

Marfan syndrome, which also caused the death this year of 6-5 Flo Hyman, America's best female volleyball player, is a congenital heart condition that affects the aorta and mainly afflicts tall people. Victims typically are tall blacks, with disproportionately long arms, concave chests and poor eyesight. But doctors and Maryland officials said yesterday they doubted that Bias had Marfan syndrome.

"If he had Marfan's, it was not a contributing factor as far as we know," said Wilson. "We always look for that."

Bias's death shocked everyone on campus.

"This is probably the saddest day in the history of the University of Maryland," said chancellor John B. Slaughter. "Leonard Bias was a wonderful young man who made a positive impact upon everyone he met. Our campus and all those who knew him are crushed by this news of his death."

Bias, regarded by many pro scouts as the best physical specimen in the NBA Draft, had shown no recent signs of feeling ill.

"He had several physicals in the last month [the Celtics administered one on May 27]," said Maryland basketball trainer Frank Grimaldi.

Bias's strength and stamina were renowned throughout the Atlantic Coast Conference, where he was routinely defended by two or three players.

"He was a thoroughbred," Grimaldi said. "Inexhaustible. He could play a whole game, nonstop, plus overtime, and within a few minutes give an interview without even breathing hard."

Kevin Paul Dupont of the Globe staff also contributed to this report.

Celtics Shock Pistons

BIRD STEALS IT FOR CELTICS

May 27, 1987 • by Bob Ryan

The message is clear. If you want to beat Larry Bird in a big game, you've got to play the full 48 minutes. Forty-seven minutes 56 seconds isn't enough.

Four seconds shy of what would have been the most meaningful triumph in the entire Detroit phase of this franchise, the dazed Pistons saw it all evaporate when Bird intercepted Isiah Thomas's inbounds pass to Bill Laimbeer, then turned and fed a streaking Dennis Johnson for a layup with one second

remaining to give the Celtics a 108-107 triumph last night and a 3-2 lead in the best-of-seven Eastern Conference finals.

Now it's Move Over, Hondo. All John Havlicek did on that April night 22 years ago was *preserve* a 1-point lead. What Bird and trusty Dennis ("The-Best-Player-I've-Ever-Played-With") Johnson did was rescue a completely lost cause and provide the battered Celtics with a pivotal triumph in what has become a tremendous battle of will.

"I thought we played a terrific game and showed great courage," said hugely disappointed Detroit coach Chuck Daly. "We basically had the game won with five seconds to go, but we made one mistake on the inbounds."

Boston had regained possession following a classic Thomas one-on-one spinner from the key that had made it 107-106, Detroit, with 17 seconds remaining. The teams had been locked in a deadly embrace for the final 4:28, or ever since a pair of Bird free throws tied the game at 95 and enabled the icy (3 for 14 to start period 4) Celtics, who again had lost Robert Parish with an ankle injury, to get the game even after falling behind by a 93-88 score earlier in the quarter.

A tough corner jumper by Bird had given the Celtics a 3-point bulge at 104-101 (1:13), but Detroit, which showed exemplary resilience all night long, calmly fought back, getting it to 1 at both 104-103 (two Thomas free throws) and 106-105 (a Laimbeer foul-line jumper in response to a Danny Ainge basket). When Bird couldn't get a little jump hook to drop, the Pistons had the ball back with 28 seconds left, trailing by 1.

Detroit called time out, and when play resumed, Isiah took Jerry Sichting and beat him on the spin move. The Celtics called time and eventually gave the ball to Bird, who drove the left base line on three Pistons. Dennis Rodman smashed the ball away. Sichting tried to save the ball from going out of bounds, but it was given to Detroit with four seconds left.

The Pistons had a timeout, and Daly wanted one. "I tried to get one," he explained, "but with all the noise, well, he [Isiah] elected to throw it in, and Bird made a great play after he had missed a shot and got the ball to Johnson for a layup."

Bird was guarding Joe Dumars at the foul line when Thomas took the ball out. "I saw Laimbeer

Dennis Johnson and Larry Bird raise their arms in triumph after Bird stole an Isiah Thomas inbounds pass and fed Johnson for the winning layup.

bounced off the Detroit center's hands and out of bounds. A grueling evening of basketball was over.

The Celtics had somehow escaped despite going 7:25 without a field goal from the 3:16 mark of the third quarter (a DJ corner shot making it 81-75, Boston) till the 7:41 mark of the final period, when Bird nailed a jumper. Boston failed to score on its first six fourth-period possessions, covering seven shots, and in so doing were fortunate to be down by just 1 at 89-88 when the dry spell ended.

But Detroit, which had come back from a first-half 12-point deficit (48-36) and a second-half 11-point deficit (69-58), was apparently ready to assert final control, going up by a 93-88 score on a fast-break dunk by Rodman before a Kevin McHale keep-alive led to a Bird follow-up three-point play (93-91). From that point on, the game was war.

The Celtics kept trying to KO the Pistons, and Detroit kept picking itself up off the canvas. At the 69-58 juncture, for example, Dantley (25), Thomas (17 points, 11 assists) and Laimbeer (16 points, 14 rebounds) led a 13-2 Detroit countersurge that eliminated any Boston blowout thoughts and made it a game once again. Detroit had responded similarly in the second quarter when Boston rattled its saber to the tune of the 48-36 lead.

And with four seconds left, the Pistons were one successful inbounds pass and a couple of inevitable free throws away from becoming the first team to defeat Boston in a 2-2 situation here in 25 years.

Bird was on the verge of being a heroic loser with 36 points, 14 rebounds, 9 assists and 11 fourth-quarter points. Until those final four seconds, however, he didn't have a steal. He does now.

With one play, Larry Bird stole a ball game and concurrently broke a few hundred thousand Michigan hearts. If the Pistons didn't know it before, they know it now: The path to the Finals goes right through Route 33.

standing there," said Bird, "and I was going to foul him real quick. But then I saw the ball was kind of lobbed up there and I saw I had a chance to steal it. As soon as I got it, I was going to shoot. I was counting four seconds in my head, and then I turned around and saw DJ cutting down the lane."

"You can see I should have called a timeout," said Thomas. "You can see I should not have thrown the pass. You can see I should have thrown the ball harder or Bill should have come in. But all I can say is they stole the ball and they won the game."

And once Bird caught the ball, he turned and surveyed the situation. Johnson, being Mr. Fundamental I, did what came naturally, which was to cut hard to the hoop. Bird, being Mr. Fundamental II, slipped him the ball. DJ stuck in a backhander as Dumars desperately tried to stop the shot.

The Pistons still had a second to go. They called time and decided to have Adrian Dantley inbound the ball from midcourt. His pass to Laimbeer

Celtics Sweat It Out, 117-114

PISTONS FINALLY SUCCUMB

May 31, 1987 • by Bob Ryan

Only two weeks after a seventh Milwaukee game that had the assembled scribes and scribettes scrambling for their thesauri; only one year after the celebrated Michael Jordan Double OT game; *only six years* after the fondly remembered Philadelphia 7th; only 11 years after the Phoenix Triple OT "Greatest Game Ever Played"; and only 30 years after Russell, Cousy, Heinsohn & Co. started this whole thing with a spectacular two-overtime victory over St. Louis, the Boston Celtics sent 14,890 people home from the steamy Boston Garden wondering if they'll ever see anything better than the transcendent basketball game that took place yesterday afternoon (and early evening).

People around here are used to seeing Boston win, of course, and the Celtics' 117-114 triumph over the Detroit Pistons had major ramifications. The Celtics for the fourth straight year are Eastern Conference champs. Injuries and all, they will be in Los Angeles Tuesday night trying for championship No. 17, a championship no one neutral and very few in Boston think they can win. The game on display yesterday will take its place with the handful of most memorable Garden events ever staged.

"You cannot see better basketball," said Detroit coach Chuck Daly. "Anybody want to talk about any other level of basketball after seeing this?"

What Daly and everyone else privileged enough to have been inside the Garden yesterday saw were two outstanding basketball teams doing something seldom seen in this level of playoff competition: They saved their most spectacular and dynamic offense for last. You could requisition the stat sheets of any other 200 playoff games you think deserved to be called "great," and you will find no others in which the winning team scored 36 points and the losing team scored 34 in the final period of play, and forget about the fact that it was 88 degrees inside the Garden when the fourth period began.

The basket that pretty much closed out the competition was delivered by Danny Ainge, who took a feed from back court partner Dennis Johnson and calmly swished an 18-footer from left of the foul line with 25 seconds remaining to make it 108-105, Boston. After that basket, Daly called his final timeout, and when play resumed, Isiah Thomas (25 points, 9 assists) missed a quick straightaway three-pointer.

Kevin McHale, who went 41 minutes on the bad foot (22 points, 10 rebounds), grabbed the vital miss and marched to the opposite end of the floor to deposit the free throws that made it a seemingly safe 112-107 lead with 11 seconds to go.

There were some scary moments left before the buzzer, and some questions, too. Why did the normally cerebral DJ immediately try to steal the ball from Joe Dumars midcourt, sending the Detroit high scorer of the day (35) to the line? Dumars made one and missed the other. John Salley dunked the rebound and it was 112-110 with seven seconds left.

That's as close as it got, however, as Ainge (114-110), Johnson (a deliberate foul at 115-111) and Ainge (117-111 before a closing Dumars three-pointer) sank the requisite free throws to guarantee one of the truly sweet victories the Celtics have ever had.

The part of the game no one will ever forget started with a pair of Thomas free throws that tied the game for the 10th time, at 91 apiece (7:21). Boston scored on its next six possessions and would go on to score on 12 of its final 14, counting all the free throw situations. But for a frightfully long time the Pistons stayed right with them.

The taut nature of this game can be illustrated by the fact that the biggest margin either way was seven points. In such a game a bad break could mean the difference, and the Pistons surely got that when, with eight seconds remaining in the third period, and the team on a roll (8 straight to make it 80-79 after Boston had gone up by 7 at 79-72), Adrian Dantley, Detroit's post-up man par *excellence*, sustained a frightening concussion when he and Vinnie Johnson banged heads while diving for a loose ball from opposite directions.

Dantley exited via a stretcher and was taken to Massachusetts General Hospital. He took a lot with him, and he was badly missed in the final quarter. "That changed us from a multidimensional team to a one-dimensional team," pointed out Detroit assistant coach Dick Versace.

It meant, too, that instead of the experienced Dantley the Pistons now had the eager, but raw,

Rodman guarding Bird, and this was no day for boys to be doing men's jobs. Bird was an Olympian figure throughout, scoring 37 points, grabbing 9 rebounds and handing out 9 assists, the most important of which was a gorgeous lefty pitch-back out of a right-to-left drive across the lane to an open Dennis Johnson. DJ may have been having shooting troubles of late, but Bird had faith.

"I knew DJ would nail that one," said Bird, and he was right. That made it 106-103 with 1:03 left.

The Garden crowd was maniacal throughout, reminding everyone of what having Game 7 at home was all about. "Like I always say," Bird declared, "the crowd can get you over the hump."

Give the crowd something to savor like yesterday's game, and they could get you over Everest.

Thomas Explains

June 5, 1987 • by Bob Ryan

INGLEWOOD, Calif.—A news conference was held so Isiah Thomas could explain his unfortunate statements following last Saturday's loss to the Celtics—and the star of the conference turned out to be Larry Bird.

Thomas insisted his endorsement of teammate Dennis Rodman's assertion that Bird was an overrated white player was made in jest. "Jokingly," Thomas explained, "I said, 'I have to agree with Rodman.' I was smiling, laughing."

The league even provided a tape of his statement, and there was laughter audible after he was through saying, " . . . if Larry Bird was black, he'd be just another good guy (in this league)."

However, according to eyewitness and earwitness reporters, the laughter was not benign. "He laughed," said Scott Price of The Sacramento Bee, "but it was not a friendly laugh. It was a 'What-can-you-do-about-it?' laugh."

Concurred Ailene Voisin of the Los Angeles Herald-Examiner, whose question initiated the Thomas response, "What you don't hear on the tape the NBA provided is my question, and his long pause while he composed an answer. He definitely was *not* joking. He meant it. I'm sure of it. He knows me. He knew exactly what he was doing."

Whether anyone else believes, or cares, what Thomas says about the incident now, Bird insists he's satisfied. "The main thing," Bird said, "is that what he said didn't bother me, anyway. If it didn't bother me, and after I explained it to my family it didn't bother them, it shouldn't bother anybody else, either."

Thomas was effusive in his appreciation for Bird's backing. "I always knew he was a great ballplayer, and I respected him as a person," Thomas said, "but now I know he's an even greater person than he could ever be as a ballplayer, simply by his being here sitting next to me. It means a lot to me."

Thomas also said that this has been an extremely unpleasant week for him. "It's been very difficult for me and my family," he said.

Bird defused much of the situation throughout his appearance. At one point, he said, "Isiah's not stupid. He knows I'm a baaad player."

When the subject turned to Dennis Rodman, Bird said, "I'm gonna bust him next year. I hope he guards me every game."

The conference did little to clarify the issue, however, since Thomas was unable to explain why he came out on Monday in a New York Times column written by Ira Berkow and said his intent had to do with the matter of black-white stereotypes. Yesterday he said his intent was to make a joke. It can't be both ways and, obviously, it isn't.

What shone through, however, was Bird's wisdom. If someone had wanted to create a scenario last Saturday geared toward improving and polishing Bird's image with the national media, he or she could have done no better than stick those words into the mouths of Rodman and Thomas.

If people now choose to believe Isiah's lame attempt to rewrite aural history, they do have that privilege. As Larry says, this is America.

To Fans, the Impossible Nightmare

June 10, 1987 • by Leigh Montville

The time was 37 minutes after 11 o'clock last night and the customers left Boston Garden as if they had seen a ghost. Silence. What was the crowd? The customary 14,890? Most of these people walked and a few of them sat absolutely still and the one sound that could be heard was an alarm from a couple of exit doors in the big building. Silence.

Los Angeles Lakers 107. Boston Celtics 106. The people walked and kept quiet. They were too tired to cry.

"What happened?" a stranger from another city might ask. "What caused this strange reaction? I have never seen anything like this. What happened?"

To explain would be a long, long story. Start from the ending, perhaps—Larry Bird's jump shot from the side at the buzzer that went up, up, hit the back of the rim and caromed back on a sad line, and go from there. Stop at Magic Johnson's drive into the heart of trouble with two seconds left that won the game for the Lakers. Go back to Kareem Abdul-Jabbar's missed foul shot that fell off friendly Boston fingers and Bird's three-pointer that had given the Celtics the lead and go back and back.

How far? Go back as far as you wish. Go back to Frank Selvy's miss for the Lakers and Jerry West's heartbreak and to all of the games and all of the ghosts and all of the stories. Go back to the beginning. Take the entire saga of these two teams in this building and bring it into this one steamy June night and fast-forward and reverse and play it all over again.

Go back to the beginning of this night, the limping Celtics needing this game so much to draw even in what had been a lopsided series coming out of Los Angeles. Go back to the third quarter of this game, the Celtics flying, rolling, winning by 16. Wasn't the game finished?

Bring the action to the final quarter as the Lakers draw closer and closer and suddenly tie the game at 93-93 with 6:14 left. Bring the Celtics ahead again, rolling, 103-95, with 3:29 left. Bring the Lakers back again to 103-102 with 58 seconds left.

Stop there. Start there. Time out. Boston.

"There's a lot of players in this league who play this game, but there are only a few who are playing in the final six minutes," Magic Johnson had said only a week ago. "It's a different game in those final six minutes. Shots that guys will take in the rest of the game, they won't take here. Only a few will. Larry will. And I will."

The time was 11:27 as the Celtics came out of their huddle. Noise. Big noise. Larry was going to take the shot. The entire building knew Larry was going to take the shot. Larry took the shot.

He was pushed into the corner by Kareem Abdul-Jabbar's long arms and he took the shot in a giant arc and missed badly. Magic grabbed the rebound and came down the floor and looked around at his options and spotted the one he wanted most of all. He threw a giant lob pass toward the basket. The giant Abdul-Jabbar cut through the air and dunked as surely as if he were going through the exact change lane.

Los Angeles 104, Boston 103. There were 29 seconds left. Time out, Boston.

"Where would the ball go now?" you would ask.

"Where else?" you would answer. "Where it always goes."

The next shot came out of the tapestry of all the stories about all the games in the building. Around and around the ball went. From Dennis Johnson to Robert Parish to Dennis Johnson to Danny Ainge . . . to Larry Bird? He was free, but he was as far away from the basket as possible on the side, one step from being out of bounds. He cranked. He threw. The ball swished through the net for a three-point basket. Have there been many happier shots than that in the building? Not many.

Boston 106, Los Angeles 104. Time out, Lakers. Twelve seconds left.

"What now?" you might ask.

"You have Magic," you might answer. "You also have the man with the most famous hook shot in basketball."

It all seemed to happen in an out-of-step blur. The ball went in to Abdul-Jabbar. The foul was called. He stepped to the line in those familiar goggles. He made the first shot in the midst of noise that equaled a jet engine leaving the ground from inside a building. He missed the second and Kevin McHale had the rebound and Robert Parish had the rebound and . . . neither of them had the rebound. The ball was out of bounds and the Lakers not only had another chance with seven seconds left, but now they had a chance to flat-out win the game.

And they did.

"What can you say?" Magic Johnson said. "In the last two minutes, you saw some of the greatest basketball ever."

Go back to Magic, putting his head down and driving to the basket and letting that soft hook loose and the Lakers going crazy with two seconds left. Speed ahead to the final inbounds pass, the ball somehow reaching Bird, his shot going through the air as everyone was stock-still frozen in the seats—"I was thinking, 'Oh no, not again,'" Magic Johnson said—and the ball hitting that rim and clanging back in the reverse direction, a leather boomerang on the way home. Finish with the people walking out of the building. Silence.

"What happened?" you might ask if you do not live here.

It is a long story. Long and suddenly, surprisingly sad.

Friends, Foes for Life

BIRD'S AND MAGIC'S RELATIONSHIP ALWAYS SOMETHING SPECIAL

June 12, 1987 • by Leigh Montville

Twenty years have passed. Thirty years have passed. Forty years have passed. Forty years and more. The sun comes through the nursing home window on a spring day.

"Checkers, Larry?" Magic Johnson asks.

"You got it," Larry Bird replies.

They set up the board—Larry is black and Magic is red this time—and the crowd gathers immediately. They are the best two checkers players in the home. Far and away. The series now stands at 2,993 to 2,992.

"Who's ahead, anyway?" Magic Johnson asks.

"You know damn well who's ahead," Larry Bird says. "Just get playing. This thing will be even when I'm through with you today."

Even in checkers. Even in everything. The two men somehow have moved along two sides of the same railroad track at the same pace for their entire lives. Frick and Frack. A and B. Even and Steven.

Name a game and the two men have played it against each other. There was basketball, of course, in the beginning and then there was softball in the summer and then there was celebrity tennis

Larry Bird shoots over Magic Johnson in the Finals.

and then celebrity golf and celebrity superstars and celebrity bowling. One game somehow led into another.

"Remember the night we both drove the sulkies at the celebrity harness race?" Magic Johnson says. "Dead heat."

"What about the celebrity auto race?" Larry Bird says. "How much did those Porsches cost? You hit me—or did I hit you?—and we made headlines across America. Hilarious."

The seed of competition, once planted, somehow grew and flourished. A black guy from East Lansing, Mich. A white guy from French Lick, Ind. They looked different, perhaps, but take a chain saw to their souls and they were fraternal, if not identical, friends.

They had the same Midwestern ideals. They had the same work habits, the same senses of humor, the same competitive fires. The same talent. That was most important of all. They had the same talent, one step above everyone else who played their game, two men linked first by the talent and then by everything else.

"Yeh, yeh, the Michigan State Spartans," Magic Johnson says. "We all know how that came out."

"Ancient history," Larry Bird says. "And if I had one other basketball player on the entire team with me, we know how the result would have been different. Michigan State. I'm sick of hearing those old Michigan State stories."

They knew each other before they knew each other. Is that the way to say it? Reputations arrived before people. Press clippings. Rumors. Magic Johnson knew about this wide-eyed scorer from Indiana State before he ever saw the real person. Larry Bird knew all about Magic Johnson. Everybody knew.

The two men—two college kids, really, at the time—finally met on some of those all-star teams. Sat on the bench together. Didn't talk much. Just acknowledged each other with a smile, a nod, some commonsense gesture.

Heck, even in the pros they didn't know each other for five or six years. Magic Johnson was on one coast. Larry Bird was on the other. How would they meet? They saw each other on the evening news. They read each other's stats. They knew each other as basketball players. They knew nothing about each other as men.

"Sometimes I wish I never made that trip to French Lick," Magic Johnson says. "I wish I never really met you. Wish I thought you were the same strange dude I did at the beginning."

"Hah," Larry Bird says. "That would have been your tough luck. I taught you everything you know about everything. Hah."

The meeting in French Lick was the start. Magic Johnson went there thinking he was going to be spending the longest days of his life filming a sneaker commercial. He wound up loving the time. He and Larry talked. He and Larry talked some more. He and Larry kept talking.

What was the subject of the talk? Everything. Everything except basketball. They found how alike they were. They found they shared the same ideas. They found they were trying to do exactly the same things. They found they liked each other. They became friends.

"So let's get started," Magic Johnson says across the checkerboard. "Is it my move first, or what?"

"Name it and claim it," Larry Bird says in return. "Spin it and win it. Name your poison."

How many championships did each man's team win after they became friends? How many MVP awards did each man win individually? One would seem to own one year. The other would seem to own the next. Back and forth. One year after another. Even. Absolutely even.

They played all of the years together and apart at the same time. They did all those things. They came into the league together. They left together. They went on all the circuits together. They played all the games together. Every game. One after another. Retirement somehow was even more competitive than their careers. There were more games to play.

"Remember that time we were on 'Hollywood Squares'?" Magic Johnson says. "Remember how I was the secret square and you were just a regular square? You were so mad."

"Are you going to move, or what?" Larry Bird says. "The game today is checkers."

Time passes and championships are won and lost, but the friendship and the rivalry remain. Magic and Larry. The best forever.

It's Magic's Kingdom, 106-93

THIRD-QUARTER BLITZ HAS CELTICS REELING

June 15, 1987 • by Bob Ryan

INGLEWOOD, Calif.—This was real life, not art.

On the printed page or in celluloid worlds, perhaps the Boston Celtics' virtue would have been rewarded with another championship. With John R. Tunis at the typewriter or Frank Capra in the director's chair, a happy ending may have been written for the saga which began June 18, 1986, when Len Bias thought it appropriate to celebrate with some white poison, and peaked Thursday night when the Celtics gave their fans a fitting farewell present with a splendid show of championship basketball.

But this story was not fictional. It was all too real. And it ended in nightmarish fashion yesterday afternoon at the Forum, with Laker Girls dancing on the floor with high-rolling front-row patrons to the tune of Randy Newman's "I Love LA" during a raucous fourth-quarter timeout: with the Los Angeles Lakers running and dunking and generally having a good time; and with the NBA championship being handed over from the best of the East to the best of the West. It was LA 106, Boston 93, and for the 18th consecutive season, the reigning titlist's string of championships ends at 1.

The Celtics became ex-champions by scoring 12 points in the third quarter and by scoring on just 8 of their first 33 possessions in the second half. In so doing, they undid all the good they had accomplished during an exemplary first half of play, a solid 24 minutes in which they led by as many as 9 (34-25, on a Greg Kite tap-in at the outset of the second quarter) and at the end of which they held what appeared to be a meaningful five-point (56-51) lead.

So what happened in the third quarter to cause an 18-point (30-12) discrepancy?

"They picked up higher and became the aggressors," explained the noble Dennis Johnson (33 points, 10 rebounds in 46 relentless minutes of play). "They took the game away from us."

The Lakers had already chopped the 56-51 lead to 56-55, and the Celtics had already missed their first five shots, when James Worthy (22) made the kind of play basketball sonnets are written about. Kevin McHale tried an entry pass to a Celtic (Worthy thought Robert Parish, others said Larry Bird and still others said DJ), but whomever it was intended for, Worthy stepped up, knocked the ball away and made a spectacular sprawling save of the ball near midcourt, tipping the ball ahead to series MVP Magic Johnson (16 points, 19 assists) for a sneak-away dunk. "It was exactly the kind of play Larry Bird makes," marveled Magic. "When one man goes on the floor like that, and everybody sees it, we all have to do it."

The Magic basket erased a lead the Celtics had attained at 11-10 (in the midst of a 15-2 spurt which peaked at 19-12), and it turned out to be the only lead change the new champions would need in the second half. For they were en route to a game-deciding run of 18-2, a spurt whose foundation was a stifling defense that so affected the Celtics it was as if

Boston had undergone basketball brain transplants with the Clippers during the halftime break.

The Celtics were 0 for 7 with 3 turnovers in the first four and a half minutes of the second half; 1 for 10 with 4 turnovers by the midway point of the quarter; and 5 for 19 with 7 turnovers by the time the horrifying period was over. The Celtics scored on just 6 of 24 third-quarter possessions and, were it not for DJ, might have been shut out.

The telling sequence came at 61-58, when first Bird (as inconsequential an offensive performance as he's ever had in a big game) and then McHale took ill-advised forced runners on successive possessions. Bird's miss turned into a second-chance Worthy dunk out of a transition (Thompson wrenched the rebound away from McHale), and the McHale miss became a Byron Scott pull-up 17-footer.

The closest Boston could get in the final period was 12, but at no time, and in no sense, were the Lakers in peril. Jabbar, whose head was freshly shaven for the occasion, came back in period four full of life, tossing in corner hooks and frolicking around like a mere 39-year-old. DJ (16 first half, 17 second half) kept taking it to the hoop, but he was playing alone. Parish fouled out with 7:32 left. McHale (20 points, 10 rebounds) wound down like a Christmas toy and Bird never did check in.

The Celtics came apart. From 50 percent first-half shooting, they tumbled to 31 percent second-half boulder-tossing. There is no doubt the one thing they wanted to avoid was being the "O's" for a bunch of stylin', high-fivin' LA "X's," but that was their fate.

They'll always have the memories of two sweet Game 7 triumphs and the satisfaction of taking a victory morsel right out of the mouths of the Pistons in Game 5. They'll soon learn, if they don't know already, that New England fans have embraced them as never before. They played to win, and they did something for which LA can never thank them enough: They made LA rise to its highest level in order to become the new champion.

They lost, and they're not happy. But they'll get over it. No NBA runner-up ever had less reason to apologize for not winning the big prize.

Reggie Lewis, the Celtics' smooth first-round draft pick selected out of Northeastern in 1987.

Lewis' No. 1 Goal: Stay Same

"I know it is more of a business now, and I have to work even harder on my game to make it. That doesn't scare me. It is another part of life I have to go through."

—Reggie Lewis

June 24, 1987 • by Jackie MacMullan

He woke up yesterday morning as a Boston Celtic.

Green veins? No, not yet. Reggie Lewis simply rolled out of bed, looked in the same mirror in the same apartment in the same city and—what a relief—saw the same face.

No changes, please. Not yet.

"The thing I liked best about Reggie," said Donna Harris, his girlfriend since his freshman year at Northeastern, "is through all the fame and glory at school, he was still the same.

"He could have changed. Kids started to hang around him more when he got really good. Because of his shy nature, he doesn't really seek people out, but he's a good judge of people. He's very sensible."

The sensible side of Reggie Lewis soothed his nerves Monday afternoon, when one NBA team after another announced their choices for the future. Be patient, his sense told him, as the 20th and 21st picks of the draft went by the boards.

Not too excited, he reminded himself, when the Celtics plucked him out of their own backyard at 22.

And now? The fun begins. There is rookie camp and, he hopes, a contract. He will be paid to play basketball.

"That is a whole lot different," Lewis said. "It's a little strange to have an agent negotiating for you, someone handling your money. But I know it's wild out there. I've talked to Mark [Haisel] and Perry [Moss], and they told me how wild it can get."

Thus, there will be no Ferraris parked on the street near his apartment, no gold chains, no Caribbean vacations. Yes, he's been drafted by the Celtics, but no, he hasn't made the team. Therefore, no changes. Not yet.

"I know it is more of a business now, and I have to work even harder on my game to make it," Lewis said. "That doesn't scare me. It is another part of life I have to go through."

So how did the newest Celtic rise to the challenge yesterday? Lewis slept until 11:30 a.m., watched a couple of soap operas and headed for NU's Cabot Gym. Just like the past two months.

"I have to make sure now that when I come in here, I come to work," said Lewis between jumpers. "I'll need to get things accomplished. No more fooling around in the gym."

Already he's begun to realize the difference between being a Northeastern Husky and a Boston Celtic. He is the same person, but his image has been altered, suddenly, his baskets count for more. Suddenly, he is legitimate.

"It's funny how people change," he said. "Four years ago there were people who said I'd never make it. Now those same people are acting like they've been there right from the beginning. It's pretty easy to figure out. I know which ones were my friends all along, guys like Andre [LaFleur], who have been there since my freshman year."

LaFleur, like Lewis, was a four-year starter. Together Monday night, the two friends toasted their futures (LaFleur was drafted in the fifth round by Houston) and the memories of Northeastern. Champagne flowed and friends dropped by, kidding Lewis that Celtic personnel had hired Secret Service agents to keep an eye on their first-round choice.

The grim reality of that is Len Bias, the Celtics' No. 1 choice last year who died from cocaine intoxication two days after he was selected by Boston. Those who heard stories of how wonderful Bias was were apprehensive when they heard the same glowing reports on Lewis. And the skepticism did not escape the NU star.

"I don't mind that," Lewis said. "I know a lot of people have Len Bias on their mind. I know people want to make sure the same thing won't happen to me.

"I understand. But it won't stop me from having a nice time."

The nicest of times will include a trip home to Baltimore next week and, shortly after that, a search for a new apartment—and a new phone number.

"I'm not the type of person that likes to be bothered a lot," said Lewis, who didn't have to worry about that a week ago. "I guess at some point, I'll have to watch where I go."

For now, the newest Celtic is easy to find. Just take a cruise down Huntington Avenue to the old Cabot Gym and look for the slender chap wearing the Northeastern T-shirt who is practicing crossover dribbles ad nauseam.

Boring? He's sorry to disappoint you. But he's not interested in anything else—not yet.

"He hasn't talked at all about buying this or buying that," said Harris. "Anyhow, the first thing he does get will be something for his mother."

As for No. 35, he realizes it all won't sink in completely until his friend Andre goes in one direction toward Houston and he heads in another toward that parquet floor he never played on in four years at NU.

Then, maybe then, Lewis will allow himself to think about what this really means.

"I honestly don't think my life will change too much," said Lewis yesterday, pulling at his red Husky sneakers. "I guess we'll have to wait and see."

The Artful Codger

HIS SCULPTURE MAY GROW OLD, BUT BIRD IS AN AGELESS WONDER

February 4, 1988 • by Leigh Montville

The face will start to develop a few cracks, a few fissures. The body tone will start to disappear. Not all at once. Slowly. Very slowly.

"What's with the statue?" visitors to the New England Sports Museum will begin to ask.

"Pardon?" the curator will say.

"The statue. It's changing. It doesn't look like Larry Bird anymore."

"Preposterous."

The changes will be small at first—visible only to the closest friends and relatives of the Celtics star—but after two years and three and four years they will become increasingly noticeable. The wooden Larry Bird suddenly will be wearing glasses. Glasses?

"Larry Bird doesn't wear glasses," the visitors will say. "No way."

"Well, this Larry Bird does," the curator will say.

"Well, when did he start?"

"Hard to say. Just noticed one day that they were there."

Change will follow change. The statue will become obviously older. A little wooden potbelly will develop. The wooden backside will thicken. A spot at the crown of the wooden haircut will begin to clear. The face will change in subtle ways. Older. Definitely.

The real Larry Bird, however, will stay the same.

"How do you feel?" the sportswriters will ask as another NBA campaign approaches. "Ready for another season?"

"Never felt better," the real Larry Bird will say. "Looks like the title if we can stay healthy."

One player after another will retire. Nights will be held for Danny Ainge and Dennis Johnson and Robert Parish and Kevin McHale. Numbers will be hoisted to the rafters next to the collection of championship flags that continues to grow. New players will arrive. Brad Lohaus will retire. Reggie Lewis will retire.

Larry Bird will be 35 years old, then 40, then 50. Still the same. He will hold every record possible. Magic Johnson will have that white hair and be working as the chief executive of some bank in Michigan. Kareem Abdul-Jabbar will be broke again and working in a record store. Michael Jordan will be president of the United States.

Larry Bird still will be sticking the 3-pointer and tossing in the running hook and diving on the floor. Fifty years old! Still the same!

"I went home for the summer, worked hard, tried to add a few shots to my repertoire," Larry will say when asked about his condition. "Well, I guess I've worked hard, plus I've been a bit lucky."

"Some luck," the general managers from the other teams in the league will ask. "Some wooden luck, if you know what we mean. Some great wooden condition he has. Woodn't it be wonderful if we all had the same wooden condition?"

The aging statue and the non-aging basketball player obviously would be subjects of great study. Who cannot fail to see what is happening? There will be a time—perhaps it will be when the wooden black Converse sneakers are replaced by fluffy slippers—when scientists become involved in the study. Scientists. Gerontologists. Artists. Psychiatrists. Whittlers of all kinds. The statue will be the most famous statue in the country. The New England Sports Museum will become the most visited museum in the country.

"How did all this come to pass?" the scientists will ask. "What happened to make this the real-life reenactment of 'The Picture of Dorian Gray'?"

The events of February 3, 1988, will be studied carefully. Wasn't that the date the statue was unveiled at the Garden? Pictures of Larry next to the statue will show that man and wood looked exactly alike. Sixteen coats of lacquer to match the blue sparkle in the eyes. Larry will be in that foul-shooting pose, that wooden Spalding basketball ready to be fired.

"He's probably got a better vertical leap than me," Larry Bird said. "He's probably faster, too. But he probably doesn't shoot as well."

It will be noted—hmmmmm—that even before the public unveilings, Rhode Island sculptor Armand LaMontagne had to give this creation a more youthful haircut and remove "10 or 15" pounds that had been lost during the summer. Was that the beginning of the process? Hmmmmmm. It will be noted that Larry mentioned he had an eerie feeling when he first saw the statue.

Films of the day will show Larry and the sculptor and some other officials standing next to the statue as it was unveiled at an afternoon news conference. A second, public unveiling will also be shown, the green shroud pulled back at halftime of a win against the Indiana Pacers and the statue rolled around the parquet floor on a little dolly to cheers of "Lar-ree, Lar-ree," surely the grandest unveiling of a sculpture this side of "Winged Victory."

"Amazing," the scientists will say. "Take a look at the sculpture's face under the microscope."

"Yes?"

"Notice how a little stubble has started to grow on the sculpture's face between the first picture in the afternoon and the second picture at night," the scientists will say. "Notice how Larry's beard somehow hasn't grown a bit. The process already has begun."

Older and older. The sculpture will sit down in a rocking chair. The sculpture will wear a hearing aid. The sculpture will smell of Vicks VapoRub and will hold a cane and will have a wooden blanket across its lap.

The person will hit that jumper. Sixty years old. Seventy years old. No different. Never better. There will be attempts, of course, to make similar sculptures of other famous athletes in their prime, but of course the attempts will fail.

The mold—it will turn out—was broken once Larry Bird was made.

He's an All-Star—
Naturally

Danny Ainge was a born athlete but worked hard to reach the top level.

February 7, 1988 • by Ian Thomsen

Had everything come easily for Danny Ainge, he would not be an All-Star guard with the Celtics today. This is his lesson, taught by a babe who was catching 30-yard football passes, in stride, at the age of 3.

Three years old, and Ainge was beating fifth- and sixth-graders.

"We would challenge strangers from other areas to a game, and we would always bring along Danny as our secret weapon," says Danny's older brother, David, an insurance man in Sacramento, Calif. "He would run down the sideline, and no one would guard him—he was, like you say, 3 or 4 years old— and we'd throw him the ball and he'd catch it. It was worth one or two touchdowns a game."

"My image of him is as a little kid with a shaved head, his ears sticking out and his two front teeth gone, at the age of 2," says Danny's oldest brother, Doug, 33, a high school teacher in Forest Grove, Ore. "The reason his teeth were gone was that he ran into

a coffee table or jumped off a couch or something. He was 2 years old and he was constantly cracking jokes and running around. He was the third kid, and third kids have to work hard to get attention."

"He found out at a very early age that if you were tough, if you didn't cry, then you could play," says his father, Don, 52. "If you cried, they sent you home. They'd tackle him, throw him down, and he didn't cry. He'd get right back up."

"It made me feel so good," Ainge says, "being able to play with the older kids."

He always has felt challenged by things he seemed to accomplish so easily. This week, Ainge should break the season record for three-point field goals: The record is 92, he has 83, and 37 games remain. He already has doubled the record for consecutive games with a 3-pointer (23). He is shooting the longest reasonable shots in the game better than anyone ever has.

This was the challenge: to find a niche in a Celtic lineup already dominated by four players worthy of the Hall of Fame. What positions remain in such a successful company? After seven years, he has found his spot in the corners, some 23 feet from the basket. Seven years it took a talented man to become all that he might have been.

"He's an athlete, see, a very good athlete," Celtics president Red Auerbach says after watching the team work out in Brookline last week. "Right now I watch him in practice, and I think he's getting to be a lazy athlete. Not during games, but in practice. I really think he could work a little harder, plan a little better.

"I'm serious when I say this. When you reach a certain level—look at Larry (Bird). People start reacting to what you do, and you have to come up with something else. You've got to go and make your own level one above it. He's got to start doing different things. But then, I'm never satisfied."

No one ever has been, not with Ainge. His athletic brothers were four and five years older. They dominated high school sports in Eugene, Ore. As a batboy in second grade, Ainge would have been good enough to start at second base for his father's American Legion team of fifth- and sixth-graders. In basketball, he handled the ball and guarded the best pivotmen. In football, he was a quarterback, a wide receiver and a defensive back. He was among the first to be named high school All-American in all three sports. On a Saturday, he might play a baseball double-header, play a summer league basketball game at night and compete in four or five events at the University of Oregon's all-comers track and field meets in between. "If there was any time, I would try to sneak in 18 holes of golf," Ainge says. "I love golf."

"He was the sweetest, nicest kid before and after games," Don Ainge says. "Just the sweetest, most loving kid. Then the bell would go off on the game, and I don't know what would happen. I remember being one of 35 parents in the stands watching these kids play baseball in the fifth grade. Danny comes around third, the catcher is standing 3 or 4 feet up the line waiting for the ball to come in, and Danny knocks the catcher down and pushes him over. All the parents are yelling at me, 'Is that the way you teach your kid to play ball?' But I know that Danny doesn't think he's being dirty. He's saying, 'Why is this dummy standing in the base line?'"

"Our mother hated it," David Ainge says. "She sat in the stands and listened to opposing fans make snide comments. They'd say something out of line, and she'd say, 'He's not so bad,' or, 'He doesn't usually do that.' She was funny about it."

She would ask Danny if he could stop pouting and whining and dramatizing his most public appearances. He could not then, though in the last few years he has become aware of his expressions. "People criticize me for the way I act sometimes, and I think it's accurate," Ainge says. "I've made a conscious effort to become a lot better. A lot of times, it looks like I'm whining at the ref when I'm really mad at myself."

"I think that's probably my fault," Don Ainge says. "His brothers were the same way, and I know when I played, I used to do that. It must be genetic. But making those faces is like Michael Jordan sticking out his tongue—it's just what you do while you're playing."

No matter what he has done, incidents and trouble have swirled around him. His coaches fought over him. One baseball coach said Ainge couldn't play basketball, too: Ainge answered by enlisting with a lesser baseball league and playing both sports. No one wanted him to play football and risk his future, but he would see the team practicing and soon that coach would be glad to see his best player returning to the team. Opponents at some high schools would build a pot of $150 or more for

the player to knock Danny Ainge out of the game. "I never got put out except once," Ainge says. "I caught a pass, had the wind knocked out of me and went out for one play, but that guy won the money. That's just the mentality of football."

Football was out, even though Don Ainge's friend from college, John Robinson, wanted to sign Ainge as a wide receiver. When he decided he would not attend the University of Oregon, his father lost insurance customers. He attended Brigham Young University in Utah, where he could practice his Mormon faith. He signed to play baseball in the summers with the Toronto Blue Jays, was married in his sophomore year, fathered a child, attended classes and drove the tired BYU basketball program into the Final Eight of the 1981 NCAA basketball tournament.

"That was funny," Don Ainge says. "When he was a kid and things got tense, he would always laugh. It was the craziest thing. In high school, when he was a junior, they went running out onto the court for the state championship game and he's got a rubber Indian mask on and a feather on his head. He was behind the other players, and none of them saw him until he'd taken his first layup in it. After that they were loose, and they won that game."

Before a BYU teammate could shoot two important free throws, Ainge pulled from his jockstrap a picture of the player's girlfriend. "What are you doing—a picture of my girlfriend in your jock?" he said before making the shots. Another player reminded Ainge of his imminent wedding night moments before Ainge made two free throws at 0:07 to win the Western Athletic Conference championship. There were huge pillow fights in meeting rooms before games, and when BYU coach Frank Arnold would yell at his team, Ainge would wrap his arm around him and say, "Come on, coach, it's not so bad."

"Coach never got upset," says Celtics forward Fred Roberts, Ainge's teammate at BYU. "At that time, Danny had already signed a $300,000 bonus with the Blue Jays. I guess coach figured Danny was making more than he was . . . I don't think he knew about the magic acts, though."

Magic acts?

"We'd be standing at the free throw line and Danny would say, 'Fred, look at this'—and he'd pull a handkerchief out of his hand like a magician. Or he'd call us all together and do it when someone had a pressure free throw to make."

Where did he hide the handkerchief?

"He never told me," Roberts says. "He was really great to have around. Once Danny left, everybody got so tensed up that we couldn't win a game."

It was during Ainge's senior year that he realized he wanted to play basketball. In public, he maintained his commitment to baseball, even though he'd never hit .250 in his minor and major league summers with the Blue Jays. As the NBA Draft approached, he told everyone he planned to fulfill his baseball contract.

"Everyone was telling me all along that the basketball travel was worse, that the lifestyle was worse," Ainge says. "Well, I've got four kids. I want to get in and out of cities and back home. I realize now that in baseball you never get a night off."

"One day, on the road, Red called me and I told him I was playing baseball. He said, 'That's b.s. You're a basketball player, and that's all there is to it. Don't worry about the contract.' He'd only seen me play a few times, but he knew—he just knew. He was the first guy to tell me that, and he was right. No one else would tell me that I would die if I gave up basketball, but that was the way I felt deep down inside."

Auerbach told Ainge the morning of the draft that the Celtics planned to take him late in the first round. In Chicago with the Blue Jays, Ainge and Toronto teammate Garth Iorg sneaked unnoticed into the Chicago Bulls' draft party at a downtown hotel.

"The first round came, and they picked Charles Bradley," Ainge says. "I was disappointed, but I saw they had the 26th pick. Then they picked Tracy Jackson. I said, 'Man, maybe they found out they couldn't draft me.' I looked at the draft order and found they were picking 31st, so I waited . . . and then I got all excited."

Soon after he was taken early in the second round, he called his father with the news he wanted to try basketball. Ainge says he was not ready to give up his career in baseball. "I just knew I didn't want to go without giving basketball a chance," he says. "Had the San Antonio Spurs (or a similar franchise) taken me, I might not have gone through everything I did to play basketball."

His idea was to try the NBA and then decide whether to make a career of basketball or baseball.

It didn't work out that way. Ainge offered to return his bonus plus interest, and his father drew a cashier's check for $328,000, payable to Toronto. However, written into his Blue Jays contract, which he had signed without an agent (NCAA basketball rules prohibit agents), was a stipulation preventing him from playing another sport. According to Ainge, Toronto general manager Pat Gillick agreed to release Ainge from the contract. "Then Pat came back and said, 'They want $1 million for him,'" Don Ainge says. "He said, 'There's nothing I can do.'"

Says Gillick, "I really can't recall. It was a long time ago . . . I still think he would have been a better baseball player than he has been in basketball."

The Blue Jays and Celtics sued each other over Boston's right to negotiate with Ainge. During the three-day New York hearing in the fall of '81, Ainge could be seen sleeping in the back row of the courtroom while the two sides argued over who owned him. His wife gave birth to their second child while he was in New York. In Utah, he was criticized for trying to break a contract, despite his claims that the Blue Jays had already told him he could leave.

"Toronto told me I could do it, Boston told me I could do it," Ainge says. "Then we got to the trial and they just started lying, just lying. People were worrying about these corporations, these machine organizations, and they're saying a 21-year-old kid is cheating these two sports conglomerates? It just didn't make sense to me."

Toronto won the ruling, and Blue Jays president Peter Bavasi—who was feuding with Auerbach—celebrated by puffing a cigar in front of the Celtics' counsel.

The two teams were forcing him into a final decision. Ainge took a cab to Marvin Miller's office and immediately retired from baseball. He returned to BYU as a junior varsity coach. The Blue Jays were still demanding $1 million from the Celtics.

"Nothing was happening," Don Ainge says. "Two days before Thanksgiving, our attorney said, 'Why don't you just wait? Danny can sit out the year, he'll go back into the draft and he'll be chosen by a team willing to pay the money to Toronto.' I talked to Danny and he said, 'I don't want to wait.'

"It was awful. He was miserable. So I called Harry Mangurian (the Celtics owner) and I said, 'Toronto wants to talk and Danny wants to play.' Then I called Pat Gillick and I said, 'Boston wants to talk.'"

The two sides met in Room 408 at the Ritz-Carlton the day after Thanksgiving. When each team realized that neither was willing to negotiate—that Don Ainge had rigged the meeting—the Blue Jays walked out of the meeting. Don Ainge chased them down the hall to the elevator.

He was crying.

"I said, 'You're talking about my son,'" Don Ainge says. "I wouldn't let them leave. I stood in front of the elevator door until they agreed to come back."

The Blue Jays returned to the room and agreed to let the Celtics negotiate a contract with Ainge. This took 45 minutes. Then, while Auerbach and Mangurian played gin, the attorneys agreed to a settlement. It cost the Celtics $400,000-$500,000 to sign Ainge.

The ensuing years have not been easy. His mother, Kay, died. After fighting cancer for a year, she committed suicide in 1983. "Danny came back for the funeral," says Don Ainge, who has trouble talking about it. "He gave one of the nicest talks I've ever heard anyone give."

He has overcome his first two NBA seasons playing for Bill Fitch. He was not the immediate star he was predicted to become. His finger was bitten by Tree Rollins, and Milwaukee coach Don Nelson called Ainge a cheap-shot artist. He was booed by opposing fans everywhere. "That flustered me," he admits. "It affected me."

No more. Danny Ainge is 28. He says he likes to hear the boos, that it means he's worth noticing. His finger has healed. He plays regularly for coach K. C. Jones. He is everything he was as a teenager in Oregon, affable away from the court, controversial on it, emotional and hyperactive always.

Again, everything seems so easy for him.

"A couple of weeks ago, he called me," Don Ainge says from his insurance office in San Jose, Calif. "He said, 'Dad, do you know any fathers whose sons are on the All-Star team?' I said, 'Congratulations, that's just great, just great.' I just feel so good about the kid."

Last week, father wrote son a poem. It concludes:
Macauley, McHale, Cousy and Bird,
Russell, Red and Dave,
Their legends live on, long after they're gone
Their names will be bronzed with the brave
Sure, Danny might fade, like a Boston
dusk shade,

And his shirt might not fly from the tiers.
But we'll remember him still,
We'll remember the thrill,
Of the Bean Town Bombardier.

Split Decision at The Garden

HAWKS KO'D BY CELTICS

May 23, 1988 • by Bob Ryan

Well. Hey. It wasn't a bad game if you're into watching athletic legends-to-be engaging in one-on-one personal combat, or if your idea of a nice seventh game is when the teams shoot a combined 59 percent, turn it over scant 15 times and just generally have the raucous Garden fans alternately jumping out of their seats and clutching the religious objects of their choice.

If there is a better brand of basketball on display somewhere, it certainly isn't on *this* planet. The Atlanta Hawks were magnificent in the biggest *game* this particular group has ever played. And they'd be the ones moving on to play Detroit for the Eastern Conference championship this week were it not for the collective team class of the Boston Celtics and the virtuoso skill level of Larry Bird, who compressed 20 of his 34 points—on 9-for-10 shooting—into the fourth quarter as the Celtics squeezed out an exhausting 118-116 triumph before 14,890 enraptured fans yesterday afternoon.

Split off the glorious whole was a spectacular fourth-quarter subplot: Larry Bird vs. Dominique Wilkins. The Hawks star threw in 15 of his frightening 47 in the final period, and there were times when there appeared to be nothing else going on. It was Larry and Nique, Larry and Nique, and it was chilling.

"They each put their team on their back and said, 'Let's go,'" said Hawks coach Mike Fratello.

Boston never trailed in the fourth quarter, but the Celtics couldn't create any daylight over the resilient Hawks until a jumper in the lane by Bird, two free throws by the inspired Kevin McHale (33 points, 13 rebounds, 4 blocks) and a typically nerveless 3-pointer (considering the context) from the left

Dominique Wilkins defends Larry Bird in Game 7 of the 1988 Eastern Conference semifinals, but neither man could stop the other during a classic duel.

all-time Garden Game 7 record to 15-2, but not before Atlanta had come eerily close to knocking them out of the playoff hunt.

Game 6 had been a legitimate playoff war, but Game 7 was majestic. Atlanta was the aggressor from the tap, emerging from the first period with a 30-28 lead and the needed confidence that it could win another game here.

The crucial juncture of the first half came at the 5½-minute mark. The Hawks, who had twice led by 6 (36-30, 40-34), were still in control at 42-39. Bird to that point was struggling (a 2-for-7 first quarter), and the only consistent source of offense for Boston had been McHale. Good defense was keeping Boston in the game against an Atlanta team that was benefiting not only from the jump shooting of Wilkins, but also the slashing drives, steely jumpers

wing by Bird left the Celtics ahead by a 112-105 count with 1:43 remaining.

Appropriately, the Hawks battled back. Wilkins hit a sensational jump hook over three men in the lane (112-107) and then worked his way back to the foul line for two more (112-109, 47 seconds to go). The right side was cleared for Bird, who backed 'Nique in and then made a running lefty drive with 26 seconds remaining (114-109).

The relentless Wilkins followed up his own missed dunk attempt (114-111), whereupon Doc Rivers goaltended a Danny Ainge sneak-away drive. It was 116-111 with 17 seconds left, and it *still* wasn't over. Before it finally did end, Rivers would make two foul shots (0:11), Dennis Johnson would make one of two at both the 10- and 5-second marks, Tree Rollins would sink a lefty jump hook and with one second left, Ainge would grab Wilkins at midcourt, sending him to the line trailing by 3 (118-115), needing obviously, to make the first, miss the second and have something positive happen with the rebound.

He did make the first. The second bounded off harmlessly to the left side. Robert Parish directed it to DJ and a memorable game and significant series were both over. The Celtics had increased their

and clever feeds of Rivers (16 points, 18 assists) and the marksmanship of the heretofore-silent Randy Wittman, who would finish the game with 22 points on 11-for-13 shooting all from the outside.

A shovel tap off the heel of his hand by McHale started the Celtics on a roll that carried them to a 59-58 halftime lead. The initial go-ahead basket at 45-44 came on a right base line post-up jumper by—are you ready?—Reggie Lewis, who would later make a nice jumper in the middle of the lane.

A brief third-quarter Boston spurt created a 67-60 lead, but that served only to ignite the Hawks, who closed quickly to 67-64. Boston needed a momentum-buster somewhere, and up stepped Dennis Johnson, who drilled three consecutive open jumpers. Even though an Atlanta countersurge briefly regained the lead (77-76), the seed had been planted that it would not be wise to leave DJ alone any longer. Take note, incidentally, that in this certified Big Game DJ did *all* of his scoring in the second half.

He also made a vital steal late in the period. It was 82-all and the Hawks were holding for one shot when DJ poke-checked the ball from Rivers and sailed in to give Boston a 2-point lead going into the fourth quarter.

Bird had been bothered again by Wilkins' tough defense, plus the usual quota of double-teams. He also had missed some open first-quarter jumpers, and entering the fourth quarter the question was, when, if ever, was Larry going to act like Larry?

He jump-started with a jumper off a pick to make it 88-86. He followed that up with a moonshot from the right (90-88). "They weren't double-teaming me as much," he said, "because of DJ. If he hits that shot, it opens it up for everybody. After you hit a couple, it gets easier."

A falling-down, driving, lefty, banked three-point drive ("a lucky shot"—Bird) was next (93-90). That was immediately answered by a Wilkins set shot 3-pointer, and the Great Shootout was a stretch of 99 seconds when it went: Wilkins deep left corner, Bird lefthanded jumper in the lane, Wilkins stop-and-popper, Bird 20-footer from the right and Wilkins tough banker, the last shot tying the game at 103 (4:38 left).

But if 'Nique could have one shot back, it would surely be the forced effort in the lane he took following a Bird bucket that broke the 105 tie. But since he had made about 12 equally improbable shots already, it's difficult to knock him for missing one.

The thing is, aside from one deep-down in-and-out, Bird wasn't missing *anything*. And he even atoned for that by promptly stealing an entry pass, heading downcourt and making a jumper. Bird finished it, all right, but in order to win this one the Fab Five all had to reach back for that Something Extra against a younger, deeper team that has matured considerably in the last 10 days. K. C. Jones substituted only once (a brief Fred Roberts for McHale) in the second half in his desperate attempt to put down the youthful insurrection and prolong his own coaching career.

No one, but no one ever dreamed the Celtics would need seven games to subdue a club they had always believed was essentially mindless and simply not on their level.

"It took everything we had to beat them," acknowledged Bird.

One look in his tired eyes answered any questions concerning the sincerity of that appraisal.

Reluctantly, the Torch Is Passed

June 4, 1988 • by Leigh Montville

PONTIAC, Mich.—There were three seconds left, and that was that. Larry Bird walked off the floor and Danny Ainge walked off the floor and Dennis Johnson and the limping, gimping Robert Parish and Kevin McHale went with them.

There were three seconds left and the celebration had begun inside the huge arena. Five starting Celtics walked and walked and . . . Kevin McHale stopped. He shook Isiah Thomas' hand.

"Go get 'em," the Celtics forward said in the middle of the noise in the middle of the floor of the Silverdome at 11:30 last night. "Neither of those teams want to play physical out there in the West. Go right after 'em. Don't be satisfied with getting there. Go get 'em. You can. You're good."

Thus the torch was passed. Go get 'em. There was not a lot of ceremony involved, but—then again—not much was needed. The Detroit Pistons were the new kings of the professional basketball East, 95-90 winners in this sixth and final game of the best-of-seven playoff series to determine a representative for next week's NBA Finals. The Boston Celtics were going home.

"The Pistons were better," one Celtic after another had to agree. "No matter how much you talk, you have to say the Pistons were better."

"You can only talk so much about what you're doing wrong before you have to talk about what the other team was doing right," McHale said. "You have to say that's a hell of a defensive team."

"They covered everything," Danny Ainge said. "There never seemed to be any open shots. They forced us to take shots we didn't want to take. They played good defense."

TORCH GETS PASSED
This final game was snipped from the same cloth as all the other games. The game was a flat-out struggle for the Celtics. Never did they seem to have a rhythm, a flow. Never did they find a secret word or code or 20-foot jumper that worked again and again. Every shot was put through the basket with a lot of hammering, a lot of Black & Decker noise.

When did scoring a basket become such a hard task? Men who are paid a lot of money to put this round leather ball through this much larger metal rim suddenly could not do the simple act that had made them millionaires.

"And it wasn't one of those 'Larry just wasn't hitting' stories, either," Danny Ainge said. "We had a lot more problems than that."

"I think we shot 10 percentage points worse in the series than we did during the season," McHale said. "You just can't do that. Forty percent (actually 41) during the series. That just won't get it done."

The individual pieces of the Celtics game had disappeared. It was as if all the pieces on a chessboard suddenly were restricted, their moves cut by half or even more. Queens and bishops and castles had become rooks. Pawns, one space, no more.

Bird seemed smothered by the Pistons' Dennis Rodman. The butterfly jumper simply would not work. WOULD NOT WORK. He was 4 for 17 in the game, 23 percent. Struggling. Even on his drives, the ball would go around the rim, spinning hard, spinning out. He looked the game by his force of will. The will could not work. Not this time.

Ainge? He scored two points in the final two games. He came out of a whirlpool in this one, troubled by a back that ached and throbbed, couldn't hit a shot. Couldn't anything. Three-point king. One for 11. Couldn't throw his dirty laundry into a clothes hamper. Dennis Johnson? Also aching. Aching worse. Brought to the city a day late from his bed at home. Walking as if he were Fred Sanford going to get the morning paper. Trying to fight through his bad back. Unable to move the way he wanted to move.

"Everybody was just getting frustrated out there," Dennis Johnson said. "We weren't hitting once again, and everybody started forcing shots. Frustrated."

Robert Parish was out of the game before the first period was finished, walking slowly on a knee bruised in a collision with the Pistons' Vinnie Johnson. McHale mostly was McHale, spinning through the middle, finding his offense, but the Pistons closed on him as if he were a mouse in a trap. How could he move? He was playing with reserves who had not played much in these games—with Mark Acres and Dirk Minniefield—and the Pistons were able to shuffle extra people to the trouble spots.

Hard. Everything was hard for the Celtics. Harder and harder, to be exact. As this game went longer—as most of the games went longer—everything become harder and harder. Too old? Too tried? Too whatever. The Pistons were the team that was flying at the end of these games. The Celtics were the ones who were not.

"You have to give them credit," Danny Ainge said. "They're the Pistons—and I don't like the Pistons, just don't like 'em—but you have to give them credit."

He sat in the locker room that was quiet and businesslike. An era was ending as tall men took showers. Red Auerbach was talking quietly about retirement. Larry Bird had a crowd around him in a corner. Robert Parish dressed without a word, no one bothering him.

"What will I do if it's Detroit against the Lakers in the Finals?" Danny Ainge asked himself—more than anyone else—as he had a sudden thought. "That would be a tough one."

"Would you watch?" a reporter asked.

Ainge thought for half a second.

"I don't think so," he said.

Bulls Edge Celtics

December 7, 1988 • by Jackie MacMullan

CHICAGO—He hoisted his club, put it atop his slender shoulders. Then hustled down on defense and tried to prevent Michael Jordan from doing the same for Chicago.

There's only one problem. Reggie Lewis, who started last night for the first time in his career, is new at this: Jordan has been carrying the load ever since he glided into the NBA as a highly touted rookie in 1984.

So Jordan's team stole a 105-100 victory over the Celtics last night in Chicago Stadium in a battle that went down to the final seconds. In those decisive moments, the Bulls' franchise player hit all six of his free throws to send Boston packing.

The Celtics exited valiantly. The battered locals took the floor with a flu-ridden Brian Shaw, without Dennis Johnson (strained Achilles' tendon) and without Danny Ainge, who was a surprise scratch because of recurring flu symptoms.

Lewis picked up the slack and was nothing short of spectacular in the process. Not only did he "hold" Jordan to 38 points. But he pumped in a career-high 33 on the other end.

"I disrespected him, and that was my mistake," said Jordan. "I played terrible defense tonight. Lewis gained my respect.

"Now, don't get me wrong, I think he has talent. But it's the first time he's ever been out there scoring for that many minutes, and I think he got tired. I've been doing it a lot longer, and I've learned to adjust."

Boston was down 1 (98-97) when Jim Paxson's jumper rolled off the rim at 2:06. Lewis leaped and hauled down the offensive rebound on the weak side, but was called for a foul over the back. The Celtics argued vehemently (the replay showed little evidence of contact by Lewis), but Jordan was awarded a pair of free throws at the other end, and it was a 3-point game (100-97, Bulls) with 2:04 left.

"[Jordan] mistimed the jump," said Lewis. "But because it's me guarding him, he's gonna get the call."

"One play doesn't lose the game, but that was the biggest one," said Kevin McHale (26 points, 10 rebounds). "I was standing right there, a foot and a half from the play, and Reggie got the ball clean. That's a four-point swing right there."

So, Micheal. Did Lewis push you?

"Somebody did," Jordan answered.

Ainge, Lohaus Dealt to Kings

GUARD'S EXIT IS NO BIG SURPRISE

February 24, 1989 • by Jackie MacMullan

Has *anyone* gotten used to the idea yet of Danny Ainge in a uniform other than the green and white of the Boston Celtics? Have Sacramento Kings fans, the same ones who booed Ainge so loudly just two nights ago, gotten used to the idea they will now applaud him in their starting back court?

Nothing was doing until late yesterday, when the Kings agreed to swap center Joe Kleine and forward Ed Pinckney for Ainge and second-year forward Brad Lohaus. It is a trade that should not send shock waves through the community, despite Ainge's longevity and popularity here.

For starters, the worst-kept secret in basketball was that Boston needed a backup center. Kleine, a burly 7-foot workhorse, is a prototype backup. His work habits are exemplary, he has developed a nice jump hook, he takes up a lot of room in the paint and works hard off the boards. In fact, he was working so hard for the Kings they recently gave the 26-year-old Arkansas alumnus the starting nod in the pivot over Jim Petersen. Kleine is averaging 6.7 points and 5.1 boards a game. He is also one of the top foul shooters in the league (91.9 percent).

Now, the big redhead should not be mistaken for anything but a top reserve, but that's exactly what the Celtics were looking for. Kevin McHale and Robert Parish can cut down on their minutes, a particularly worrisome problem of late since Parish's chronic elbow problems have flared up.

Pinckney, the slender 6-9 forward who helped Villanova to its dream national championship in 1985, is a little harder to figure. He is obviously talented, yet has not flourished in the NBA. His offensive output has varied from night to night, and he has not improved on his perimeter shooting since he came into the league.

On the upside, Pinckney is only 25 and the sight of Pinckney, Brian Shaw, Reggie Lewis and Parish running the break together conjures up just the kind of images Coach Jimmy Rodgers has been trying to create. The kid also has some sweet inside moves, when he has a notion to unleash them.

Now for the most pressing question: Why was Ainge the one to go?

There are a few reasons. No. 1, he and McHale were the most marketable and the Celtics view No. 32 as too valuable a commodity to give up.

Of all the veterans, Ainge was struggling the most under the new regime of Jimmy Rodgers. The two differed greatly in their approach to the game, a fact that became public when the two clashed over Ainge's shot selection during a game in Charlotte.

Ainge, a fiery competitor, wasn't thrilled about coming off the bench, and he was adamant about

Danny Ainge embraced his reputation as an agitator during his eight seasons with the Celtics.

his right to shoot the 3-pointer, despite often being discouraged.

In the last couple of weeks, Ainge met with general manager Jan Volk to discuss some of his concerns. As the trading deadline approached, Ainge joked that if he did stay in Boston, "it could be worse."

Doesn't sound like a guy who's dying to stick around, does it? With Brian Shaw coming along at point guard and Reggie Lewis able to fit in at the 2 slot, the Celtics finally determined Ainge could be expendable.

That is the gamble of this whole deal. With Larry Bird out, and Lewis still logging most of his time at forward, Boston has traded its only true outside shooter. Together the starting back court of Shaw and Dennis Johnson are shooting 42.6 percent from the floor.

Ainge was also one of the best athletes on the team and could never be criticized for lack of effort. He was pesky, relentless, knowledgeable and emotional. He will be missed.

Will Boston miss Ainge's outside shooting? Definitely. How much will depend on the development of their *remaining* personnel.

Finally, is this a deal that could ultimately take the Celtics back to the top? The answer is the same as it has been for months: not without Larry Bird.

Brown Incident Another Case of Area's Prejudice

September 23, 1990 • by Bob Ryan

Right now Dee Brown has got to believe that the folks back home in Jacksonville were right.

"They told me Boston was a prejudiced city," he explains. "They said, 'You're not going to be happy there.' I'm sure the people who told me this are patting themselves on the back."

Surely, you've heard the news, about how the Celtics' No. 1 draft choice was sitting in his car with his fiancee across the street from the Wellesley post office reading his mail Friday afternoon when he was accosted by seven police officers, who produced firearms, ordered him from the car and made him either lie face down (his version) or kneel (theirs) while they tried to determine if he was the man who had robbed a branch of the South Shore National Bank Tuesday. It took 20 agonizing, humiliating minutes before Dee Brown was cleared.

The police officers, like most everyone in Wellesley, are Caucasian. Brown is an African-American. This is a front-page story for one reason only, the celebrity of Dee Brown. If Dee Brown happened to be the young IBM trainee he is capable of being rather than a large part of the Boston Celtics' future, you would be unaware of the incident.

It would just be another Day in the Life of an African-American in a troubled society.

The Wellesley police can say what they wish, but white people don't have to put up with this. At least when white people are involved, a description is worth something.

"I don't look anything like the guy they're after," Brown sighs. "I've seen a picture in the Wellesley paper of the guy they want. When I saw it, I said, 'Wait a minute. That doesn't make any sense.' They're describing a light-skinned guy with green eyes between 25 and 30."

Suffice it to say that 21-year-old Dee Brown is darker-skinned than 95 percent of the African-American population. The Crayola box must have been a real challenge to these Wellesley officers.

Says Brown, "I spent a lot of time on Friday night looking in the mirror and saying, 'Am I crazy? Do I look like this guy?'"

Meanwhile, local Blacks simply say, "Welcome to the club, kid."

"I wasn't surprised to hear about this," says veteran broadcaster Maurice Lewis. "I've had three major incidents of this nature in the 20 years I've been here. It's just business as usual."

Just as the people in Jacksonville warned Dee Brown about the perils of Boston two months ago, so, too, did Maurice Lewis receive a going-away message when he left Chicago in the late '60s.

"One old gentleman said when he heard I was going to Boston, 'Oh, you goin' up South, huh?'" laughs Lewis.

"I said, 'What do you mean by that?'"

"He said, 'You'll find out.'"

And so Lewis did. He discovered that being impeccably dressed and driving a nice car is enough to arouse suspicion on the part of some police departments. He learned that you're never safe. You never know when, without any provocation whatsoever, police harassment can humiliate you and badly upset your equilibrium.

"This incident will affect Dee Brown subconsciously," points out Lewis. "It's lashing out at your manhood, and it definitely knocks you off balance emotionally."

It's already taken a toll on a buoyant young man. "It affects you in all kinds of ways," Brown says. "I'm feeling paranoid already. I was used to having people look at me in this town, but that was OK because when they'd find out who I was, they were very nice and wanted to talk basketball. Now I'm going to wonder, 'What are they staring at me for?'"

Until Friday afternoon, Dee Brown had been very happy in Boston/Wellesley. He and fiancee Jill Edmondson had discovered Wellesley during the Celtics' rookie camp conducted at Babson College. "It seemed like a nice quiet town, and I decided that's where I wanted to live," Brown explains. They found a house and were busy getting it ready. Now he wants out. He won't be living in Wellesley.

"I was very comfortable here," he says. "I was having a great time. The house was perfect. We were looking forward to living in it. But one incident can change your whole attitude. None of this is relevant to my contract. It's a personal matter. I am having a hard time getting over the fact that not one, not two, but several guns were waved in my face, and I never received a real apology. It's not enough for someone to say, 'Sorry, but you don't understand the situation.' No one sincerely apologized, either to me or to my fiancee."

So once again, it's all over the wires, and it will be in every newspaper in America. The entire country can laugh at Boston, the city that refuses to join the 20th century. Thirty-three years after Bill Russell couldn't buy the house he wanted in the locale he wanted, the latest No. 1 Celtics draft pick is reminded forcibly that to be non-Caucasian in Greater Boston is to be vulnerable to authority. Your civil rights begin and end with the whims of some badge-toting white guy.

One solution might be for each Boston team to send photos of all their African-Americans to every metropolitan area police department (the Red Sox would not need a particularly large envelope). Someone could administer periodic identification tests, and maybe there could be Dunkin' Donuts gift certificates for the winners.

As for Greater Boston's remaining African Americans, the 99.9 percent who aren't professional athletes, and whose routine harassment stories won't be major news stories, I guess all I can recommend is to get yourself a good civil rights lawyer. Sooner or later, you'll need one.

HAPPY IN HIS WORK

Kevin McHale's carefree demeanor belies his dedication to peak performance—performance often overshadowed by his superstar teammate

January 20, 1991 • by Jackie MacMullan

If he concentrated, the image would float into focus. There it was. John Retica pulling down the rebound. John Retica scoring another basket.

OK. Now Kevin McHale could open his eyes and get to work. He would not stop until he, and not John Retica, was the best junior high school player around.

"I used to play against him summers," McHale said. "He was a very good player. My goal was to be better, and I wasn't going to be satisfied until that happened."

It did happen, of course (who in the NBA has ever heard of John Retica?), and the objective became a habit, a pattern. As the gangly young man from Minnesota moved up the basketball ladder, he would choose a player he admired, then play and play and play until the player he admired was a rung below, wondering how McHale floated past him.

In college, the role model was Minnesota teammate Mychal Thompson.

"He was a phenomenal college player," McHale gushed.

Today Mychal Thompson is a steady NBA backup center in Los Angeles. McHale? He is an ageless NBA All-Star whose No. 32 jersey will reside in the Hall of Fame whenever he decides to relinquish it.

Notified that he was once a role model for McHale, whom Thompson rates as one of the 10 best forwards ever to play the game, Thompson sounded genuinely perplexed.

"I was never aware of that," Thompson said. "He certainly never outwardly looked to anyone for advice or guidance. He was a kid who came in thinking he was the boss, even though he was a freshman.

"When he left, he was the boss. I'm flattered he ever emulated anything I did."

This notion of McHale as a thinking man's basketball player, an athlete with an obsessive work ethic, is foreign to many. He will forever be known as a character, a wisecracking star with talent that

enables him to make the game seem effortless. McHale has never bucked the image, never bothered to correct people. He knows himself. Nothing else matters.

"People only see the jovial side of Kevin," said former Celtics coach K. C. Jones, "but behind the laughter and the fun is a very perceptive, very intelligent person. Behind the laughter is one of the most hardworking players I've ever coached."

McHale says his teachers were his Celtic teammates in his rookie season, when he established himself in the vaunted sixth-man role.

"We had a bunch of great guys," he said. "I learned about sacrificing, about playing hurt, things that never showed up in the box score. You never saw any of those guys miss a game with a bruised thigh.

"I'm sure things would have been a lot different if I got drafted by another team. I probably would have gotten a lot more exposure, a lot more playing time. But I liked the way it evolved for me. I came in with great players as a role player, then made a transition into one of those players myself."

In those days, he focused on Cedric Maxwell, the beanpole forward who wiggled and rattled and rolled his way to the basket. The understudy watched carefully, learned to wiggle. By the time McHale was anchoring the post, Max's moves had been dissected, refined, and perfected into the most devastating low-post repertoire in the game.

"I got a lot of my ideas from Max," McHale said. "He's the guy who always stands out. The other is M. L. Carr. There are two different aspects to a person: who they are on the court, and who they are off it. M. L. was a great influence that way. He could turn it on and off as well as anyone."

McHale has carried on that legacy, having little trouble separating his professional and personal lives. For that, he has been criticized by some, admired by others.

"We beat Boston in their place one year during the playoffs," said Detroit captain Isiah Thomas. "After the game, I saw Kevin with his wife and his kids walking out laughing, having a good time. I knew inside he was hurting because of the game, but he was able to put it aside.

"I told someone, 'That's how I want to be. If I can get it down that good, to play, leave it on the court

Kevin McHale high-fives Cedric Maxwell during Game 5 of the 1984 Finals.

So what if he never gets the same recognition as Bird? He has never had any illusions about that.

"One mistake I've never made," said McHale, "is comparing myself to Larry Bird."

—

Since the Big Three came into existence, there has never been a question about the order in which they are introduced: It's Larry, then Kevin, then Robert, and don't you forget it. McHale and Parish have never bucked the notion, never allowed it to eat at them the way others might have. Instead, they have graciously tipped their hat to No. 33.

"No one will be considered the same as Larry—except Red Auerbach," said Parish. "But that's OK with Kevin. His concerns are the same as mine. He wants to win."

The media is to blame, in part, for deifying Bird and downplaying the other two. Larry is appealing because he is a mysterious figure; at times aloof, at times hilarious,

and spend time with my kids, then I'd be OK. I'd be living.' That's what Kevin does."

What Kevin does is pull up for a 3-pointer with the same unabashed confidence with which he wiggles his way out of a triple-team. Fun? McHale is the Fun Master.

Sometimes teammates such as Larry Bird get frustrated with the Fun Master. Bird has often said if McHale really wanted to work, he could have a few MVP trophies of his own. It was Bird who said what his longtime teammate does looks "effortless."

McHale believes his longtime teammate is wrong, but he won't ever say that. He knows himself. That's all that matters.

at times totally inexplicable. His tremendous talent has made him larger than life.

Kevin? Well, he's just Kevin. He always talks to the media. He never complains about his sixth-man role, a huge concession that most stars simply would not make. Most writers who cover the NBA beat have his home phone number. He's scored so many improbable turnarounds we've come to expect them.

While Bird has chosen to be reclusive during the season, McHale pops up all sorts of places with his wife, Lynn: at the Pops, at Charles River Country Club, at the grocery store.

He never misses a team function, and has retired the trophy for donating his time to the endless number of charities that besiege the Celtics.

"It's hard to keep track of specific examples," said Tod Rosensweig, vice president of marketing and communications for the Celtics, "because Kevin does something for me every day."

Yet for all their obvious personality differences, Bird and McHale always maintained a healthy respect for each other's talents. Their approach to basketball had always been in sync.

That changed last season when Bird, recovering from double heel surgery, struggled to regain his place with the team. He became the primary offensive option again, yet the results were not always successful. After a game in Detroit in which he deliberately passed up offensive opportunities, Bird declared himself a "point forward."

Soon thereafter, the New York Post quoted unnamed teammates saying that Bird, among other things, was "ripping the team apart." The Boston Herald followed the next day with a similar report. Bird later implicated Jim Paxson as one of the unnamed teammates. Paxson was the only player whose name became public, although many close to the team believed McHale, too, had made comments.

"I said what I said," McHale said. "Larry was trying too hard last year. He was trying to make us better by single-handedly saying, 'I'm going to take over.' He wasn't trying to be negative, but he was hurting the team.

"That's nothing I wouldn't have said to Larry's face. Five years ago, that approach might have worked. But the league has changed, and we have changed. Larry knows that, too. Look how he's playing now. He's been the biggest reason for our success this year.

"The whole thing got blown way out of proportion. At one point, I said, 'Let's get the names out there. Let everyone take responsibility for what they said.' That never happened, and it turned into a bad feeling."

The bad feelings have dissipated during this campaign. The team is winning again, Bird resumed his role as the consummate team player before being sidelined recently with back trouble, and he and McHale appear to have put the past behind them. In fact, during a television interview last month, Bird said he didn't want to come back and play next season unless McHale was aboard as well.

Kevin, meanwhile, said he appreciates his tenure with Bird more and more each day.

"It's been a joy to play with him," McHale said. "I actually enjoy this role more than if I had to be the main focus myself. Larry has a will of iron. If the game is close, I want him to have the ball."

—

On Dec. 19, 1990, the ball should have belonged to Kevin McHale. In the waning minutes of a victory over Philadelphia at Boston Garden, he scored his 15,000th point.

The milestone passed virtually unnoticed. In fact, most Celtic officials didn't even realize it had occurred until the next day.

"Can you believe that?" said an angry Parish. "I thought that was a bunch of [expletive]. If it was Larry, they would have given him the ball, stopped the game, the whole thing. But because it's Kevin, it's OK to do nothing? I'm sorry. That's [expletive]."

Brian Shaw offered his congratulations, then wondered aloud how the Celtics could permit the Nuggets to stop a game at the Garden for Orlando Woolridge when he scored his 10,000th and not remember their own forward.

The embarrassed Boston staff (not to mention a few media members) tried to make amends, but the gangly forward with the coat-hanger shoulders and deep-set eyes merely shrugged.

"It hurt for a second," McHale admitted. "But maybe it's better this way. Now I can bust Doc, coach Chris Ford and Tod Rosensweig about it forever. The fact they feel so awful about it means I'll get that much more mileage out of it."

Yet the perceptions are already in stone. The documentation of Bird's fastidious work habits are lengthy. Who in the city of Boston doesn't know that Bird used to arrive two hours before game time for extra shooting? But how many know that McHale also does extra shooting, or that he stays at least an hour after every practice working with young McHale wannabes?

"Kevin is Rodney Dangerfield," said former teammate Danny Ainge. "Larry has gotten so much attention, and deservedly so, but the attention has been unbalanced.

"People always talked about Larry coming out to shoot at 5:30 before the game, and how that made him such a hard worker. Well, Larry went out at 5:30 because he likes to shoot by himself. Kevin comes out at 6 and spends just as much time working. It's just that he likes to shoot with people around him. He likes to talk trash to the other team. The time he put in is the same. It's just two different approaches from two great players."

McHale dismisses talk of work habits. Unless you produce, he said, they are a moot point.

"You are judged by your play, not if you stay after practice," he said. "Greg Kite stayed after practice every single day and it didn't make him any better."

McHale is aware of his breezy reputation but makes no apologies. He knows himself. That's all that matters.

Thomas still marvels at the appearance and reality of his Eastern Conference rival. He first met McHale as a 17-year-old high school graduate, freshly signed at Indiana and the youngest member of the 1979 Pan American Games team. His future college coach, Bobby Knight, was in charge. McHale, who teased Thomas endlessly for not choosing Minnesota, was on the team.

"Kevin and I were the whipping boys," said Thomas. "Me because I was young, and Kevin because he was Kevin. He'd be out there abusing guys, yet laughing about it. It sort of gave the illusion he wasn't playing that hard.

"He got Knight so mad he started Danny Vranes in front of him."

McHale also became a famous antagonist of former Celtic coach Bill Fitch. He is credited with giving Fitch the nickname "Captain Video" for forcing the team to watch so much film. McHale never bothered to explain he didn't need the VCR; all he had to do was concentrate, and the images came into focus.

"The only time I didn't stay after practice in my whole career was when Bill Fitch was in charge," said McHale. "If you stuck around, he made you do full-court crossover dribbles. If Bill ever saw me take a 3-pointer, he would have gone nuts. He would have started yelling, 'Game shots, game shots!'

"That was Bill's biggest problem. He couldn't shut it off. He even coached on planes."

—

The ability to leave basketball behind when the buzzer has sounded has long been considered McHale's forte. Last summer, however, he failed miserably.

A season that began with Brian Shaw's exodus to Rome and ended with the firing of Jimmy Rodgers left McHale depressed, uncertain of his future.

"I'd call to say hello," said Ainge, "and all he talked about was retiring."

McHale says now retirement was a real possibility. He injured his thumb in Game 5 of the playoff series with New York and was facing offseason surgery. He was tired, beat up and pessimistic about the future of his once-proud franchise.

"I asked [team physician] Arnie Scheller to give me 10 days to relax and play golf before the operation," McHale said. "I was going to be put in a cast, and I just hated that.

"In those 10 days, I thought a lot about not coming back. It was such a depressing year, and truthfully, the prospects of being better weren't too bright. Even though we won 52 games, it was obvious we had problems. We couldn't beat Washington, we couldn't beat Indiana, and they couldn't beat anyone else.

"I thought about all the fun we had with the guys and I wondered, 'Where did it all go?'"

Part of it was that McHale was no longer the brash rookie running through the halls of the Garden smoking Red's cigars and drinking champagne. The last championship flag was hung in 1986, when he was still a kid. Somewhere along the way, he became the veteran.

"When I came in, I was the young guy everyone was excited about," McHale said.

"Then, for a four- or five-year period, people just expected you to get the job done. You were taken for granted. Now that I'm older, it's all going by fast.

"I remember Mychal Thompson's senior year at Minnesota. We had a great season, mostly because of him, and after his last game, we had a team meeting to discuss next year. All of a sudden, it was 'Mychal, you don't have to come.' That was the first time it hit home to me how temporary all of this is."

He wanted to go out on his own terms, at the top of his game, much the way John Havlicek did. But all of a sudden, good friend Chris Ford was the new coach, and Dave Gavitt was in place as the new chief officer, and wait, Brian Shaw was coming back, and boy, that kid Dee Brown looks like a player. So he returned—much to the dismay of 26 other teams in the NBA.

"Our biggest concern when we play the Celtics," said Thomas, "is defending McHale."

"I knew he'd be a great one," said Parish. "I remember one game when we were down one, playing the Bullets. Bill Fitch called a timeout and said, 'Who wants to take the last shot?' Kevin said, 'I do.'

"He was a rookie, but he wanted the load. He made it, too."

The Celtics find it hard to envision life without Kevin, Larry and Robert. McHale makes $1.4 million this year, and has an option next season that would pay him $1.6 million. By today's standards, he is a bargain-basement deal. Yet money, he insists, is not the incentive. He has four growing children and a wife who would like to spend more time with him.

"I won't make a decision until this summer," McHale said. "But right now something would have to happen to cause me not to come back."

Gavitt is planning on having McHale for next season and would like to explore the possibility of securing him beyond that.

"I've already told Kevin one of the first things I want to do this summer is sit down and extend his contract," Gavitt said. "He's due for a big hit, and he'll get one."

The Fun Master will have decisions to make soon. He is encouraged by the fast start of this team and is hopeful about the future young players such as Shaw, Brown, Reggie Lewis and Kevin Gamble represent. He is also appreciative of his standing in the Big Three, even in the No. 2 spot.

"The special part is not playing together so long, but the respect for each other we've maintained," said McHale. "That's why last year was so hard. The memories were getting tainted, and I didn't want that.

"Whenever I see Robert do that spin move, or Larry make one of those unbelievable passes, I ask myself, 'Will I ever get tired of that?' I don't think so."

He will ride out the tide as the carefree, breezy All-Star forward. He won't linger at 15,000 points. Who needs a game ball, anyway? Kevin McHale knows what he's accomplished. He knows himself, and that's all that really matters.

Pumped-Up Brown Wins Slam-Dunk

February 10, 1991 • by Jackie MacMullan

CHARLOTTE, N.C.—Dee Brown came to All-Star weekend as a quiet rookie with a quiet game plan.

He leaves today as the NBA's reigning slam-dunk champion with instant visibility, a shiny gold trophy and a check for $20,000.

He also leaves making good on his promise that he wasn't coming just to show up, but to win.

Brown edged favorite Shawn Kemp in the finals, 97.7 to 93.7, clinching the competition with a lefthanded leaner dunk that Kemp himself termed "the most creative dunk I've seen in this competition."

Yet for all his acrobatics, Brown did not cart home his trophy without some controversy.

At issue was his blatant commercialism of his sneakers, the Reebok pumps.

Brown put a smile on the face of the judges (not to mention his sneaker company) when he began his routine by bending down and pumping up his shoes. After his first dunk, which scored a 48.2, second only to Kenny Smith, Brown bent down and deflated his sneakers. The crowd laughed the first time, but when Brown continued the ritual through the competition, the chuckles turned to boos.

Afterward, the rookie came under fire from a skeptical national media, which wanted to know if he was paid to pump up. Brown denied receiving any compensation for giving Reebok the publicity.

"It was just an idea I thought up myself," he said. "I mentioned it to Kevin McHale, and he said to go ahead and do it.

"I knew the crowd might not like it, but I wasn't the crowd favorite anyway. Rex Chapman was."

In fact, it was Brown who deflated the hopes of the partisan Hornet crowd in the semifinals with a spread-eagle reverse jam that scored the highest two-dunk total of the round (98.0) and eliminated Chapman. Smith, the other semifinalist, finished fourth.

Brown's dunks brought spectator John Salley to his feet, and left the rookie high-fiving with the likes of Kevin Johnson and Magic Johnson.

Judges Julius Erving, Dan Roundfield, Bobby Jones, Maurice Lucas and George Gervin also were suitably impressed with the first Celtic slam-dunk entry.

Legend Became the Story

BIRD LIFTS CELTICS AGAIN

May 6, 1991 • by Bob Ryan

The Indiana boys aren't stupid. In their minds, Larry was coming back into the game and there was no doubt that when he did it would be like George Bush welcoming General Schwarzkopf back from the gulf, only somewhat louder.

"At halftime," recalled Indiana coach Bob Hill, "I said, 'Look, he's coming back into the game and the place is going to go crazy. They'll be pumped up.' Then I said, 'But he still has to play. Just being there will only take them so far. We've got to make him make his shots.'

"Well," sighed Hill, "he made 'em. And he passed. And he rebounded. All I know is that they'll be talking about him in Boston for the next hundred years."

In the world of sports, there are greats, greatests and there are legends. Ted Williams hitting a home run in his final at-bat is a legend. Nolan Ryan fanning 16 while throwing no-hitter No. 7 at age 44 is a legend. And right here on our stage, as Ed Sullivan used to say, Larry Bird continues to live out and expand his own legend.

With 4:23 remaining in the second quarter of this splendiferous NBA affair between the Celtics and Pacers, which Boston won, 124-121, to advance to the second round of the playoffs, Bird lost control of his dribble. The ball squirted loose. Larry went diving for it, landing not on his shoulder or stomach, but squarely on his right cheek. The other nine players ran to the opposite end of the floor. Larry Bird

lay face down, motionless. The universal assumption was, "Omigod. It's the back. Larry's gone for good."

But it wasn't the back. It was his face. Larry Bird was groggy. The word after the game was "bruised right cheekbone." In Australia, they would probably say he was "concussed." OK, it wasn't the back, but it wasn't good news, either.

The Celtics were up by 48-46 when he left. When he came jogging out of the runway at the 6:46 mark of the third period, the lead was the same (73-71), thanks mainly to Reggie Lewis and Robert Parish. Let's just say the fans took note of his arrival. He told Boston coach Chris Ford he was ready to go, so in he went.

"When he first went out," said Ford, "I didn't know what to expect. He was back day-to-day again. I didn't know how many more minutes he could play, or even if he could come back out at all."

Concussed or not, this was Larry Bird, legend extraordinaire. In the last four minutes of the period, Larry was the '81, '84 or '86 Larry, the Larry whose omnipresence and basketball omniscience made him the individual personification of all basketball has to offer.

His deep jumper gave Boston a nonrefundable lead. He ripped down rebounds. He started the first three fast breaks the Celtics had managed since the opening period with artful lead passes. He conducted a "How-To" post-up clinic on all Indiana comers, driving base line for a reverse layup 3-point play out of one spin move and then turning to the base line for a spinning runner for another 3-point play. He triggered the Celtics to a 21-9 run in the final 4:46 of the period and a 9-point lead.

He would not discuss the injury, other than to say he had been knocked groggy. He just knew that as long as it wasn't his back, he was coming back in. A game like this is what he lives for.

And who knows about the back? We can't forget the back.

"You don't worry about that stuff when you're on the court," he said. "You just go out there and play as hard as you can."

The Celtics needed every bit of Larry Bird's skill and guile to defeat a talented, well-coached and oft-inspired Indiana team. This was a championship series disguised as a first-rounder.

"It was a great game," allowed Bird, "because I was playing against the Pacers."

Life does get back to the basics, folks. Larry takes all this Hoosier stuff seriously. He had waited for 12 years to play in the postseason against the Pacers, and he wanted to be out there. Old wounds and feelings run very deep in the Bird psyche. He wanted to show those people in Jasper, Paoli, Loogootee and assorted other locales in southwest Indiana that he was still Larry Bird and that the Celtics were still the Celtics. And he wanted to win any woof-off with Chuck Person (each, appropriately, finished with 32 points). What Larry Bird is doing now has no Celtic parallel. He has not practiced in any real sense for over a month. Repeat: bad back, no practice, no chance to sharpen skills. He submits a triple-double in Game 1 and then heads to New England Baptist for traction. He goes out in the deciding game of an NBA series against a team playing superb basketball and hangs up a 32-9-7 line while shooting 12 for 19 (12 for 14 on twos). And he damn near breaks his face while doing it.

"Larry Bird," said Chris Ford, "is spectacular, amazing, stupendous."

He's a legend. You can only hope the kids are taking notes.

Just Like Old Times

BIRD ADDS TO HIS LEGEND; CELTICS SINK BLAZERS IN 2 OTS

March 16, 1992 • by Peter May

This was not a game to shatter images. Reinforce them? Absolutely.

Larry Bird only added to his status as Maker of Miracles with a 49-point effort that virtually everyone in Boston Garden felt was one point more than he deserved. But who's counting? And the Portland Trail Blazers did nothing to shed their reputation as the NBA's version of Maynard G. Krebs.

It took both of those ongoing plots, plus more twists than Lombard Street in San Francisco, to finally produce a winner yesterday. In a game that took longer than the Orange Bowl halftime ceremony, the Celtics outlasted the Trail Blazers, 152-148, in double overtime, ending a three-game skid and snapping Portland's seven-game winning streak.

The game featured 220 shots, 68 fouls, 100 free throws, one ejection, six disqualifications, a number of incredible calls (and non-calls) and one injury (Dee Brown), all packed into 199 entertaining minutes. The Blazers had easy chances to win it in regulation and in the first overtime but started shooting free throws like a college team. And they paid for it. Above it all, however, stood Clyde Drexler (41 points, 11 assists, 8 rebounds) and Terry Porter (29 points).

But even those efforts paled in comparison to Bird's. Because he was bothered by an inflamed right Achilles' tendon and a sore right thigh, the Celtics weren't even sure Bird would be able to play until late morning. He hadn't even practiced Saturday.

All he did was register his first triple-double of the season with 49 points, 14 rebounds and 12 assists. He also had five steals in 54 minutes, but left open the most appropriate postgame thought: Does MGM Grand fly to Brookline?

Bird produced the most controversial play in the afternoon epic. The Blazers had forged a 118-111 lead with 1:52 to play and seemed in excellent shape. And the Celtics looked cooked.

"I thought it was over," Portland's Danny Ainge said. "I really thought it was over."

But the Celtics fought back to 122-119, and then Jerome Kersey cooperated by missing two free throws with 7.2 seconds left. The Celtics had a chance to tie and needed a 3-pointer. And when coach Chris Ford didn't insert hired gun Joe Kleine, do you suppose Bird might have been the guy they were looking to?

Bird squirmed around Drexler and launched a frozen rope . . . from where? Was it a trey? His left foot may have scraped the line. His right foot looked well inside the arc.

Most of the Celtics tiptoed around the obvious, noting it was one of many blown calls by a crew that bore a striking resemblance to Wynken, Blynken and Nod. At one point during the game, Ford had turned to the press table and said, "Whoever gets the worst last call wins." Afterward, [Rick] Adelman simply said, "I thought Bird was inside the line."

Robert Parish said of Bird's trey: "It was a 2. And a prayer."

And it rattled in.

"It was luck," Bird admitted. "But I thought I was fouled. I was surprised it went in."

Portland protested to no avail but still had a chance to win in regulation, since there were 2.0 seconds on the clock. But Drexler missed at the buzzer, and it was into overtime. Again, the Blazers looked in good shape, leading by 4 and by 134-132 after Bird (who was 19 of 35) missed two treys.

Drexler missed, but Buck Williams got the rebound. Instead of running out the clock, however, Williams got himself fouled. And, like Kersey, he missed them both.

There were 4.4 seconds left. The Celtics by now were committed fully to their revolutionary Offense of the '90s, which involves dropping it in to Bird on the right block on every possession. That was the call again, but John Bagley (a superb game) instead found Kevin Gamble wide open on the right base line.

The shot swished through as the horn sounded.

In the second overtime, the Blazers stopped making shots (4 of 13) and the Celtics went on an 8-0 run to lead, 144-136, on an Ed Pinckney reverse dunk off a Bird feed. Portland never caught up, although it made things interesting.

But the Celtics made enough free throws to stay in control and left the floor gratified, exhausted, and relieved. They needed this one.

Now He Sits at Head of Table

May 9, 1992 • by Bob Ryan

If you're into Celtic torch-passing, this was a special moment. Reggie Lewis was holding court on the big ol' table planted right in the middle of the overflowing, steamy, antiquated Celtic locker room, having just surgically removed Cleveland's heart and Hannibal Lectored same, minus the good doctor's preferred chianti.

Out from the shower came Kevin McHale. He saw Reggie sitting on The Table. In normal times, only Larry Bird and Kevin ever sit on The Table. It is where legitimate Boston superstars accommodate the press.

"Hey," yelled McHale. "You killed those guys, but DON'T STEAL MY TABLE!"

A smiling McHale then walked over, sat down and put his arm around Reggie. "Put that hand in a cast," he advised. "At least put a towel around it."

That hand, that arm had just defied every conceivable Cleveland defensive tactic. The Cavs can play some nice individual D and they can play some serious team D, but they could do nothing with a spinning, twisting, floating and downright wondrous Reggie Lewis, who basically broke open a tight ballgame all by himself.

"Our fourth-quarter offense?" inquired Dee Brown. "Get the ball to Reggie, basically."

Any more games like this and Reggie will not only have his own table, he'll have his own room. Hell, give him his own building, block, city, state, country, continent or planet. In the most intense playoff pressure, the kid from Baltimore buried the Cleveland Cavaliers—a very, very good team—with a shooting performance that no Celtic guard has submitted since, well, a Long Time Ago. Reggie scored 13 points in the third period and 13 more in the fourth, with the final 11 coming in a span of less than five minutes to provide his team with a 110-107 victory and a 2-1 lead in this very competitive and entertaining series.

Reggie came into this season as a basic 20-points-per-game man. He made his first All-Star Game this season. He's clearly been on the upswing for the past three years. But what we're seeing now is a man around whom defensive game plans must be designed.

"It's like it all just happened," said a dazed Wayne Embry, the Cavs' general manager. "And late this year, he's like a damned superstar. He's . . . Sam Jones!"

That, in truth, is about how far back a Celtic historian must wander before finding a Boston back court man as explosive as Reggie Lewis is now. I mean, guys have had great moments and careers. Jo Jo White could fill it up. Paul Westphal would have, had he stayed. Charlie Scott did, every once in a while. Scoring like this wasn't Dennis Johnson's thing. You throw in John Havlicek in some of his back court moments, but that's it. And John did most of his damage running off picks. Reggie doesn't need any help. All Reggie needs is the ball. Reggie is busy writing new chapters in all the Celtic history books.

It was 93-93 when Reggie began his hostile takeover of this ballgame. He began with an open

18-footer. Then a 21-footer. Then a feed (he also had 7 assists) to Robert Parish for a corner jumper. Cleveland, which shot 57 percent and still lost the game, was matching, but at 99-all, Reggie took the ball again, went one-on-one from the right, stuck a very difficult 12-footer, and picked up a foul from Mike Sanders. The 3-point play tipped the scales irrevocably in Boston's favor.

There's more. For when Craig Ehlo, the main Lewis torture victim, attempted a three at the other end, Reggie deflected the shot. Mark Price picked up the loose ball and missed a three, whereupon Reggie made them pay with a spectacular driving layup high off the glass. Reggie next fed Dee Brown, connected on another jumper and found McHale for a corner turnaround. He had just scored or assisted on eight consecutive Boston baskets.

"I just felt like there wasn't anything the defense can do," said Lewis. "I was going to score, regardless." He says this in a disarming, almost apologetic way. We are not talking about Chuck Person II here.

Not too very long ago, Reggie was a completely one-dimensional offensive player. If he put his head down, he was going to the basket—period. If he got the ball coming off a pick, it was going up—period. Now Reggie poses major problems for the defense.

"He absolutely carried us offensively," saluted McHale, now safely perched on his throne in the middle of the room. "He's getting very reminiscent of another guy we've had around here. There are times you feel good offensively yourself, but you just get out of the way and let him go.

"The big thing," continued McHale, "is that now he is doing something I wasn't sure he could do. He is passing off the dribble. And he's learning to read the defense. Those seven assists are the key. He used to make shots for Reggie, but now he is taking the rest of us along with him. He's making us better with his ability to pass the ball."

Most of all, however, he is making these amazing shots. This is a guy you don't just go to. He's someone you build around. He's a guy who deserves to sit at The Table.

THE END OF AN ERA: LARRY BIRD RETIRES

INEVITABLE CAME A BIT EARLY

August 19, 1992 • by Peter May

He went out as he wanted to. Almost. There was no rocking chair, gifts, fanfare, hoopla or adoration, all of which Larry Bird detested. He scripted it to the very end, though there was one rather significant omission: time. He would have liked to have made yesterday's announcement in 1993 or 1994.

Having reluctantly but realistically come to the inevitable conclusion that he couldn't play professional basketball anymore, Bird made it official: He is retiring from the Celtics after 13 years as the team's conscience, savior and hoop ambassador. He will remain with the team as a special assistant to basketball czar Dave Gavitt.

The decision to retire was not a shocker; anyone who saw him struggling through last year and the Tournament of the Americas could not have been stunned. And, Bird added, it was final and irreversible. The decision to stay with the Celtics was somewhat of a surprise, although it won't be a 9-to-5 job and Bird probably won't be required to wear a suit and tie.

The culprit was Bird's increasingly troublesome back. During the last two seasons, he had missed 59 games because of the back, undergone surgery and still couldn't endure the rigors of an NBA season.

"I would have liked to play a little longer, but I've had enough pain to last me a lifetime," he told an overflow news conference at Boston Garden. "I can't shake it. I don't care if I could go out and score 60 points each night. It just is not worth it.

"Emotionally, it's very tough for me right now because I'm giving up something I love, something I have been doing for a long time. But I have to give it up. I don't want to go out this way, but I have to."

Larry Bird won three championships in his 13 years with the Celtics, with the pinnacle being the spectacular 1986 season.

a loose ball. I had to compete at a high level. I played one way—as hard as I could—and my body held up pretty well over the years. I played in over 1,100 games. I gave my heart, body and soul to the Celtics. I hope that's how they remember me."

The decision to retire was made about a week ago, Gavitt and Bird said. The two had had sporadic talks during both the Tournament of the Americas and the Olympics, then chatted more formally on the plane back from Barcelona. They met for four hours last Tuesday, and most of the time was spent finding something for Bird to do.

"He had made up his mind then," Gavitt said. "I asked him if he was 100 percent sure. I wasn't going to try and talk him out of it. I was hoping he'd want to stay involved, and I was thrilled that he did."

With Bird's retirement, he forfeits his $3.75 million salary for next season. He'll be working for considerably less as Gavitt's assistant, and Gavitt joked, "It'll be a race to see who's working for who." The Celtics will get a $1.65 million slot to replace Bird, a slot that will be open for 365 days.

The impact of Bird's retirement sent shock waves throughout the NBA. Indiana Pacers president Donnie Walsh said, "It's kind of like when Alexander the Great decided he wasn't going to conquer any more countries." Gavitt said Bird will go down as one of the five greatest players ever and, "from shoulder to head and from wrists to the tips of the fingers, there was no one better."

When Bird joined the team for the 1980 season, the Celtics were coming off a disastrous year (29-53) and were in chaos. But with Bird, the team made what was then the greatest single-season turnaround in NBA history, winning the Atlantic Division with a 61-21 record. Bird was named Rookie of the Year and made first-team All-NBA, the first of nine straight such honors.

The Celtics won three championships with Bird, in 1981, 1984 and 1986. He said yesterday, "I thought we'd win five championships when I came here. I guess we'll have to get the next two while I'm working with Dave." The team has made the playoffs in each of his 13 seasons, the second-longest streak in the NBA.

In the last week, there was talk of Bird having a reduced workload or even limiting his appearances to home games. No one who knew Bird seriously believed he would have any part of that. "That's not the way I approach things," he said yesterday. "I want to play every minute of every game."

Bird stayed composed throughout the news conference, though at times he seemed on the verge of breaking down. He said that he had shed his tears the night before, when the reality of the decision hit home. His wife, Dinah, did not come to the news conference for that very reason, he said.

He frequently mixed in one-liners with moments of serious reflection, an attempt to avoid, or at least delay, the intense emotion of the hour. Asked how he wanted to be remembered, he cracked, "That he didn't weigh as much as everyone thought he would." After the obligatory laughs, he got serious.

"One thing I know—I played as hard as I could every time I was out there," he said. "I wasn't going to let an injury stop me from diving on the floor for

Bird's back problems surfaced at the beginning of the 1992 season. Prior to then, he had had only one serious injury, missing 76 games in the 1989 season after double heel surgery for the removal of bone spurs. The year before, he had looked as good as he ever had before the ankle problems.

His last year started out on an encouraging note. After summer back surgery, he reported to training camp on time, signed a two-year, $8 million extension, went through the exhibition season without a hitch and played in 28 of the first 29 games. But the back was bothering him again, and he missed all of January and February.

He returned March 1 and two weeks later delivered his greatest performance of the year, a 49-point, 14-rebound, 12-assist gem against Portland. Three weeks later he was on the shelf again, missing the last eight games of the regular season and the first six of the playoffs.

His last game? An eminently forgettable 12-point, 5-rebound performance in a blowout loss to the Cleveland Cavaliers in Game 7 of the Eastern Conference semifinals.

"None of us will know how bad the pain was," Gavitt said. "And no one had the right to ask anyone to go through that again, including Larry himself."

And so, Bird decided that enough was enough. He said he wasn't sad—few believed him—and made it clear this was as much a time of celebration as condolences. "This is the greatest life in the world," he said. "If you know how to play basketball, it's the easiest game in the world. Don't feel sorry for me. I had a great life the last 17 years. I've had nothing but highs."

A Special Bond Between Country Boy and City Slicker

August 19, 1992 • by Will McDonough

The stretch limousine worked its way tediously up the back ramp of Boston Garden stuffed with the Celtics brass and Larry Bird.

"Think this thing is going to make it?" Celtics owner Don Gaston asked as the sleek vehicle worked its way precariously over the aging, wooden ramp at a severe angle.

"I've been worried about this for 13 years," laughed Bird, before a voice from the back offered, "Try it for 42 years."

Red Auerbach had been here before, for all of the Celtic greats. He worried about them not only making it safely into the building but also through their careers and on with the rest of their lives, when they could no longer be what they had been in the green and white of the legendary Boston franchise.

But this one was different. Auerbach may be just about a month short of 75 years old, but his fastball has lost little of its zip. Yesterday, though, those who know him best could see that he wasn't his usual upbeat self. Another great one was leaving, one he had nurtured from Day 1 and had a special feeling for. "You know how much I care for Cousy and Russell," says Auerbach, "and that I would never say a bad word about them. Never. Not word one. But this kid . . . Bird."

That last word stops him as he tilts back in his chair, looking wistfully at the ceiling in his office, searching for the right words to fit the moment. Auerbach and Bird have just returned in the limo from Bird's retirement press conference just 200 yards down the street. Over the past 13 years, Auerbach ("The Mentor," as Bird calls him) and Larry have developed a mutual respect few thought could ever develop when they first came together— the self-proclaimed "hick from French Lick" and the basketball mogul from the streets of Brooklyn.

"He was no hick," says Auerbach, warming up with a cigar. "He is bright. He is intelligent. Not putting down any other player that ever played here, but Bird was the most self-motivated player ever. He was the best I ever saw getting himself ready for every game and doing things to get his teammates ready.

"I never hang around the dressing room that much, but I saw things from time to time. One night before a game, he'd be funny and loose. The next night, he'd give a little speech almost like a coach. The third night, he'd be on the back of one of the players, giving them a little needle.

"He was completely into playing. Into winning. That's how I remember him. Wanting to win, and playing through pain more than any other player I have ever seen. No one will ever know the pain he has had to endure to play these last four or five years for us. The guy has lived on the floor so that he'd be able to stand up and try to play for us.

"I'll never forget those things, or what he has done for this franchise."

—

Others talk about games, and statistics, and Larry and Magic, and what Larry did for the NBA, and the spectacular growth of the game in the past decade. But Auerbach looks at other things. The dedication to staying in shape. The unselfishness to help the team. The caring for the Celtics family, as Larry grew to be the big brother in it.

"He does tremendous things for charity and other people, and never says anything about it," says Auerbach. "I remember one year we won a championship and a few weeks later he says to me, 'I want to buy a championship ring.' I knew he knew he didn't have to buy one, so I asked him what he wanted it for. He wanted it for Randall, the guy that worked so many years in our locker room that no one ever paid much attention to.

"Bird wanted to buy Randall a championship ring and you know that thing costs thousands of dollars. But I said no, the club would buy it. It was an oversight on our part. Randall should have had a ring long before that, but Larry wanted to buy it, give it to Randall, and no one would have known about it."

—

It is 60 minutes after Bird has said his official goodbye at the Garden. Auerbach and Dave Gavitt are sitting with a few friends, munching on cold cut sandwiches in the Celtics' boardroom, telling each other when they first knew Bird would not be back for the 1993 season.

"I was watching one of those Olympic games on television and they showed a close-up of Larry on the bench," says Auerbach. "And I saw this expression on his face. I don't quite know how to describe it, but it wasn't Larry—know what I mean?—and then the camera stayed on him as he left the bench and went into the game. When I saw him walking, the way he was walking, I said to myself, 'This is it. He won't be back.'

"I had the feeling, and I knew he was right."

Gavitt and Bird have become exceptionally close in a short time. There is nothing that has happened to Larry in the last couple of years that Dave does not know about.

"Last season," says Gavitt, "Larry got hurt early and was trying to come back again. One day he worked out at Brandeis, and the pain was getting worse, so after practice, he got in his car and drove down here to be treated by his guy, physical therapist Dan Dyrek.

"In the ride in the car, the pain got worse, shooting down his leg like a knife, he told me. Dyrek saw what kind of shape he was in and wouldn't touch him. He told Larry to see the doctor [Arnold Scheller].

"Larry got back into his car, and he told me later he had to stop five times between the Garden and Brookline because the pain was so bad. A couple of times his back seized up and he had to get out of the car. It hurt so bad it brought tears to his eyes. He couldn't tell whether he stopped on Storrow Drive or the Mass. Pike, that's how much pain he was in.

"He told me later that he never wanted to go through that kind of pain again, that he didn't know if he could go through that kind of pain again. I knew then it was over. Larry couldn't stay in shape without practicing, and if he practiced and played both, the pain just had to come back again and get worse as time went on."

—

The talk drifts away from the back, and Bird comes into the room and joins the conversation. It is mentioned that in his first press conference ever, after signing a Celtic contract, the press wondered if he would talk to them, because he didn't during his senior year in college. Bird, after a masterful one-hour performance in his finale yesterday, laughs at the memory and at how his life has changed.

He came to Boston not knowing what to expect about the Celtics' tradition or the family aspect of the franchise, but he had totally bought into it by the end. Bird came to Boston to play ball and make money.

"The first day I came here, I said I was going to have every cent I ever earned when it was all over, and I did that," said Bird proudly.

Quietly, Bird has handled himself better than perhaps any athlete of the modern era. Auerbach and Bird's agent, Bob Woolf, speculate that he has more than $20 million in the bank, with all of the taxes on it paid, and very little debt. Not bad for a hick from French Lick.

—

"Bill Russell is on the phone, Mr. Auerbach," a secretary is saying, as Red tells her to put the call through to the boardroom.

Russell, in Seattle, has heard about Bird and calls Red for the inside story. "Ask him yourself," says Auerbach. "He's standing right here."

Bird walks across the room, picks up the phone and says, "How are you, Mr. Russell?" with the proper respect, as the two greats talk for five minutes. Bird says "thank you" five or six times, and Russell obviously pays the respect back in turn.

Auerbach is obviously pleased that two of his greatest have come together at another important moment in Celtic history—even though they never played a single game with each other—and proud that it is moments like this that have made the Celtic history what it is.

LARRY! LARRY! LARRY!

BIRD BIDS ADIEU AMID ADULATION

February 5, 1993 • by Bob Ryan

"I never put on a uniform to play a game," he said. "I put on a uniform to win.

"I'm going to miss running the pick-and-roll with Robert Parish," he said. "Yes, I'm going to miss throwing the ball down low to Kevin McHale and watching him go to work. I'll miss those back-door passes from Dennis Johnson. Most of all, believe it or not, I'll miss the fans."

It was the climax of a unique evening. Oodles of players have had jerseys or uniforms retired. But last night's affair, with more than 15,000 on hand, was the first time in known American professional sports history in which the ceremony was not tucked inside a game. Larry Bird was too big, too special and too singularly bonded with his fans for that. Bird's No. 33 went up to the Garden's famed Rafter Heaven during a 2½-hour presentation which took advantage of modern technological expertise not imaginable when the likes of 14 (Bob Cousy), 6 (Bill Russell) and 17 (John Havlicek) were honored.

No one is happier that this much-anticipated evening is over than Larry Bird. "I was nervous coming out here," he admitted. "I was kind of emotional before I walked out. Scared." He even likened the pre-ceremony feeling to one he would have before a big game.

It was not just a tribute for Larry Bird. It was also, as CEO Dave Gavitt put it, a "Celtic family reunion." Among the Retired Numbers and/or Names in attendance were Tom Heinsohn, Satch Sanders, Dave Cowens, Frank Ramsey, John Havlicek, Jungle Jim Loscutoff, Jo Jo White, Bill Sharman, Ed Macauley and, of course, K. C. Jones, a.k.a. The Man With All The Rings, who made his appearance as a Retired Number, assistant coach on the '81 championship team and coach of the '84 and '86 titlists.

The format was a mixture of introductions, tributes and, of course, video examples of just exactly why everyone was summoned to the Garden in the first place. The fans and assorted guests were able to see the Young Bird, the Middle-Aged Bird and even the Dream Team Bird. They got to see a cross-section of some of the more amazing shots and passes the NBA has ever seen. They also got to see some bloopers, and even some of his commercials.

Invited to the celebration were members of Bird's family, assorted friends (Brad Lohaus, for example) and various dignitaries, such as NBA commissioner David Stern.

Master of ceremonies Bob Costas conducted interviews with small groups, or in the case of Magic Johnson and Red Auerbach, solo sessions. The fans heard Cedric Maxwell, making his first visit to the Garden since his retirement, say how he remembered thinking early on, "Boy, this white guy can really play, can't he?" They heard Red Auerbach reveal his one regret: "I never got to coach him."

There was also a video hello from Danny Ainge, as well as video tributes from Dominique Wilkins,

Magic Johnson opens his Lakers warm-up jacket to reveal a Celtics T-shirt on Larry Bird Night.

Michael Cooper and Dream Teamers Patrick Ewing, Chris Mullin and Charles Barkley. Sir Charles was positively eloquent. "I'm glad you were born in my lifetime so I can tell my kids I played against such a great player," Barkley said. "If it wasn't for you and Magic Johnson, the NBA wouldn't be where it is today."

Magic spoke the longest, and it was worth waiting for. The two exchanged signed jerseys, embraced twice and told the world how each had forced the other to become a better player. "Larry," Magic said, "you only told me one lie. You said there will be another Larry Bird. Larry, there will never, ever be another Larry Bird. You take that to the bank. I love you. I respect you. I admire you."

Unlike the old days, when players were feted with cars, boats, golf clubs and the like, the modern player doesn't need, you know, stuff, since he can buy back the team and maybe even the entire city. Thus the gifts:

From Maxwell, representing the '81 team, a commemorative coin ("very expensive"). From Quinn Buckner, representing the '84 team, a watch. From Kevin McHale, representing the '86 team, a piece of the parquet floor. And from Magic, representing everything Larry Bird himself admires in a basketball player, a piece of the Forum floor, signed,

"By Kareem Abdul-Jabbar, Jerry West, Elgin Baylor and a lot of other people you probably don't want to hear about."

The fans wanted to hear everything Magic had to say, however, just as they enjoyed hearing the remembrances and anecdotes of Bird's old teammates and coaches. About the only downer was actually hearing Larry say, "My basketball career is officially over."

If anyone doubted the necessity of Bird's decision to cease active participation, the sight of Bird being forced to get up from his stool to alleviate his incessant back pain while the videos were being shown on the specially constructed four-sided screens was a grim reminder of Larry's current physical reality.

A relaxed and relieved Bird drove home that point when the ceremony was complete. "Those days are over for me," he declared. "I can't play no more. I can't play and I have no desire to play. I've finally put basketball to rest.

"I played hard. I practiced very hard to develop my skills. I had a career with fulfillment, and it was a fulfillment with gratitude and a lot of emotion."

Who could ask a man to give anything more for the price of a ticket?

5 THE LOST YEARS

(1993-2001)

As the Larry Bird, Big Three era hobbled to its conclusion in the early 1990s, there was some comfort to be found, some real hope, in knowing that the next Celtics star was already on the roster and thriving.

The Celtics were going to become Reggie Lewis's team. In a way, they already had. Lewis, who had played his college ball just a couple of T-stops from Boston Garden at Northeastern University, carried himself with a gentle demeanor off the court—he had created a tradition of providing turkeys for needy families at Thanksgiving—that belied his fierce competitiveness on the parquet.

Lewis made his first All-Star team in 1992, Bird's final season, while leading the Celtics in scoring at 20.8 points per game. In a matchup with the Chicago Bulls in March, 1991, he blocked Michael Jordan's shot four times. He wasn't merely on his way. He was already there.

When Lewis was named Celtics captain in training camp before the 1993 season, it was both an obvious choice and a reassuring one. "There is a tradition on the Celtics of passing the torch," executive vice president Dave Gavitt told the *Globe*. "And it is quietly being passed to Reggie."

Lewis could have been a legend. Instead, like Len Bias, he became a tragic what-if. On April 29, 1993, Lewis—who had averaged 20.8 points per game again in 1993—collapsed during Game 1 of a first-round playoff series with the Charlotte Hornets. On May 2, the Celtics announced that what the team called a "Dream Team" of 12 heart specialists had determined that Lewis suffered from a condition called cardiomyopathy. There were reports that it had been recommended that he have a defibrillator implanted. The Dream Team advised the Lewises that Reggie retire from basketball.

Lewis and his wife, Donna, did not take their advice. In the middle of the night, they switched hospitals from New England Baptist to Brigham and Women's, where a doctor named Gilbert Mudge offered a different diagnosis, and one surely more welcome to their ears. Dr. Mudge said there was no evidence of cardiomyopathy. He said that Lewis had a normal athlete's heart. Lewis accepted the 13th opinion, hopeful of resuming his career.

On July 27, 1993, while shooting baskets at Brandeis University, Reggie Lewis collapsed, suffering cardiac arrest, and died. The captain of the Celtics was 27 years old.

❮ A bird's-eye view of the FleetCenter—now known as TD Garden— during a Celtics-76ers game, April, 1995.

Lewis's death, seven years after Len Bias died of a cocaine overdose two days after the Celtics selected him with the No. 2 pick in the 1986 NBA Draft, was too much for the franchise to overcome. Kevin McHale, the health of his feet sacrificed to the game, retired after the Celtics were eliminated in that fateful 1993 series with the Hornets, and Robert Parish joined Charlotte as a free agent in August, 1994. The Celtics even changed their home, playing their final game at the Garden—a season-ending playoff loss to the Orlando Magic—on April 21, 1995. The Celtics moved the famous parquet floor to the brand-new FleetCenter (now TD Garden) for the 1996 season on.

To fill the various voids, a layup line of flawed or fading players, among them Dominique Wilkins and Xavier McDaniel, along with skilled but defense-averse Dino Radja from Croatia, were brought on board. But nothing could stem what would become the least successful stretch in Celtics history. In 1996, the Celtics missed the playoffs for the first time since 1979. They would not make the playoffs again until 2002, a six-year drought, longest in the franchise annals.

With the No. 6 pick in the 1996 NBA Draft, the Celtics selected skilled but undisciplined University of Kentucky forward Antoine Walker. He would become a star despite his maddening ways, but his rookie season, by design, was the ultimate lost cause. The Celtics won just 15 games in 1997, losing 34 of their final 38, under coach M. L. Carr, the Celtics tanking long before such a thing became a trend in the NBA.

The plan was to position the team to draft Wake Forest All-America big man Tim Duncan, a sure-thing, franchise-altering prospect. In May, 1997, the Celtics made Kentucky coach Rick Pitino the highest-paid coach in basketball history with a 10-year, $70 million deal that also included his shameless seizure of Red Auerbach's team president title. Pitino was hired before the NBA Draft lottery, when the Celtics had the best odds of landing the top pick, albeit at just 36 percent.

The ping-pong balls, like so much else in this period, refused to bounce the Celtics' way. While Duncan went to the San Antonio Spurs, the Celtics ended up with Colorado guard Chauncey Billups at No. 3 and Kentucky's Ron Mercer at No. 6. They were consolation prizes, and the consolation was minimal.

The high point of Pitino's tenure was his first game, when his Celtics defeated Jordan and the champion Bulls in the 1998 season opener. He would prove to be an arrogant, notoriously impatient flop. Among his worst moves: He renounced the rights to steady veterans Rick Fox and David Wesley to lavish backup center Travis Knight with a seven-year, $22 million contract, and traded future Hall of Famer Billups after 55 games for veteran Kenny Anderson.

Pitino did get one crucial thing right, drafting Kansas forward Paul Pierce—who was projected to go much higher—with the No. 10 overall pick in the 1998 NBA Draft. Pierce, who even as a young player had the crafty game of a 10-year veteran, was an immediate star, making the All-Rookie team in 1999.

On the night of September 25, 2000, Pierce nearly became a tragic chapter in Celtics lore in his own right. While playing pool at the Buzz Club, a nightclub on Stuart Street in Boston, he was attacked, hit with a bottle, and stabbed 11 times. Teammate Tony Battie and his brother Derrick rushed Pierce to the nearby hospital, where he underwent surgery to repair damage to a lung. Pierce was told that his leather jacket had probably saved his life and that he would have died had the knife entered his body a fraction of an inch in a different direction.

Pierce's, and to a lesser degree Walker's, development into stars were not enough to help Pitino, whose lasting contribution to Boston sports lore was an epic rant after a loss to the Raptors in March, 2000. "Larry Bird is not walking through that door, fans. Kevin McHale is not walking through that door, and Robert Parish is not walking through that door. And if you expect them to walk through that door, they're going to be gray and old . . . " Pitino lasted until January 8, 2001, when he quit in quiet ignominy after a Celtics loss in Miami, his defensive-minded assistant Jim O'Brien taking over. Pitino walked out that door, and the worst of times were over.

Captain's Brilliance Is Tempered by His Collapse

April 30, 1993 • by Dan Shaughnessy

It was a strange night for Reggie Lewis. Strange and scary.

It was midway through the first quarter of a playoff game with the Charlotte Hornets. He was

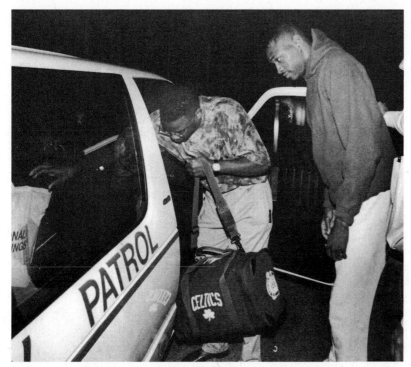

Reggie Lewis leaves New England Baptist Hospital for Brigham and Women's Hospital on May 3, 1993, for a second opinion on the condition of his heart.

Lewis simply passed out, and the Celtics don't know why. He will be evaluated today at New England Baptist Hospital and his status for Game 2 is very much up in the air.

Celtic CEO Dave Gavitt said after the game, "Basketball games are very insignificant when compared to someone's health."

It would seem that the Celtics were not totally cautious with Lewis after his initial episode last night. Three minutes five seconds (of game time) after he passed out, Lewis was back in the game. He didn't stay on the court very long. He missed a 3-pointer and was lifted after 1 minute 4 seconds of action. This time he went to the trainer's room, where he was visited by his wife, Donna.

He came back to the bench for the final minutes of the second half, and at this time, the Celtic PR staff again made the rounds to inform the media that Lewis simply had "his bell rung."

One team official told a reporter that Lewis had been hyperventilating in the locker room. Celtic publicist Jeff Twiss denied the rumor.

Lewis was all smiles when he came out after intermission. He participated in a midcourt halftime ceremony with Red Auerbach.

He started the second half. He buried a jumper from the perimeter in the second minute of the third period to give the Celtics a 57-53 lead. Then he made a foul shot. It seemed everything was normal.

With 6:08 left in the third, Lewis missed from the right side, followed his miss and made a nice conversion after gathering the rebound. Seconds later, players on the Celtic bench alerted coach Chris Ford that something was wrong with Lewis. Ford frantically called time out. Lewis came out for good. He was assisted to the bench. Lewis sat down, put a

hot. The basket looked very big. Ten points. Four for five from the floor. Twenty-seven years old. Forever young and strong.

It was 16-16, and he was running his lane, doing his thing, when suddenly, he passed out. He was flat on his back. By himself. In the middle of the famous parquet floor.

"Yeah, I was scared when it happened," Lewis told the Globe's Jackie MacMullan after the game. "I started having flashbacks to that Hank Gathers thing."

For those of you with short, or maybe selective memories, the "Hank Gathers thing" was that awful moment March 4, 1990, when Loyola Marymount's star forward collapsed in a heap and died on a basketball court in California. We all saw it on television. Awful. The worst. When Lewis last night came off the court, ice was applied to the back of his neck. Celtic publicists came around press row to announce that Lewis "got his bell rung" by a Kendall Gill elbow. This was erroneous information. After the game, Celtic physician Arnold Scheller said Lewis was not hit.

towel to his mouth and breathed into the towel. The towel stayed at his mouth for most of the remainder of the third.

While the game was still going on, Scheller was asked if he considered Lewis's problem serious.

"We are keeping a very close eye on him," said Scheller. "But I'm concerned. I'll tell you, I'm very, very concerned."

They put ice on the back of Lewis's neck again as he sat on the bench in the fourth. The Celtics built a lead. He would not be needed. Captain Reggie Lewis scored 17 points and played only 13 minutes of this Game 1 victory.

Just over a month ago, at home against the Miami Heat, Lewis suffered a dizzy spell in the middle of a game. Scheller last night said he believed that fatigue was Lewis's problem in the Heat game.

Lewis left the locker room quickly after last night's victory. Scheller and Gavitt were left to answer the questions. They are concerned. They should be.

The doctor said that it was "unusual for an athlete of this caliber" to have a problem like this. We know Lewis was having problems breathing, but Scheller said, "It's not obvious what the problem was."

When Scheller was asked if he'd have been comfortable putting Lewis back in the game, he said it wasn't a factor because the Celtics had a big lead.

And if the Celtics had needed Lewis down the stretch?

"That would have been pushing it," said Scheller.

Gavitt said, "I'm not a doctor, but one thing I have to disagree with what Arnie said is about taking him out because of the score. That's never a consideration."

The Celtics won last night. They won even though their captain played only 13 minutes. Lewis is at the hospital today while the Celtics practice for Game 2. There is much to consider.

McHale Makes It Official—and Heroic

May 6, 1993 • by Jackie MacMullan

CHARLOTTE, N.C.—He wanted to do it on the court. Kevin McHale had this retirement thing all planned

out: have a chat with the reporters who had covered him for all those glorious years, tell a few jokes, reminisce a little, then pull off the No. 32 jersey and end it.

But it wasn't that easy; no, it wasn't easy at all. Thinking about retiring is one thing; saying it out loud is quite another.

Kevin McHale finally admitted it after the Celtics were eliminated by the Charlotte Hornets last night: His career is over. No more twisting scoops under the basket, no more arching fallaways, no more octopus rebounds, no more blocked shots, no more wisecracks.

No more pain.

"This has been a very tough year for me," he said. "I've had a lot of injuries, but this is the first time in my career I lost my mental edge. That was the really frustrating part.

"I played so passive in so many games because I was afraid to get hurt. I was afraid of doing anything. I had to dig deep, deep, deep for what I gave in the playoffs."

He confirmed what we have suspected all along, that he made his decision to retire at the start of training camp. In fact, when McHale reported for the grueling preseason workouts, and his feet became wracked with pain within days, he decided he would not play the 1993 season.

"It was hard, because my feet were really hurting," he said. "So I told wife, Lynn, and we sat on the bed and talked about it.

"Then I went down and told the kids, Kristen and Joey and Mikey and Sasha, and they were so disappointed, because they couldn't be ball boys and stuff, so I figured, 'I guess I can strap it up and go again.'"

But this season was not like all the others. He was inconsistent offensively and was embarrassed at his lack of mobility defensively. He played in pain constantly.

In January, the mixture of pain and doubt and frustration and resignation sent him into a tailspin, and he was virtually incommunicado for several days. He had decided it was time to quit—right now—and he would have done it if CEO Dave Gavitt hadn't convinced him otherwise.

"I talked to Mr. Gavitt, and I told him I was done," said McHale. "But he talked me out of it. He said the team needed me."

Kevin McHale sits courtside with his kids during a game against the 76ers on November 13, 1992.

Gavitt was right. As January turned to February, and the snow melted and spring came around, the playoffs jolted McHale into a realization.

"I decided I had to stop worrying about my feet and just play," he said.

He was the flashback he had been joking about all season. He was energetic and active, and effective. Last night, in his final performance, he scored 19 points in 33 minutes and grabbed 6 rebounds. McHale and Robert Parish gave the Celtics hope.

"One thing I wanted to do was go out with pride," said McHale. "I'm disappointed in the game. If we lost, I wanted to lose in Boston Garden. The fans have been so great there. I always played before sellout crowds.

"I went through so much in Boston. I've run the gamut of emotions on that floor. I've cried, been jubilant, been frustrated, been happy.

"But there is a time for everything, and it's my time to step down."

Celtics Captain Lewis Dies after Collapse while Shooting

CARDIAC ARREST DEATH COMES 3 MONTHS AFTER PLAYOFF ILLNESS

July 28, 1993 • by Peter May

WALTHAM—Boston Celtics captain Reggie Lewis collapsed while shooting baskets at Brandeis University yesterday and was pronounced dead 2½ hours later at Waltham-Weston Hospital.

Lewis, who had been slow to return to any kind of vigorous basketball since he collapsed in a play-off game three months ago, was pronounced dead at the Waltham hospital at 7:30 p.m. The official announcement was delayed for almost three hours, sources said, because the Celtics had trouble locating Lewis's mother, Inez, who lives in Baltimore.

Witnesses at Brandeis said Lewis, 27, was doing some light shooting with a ball boy rebounding for him when he suddenly slumped to the floor about 5:05 p.m.

Amir Weiss, a Brandeis junior shooting baskets on the adjacent court, said Lewis seemed content until he suddenly slumped to the floor and stopped breathing.

Brandeis police were summoned and arrived about 10 minutes later; seven minutes after that, paramedics arrived and found Lewis in cardiac arrest. They administered advanced cardiac life support measures until 5:30 p.m., when they took Lewis by ambulance to the hospital's emergency room, less than ¼ mile from the gymnasium, arriving at 5:41 p.m.

Resuscitation efforts continued unsuccessfully for 1 hour and 50 minutes. Dr. Mary Anne McGinn of the hospital staff made the announcement of Lewis's death. Hospital staff declined to take questions from the media, saying the family had requested that they not do so.

Brandeis officials said Lewis showed up at 4 p.m. to shoot, which he had been doing on an irregular basis for the past two weeks.

"I don't think he was breathing on the way out," said Tom McDermott, who was working the security desk. "I saw the look on his face; it looked like someone who wasn't in very good condition."

Lewis's death comes seven years after Len Bias, the team's top draft pick in 1986, died of cocaine intoxication two days after being selected in the draft.

McGinn made the official announcement of Lewis's death at 10:19 p.m. and, at the request of the family, provided no further details.

Lewis's wife, Donna Harris Lewis—who is pregnant with the couple's second child, according to radio station WEEI-AM—was at the hospital when her husband died and later left with a police escort. Lewis was the father of a 10-month-old son, Reginald.

"We lost a very treasured member of our family today," a somber Dave Gavitt, the team's senior executive vice president, said from team offices on Merrimac Street after the announcement of Lewis's death. "This is a time of incredible grief."

"We had players and coaches come in and they didn't know what to do," he said. "So many players called in from all over the country. Our hearts are with the Lewis family.

"Reggie was not only an outstanding basketball player, but also an outstanding human being," continued Gavitt. "He was a gentle, kind and wonderful guy. He had so much to give to the city of Boston and to his family."

Already Lewis's death has spurred renewed debate about the conflicting medical advice Lewis received in May and the favorable diagnosis he and the team apparently embraced.

Both Lewis and the Celtics dismissed the findings of several prominent Boston cardiologists, who diagnosed the Celtics' captain as having heart trouble, and instead accepted the conclusions of another heart specialist, Dr. Gilbert Mudge of Brigham and Women's Hospital, who said Lewis had only a fainting condition that was treatable and should not prevent him from returning to the NBA.

No one answered the door at Mudge's house last night.

Lewis collapsed early in Game 1 of the Celtics' playoff series with the Charlotte Hornets on April 29 but was allowed to return in the second half. He quickly was removed when he became noticeably woozy and was taken to New England Baptist Hospital for tests.

Over the next 72 hours, the Celtics assembled a group of Boston heart specialists, dubbed "The Dream Team of Cardiology," who reviewed Lewis's test results and concluded he had a serious heart problem. But on the heels of that diagnosis, Lewis abruptly left New England Baptist and admitted himself to Brigham and Women's, where his wife had formerly worked.

After an extensive series of tests over more than a week, Mudge decided Lewis suffered from neurocardiogenic syncope, a nerve disorder. Mudge also said Lewis had a normal athlete's heart, and that Lewis could expect to resume his NBA career without restrictions.

The hospital switch, however, removed Lewis from the oversight of the Celtics' medical staff. The Celtics subsequently deferred all medical decisions instead to Lewis and Mudge.

Only two weeks ago, while the Celtics were staging their annual rookie camp at Brandeis, Mudge said Lewis had medical clearance to participate. He did not play, however. Lewis's agent, Peter Roisman, said his client was "struggling internally" with the prospect of returning to the court. It was not known when, or how vigorously, Lewis resumed his basketball workouts. He refused numerous interview requests over that span.

Lewis had just completed his sixth season with the Celtics, his first as the team's captain following the retirement of Larry Bird. He was a quiet presence both on the floor and in the locker room and distinguished himself in the last two years as one of the NBA's top shooting guards. He was named to the Eastern Conference All-Star team in 1992, the last Celtic to be so honored.

Lewis was one of four children raised by a single working mother in East Baltimore, where he began his basketball career using rolled-up socks and makeshift baskets on the doors. Originally, he wanted to play football. But his slender body and his mother's objections led him to basketball instead. Often, he would leave his row house on North Rose Street after midnight in the summer to practice with his brother Irving. The courts weren't crowded then and the air was cooler.

He first displayed his basketball prowess as the sixth man on the famed Dunbar High team, which won 59 straight games and also included future NBA players David Wingate, Tyrone (Muggsy) Bogues and Reggie Williams. Northeastern University discovered Lewis while recruiting another player and he played four years there, leaving as the ninth all-time scorer in Division I history.

The Celtics made Lewis their No. 1 draft pick, 22d overall, in 1987. After a rookie season spent on the bench, Lewis emerged as a starter in his second year. He finished second to Kevin Johnson in balloting for the league's Most Improved Player as he improved his scoring average from 4.5 to 18.5 points a game. He improved each season, capped by the All-Star berth in 1992. Last year, he led the team in scoring for the second straight year.

Reggie Lewis, pictured with his son Reggie Jr. at Celtics rookie camp in Waltham, Mass., on July 13, 1993.

Poignant Memories Remain

July 28, 1993 • by Jackie MacMullan

He was just a kid when he came to Boston, a gangly colt with doe eyes and an innocent smile.

Reggie Lewis was Northeastern's secret. He showed up the first day of practice, his shorts drooping off skinny legs, his long, long arms dangling by his side. But when he stepped on the court, those arms swooped to life and those skinny legs launched him to heights never before seen at the school.

Jim Calhoun, who coached NU then and is now at the University of Connecticut, is an excitable man by nature to begin with, but he was so juiced up about this player that he couldn't put sentences together fast enough.

"You've got to see him," he told me. "I'm telling you, he's terrific. And he's such a great kid."

So I went over to meet this Reggie Lewis. He hadn't done an interview in Boston yet, and he was nervous, and he was shy, and I walked away with an empty notebook—but with a smile on my face.

You couldn't help but like him. You couldn't help but smile at that silly little chuckle he had, or warm to the friendly grin that stayed with him nearly all the time.

He wore his high school jacket from Dunbar to the interview. The nickname of his team was the Poets, and he wore that jacket all season long. His new Northeastern teammates rode him about it all the time, but he didn't care. He was a Poet. He would always be a Poet.

They didn't play him much at Dunbar, but they played him all the time at Northeastern. He was a special player with a special gift—the ability to dominate a game yet still leave the court with every one of his teammates enormously happy about his success.

I was privileged to cover Reggie Lewis for his entire college career. Often he played in half-empty gyms with only a core of diehard fans watching his every move.

He did some remarkable things in those years. He went to the NCAA Tournament as a freshman, and in the cavernous Meadowlands he nearly led Northeastern to a stunning upset of Virginia Commonwealth by shooting a remarkable 15 of 17 from the floor. He played an entire postseason with a broken wrist. He did not lose a league game in his senior season.

He didn't forget his friends when the Celtics made him their first-round draft pick. His college point guard, Andre LaFleur, never made it in the NBA, but his dreams were kept alive by the encouragement—and recommendations—of his famous teammate.

I saw LaFleur one day during a Celtics practice. He was riding the stationary bike, and he said Reggie got him in to use the facilities. "He's putting in a good word for me," said LaFleur. "He hasn't changed. Not one bit."

There was some initial doubt about whether Lewis would be an NBA first-round draft pick, and

of course he didn't say much about that. But years later, he told me he was so sure he'd get picked that he went out three days before the draft and bought his first suit.

When Boston called out his name, Lewis appeared at the Garden wearing pinstriped black, looking so grown up, so professional, that I caught myself wondering when he had stopped being that shy, gangly colt with those wide, innocent eyes.

He waited his turn with the Celtics and kept his frustrations to himself, just as he had done at Dunbar. When his turn came, he unleashed those long, long arms and those legs that had somewhere along the way gotten a little bit bigger, a little bit stronger. He wouldn't stop playing until they noticed.

He made the All-Star team two seasons ago, and when I bumped into him in Orlando, he was distracted because he needed more tickets for his family and somehow his sweatsuit hadn't made the trip with him. So he showed up for his first All-Star Game without his Celtics team jacket, but that didn't diminish his exuberance. The smile didn't waver. He finally had made it.

Reggie Lewis promised to give back to the community, and his words were not hollow. He started an annual turkey giveaway for underprivileged families. He appeared at countless charity events. He was in the process of starting his own foundation to provide scholarships for student-athletes.

He was on the cusp of stardom, but this past season was a difficult one for Lewis. Larry Bird had retired, and Lewis had been chosen team captain. All of those double- and triple-teams that used to chase Bird around every night were chasing him now.

His numbers were off, his legs were bothering him, his back was tight, and when the All-Star selections were made, he wasn't included.

It was a major disappointment, but it seemed so small after what happened in the playoffs, when he collapsed without warning in Game 1 against the Charlotte Hornets. He likened the experience to "that Hank Gathers thing," and in all the years I had known him, I had never seen Reggie Lewis look so frightened.

I do not wish to remember Reggie Lewis that way. I want to remember him as a shy, gangly kid who grew to be a man before my eyes.

I want to remember him as a new father apologizing profusely for being tardy for an interview because he fell asleep on the couch with his newborn son.

I want to remember the confident athlete who assured me he would be on the 1994 All-Star team, "and would you care to wager a bet on that?"

I want to remember the easy smile, that silly little laugh. I want to say Reggie Lewis was once a Celtic, always a Celtic, but then I find myself thinking about that little boy who will never take another nap with his daddy, and I wonder why a 27-year-old man and his family, who had their whole lives in front of them, deserved this.

I want Reggie Lewis to be in the 1994 All-Star Game. I want somebody to tell me this just isn't true.

Parish's Pivotal Assistance Was Too Often Overlooked

August 5, 1994 • by Bob Ryan

Bad enough for Robert Parish there was Larry Bird. There was also Kevin McHale. In the Big Three, he was considered to be, well, Three.

Pity. Many a franchise would this morning be in mourning, bemoaning the loss of The Best Player We've Ever Had. Oh yes, Robert Parish was/is that good. Only in Boston would there be a spirited debate about whether he is the second- or third-best center in the team's history. It's either Robert or Dave Cowens for the second spot. (If you don't know who Numero Uno is, ask your daddy or mommy.)

And as for that was/is business, the Charlotte Hornets and their fans will soon be discovering that Robert Parish is very much an is. He is, in fact, a unique figure in the game's history. Only Kareem Abdul-Jabbar was functioning at all at such an advanced age, and then only as a partial player. Kareem's last couple of seasons were spent shooting that deadly hook shot and passing the basketball. Defense? Sorry. Rebounding? Surely you jest. Kareem The Elder was not really a full-time participant.

The folks in Charlotte will quickly learn that Robert Parish remains a fully functioning basketball player. There are no caveat emptor provisos attached thereto, save for the obvious reality that

Robert will do what he does for no more than, say, 25 minutes in any given game. If all goes well, of course, he won't be doing it for more than 15-18 minutes a night, if that. Alonzo Mourning barely shaves, correct? So his young legs have to be good for 30-plus minutes, easy.

Ah, but wouldn't you love to be in the Charlotte Coliseum to see and hear the reaction the first time some young stud who had yet to learn his A-B-Cs when The Chief first laced 'em up for Golden State (pre-MTV, pre-ESPN, pre-compact disc, pre-microwave, pre-velcro, but not, smarty-pants, pre-electricity) turns his snotty little head when the shot goes up, fails to do a U-turn from offense to defense, and now finds Mr. Parish sprinting downcourt for a lead pass and a dunk? At age Four-One.

Book it. You and I both know it will happen. Often. Sadly, the treat will now be Charlotte's, not ours.

We in Boston will truly miss Robert Parish. Remains there a more stylish pivot entrepreneur in the NBA? I don't think so. There are so few true centers left, anyway, with legitimate pivotmen—players who thrive while playing with their backs to the basket—fast becoming the drop-kickers of hoop.

We've now seen our last amazing, high-arc Parish turnaround jumper. 'Fess up: Over the entire 14-year Parish era, you never once really expected any of those things to go in, did you? There have been one or two moonshot specialists aside from Parish (remember Purvis Short?), but Robert is the only one who has consistently made them with convoys of Very Large People hanging on his right arm. Robert is the only one who has made them night after night, year after year, from the first quarter till the last, regardless of game time or circumstance, again in the annoying company of all those Very Large People.

But Robert Parish does more than just shoot turnaround jumpers.

The repertoire also includes a very nice running hook, ambidextrous short jump hooks, a spiffy finger roll, a drop-dead spin move from the right box and, finally, a terrific face-up move with a crossover dribble he really should have used more often.

Then there's the matter of Robert's astonishing agility. I will state categorically that no big man in history has ever continually executed more acrobatic moves at the end of sneak-away touchdown passes than this man. We are talking about shaking and baking and hanging in the air and contorting that angular frame this way and that after receiving the ball on the fly.

Oh, and have we mentioned the vaunted pick-and-roll? History might record Bird and Parish as the most devastating executioners of this art who've ever played the game, especially when you consider that we are talking about the feeder being 6 feet 9 inches and change and the pick-and-roller being a shade over 7 feet tall.

None of us appreciated Robert Parish early enough. He was a great force during his first three or four years, back when someone would actually give him the basketball. The problem is that few of us could ever see far beyond Larry then. But Larry himself always knew. Let the record show that right from the beginning of his Celtic career, Parish had no stauncher supporter than Larry Bird, that no one was more appreciative of both Parish's all-around skills and his wonderful athletic temperament than No. 33. Bird always had faith in Parish, in all situations.

The mind drifts back to April 20, 1986, the Michael Jordan 63-point game. In a key situation late in the second overtime, Bird elected to run a pick-and-roll with Parish, despite the fact that Robert hadn't hit a jump shot all day. Bird came off the pick, Parish rolled, and Bird hit him—swish.

"You've got to give Robert the ball if he's open," Larry shrugged.

Robert Parish leaves Boston in the knowledge that he did what he was originally brought here to do. Bill Fitch pushed to get him because he needed to get bigger in order to beat Philadelphia. Fitch believed that Parish had not been properly utilized by the Warriors, and he was proven correct. Robert Parish can say he put three rings on Larry Bird's fingers as easily as Larry Bird can say the same about Robert.

In a better athletic world, The Chief wouldn't be going anywhere. It is somewhat easy to rationalize since the man himself is notoriously unsentimental, and it is easier still since he winds up in a better place, professionally speaking. Yet we never got a chance to give him a proper Boston Celtic-Boston Garden send-off, and that is sad.

The Chief gave us enormous pleasure for 14 seasons. Now he can be the first man to have his number raised in the new Boston Garden. In that sense, he will not be No. 3, he will be No. 1. I rather like that idea.

THAT'S ALL, FOLKS

FANS RELIVE FAVORITE PAST TIMES

May 6, 1995 • by Dan Shaughnessy

It was a night for collectibles. Folks actually bought programs. About a thousand flashbulbs popped when Shaquille O'Neal and Eric Montross went up for the opening tap. Like high school prom dates pressing flowers inside wax paper, fans carried home leftover popcorn to store for the ages. They will be able to say, "I was there."

Red was there. Larry was there. A handful of red-coat ushers who saw Chuck Connors play in the 1940s were there, too. This was the night the Celtics bid adieu to Boston Garden. Never again will we see the Green Team play in the old barn on Causeway Street.

The Orlando Magic last night defeated the Celtics, 95-92, eliminating Boston from the 1995 NBA playoffs. In the short term, this means that the 49th season of the Celts is over, and coach Chris Ford may soon be looking for a new job. But this game takes its place in local sports history because it was the final night for the Celtics in the old Garden.

There were plenty of last, loud roars. When the Celtics took their first lead on a Dee Brown break-away dunk with 53.3 seconds left in the third, it was as noisy as it ever was in the days of John Havlicek or Larry Bird.

It was like the old days. Bird stood and cheered. Red stood and hollered at referee Mike Mathis. The traditional 14,890 rattled the rails of the train station below. One last time.

For a few moments late in the fourth, it seemed the Celtics were going to pull off one last Garden miracle. Sherm Douglas threw up a shot that bounced high off the rim—the ghost of Don Nelson—then dropped through the strings. A Douglas 3-point heave from the shootops with 2:35 left gave the Celts a 91-90 lead.

More than 1,000 fans and players linger on the floor of Boston Garden after the last game in the building.

Not yet, the building seemed to be saying. The old Garden would not lose its basketball breath. Not yet.

But in the end, the Magic were too young and strong. They were better, and not even the magic of the Garden could bring victory in this final game.

When it was over, many fans wouldn't leave. More than 1,000 Green people milled around the parquet for a good half-hour. A woman wrote her name in lipstick on the foul line. A young man scraped at the oak floor until there was blood under his fingernail. Some fans made off with bolts, and two floorboards were snapped from one corner of the court. In the stands, fathers sat with their children, watching the scene, saying little.

It's official. There'll be no more basketball in the best hardwood house the world has ever known. Progress has its price. This time air-conditioning takes a toll on our city's soul.

The Celts have played in the Garden since they were born in 1946, and watching them play their last Garden game was a little like eating your last meal before the wrecking ball hits Durgin-Park.

It's been a weird spring ripe with long goodbyes. We've had the last Beanpot, the last Tom Petty concert and the last Celtic and Bruin regular-season games. Your local newspaper has furnished enough commemorative pages to wallpaper the outside of FleetCenter. Waiting for the Garden to close has become like waiting for Franco to die.

Folks brought their cameras last night. Every fan wanted a commemorative photo with the banners and/or parquet in the background. It's not as if Celtic fans didn't have faith in their team, but rational locals knew that there was every likelihood that this would be the famous farewell scene for the Green in the Garden.

Soon the Bruins will have their chance for the final skate on the small ice. And the Grateful Dead will be truckin' through the Garden before it's dismantled. But hockey games and rock concerts didn't put this building on the map. It was the local professional basketball team that made the Garden internationally famous. The Celtics of the 1960s were the best-known sports team on the planet, and Everyfan wanted to visit the House of Auerbach and Russell. Just once.

Bill Walton, here last night in his capacity as an NBC commentator, said, "This is the building that brought me into basketball. Even though I grew up in California, it was the Celtics playing in the Garden that I watched on television. I can't believe what a basketball building this is. It's a temple. It's a shrine. It's a place where people make religious pilgrimages."

It's also a dump. But it's our dump. And it's a place where so many things happened. Boston Garden has more basketball history than the aggregate resumes of Madison Square Garden, Chicago Stadium, Pauley Pavilion and the Palestra.

Last night the Celtics citizenry walked up the smelly ramps one last time. And they rocked the arena. One last time. They came out to say goodbye to a team that wasn't good, and to an ugly old building that served as the Sistine Chapel of professional basketball.

It's over. Never again will fans be as close to the action. No matter how loud it gets, it won't seem as loud. The new place just won't be a gym.

The old Boston Garden was a gym—the best gym there ever was.

This Is the Perfect Home for Rebuilding Team

November 4, 1995 • by Bob Ryan

Well, we here in Boston are in the 20th century now, boys and girls. A timeout comes in the NewPlace and we get a car commercial up on the Sony Jumbotron hanging at midcourt. How did we ever get along without that?

We've got music now, and we've got plush, comfortable seats with drink-holders. We've got escalators. We've got hamburgers, frozen yogurt, waffles and lots of pizza. We've got $125 courtside seats. We've got suites, club seats and waiters and/or waitresses in the stands to make the high rollers feel even more special.

What we don't have, of course, is a good basketball team, but at least last night it didn't, you know, stink, if you'll pardon the expression.

It didn't win, either, but it didn't stink.

Let history record that in the first NBA regular-season game ever played in the NewPlace, the Milwaukee Bucks defeated the Boston Celtics, 101-100. And let history also record that new coach M. L. Carr stepped up to the podium afterward and took the blame for a disastrous second quarter, during which his team was outscored by 15 points (31-16). If you want to break this game down, start with the fact that the Celtics outscored the Bucks by 9 in the first quarter and 6 in the fourth, with the teams breaking even in the third.

M. L. is trying to figure out what he's got and hasn't got. In the second quarter, he was trying to fool around with a dash of Eric Williams, a pinch of Doug Smith, a dollop of Charles Claxton and a soup-con of Junior Burrough. The mixture never exactly jelled. The Celtics lost control of the game and never really regained it (don't be fooled by the final score).

This wasn't exactly a preview of the 1996 Eastern Conference finals. This was a confrontation between a team whose big goal is to make the playoffs (and perhaps finish above .500) and a team whose goal is to avoid embarrassment. The Bucks looked at this affair as the kind of game they should win and, indeed, have to win if they are to achieve middle-level status. The Celtics looked at this game as one of the few in which they actually had a chance during what promises to be a rigorous November.

The Celtics did play hard. They didn't always play smart, but they did play hard. They seemed to feed off the energy provided by rookie forward Williams, a young man in clear possession of the proverbial "live body." Williams submitted 14 of his 16 points and all six of his rebounds during the second half. Fans always love aggressive youngsters, and he brought them out of those cushy seats a few times with some hustle plays.

The crowd hasn't changed, NewPlace or OldPlace. We can forget the idea of the crowd ever doing anything for the team. If the team is down, or not playing well, it can forget about hearing a clap or encouraging word. If the team does something, then the fans get jolted into action.

So there was noise when a Rick Fox pull-up banker made it 77-74, and there was noise when an Eric Montross keep-alive led to a Williams tip at 88-83. But the noise was never sustained.

As for the music, consider that during a Celtic timeout with 44.7 seconds left (98-95, Bucks), the tune taking the fans through the interlude was "Taking Care of Business," and that as soon as the team broke from the huddle, it most decidedly did not take care of business. Instead, Dee Brown, capping off a dreadful evening (2 for 11), lost the ball out of bounds.

Look at it this way: For 35 years or so, Celtic fans were proud parents of honor students. And the schoolhouse was old and uncomfortable. Now Celtic fans are not-so-proud parents of D-plus students who at least stay out of jail. And the schoolhouse is lovely.

Bird Has Word on Walker

THIS DRAFT PICK IS A REAL KEEPER

June 27, 1996 • by Bob Ryan

Larry's loyal, so you'd expect him to sign on to whatever they do. But Larry's also Larry, which means he's not going to insult our intelligence by running any jive by us.

"I think this is going to be a special player for us," swears Larry Bird.

He is talking about Antoine Walker.

That's strong. Larry could cover himself by simply saying, "He's a nice pick," or "He's got good skills," or some other polite, tepid, meaningless assessment that would hide his true feelings.

Larry isn't doing that. Larry is putting his professional credibility on the line. Larry is the 1992 Frank Rich pulling out the superlatives for a Broadway show, thus ensuring a solid year's run.

He thinks Antoine Walker has a chance to be a major keeper, a true All-Star.

"We got a very good player," Bird says. "People are going to enjoy watching him play."

But now hear this: Larry says he would have been equally effusive had the Celtics wound up with Ray Allen.

"At the end of last season, I said Ray Allen would be the No. 1 or No. 2 pick if he were to come out," Bird declares. "That's how much I liked him. Guys here were teasing me all week. They said, 'We're gonna go and find something wrong with him'—and they came up blank every time."

Bird sees no real negatives with Walker. For example . . .

Shooting? "He's not a bad shooter. He shot about 47 percent from the floor. He's a little bit of a streak shooter, but he'll improve. The pro game is different, and when he gets out on the floor and gets a few easy baskets, his confidence will improve."

Stamina? Walker probably played fewer minutes (27 a game) than any of the premier players in the 1996 draft. "He may only have played 23 a game in college," Bird says, coming close enough to the actual figure. "But that's like 35 down in Kentucky, the way they play."

Maturity? Walker won't turn 20 until next month. "He's obviously more mature than I was at 19," says Bird. "I can't imagine coming out after my freshman year, like a few of these guys. At 19, I wasn't even old enough to drink a beer. Although I did."

Attitude? "He likes to play," Bird maintains. "He really likes to play. It's like Walter McCarty. He's always happy on the basketball court. Rick Pitino did a real good job recruiting these players. You need guys who'll be ready to play 82 games, not 40."

This is Year 4 of the Executive Bird, as opposed to the Athlete Bird. This is the only time of the year *vox populi* is reminded that Larry is indeed on the payroll, and not just a number hanging in the rafters. The fact is that he is active in the scouting process. He does get out there during the year and during the NCAA tournament. He does sit home and watch college game after college game on his TV. And he is very much an active participant in the selection process.

"It's amazing," he says. "I will go see a player and either he can score and rebound and run and jump, or he can't. Then I will look at these scouting reports and I'll go half crazy. They keep changing. After I see what I want to see, I make a few notes and then go on to the next one. People like to find the smallest thing wrong with these guys and focus on what they can't do, rather than what they can do."

After a decade of disappointment and much more than their share of heartache, the Celtics are finally walking around with smiles on their faces. Eric Williams has a chance to be a decent player. David Wesley took a huge step upward last year. Walker is a very intriguing player. And there are the two 1997 first-rounders on the horizon. Is the Celtic sky finally turning a little blue?

"I hope," says Bird. "God, I hope so. It's time to buckle down and give the fans what they really deserve—a winner."

So Larry will be back in the hunt next year, scouring this great land of ours for the next quasi-savior—wherever he may be. "Things are moving forward here," Bird says. "We've got the opportunity to get at least one great player next year. He might be in eighth grade."

Eighth grade like Mr. X or 14th grade like Antoine Walker, anyone who can play a little can help the Boston Celtics.

Look of Leadership for Celtics

PITINO COULD SPUR A REBOUND

May 7, 1997 • by Bob Ryan

Bill Parcells was in New England, but not of it.

Rick Pitino, two months ago, on the feasibility of coaching the Boston Celtics, now or ever: "Nobody will have to sell me on Boston. I love that city."

Bill Parcells came to create a winning tradition for the New England Patriots. Rick Pitino comes to restore one to the Boston Celtics.

"It's a franchise full of glory, full of tradition, and full of wonderful pride," he declared yesterday. "I would like to take it back to a championship level."

Rick Pitino could have remained at the University of Kentucky for the rest of his life, becoming a combination Mr. Chips/Dean Smith. He conceivably could have presided over the opening of the mythical 25,000-seat Rick Pitino Center on campus. He could have repeated himself many times over, and he could have been happy. But yesterday he delighted Boston and deflated Lexington by announcing that he had accepted the position as head coach and head of basketball operations of the Celtics.

Boston represents the perfect package for Pitino, 44, at this stage of his life. His coaching and talent evaluation skills have never been better. He is truly at the top of his game. The Celtics have a tradition that he respects and they truly need him. He has

been given both the time (10 years) and the power (virtually unlimited) he needs to get the job done.

He downplayed the money yesterday, but of course, those people who are already making more money than the rest of us could ever imagine (in his case, close to $3 million a year) always downplay the money as an abstract in explaining their decisions. The guessing is that the package is worth $65 million-$70 million for the duration, so any Pitino family financial worries should be alleviated.

What Pitino means for the organization is credibility. He is a great coach, but there are low-profile people out there who could coach the team in a professional manner. Pitino happens to be the one man not currently already in the employ of an NBA team who is both the steak and the sizzle. He is, his recent protestations to the contrary, totally comfortable in the spotlight. He will coach, and coach darn well, but he will also be the public face of the organization. Over the next 10 years, when you think "Boston Celtics," you are going to think "Rick Pitino." He will work awesomely hard, but he will not be a hermit. Sooner or later, he will have his picture taken with Keith Lockhart; count on it.

Pitino has made a career out of taking handyman-special teams and turning them into glittering mansions Bob Vila would be proud of. He did it as a 26-year-old wunderkind with Boston University (a pre-Pitino 7-19 to 17-9 in two years); he did it at Providence College (a pre-Pitino 11-20 to 25-9 and the Final Four in two years); he did it with the New York Knicks (a pre-Pitino 24-58 to 52-30 and an Atlantic Division title in two years); and he did it with the University of Kentucky (a pre-Pitino 13-19 to 22-6 in two years and 29-7 and the Final Four in three).

He now assumes control of an under-coached—some would go so far as to say non-coached—15-67 team, and it could be argued that this is his biggest challenge yet, although it should be pointed out that the Pitino viewpoint on just how difficult it will be to rebuild in a 29-team league is a bit different from most people's.

"In some ways," he said, "it may be easier to win 45 games in this league than it was when I was in the NBA before. When we won 52, there were a lot of good teams. The division was very good. The Central Division was an absolute killer. The Texas trip was brutal. When we won 52 games, it was wholly legitimate."

He needn't finish the thought. The NBA is an expansion-ravaged league in which most teams have no bench strength whatsoever. If the Celtics are fortunate enough to win the draft lottery May 18, they would be in position to get a potential impact player in Tim Duncan, a shot-blocking/rebounding/passing center who, almost by definition, makes other players better. If they don't win it, well, they'll at least get two decent young players, and whatever group emerges from training camp next year will be professionally prepared to play an 82-game NBA schedule.

Rick Pitino represents that most precious of all human virtues—hope. Paul Gaston, the Celtics' frequently (and rightfully) maligned chairman of the board, has addressed the business needs of his team and the psychic need of the fans with this one hiring. He gets a highly qualified coach and chief executive who not only wants to succeed, but who wants to succeed here.

The long local nightmare is over. Rick Pitino will make the Celtics relevant again.

Celtics' Draft Dreams Fizzle

May 19, 1997 • by Michael Holley

SECAUCUS, N.J.—You could see the disappointment on his face yesterday, even if it was a smile the Celtics' M. L. Carr flashed for the cameras.

And you could practically hear the entire Celtics organization groan as it was announced that Boston hadn't won the No. 1 pick in the NBA Draft, even though it had had the best odds of any team (36 percent) to win the right to select Wake Forest center Tim Duncan, the best player in college basketball.

Instead, the Celtics came away with the No. 3 and No. 6 picks. The San Antonio Spurs, a team that already has a star center in David Robinson, won the No. 1 selection.

Not being able to land Duncan was a big blow to new Celtics coach Rick Pitino as he tries to rebuild the 15-67 team. Barring a trade, Pitino will start this new Celtics era without a dominant center.

Instead, the Celtics have two of the draft's top six picks. That wouldn't be so bad if this were 1984, when Michael Jordan went third and Charles Barkley was

fifth. But this is 1997, and, as Pitino said, "The No. 7 pick could be better than the No. 2 pick."

And the No. 1 pick? "The only way I could see us trading Tim Duncan is if someone offered us Michael, Magic, and Larry," Spurs coach and general manager Gregg Popovich said.

No one was surprised when deputy commissioner Russ Granik pulled the Celtics' logo out of the No. 6 envelope. That was the pick the Celtics received from Dallas last summer; since the Mavericks were the league's sixth-worst team, that meant the lottery was going as could have been predicted. But when Vancouver's logo came out of the No. 4 envelope, Carr, now the team's executive vice president for corporate development, looked as if he wanted to faint. He turned to Grizzlies general manager Stu Jackson and said, "It just turned."

He was right. The next envelope also contained a Celtics card. The Grizzlies, not eligible to pick first, had a 45 percent chance of landing the No. 2 pick. Vancouver and Boston, the two worst teams in the league, were nowhere near the No. 1 pick.

Carr tried to laugh. It sounded hollow.

"I can tell you this," he said, "Coach Pitino will do the right thing with the picks. He knows what he's doing, he knows college basketball." Pitino, who did not attend the lottery selection show, said he wasn't depressed by the outcome, either.

"The only thing I'm disappointed in is that we can't start practice tomorrow. I'm very anxious to get started," he said.

The Deal: New Backcourt
CELTICS MAKE BILLUPS, MERCER THE CHOSEN TWO

June 26, 1997 • by Michael Holley

CHARLOTTE, N.C.—Both of them sat in a place called the Green Room last night, hoping Rick Pitino would not pass them by. Chauncey Billups and Ron Mercer knew they wanted to play in Boston. They also knew it wasn't up to them. So they sat in Charlotte Coliseum and waited.

They didn't have to squirm for long. Forty minutes after last night's NBA Draft began, Billups and Mercer were officially Celtics. Pitino had considered trading the No. 3 and No. 6 draft picks to Chicago for Scottie Pippen, but the Celtics' president and coach settled instead for a new back court. With the third pick, Billups, a 6-foot-3-inch point guard from Colorado, was selected. Three spots later, 6-7 shooting guard Mercer was reunited with his head coach at the University of Kentucky.

"That's where I wanted to be," Billups gushed last night. "I think everybody in the draft right now was a Celtic fan growing up because of how much they won. Those guys and the Lakers. I mean, it was like the Bulls right now. I saw a lot of them and they had a lot of great players; teams that kids would always admire."

Last night, Pitino stated the obvious: Billups and Mercer will have to be ready to contribute. Especially Billups. Since he was 11, he has been nicknamed "Smooth." He has the moniker seared into his flesh. He'll have to live up to the name because he will be the only true point guard on the roster.

"If we re-sign David Wesley, then we will have three point guards making more than $10 million combined," Pitino said. "That does not bode well."

Billups, who averaged 18 points per game in two seasons at Colorado, says he is ready to start. He also says you can check his resumé for experience with team makeovers.

"My first year at Colorado, we were 9-18," he said. "That really helped me out in Year 2 because it made me appreciate winning a lot more."

Mercer's first year of college was different. As a Pitino-coached freshman, he and Walker contributed to UK's national championship. Last season, with Walker moving on to the Celtics, the Wildcats were national runners-up. Mercer thought of that last night. The Denver Nuggets had just selected Tony Battie fifth. That meant Boston had five minutes to make a choice. As an electronic clock approached zero, Mercer sat at a table with his family. His head was bowed. No secret: he wanted Boston.

"I've been with Coach for two years," he said. "I really didn't think he would pass on me."

Earlier in the day, Mercer sat uncomfortably in a downtown hotel as he listened to rumors of the Pippen trade. He said he was scared. He would be satisfied to be a part of any NBA team, but if the question is where did he want to be, the answer is Causeway Street.

He was the Southeastern Conference Player of the Year last season, averaging 18 points and shooting 49 percent from the field.

Taking Bulls by Horn

CELTICS GET OFF TO A ROLLICKING START IN STUNNER

November 1, 1997 • by Michael Holley

You kept expecting the kids to trash the 18,624-seat house last night. At some point you thought they would disrespect the expensive FleetCenter parquet, recklessly throw around basketballs, or simply allow their visitors from Chicago to run all evening and hang on the rims.

A national cable TV audience waited for a while, too, until it became obvious: it was not going to happen. The Kid Celtics, the youngest team in the NBA, handled themselves like grown-ups and defeated the defending NBA champion Bulls, 92-85. It was the first win of the Rick Pitino Era. It was the first time the Celtics have been over .500 in two years. It was the first time since coming out of retirement that Michael Jordan had to come to Boston and analyze a loss to the Celtics.

"Once we realized the Bulls were human like we are, we settled down," said Antoine Walker, who grew up a Bulls fan, just like the five young men and women in the FleetCenter seats who grew up with him on the South Side of Chicago. But his brothers and sisters were rooting for their big brother last night. It was hard not to like what he was doing.

"He didn't just play like an All-Star," said Chauncey (15 points) Billups, who admitted he had butterflies before the game. "He played like he was All-NBA."

Walker finished with 31 points and 8 rebounds. He only had two assists, but one of them, a touchdown pass to Ron Mercer in the fourth, secured the win. Walker's fingerprints could be found all over the third quarter. That was necessary considering the Celtics entered the period trailing, 43-34. Of course, that was much better than the 20-point deficit they faced after one and the awful 17 turn-overs they had after two.

Two things won this game: the Celtics' trap and Walker's demands for the ball.

First there was Walker. After the Celtics quickly tied the Bulls at the beginning of the third, their power forward went to work. He pulled up for a 27-foot 3-pointer with the game tied at 49. Swish. Exactly one minute later, with 5½ minutes remaining in the quarter, he pulled up for a 26-footer. Swish. The Celtics wouldn't trail again. They wouldn't lack for confidence, either, because you should have seen the look on Walker's face. It was a sneer. He did his dance, a shoulder-shaker called The BK Bounce, and did chest bumps with everyone who came his way.

By the time the dancing and celebrating was over by the end of the third, the Celtics led, 68-58. They were calm going into the fourth.

"Before the game I was thinking, 'Man, I'm about to guard Michael Jordan,'" said rookie Ron Mercer, who was assigned to The Great One. "Then I started thinking, 'I've just got to play.' I'm not into grading my performances, but I think I did all right. I just didn't want to get embarrassed."

He wasn't. It was the Bulls who had to answer why they lost to a team that won 15 games last season. It was the Bulls who were prodded and questioned until Jordan finally said, "One game early in the season doesn't mean we're not going to win No. 6."

Pitino Plies Trade Again

CELTICS AND RAPTORS MAKE 7-PLAYER DEAL

February 19, 1998 • by Michael Holley

VANCOUVER, British Columbia—They liked to call themselves a family. Not only did the Celtics have the youngest team in the NBA, you could argue that they had the closest one, too. But the young Celtics received a lesson in NBA family structure yesterday. Simply—kinship can dissolve quickly when the trading deadline is approaching.

Chauncey Billups, Dee Brown, Roy Rogers, and John Thomas arrived here early yesterday morning with the rest of the Celtics. None among the quartet

unpacked his bags. A few hours after arriving at the team hotel, all were notified that they had been traded to Toronto in exchange for 6-foot-1-inch point guard Kenny Anderson, 6-8 power forward Popeye Jones (out for the season), and 7-foot center Zan Tabak.

What happened yesterday was the completion of a deal that had been agreed to in principle Tuesday night. One hour before the Celtics' game at Sacramento, Pitino was told that a deal was in place and all he had to do was give his OK. He thought about it for a while, told Billups that something could happen, and, a few hours later, officially made his fifth trade in nine months as Celtics president and coach.

So Pitino said goodbye to his first Celtic draft pick (Billups) and one of his first Celtic captains (Brown). He will now coach a 27-year-old point guard known for his ability to quickly penetrate and create. "In some ways, he reminds me of Tiny Archibald," Pitino said of Anderson. Pitino's son Richard went to school in a funk yesterday morning because his father traded his favorite player, Billups. "He said to me, 'Dad, don't do it; don't do it,'" Pitino said. "He's going to kill me." But the coach was impressed that he could get an All-Star point guard (1994) and clear cap space at the same time.

Not many Celtics could argue with the basketball side of the deal. Most of them were hurt because their close friends were going to work somewhere else. It was only two weeks ago that Billups was saying he wanted to spend his entire career playing with Ron Mercer. But the rookie guards had their dream ended at 51 games.

"I feel bad for Chauncey," Brown said. "He was Coach Pitino's first pick and it's like he's always going to be traded. He told me he was glad I was going with him. Somehow I think I'll be able to deal with this a little quicker than he will."

Walking the Walk

Actions and numbers speak louder than talk for this Celtic.

March 31, 1998 • by Michael Holley

MIAMI—The noon sun is in Antoine Walker's eyes, so he squints as he considers the question. The brim from his baseball cap could shield the rays, but it is turned backward on his head. He doesn't care about that. He has a few subjects on his mind: The state of the Celtics, his game, and food.

Right now, the food comes first.

"How do you get to the Cheesecake Factory?" he asks. He is given directions. Soon a cab will be here to take him to a trendy place known as the Coco Walk.

Now, back to that original question.

No, he replies, he doesn't listen to much talk radio in Boston. So, no, he hadn't heard about the caller who insisted that the Celtics forward doesn't have a "butter" move. You know, no sweet move that is so distinctly Walker that you could identify it and him even if you were watching only a silhouette.

"That must be somebody who doesn't watch a lot of the games," Walker said, smiling. "Every great player has to have a go-to move when they get in trouble. Hakeem Olajuwon told me that last year. But people who only see a few games have to realize that great players aren't going to have it every night."

Later Walker will look at Stephon Marbury's name in a box score. "He only had 2 points," Walker will say, "but he had 10 assists. And his team won. I like players like that."

Walker is not shy about mentioning himself in the same sentence as great players such as Olajuwon. He will tell you that he isn't there yet. But the day is coming fast, faster than most people who watch him daily might expect. It seems as if there is always some poking at the perceived flaws in Walker's game. No butter move. Poor free throw shooting. Poor shot selection. Poor treatment of officials. Too much early Dominique Wilkins in his game.

But then you look at the numbers.

You find that Larry Bird was 24 when he won his first title and 27 when he first averaged at least 24 points per game. You find that Tom Heinsohn shot 39 percent from the field in his first two pro seasons and was 25 before he ever averaged 20 points per game. You see that John Havlicek was a 73 percent free throw shooter his first two seasons, averaged 20 points his fifth season and, when he was 29, became a terrific 500-assist man. And while Walker never will have as many rebounds in a season as Bill Russell had in his second year (1,564), his two-season scoring and shooting percentages are comparable with those of the greatest center in franchise history.

Antoine Walker had an advocate in Larry Bird, who selected him to the Eastern Conference All-Star team in 1998.

Stir those numbers around and remember this: Walker is 21. He will finish this season averaging more than 21 points and 10 rebounds. He will be second- or third-team All-NBA. He is the youngest All-Star in team history. He never has missed a game in his 153-game career. And if he had stayed the course at the University of Kentucky, he would have been in San Antonio last night, playing in the NCAA championship game.

"When I was growing up, I just thought of being in the NBA," he said. "I thought I'd make $2 million or $3 million. I still can't believe it when people start talking about me getting $14 million, $15 million, $20 million a year."

He'll get one of those numbers this summer from the Celtics, unless something strange happens.

"I want people to understand that I want to stay in Boston," he said. "I love playing here. But once April 18 hits, the business side takes over. I think

Coach Pitino and Paul Gaston understand that they'll have to pay market value. I'm not saying I want to play somewhere else, but I'm comfortable doing that if it comes to that."

You can tell it is not natural for him to speak that way. He is a Celtic.

"I don't think we need to go out this summer and pick up five new guys," he said. "I don't think that would be a positive for us at all. We need a dominant big man and one more player. The big man will change all of our games.

"Look at Miami, tonight's opponent. I don't think you could say their guys are classic defensive players. But they've got Alonzo Mourning, who is a great shot blocker. And they've got P. J. Brown."

Ah, the Heat. They also have a reserve named Mark Strickland. He had 23 points against the Celtics last week. Afterward, he stood in the line of critics and also poked at those perceived flaws of Walker's. He made a point of mentioning that Heat assistant Stan Van Gundy told him Walker doesn't get back on defense consistently.

"Well, I don't know how much he got back either because I remember having 29," Walker said. "See, I don't respect guys like that. He's a 12th man talking trash. He barely even shows up on the scouting report. I'm not even going to get into anything with him. I don't respect him."

He tells you that he respects guys like Grant Hill, Michael Jordan, and Kevin Garnett. Fierce competitors who are also team-minded. He's like that, too. You understand that when a man approaches him with a pen.

"Can I have your autograph?" he says.

The man reaches for a napkin. Walker signs it, "Antoine Walker No. 8." Then he adds another line, "Boston Celtics."

Pleasant Surprise

CELTICS LAND A PRIZE, PIERCE, WITH 10TH PICK

June 25, 1998 • by Michael Holley

The nature of the NBA Draft is such that in the last month, the Celtics worked out several players all over the United States and, in one case, Italy. But they never thought about interviewing the player they wound up drafting. It's not that they didn't like him. They just thought he was too good for them.

As far as the Celtics could see, their math wasn't working. They knew they held the 10th pick in last night's draft and that Paul Pierce was supposed to go in the top seven. That would leave the Celtics three draft slots away from being able to get the University of Kansas forward. Or so you would think. So why did the Celtics leave the second draft of the Rick Pitino Era smiling about the acquisition of a 6-foot-7-inch forward who grew up rooting for the Lakers?

That's a question that could not be answered by Pierce, Pitino, or most Celtic fans last night. All the Celtics know is that they entered the night thinking about Keon Clark and Dirk Nowitzki. Instead, they came away with a 20-year-old forward who averaged 20 points per game for Roy Williams's Jayhawks.

"To be honest with you, I'm in shock right now," Pitino said after Pierce had become a Celtic. "I didn't expect this."

As for Pierce, he thought he wouldn't get by the Warriors, who picked fifth. But "after that Golden State pick, I was wondering, 'Where can I end up?'" he said. "I was sort of holding my breath after each pick. I really didn't have a clue coming into the draft whether I'd be drafted in the top five or not."

Lester Conner, the Celtics' newest assistant coach, had raved about Pierce to Pitino. He told the coach he and Magic Johnson—who works out with Pierce in Los Angeles—always said Pierce would be an All-Star. They said Michael Olowokandi, who was taken first by the Clippers, would be a fine pro. But Pierce wouldn't be far behind.

"We just changed the subject and didn't follow any of that up," Pitino said. "We didn't think we had a shot."

But they got their shot, and once again, they should thank a team formerly known as the Southwest Celtics (the Dallas Mavericks) and the Sacramento Kings. It was the Mavericks who allowed the Celtics to draft Antoine Walker and Ron Mercer in 1996 and '97. In '98, the Mavericks took Robert Traylor with the sixth pick, which led to the Kings shocking everyone and taking Florida point guard Jason Williams, who wasn't projected in the top 10. That upset the order of the draft and began the buzz: Could the Celtics get Pierce?

First, they had to get by the 76ers, who took Larry Hughes. Next, Pitino got word that the Bucks would take Nowitzki, whom the Celtics worked out in Italy. That left the Celtics with a chance to take Pierce.

"We were a little unlucky last year," Pitino told a group of cheering fans at the FleetCenter. He was referring to the '97 lottery, an event that led to the Celtics getting the No. 3 overall pick (Chauncey Billups) while the Spurs finished first and took draft prize Tim Duncan. "We got lucky this year. We will take, from the University of Kansas, Paul Pierce . . . "

The crowd erupted as the NBA wondered why Pierce slipped so low. Some suggested that he did not arrive at all his workouts in the best shape. He worked out for the Clippers, Warriors, Raptors, Grizzlies, and Nuggets. Any of them could have used the 220-pound forward from Inglewood, Calif., who sharpens his game daily by working out with Johnson.

But no one was talking about wind sprints and "suicides" last night. Most were imagining a starting five which includes Pierce, Antoine Walker, Kenny Anderson, and Ron Mercer. "We've got four pieces to the puzzle in place," Pitino said. "I'll tell you, this young man will have all the ingredients. I don't have to get him on my program. Roy Williams already has him on it. So we're extremely lucky as far as that's concerned. We're getting somebody who is going to be well schooled in all phases of our style."

PITINO PLAYS DEFENSE

HE CHASTISES 'NEGATIVE' FANS

March 2, 2000 • by Frank Dell'Apa

Celtics coach Rick Pitino vented his frustration with a combination lecture/pep talk following the Celtics' 96-94 loss to Toronto last night.

In his postgame press conference, Pitino defended the Celtics' defensive play on the deciding last-second shot by Vince Carter, who converted a 3-pointer over Adrian Griffin. Then, Pitino went to the defense of his team, accusing the media and "some fans" of excessive negativity and of comparing the current team to past, more successful teams. He also compared criticism of the Celtics to that of former Red Sox players Jim Rice and Carl Yastrzemski. "We've been unlucky with getting the breaks," Pitino said. "We played our asses off and had a good chance to win until the last play, which we played perfectly. Adrian played great defense on him. [Carter] knocked down a fadeaway 3-pointer going out of bounds and you have to give him credit for making that shot."

Pitino then was asked what he told his team, and he launched into a diatribe. "We've played hard the whole year and we are being positive every day," Pitino said. "You're the ones who are being negative. Larry Bird is not walking through that door, fans. Kevin McHale is not walking through that door, and Robert Parish is not walking through that door. And if you expect them to walk through that door, they're going to be gray and old.

"What we are is young and exciting and hard-working and going to improve. People don't realize that. And as soon as they realize those guys are not coming through the door, the better this town will be for all of us."

Celtic players said they were affected by the booing crowd.

"It's frustrating, but it's something that we've been through," Antoine Walker said. "The fans want W's and we are in the process of rebuilding and it's a tough process. But we are giving 110 percent every night and working hard. We need this place to be an intimidating factor. And when things are not going well, they turn on us a bit. They need to understand we are giving 110 percent and it's not a process that will happen overnight."

Walker also defended Pitino, his coach at the University of Kentucky. "Coach gives us total freedom," Walker said. "Coach gets us prepared for every game. He's changed. He's a players' coach and he has changed the system around and he communicates with the players.

"You have to understand what he is going through. He prepares us for every game and he has to motivate 12 or 13 guys. I've known him the longest. He comes to work every day and pushes us and he doesn't point fingers. He keeps everything in house."

CELTIC PIERCE OK AFTER STABBING

ATTACKED AT CLUB; HAS LUNG SURGERY

September 26, 2000 •
by Francie Latour and Shira Springer

Boston Celtics forward/guard Paul Pierce was stabbed repeatedly early yesterday while playing pool in a downtown nightclub during a packed after-hours party.

Wrapped in gauze and bleeding from at least seven stab wounds, including one that pricked his lung, Pierce staggered into the emergency room of nearby New England Medical Center, where friends had driven him.

According to sources close to Pierce, the leather jacket he wore to the private party at the Buzz Club / Europa helped save his life, protecting his vital organs when he was stabbed in the neck, back, and face.

The sources also said Pierce, 22, was hit over the head with a bottle at the Stuart Street club.

Derrick Battie, brother of Celtics player Tony Battie, and Pierce's half brother, Steve Hosey, were at the party with Pierce and drove him to the hospital moments after the stabbing, according to sources close to Pierce.

Hospital officials yesterday said they expected Pierce—the team's top draft choice in 1998 who is regarded as a key player in the rebuilding of the Celtics—to recover fully from his mostly superficial wounds. He was in fair and stable condition after undergoing surgery to repair his damaged lung.

Early reports of the stabbing had Celtics fans fearing the worst, calling to mind the untimely deaths of other young, promising players such as Len Bias and Reggie Lewis.

In a family statement yesterday, Pierce's relatives said, "We would like to thank everyone in Boston and the Celtics fans for their thoughts and prayers . . . Paul is in good spirits and is looking forward to putting this ordeal behind him and returning to doing what he does best, playing basketball."

As Pierce recovered, police yesterday focused on two separate targets: associates of a Roxbury-based rap group identified by witnesses as the alleged stabbers, and a nightclub with a history of violence and code violations.

Investigators had no suspects or motive in the stabbing, which occurred at 1:10 a.m. yesterday, but were investigating associates of the rap group Made Men, Boston police spokeswoman Mariellen Burns said.

But according to a police report, a witness who was working as a security guard for the party said he recognized the suspects as members of Made Men.

In April, a member of the Made Men trio, Marco Ennis, was among several stabbing victims when a brawl broke out backstage at the FleetCenter during a national tour of rap artists. The group has been linked to several melees in the past, and one of its former members was stabbed to death in a Roxbury nightclub in 1990.

But a lawyer representing Made Men said none of the rap group's three members were involved in Pierce's stabbing and accused Boston police of having a vendetta against them after the group recorded a controversial song criticized by police as an anti-cop rant.

"My clients had nothing to do with [Pierce's stabbing]," said John Swomley, who represents Ennis, Raymond "Ray Dogg" Scott, and Anthony Grant. "Whether or not anyone who is wannabe [Made Men] did, I don't know."

Swomley said he had contacted investigators in the stabbing and asked if they wanted to speak to his clients, but the investigators declined.

Scott and Ennis, through Swomley, said they were at the party but had nothing to do with the brawl. Grant, they said, was recording in New Jersey at the time. They said they didn't know Pierce.

Ennis, who owns a Newbury Street clothing store, was at the party because he outfitted models who had appeared in a hairdressers' show earlier in Symphony Hall. The party at the club followed the show.

As police searched for suspects and a motive, attention also focused on the Buzz Club/Europa, whose liquor license has been suspended five times in five years. The club is also the target of a lawsuit by a former employee who was stabbed in the heart and lungs in 1996.

According to a police source, a club manager who helped bandage Pierce refused to call 911 and later denied having any knowledge of the stabbings when police questioned him.

Sources close to Pierce said the player, who is from Inglewood, Calif., had resisted the lure of the streets at an early age and was careful to avoid violent situations.

"Paul is the type of individual who's very selective of who he hangs around with and where he goes out," said Patrick Roy, his coach from Inglewood High School. "Inglewood was a tough area to live in. If you can survive in Inglewood, you can survive anywhere. If people or places present a remote chance of something bad happening, he wouldn't go."

THREE AND EASY

IMPROBABLE SHOT GIVES CELTICS WIN

December 29, 2000 • by Shira Springer

EAST RUTHERFORD, N.J.—With 1.8 seconds left and New Jersey's Lucious Harris prepared to inbound the ball, the Celtics, trailing by 2, knew only the most improbable of plays could give them a shot at victory. Players staggered themselves across the midcourt line. Harris looked down the row at his teammates, thought he saw center Aaron Williams swing free, and sent the ball into the back court. But Williams could not reach the pass and unintentionally tipped it backward to Milt Palacio.

The Celtics' backup point guard extended his right arm to collect the ball. He saw Paul Pierce open on his left and briefly considered giving Boston's leading scorer a chance to win the game. But there was no time, and Palacio took the last-second shot. With his first and only field goal attempt, Palacio awkwardly hoisted a 30-foot jump shot. He had one thought in mind, "Get it to the rim."

Palacio was so off-balance when he took the shot that he tumbled to the floor after he released the ball. He never saw his 3-pointer go through the hoop with six-tenths of a second left. Palacio sat up and saw Pierce running toward him and knew he had given the Celtics a 112-111 win.

Soon, a pile of Celtics fell on top of Palacio in a wild celebration. The final sequence had even the most seasoned observers shaking their heads and searching out replays.

"We were going for the steal and Coach said their biggest mistake was going to be throwing it to the back court," said Palacio. "When I saw that, my eyes kind of lit up. I just went after it and threw it to the rim. To be honest, I didn't even see it go in . . . I'm going to have my parents put on 'SportsCenter' and tape it a couple of times."

HIS FAREWELL WASN'T FOND

January 9, 2001 • by Michael Holley

All he left was three paragraphs. That was it. He treated the Celtics like an anonymous lover, leaving them with a terse note on the nightstand. He didn't even promise to call.

Rick Pitino flew to South Florida and played a round of golf with Bob Lobel. Apparently the former Celtics coach/president decided it was better to listen to music rather than face it on his resignation day, so he spent Sunday afternoon relaxing, an oldies station providing the lazy soundtrack.

No one is surprised that Pitino left, but did anyone expect him to depart in such a cowardly fashion? Leaving on Jan. 8, with a three-paragraph send-off?

Just.

Like.

That.

Weak. He'll have a hard time looking at his former players now because he has taken disrespect a rung lower. It was clear that the coach and players didn't respect each other by the way they didn't respond to him and the way they threatened them. But history will show that he was the first to take his loot and go home.

Pitino said last week that he can "take all the abuse in the world," but it's not true. Criticism bothers him deeply and often has led him to wade into wacky waters.

He once traded insults with a drunk heckler in Cleveland; he told critics behind the Boston bench to watch the games at home; he called for FleetCenter

Rick Pitino reacts after the call doesn't go the Celtics' way during a game against the 76ers.

security to remove an anti-Pitino sign that a young fan was holding during a game; and, in his most famous rant, he reminded everyone that Larry Bird, Kevin McHale, and Robert Parish would not be walking through the door.

Now there is his bizarre short story. It won't tell you why he had to run away, but read between the significant white space and you'll understand.

For someone who claimed not to read the sports pages, watch the late-night sports TV shows, or tune into talk radio, Pitino always seemed to know what was being said about him. Image and perception held more weight than the facts.

This obsession was fascinating to watch because the obvious question was, "Rick, baby, why do you give a damn?" And that is one of the coach's professional weaknesses. He gives a damn about things that rarely cross the minds of NBA head men. The best ones realize that baseball got its titles right and that NBA coaches are actually NBA managers, and semi-aloof managers at that.

But Pitino never could divorce himself from the college game, in which coaches feel they have the

right to hover over players' personal lives. Pitino tried to do that in the pros and, no matter what he says now, many of the Celtics mocked him for it.

They mocked his heavy-handed rule book, which outlines 36 violations for which a player can be fined. You've heard of hands-on coaches? Pitino was so hands-on that he wanted to know who his players had their hands on behind closed doors. If any Celtic wanted to have a guest in a hotel room, no matter who that guest was, he had to have advance permission from the coach. Players who failed to do that were fined, in this case $3,000. That might be a sensible rule for eighth graders on a field trip, but not in the NBA.

There was also a $500 fine for players who didn't have an extra pair of contact lenses with them on the road. The coach stopped short of inserting a clause stating that every player always should have boxers, crew socks, and a copy of "Success Is a Choice" in a Celtics duffel bag.

His quirks don't make him a bad man or a bad coach. What they illustrate is that he is like all of us: complex, flawed, hypocritical, mortal. If Genius

Grants were given to basketball coaches, Pitino would qualify for one. But he didn't seem to realize that luck was attached to his unusually high basketball intellect.

There are other coaches, equally as smart and as prepared, who haven't been as fortunate as Pitino. Let's hope the coach realizes that people cannot always choose their success. But then, if fate can be steered, Pitino is in Miami now because he chose a path of bad karma, with the blessing of Celtics owner Paul Gaston.

They threw a hex on the Celtic family when they insisted on taking Red Auerbach's title of president and giving it to Pitino. That should have been the first clue that Pitino didn't have the proper amount of respect for the organization or the 83-year-old man responsible for building it. Pitino and Gaston also proved that their egos can push fairness and honesty aside.

When Pitino came to Boston, he fired his salary-cap expert even though Pitino hadn't dealt with a salary cap in 10 years.

That's arrogant.

He met with M. L. Carr, claimed to listen when Carr told him to hold on to David Wesley and Rick Fox, and then watched both players walk away even when he should have known he couldn't replace them with anyone better.

That's stupid.

Gaston made overtures to Larry Brown and promises to Carr. He backed away from both men, showed that his word is not his bond, and linked up with Pitino. He then proceeded to ink Pitino to a 10-year contract, a deal so powerful that the owner couldn't fire the coach, even though he deserved to be fired.

Pitino, meanwhile, spent an entire summer trying to trade Antoine Walker. When he realized he wouldn't be able to do it, he called Walker on Sept. 15—two weeks before training camp—and tried to smooth things over. He then became a coaching Hamlet, becoming indecisive on his next moves, always threatening to leave.

That's bad business.

Don't let anyone tell you that this is a good week for the Celtics, just because Pitino is gone. He already has begun spinning his departure to his friends in the media, but don't believe it. There are no villains and heroes in this, just parts of problems.

Yesterday, a large section of the problem was playing golf in Florida. He demanded patience and toughness, but was unable to display either. He quit on the team that he claimed to love, and then sent a sorry goodbye to Boston via fax. He said he loved Boston, but he never mentioned the city or its fans in his resignation letter.

He said he loved the Celtics, but he didn't mention one current player in his three-paragraph salute.

He should have invited Gaston and the players to come to his Miami home with him, because all of them have to leave anyway. Gaston should sell the team as soon as possible. Walker should pack his bags, because the next management team is going to trade him away. What we have now is Boston's lesser-known Big Dig project, also known as the Boston Celtics. A new owner is needed. A patient, measured personnel man is needed. The three first-round picks the team has are needed to entice teams to take away bad contracts.

Pitino could have corrected some of his errors by listening to his staff and admitting that he needed help. Instead, he left a paper trail: a three-paragraph piece of paper with the Celtics; green paper— with pictures of dead presidents on them—in his bank accounts.

6 RETURN TO RELEVANCE

(2001-2006)

anny Ainge couldn't have received a better endorsement when he was hired in May, 2003, as the Celtics' president of basketball operations. "He bleeds green," said Red Auerbach, who had drafted Ainge in 1981 and watched him develop into a member of arguably the finest starting five in NBA history on the 1984 and 1986 champions.

Ainge, who had worked as coach and general manager of the Phoenix Suns and done some television work after his playing days ended, was brought back to the Celtics family by newer members. Eight months before his hiring, a group led by Wyc Grousbeck and Steve Pagliuca had purchased the Celtics for $360 million, a deal that looked more and more like a steal with each passing year.

Before Ainge's arrival, the Celtics had begun emerging from the Rick Pitino-induced malaise under Jim O'Brien, Pitino's longtime assistant who took over for his former boss and brought a stabilizing presence and a demand for defensive commitment. Paul Pierce emerged as an elite scorer and perennial All-Star, and along with the talented if undisciplined Antoine Walker, gave the Celtics a 1-2 punch that, with the contributions of veteran point guard Kenny Anderson and role players such as Eric Williams, Walter McCarty, and Tony Battie, brought some unanticipated success. A February, 2002, trade with the Phoenix Suns brought quality depth in rugged forward Rodney Rogers and guard Tony Delk, though the price—rookie forward Joe Johnson, who would blossom into a star—would become regrettable in the long term.

In the 2002 season, the Celtics made their first playoff appearance since 1995 and first in the Eastern Conference finals since 1988, losing in six games to Jason Kidd and the New Jersey Nets. They won 49 games that year— their most since 1992, when they went 51-31 in Larry Bird's final season— and provided an assortment of highlights and hopeful moments along the way. The first win-or-go-home challenge of Pierce's career came in the decisive Game 5 of a first-round series with Allen Iverson and the Sixers. Pierce had the answer for The Answer, scoring 46 points, a victory that suggested he had the moxie to be a player who would consistently thrive in the highest-pressure situations.

‹ Paul Pierce confers with the legendary Bill Russell at a Celtics practice.

In a December 1 win in the regular season versus the Nets, Pierce scored 48—an astounding 46 coming in the second half and overtime. No one would have believed it then, but that would not stand as the Celtics' most impressive performance against the Nets that season. In Game 3 of the conference finals, the Celtics outscored the Nets 41-16 in the fourth quarter, overcoming a deficit that had peaked at 27 points, to earn a 94-90 victory and take a 2-1 advantage in the series. It felt like a turning point. It turned out to be the high point. The Nets won the next three games.

The 2003 season also ended with a postseason loss to the Nets, but it was a step back. This time, New Jersey swept the Celtics in the conference semifinals, a round sooner and with greater ease than the year previous. The Celtics had dipped to 44 wins, with the July, 2002, acquisition of former All-Star Vin Baker quickly going haywire, and no other significant roster additions to speak of.

Still, it made for odd timing when Ainge was hired *during* the Nets series, and with typical candor essentially described the Celtics' modest success in a weak Eastern Conference as a mirage. "I can't sugarcoat what's not there," he told the *Globe*'s Jackie MacMullan. Three days after he was hired, the Nets completed the sweep with a 110-101 double-overtime victory in Game 4.

As he began reshaping the roster, Ainge made it clear that while the Celtics may have two All-Star caliber players in Pierce and Walker, he saw just one as a building block. In October, 2003, Ainge stunned Celtics fans by trading Walker to the Dallas Mavericks in a deal that brought forward Raef LaFrentz to Boston. Walker, known for his trademark "Walker Wiggle" after highlight-reel plays, would return to the Celtics in the 2005 season for a brief reunion.

Methodically, Ainge began assembling pieces that would either be significant contributors on the next great Celtics team—or pieces that would help acquire such players. A draft day trade with the Grizzlies in June, 2003, landed 18-year-old Kendrick Perkins, who became the first player straight out of

high school to play for the Celtics. In the following draft, Ainge took another high school big man, Al Jefferson, along with college guards Delonte West and Tony Allen. In 2006, a swap with the Suns brought Kentucky point guard Rajon Rondo to the Celtics on draft night. Their coach would be former Hawks, Knicks, and Spurs guard Doc Rivers, who was hired by former on-court rival Ainge in April, 2004, and had won a coach of the year award with the Orlando Magic in his first head coaching stop.

The build was not painless. The Celtics failed to get out of the first round in 2004 and 2005, won just 33 games and missed the playoffs in 2006, and bottomed out in 2007, winning just 25 games while suffering a franchise-record 18-game losing streak that finally ended on February 14, 2007, with a win over the Milwaukee Bucks.

That season brought personal pain to the Celtics family, too. Auerbach, the franchise patriarch, died on October 28, 2006, at age 89, and Dennis Johnson, Ainge's fearless back court partner on the 1984 and 1986 champions, died of a heart attack at age 52 on February 22, 2007.

It was fair to wonder whether luck and good fortune had abandoned the franchise, that Celtics Pride was a concept with no intention of returning anytime soon. The hope was that there would be a payoff for the misery, that the draft lottery ping-pong balls would cooperate in a way that they had refused in 1997 when Tim Duncan was the prize, and the Celtics would have the opportunity to select one of two freshman phenoms expected to be available: Ohio State center Greg Oden, the consensus top pick, and Texas forward Kevin Durant, whom Ainge had shown the most affinity for.

Once again, lucky bounces of the ping-pong balls eluded them. Oden went to the Portland Trail Blazers first overall, while Durant went second to the Seattle SuperSonics. The Celtics ended up with the fifth pick, selecting Georgetown forward Jeff Green. With the best-laid plans through the draft falling apart, Ainge activated another strategy and made a pair of trades that would, sooner rather than later, elevate the Celtics back to the top of the basketball world.

A STAR TURN BY PIERCE

POST-HALFTIME BURST NETS HIM 48 IN WIN

December 2, 2001 • by Peter May

EAST RUTHERFORD, N.J.—Only when the game ended did the double-team finally come. By then, of course, it was too late.

The final buzzer had sounded, ending a remarkable afternoon for Paul Pierce and the Celtics. Pierce was quickly accosted by radio men Sean Grande and Cedric Maxwell. Then came the television double-team from Mike Gorman and Tom Heinsohn.

If the Nets had done that in overtime, we might still be playing. But they didn't and Pierce made them pay for it.

Pierce delivered a jaw-dropping tour de force even by his exalted standards before 11,379 at Continental Airlines Arena yesterday. He had a career-high 48 points, all but 2 coming in the second half and overtime. He had 13 points in the extra period, personally outscoring New Jersey by 5 points, as the Celtics rallied for a richly rewarding 105-98 victory. It was their third straight road win.

All this came after a 1-for-16 first half—Pierce eventually would miss 16 consecutive shots—and then a complete 180 in which he took over the game, leaving deflated Nets everywhere in his wake. If he wasn't hitting from the perimeter, or knocking down treys (he had five), he was going to the line. He made 17 of 18 free throws, all after halftime.

"That," marveled Maxwell, "was past Bird-like. Larry never had the physical tools that Paul has. He couldn't get to the hole like Paul can. He was beating them inside, outside. After a while, I didn't have anything left to say. It really was more Jordan-like. It was like he was out there playing with some kindergartners."

And how did Pierce feel?

"You feel head and shoulders above everybody," he said. "You feel like everyone else is playing in slow motion and you're the fastest guy out there."

CELTICS GET DELK, ROGERS

February 21, 2002 •
by Bob Ryan and Shira Springer

The Celtics yesterday sent a clear message to the NBA that they take themselves very seriously in any discussion of Eastern Conference contenders by executing a significant trade with the Phoenix Suns.

The deal almost enters the "too-good-to-be-true" category. Boston gave up rookie forward Joe Johnson, veteran guard Randy Brown, backup point guard Milt Palacio, and their first-round draft pick for 2002. In exchange, they acquired the services of 6-foot-7-inch forward Rodney Rogers and 6-2 shooting guard Tony Delk.

In other words, they traded three people who weren't playing, plus a draft pick that could be in the 20-plus range, for two players who make them a vastly better team than they were 24 hours ago. It's the sports ultimate: addition by addition.

"This is like one of those baseball trades that you see in the second half of the season with the purpose of trying to bolster your team," said Celtics general manager Chris Wallace. "We acquired two veterans who are proven scorers. We'll have more offensive punch than we've ever had for the stretch run. Looking at the Eastern Conference, it's so wide open, why not take a shot?"

Rogers, 30, is a rugged, versatile player who won the NBA's Sixth Man Award in 2000. He can score from inside and out, and when he flexes his massive biceps small mountains in neighboring states have been known to move. He was averaging 12.6 points and 4.8 rebounds for the Suns.

Delk, 28, is the answer to a prayer Celtics fans have been aiming skyward for anywhere from 12 to 20 years. One of the great ongoing team needs has been a man who can come off the bench and provide instant offense. This is Delk's game. He is a jump shooter supreme. He is a tweener size with the reputation of being "a shooting guard in a point guard's body." But a shooting guard is what he is. Delk once scored 53 points in an NBA game.

Johnson, the Celtics' first of three first-round draft picks in 2001, started the season in tremendous fashion but ran into problems before the month of November was concluded and before long was surpassed in the eyes of Celtic brass by fellow rookie Kedrick Brown. The 6-7 Johnson entered the NBA with the reputation of being a passive young man who is too polite and deferential for his own good. That scouting report now looks pretty sound.

UNBELIEVABLE!

CELTICS STUN THE NETS WITH HISTORIC FOURTH-QUARTER COMEBACK IN PLAYOFF

May 26, 2002 • by Jackie MacMullan

There was absolutely no reason to think it was possible. The Boston Celtics were down 21 points with one quarter left to play and their star, Paul Pierce, had missed 12 of his 14 shots. Boston's defense, the pulse of its basketball team, was weak and barely detectable amid the groans of a capacity FleetCenter crowd that could not bear to watch the New Jersey Nets pummel their beloved franchise for another second.

Boston trailed, 74-53, and was about to relinquish home court advantage in this critical Game 3 of the Eastern Conference finals.

The Celtics simply could not win this basketball game.

"I'm sure that's what everybody thought," agreed point guard Kenny Anderson. "But we've been doing stuff all year long. Why not this, too?"

Why not? Buoyed by an emotional plea by forward Antoine Walker in the huddle just before the final quarter started, the Celtics submitted the single most incredible fourth-quarter performance in playoff history last night, ripping a sure victory from New Jersey's hands with a spectacular, improbable, truly unimaginable 94-90 win.

Nobody in NBA history had ever come back from a 21-point deficit in the final quarter of a playoff game.

"But nobody has the kind of heart that we have," said a euphoric Walker, who capped off this amazing feat by jumping atop the scorer's table and pounding his chest emphatically.

As coach Jim O'Brien turned to his players in the huddle, and began to give them instructions for the final 12 minutes, Walker, the co-captain, interjected.

"I cut him off," Walker would confess later. "I had to. I saw some things. I saw New Jersey over there smiling, and laughing, and the game wasn't even over.

"I looked right at Paul, and I told him he wasn't playing his kind of basketball. He wasn't aggressive, and he was settling for jump shots.

"I told him, 'You're letting guys stop you that can't even guard you.' I told him, 'You've got to be aggressive, or we can't win.'

"I looked at our team, and I told them we needed to send New Jersey a message. Even if we didn't win the game, we needed to show them something to carry over to Game 4.

"We had to show them what we were made of."

You want to see what makes these Boston Celtics tick? Watch Pierce's eyes widen as his friend and teammate challenges him to make a difference down the stretch. Watch Pierce snatch the ball on the first possession of that final quarter and drive to the basket, his teeth gritted, his face taut with emotion.

"I don't know what I'd do without Antoine Walker as my teammate," Pierce would say softly when it was over. "He's one of our emotional leaders. I just saw it in his eyes. He took control of this whole game.

"Guys [in the huddle] were tuned in and listening. He felt it, and once he got it all out, we felt it, too."

You want some heart? Watch Kenny Anderson, who was 3 for 10 up to this point, step up to the foul line and knock down the jumpers New Jersey had dared him to make all day. Watch Anderson pick up Nets superstar Jason Kidd under his own basket and harass him up the court, playing the kind of defense everyone said he wasn't capable of playing.

Celtics president Red Auerbach has seen it all in basketball, yet the proud patriarch said last night he can't recall a more stunning comeback.

"This rates as one of the greatest I've seen," Auerbach declared. "We were so bad, for so long in that game, I never dreamed we could make it all the way back.

"But that ought to tell you something about this team. They're special.

"A great deal of the credit for that goes to Jimmy O'Brien. I don't know how he kept his sanity on the bench, but he did.

"I probably would have gotten thrown out."

In the midst of this surreal turnaround, which sent the FleetCenter crowd into such a frenzy that O'Brien couldn't even hear instructions from his assistants sitting directly beside him, the Celtics coach adopted an air of calm that was duly noted by his players.

How many other coaches would have stepped aside and allowed one of his stars to address the most critical huddle of the season? Would Pat Riley's ego have allowed that? Phil Jackson's?

That is a moot point with your Boston Celtics. Nobody's ego comes ahead of the team, not even the coach.

"This is the greatest comeback I've ever been a part of," said O'Brien. "Especially from the standpoint of what was riding on this game.

"And it was so impressive to be in a building where nobody leaves. The team was down 26 (in the third quarter) and nobody leaves."

CELTICS SOLD FOR $360M

LOCAL GROUP PAYS RECORD PRICE FOR NBA TEAM

September 28, 2002 • by Shira Springer

WALTHAM—Paul Gaston sold the Boston Celtics to a local private investment group for $360 million, the highest price ever paid for an NBA franchise, in a move that shocked the New England sports world yesterday.

The new ownership group, which includes Wycliffe Grousbeck, his father, H. Irving Grousbeck, and Stephen Pagliuca, must be approved by the NBA. The three are venture capitalists who had not been involved in professional sports.

Once the group officially assumes ownership, Wycliffe Grousbeck said, he will be "on the scene full time" and oversee day-to-day operations. The partnership anticipates additional investors to the management group, and Pagliuca suggested that

former Celtic superstar Larry Bird would make a nice fit.

"We haven't thought through the specifics of that yet," said Pagliuca. "But he's one of the best basketball minds in the country. We would welcome him to be a part of this."

"It's a tremendous honor to be here representing my partners with the announcement of our agreement to buy the Boston Celtics," said Wycliffe Grousbeck. "As we all know, this is the greatest team in NBA history and one of the greatest teams in sports history. The team, of course, belongs ultimately to Boston and New England fans and Celtics fans everywhere. The Celtics also belong to the players and coaches who brought 16 world championships to the city. Our goal as an ownership group is to raise more championship banners . . . I wasn't sure if [the Gaston family and Celtics] could keep a secret, but we pulled it off."

Although the Celtics' coaching staff and management learned of the deal only hours before Gaston and the local investors held a news conference yesterday afternoon at the team's practice facility, the announcement marked the culmination of a six-month quest. In late spring, the Grousbecks asked business advisers Robert Caporale and Randy Vataha to work toward buying a professional sports team. The Grousbecks laid out their preferences for location, and Boston was their first choice.

Caporale called Gaston, who initially said the Celtics were not for sale. But once Caporale told Gaston whom he was representing and discussed the price range, the conversation became more serious. Gaston has maintained he would sell the franchise if a blockbuster offer came along. And the Grousbecks and Pagliuca were not the only suitors. According to sources, Bruins owner Jeremy Jacobs's company, Delaware North, also made a recent "aggressive bid."

The new owners, called Boston Basketball Partners, L.P., entered a confidentiality agreement with Gaston in July, and the franchise supplied the local investors with the necessary financial information for due diligence. The $360 million offer was put on the table in August. Details were worked out yesterday morning, when the papers were signed in New York. Now, after a quick and quiet sale, the new owners are looking forward to a long and successful run with the Celtics.

"In any kind of endeavor like this, you really have to have a long-term perspective," said Pagliuca. "If the team doesn't perform up to expectations next year, that's not the end of the world. We think it will. But you really have to get a program that works for the long term, five- to seven-year period. It may take that long to get back on top. You can't make a purchase expecting instant gratification."

The new owners made a point to emphasize their connection to the Boston community. Both Wycliffe Grousbeck, a general partner at Lexington-based Highland Capital Partners, and Pagliuca, managing director at Boston-based Bain Capital, are avid Celtics fans.

"I grew up wearing Celtics, Bruins, Patriots, and Red Sox jerseys, season tickets to all four teams," said Grousbeck, who was born in Worcester and resides outside Boston with his wife and two children. "It's about as fun as it gets. [My favorite players] start with Bill Russell and goes on from there. I don't want to name any players and leave any out. But what a tradition."

AINGE WILL HAVE RUN OF THE PLACE

HE SPEAKS HIS MIND, HONEST

May 10, 2003 • by Jackie MacMullan

He had been running the basketball team for all of 10 minutes, and already the doubters were jamming the talk radio airwaves with questions about how Danny Ainge had come aboard as executive director of basketball operations for the Celtics, and what he said once he did.

Why now? The timing was abominable, wasn't it? And why, in his inaugural press conference, did he fail to pump up the fans with declarations that banner 17 was just around the corner? Why was Ainge talking about "turning this thing around" just hours before his club was to take the floor in the Eastern Conference semifinals? What about the reference to the "tough road ahead" and the fact this team that was battling for its postseason life was a group of "overachievers"? Apparently, those references were offensive to diehard fans who have been pining to

return to the glory days that included No. 44 in your program, Danny Ainge. They wanted peppy, positive, pompom rhetoric. They wanted guarantees.

Here's my question: Are you people serious? If you want coronations, then let's bring back Rick Pitino. You all remember how well that went, don't you? Or perhaps you'd prefer M. L. Carr promising us the Celtics were "championship driven," even as his ownership was ordering him to lose games to get a better shot at Tim Duncan. That worked out really well, too, right?

Sometimes the truth hurts. All Ainge did yesterday during his introduction as the Celtics' president of basketball operations was say out loud what's whispered in the halls of the FleetCenter every day. Telling it like it is will be what Ainge will do best, consistently and unfailingly, so get used to it. The bottom line is, if the Celtics want to advance further than serving as fodder for the Nets in the playoffs, they need to make some changes. Because of their difficult salary-cap situation, the number of maximum contracts they carry, and the value (or lack thereof) of some of their personnel, it will be a tough road ahead to alter this roster. And since when is the fact that Boston is a bunch of overachievers a news flash? Do you think this will shock Walter McCarty? Mark Blount? They make their living overachieving, and I bet if you asked them, they're darn proud of it, too.

Ainge can be diplomatic, for sure, but he won't toss around hyperbole, and he is going to say things the fans don't like, the coaches don't like, and the players don't like.

Even so, he was mildly surprised to hear his press conference was not unanimously endorsed. "As I've been walking around the streets, people have been really positive," Ainge said. "They are all asking me, 'Is this the year?' I love how much they care.

"But it's not going to stop me from being honest. I can't sugarcoat what's not there."

One of the first major decisions Ainge should make is to lock up coach Jim O'Brien for the long haul. He has the trust of his players, has made the most of his personnel (hence, the reference to overachieving), and knows the league. He is also at the bottom of the barrel as far as salaries for head coaches go ($1.5 million) and won't be looking for George Karl money. Sure, O'Brien could use some help, at times, in the department of communicating with others, but that's where Ainge comes in.

Danny Ainge got right to work when owner Wyc Grousbeck (left) and the Celtics hired him as executive director of basketball operations on May 9, 2003.

SELECT COMPANY

CELTICS GET BANKS, PERKINS VIA MEMPHIS

June 27, 2003 • by Shira Springer

WALTHAM—It took making a deal with savvy Memphis president Jerry West, but Celtics director of basketball operations Danny Ainge got the players he wanted in last night's NBA Draft.

Once Memphis made the 27th pick of the first round, Boston announced a trade. The Celtics received the No. 13 pick, Marcus Banks, and No. 27 pick Kendrick Perkins from the Grizzlies in exchange for Troy Bell (No. 16) and Dahntay Jones (20). The teams had simply picked for each other in the first round.

"This was Plan A," said Ainge. "We put a lot of work into studying these guys—Marcus Banks is a four-year player, a national champion out of Dixie Junior College and went to UNLV and was a great player in that conference, the defensive player of the year. He is one of the most explosive guards in this whole draft and he was a guy that we felt we were not going to get at 16 as the process went along."

Looking more long term, the Celtics hope Perkins can also be the "man for the job" at center. In a historic first for the franchise, Boston drafted a high school player. The 18-year-old out of Clifton J. Ozen high school in Beaumont, Texas, impressed Ainge with his workout. At 6 feet 10 inches, 285 pounds, with a wingspan of 7-6½ and a standing reach of 9-4½, Perkins has a lot of the proverbial upside. But both Ainge and coach Jim O'Brien know he will be a project for the next three or more years. At the end of that development period, the Celtics could have a solid—and still very young—center. The real question about Perkins: Do fans, O'Brien, and others within the franchise have enough patience to develop a high school player?

"You're taking a shot with a high school young man, but he's been thoroughly investigated," said O'Brien. "If he hits, we're hoping that at some point in time somebody will describe him as a guy that the Celtics got late in the first round and could've been in the lottery."

He could serve as the ideal buffer for O'Brien with ownership, players, and maybe other staff members. O'Brien, meanwhile, finally has someone who has the power and the basketball pedigree to serve as an advocate for him and his team. General manager Chris Wallace simply never had, by his own admission, the clout he needed to make courageous decisions, and to stick by them.

Ainge will not even discuss O'Brien or the draft or anything like that until this season is over. He admits the timing of his hiring "was not ideal," but then quickly added, "I've been a player when things have happened during the playoffs, and it means nothing. Players don't care in the least about this stuff. They're getting ready. I think this has been a zero distraction.

"Still, I am sensitive to the fact it would have been better to wait. But, the other thing is, I've got a lot to do in a short amount of time. We've got two draft picks, and I've got to get out there and evaluate the high school kids, the Europeans, the college players."

He is aware he will not always be popular. He wasn't always that way as a player, either. Be prepared. Ainge is not going to say what you want to hear, only what he believes.

CELTICS DEAL WALKER TO DALLAS

HE HAD NO WIGGLE ROOM HERE

October 21, 2003 • by Bob Ryan

No one in this town who cares about basketball is neutral on the subject of Antoine Walker.

If you're 40 or older (perhaps even 35), and your basketball frame of reference lies somewhere between The Cooz and Larry, yesterday was a day of rejoicing. You decided long ago that it would be a happy day when you no longer had to put up with those hideous threes, those foolish coast-to-coast excursions, and the theatrics that were the hallmark of Antoine's game. You knew this long before last spring's crash-and-burn against the Nets, when Kenyon Martin treated 'Toine like some 12-year-old camper called out for a demonstration at a summer clinic.

If you're 30 and under, 'Toine was your man. You parted with the cash for that No. 8 jersey and you reveled in the full scope of His 'Toineness. You loooooved the killer threes—he did have a number of game-winners, you like to point out—and you freaked out on his crossover moves, and you thought it was a completely acceptable practice every time he went into the Antoine Wiggle after nailing a big three, or cupped his hands to his ear every time the other team called a timeout when things were going the Celtics' way.

We know one thing. Jim O'Brien slept better last night than he did the night before, because Antoine Walker is now Dallas's problem, and no longer his.

When he was at his best, Antoine Walker could get the Garden faithful on their feet.

Anyone who appreciated O'Brien's Philadelphia Big 5 pedigree, his marriage connection (he wed Dr. Jack Ramsay's daughter), and his general orthodoxy always suspected that he was putting on a magnificent act, when, night after night, day after day, season after season, he would stand before his postgame inquisitors and lavish praise on a player who you just knew offended his professional sensibilities. It never made the slightest sense, and those of us for whom the NBA is not just a necessary assignment felt embarrassed for him.

Jim O'Brien had no choice. Antoine Walker was a daily reality. He had the capability of making or breaking O'Brien and the team, so the mentor was obligated to make some kind of a pact with this man that would allow the team to function. It may even be that Jim O'Brien came to like Antoine Walker the person. But there was never the slightest chance he would be able to embrace Antoine Walker the player.

Walker is, in so many ways, the quintessential modern player. He wasn't really ready to leave school, but he left anyway. He went to a sorry team where the permissive coach (that would be M. L. Carr) allowed him to do absolutely anything he wanted on the court. He was barely two months past his 20th birthday when he played his first NBA game, and he had to do all his growing up in public.

He made an All-Star team in his second year, and that was a disaster because it confirmed his judgment of himself and led to his infamous "veteran All-Star" quote in the summer of 1998, when he had not yet turned 22. The silly system being what it is, he was ludicrously rewarded at the pay window, further confirming his overblown opinion of his game. Now he thinks he deserves the maximum. Perhaps someone should send him a full set of tapes from last spring's Jersey series.

He was made—and this always amazed me—"captain" of this team. Bob Cousy . . . Bill Russell . . . John Havlicek . . . Larry Bird . . . Antoine Walker. One of these things is most definitely not like the other. Did he want to win? Sure. Did he use his position to prod and motivate his teammates at certain times? Apparently. But did his entire package remotely merit the exalted designation of "captain"? How can we even go there?

Look, he did some good things here. I wouldn't have any trouble quoting my own self after some of his better games. But I was always pleasantly

surprised when he did these things. They were not the norm.

My own daughter is from the Antoine generation, but her basketball memories begin with Larry, Kevin, and Robert. "Is this a good idea?" she asked me. "I kinda liked him."

"Think about it," I said. "How many times did you like what he did? Two out of five? Three out of seven? Eight out of 20?"

"I guess you're right," she said.

The only surprise here is that Danny Ainge was actually able to find a buyer. It wasn't easy. I heard him tell Glenn Ordway on WEEI yesterday, "I talked to every team in the league, and, believe me, there are people out there who, even if he averaged 20 points, 10 rebounds and shot 50 percent from the floor, would not want him on their team."

There may be other players in the league about whom the same can be said, but not many. I'd have to say that Danny has just done some very nice GMing.

MOVIN' ON UP

HIGH SCHOOLER JEFFERSON WILL MAKE LEAP TO CELTICS

June 25, 2004 • by Shira Springer

WALTHAM—Call it Plan 1 and Plan 1A.

The Celtics had two players in mind for the No. 15 pick, the first of three they exercised in the opening round of last night's NBA Draft. With 7-footer Robert Swift off the board and headed to Seattle at No. 12, Boston went with power forward Al Jefferson. With the Nos. 24 and 25 picks, the Celtics added guards Delonte West (Saint Joseph's) and Tony Allen (Oklahoma State). In the second round, Boston selected forward Justin Reed (Mississippi) with the No. 40 pick.

"We're not as talented at the big positions as I'd like us to be, but we have opportunities now," said executive director of basketball operations Danny Ainge. "We have pieces to move. We're not near where we need to be to be a championship team, but we've improved. We're deeper, we're tougher, we're more athletic, and we're better shooters."

When Ainge talked after making the No. 15 selection, it was with a certain amount of relief. He feared both Swift and Jefferson would be gone by the time Boston was on the clock at Madison Square Garden.

"He's one of the few big, young guys in the draft," said Ainge. "He's got a ways to go. He's not ready to make an impact, but he's got great basketball instincts. He has not been very well coached fundamentally. Everything he's done he's done on instinct. The thing I like about this guy is he loves to play basketball and he's tough, and he has an NBA body. We're very excited."

While the 19-year-old may have an NBA body at 6 feet 10 inches and 265 pounds, the numbers he recorded while competing for Prentiss (Miss.) High School were even more impressive. After averaging 42 points and 18 rebounds as a senior, Jefferson earned Mr. Basketball honors. He collected numerous All-America honors. He rated a spot on the 2004 USA men's junior national select team. Now, after finding himself a so-called man among boys in high school, Jefferson will be a boy among men in the NBA.

EVERYBODY'S FAVORITE BIG MOUTH

WITH THE CELTICS STRUGGLING TO RECLAIM THEIR GLORY, THE PASSION OF THEIR ANIMATED COMMENTATOR, TOMMY HEINSOHN, REMAINS AS STRONG AS EVER FOR THE GAME, FOR HIS ARTWORK, AND MOST OF ALL, FOR HIS WIFE THROUGH HER FIGHT WITH CANCER.

January 16, 2005 • by Shira Springer

The redhead in Needham, as Tommy Heinsohn affectionately calls his wife, casually passes a portrait of herself hanging just outside the master bedroom. The grand tour of the Heinsohns' ranch house does not ordinarily include this particular, private painting. But it's nearly impossible not to stop and stare at the young knockout with flowing, fiery red hair framed against a black background.

Draped in an unbuttoned peach blouse over tight blue jeans, the subject sits in a chair and looks downward with vulnerable reserve, uncharacteristic for those who know Helen Heinsohn as fearlessly independent and outspoken. The painter has captured her softer side in the simple composition and hazy focus, bringing sensitivity and tenderness to the portrait. In the lower-right-hand corner, Tommy Heinsohn has signed and dated this 1975 tribute to his wife.

"It captured who Helen was to me," says Heinsohn. "I wanted to show a quiet person. She's deeper than you think. It conveyed my message, but it left a lot of things to the imagination. It fades out in different spots, loses the edges."

The portrait departs from the landscapes, buildings, and still lifes Heinsohn usually draws and paints. His sketchbooks look like pictorial travelogs, as he spends time on the road filling pages with what he sees through hotel windows. The state capitals in Indianapolis and Sacramento. The River Walk in San Antonio. Rooftops and brick walls. He has sketched scenes on the team plane from his perspective as a broadcaster and in the locker room when he played for the Boston Celtics from 1956 until 1965. He prides himself on capturing what is, rather than what is merely pretty. An artist without artifice.

But with Heinsohn behind the microphone as color commentator for Celtics broadcasts on Fox Sports Net New England, games come across in broad strokes filled with unapologetic loyalty to the team he covers. "He's a homer," says his friend, former Celtic, and current Cleveland head coach Paul Silas. "He's in the Johnny Most mold. They bleed Green. To me, that's to be expected." After all, Heinsohn played an integral part on eight championship teams and coached the Celtics to two NBA titles. In the pantheon of Boston basketball greats that includes Bob Cousy and Bill Russell and Larry Bird, Heinsohn remains the only Celtic who returned to the league after his playing days and never worked for another team.

"I learned way back that what you're there for is to be you," says Heinsohn. "I try to put all I am as a person into what I do. My intelligence, my emotion. I've done that in everything. That's the way I believe people should do what they do."

With an accent that echoes both his hometown of Union City, New Jersey, and adopted home of Boston, his distinctively raspy voice bellows out the finer points of the game and bestows "Tommy Points" recognizing hustle, toughness, and team play. Heinsohn

Tommy Heinsohn was an animated analyst on game broadcasts for more than 40 years.

started the unofficial Walter McCarty fan club, coining the catchphrase "I love Waltah" and creating a national following for the reserve Celtic forward. He elevated the harassment of referees to an art.

His broadcasts are peppered with complaints that begin, "You've got to be kidding me" and "You call that a hard foul?" as he bemoans the injustice of calls against the Celtics. It is the sincerest kind of shtick.

Celebrated with a bobblehead doll, Heinsohn, 70, sits courtside as an easily recognized cult figure on the NBA circuit, inspiring imitators who shout his most famous slogans from the stands. At home and road games, teenagers and older fans alike ask Heinsohn for his autograph and hope for 10 seconds of conversation. They usually get much more than that from a man who never tires of dispensing opinions or expertise.

In passion, humor, and feistiness, Heinsohn met his match in his wife, Helen. Their nonstop banter never lacks colorful language, sarcasm, innuendo, or laughter. A conversation about a problematic cable television connection quickly devolves into a ribald romp, quips flying. Heinsohn loves Helen's quick wit and "mouth and a half," which can end a mock argument by teasing, "Go ahead, darling. Tell how much you love me." And the two are back laughing at themselves again.

Since July 5, 2002, when Helen was diagnosed with brain and lung cancer, the laughter in their relationship has meant even more. Initially, the prognosis was grim. Swelling of the brain forced the Heinsohns to the hospital over that holiday weekend, where Helen was immediately sent to intensive care. During the following six months, she would undergo one brain surgery, two lung biopsies, and 14 chemotherapy treatments concurrent with 55 radiation treatments. She lost her trademark red hair, her appetite, and about 20 pounds. She gained an impressive collection of hats and headscarves. She maintained her sense of humor, though it sometimes showed a darker edge during the toughest months.

"My joke was always: Nothing can happen to me, because Tommy won't be able to find his socks," says Helen, whose cancer is currently in remission.

A funny line here, a funny line there helped Tommy get through the ordeal. "She has difficulty remembering some of the things I said when she first went into the hospital," says Heinsohn. "But the circumstances engendered in me the thought 'What is this all about if you can't be meaningful to the person you care about?' That's what I try to be. She's always been that to me. She just entered into [the treatments] like, 'I'm going to have my life, and that's it.' And that included humor. That was the way our life was. There was humor."

Tommy and Helen never looked for an escape from reality. They face cancer with unflinching honesty. Trying to explain the tests and treatments involved in Helen's ongoing fight, Heinsohn sounds very much like a clinician, the booming theatrics of the broadcaster replaced by a slower cadence and softer tone. But he does borrow from his broadcast style. He talks about PET scans and biopsies and survival rates, breaking down the doctor-speak like so many replays. He accompanies Helen to as many tests as possible. When the two discuss dealing with the disease, Heinsohn often takes over the narrative, though he always uses "we," as if the couple has cancer.

"We had the lung scan today," says Heinsohn. "And yesterday, we had the MRI on the brain. . . . We go through this thing every three months with something. Everybody hopes initially that it's going to go away. Cancer doesn't go away. You just hold it in retreat as best you can. We're 2½ years into the deal."

When the treatments began, Heinsohn started a nightly ritual. As the pair went to bed, Heinsohn would always ask Helen, "Did you have a happy day today?" It was his way of reminding Helen to take the fight day by day, to try to pull something, anything, positive from the situation. Usually, Helen would say, "Yes, dear, I had a happy day," and they would fall asleep with that thought. But after one particularly difficult lung biopsy, Helen could not kid herself. "I told Tommy, 'Let me think,'" says Helen. "'I had my throat cut. They sawed through several ribs in my chest. I almost threw up in the recovery room. Are you out of your [expletive] mind? Did I have a happy day today?' Then I told him, 'Yeah, I had a good day today. I'm here to discuss it.'"

It comes as no surprise when Heinsohn mentions he was the class cutup at St. Michael's High School in Union City. As Heinsohn politely puts it, he never devoted the proper attention to daily prayers. But his 10th-grade homeroom teacher, Sister Eleanor, kept the antics to a minimum by encouraging his growing passion for art. "I've always been interested in art since I was a kid," says Heinsohn, "before I even knew there was such a thing as basketball."

In grammar school, he began drawing Christmas scenes in colored chalk on the blackboard. He bought how-to books. He begged his parents for the pastel sticks displayed in the window of a Union City five-and-dime store called Cheap Sam's. The family could not afford a set of pastels, but Heinsohn's interest in art continued undiminished though largely unacknowledged, until Sister Eleanor sent him upstairs with drawing assignments. She was studying for a master's degree in biology at Fordham University, and Heinsohn would sketch the amoebas, frog legs, and cell parts needed to complete her homework. "That was the first time anyone encouraged me to do anything, really," says Heinsohn.

After decades spent honing technique, Heinsohn calls himself a "decent amateur," with dozens of exhibits across the country to his credit and a basement studio cluttered with hundreds of unframed canvases. He once participated in a show called "Twice Gifted," which featured the artwork of celebrities who had earned fame in another field, including Winston Churchill, Marilyn Monroe, Frank Sinatra, Katharine Hepburn, and James Dean. Heinsohn remarks with admiration that Dean "was probably the best artist of everybody."

Heinsohn has "painting buddies" the way many men have golf buddies. They travel New England three times a year, a mix of professionals and avid amateurs, in search of picturesque scenes to paint. An original Heinsohn landscape once fetched $2,500, much to the surprise of the artist.

"The first time I sold a painting, Helen took it to this guy who's a friend of ours to have it framed, and I didn't pick it up," says Heinsohn. "The guy asked, 'Do you want to sell this painting?' I said, 'No, I don't want to sell it.' The guy said, 'Well, I'm gonna tell you how much someone wants to offer: $800.' I said, 'All right, sold.'"

Until Helen became sick, she organized annual exhibits of Heinsohn's paintings, first at a Brookline framer, then at Joseph's restaurant in downtown Boston. They were invitation-only affairs designed to sell off pieces the Heinsohns had no place to store. Now, Heinsohn occasionally shows paintings at the Bryant Gallery in Jeffersonville, Vermont, and with Gloucester's North Shore Arts Association. But he derives greater satisfaction from giving his art to friends.

At one invitation-only exhibit, Heinsohn placed a special painting at the center of the showroom, cordoned off by velvet ropes. The piece, Wedding Day, depicts the Stone House Inn, where broadcast partner Mike Gorman got married 17 years ago in Little Compton, Rhode Island. When Gorman and his wife arrived at the exhibit, Heinsohn escorted them to the center of the room and presented their wedding gift.

"When I first started, it was something I could do by myself," says Heinsohn. "It really is like a friend. It keeps me involved in something. It's soothing. It's fun. It's a social exercise. It's an intellectual exercise."

Covering the Celtics these days, Heinsohn can be heard voicing wild enthusiasm for the team's return to a running game. Celtics coach Doc Rivers does a humorous impression of Heinsohn exclaiming, "That's the basketball I'm talking about." It's the refrain Heinsohn favors whenever Boston scores on the fast break. A steadfast belief in the running game represents the Celtics birthright as passed down directly by patriarch Red Auerbach. It was the style Heinsohn played and coached. He delights in the tradition continuing.

"Tommy doesn't really do color," says Celtics play-by-play man Gorman. "In his heart, he's still coaching the Celtics, and he always will be. It doesn't matter who the coach is, and it's no disrespect to the coach. This always will be Tommy's team. Tommy will be coaching this team till he takes his final breath. If it was possible to still be playing for this team, he would be."

Watch Heinsohn work a game: He expends more emotional energy than any Celtic in uniform. Gorman has long suggested that Fox add a "Tommy cam," a small picture-in-picture feed to capture the emphatic gestures and cartoonlike facial expressions that punctuate all Heinsohn commentary. He makes his points with hands flying, eyes popping. The audience at home misses half the entertainment.

Pregame, halftime, and postgame stand-ups showcase a more subdued Heinsohn in suit and abstractly patterned tie. He looks younger than his age, with his gray hair barely receding. But time has slightly bent and added weight to his 6-foot-7-inch frame, rounding out his features. Deep, frequent laughter reinforces Heinsohn's jolly presence.

For all the fun and frivolity Heinsohn brings to Celtics broadcasts, with Gorman serving as straight man, the former NBA coach of the year views his job with a surprising seriousness behind the scenes. Heinsohn sees himself as both entertainer and educator. "I came to the conclusion that the way I wanted to present it is that every game was a murder mystery," says Heinsohn. "And I would like the producer and director to help me lay down the clues so that by the end of the game the people would know how the murder took place. What I managed to do was take the games like a coach, pull them apart, and choreograph the camerawork to get key replays. Each one of these replays was a clue."

Critics accuse Heinsohn of coming across as a bombastic know-it-all: too much theater, not enough insight. They look to the impartial, analytical, and more dispassionate national broadcasters as role models. Unquestionably, Heinsohn goes over the top when it comes to commenting on the performance of officials. "I have a thorough belief that there are three teams involved in a game," Heinsohn explains. "There are the two basketball teams and a team of officials. They all have a bearing on how the game is played. . . . Officials have to be held accountable like the players."

A really bad call can provide color for an entire broadcast. With an official in his sights, Heinsohn cannot be distracted or dissuaded from his agenda. When veteran official Kenny Mauer became the target of a tirade for the better half of a game, he collected his jacket from the scorer's table at the end of the contest, smiled wryly at Heinsohn, and said, "Merry Christmas."

"Tommy never has a nonfeeling moment," says Gorman.

When the subject turns to Helen, art, or basketball, Heinsohn is most open and most passionate.

With Helen too sick to join him for games at the FleetCenter in the months after her initial diagnosis, Heinsohn devised a special on-air tribute. "The redhead in Needham sure would have hated that shot," he said, and at first, only people close to the couple knew whom Heinsohn had in mind. "The redhead in Needham would have gotten all over the referee for that one." The tradition continues for road games. Watching from home, Helen enjoys the private acknowledgment. It is like that heartfelt tribute hanging nearby in the hallway.

IT FITS LIKE A GLOVE

March 5, 2005 • by Dan Shaughnessy

Meet the new point guard. Same as the old point guard.

Gary Payton is back. Turns out he was unofficially the player to be named later in the deal that brought Antoine Walker home to Boston. For all practical purposes, Payton was traded for . . . Payton. Something like that.

The Celtics dealt Payton to the Hawks (along with Tom Gugliotta, Michael Stewart and a first-rounder in 2005 or 2006) in the mega-deal that brought Walker back to the New Garden just nine days ago. And last night Payton, who signed with the Celtics after being waived by Atlanta, was starting at the point, just as he did in his first 54 games with the Green. He scored 10 points and had 4 assists in 21 minutes in a 104-84 win over Charlotte. It was Boston's fourth straight victory since Danny Ainge traded Payton for Payton and got that other guy, Walker.

Say what you want, but the Celtics have a pretty formidable starting five these days. Payton is going to the Hall of Fame. Walker and Paul Pierce are, or have been, All-Stars. Ricky Davis has all-world skills and has been a team guy all season. And Raef LaFrentz is more than serviceable when healthy.

They are certainly more interesting than they were last season without Payton and Walker (not to mention Al Jefferson, Delonte West, and Tony Allen). You might even say they have a new identity.

"Ricky Davis looked around at practice this morning and said we're like the Oakland Raiders," said coach Doc Rivers. "I think I know what he means. Gary was basically an outcast. Gary . . . Ricky . . . Antoine."

Davis expanded on the thought briefly before playing the mighty Bobcats. "It's just guys who can play that have a bad rep," said Davis. "But everybody's a good person."

Payton had options after he was waived. The Suns, Kings, and Timberwolves allegedly were interested. But Boston was the choice. He said he was lured back by the prospect of further contributing to the hardwood educations of Jefferson, West (no turnovers in 29 minutes), and their young friends.

"I started here and I got a relationship with these kids," said Payton. "This is the right opportunity for me. It's a good fit. We can go far. The young kids were calling me every day."

Some of the kids scratched their heads when asked about making calls to the old guy, but Jefferson looked across the locker room at Payton and said, "I can't live without you, man. Who else is gonna cuss me out?"

CELTICS STRETCH THE POINT WITH TELFAIR, RONDO

June 29, 2006 • by Shira Springer

NEW YORK—On his master rankings list, Celtics executive director of basketball operations Danny Ainge placed Kentucky point guard Rajon Rondo seventh overall, according to team sources. Other organizations did not assign the same value to the fast, but undersized point guard generously listed at 6 feet 1 inch, 171 pounds. That left Ainge with an unexpected opportunity last night as the NBA Draft progressed. He finished the first round just the way he started it, making a deal to acquire a floor general for the future.

The Celtics traded the rights to the No. 7 pick, Raef LaFrentz, Dan Dickau, and cash to the Trail Blazers in exchange for Sebastian Telfair and Theo Ratliff and a 2008 second-round pick, finalizing the deal shortly before the draft started last night at The Theater at Madison Square Garden. Then, the Celtics sent a 2007 first-round pick (from the Cleveland Cavaliers) to the Suns for the draft rights to Rondo and Brian Grant. Don't expect Grant in a Boston uniform. The Celtics will simply pay the remainder of his contract worth $1.8 million for next season (player option) and a 15 percent trade kicker. In the second round, Ainge acquired forward Leon Powe from the Denver Nuggets for a future second-round pick.

With the three deals, Ainge appeared to pull off the draft equivalent of having your cake and eating it too, with Rondo the icing.

"We've had Rondo rated very, very high in this draft," said Ainge, who started making calls in an effort to acquire Rondo when the point guard slipped past No. 15.

When asked if he would have taken him at No. 7, Ainge added: "It was a consideration for us, but the way the draft fell, probably not. But he was a consideration."

"I don't think you can have too many [point guards]. We feel like speed is the way the game is going now. You see in Chicago and you see in Dallas all those teams playing multiple point guards at one time. And we think [Rondo] has a chance to be a special player. We wouldn't have done the deal if we didn't think that he has a chance to be the quality of a player of an Al Jefferson, a Gerald Green, those kinds of players. We think he has that kind of upside."

Doc Rivers is third among Celtics coaches with 416 regular-season wins in his nine seasons.

FAMILY DOC

TO RIVERS, MORE IMPORTANT THAN WINS AND LOSSES ARE TIES—THE TIES THAT BIND AT HOME, WHICH IS WHY EXTRA ROAD TRIPS ARE JUST PART OF THE SCHEDULE.

October 1, 2006 • by Jackie MacMullan

WINTER PARK, Fla.—He didn't grasp the significance of it at the time. When Glenn Rivers was growing up on the West Side of Chicago, long before he became an NBA star, a millionaire, the coach of the Boston Celtics, he didn't stop to consider how his father, Grady, a police patrolman, also found time to be his baseball coach.

During practice, Grady would pull his squad car onto the field and crank up the volume on the dispatch radio. If a call came in, he'd yank off his baseball cap, straighten out his blue uniform, and peel out, lights flashing.

By the time Glenn wore the basketball uniform of Proviso East High School, his father had made lieutenant.

"Then I never missed a game," Grady said, "because I made out the schedule."

Grady positioned himself courtside, in full uniform, his badge gleaming. His wife, Betty, preferred the last row, so she could rest her back against the wall.

Did the boy appreciate his parents? No, not fully. Sometimes, he was even embarrassed by the way Grady harangued the officials.

It never occurred to Glenn Rivers that many of the fathers of his teammates were incarcerated, dead, or gone, just gone. You don't think of those things when your parents are always, always there.

"We were there," said Grady, "because so many parents weren't."

Glenn "Doc" Rivers wants to be there for his children. He insists on it, in fact. And if it means spending $200,000 of his own money, as he did last season, his first as Celtics coach, to fly private charters between Boston and Florida, where his family resides, then he'll do it.

If it means flying all night from Portland to Florida to see his son Jeremiah's basketball play-off game, then turning around and flying back to Los Angeles that night so he can coach against the Lakers the next day, then he'll do that, too.

"That was the toughest one, that West Coast trip," Doc said. "We were coming off three games in four nights. We played Portland in Portland on a Friday night. I gave the guys the next day off. Right after the game, I chartered a plane.

"I got to Lakeland Saturday, watched my son's game, then flew right back to Los Angeles. I landed around 11:30 Saturday night. The next morning, we had a team meeting at 10 a.m., then went out and beat the Lakers. Then we flew home to Boston."

That utterly absurd weekend schedule was an aberration. Most times, Rivers would fly to Orlando after Celtics practice, attend his children's games, and fly back to Boston either later that night or at 5 a.m. the following morning.

"It's not the perfect way to live, but it's the right way," he said. "I know there are Boston fans out there who think I should live up there. But if it comes down to upsetting a million people in Boston, or the five people in my family, I'll figure out a way to deal with the million."

His kids and his wife, Kris, are settled. He couldn't—no, he wouldn't—disrupt their lives. They have moved too many times, been through too much. And the fire . . . it was a cowardly act of racial hatred and changed everything. It happened in 1997, in San Antonio, and it destroyed their house, but the damage went deeper. For a time, it destroyed their trust and faith in the goodness of those around them.

LIFE-ALTERING EVENT

Doc Rivers is wearing shorts. He is sitting in his kitchen in Winter Park, Fla., and he asks if it's cold yet in Boston. He loves the Florida weather. He loves the club where he plays golf and shoots the breeze with former Mets manager Davey Johnson. He loves throwing a football with his 11-year-old son Spencer in January.

He is making some notations in his basketball notebook before his daughter Callie's volleyball game. Her 17th birthday is coming up, and her friends are soliciting ideas on favorite restaurant venues from her dad.

"It's nice here," said Rivers, gesturing throughout his home. "Comfortable."

They have regained a sense of community in Florida. They have lived there seven years now, and for the first time Glenn and Kris Rivers have a home base.

So it's difficult to juggle Doc's schedule sometimes. It is a price he gladly pays, just as his parents did before him.

Grady and Betty couldn't make everything perfect for their two boys. The streets of Maywood, Ill., could be cruel, dangerous. Racial tensions were simmering, just one hurled brick—or insult—away from bubbling to the surface. There were riots, and incidents at their so-called integrated school. As Glenn became older and walked into a department store, he would often be shadowed, stared down, because . . . why? Because he was Black. The "routine traffic stops" he endured as an African-American would have been comical if they weren't so horribly sad.

Glenn didn't have Grady's fiery temper. The injustices ate away at his father, but Glenn was more like Betty; calm, rational, capable of moving on.

His temperament would serve him well at Marquette, when someone slashed the tires and keyed the car of his girlfriend, Kris Campion, because she was white and had the audacity to date a Black man.

Kris was born and raised in Wisconsin, a stone's throw from the Marquette campus. She went to college 72 miles away at the University of Wisconsin, but transferred to Marquette and lived with her parents after her freshman year.

"I'm a homebody," Kris explained. "Always have been."

She met Glenn one day after class. He walked past her and said, "You know, you'd be kind of pretty if you washed your hair once in a while." Kris Campion was too astonished to be offended.

"He came back and said, 'Now I don't want to give you the wrong idea. I don't want to date you. But I have a friend I might want to fix you up with,'" she said.

The friend was basketball teammate Marc Marotta. He and Kris dated for a year or so, but one summer, he went overseas, and when he came back, Kris and Glenn had fallen in love. The development did little to improve Marquette basketball's team chemistry. Glenn, mindful that his interracial relationship with Kris could be socially volatile, asked the Campions for permission to date her.

"People were so startled," Kris said. "Friends asked me, 'What's it like dating a Black guy?' I told them, 'That's the problem. You see him as Black. I see him as a man.'"

Some people were offended that the blond, fair-skinned girl and the Black basketball star were together. They found out where Kris lived—where her parents lived—and spray-painted their home. The crank phone calls were crude, frightening.

"It divided the campus," Kris said. "It was horrible. It was also the main reason Glenn left school early.

"When all that stuff happened at Marquette, my father [Bill] told me, 'You've done nothing wrong. We're right with you.' Then he said, 'This seems like a big deal now, but tomorrow morning the sun will come up and you will be fine.'"

Her father was right. She married Glenn, had a son, and embarked on the nomadic life of an NBA family. Doc's career included stops in Atlanta, Los Angeles, New York, and San Antonio. When he retired, he signed on as a Spurs television broadcaster and bought his growing young family a big, rambling house.

On June 28, 1997, Kris made a last-minute decision to pack up her four young children and join her parents at their lake home in Wisconsin while Doc attended Detlef Schrempf's charity golf tournament in Washington.

"It was a Friday night," Kris said. "I only told one person I was going. She was a friend. She went by to check on the dogs and the cats."

The animals were fed, the house locked. Sometime during the night, under the cover of darkness, the Rivers's home was torched. The firemen said it was arson, and suspicion quickly centered on some kids who went to school bragging about how they reduced the house of the Black guy and the white lady to ashes.

"It was so devastating," Kris said. "Everything melted. And our pets. Two dogs and three cats. All killed.

"They never convicted anyone for it, but we know it was racial."

Upon hearing the news, Grady and Betty Rivers winced from an old, familiar pain. In Wisconsin, Ginger and Bill Campion grimaced along with them.

"That bothered me even more than what happened at Marquette," said Ginger. "To think someone could do that . . . it changed Kris. How could it not?"

Doc waited for things to settle down, for his wife to come to grips with the horror of what could have been had she and the children been home, asleep.

"One day Glenn said, 'We're going back to San Antonio,'" Kris said. "My response was, 'Are you crazy?' He said, 'Kris, we're not running from anybody.'"

Seven months later, the Rivers family moved into a renovated home just miles from the rubble of their previous address. By then, Jeremiah was 11 years old and had lived in six places.

"One day he looked up at me and said, 'So, Dad, when are we moving again?'" Doc said. "I didn't like that. I didn't like that at all."

A SENSE OF BELONGING

In 1999, Rivers was named head coach of the Orlando Magic. He bought a piece of land and built an elegant, spacious home on a lake. It's perfect. The kids have a pool, Doc has a television in nearly every room, and Kris has a place to water-ski, just like in her beloved Wisconsin. They constructed a boathouse where friends and family could stay, and it immediately became the favorite vacation spot of Bill and Ginger Campion, who loved to watch the birds dry their wings on the deck.

Glenn and Kris immersed themselves in the community. Kris helped with charitable fundraisers; Glenn was a fixture at his kids' games and conducted hundreds of clinics. They threw their support behind Shepherd's Hope, a wonderful nonprofit organization that provides free medical care and prescriptions to those who can't afford it. They discovered a favorite restaurant, 310 Park South, where Doc always ordered the salmon bites. They took in stray cats, stray dogs, and occasionally even stray kids who needed some temporary guidance.

Even when Rivers was fired from the Magic in 2004, which was a trying time, Orlando still felt like home. Kris knew another job would come along, and when the Celtics hired her husband, the family discussed moving. But Jeremiah was a junior in high school, on a basketball team that had a chance to win it all. Callie was a sophomore, a nationally ranked volleyball player who would have difficulty finding the same elite programs in Boston. The two youngest, Austin and Spencer, were thriving in the only environment they had really known. The discussion didn't last long. Glenn would go; Kris and the kids would stay.

"The fire . . . it changed my personality," Kris acknowledged. "I've become incredibly protective of my kids. So when we moved to Orlando, and we found this great home, this safe place, I didn't want to leave.

"I know there are wonderful people everywhere. We discovered that every time Glenn got traded. But it takes time to develop that network of friends.

"It wasn't about moving to Boston. It was about moving anywhere."

Doc's frequent trips to Orlando became topical last season as the Celtics swooned. His work ethic was questioned. How can someone who is spending so much time shuttling back and forth be dedicated to his job? Rivers smiles. He is a poor sleeper, so he watched film and filled his playbook with notations during his charters south. He rented an apartment in Boston, and after practice he went home and spent countless hours on strategies to improve his basketball team. With no family to distract him, Rivers figures he's put in more time on this job than any other.

He does not deny that his employer was, and probably is, uncomfortable with his family arrangement. He solicited advice from Red Auerbach, who commuted from Washington during his tenure as Celtics coach, and Miami coach Pat Riley, who stressed the need to find a haven outside the market he was coaching in.

"Our major concern was we feel the family is a great support system, which is why we were always high on him bringing his kids up here," said Celtics managing partner Steve Pagliuca. "But we respect Doc's decision not to disrupt his children.

"He's a very prepared guy. There has been no drop-off in our play or execution because he does the occasional thing with his family."

A TOUGH STRETCH

The initial plan was for Ginger and Bill to come down to Orlando for a couple months so Kris, who does not like to leave her children with anyone but family, could shoot up to Boston to see Glenn.

But Bill's throat was bothering him. He went to the doctor, who asked if he was a smoker. He said no, and the physician assured him he'd be fine. He never did a biopsy. If he did, he would have discovered the cancer and might have saved Bill's life. By the time Bill went back a second time, the disease was too far along.

"It was difficult to watch," Doc said. "Kris's dad was the healthiest person in the family."

The Campions did spend several months last year in Orlando, but by early March, those days were spent preparing Bill to die comfortably.

Jeremiah's team was in the state finals, and somehow, Bill Campion dragged himself out of bed to go to the game. Ginger, in her attempt to help Bill into his wheelchair, fell and tore her ACL. Betty Rivers, so excited about her grandson's game, forgot to eat and take her medication for diabetes. As they walked out of the gym after Winter Park's loss in the title game, she fainted.

"One of the worst nights of my life," said Doc, who had flown in for the game. "My father-in-law was so sick, my mother-in-law tore up her knee, my mom fainted, and my son's team lost by 14 points. They missed 16 free throws. Then, as we were trying to get everyone back to the house, Kris lost the keys to the car. By the time I got on the plane back to Boston that night, I was scared. I'm thinking, 'What next?'"

Six days later, Bill Campion died in the boathouse, surrounded by family. His son-in-law left the Celtics and flew home. According to Pagliuca, it was one of only two practices Doc Rivers would miss all season.

SETTLING INTO THE ROUTINE

Kris Rivers is sitting in the boathouse, squinting out at the empty deck where her father once sat in his rocking chair enjoying the birds basking in the sun.

A new Celtics campaign will begin Nov. 3, and Doc will move back to Boston without his family. He expects his schedule to be far less hectic this year. Callie's volleyball season is almost completed. Jeremiah is a freshman at Georgetown, and 13-year-old Austin has a shot at playing varsity basketball as an eighth-grader. Spencer, a budding football star, has already shared a number of game days with his dad this fall.

Kris believes they are all where they should be.

"I'm immature [about criticism]," she acknowledged. "I was never good at sports. I don't understand why they adore you when you are winning and criticize you so harshly when you lose. I take it very personally when fans are just being fans, and the media is 'just doing their job.' I think it's probably better I'm down here."

She remembers how she felt when Doc had lost 11 straight as the coach of the Magic, and the pressure began mounting.

"I said to Glenn, 'There's no amount of money that is worth this if you want out,'" she said. "He said to me, 'Kris, I love this. It's more fun than playing.'"

The coach of the Celtics is hopeful that one of his young players will shed the "potential" tag and emerge as a No. 2 star alongside Paul Pierce. He believes his team must go with a small lineup and apply pressure to be successful.

"I love Boston," he said. "The fans are demanding and knowledgeable. I know if we ever get this right, it will be the most amazing experience of my life."

It is getting cool in New England. In Wisconsin, too. Ginger Campion plans to bunk alone in the boathouse this fall, drawing comfort from her daughter and her grandchildren. She hopes Callie will be playing in the state championship Nov. 8-10 and plans to be there when Georgetown opens its season Nov. 11.

Doc has home Celtics games Nov. 8 and 10, and a road game in Cleveland on the 11th. It's possible Austin and Spencer will fly up to Boston and spend that weekend with him.

Perhaps Glenn and Kris will revisit their family plan when Callie graduates. She has been accepted to Florida on a full volleyball scholarship. But Austin will be a freshman next year, so there probably is no good time to move.

Betty Rivers, who still attends most East Proviso basketball games, hopes to visit Orlando in the fall while her dear friend Ginger is there. Grady stopped flying after Sept. 11.

His son flies so much that he's thought of buying his own aircraft.

It wouldn't have to be spacious. All Glenn needs is room for six.

Auerbach, Pride of Celtics, Dies

PRO BASKETBALL LEGEND WAS 89

October 29, 2006 • by Peter May

Arnold "Red" Auerbach, who for more than half a century was the combative, competitive, and occasionally abrasive personification of pro basketball's greatest dynasty, the Boston Celtics, died yesterday in the Washington area. He was 89.

He died of a heart attack, the Associated Press reported, according to an NBA source who did not want to be identified.

In two decades of National Basketball Association coaching, Auerbach won 938 games, a

Ever-present cigar in place, Red Auerbach proudly holds the championship trophy at Boston City Hall on June 10, 1986.

record when he retired in 1966, as well as a record nine NBA championship titles, a number he shares with Phil Jackson. In those 20 years, 16 with the Celtics, Auerbach had only one losing season while winning almost two-thirds of his games.

Auerbach was inducted into the Basketball Hall of Fame in 1968 and, 12 years later, was recognized as the greatest coach in NBA history by the Professional Basketball Writers Association of America. That same year, 1980, he was inducted a second time into the Hall of Fame in recognition of his contributions to the game.

In 1996, he was honored on the 50th anniversary of the NBA as one of its greatest 10 coaches. His coaching achievement is recognized annually with the awarding of the Red Auerbach Trophy to the league's Coach of the Year.

Auerbach himself won the award only once, in 1965. The award was named in his honor in 1967.

Auerbach's genius extended well beyond his coaching. He moved into the Celtics' front office, starting in 1966, and by then already had shown his ability to judge talent with the acquisitions of future Hall of Famers such as Bill Russell, John Havlicek, and Sam Jones through trades or the NBA Draft. Later, as the team's general manager, he would engineer deals for Larry Bird, Kevin McHale, and Robert Parish—all of whom also are in the Hall.

Proof of Auerbach's impact on the game as both a coach and talent evaluator is the number of his players who made it to the Hall of Fame (14) and the number of his players who became coaches (30), including eight of the 12 players on his 1963 championship team. Three of his players, Tom Heinsohn, Bill Sharman, and Don Nelson, later won Coach of the Year honors. Nelson won it three times.

He was also a social force in the NBA, drafting the league's first African-American player in 1950 in Chuck Cooper, hiring the first African-American head coach in pro sports in 1966 in Russell, and having five African-Americans as the Celtics' starting lineup in 1964, an NBA first.

"I never thought he'd die," author John Feinstein, who last year collaborated with Auerbach on "Let Me Tell You a Story: A Lifetime in the Game," told the Associated Press. "He was a unique personality, a combination of toughness and great, great caring about people. He cared about people much more

than it showed in his public face, and that's why people cared about him."

Auerbach was fiercely competitive, sometimes to the point of boorishness. It was Auerbach who would break out a celebratory cigar during Celtics home games—never on the road—when it was clear his team had won. He once had a writer's seat moved from the floor to an upper box at Boston Garden because of an unfavorable story. He ordered a complimentary mention of Cedric Maxwell to be excised from one of his books after he felt Maxwell betrayed him.

In 1984, Auerbach was invited to coach an old-timers team in the All-Star Game and was ejected for arguing with the officials. In his early years as the commissioner of the NBA, David Stern would joke to friends that he felt his real first name was "Stupid" because of all the conversations he had with Auerbach.

Whether it was tennis, racquetball, basketball, knowledge of Chinese cuisine, or simply having the final word, Auerbach was relentless. As former player agent Ron Grinker once said of Auerbach, "Red plays chess. The other general managers play checkers."

TOOK OVER IN '50

Auerbach took over as the team's head coach in 1950. He retired from coaching after the 1966 season, having won his eighth consecutive NBA title and ninth overall. He served as the team's president and GM for another 14 years and as the president solely from 1984 until 1997, and again from 2001 until his death.

In his long tenure in Boston, he built three distinct Celtics championship teams: the dominating group that won all but one title in the 1960s, a second team that won two titles in the 1970s, and the last, great Celtics team, which won three championships in the 1980s.

The team he took over in 1950 was in last place, but seven years later, he had the first of his nine championships, all anchored by the indomitable Russell. The Celtics won world championships in 1974 and '76 with a nucleus of Auerbach draftees, Havlicek, Cowens, and Jo Jo White, and triumphed in 1981, 1984, and 1986 with the so-called Big Three: Bird, McHale, and Parish, arguably the greatest frontcourt in NBA history.

In the 1990s, the Celtics became something they never were when Auerbach was either coaching or involved on a day-to-day basis in the front office: irrelevant. Bird and McHale retired prematurely because of injuries. Reggie Lewis, an Auerbach draft pick and emerging star, died of cardiac arrest. The team had a stretch where it made the playoffs only once in eight years.

And when the Celtics briefly made what looked to be a significant move in 1997, the hiring of Rick Pitino as coach, it quickly backfired on Auerbach when Pitino insisted on having Auerbach's long-held title of president. Four years later, Pitino left in disgrace and the team quickly moved to reinstall Auerbach's favorite title (other than coach).

Auerbach's record for identifying talent and then acquiring it was remarkable. He convinced two teams in 1956 not to draft Russell, getting one of them (St. Louis) to trade its pick to him for two players, and getting the other to bypass Russell entirely in return for some arena-filling Ice Capades dates. In 1978, five teams passed on drafting Bird, either because Bird would cost too much or would not be available to the NBA for another year because he was still a junior at Indiana State. Auerbach didn't hesitate, and then managed to sign Bird and keep him in Boston throughout his career.

Where others saw impediments or obstacles, Auerbach saw opportunity. In 1969, several teams shied away from Jo Jo White because of a supposed military commitment. Auerbach drafted White, who went directly to the NBA and fulfilled his military service in the reserves. In 1981, Danny Ainge, then a professional baseball player, was said to be firm in his decision not to play in the NBA. Auerbach drafted Ainge, now the Celtics' executive director of basketball operations, in the second round and had him in a Boston uniform for 53 games the following season.

Auerbach was also the mastermind in what is still considered by many to be the most lopsided trade in NBA history, a deal that brought the Celtics Parish and the chance to draft McHale. The Warriors, who made the deal, ended up with Joe Barry Carroll and Rickey Brown, two NBA journeymen of limited value.

Auerbach was among the first to cultivate the team as family concept, using loyalty as his linchpin. Hall of Famer Bill Walton, who really had only one season playing with Boston, still considers himself a Celtic, first, last, and always. Players occasionally felt the coach's public wrath, but there was always a method to the motive. Agents became a favorite target; he only gradually and reluctantly revised his opinion of them from scum to lowest possible life-form. Others, be they referees, judges, opponents, advisers, or even colleagues, would feel his wrath if he detected the Celtics were being scorned or spurned. No one played the us-against-them dynamic more adroitly.

He could also be crude, abusive, and hostile. He once sought out Ainge after Ainge played a particularly bad game in Washington. "What, were you out drinking with your other wife?" Auerbach said to Ainge, a Mormon. One longtime acquaintance called Auerbach a terminal juvenile delinquent—and Auerbach did little to dispel the image. Yet it also, undeniably, was a shtick that he cultivated.

"In whatever he did, he wanted to win," said Harry Mangurian, one of many Celtics owners who worked with Auerbach. "There was no letup in him at all."

BORN IN 1917

Arnold Jacob Auerbach was born Sept. 20, 1917, the second of four children of Hyman Auerbach, who ran a dry cleaning business in Brooklyn, and Marie Thompson Auerbach. Hyman Auerbach immigrated to the United States from Minsk, Russia, at the age of 12. He took a job working the counter at Rosoff's Restaurant in Manhattan and met Marie Thompson there. They married and opened a delicatessen on Sixth Avenue, across from Radio City Music Hall. In 1931, Hyman Auerbach sold his delicatessen and started a dry cleaning business.

Arnold had an older brother, Victor, who succeeded his father in the business. A younger brother, Zang, became a commercial artist and designed the Celtics' leprechaun logo. A younger sister, Florence, was born two days before his eighth birthday.

The family lived in the Williamsburg section of Brooklyn, which in the 1920s was a true melting pot of both color and creed.

Auerbach attended P.S. 122 and then Eastern District High School, where he captained both the basketball and handball teams. His grades were not quite good enough to get a scholarship to New York University, but the basketball coach at Seth Low

Junior College, a Brooklyn offshoot of Columbia University, offered him a $100 scholarship.

Two years after enrolling at Seth Low, Auerbach moved on to George Washington University in Washington, D.C., after the basketball coach spotted him during a scrimmage and gave him a scholarship. The move to Washington turned out to be a permanent one for Auerbach, who maintained a residence there until his death. Even when he coached the Celtics, his wife and daughters lived in the nation's capital while he stayed at the Lenox Hotel and later in an apartment in the Prudential Center.

Auerbach played three seasons for George Washington, averaging 6 points in 56 games. But while there, he established two relationships that would guide him for decades: a love for his wife and a visceral hatred of Madison Square Garden, then the Mecca of college basketball.

His wife was Dorothy Lewis, a third-generation Washingtonian and daughter of a local pediatrician. The two were married when Auerbach graduated in 1941 with a bachelor of science degree in physical education. He also got a master's in education, leading him one time to chastise a heckler by saying, "I'm not a bum. I'm an educated bum!"

The issue with Madison Square Garden came about because the National Invitation Tournament, then the best of the college tournaments, slighted George Washington in Auerbach's first season. He blamed the folks at MSG, where the tournament was played, for the snub, and throughout his pro career he relished wins in that building more than in any other.

Auerbach's first two coaching jobs were high school assignments. The first was at an exclusive private school in Washington, St. Albans, and the second was at Roosevelt High School in the city. The second job also included teaching history and hygiene (this was before he became addicted to cigars) and coaching handball. In May, 1943, he joined the Navy. Auerbach was spared active duty in World War II, although he became a third-class petty officer.

ENTERS PRO BASKETBALL

After discharge, Auerbach, at 28, entered professional basketball, which would occupy the rest of his life and make him wealthy and famous. A new league was beginning in 1946 that, eventually, became the NBA. One of the franchises was located in Washington, and Auerbach summoned all of his bravado to present himself to the owner as the best candidate for the job. He accepted a one-year deal for $5,000.

As the coach of the Washington Caps, he assembled a team from all over, using his military and coaching contacts. One of his signees, a player from the University of North Carolina named Bones McKinney, agreed to terms in the men's room of the Blackstone Hotel. McKinney finished his career with the Celtics and later became a trusted adviser and confidant to Auerbach, responsible for the Celtics' drafting of Hall of Famer Sam Jones in 1957.

His first professional team won 49 of 60 games, including 17 straight, a streak that would remain a league record until 1969. The team, however, was eliminated in the playoffs. In his next two years with Washington, he went 28-20 and 38-22, the second year making it to the NBA Finals before losing in six games to the Minneapolis Lakers.

But there were rumors of discontent on the team and Auerbach went back to ownership and demanded a three-year contract. When he was offered only one year, he left to accept a profitable job for $7,500 at Duke University as an assistant and adviser to coach Gerry Gerard. This was Auerbach's only flirtation with the college game—and it was over almost as soon as it began. He felt uneasy about the job, mainly because Gerard was terminally ill with cancer. Three months after arriving in Durham, N.C., owner Ben Kerner of the Tri-Cities Blackhawks of the NBA called. He had just fired his coach, Roger Potter, after a 1-6 start, and needed a new coach. Auerbach accepted a two-year deal for $17,000.

He finished out the 1950 season in Tri-Cities, going 28-29. It was the only time he coached a team with a losing record. He then left, furious that Kerner traded one of his starters without his knowledge.

Auerbach wasn't out of work for long. The owner of the last-place Celtics, Walter Brown, inquired if Auerbach would coach the team. Brown had come across Auerbach's name after talking to local sportswriters.

Auerbach demanded a three-year deal. Brown told him it would be a one-year offer because the team's situation was so precarious there might not be a second year. The Celtics had finished 31 games out of first place with a 22-46 record. Auerbach took the one-year offer for $10,000 and began a long, amicable relationship covering 13 years with Brown that always involved a handshake deal. One year, Auerbach estimated it took 70 seconds to agree on a new contract.

BUILDS CELTICS DYNASTY

Auerbach had two new players around which to build—one of which they got by luck. The team acquired 6-foot-8-inch "Easy" Ed Macauley in the 1950 dispersal draft and a local back court whiz from Holy Cross named Bob Cousy. The Celtics could have had Cousy in the draft, but Auerbach was wary of the local pressure to play the popular Cousy and also thought Cousy's unrefined game might not make it in the pros.

The 1950 draft also produced a first: the NBA's first Black player. Auerbach chose Chuck Cooper of Duquesne, who played four seasons with the Celtics.

Cousy and Macauley started the Celtics on their way. The 1951 Celtics went 39-30 and made the playoffs. In 1951, Auerbach acquired a shooting guard named Bill Sharman and a bruiser named Bob Brannum from Fort Wayne, and the team had success each year.

Then, in the summer of 1953, while working at a resort in New York, he got his first glimpse at Wilt Chamberlain, then a gangly high school center from Philadelphia. Auerbach was infatuated with the teenager. He knew he had no chance to get Chamberlain, but it made him realize he needed a big man to complete the Celtics' puzzle. Two years later, while in New York to scout the Holiday Festival, he laid eyes on Russell.

Auerbach made a deal with St. Louis to move up in the draft to select Russell, then fended off advances from the Harlem Globetrotters and signed the franchise center, starting a 13-year partnership that would produce 11 world championships.

Simply, there is no more successful professional team athlete than Russell. In his college and pro careers, he played in 21 winner-take-all games. His record in those games: 21-0.

The Celtics teams of the Russell era were built on defense and running. Russell dominated the boards and blocked shots. Cousy ran the break. Sharman, Heinsohn, Frank Ramsey, and Sam Jones delivered at the other end. Gradually, new pieces were added to the mix. K. C. Jones, drafted in 1956, came aboard in 1958 and Tom Sanders in

1960. In 1962, Auerbach drafted John Havlicek, who had played in Jerry Lucas's shadow at Ohio State University, and then sweated out Havlicek's ill-fated tryout with the Cleveland Browns of the National Football League.

FACE OF TEAM'S SUCCESS

As the Celtics continued to win, Auerbach become the embodiment of their success, which, given his legendary arrogance, inevitably led to some clashes. He was never a favorite of the referees and was fined more than $17,000 in his career. Even when he returned in 1974 to coach for one game during an emergency, he couldn't control himself and got ejected. He was suspended for three games in 1951 and got into a fight with Kerner during the 1957 NBA Finals, the only playoff series he lost after Russell arrived. In 1961, three fans in Syracuse invaded the Boston huddle and fists started flying. Auerbach was served with a summons the next day.

"I've been accused of being competitive, but [Auerbach had] total and absolute commitment," said Cousy. "He was the most relentless person I've ever met in terms of achieving his goals. He did back then what it takes about eight people to do today. I've never seen such dedication. You can argue about this, but I think he produced the greatest dynasty in the history of sports, certainly in basketball. He knew talent. He knew how to acquire it. He knew how to coach it. He knew how to motivate it. His legacy in terms of sport achievement is unparalleled."

The 1966 season was his last as coach, and the Celtics rewarded him with an eighth straight title, defeating the Lakers in seven games. Auerbach then made the leap and named Russell as player-coach while Auerbach went into the front office as general manager. The first year, the Celtics relinquished their title despite the additions of Wayne Embry and Bailey Howell. But Russell led Boston to championships in the next two seasons—both upsets—before retiring unexpectedly in 1969. Auerbach, who had built the team from scratch in 1950, now had to rebuild again. Sam Jones also was leaving.

It took five years, but another flag was raised to the Boston Garden rafters in 1974. A year after Russell retired, the Celtics won 34 games under coach Heinsohn and ended up with the fourth pick in the draft. Needing a center, Auerbach had scouted a 6-8 dervish from Florida State named Dave Cowens. The first three teams passed on Cowens, who would anchor the 1974 and 1976 championship teams, win the Most Valuable Player award in 1973, and go on to be named one of the top 50 NBA players of all time in 1996.

In 1978, Auerbach pulled another coup, drafting Bird, then a junior eligible at Indiana State.

The contract negotiations with Bird's agent, Bob Woolf, were historic both for the contentiousness and the time constraints. Woolf knew his client had extraordinary leverage and tried to milk it for what he could. Auerbach became so exasperated he turned things over to Mangurian and a deal was reached. Bird then proceeded to lead the Celtics to a 31-game turnaround, largest at the time in NBA history.

The Celtics won another title, first of the Bird era, in 1981 under Bill Fitch, but by 1983, the team was coming apart. Auerbach named placid K. C. Jones to replace Fitch and then convinced Phoenix to part with guard Dennis Johnson for the no-longer-needed Rick Robey. Johnson gave Boston a stabilizing and defensive presence in the back court and the Celtics beat Magic Johnson and the Lakers in a thrilling seven-game series in 1984.

Two years later, Auerbach experienced the high and low of his Celtics career. In early June of '86, he again accepted the league championship trophy after the Celtics steamrolled through the league with a 67-15 record and through the postseason at 15-3. It was probably the greatest Celtics team ever. Walton, who had come over the previous summer in a trade for Maxwell, won the Sixth Man Award and was a huge presence on and off the floor. Bird won the third of his three consecutive MVPs. The team went 40-1 at home.

But soon after defeating the Houston Rockets for the NBA title, the bottom fell out. The Celtics had the second pick in the draft, courtesy of a deal with Seattle in 1984. Auerbach had his heart set on an athletic, mobile, gifted forward from Maryland named Len Bias. Auerbach had scouted Bias and was good friends with Maryland coach Lefty Dreisell. By all accounts, Bias was a can't-miss prospect and Auerbach gloated when he announced the pick. Two days later, Bias was dead of cocaine intoxication. Auerbach cried in the Celtics' office.

REMAINS A PRESENCE

Even after Auerbach ceded control of the day-to-day operation of the team, his reputation and presence still loomed large, even from afar. In the early 1990s, Dave Gavitt, now the Celtics' senior executive vice president, and another general manager had agreed on a trade. But when the opposing owner was asked to approve, he shook his head and said, "If Red is for it, I want no part of it."

Gavitt was forced out in 1994 and former Celtic player M. L. Carr was brought in to run the day-to-day operations. He stayed there long enough to pave the way for Pitino by engineering a 15-67 record in 1997, all designed to get the No. 1 pick in the 1997 draft, Tim Duncan. But the Celtics ended up with the third pick (and No. 6) and Pitino never recovered. Auerbach was still consulted, but Pitino was the

Red Auerbach watches the Celtics practice at Hellenic College in Brookline, on October 31, 1991.

Red Auerbach and Larry Bird walk the court together after Bird's retirement press conference on August 18, 1992.

unquestioned power, as evidenced by his insistence on stripping Auerbach of the club president's title.

Pitino left in 2000. Yet another new ownership group came on board in 2002. Ainge was hired in May 2002 to rebuild the team. On the podium that day, Auerbach was asked what he thought about Ainge. "He bleeds green," said Auerbach, who was passed for career wins by Lenny Wilkens in the 1995 season. Ainge knew there could be no greater compliment.

On Wednesday, Auerbach proudly received the US Navy's Lone Sailor Award in front of family and friends at ceremonies in Washington.

Auerbach's wife, Dorothy, died in 2000. He's survived by his two daughters, Nancy Auerbach Collins and Randy Auerbach. He also leaves a granddaughter, Julie Auerbach Flieger, and three great-grandchildren.

Tough Man Had a Tender Side

October 29, 2006 • by Jackie MacMullan

The first time I met Red Auerbach, I was 22 years old, and I was terrified.

It was January, 1983, and I had been working at the Globe as a full-time writer exactly two months. My assignment was the Boston College-St. John's basketball game, which seemed manageable enough until five minutes before tip-off, when this silver-haired gentleman in a blue blazer plopped himself down next to me and lit up a cigar.

Of course. What else would he do?

No one dared to instruct Arnold "Red" Auerbach to extinguish it. We were in Boston Garden—the

Red Auerbach and John Havlicek celebrate the latter's birthday during a game against the New Orleans Jazz on April 8, 1977.

house Red built—and he did whatever he wanted when he roamed that creaky old arena with the hallowed banners hanging from its rafters.

I wanted so desperately to impress him, but I couldn't think of a single intelligent thing to say. Instead, I diligently took notes while BC and its water bug point guard, Michael Adams, wreaked havoc on Mark Jackson and the heavily favored St. John's team. Red didn't say much to me, other than offering to buy me an ice cream midway through the first half.

At the intermission, as the cheerleaders sprinted to center court to begin their spirited, peppy routine, the greatest coach in basketball history gestured toward the parquet—his parquet—and asked, "So . . . what do you think?"

It was the moment I had been waiting for. I immediately explained how I thought BC's full-court press was particularly effective, and if St. John's didn't begin to respect the Eagles' perimeter shooter soon, maybe BC could pull off the upset.

"No, no," Auerbach interrupted. "I meant the girls. Aren't you the cheerleading coach?"

Well, no. I wasn't. Red would learn that soon enough. Over nearly 24 years, our paths would cross on a regular basis. I was a young reporter trying to capture the Celtics' mystique, and he was the man who invented it. In the beginning, he vociferously objected to everything about me, particularly when I entered his team's locker room.

"You don't belong in there," he'd bark.

"What if you were trying to decide whether to draft a player, and everyone got to talk to him but you?" I'd retort. "Would that be fair?"

"It would never happen!" he'd bellow. "I would already know more about the kid than everyone else anyway!"

This, of course, was true. Back when Auerbach's staff consisted of himself, and, well, himself, he relied on a Rolodex full of numbers for nearly every prominent college coach in the country to glean his scouting reports. He was always one step ahead of the competition. And, when he'd fleece his fellow NBA executives, he did so without a trace of humility.

"If you do something great, kid, then don't apologize to anyone," he told me. "If you're a winner, then act like one."

He called me "kid" right up until yesterday, the day he died of a heart attack. He had battled respiratory problems in recent years, and I suppose none of us should have been shocked that an 89-year-old man's time finally had come.

Still, the news took my breath away. Forgive me. Red was so stubborn, I assumed he would live forever.

Or maybe I just hoped that was true.

I know how people felt about him outside of Boston. They felt he was arrogant, superior. They hated the fact he lit up that cigar in the waning moments of a sure victory. It was showboating, they said, a galling lack of sportsmanship. The book on Red outside of our city was that he was a graceless winner and sore loser.

Maybe so. I asked him about it once. He smiled, took a puff, and blew it in my face.

Our relationship was a work in progress, but over time, I grew to love Red Auerbach. We developed a quirky sort of professional friendship that included spirited debates on women's issues, on the merits of different eras, on the best blacktop playgrounds in the country. He grew to appreciate my love of the game and became one of my most trusted sources.

In the early '90s, he fell ill and almost died. Naturally, the Celtics insulated him, so the public (and most of us in the media) didn't completely grasp how close he came to leaving us. I didn't realize it myself until I went to see him in his native Washington after he had recovered. I was asking him how Reggie Lewis's shocking death affected him, and, after taking a long draw of his cigar, he admitted he was so sick during that time he had little or no idea what had happened to the young star.

It was a beautiful spring day in Washington, and he asked me when my flight was leaving. I told him I had some time. We hopped into his Saab convertible (really now, how many senior citizens do you know drive a Saab convertible?), and he took me to the Smithsonian. There was a great Duke Ellington exhibit, he explained, and he felt I should see it before I left.

Who knew? Red loved Chinese food and owned an eclectic collection of letter openers ("Go to the back of the store," he always insisted. "The best stuff is always in the back."), but until that day, I didn't realize he was tuned into Sir Duke as well.

As we pulled up to the entrance, he parked his car in the little cul de sac in front of the building. A uniformed guard immediately approached us and said, "I'm sorry, sir. There's no parking here."

Red got out of the car, patted him on the shoulder, and said, "That's OK, son."

Then he walked inside. One hour later, we returned to the cul de sac, where his car remained, untouched.

You know most of the facts concerning Red. You know about the championships, his willingness to hire the first African-American coach, his unparalleled tenure as a cunning and ruthless general manager.

I wish he showed his softer side more. It was there, particularly when discussing the two daughters who made him so proud, or his wife, Dorothy, whom he missed terribly after she died in 2000, or when he called to console a young reporter who had experienced her own devastating personal loss, not six months after he had blown smoke in her face.

In recent years, the trip to Boston was increasingly difficult for Red. He walked with a cane, which he hated ("Ask me about it and I'll hit you with it," he groused). He couldn't quite keep up with the team as he once did.

Two years ago, I stood with him in the hallway of the FleetCenter outside the locker room when one of the young players (who shall remain nameless to save him the embarrassment) came up to the Celtics patriarch.

"Coach Auerbach," he said. "I just want to shake your hand. It is such an honor to meet you."

As the player walked away, Red turned to me and said, "Who the hell was that?"

In his final years, he spent most afternoons at his club in Maryland, where he played cards and held court. He still attended games at his beloved George Washington and took in some of the Atlantic Coast Conference tournament last spring.

"If you come down, we'll go together," he told me.

"I should do that," I said.

I didn't. I got busy with my life and my work and my kids. It sounded good at the time, but I couldn't get there.

I talked to Red for the last time about three weeks ago. I had written a story on Doc Rivers and his attempts to balance his job with commuting to Orlando where his family lives. Red had done a similar juggling act when he was coaching the Celtics in Boston, and his family remained in D.C.

"I don't blame Doc," Red told me. "At the end of the day, your family is the only thing that matters."

He told me he was flying up for the season opener, which is Wednesday.

"Are you coming?" he said. "I'll see you there."

I wish.

Bucking the Trend

CELTICS PUT END TO TEAM-RECORD 18-GAME SKID

February 15, 2007 • by Christopher L. Gasper

The words of public address announcer Eddie Palladino echoed throughout TD Banknorth Garden last night, words that hadn't been heard in these parts for 40 days and 40 nights: "Celtics win!"

Surely, some of the generously estimated 14,482 fans who braved the rain, sleet, and snow to watch the Celtics thought they must have been hearing things. But Boston finally decided that 18 was enough.

With both Paul Pierce and Wally Szczerbiak in the lineup for the first time since Dec. 16 and a sense of urgency befitting the playoffs, not the NBA Draft lottery, the Celtics snapped their franchise-record 18-game losing streak with a 117-97 win over another woebegone Eastern Conference team, the Milwaukee Bucks, losers of 19 of their last 23.

With a victory in their final game before the All-Star break, the Celtics avoided potential NBA infamy, as with a five-game Western swing looming after the show in Las Vegas, Boston was perilously close to challenging the league's all-time mark for consecutive losses (24) and consecutive setbacks in a season (23).

"We won't be a topic of conversation each and every night," said Pierce. "I saw everybody talking about the longest losing streak or possibly the longest losing streak in NBA history, so it feels good to finally get past that, especially with such a tough road trip coming up, because we could have easily fallen into that."

Pierce, who yesterday morning on WEEI expressed dismay at the plight of the team at this point in his career, went out and did something about it, scoring a game-high 32 points on 12-of-19 shooting.

The win was the team's first since Jan. 5, when Boston upended Memphis, 128-119, on the road. It also was the first in front of the home crowd since Dec. 15, snapping a 13-game skid on the parquet.

Still, some may have left disappointed. It's all about Greg Oden and Kevin Durant at this point, right?

He Always Rose to the Occasion

February 23, 2007 • by Jackie MacMullan

He was the guy who would miss 11 straight shots, then come down the court with everything on the line and drill the game-winner without blinking.

That's how I will remember Dennis Johnson, the freckle-faced bulldog who joined the Celtics in 1983 and was a pivotal member of the 1984 and '86 championship teams. DJ's role was often diminished amid the long shadows of Larry Bird, Kevin McHale, and Robert Parish, yet he was the one Bird singled out as "the best teammate I've ever played with."

Johnson collapsed and died yesterday in Austin, Texas, where he was the coach of the Austin Toros of the NBA Development League. He was 52 years old, too young to have his life cut so terribly short.

"What a sad, sad day," said McHale. "I tell you, this one really hits you. I was just talking to a friend who had just talked with DJ, and he was telling me how excited DJ was about his team. I guess his guys had started out losing eight in a row, or something like that, but lately they had been winning, and no one was happier about that than him.

"I can't believe this has happened. First Reggie [Lewis] and now him. We're too young to be losing teammates like this."

DJ was memorable on a number of fronts, but mostly for his ability to rise to the occasion when the games mattered most.

"That's when you really appreciated him," offered Bird. "Not during a regular-season game in Cleveland in December."

Johnson's career averages of 14.1 points and five assists per game don't begin to explain his value. He was an unorthodox point guard, a below-average shooter who was a tenacious defender during critical moments, who used his strength, moxie, and high basketball IQ to make exactly the right pass at exactly the right moment, or drill the big jumper when his team needed it.

"I remember that time in the '85 Finals against the Lakers in [Game 4]," said Bird. "I got the ball on the right side at the top of the key, and they sent two guys running right at me. Out of the corner of my eye, I saw DJ was open and I said, 'Thank God.' I knew he'd hit it, and of course he did."

One of Johnson's more memorable hoops was during the 1987 Eastern Conference finals against the Detroit Pistons, when Bird intercepted Isiah Thomas's inbounds pass and relayed it to a streaking Johnson.

"He was stretched out on that play," Bird recalled. "He was using his right hand going in on the left side of the basket. But it never occurred to me he'd miss it. Not DJ. He told me once, 'I'm a horrible shooter. But give me the ball down the stretch and I'll hit it every time.'"

"He joked about that a lot," McHale said. "I can remember one season when he was going through a really bad stretch of shooting. Danny [Ainge] was always messing with him. He said, 'DJ, you miss every time. What are you doing?' DJ said, 'I'm just setting them all up for the playoffs. If I shoot bad now, they'll lay off me in the postseason, and I'll light 'em up.'"

For all his offensive heroics, though, it was his defense that set him apart. Johnson was acquired by Boston, in part, to slow up Lakers superstar Magic

The crowd catches Dennis Johnson—known as DJ— during a game against the Trail Blazers on December 6, 1985.

Johnson. A six-time NBA All-Defensive first-team selection, he became Magic's most formidable defensive adversary and haunted him the way Lakers defensive specialist Michael Cooper haunted Bird. Magic has often said no one bothered him more on the basketball court.

"That was the thing about DJ," said Ainge. "He found more ways to help us win than any other player I've ever played with.

"Whether it was hitting the shot, coming up with a steal, blocking a shot, or shutting down the team's best player, he would do it. I've said this many times: He was a true Hall of Famer."

The fact that Johnson was not chosen for basketball's highest honor was one of a number of disappointments he endured after his playing days. DJ dreamed of being an NBA coach, but a messy domestic-abuse incident involving his wife, Donna, hampered his efforts to earn a legitimate shot at such a job. Johnson was an assistant with the Celtics in the early '90s and coached the Clippers in 2003, and was trying to work his way back to the big leagues when he collapsed.

Bird said he was prepared to hire DJ as a scout for the Pacers when the NBA Development League job opened up. "He liked the idea of coaching," said Bird, who last saw his former running mate at his annual golf tournament in Terre Haute, Ind., last summer.

Although Johnson won an NBA championship with the Seattle SuperSonics in 1979 and was named the Finals MVP, he was branded a "cancer" by Seattle coach Lenny Wilkens and traded to Phoenix. Upon his arrival in Boston, a loose bunch of Celtics were waiting with their own good-natured barbs to break him in.

"I used to call him 'Chemo,' because I told him I didn't want him to spread his cancer," Ainge said. "And we called him 'Spot' because he had all those freckles on his face. DJ was a lot of fun. He took jokes well and he gave jokes well. He was a happy-go-lucky guy most of the time. And we all knew how much basketball meant to him."

DJ came to Boston with a reputation as a difficult player, yet that dissipated early on in his tenure with the team.

"We weren't worried," Bird said. "Who can't get along with [former coach] K. C. Jones? There were some days DJ would come into practice at [Hellenic College] and he'd say, 'I don't feel like doing this today.' We'd say to him, 'Then go sit down on the stage over there. You're not going to ruin our practice.' That's how we handled it. He only did that one day out of 10. The rest of the time he was a great, great teammate."

Ainge said he spoke to Dennis Johnson about a week and a half ago to prep him on the arrival of Celtics rookie Allan Ray, who was assigned to his team.

"He was excited to help," Ainge said. "He was excited about his job."

It has been a tough season for Celtics fans. They've lost Red Auerbach, a ton of basketball games, and now one of the most clutch performers in their storied history.

"I loved playing with him," said McHale.

The rest of us loved watching him.

Early Disappointment

May 23, 2007 • by Shira Springer

SECAUCUS, N.J.—Celtics owner Wyc Grousbeck did not flip through the listings of winning combinations when the first set of four Ping-Pong balls were announced last night. Unlike other team representatives sequestered in conference room 3A at the NBA Entertainment Studios—where the actual lottery drawing took place—Grousbeck knew almost immediately Boston would not receive the No. 1 pick. It would go to the Portland Trail Blazers.

As the second set of Ping-Pong balls were plucked from a tumbler, Grousbeck rocked ever so slightly in his chair, slowly realizing the Celtics would not land the No. 2 pick, either, as numbers 14, 4, 11, and 10 were pulled. That choice would go to the Seattle SuperSonics. Although Grousbeck didn't say anything, it was easy to read his mind—and that of everyone else not affiliated with Portland or Seattle.

Goodbye Greg Oden and Kevin Durant.

Moments later, when the Atlanta Hawks took the third pick, Grousbeck forced a smile, disappointed that Boston will pick fifth in the 2007 NBA Draft June 28. Then, he turned around to shake hands and congratulate the three men sitting behind him: Portland general manager Kevin Pritchard, Seattle (assistant GM) Rich Cho, and Atlanta owner Ed Peskowitz.

"I knew the numbers," said Grousbeck. "I had a general idea a 1 or 2 had to show up or we weren't getting a pick and they didn't show up. The first thing I thought of is that Danny [Ainge] has been hammering into me that there's five or six guys he likes. I was probably looking for something to cheer me up, but that's what we've been talking about for a month and we're going to go with that plan. It would have been fun [to win]. It was like the feeling of watching a Paul Pierce last-second 3-pointer go toward the net except it took a month and a half to not fall, instead of a second and a half.

"In five or six years, it will probably be seen as a draft that is probably pretty deep, but right now all the flow is with 1 and 2. You can't fight that, but we will make pick No. 5 work."

7

THE NEW BIG THREE

(2007-2013)

The construction of the Celtics' first championship team in 22 seasons first required the alteration of two well-worn sports adages. The best-laid plans . . . sometimes lead to an even better plan. And: The best trades are sometimes the ones you *do* make.

After the ping-pong balls in the 2007 NBA Draft Lottery refused to cooperate, causing the Celtics to miss out on a chance to draft presumed franchise-altering talents in Ohio State's Greg Oden or Texas's Kevin Durant, President of Basketball Operations Danny Ainge swiftly activated Plan B. On draft night, he dealt the player selected fifth overall, Georgetown forward Jeff Green, along with guard Delonte West, forward Wally Szczerbiak, and a second-round pick to the Seattle SuperSonics for sweet-shooting veteran All-Star Ray Allen and the draft rights to burly LSU forward Glen "Big Baby" Davis.

The Allen move was essential for two reasons. Paul Pierce had become disenchanted during the 24-win 2007 season and requested a trade. "I'm in my prime, and I'm watching all these other guys in the playoffs," Pierce later recalled. "It was depressing." The acquisition of Allen, who had averaged 26.4 points per game for the Sonics the previous season and would become, during his time with the Celtics, the NBA's all-time leader in made 3-pointers, gave the Celtics a second All-Star.

More important, it opened the door for the acquisition of the most essential piece of what would become known as the New Big Three. Kevin Garnett, drafted out of a Chicago high school in 1995, had developed during his 12 seasons with the Minnesota Timberwolves as one of the NBA's premier stars, an intense two-way force who won the Most Valuable Player award in 2004. But after more than a decade of loyalty to the middling franchise, he decided a change of scenery would do him good.

Initial interest by the Celtics did not appeal to him, and his preferred destinations included Phoenix and Los Angeles. But the Allen trade, and some cajoling by the likes of Pierce and others with Celtics ties, convinced him that Boston was the place to be.

On July 31, 2007, in a swap between Ainge and his good friend and former teammate, Timberwolves General Manager Kevin McHale, Garnett became a Celtic, with Al Jefferson and an assortment of second-tier players and picks

‹ Kevin Garnett celebrates after winning the Finals on June 17, 2008.

headed to the Timberwolves. It was a seismic move, one that made the Celtics genuine contenders if not front-runners for the NBA title.

Wrote Bob Ryan that day: "Garnett is a legitimate NBA force. There never has been anyone quite like him. He's a 6-foot-11-inch, backboard-eating, perimeter-roaming, jump-shooting former Most Valuable Player. And his arrival gives the Celtics a shot to make one of those turnarounds that accompanied Larry Bird's first year in Boston (29 wins to 61 wins)."

(The front page of the *Globe* the following morning greeted the deal with a fitting headline, "Trade Wins," though it should be noted, with more amusement than regret, that the Red Sox's acquisition of relief pitcher Eric Gagne received near-equal billing.)

The press conference introducing Garnett and Allen, alongside beaming holdover Pierce, was a giddy occasion. "We still have things to prove," Garnett cautioned in between smiles. "But I will say this: We'll be a force to be reckoned with."

Apparently his vast skill set included prescience because he could not have been more correct about that. With second-year point guard Rajon Rondo emerging as a delightful playmaker, Kendrick Perkins providing the muscle, and veteran free-agent pickups James Posey and Eddie House bolstering the bench, the new-look Celtics tore through the NBA from the first time they took the parquet together.

A preseason European trip—during which the team embraced the spirit of "ubuntu," an ancient African term defined as "I am what I am because of who we all are"—accelerated the development of their bond. The Celtics won their first eight games and 29 of 32 to begin the season en route to 66 victories, third-most in Celtics history and a 42-win improvement over the previous season. A first-round matchup with the pesky Atlanta Hawks and a rookie forward named Al Horford brought some unexpected tension. But the Celtics finished off that series in seven, then defeated LeBron James and the Cavaliers in the conference semifinals, with Pierce coming up with a crucial loose ball and scoring 41 points to James's 45 in an epic Game 7 showdown. The Celtics required six games to dispatch the Detroit Pistons in the conference finals, setting up their first Finals showdown with the rival Lakers since 1987.

The Celtics won the series in six games and in a remarkably fulfilling way. Each of the four Celtic

victories provided a performance or achievement that would register forever in franchise lore. In Game 1, Pierce left the court in a wheelchair after an apparent knee injury, only to return and lead the Celtics to a 10-point win. In Game 2, reserve forward Leon Powe scored 21 points in 15 minutes in a 108-102 victory. After dropping Game 3, the Celtics rallied from a 24-point deficit—the largest comeback in Finals history—to take Game 4 and a commanding 3-1 lead. The Celtics' 17th championship was secured in an utterly suspense-free 131-92 rout in Game 6 at the Garden.

The champs looked more than ready to defend the crown in the early weeks of the 2009 season, jumping out to a 27-2 start, the best in franchise history. But Garnett, the reigning defensive player of the year, injured his knee on an innocuous-looking dunk in February against the Jazz. He missed a month, returned, reaggravated the injury, and missed the postseason, which saw the Celtics survive a thrilling seven-game series with the Bulls before falling to the Magic in the second round.

The Celtics became a Big Four in 2010 with the full emergence of Rondo as a genuine star. In Game 4 of the Celtics' win over the Cavaliers in the conference semifinals, Rondo delivered 29 points, 18 rebounds, and 13 assists, leading Cleveland's LeBron James, among other observers, to comment that Rondo was the best player on the court. The Celtics eliminated the Cavaliers in six games, ending James's first run with Cleveland, then defeated the Magic in six games in the conference finals, setting up another duel with the Lakers again in the Finals.

The Celtics seized a 3-2 lead in the series—Allen hit a Finals-record eight 3-pointers in Game 2—and Banner No. 18 appeared on the horizon. But the Lakers did not fold, and a Game 6 injury to Perkins cost the Celtics needed toughness and rebounding. The Celtics led for much of Game 7, including by as many as 13 points in the second half, but the shots refused to fall down the stretch, and the Lakers earned their 17th banner with an 83-79 win.

The Celtics didn't know it then, but the championship window had closed. Texas guard Avery Bradley, the first-round pick in 2010, added a defensive presence at guard, and Shaquille O'Neal arrived for what would be the final season of his career. But a February 2011 trade of Perkins to the

Thunder for former Celtics pick Jeff Green affected team chemistry.

James had taken his talents to South Beach to create his version of a Big Three and join forces on the Heat with Dwyane Wade and Chris Bosh. The loaded Heat wiped out the aging Celtics—further limited when a Wade cheap shot dislocated Rondo's elbow in Game 3—in five games. A season later, a transcendent 45-performance by James in Game 6 of the East finals, followed by a 13-point win in Game 7, put an unofficial end to the New Big Three.

The official end came little more than a month after the East finals, when Allen, who had lost playing time to Bradley and was bothered by a near-trade during the season to the Grizzlies for O. J. Mayo, signed with the Heat, a decision that caused tension between him and Garnett for more than a decade. The 2013 Celtics were eliminated in the first round of the playoffs by the Knicks, the sort of outcome that made everyone see how murky the future had become.

Exactly a month after being dismissed by the Knicks, coach Doc Rivers, who had no interest in participating on a rebuild, was allowed out of his contract so that he could coach the Los Angeles Clippers for the price of a first-round pick.

The truly seismic move was still to come. On June 28, 2013, Ainge sent Pierce, Garnett, Jason Terry, and D. J. White to the Brooklyn Nets in exchange for five veterans of little magnitude, three first-round picks, and the rights to a pick swap. The deal was as necessary as it was unsentimental, ending the New Big Three era, but bringing draft capital that if deployed properly would result in the arrival of the next generation of Celtics stars.

Celtics Pick Trade

NO. 5 CHOICE SENT TO SONICS FOR ALLEN

June 29, 2007 • by Shira Springer

Choosing veteran talent over youth, the Celtics completed a trade with the Seattle SuperSonics during the NBA Draft last night, acquiring 31-year-old shooting guard Ray Allen and the No. 35 overall

pick in exchange for small forward Wally Szczerbiak, point guard Delonte West, and the No. 5 pick.

Selecting for Seattle, Boston picked Georgetown forward Jeff Green at No. 5. Seattle general manager Sam Presti confirmed the deal midway through the first round.

"Boston really pursued this," Presti told reporters in Seattle. "What started as a smaller conversation became fulfilled. Their pursuit was impeccable.

"We're thrilled to have [No. 2 pick] Kevin [Durant], but at the same time, to make the decision to move a player and a person like Ray Allen was tremendously difficult."

In the second round, the Celtics selected Southern Cal guard Gabe Pruitt 32d overall, and will receive Louisiana State forward Glen "Big Baby" Davis, who was selected by the Sonics at No. 35.

Allen gives the Celtics one of the best shooters in the game, though scoring has not been a problem for the team. While Paul Pierce may be smiling knowing the Celtics listened to his long-held preference for an experienced player, it remains to be seen how the All-Stars will work as teammates. Both Pierce and Allen like the ball in their hands. The other question about Allen concerns his health, considering he underwent surgery on both ankles in early April to remove bone spurs.

"I wasn't surprised," said Allen, who learned yesterday that a Seattle-Boston deal was becoming increasingly likely. "I took it in stride. I know the team has been floundering in the Northwest the last couple seasons. It almost seemed appropriate for a change at this point. It seems like this organization is heading in a different direction."

With regard to playing alongside Pierce, Allen, reached by telephone, added, "I'm a chameleon. I'll adapt wherever I go. One of my best attributes is to assess the situation and not try to force my personality on the team. I know it's Paul Pierce's team. I just want to fit in and make the team better the best I know how."

While Allen has averaged 21.5 points over an 11-year NBA career and shot 45 percent from the field, including 45 percent from 3-point range, the seven-time All-Star believes he can contribute more than offense.

"There's more to me than the ability to shoot it," said Allen, who has three years worth $52.2 million remaining on his contract. "It's about being professional and doing your job every day. I can teach young players to step up and be great at their jobs. I can [be a part of] providing leadership, giving Paul that help.

"We both can score, but I don't think we have to have the ball in our hands to score. I can score without the ball. I look at scoring in different ways. The ball doesn't have to be in my hands. I have a responsibility when I'm on the floor to know what every other player can do and put them in good situations."

Trade Wins

GARNETT: CELTICS BELIEVE THEIR SHIP HAS COME IN

August 1, 2007 • by Peter May

It may be hard to remember a recent Celtic scene with more sheer optimism. Kevin Garnett, fresh in from the Twin Cities (and not from a cruise) in the middle of the table, a broad smile, flanked by a beaming Paul Pierce and Ray Allen. No, they're not the new Big Three yet; Danny Ainge made that clear yesterday. They haven't won anything.

But the mere addition of the 6-foot-11-inch Garnett, who is under wraps for five years, has shaken the foundation of the Eastern Conference and awakened a somnolent Celtic nation like a 7.5 Richter scale earthquake. Sportsbook.com has put the Celtics at 5-2 to win the Eastern Conference (the favorite) and gulp—5-1—to *win the 2008 NBA championship*, trailing only the Mavericks, Suns, and Spurs. "From low expectations to high expectations, that's what we want," Doc Rivers said.

Or, as Pierce noted, "I asked for veterans. I didn't expect to get a 12-time All-Star."

Hey, he's only been to 10 All-Star Games, but who's counting?

Garnett made his first appearance as a Celtic last night, capping a whirlwind 72 hours that he described as "like being in a Lamborghini driving 200 with your head stuck out of the window." He passed his physical at New England Baptist Hospital, signed a three-year extension (for roughly $60 million) to the two years he had remaining, and then was hoping to find a quiet spot in the

North End for some dinner after his dinnertime news conference.

He will wear No. 5 "because I was the No. 5 pick in '95." He also considered No. 4. He really wanted No. 2 (in honor of his former teammate, the late Malik Sealy) but it wasn't available. You can see his face in a Celtics jersey (sort of) on the team's website in the link for tickets. As one season ticket-holder said last night, "My seats will finally be worth what I'm paying."

Getting Garnett was a monumental coup for Ainge and the Celtics, as was the go-get-'em attitude by ownership, which now will have to deal with the dreaded luxury tax down the road. So what? This is Kevin Garnett. "This was an opportunity that came along," said Robert Epstein, one of the team's owners. "How do you let something like this go by?"

They couldn't. They didn't. They had Garnett in their grasp a month ago, but the situation wasn't right. He didn't want any part of joining a 24-win team. But after the draft-night addition of Ray Allen, and with the rather transparent rebuilding effort about to happen in Minnesota, Garnett started to think about moving for the first time in his career.

"Initially, I had no interest in leaving Minnesota," he said. "But after talking with [owner] Glen Taylor, his vision of the future was very different from mine. And when Boston [traded for] Ray Allen, the whole thing changed for me. I could see myself in a Celtics jersey. I went to my summer home [in Malibu, Calif.] and played some ball with Paul. He didn't say much.

"I guess at the end of the day, I'm loyal to a point where I feel if someone's loyal to me, then I have no problem with that. But when that changes, it's pretty easy for me. But I got to thinking this may be the best opportunity for me to win a ring. So, here we are."

It wasn't easy. He had been unflaggingly loyal to the Timberwolves for his entire career, but, as he noted, "I can't do young." And Minnesota is definitely doing young. So he did some due diligence. He said he left messages on all four of Pierce's cellphones, but didn't get a response. "I didn't recognize the area code," Pierce said, rather lamely. "It was the same on all four phones," Garnett quipped. He talked to Allen, with whom he had played on the 1999 US Olympic qualifying team and the 2000 Olympic team.

He sounded out former Celtics like Antoine Walker and Gary Payton for their views on life in Boston. He liked what he heard. He talked once more to the Timberwolves. He didn't like what he heard. So he made the call to get the process rolling again.

"Slowly, but surely, I got more comfortable with the situation," he said. "It feels good to be appreciated. It's good to recognize that."

Ainge and Rivers did the appropriate keening for the losses of the players dealt to the Wolves, Al Jefferson in particular. But even though the Celtics surrendered five players and two draft picks, they looked and felt like the winners last night. Garnett has put up frightening numbers in Minnesota, been a perennial All-NBAer, will be a dead bolt lock for the Hall of Fame, and—shock to the system—is usually a representative on the league's All-Defensive team. And he's going to be in Celtic green for five years.

Pierce said he was so excited that he felt like a rookie again. "A big load has been taken off my back," he said. Garnett and Allen are only too willing to take that load off Pierce's back and share it—and take the Celtics where they haven't been in two decades and where none of the three ever has been.

"We still have things to prove," Garnett cautioned. "But I will say this: We'll be a force to be reckoned with."

That's something no one could have said 48 hours earlier without a laugh track. Now, thanks to one man, it's pretty much gospel.

'BASKETBALL IS MY SPINE'

High school season in Chicago forged Celtic Garnett's game

October 30, 2007 • by Shira Springer

Scanning the crowd of NBA representatives awaiting his predraft workout at the University of Illinois-Chicago, Kevin Garnett saw a group of men holding lottery picks for the 1995 draft with better places to be. Garnett leans back and feigns glassy-eyed boredom to reenact what he remembers most about the invited audience on that fateful June day. He stares blankly into the distance for more than a minute, making his dramatic point.

"I'll never forget they all came in and they were looking like this," said Garnett. "They were thinking, 'Man, we're coming in here to watch this [expletive], wasting our time.' When I saw that there, that irked me."

Minnesota vice president of basketball operations Kevin McHale was among the group of skeptical NBA representatives gathered at UIC, wondering if Garnett would be the first high school player in two decades to go straight to the NBA. It took an hour to convince the gathering that Garnett was the future. In a gym McHale recalled as "beastly hot," a sweat-drenched Garnett did everything that was asked of him during the workout by NBA executives and coaches shouting instructions.

Let's see him dribble down the court righthanded. Lefthanded. Let's see him pull up for a jump shot at the elbow. Step farther back and shoot again. Let's see him jump and reach as high as he can on the backboard. Again. Again. Again.

"They were just yelling stuff out and I was going and going," said Garnett. "Man, what do you want? Let's see him chili sauce. Let's see him breakdance. Let's see him do the salsa. That's how it was.

"Then, Bill Fitch [then coaching the LA Clippers] was like, 'You need a break?' I felt he was looking at me like, 'Hey, boy, you need a break?' Even though he didn't say it like that, I took it like he was looking at me like, 'Are you tired? Are you tired?' I was like, 'Hell, no. I don't need no break.' But I was about to faint."

Garnett threw down a showstopping dunk and released whatever aggression remained with an emphatic yell directed toward the duly impressed scouts, then walked off the court. The NBA crowd left wanting more from the high school kid. McHale left worrying Garnett would be gone before Minnesota exercised the No. 5 pick.

"That workout was one of those deals where you get a snippet of a guy and it ends up being who he is," said McHale.

The predraft workout also served as testament and tribute to the competitor Garnett became in Chicago, where he spent his senior season playing for Farragut Academy, frequented the city's toughest spots for pickup games, and earned National High School Player of the Year honors. All the lessons learned from that year were on display. The attitude. The relentless drive. The intensity.

While the 6-foot-11-inch body may have been underdeveloped and the jump shot a little loose when Garnett auditioned for the NBA, he was, in the most important respects, the same player who would carry the Minnesota Timberwolves for 12 seasons and give the Celtics legitimate hope for a 17th championship this season.

After all, the first big move Garnett made from Mauldin, S.C., to Chicago showed the kind of transformation that can take place within one year with a change of scenery.

"Chicago embraced me when they didn't have to," said Garnett. "They embraced a young soldier. They embraced a person who embraced them. That's why I have a rubber band that says, 'Embrace change.'

"Chicago gave me a different flair. Chicago gave me attitude and swagger and confidence, like, 'This is how you have to be out here on the court. It's kill or be killed.' You learn that right away. Someone's always looking to embarrass you or say that they kicked your [butt] or something . . . Now that I look back on it, I was a young boy turning into a man. It was definitely a grow-up kind of year for me."

FARRAGUT A FACTOR

When William "Wolf" Nelson met Garnett for the first time, the Farragut Academy coach could not conceal his disappointment. Waiting for big men to complete his roster at the 1993 Nike Camp, Nelson first thought he was assigned Garnett as a joke. By Nelson's estimate, Garnett arrived at camp measuring 6 feet 10 and weighing 217 pounds. Garnett disputes the numbers, confessing he was closer to 200 pounds.

"I see Kevin and I'm like, 'Stop playing. How you all give me the little guy?'" said Nelson. "Kevin told me, 'C'mon man, quit tripping.' I said, 'Quit tripping? You skinny, man.'"

Undeterred with a roster led by Garnett and Antawn Jamison, Nelson told his players to run. They did and finished the week of tournament play atop the standings. During the camp, Garnett liked what he heard and saw from Nelson, appreciated his passion for the game. Garnett also clicked with Farragut Academy star Ronnie Fields. There was talk about Garnett transferring to Farragut.

"I heard it, but I didn't hear it," said Nelson. "I had trouble getting a transfer from across the city and Kevin lived in South Carolina."

But circumstances in South Carolina changed as Garnett neared the end of his junior year at Mauldin High School. When a white student was beaten by Black assailants in a school hallway, Garnett found himself among those arrested. Garnett asserted his innocence in the matter that, according to some accounts, started when the white student hurled racist taunts at the Black students. After pretrial intervention for first-time offenders, the charges were dropped, though expulsion from Mauldin High remained a distinct possibility. Chicago, Nelson, and Farragut Academy reentered the picture.

"I went to Wolf and was like, 'I'm trying to figure this out, help me out here,'" said Garnett. "He was like, 'We can make it work. It's going to be different, but man, we can make it work.' I didn't even see Farragut. I didn't see no pictures, none of that. I didn't need to. I just knew Wolf.

"When I got to Wolf, he was all of [the fundamental instruction]. But you know what else? He said, 'If you can give 'em 40, give 'em 40. If you can give 'em 50, give 'em 50.' He gave me goose bumps. He said, 'When they see you, beat your chest. You let him know that you dunked on him.' . . . That was the first time I got that from a coach who was promoting me to go out here and be an animal. If you're a beast, be a beast. You're not like everybody else, go out here and prove it. I loved it."

During his senior season at Farragut, Garnett led his new team to a 28-2 record and its first city championship, averaging 26 points and 18 rebounds. At one point, he had more assists than all the Farragut guards combined. As stories of his dunking, dribbling, and passing ability strained credulity for a player his size, Farragut games became one of the toughest tickets in town.

Navigating the crowded halls of Farragut at the end of the school day, Nelson pauses before an impressive collection of Garnett memorabilia, documenting the forward's rise from precocious NBA prospect to 10-time All-Star to 2004 NBA MVP. Game-worn shoes, jerseys. A Wheaties box and autographed magazine covers. Inside the gym, a giant mural captures Garnett completing a reverse dunk wearing the Timberwolves uniform in which he amassed career averages of 20.5 points per game, 11.4 rebounds, and 4.5 assists before the blockbuster trade that sent him to Boston in July.

From left, Paul Pierce, Kevin Garnett, Ray Allen, Danny Ainge, and Doc Rivers were all smiles at the press conference introducing Garnett and Allen as Celtics.

"People still say today, 'I missed work to go see him play and I'd do it again. I had to see it. I couldn't believe it,'" said Nelson. "At the city championships, they were scalping $2 tickets for $50 and $60. I witnessed this. It was crazy. They were paying because they were like, 'I've got to see this.' The stuff he started to do in the NBA with numbers that are real ridiculous, all the triple-doubles, he was doing that to high school guys. It was a show all the time. My problem was, coaching that team was like leading a three-ring circus."

TOUGH COMPETITION

More than a decade later, the 31-year-old Garnett vividly recalls the places and players in Chicago where he sought competition he could not find in high school games. He lists the places slowly, reverentially. Kennedy King College. Saturday mornings. Oooh, Lord. Franklin Park. Man, the midnight league. LeClair Courts. Some battles there. Malcolm X College. The Boys and Girls Club on Roosevelt. He lists the players with equal respect. Pros and college stars home for the summer like Antoine Walker, Juwan Howard, and Rashard Griffith. "Hood cats," as he called them, like Big Hammer and Helicopter.

"All those places he named are basketball sites where they're going to be hacking," said the Celtics' Tony Allen, a Chicago product who followed the growing legend of Garnett around the city as a 12-year-old. "There are going to be Dennis Rodman-type fouls. He played through all that. That's what makes him who he is now. He got that heart from Chicago, playing through the grimiest places, the toughest places, where you think you might not come up out of there. But your game on the court makes everybody love you."

At the well-known spots on the west and south sides of Chicago, Garnett quickly made a name for himself, becoming an attraction the basketball community adopted as its own. Everyone wanted to see the "Big Fella." Anytime, anywhere, Garnett took on challengers. He learned respect and bragging rights were earned every day, every game. Nothing came easy in Chicago, and Garnett would have it no other way.

"I embraced it," said Garnett. "You know how they say dope fiends chase a high? I was chasing that. I wanted to see who was the best in the city. If you want to be the best, you have to play against the best. You have to experience that. I've always searched that out.

"Home wasn't a great place for me, and I found my sanctuary to be basketball to where I could disappear on the court. It's almost very similar to people who read. They take a good book and get lost in the book. I take my ball and I get lost on the court. I can be whoever I want to be at that time. It don't matter if it's 12 in the morning, 2 in the morning. That was my sanctuary."

Basketball offered Garnett an escape from the memories of his "trouble" in Mauldin and the betrayal by close friends that followed, from the strained household back in South Carolina where his mother went "through some difficulties" with his stepfather, from the "hustling and bustling" and "grind" of life in Chicago that left him longing for the freedom and familiarity of his small hometown. Basketball was the reassuring constant when questions about turning pro grew more insistent.

"At the end of the day, I'm a regular person like anybody else," said Garnett. "I just so happen to have a talent that I manage pretty well, and I love what I do, even without the glitz and the glamour parts of it. When I'm done in these next four or five years, I will still have my basketball. I will still have my court. I'll still go to it when I need to figure something out, or I'm going through a little something. I'll still go to the court and just get lost. It will always be my book. Basketball is my spine. It's my heart. It's my blood. It's my makeup."

GOING ALL-OUT

While other NBA executives filed out of the UIC gym after the predraft workout, McHale made his way down to the court to talk with Garnett. McHale offered a few tips on shooting form, squaring the shoulders, tightening the mechanics, avoiding the tendency to drift. Garnett was touched and impressed by the gesture, though McHale didn't think much of it at the time. McHale was more focused on the talent before him.

"I just wanted to share a couple of thoughts and thank him," said McHale. "He put on a hell of a show."

When all the NBA representatives left the gym, Garnett fell asleep for three hours on the court. He was emotionally and physically drained. He does nothing in half measures, whether playing or pursuing a better future.

"What they loved about me in Chicago was that I'm loyal," said Garnett. "I don't make friends easy. I don't trust easy. But once I do trust, once I do commit, it's a commitment for life. It's blood in. It's blood out. It's not anything watered down. That's just who I am. Chicago was a whole other level.

"So, when they were talking about, 'Could he survive in the league? How's this kid going to deal with it, living with grown men?' They didn't even know.

They had no idea what the hell I was coming from. They had no earthly idea what they were getting into, who they were drafting and what was coming into the league."

Boston knows exactly what it is getting into, embracing Garnett in much the same way as Chicago. Now, with the regular season starting, the city can hardly wait to see what he does with his next big move.

Routine Excellence Is Allen's Secret

April 20, 2008 • by Jackie MacMullan

WALTHAM—The routine is paramount. People don't understand that. They see Ray Allen, his head meticulously shaved, his jersey tucked carefully into his shorts, his socks pulled up to precisely the same length, and they are drawn to his silky jumper. Can you blame them? It is so smooth, so fluid, so seemingly effortless.

Everyone wishes they could shoot like Ray. They tell him that all the time. They are envious, they say, of his God-given talent.

"An insult," says Allen. "God could care less whether I can shoot a jump shot."

As the Celtics kick off their campaign for an NBA championship tonight in the opening round of the playoffs against the Atlanta Hawks, Allen will leave nothing to chance. He will line up for the tip exactly as he has for his other 73 games. His pregame ritual does not waver: a nap from 11:30 a.m. until 1 p.m., a meal of chicken and white rice at 2:30, an arrival time at the gym at precisely 3:45 to stretch. Allen will shave his head, then walk out to the court at exactly 4:30. He will methodically take shots from both baselines, both elbows, and the top of the key.

Allen is second all-time in 3-pointers, 460 shy of Reggie Miller. He has a chance of surpassing Miller, provided he stays healthy, but if he does, it will not be by divine intervention. It will be the result of years of painstaking preparation.

It will also be the byproduct of learning to strike a delicate balance between routine and superstition.

Ray Allen drives against Josh Smith of the Hawks during the 2008 NBA playoffs.

He requires the same symmetry in his basketball universe. That's why, when Paul Pierce suddenly began doing 360 dunks in warm-ups earlier this season, Allen demanded an explanation.

"We were winning," Allen says. "Why would he change it up when we were winning?"

"I was just trying something new," Pierce says. "I missed the shot. So Ray tells me I have to miss it the rest of the year."

COMMUNICATE, COMPROMISE

There was considerable discussion before the season on how Pierce, Allen, and Kevin Garnett would share shots.

It didn't occur to anyone, except their coach, to consider how they would share their personal space.

The wildly divergent rituals of the three superstars was a surprise—and, initially, a problem.

"As a team," Allen concedes, "we're all inside a bubble. Each of us only has so much room to operate. You have to carve out your space and recognize that because of someone else's needs, you might have to compromise a bit."

There's the free-wheeling Pierce, who never does anything quite the same from game to game. There is Allen, who needs to complete a specific checklist of chores before tipoff. And then there is Garnett, a brooding pregame figure who requires an intense period of introspection to prepare himself.

It was inevitable that their approaches would collide. In early December, Garnett was at his locker, alone, silently visualizing his responsibilities for the game. Allen, who had long ago completed his pregame tasks, was joking with Kendrick Perkins and Rajon Rondo. The noise interrupted Garnett's concentration. He barked his objections; his veteran teammate barked back.

"They got into it with each other," reports Rondo. "Me and Perk were sitting there going, 'Whoa, what's this about?'"

When Allen was small, he recited a familiar rhyme: Step on a crack, break your mother's back. So what happened if you stumbled onto the line? You'd groan, lament your misfortune, then go home for supper.

Not Ray. He would retreat to his room and wait for the sky to fall.

"I had a borderline case of OCD [obsessive compulsive disorder]," Allen explains. "I was never diagnosed, but it was something I was aware of."

This is how Ray Allen's mind works. If there is a speck of paper on the floor in his house, he cannot walk by without picking it up. He has tried. He has purposely marched up the stairs without correcting the glaring imperfection, but he's unable to eliminate the image from his mind until he goes back down, throws the scrap in the wastebasket, and restores order in his home.

Pierce observed the verbal skirmish with amusement.

"Stuff like that happens on teams all the time," Pierce insists. "Different personalities. But Ray's to blame. He's crazy. One night he gets on the plane and says, 'Paul, you're in the wrong seat.' I told him, 'Man, there's a hundred seats open. Leave me alone.'"

Ray's obsession with routine has struck a chord with Rondo, who confesses, "I probably have OCD myself." The point guard must wash his hands twice at the nine-minute mark of every game. When teammates and fans high-five him, he offers a closed fist to ward off germs.

Allen has become his role model, and Rondo has started showing up at the arena three hours before the game to mimic Ray's routine.

"I want to be consistent," explains Rondo, "and Ray is all about that."

Allen's mantra is that you must walk, talk, eat, and dress as though you are the best. Garnett concurs—to a point. KG does not feel obligated to wear tailored suits to prove his commitment, as Allen does.

"Ray is very strong-minded," Garnett says. "When you have other guys who are as strong, obviously you are going to have debates. But I think the young guys can see we can challenge one another without being destructive.

"I'm not going to say it was easy, but it was simple. Communicating is the best thing we do. A lot of people talk to hear themselves talk. Here, guys talk with their soul."

But coach Doc Rivers needed his trio to *listen* with the same fervor. His three stars were used to going about things in their own way, with teammates who deferred to them. That was no longer possible, and Rivers knew who would suffer the most.

"Earlier in the year, Ray would come to me and say, 'This is the way I used to do it,'" Rivers says. "I'd tell him, 'That's in the past.' Ray is a military guy. It was hard for him.

"But I told him if we were going to win this thing, he had to change."

'HOLLYWOOD' TO SEATTLE

When Ray Allen was 8, he had to drop in five lefty layups and five righty layups before he could leave the gym. Sometimes another team needed the floor and he'd run out of time before he could complete his ritual.

"I cried," Allen says. "It messed up my day."

He did not discuss his compulsion with his teammates, his coaches, his siblings, or even his mother.

"I was almost embarrassed by it," Allen says. "It was just always beating inside my brain when I was young and trying to make sense of who I was."

They nicknamed him "Hollywood" when he arrived at the University of Connecticut because he was always color-coordinated, always meticulously groomed. He looked like someone important.

"I got that from [Michael] Jordan," Allen says. "When I was a kid, every time he did an interview on television, he was wearing a suit. He looked professional. I told myself, 'That's the way to go.'"

Ray roomed with Travis Knight at UConn. Knight was disorganized, messy. Worst of all, he squeezed the toothpaste tube from the middle.

"We said they'd never last together," says UConn coach Jim Calhoun, "and they didn't."

Ray plotted his workouts as if he were one of the coaches. Calhoun would show the team game film and Allen would ask to see it again, not because he needed to, but because he knew his teammates hadn't paid proper attention.

"It's internal," says Calhoun, "but it's there 24 hours a day. Ray does things the right way, and expects others to do them, too. People are sloppy—in their preparation, in the way they present themselves.

"Not Ray. Never."

So Allen harangues Garnett about his sweater-and-tie combos, and the omnipresent Adidas logo on everything he wears. He chastises Eddie House for shooting halfcourt shots at intermission at the opposing team's basket.

"Bad luck," Ray says. "Everyone knows that."

He talks to Perkins and Glen Davis about their social life. Allen doesn't drink alcohol. He reminds the young big men, "You have all summer to go out. Do it then. Not now. Not with so much at stake."

"Ray says he always packs light," Perkins says, "because he leaves his nightclub clothes at home."

Allen is certain his philosophy works. When he played in Seattle, a veteran leader among a mass of young, floundering talent, he would complete his pregame pattern, then retreat to the locker room where he'd read, often for more than an hour, before anyone else showed up.

Rashard Lewis, a young forward who jumped to the NBA from high school, began quizzing Allen about his routine. Soon he started showing up early, too. Before long, Damien Wilkins, Chris Wilcox, and Luke Ridnour joined them. Ray was the pied piper of preparation.

"It got to the point," says former Seattle coach Nate McMillan, "where the first bus was more crowded than the second bus. And that never happens."

Not everybody in Seattle bought into Allen's plan. One day, when he arrived at the arena, Allen's regular parking spot was occupied. The owner of the car was Antonio Daniels, who had recently latched on to the early-bird shooting.

"I walk in and say, 'Why are you parking in my spot?'" Allen says. "He is acting like he doesn't know what I am talking about.

"We are playing the Knicks that night. I think I had about 40 points, but I'm still mad. I'm at the free throw line and Daniels comes up to me and says, 'You need me to take that spot more often.' I hit the free throw, then turn to him and shout, 'You stay out of my spot!'"

McMillan was worried after so many losses that his young players might abandon the Allen plan. But even after a double-digit loss, there was Allen, his head shaved, his shirt tucked in, reading a book, prepared to fight again.

"He made my job easy," McMillan says. "No matter what happened the night before, I could always say, 'Ray's here. He's ready. How about you?'"

BUYING INTO CONCESSIONS

The Celtics have asked Ray Allen to reinvent himself this season. He plays fewer minutes, takes fewer shots, is no longer the focal point of the offense.

"You see him sacrifice," says Perkins, "and you think, 'If he can do it, then I can do it, too.'"

Those changes were palatable for Ray. But he blanched when Rivers changed the team shootaround from the morning of the game to three hours before the game. And when Davis's minutes dwindled, and the coaches asked him to put in workouts before and after games, that cut into Allen's alone time on the floor.

"The last time I talked to Ray, he was ticked at Big Baby for not playing better, because he was messing up his pregame," Calhoun says. "I said to Ray, 'You've been in this league 12 years. Don't you have this down by now?'"

Allen is pleased that Rondo has become his pregame partner. He noted that Pierce, who ribs him the most about his eccentricities, has showed up early himself from time to time. In the meantime, Allen has worked to respect KG's ritual from afar.

"I've watched Ray," Garnett says. "I've watched Paul, and I've watched Pose [James Posey], and we all have our own way of preparing. All of us are excessive in how we go about it. It makes sense to me. Everybody is a little over the top in what they do, because it means so much."

When the Celtics played in Orlando earlier this season, Allen was at the arena at his customary time. He was surprised to see a lone Magic player working down at the other end of the floor—until he realized it was Rashard Lewis.

The word in Seattle is that Ridnour, Wilkins, and Wilcox have continued their pregame routine. McMillan, now the coach of the Portland Trail Blazers, reports that he imparted Allen's pregame wisdom to young All-Star Brandon Roy, who is so pleased with the results that he doesn't even wait for the first bus anymore. He goes a half-hour earlier by cab with an assistant coach.

The Celtics have benefited most from Allen, who admits he's made more concessions this season than all the others combined.

"I'm so happy with Ray," says Rivers. "He hasn't fought it.

"Our young guys are lucky to be around him. Too often these kids make it to the NBA and they settle. Ray won't let them."

Pierce says he plans to adopt some of Allen's eating habits and offseason workouts. But that's where he draws the line.

"If I had to stick to the exact same thing every day, I'd kill myself," Pierce says. "What happens if you go for your pregame meal and there's no more salmon in the freezer?

"I love Ray, but I don't get it. I'm not ever going to be at the free throw line saying, 'Damn, I didn't get my parking spot today.'"

The trio of stars has banged into each other throughout the long NBA season. Sometimes, they've even traded elbows. But, when that happens, Ray Allen has learned to retreat to his corner, regroup, and find a way to adapt.

The bubble he calls the Boston Celtics can get cluttered. Very cluttered. But, according to Ray's careful calculations, there is still plenty of space inside for a championship trophy.

Double Clutch

PIERCE STARS IN HIS MOMENT OF TRUTH

May 19, 2008 • by Bob Ryan

"The Truth" may be a reach, but he sure lived up to his Captain's title yesterday.

Paul Pierce brought his certified 'A' game to a deciding seventh game against the Cavaliers. He stood tall in the Cousy-Russell-Havlicek-Bird sense, picking the most propitious moment to play his best game of the 2008 playoffs.

"He just willed his team to victory," said Cleveland's LeBron James. "I know that was the breakout game he was waiting for."

Pierce could have said the same thing about LeBron, the ridiculously precocious 23-year-old who scored 45 points. With Pierce scoring 41, there were serious overtones of a much-discussed Game 7 against Atlanta 20 years ago featuring two Hall of Famers fully recognizable by first names only. But this personal shootout will stand on its own merits, given that they combined for a fairly amazin' 45 percent of the points in a 97-92 Celtics triumph that sends them into the Eastern Conference finals against those hardy perennials, the Detroit Pistons.

Pierce was not having a great series. He was held to 4 points in Game 1, and he averaged a mere 14 points a game in the three fruitless trips to Cleveland. The only reason you didn't hear all that much about this business was that everyone was focusing on Ray Allen's astonishing (ongoing) futility.

But Pierce took charge immediately yesterday, opening the day's scoring with a very difficult foul line jumper that, by any reasonable measure, was a force. But it went in, and so did the next one, and the next one (a second-chance three). He had 9 of the

first 14 Boston points as the Celtics moved to a 16-4 lead, a cushion they would exploit for the rest of the peculiar game in which the Cavaliers never led, were never even tied past 4-4, and yet were never out of.

This was an aggressive, but not reckless, Paul Pierce. You know how he goes into those wild spin-o-ramas, crashing into people in the vain hope of getting to the line? Nope, there was none of that yesterday. His six trips to the line (11 for 12) were the result of intelligent, confident, I'm-a-star-and-I-know-what-I'm-doing excursions to the hoop. And his shot selection? Just outstanding.

He had 26 by halftime, and that represented more than half of the Boston points as the Celtics moved to a 50-40 lead by intermission. He had 35 after three quarters, and, after sinking two professional jumpers in the first six minutes of the fourth, he concluded his afternoon and early evening's work with a pair of free throws with 7.9 seconds left (the first an up-and-in job he said must have been guided in by the "Ghost of Red") that closed the deal.

"Tonight was very simple," quipped Kevin Garnett. "Get the ball to Paul Pierce and get the hell out of the way. That's exactly what it was. No need for you all to ask me no questions. That was the game plan; this is what we did."

Garnett was only being mildly facetious. While there was never any intention for Pierce to score 42 percent of the team's points, it was in the head of Pierce and his coach that he be a bit more assertive than he was in most of this tedious series.

"I took a number of 15-footers I know I can make right there off the dribble," Pierce explained. "So I thought I was well within the flow of the offense. The ball was just coming to me. I felt great, and I was just letting it ride."

Every once in a while Pierce reminds us that he is the greatest pure scoring machine in Celtics history. Many old-timers bristle when you say that, citing John Havlicek, Sam Jones, Larry Bird, Kevin McHale, or whomever. But it just happens to be the truth.

He can get his own shot, which is a major plus. He is an extremely proficient, highly ambidextrous, driver. He takes a lot of free throws. He is a constant 3-point threat. And he is the best fast-break finisher the team has ever had. No argument.

"Before I came here I couldn't understand how he scored so well," acknowledged coach Doc Rivers.

"He didn't look that quick. But he's very strong, and he has great fundamental footwork. He's never in a hurry, and he knows exactly what he's trying to do. And he can shoot."

We might quibble with the "never in a hurry" part, but not with anything else. The man is simply a magnificent scorer.

"Paul Pierce is one of my favorite players," said James. "I always say, second to Kobe Bryant, he has some of the best footwork I've ever seen in a player. I love going against the best, and Paul Pierce is one of those guys."

His contributions were hardly limited to points. He had five assists and he provided the Celtics with a vital possession when he sniffed out man mountain Ilgauskas's intentions on a jump ball with James Posey, knocking Big Z's intended tip toward a teammate away, diving on the floor, and getting a necessary timeout with 58 seconds to play and the Celtics leading, 91-88.

"That was a big possession at the time," Pierce noted. "In the playoffs, you've got to treat every possession as if it's your last."

In a better world, Paul Pierce would be able to put his feet up and rest a spell. This Cleveland series was hard work.

"This is one of the tougher, if not the toughest, guys I guard," he said in reference to LeBron. "I'm glad this series is over. He wears you out. Your body is sore. It's massages. Hot tubs."

But the problem with going seven is that there is no rest. Detroit is here tomorrow night. Perhaps this time, a simple 20 or 25 will get the job done. But if any Celtic can get 40, it's Captain Paul Pierce.

A Return to Glory at The Garden

PIERCE SHAKES OFF INJURY TO PACE CELTICS, 98-88

June 6, 2008 • by Dan Shaughnessy

It goes down in Hub hardwood history as the Miracle on Causeway Street. Paul Pierce and his chariot of fire.

Bill Russell, Bob Cousy, and Larry Bird enjoyed some great moments in the old Boston gym, but not one of those Garden gods ever vaulted out of a wheelchair to lead the Celtics to victory in the NBA Finals.

That's what Paul Pierce did in Boston's 98-88 win over the Lakers in Game 1 last night. Carried off the floor midway through the third quarter, placed in a chair that made him look like an ER patient at Massachusetts General Hospital, Pierce returned after a 1-minute-45-second absence, drilled a couple of stake-driving 3-pointers, and willed the Green to victory.

Pierce clutched his right knee after collapsing in a heap under the basket near the Celtic bench.

"Once I heard a pop, I couldn't move it at first," said Pierce, who scored 22 points. "It went through my head—'Man, it can't be over like this.' . . . I thought that was it."

He rode a wheelchair to the Celtics' locker room, only to emerge seconds later to hit the crucial jumpers as the Celtics took the lead for keeps. Pierce made 5 of 5 from the floor in the same quarter in which he rode in the wheelchair.

"The guy grabbed his knee," said Celtics coach Doc Rivers. "It was great to see him come back. Him coming back lifted us up."

Seeing the Celtics and Lakers back in the NBA Finals triggered memories of bygone days when dinosaurs ruled the earth and basketball royalty ran on the parquet floor of the Old Boston Garden. Pro basketball's championship round has inflated to World Series/Super Bowl proportions since Boston and Los Angeles last met in the Finals in 1987, and there was considerable star power on the court and the sidelines when the Celtics and Lakers tapped off just after 9 p.m.

The pregame festivities were electric. Waiting 21 years will do that; the NBA is big on presentation and Boston was treated to all the trimmings in the Celtics' return to the Finals. It amounts to an audio/video assault of the senses, but nobody minds when the Celtics are being celebrated. Bill Russell and John Havlicek were among the Boston basketball royalty in the house. It was nice to have a championship game played on the Red Auerbach court.

Pau Gasol broke the lid for the first basket of the Finals. Garnett (24 points) tied it a minute later. A spectacular drive and dunk by Garnett made it 10-10 midway through the first as the crowd settled in for a night of thrills, chills, and spills. The Celtics led, 23-21, after one.

The benches went at one another at the start of the second and held serve until the starters returned. The Lakers led, 51-46, at intermission. Boston's vaunted defense allowed the Lakers to shoot 50 percent in the first half. The signs were all bad.

"We didn't play the defense that we played all year in that half," said Rivers. "They got a lot of open shots. We can be better defensively for two halves."

Pierce came out flying after halftime, scoring 7 straight points, but he went down when teammate Kendrick Perkins crashed into him on a Kobe Bryant drive to the basket. Pierce appeared to aggravate his right knee and things looked dire when he was carried off the floor.

Precisely 1:45 after leaving the court, Pierce reappeared from the tunnel and checked back into the game. A Festivus miracle. It was mildly reminiscent of Bird's return after slamming his face on the floor in a home playoff game against the Pacers in 1991.

"I thought he moved pretty well, but I was watching him closely," said Rivers. "He moved OK, so it was no big deal."

Pierce's crucial threes came in a span of 22 seconds. Boston led the rest of the way.

"What helped them out were those two threes that he hit, not coming back on the floor," said Lakers coach Phil Jackson.

That's not the way history will be written. In Game 1 of the 2008 Finals, Pierce created a memory worthy of the best of Kareem, Magic, Larry, or the Cooz.

'X' Marks the Spot for Powe

June 9, 2008 • by Bob Ryan

The X-factor guys are the ones who make it fun.

Everybody knows what the Pierces, Garnetts, Allens, and Bryants can, and probably will, do. That's why they get the eight-figure paychecks. But winning teams always, always, always need more than that.

Leon Powe is an X-factor for the Boston Celtics. That's when he's even given a chance to be the "X."

In the 10 games leading up to the NBA Finals, the 6-foot-8-inch kid from Cal played a total of 36 minutes, including three DNPs.

But last night he was needed, and boy, did he deliver.

Powe was the one-man energy source off Doc Rivers's bench, powering his way to 21 points in a mere 14:39 of playing time as the Celtics took a 2-0 lead with that roller-coasterish 108-102 triumph over the Los Angeles Lakers.

Long before the Lakers staged a sensational finish that almost stole the game from the home side, Powe had punished them inside with his relentless play.

Powe left the game after picking up his fourth foul with 5:56 to go, the Celtics leading, 96-80. And it was a bogus exit, too, since replays showed that referee Ken Mauer had completely blown the call. Powe had reached in to strip the ball from Derek Fisher, making no contact whatsoever.

This was his coming-out party for the national audience, but Celtics fans have known for two years now what an exciting, if still somewhat raw, talent he is. Powe can get a lot done, and it really doesn't matter who the foe is. He plays with a healthy disrespect, no matter who's on the other team.

Powe was the focal point of a Boston bench effort that turned a 22-20 deficit coming out of the first period into a 10-point (36-26) lead in the first four minutes and change of the second quarter.

That's when the game seemed to revolve around Powe. He got himself to the line three times in the first two minutes of period two, the third time the result of being fouled on one of his beautiful spin moves. He made five of those six freebies. And it was his traffic layup 3-point play that created the aforementioned 36-26 lead.

"Leon was terrific," said Rivers. "I thought he was terrific in Game 1, too. We made a concerted effort to get him the ball. We needed to start out the game that way. In the first six minutes, we established no post game. We actually had to go to Leon to establish a post game. So I was happy that Leon could do it."

Powe was on the floor for the game's most crucial sequence, a dazzling 11-0 blitz (consuming just 2:18) emanating from a timeout after the Lakers chopped a 16-point lead (65-49) to 9 at 68-59, his contribution being an alley-oop layup from Rajon Rondo that made it 79-59.

He followed that with two soaring dunks, the first on a fast break (81-59) and the second with 0.8 seconds remaining on a Rondo penetration feed. This one was in serious traffic.

That was all prelude to the "Leon Powe Show" in the first 4½ minutes of the fourth quarter. Powe brought the crowd to its feet on the first Boston possession when he beat the shot clock with an artful, running right-hand hook off the glass.

Then came two more hard-earned free throws, and then came the showstopper.

Taking a pass from Rondo in the backcourt, he headed straight for the basket against a Laker team that was supposed to be trapping. With just three dribbles he took it to the hoop, flew past Sasha Vujacic and Pau Gasol, and threw it down for points 19 and 20.

Phil Jackson was not pleased.

"Vladdy [Vladimir Radmanovich] had a trap in the backcourt and opened it up and Gasol was afraid to leave Kevin Garnett for an easy basket," said Jackson. "But it was a poor play, an awful play."

The Zen master wasn't too pleased about a whopping free throw discrepancy (38-10 FTAs in favor of Boston), submitting Powe as a reference point.

"I'm more struck at the fact that Leon Powe gets more foul shots than our whole team does in 14 minutes of playing time," he said. "That's ridiculous."

Phil can argue that his team should have gotten to the line more often, but he can't begrudge Powe his 13 free throws. He was Exhibit A of what effort, plus strong inside moves, can do for someone. There are times you look at him and say, "If only he were 6-11, he would be a monster," but it doesn't always work out that way. In all likelihood, he plays harder at 6-8 than he would at 6-11 or 7 feet. He has developed a game that suits Leon Powe, and it will keep him gainfully employed in the NBA for the next 10 or 12 years.

His resilience is amazing. He has stretches when he plays and stretches when he doesn't play, but he always keeps his spirits up and he is always ready when his number is called. This was the biggest game of his life, but he made it look like a January game against Charlotte.

He was last night's X-factor, and you can't win a title without them.

Seeing This Was Believing

June 13, 2008 • by Bob Ryan

LOS ANGELES—Now I've seen it all.

All season long this Celtics team has done improbable things, but this was the absolute showstopper. Did I really just see the Boston Celtics come from 24 points down after submitting a horror show of a first half and come back to defeat the Lakers in their own building?

I believe I did.

They did it by obliterating the Lakers by a fairly amazing 57-33 score in the second half. They did it by taking control of the game in the final six minutes, coming back from their last deficit (81-77) with a 15-6 run, capped by an icy left corner 3-pointer from James Posey, who lived up to the praise heaped upon him way back in the early part of the season by Pat Riley, who informed the Boston media that the Celtics would really come to love Posey when they saw him raining threes in the playoffs.

The 97-91 Celtics triumph gives them a 3-1 series lead and means that the 17th Boston championship, and first in 22 years, could come as early as Sunday night. But Doc Rivers doesn't want to talk about that.

"It's a great position to be in," Rivers pointed out. "But you have to win one game four times, you know what I'm saying?"

Yes, Coach, everyone knows. And everyone also knows that in order to win a championship, a team needs contributions from more than its stars, and last night's astonishing comeback was fueled by a pair of bench performers who picked a very nice time to have their best games of the playoffs.

First, there was Posey. The 6-foot-7-inch swingman threw in 18 points, 12 of which came on threes, the largest of which was that aforementioned shot from the left corner with 1:13 to go. That gave the Celtics a 92-87 lead, and if a good team is up by 5 with a little more than a minute to play, it generally knows how to close the deal.

And how about Eddie House? This guy had, in his own words, "fallen off the face of the earth" during these playoffs, racking up five DNPs and four other abbreviated situational appearances. But he never stopped working in practice, never complained (publicly, anyway), and, most importantly, never lost faith in himself. He kept telling himself that his time would come.

Last night was House's time. With 8:22 remaining in the third quarter, his team trailing by 18, Rivers made a decision. He put Posey in for P.J. Brown (who had himself replaced the injured Kendrick Perkins). A minute later, Rivers took out Rajon Rondo and put in House, which gave the Celtics a small lineup in which all five men were offensive threats. And that's the way it remained for the duration of the game.

"They were just trapping all over the floor," Rivers explained. "You know, they were trapping off Rajon, they were trapping off Perk early. I brought it up to our staff yesterday, probably a 50-50 split, and I just did it, honestly, because I thought we had to have floor spacing. Whether we made those shots from that point was up to us. But the trap stopped, the floor was spaced, and once the floor was spaced our scorers could score."

House was one of those scorers. He hit a 3-pointer as the Celtics closed the third with a ferocious 21-3 run in the final 6:04. And he hit a difficult right corner jumper with a hand in his face to give the Celtics their first (and nonrefundable) lead, 84-83, with 4:07 to play.

At that point it was rather difficult to comprehend that the Celtics had trailed in the first half by such scores as 20-6, 26-7, and 35-14 after one, or that they trailed by such scores as 37-17 and, finally, 45-21 in the second quarter.

The one word on everyone's lips was defense. It is the main reason the Celtics won 66 games during the regular season, and it was the best rationale for anyone to pick them to win this series. Every great comeback—and this was not only the greatest comeback win in Celtics playoff history but also the biggest known comeback in the 62-year history of the Finals—must begin and end with great defense.

The last possession of the third quarter might have exemplified it all. The Lakers had absolutely nowhere to go and the possession ended with Jordan Farmar, who had beaten the first-half buzzer with a banked running three—missing the basket by about 3 feet.

So what's not to like about this team? What other questions do the Celtics need to answer? "Just great mental toughness," said Rivers. "They just hung in together. We've been preaching 'leaning in.' When things get bad, lean into each other, all year, and tonight we did."

When the playoffs started, they needed 16 wins. Now they only need one. But this one should have counted as two.

Back on Top

17TH TEAM TITLE, FIRST SINCE '86

June 18, 2008 • by Bob Ryan

131-92.

Embrace it. Ogle it. Relish it.

But, above all, believe it.

The Boston Celtics did not just win franchise championship No. 17 last night. They snatched it. They swallowed it. They *demanded* it.

So they've done it. They have claimed the honor of having the greatest single-season turnaround in NBA history. One year ago today, the franchise could accurately be described as forlorn. The Celtics were coming off a 24-58 season punctuated by an 18-game losing streak. They had been cruelly treated by the draft lottery, which left them with nothing better than the fifth pick.

And now they are champions. Again.

Lordy, Lordy, what hath Danny and Doc wrought?

It was a wire-to-wire championship that began with a 103-83 dismissal of the Washington Wizards back on Nov. 2 and came to fruition at the TD Banknorth Garden with perhaps their greatest combination of offensive play, defensive play, bench play, and just plain basketball in any game of the entire 116-game exhibition/regular season/playoff season.

131-92.

The Celtics started the season 8-0. They had such records as 20-2, 40-9, and, finally, 66-16. They never trailed in any playoff series. They won every playoff game they *had* to win. And they saved their absolute best for last, blowing away the Western Conference champion Lakers with a truly phenomenal display of

While Paul Pierce clutches his Finals MVP trophy, the Celtics exult after clinching the franchise's 17th championship.

all-around basketball that left no doubt just which was the best basketball team in the known universe.

It was over at the half, when the Celtics went into the locker room up by 23 (58-35) after ending the second quarter with a 26-6 run. The second half was simply a glorious celebration of Boston Celtics basketball, and, specifically, of Three Amigos basketball. The lead grew and grew until the standard sellout crowd of 18,624 found itself looking at a scoreboard bearing the unimaginably happy news that the Celtics were actually 43 points ahead of the hated Left Coasters (129-86 on a Tony Allen reverse alley-oop dunk off an Eddie House feed with 1:22 remaining).

Even in a game with such a lopsided final score, there are key moments. The first key to this game was a first-quarter flurry from Kevin Garnett, who scored three straight baskets (a tough turnaround, a face-up jumper, and another tough turnaround) when LA led

by an 18-16 score. When he was done, the Celtics were up, 22-18, and they would never trail again.

The second key juncture came a little more than four minutes into the second quarter, with the Celtics clinging to a 32-29 lead. That's when bench energizers James Posey and Eddie House hit back-to-back threes to ignite that extraordinary 26-6 demonstration of Celtics basketball superiority.

Soon it was 43-29 and the building was reverberating with the vaunted "Beat LA" cheer. And then it was 53-35 on a scoop shot by the effervescent Rajon Rondo, who rebounded from an injury-plagued, almost wasted trip to Los Angeles with as spectacular a game as anyone could ask from a 22-year-old point guard (21 points, 7 rebounds, 8 assists, and 6 credited steals).

And then came the play that resoundingly emphasized it was Boston's night, and not LA's. Garnett (26 points, 14 rebounds, 4 assists) was

Paul Pierce, Doc Rivers, and Kevin Garnett embrace after clinching Banner 17.

already in a transcendent mode when he took a pass from series MVP Paul Pierce and banked home a pumping, hanging something-or-other for an old-fashioned 3-point play. It was Pierce's ninth assist of the half, and you want to talk N-O-I-S-E . . .

You've heard about two of the Three Amigos. The third wasn't bad, either. Ray Allen was off to a solid start when he was accidentally poked in the eye by Lamar Odom in the first quarter as he drove baseline. He went to the locker room and didn't re-emerge until the 6:05 mark of the second quarter. Allen finished with a Finals-record seven 3-pointers. That 13-game, 9-for-51 drought he had back in the middle of the playoffs seems like so much science fiction now, doesn't it?

But the most intriguing story of this game might very well have been the Other Guys. Rondo, of course, was magnificent. Kendrick Perkins didn't get much love from the officials, but he made himself known. That leaves the bench.

One great constant in this series was the way the bench play helped dictate the outcome. That was once again the case last night, as Doc Rivers's substitutes totally outplayed Phil Jackson's, with a particular emphasis on the second quarter. At the half, the Boston bench had 15 points, 9 rebounds, and 4

assists, compared with LA's totals of 9-0-0.

After 116 games, Rivers is still searching for a so-called rotation. Guess he doesn't need one. Old Reliable James Posey was his only bench staple, and Posey came through once again last night with 11 points (4-for-4 shooting) and flypaper D on the ineffective Kobe Bryant, who started off by scoring 11 points on 4-for-5 long-distance shooting in the first 6:31 and who shot 3-for-17 thereafter. Kobe went 22:20 without a field goal. He scored field goal No. 4 to put LA ahead, 13-12. When he scored field goal No. 5, it reduced the Laker deficit to 25 (73-48). You can supply your own punch line.

So there was Posey being Posey, but as the Celtics were putting the game away in the second quarter, guess who else was out there. Try Eddie House, who had been a completely forgotten entity for long stretches of the playoffs, and then try none other than Glen "Big Baby" Davis, who was summoned when P.J. Brown picked up his second foul in relief of Perkins, who, naturally, already had two himself.

Between them, House and Big Baby had racked up a combined 15 playoff DNPs. Big Baby had been DNP'd eight consecutive games, not seeing action since Game 4 against Detroit. But the beefy lad from LSU gave his team 14 valuable minutes, laying that big body on Pau Gasol, just as he had put it on luminaries such as Tim Duncan during the regular season.

What we had, ladies and gentlemen, was the first six-game sweep in NBA Finals history. The Celtics dominated the three games in Boston, and they absolutely, positively could have won all three games in LA. But isn't it fortunate for the fans that they didn't? How many times do home fans get to see an NBA coach get the Gatorade bucket treatment, as Rivers got from Pierce with 30 seconds to go?

131-92.

That's a score you'll never, ever forget.

The Survivor

After a decade of losing and a lifetime of obstacles, Paul Pierce finally vanquished his doubters and his attackers by winning on the court and growing up off it.

December 21, 2008 • by Neil Swidey

As the night winds down and the TV cameras and most of the A-list athletes and C-list celebrities have left, Paul Pierce makes his way out of the VIP room, its crimson walls covered with flat screens playing an endless loop of his late-night talk-show appearances. The hip-hop on this November night is still thumping at Kings, in the Back Bay, which is either supposed to be a bowling alley dressed up as a nightclub or a nightclub dressed up as a bowling alley. But for the first time during his charity bowl, Pierce has managed to break free from the coterie of female handlers and event planners who've been covering him better than Kobe or LeBron ever did, all the while furiously thumbing on their BlackBerries with the urgency of National Security Council staffers arranging a crisis briefing.

Wearing a black, military-style commando shirt that accentuates his career-best physique, Pierce is heading back to the lanes when he spots a tall white-haired gentleman carrying a bowling bag the same shade of tan as his slacks and walking alone toward the exit. Pierce pivots and heads over to the man.

Wrapping his arm around him, Pierce smiles and says in his raspy voice, "Thank you so much for coming, *Mr.* Havlicek."

John Havlicek's eyes light up behind his boxy glasses. He sets down his bowling bag and returns the hug.

It's a small moment. But it's more telling than the hug they had shared a few weeks earlier. On October 28, over the cheers of a packed Garden crowd, Havlicek handed over the NBA championship trophy to Pierce before the Boston Celtics' 17th world-title

banner was raised to the rafters. That moment was genuine, too, of course. No one without a SAG card can cry as uncontrollably as Pierce did during the banner-raising ceremony without it being genuine. But that exchange was also impossibly portentous and public. Havlicek, an undisputed legend who helped secure eight of those 17 banners, was officially welcoming Pierce into the club.

In contrast, this moment in the bowling alley was quiet and, as far as they knew, unrecorded for posterity. After his 10 long, mostly lean years as the face of the franchise, when all those banners looked down on him, a burden more than a benefit, Pierce was telling Havlicek how honored he was to have been granted admission.

"I respect our greats. I admire them," Pierce tells me later. "Now I'm part of that."

The 31-year-old laughs when I ask him if he expects the rest of us to address him as *Mr.* Pierce now. After all, it wasn't too long ago that he was known as much for his hotheaded moments on the court and his clubbing ways off it as he was for play so dazzling it would earn him the NBA Finals MVP trophy. But through all those years, he never stopped playing hard, never faked injuries like other high-salaried star athletes in this town who need not be mentioned by name (Manny), and never gave up on his community involvement or his ferocious desire to win. For his pivotal role in bringing green glory back to New England and for his perseverance through a decade when that seemed like a hopeless cause, he is our Bostonian of the Year.

We've seen him grow up right before our eyes, and it hasn't always been pretty. But in 2008, when the championship was only the capstone to a transformative year that made him a father and gave him new insight into the long-buried pain he felt as a son, we finally got to The Truth.

HE'D HAD ENOUGH.

Going into the 10th grade, Pierce wanted nothing more than to play varsity ball. He'd played JV his freshman year and barely got off the bench during summer league play. His friends told him he should be a starter. This is what high school ballplayers tell one another. So he transferred. He left Inglewood High School, down the street from where the Los Angeles Lakers played, and enrolled at nearby Crenshaw High.

His mother and his two brothers were having none of it. Jamal Hosey was older than Paul by 14 years, Steve Hosey by eight. They had a different father than Paul, but were brothers just the same. Their mom, Lorraine Hosey, had raised all three of them on her nurse's salary. And because the two older boys had used sports to avoid the minefields of their neighborhood and get to college on scholarship, they were Paul's role models. They never worried about their little brother's toughness. Once when Jamal put 6-year-old Paul in a headlock and demanded he cry uncle, the boy shot back, "You might as well just break my neck now, 'cause there's no way I'm gonna say uncle." But they did worry about his decision making.

"I came to a bump in the road, and my first instinct was to try to go around it," Pierce says now. "They encouraged me to face that bump and try to go over it."

Two weeks later, he transferred back to Inglewood High.

Flash-forward to the spring of 2007. Pierce had been with the Celtics for all nine of his NBA seasons. He'd seen players, coaches, and owners come and go. When Doc Rivers took over as coach in 2004, he'd demanded that Pierce, an All-Star, change his style of play. After half a season of shooting icy stares at his new coach, Pierce relented, agreeing to pass the ball more to all the untested young players around him. And where had it gotten him?

When Pierce went down with an injury, he was forced to watch from the bench as the storied Celtics became an NBA joke, losing 18 in a row. His friends were telling him it would never happen for him in Boston. If he wanted a ring, he'd have to leave.

He'd had enough.

He and his agent called a meeting with managing partners Wyc Grousbeck and Steve Pagliuca and general manager Danny Ainge. "I went into that meeting with a lot of fear," Pagliuca says now. "We didn't have a vision for winning here without Paul."

Grousbeck, known to wear a Pierce jersey to games before he bought the team in 2002, loved the guy's intensity. He liked to talk about the game against Phoenix that same year when Pierce got his two front teeth knocked out—the dental fragments landed next to Grousbeck's wife's courtside shoe—and he simply grabbed a mouth guard and went back in the game. (Pierce downplays the incident with a laugh: "It was more embarrassment than pain. I'm like, 'My goodness, I just lost my grill right here in front of 16,000 people!'")

But during the meeting, Pierce took the tack of the GM he hopes to be after he retires. A high draft pick at the end of the losing season could bring a title several years down the line. But that would be too late for Pierce. "If I was you all," he told them, "I'd take the pick and trade me for some other young pieces, and you've got your foundation."

The owners shot that down. Ainge vowed to find Pierce help, and the partners vowed to pay for it. The assurances were enough for Pierce. To the relief of his family once again, he faced that bump in the road head-on. Ainge then engineered the trades that replaced youthful promise for All-Star experience in the form of Ray Allen and Kevin Garnett. "The worst thing that could have happened for Paul was to get traded," says brother Jamal. "He didn't want to leave Boston as a loser."

Before this year, Pierce didn't know many perfect days. That had less to do with winning and losing than with how he defined perfection: being at practice. "The gym was my sanctuary," he says. "The place where you could forget about all your worries, your problems, people asking you for money, people asking you to do this, do that." Still, practice lasted only so long.

This year, his definition of perfection changed. "Now it's lying on the floor with my daughter, rolling around, playing with her. When she looks at me and starts smiling, I forget that I went 0 for 15, or I lost the game."

Prianna Lee was born eight months ago. Pierce's fiancee, Julie Landrum, had been set on the name Piper, until Pierce came up with Prianna. Pierce and Landrum began dating during All-Star weekend in Houston in 2006. Both Pierce and his family credit her with helping bring stability to his life.

"He's just a much more settled person," says brother Steve. "Now," Jamal says, "he prefers to be around his family rather than his boys."

When he cradles Prianna in his arms, the troubles of the day magically go away, but he can't help but ponder the biggest unanswered question from deep in his past: Why did his father, George Pierce, walk out of his life when Paul was just a few years old and never come back?

"It's crazy," he says, "how people just don't care sometimes about the kids they have."

When Pierce was a college star at Kansas, he received a letter from his father's sister, saying she wanted to help him. Pierce was widely predicted to be a high lottery pick in the NBA Draft. "At the time, you got so many people coming at you. They want to give you gifts, want to do things for you," he says. "And she was just one of them. I felt that was his way of using her to creep back into my life."

Pierce ignored the letter. He didn't need any help then.

In September 2000, when Pierce was attacked and stabbed nearly to death after an argument at a Boston nightclub, his family rushed to his bedside at what is now Tufts Medical Center. (He would later help fund the hospital's Center for Minimally Invasive Surgery, which bears his name.) Cards and phone calls poured in from around the country. But nothing from his father. "That's what hurt me the most," Pierce says, his eyes filling with tears that somehow manage to stay in. "Not hearing from him at all. Like it didn't matter if I had died or not." He finds himself wondering how his life might have been different if his dad had been involved in it. For the first time, his father is helping serve as a model—but not in the usual way. "I want to be the dad that my father never was."

Still, this past summer he told his mother he wants to reconnect with his father one day. "There's definitely some things that I want to ask him," he says. "If I didn't have a daughter, I probably wouldn't do it. But one day she's going to ask about who her grandfather is, and I want to be able to tell her something." (From his home in California, George Pierce told me, "Paul wants to call me, he can call me. I have no problem with that.")

When Pierce was in the ninth grade, Magic Johnson drove past him in his black Mercedes with tinted windows. Magic didn't see Pierce, but Pierce saw him. "I was like, *Dang!* I got all excited, just because I got a glimpse of him."

Pierce, who now drives his own Mercedes—white, with tinted windows—thinks about that experience whenever he talks to kids. "Going into a classroom, you know they're going to listen," he says. "If my mom had told me, 'You go to school and you can be president,' I'd be like, 'Yah.' But if Magic had told me, I'd be like, '*For real?!*'"

The charity bowl in November was the official launch of his new health initiative aimed at reducing obesity among inner-city kids. It was also a relaunch of Pierce himself. After a decade of viewing him as the embodiment of unrealized potential, of towering talent that could somehow never measure up, it was finally possible to envision Paul Pierce as a Celtics Legend of tomorrow. Close your eyes, and you can picture him with gray hair, attending the charity event of some as-yet-unborn Celtics star, doing his best to groove to another generation's music as the 68-year-old Havlicek had done earlier in the night, when he wasn't trading fist-bumps with the 20-somethings crowded around him.

Mr. Pierce.

Great Lengths

Celtics establish team mark with 19th win in a row.

December 24, 2008 • by Frank Dell'Apa

Among the Celtics' mantras this season is taking games one at a time. But their fans were not buying into that last night, chanting "Beat LA" late in the final quarter of a 110-91 win over the Philadelphia 76ers, the Celtics' franchise-record 19th consecutive victory.

At 27-2, the Celtics also surpassed the NBA record for best start shared by Philadelphia (1967) and New York (1970), which began seasons with 26 victories in 29 games.

There was some symmetry to this milestone, the Sixers having snapped the 1982 Celtics' 18-game streak with a 116-98 win March 22, 1982, then going on to eliminate them in a seven-game playoff series.

The Celtics improved to 17-1 at home with their 12th straight win at TD Banknorth Garden, a sendoff for a four-game trip that begins tomorrow against the Los Angeles Lakers.

A Kevin Garnett 18-footer signaled the start of a 10-2 Celtic spree that gave them a 58-44 lead at the half.

The Sixers pulled within 60-50 on Samuel Dalembert's jumper 2:55 into the second half. Then a 14-2 Celtic run over a 3:24 span extended the lead to

74-52, capped by Garnett's left-handed tip of a Paul Pierce lob with 4:32 left in the third quarter.

The Sixers responded with 10 successive points and a 14-4 spree, concluding the quarter with Marreese Speights's dunk to cut their deficit to 78-66 with 21 seconds to play.

The Celtics' second unit, plus Ray Allen, got off to an 11-4 start in the first 4:26 of the final quarter. Leon Powe's free throw for an 89-70 advantage with 7:47 remaining made Doc Rivers feel secure enough to replace Ray Allen with Gabe Pruitt, who confirmed that faith with a 3-pointer for a 93-71 lead with 6:57 to play.

The "Beat LA" chants started soon after that.

Taking Charge of It Is Cool with Him

April 29, 2009 • by Marc J. Spears

Walking with a slight limp while dressed in expensive blue jeans, a lime polo shirt, and a hard-to-find Louis Vuitton fisherman's hat, Paul Pierce was an interesting vision of cool after he got off work last night.

The mother of teammate Ray Allen ran up to him and gave him a hug. Several fans behind barricades begged for his autograph. One even began clapping as Pierce was whisked away from TD Banknorth Garden by Celtics director of security Phil Lynch.

As cool as The Truth may have played it, the excitement of the people he passed on his way out was more than warranted, as his latest in a long list of great performances may have saved the defending champions' injury-riddled season.

Pierce scored 15 of his 26 points in the fourth quarter and overtime to spark the Celtics to a 106-104 victory over the Bulls in Game 5 of a wild first-round series. The Celtics enter Game 6 in Chicago tomorrow with a chance to end this amazing series in large part because of the cool Pierce's late hot hand.

"Obviously, Paul, the shots he made down the stretch were huge," said coach Doc Rivers. "He got to his spots."

Sure, Pierce also had a great performance with 24 points in a Game 3 victory at Chicago. But other than that, he hasn't been his normal unstoppable offensive self for most of this series.

Pierce entered Game 5 averaging a team-best 23.5 points in the series but was shooting only 43 percent from the field, averaging just 5 free throws per game, and with a total of 15 turnovers. Even with the Bulls missing supposed Pierce stopper Luol Deng, he seemed affected by the athleticism of the Chicagoans.

The Celtics were down, 70-66, entering the fourth quarter with Pierce struggling to find his game. He had 11 points on 5-of-13 shooting and hadn't attempted a free throw.

"I don't think it was something that was taken away," Pierce said. "If I go back and look, I know there were a couple shots where I was mad at myself that were open shots that I know I could make. I missed a layup at the end of the second quarter. I wasn't able to get to the line."

The Celtics' season looked to be in serious jeopardy when the Bulls jumped ahead, 77-66, after a Noah lay-in with 9:28 remaining. Though the gritty Celtics trimmed it to 83-80 following an Allen 3-pointer with 5:45 left, the sharpshooter fouled out of the game 18 seconds later.

From that point on, Pierce felt it was time to take over in solo fashion, as he did in the days before the Big Three.

"I thought I had some great looks," Pierce said. "I missed a couple wide-open threes that I had, missed a couple layups. I never got down over the shots I missed because I thought a lot of them were good shots. I just knew before long they would fall."

His lay-in with 1:13 remaining in the fourth quarter tied the game at 91. With Boston down, 93-91, and 10.5 seconds left, he nailed a 15-foot jumper to tie the game again. He scored 9 points in the fourth and nailed all three free throws.

Two stepback jumpers of 16 and 19 feet over John Salmons pushed Boston ahead, 104-101, in OT, and with the game tied in the final seconds, Pierce continued hitting his trademark midrange jumper with a 19-foot pull-up game-winner with 3.4 seconds left.

"I just thought I didn't overpenetrate tonight," Pierce said. "I took my time. I got some space off the dribble. I got into my sweet spot and got the shot."

Said Salmons, "He hit some shots. He hit three contested shots. They went to him a little bit more down the stretch."

After a postgame interview, Pierce ran through the tunnel, with adoring fans hoping to get a high five or some other type of acknowledgment. In Joe Namath fashion, he ran by as if it all was supposed to happen that way, while holding up a No. 1 sign.

Other than Kobe Bryant, there may not be a player in the league more confident than Pierce. So even with his offensive struggles in this series, deep down the captain always felt he would figure it out when it counted the most. No wonder he seemed so cool on his way home.

Raging Bulls Drop Celtics, Force Game 7

May 1, 2009 • by Frank Dell'Apa

CHICAGO—The gods of overtime got some payback on the Celtics last night. Or maybe just the odds of overtime are playing catch-up.

In their first triple-overtime game in the playoffs in 33 years, the Celtics fell to the Bulls, 128-127, and extended their first-round playoff series to tomorrow's climactic Game 7 in Boston.

This is the first NBA playoff series to include four OT games, and Game 6 showed once again how evenly matched the teams have become, and also how the Celtics' killer instincts seem to have deserted them.

Ray Allen scored 51 points, converting a team playoff record nine 3-pointers, including one to tie the score, 118-118, sending things to a third overtime.

The Celtics lost three starters—Glen Davis, Kendrick Perkins, and Paul Pierce—to disqualifications, and squandered chances to make an improbable rally in the final OT.

Brad Miller provided the deciding point with a free throw with 28.3 seconds remaining. The Celtics cut the deficit to 1 as Rajon Rondo followed his own miss 4.6 seconds later. Then the Celtics had two chances to recover. After Kirk Hinrich missed a layup on an inbounds play, the Celtics called time

out with 16.7 seconds to go. Derrick Rose blocked Rondo's shot, then was fouled by Brian Scalabrine with 3.2 seconds on the clock. Rose missed both free throws, and Rondo launched a shot off the backboard at the buzzer.

The Celtics had seemed on the verge of concluding the series with an 18-point run over a five-minute span late in regulation. But they squandered a 99-91 advantage, Miller providing the tying points on a 3-pointer with 1:06 remaining and a layup with 29 seconds left.

"With an 8-point lead, if you're a good defensive team, all you have to do is play defense," Celtics coach Doc Rivers said. "You don't have to score again. You literally don't have to score again. But we didn't do that.

"We just stopped playing. We had a chance to close it out. We saw that score and we just stopped playing."

The Celtics took the lead in all three overtimes. But unlike their 128-126 win over the Phoenix Suns in the 1976 NBA Finals, they could not hold on.

Enjoying Sights of the Seven C's

May 3, 2009 • by Dan Shaughnessy

Did Derrick Rose and friends really have a chance last night? This was, after all, a seventh and deciding game in Boston against the Celtics.

There's Game 7 magic in those parquet panel floorboards. If you take it to the limit against the Celtics, you should be prepared to suffocate in the North End Vault. Beating the Celtics in a Game 7 in the Garden is like beating a Kennedy in a Massachusetts election.

After six games of blood and thunder—including seven overtimes, multiple sutures, and 108 lead changes, the Celtics gored the Bulls in the finale, 109-99, in a game that lacked the drama of most of the series.

"We've done it before," said captain Paul Pierce. "We were confident coming into our building in Game 7."

Since 1957, the Celtics are 17-3 at home in seventh games. Bill Russell was 10-0 in Game 7s.

Blessed with hearts as large as Big Baby's head, these depleted defending champs now advance to the Eastern Conference semifinals. After the Bruins play Game 2 of their series with Carolina tonight, the Celtics open Round 2 tomorrow night at home against Superman Dwight Howard and the Orlando Magic. So even though the Bulls are done, the bull gang is going to be very busy in the big barn on Causeway Street.

"I'm proud of our guys," said Doc Rivers. "The Bulls were phenomenal in this series, but I'm really proud of our entire team. Our bench hadn't given us much, but they came through tonight."

Amen, Doctor. Eddie House torched the Bulls, hitting 5 of 5 floor shots, four of them from 3-point range. Pine brother Jackie Moon Scalabrine added 8 points and the Celtics got unexpected help from missing persons Stephon Marbury and Mikki Moore.

There is no "I" in ubuntu.

There was significant pregame anxiety about the finale because Chicago proved to be perhaps the toughest No. 7 seed in the history of basketball and the Celtics were again playing without their 21st century Russell: Kevin Garnett.

The faux ambiguity regarding Garnett's status dominated the 36 hours leading to Game 7. It was wacky and ridiculous. Based on all statements and evidence, there was no way Garnett was going to play. Still, we wondered. No matter how many times Danny Ainge and Rivers closed the door on Garnett's return, the topic resurfaced. It was downright Elvis-like. Would KG burst out of the locker room at 8 p.m. and carry the Celtics into the second round?

No. There was no KG during warm-ups. There was no KG running out for introductions. When he finally appeared he was dressed in a beautifully tailored suit.

Garnett had a front-row seat to see the Celtics fall behind by 9 early in the second quarter. Scal

kick-started the comeback with a missile launched from international waters and the Celtics took the lead for good when House stole a Ben Gordon pass, then drained a trey off a give-and-go play with Rajon Rondo.

That was it. The Bulls never got closer than 3 the rest of the way, which made this game an absolute aberration . . . and a reprieve for Ainge and the rest of us who got heart palpitations watching the first six games. Ultimately, it looked like both squads were somewhat spent.

It ended at 11:03 p.m. with House tossing the ball high above courtside in the general direction of the 1968 championship banner.

So what did we learn from these seven games spaced over 15 days?

We learned that the Celtics are worthy champions. With Garnett sidelined and Leon Powe KO'd in Game 1, the 2009 playoffs have the feel of a quixotic quest, but that has not deterred the C's. We all know that the conference finals are going through LeBrontown this year and the Cavaliers look unbeatable. But the Celtics refuse to die.

We learned that Rajon Rondo is officially one of the best point guards in the NBA.

We also learned that anything is possible in this world of video review. Chicago's Ben Gordon canned a long-range jumper in the first quarter, which was ruled a 2-point shot at the moment of execution. Amazingly, with 5:44 left in the game, it was announced that Gordon's first-quarter shot was actually a 3-pointer and the fourth quarter score was changed from 89-83 to 89-84.

This is somewhat akin to Bud Selig tomorrow announcing that the St. Louis Cardinals actually won the 1985 World Series because video shows that Don Denkinger messed up a call in Game 6. Scary stuff, no?

But we digress. The Celtics are moving on. The Bulls are done and the bull gang is just getting warmed up.

The Stubborn, Impatient, Self-Centered, and Absolutely Essential Rajon Rondo

Even on a team full of superstars, the 23-year-old point guard has quickly risen to the status of indispensable. But he still has a lot of growing up to do. Now that the Celtics have put their faith in him with a new contract extension, can he emerge as the player they need him to be?

November 15, 2009 • by Charles P. Pierce

All great athletes create a permanence within themselves. So much else is out of their control. From the time they show promise, they are judged from afar, their future writ in scribbles on some distant clipboard. What other people think of them can be more important than what they know about themselves. Their professional lives can depend on the whim of a coach or the thin, fragile strands of the ligaments in the human knee. What is often decried as selfishness or stubbornness in an athlete is nothing more than an attempt to assert something solid at the heart of a world they cannot control. They create the permanence in their lives within themselves—*their* game, *their* talent—as a hedge against the gleaming evanescence of the careers those talents have brought. And, of all our sports, basketball is the least permanent.

People who are old enough to remember the first National Basketball Association championship won by the Boston Celtics, in 1957, also are old enough to remember that the team's point guard, Bob Cousy, was regularly derided as a "showboat" because he had the audacity to dribble the ball behind his back. Today, given the strength and speed of modern NBA players, someone like, say, Rajon Rondo—who plays the same position for the Celtics that Cousy did— cannot function as an NBA point guard without being able to do that. Someone who dribbles behind his back doesn't even draw a gasp from the crowd anymore. It took less than 40 years for the NBA to get from the two-handed set shot to Michael Jordan. By contrast, it took baseball nearly a century just to develop the relief pitcher. Even basketball's

fundamentals are not fundamental. They evolve. It is harder for basketball players to create that permanence within themselves, so when they do, they hold tight to it against an accelerated existence.

It's mid-October, and Rajon Rondo was still negotiating his future with the team. "This is a business," Rondo explains, his eyes flickering over the shoulder of the person to whom he's talking, taking in everything going on as his teammates shoot free throws and crack wise with one another out on the court beyond. There is a shrewdness in the compass of his gaze, and a kind of universal comprehension. And he measures every word, every thought by the syllable. He reveals very little, but he misses nothing.

"It's never permanent," he continues. "The next generation of Celtics? Naw, I don't think like that. You can't guarantee anything in this league. There's a total of, I think, six guys who have played their entire careers for one team. I mean, Kevin [Garnett, his Celtics teammate] has been traded. It may have been his option, but he got traded. Ray [Allen] got traded. Those are future Hall of Fame players. A couple of summers ago, Kobe [Bryant, the star of the Los Angeles Lakers] was about to be traded, supposedly to Denver. Nobody in this league is guaranteed to be in one place."

By most standards, these shouldn't have been matters of any concern to him. Rondo is 23 and starting his fourth year with the Celtics. Since battling his way into the starting lineup as point guard—the player responsible for controlling the offense that must flow through Garnett, Allen, and Paul Pierce, the team's three stars—Rondo has developed into a recognized force in the NBA. During the 2008 championship season, he blossomed most fully in the playoffs; in the deciding sixth game against the Lakers, Rondo was clearly the best player on the floor, with 21 points, seven rebounds, eight assists, and six steals. That continued through last season, when he almost single-handedly got the Celtics through a surprisingly tough opening-round series against the Chicago Bulls and became the only Celtic besides Larry Bird to put up three triple-doubles—points, rebounds, and assists—in the same postseason. He has the big house in Lincoln and the baby daughter. He is settled, it seems, at first glance.

And throughout, he has become unquestionably the most vividly athletic player on the team. Garnett

Rajon Rondo was both extraordinary and enigmatic during his nine seasons as a Celtic.

$2.09 million this year. On October 27, Rondo's agent announced that the Celtics and Rondo could not reach an agreement to extend his contract with the team. It appeared that Rondo would be a restricted free agent at the end of this season. However, on November 1, the two sides agreed on a five-year extension that will pay Rondo the $55 million he was asking for in the first place. For a month, Rondo seemed to be in a preposterous position—a young man who is absolutely vital to a team's success, yet about whom the team seemed to have had amorphous, long-term doubts.

The roundelay about his future began in June, after the Celtics were eliminated from the playoffs by the Orlando Magic. There were rumors that Rondo had arrived late

is an emotional cyclone and Allen has his spun-gold jump shot. Pierce has a dozen ways to score he hasn't tried yet. But it is Rondo who brings people out of their seats. Defensively, he appears to be possessed of the same kind of athletic clairvoyance—in reality, a kind of hyperattuned anticipation—that Bird once had on offense. There were plays in which Bird would throw a pass, and the lane that he saw instantly was visible to the casual viewer only in the slow-motion replays. Flashing for an interception, Rondo can be just as sudden and startling. With Garnett, Allen, and Pierce all over 30, Rondo would seem to be perfectly positioned to be the unchallenged star of whatever is the next iteration of the Boston Celtics.

And yet . . .

With him, there is always "and yet."

He began training camp this fall in the last year of a rookie contract that would have paid him

for a playoff game and that he'd had something of a chronic tardiness problem throughout the season. (Enterprising souls then dredged up difficulties Rondo had playing for Tubby Smith at the University of Kentucky.) Celtics general manager Danny Ainge took the unusual step of confirming the rumors. He went on the radio and said that Rondo had to grow up. Rondo's agent fired back at Ainge, who also had said that Rondo was "a player we want to have on our team." This is, of course, a very interesting statement. It has a loophole in the middle of it through which you can drive a luxury automobile. To New Jersey, say. Or Memphis.

As the 2009 NBA Draft approached, talk intensified that the Celtics were trying to deal Rondo. The most plausible scenario involved a multi-player package with the Detroit Pistons, but there were others, and Rondo was aware of them. The NBA grapevine is hung thick with BlackBerrys, and every player has one. Rondo heard about the Detroit deal while he was returning to Boston on the train from New York. "I wasn't really bothered by it," he says. "I heard about a lot of trades that didn't get to the media; I heard Sacramento, New Jersey. A lot of them were just rumors, probably from other players."

There is more to him than there appears to be at first glance. On the court, headband slung low, he seems to be someone's skinny younger brother. Up close, at 6-1 and 178 pounds, he is considerably more formidable. He seems to be wired together with iron cables. His hands are huge and supple. And his eyes miss absolutely nothing. "I'm pretty secure," he muses. "It might not be here, but I'm pretty secure that I can play in the NBA for 10 or 14 more years."

In the end, there was no trade, and he is still in Boston. He won.

It looks very much like the place he belongs. It is one of the first practices of the year, and someone drains a long jump shot to win for Rondo's team, and the guard goes bouncing around to all his team-mates, dropping his head on their shoulders and laughing at everyone on the other team.

"Rondo's fine," Doc Rivers says during that mid-October practice, as the point guard ducks down the hallway, trying to avoid paying the coach what he owes on a truly terrible college football bet. (Rondo took Kentucky. Rivers took Florida. Kentucky should give Rondo an Alumnus of the Year Award for that kind of loyalty.) "Unfortunately for Rondo, he's on a high-profile basketball team. The reason we lose is never going to be Kevin, or Paul, or Ray. Who's the next guy? Rondo," Rivers says. "Unfortunately, it seems that people look two ways at him—the reason that the Celtics win is because of the way that Rajon Rondo plays, and the reason that the Celtics lose is because of the way Rajon Rondo plays. He has to answer to both of those all the time, and that's a bind, because there's no way around that. Truth be told, the reason we win is because the Big Three play like the Big Three.

"But it goes to that fourth guy because he's who everybody targets, even the opposing team. Like Orlando, in the playoffs last year. They said, 'We're going to make him beat us.' He'll get that this year, too, and each year he's handled that better.

"Rondo's a good kid," Rivers adds. "That's one thing people don't get. He's a stubborn kid, a moody kid. He's all of these things, but I've dealt with a lot

of kids so far in coaching who were like that, and they weren't good kids. That's the saving grace for him—he's a good kid, and he wants to do right, so I'm not concerned by the times he's stubborn and immature. He's still young."

Rivers was frustrated when the trade rumors leaked in June, not least because they threatened the special relationship he'd been building with his point guard. In 1983, as a rookie point guard with the Atlanta Hawks, Rivers struggled to please coach Mike Fratello, a martinet who since has gone on to a career as a broadcaster. "I remember feeling picked on," Rivers recalls. "Fratello used words toward me that I'd never heard before. What you realize is that I'm that important. If I can take it, everybody can take it. I probably am tough on point guards because I am one.

"If we can win, the point guard did something right," Rivers says. "That's one thing I always stay on Rondo about—it can't ever be about your show. It can't ever be about you establishing yourself as one of the great point guards. Winning will establish that. This year, he has a chance to do that. Now, if we win it, it'll be because of Rondo's play."

The two of them hash out their differences in the open, along the sidelines, in full view of the entire crowd. "I don't know what it's like anywhere else, because he's the only coach I've played for at this level," Rondo says. "It's just being the point guard. It comes with the territory. Not just at this level, either, although this is a bigger stage. It's the role I've played throughout my entire career in sports. I just got a bigger stage now."

That's only one of the relationships, however, albeit a vital one, in the life that Rajon Rondo is living today. There is also the one he has with the business institution that is the Boston Celtics. There is also the one he has with his own history, throughout which he has clung fiercely (arguably, too fiercely) to the permanence that he has built within himself—through his game, his talent—as his life sped up around him.

Amber Rondo worked the third shift, 11 at night until 8 in the morning, making cigarettes for Philip Morris at the company's plant in Louisville. Each day, she left her three sons with one unbreakable rule. Once the street lights came on in the neighborhood of College Court, the outer boundary of their world became the front porch of the house. So the front porch of the house at Seventh and Kentucky became the de facto recreation center for Rajon, his two brothers, their cousin Jermaine Bentley, and all their friends. And central to everything was Connect Four, a Milton Bradley game from 1974, an upright version of tic-tac-toe checkers in which the first player to get four of his pieces in a row—vertically, horizontally, or diagonally—is the winner. The sessions went on for hours. If Rajon was losing, they went on ever longer. "Connect Four, I was pretty much the man," he says today. "I ran a couple guys here. You can ask Mr. Allen—talking about Ray there. You can ask a couple of kids. They came to watch practice, and they ended up getting beat."

"He just wants to be the best at everything," Jermaine Bentley explains. "I remember that from Connect Four."

When they all hit Meyzeek Middle School, it was Bentley who was the basketball star. Rondo's heart was in football. He lived for the contact, and he loved how, as the quarterback, he was the focal point of any team on which he played. However, when Bentley began to play basketball in an open gym program run at Eastern High School by Doug Bibby, the school's coach, Rondo tagged along. "The first time I saw him," Bibby says, "I knew he could be an incredible ballplayer, because it was open gym, and he was in eighth grade, and he was pretty much dominating the game against young adults."

Bibby came from a basketball family. His uncle Henry Bibby was an NBA point guard and the coach at the University of Southern California. His cousin Mike Bibby was a first-team All-American at Arizona and currently plays the point for the Atlanta Hawks. Also, at the University of Richmond, Bibby's father coached Kevin Eastman, who is currently a Celtics assistant coach, and another cousin is married to Eddie House, who backs up Rondo at the point in Boston. "Rajon was real thin, but he was wiry strong," recalls Bibby, who brought Rondo to Eastern to play. In one week of informal summer pickup games, Rondo absorbed Bibby's entire system, but he bristled at criticism, and Bibby had to suspend him a couple of times.

"At first it threw me," Bibby admits. "But I recognized how intelligent the kid was. Some coaches can look at that as bucking the system, but what I had to do was to step back. By the beginning of his

sophomore year, he wasn't just an extension of me. It was like he was my assistant coach."

However, after three years, Doug Bibby left Eastern High, and he and Rondo decided that the latter would play his senior season at Oak Hill Academy, a legendary basketball power tucked away in rural Mouth of Wilson, Virginia. "I didn't know how difficult it was going to be until I went there," Rondo says. "It was kind of like a boarding school, and the first few months were difficult, because we couldn't go off campus. It was a nine-hour drive from home. You had to grow up and be a man, because there was no family at all, so we had to become accustomed to each other. It was the middle of nowhere. Nothing works. The closest airport was Charlotte, which is two hours. The closest McDonald's was an hour and a half."

Nevertheless, Oak Hill's reputation as a finishing school for basketball players guaranteed that college coaches found out how to get there. The first time that Rondo played a pickup game, there were 30 coaches in the gym, most of them looking at Josh Smith, a vastly talented forward who'd already made it clear he was going to forgo college and move right into the NBA Draft. (Smith now plays for the Atlanta Hawks.) For his part, Rondo managed to turn heads mostly through his speed and toughness, and his defensive ability.

"When he came to us," recalls Steve Smith, the longtime coach at Oak Hill, "he was probably borderline Top 100. After about a month, I thought, 'This guy's really good.' He had those huge hands and that long wingspan." During that season, Smith took Oak Hill to Barcelona to play against some Spanish teams. In one game, with Josh Smith in foul trouble, Rondo put up 55 points, many of them against Sergio Rodriguez, a Spanish star who now plays for Portland in the NBA.

"You try to go into a game figuring any guy can embarrass you," Rondo explains. "He can be better than you on a single night if he's on. You don't want that to happen to you."

In 2004, Rondo was recruited by the University of Kentucky, and he played two seasons there, chafing under the patterned offensive system favored by then-coach Tubby Smith. Rondo wanted to run, and Smith didn't want him to, and the two clashed regularly, with Smith benching Rondo for six games. It was here that Rondo's reputation for stubbornness, and for uncoachability, was born, even as he led the Southeastern Conference in assists as a sophomore. (Now at the University of Minnesota, Smith declined to return phone calls for this story.) When Rondo decided to declare for the 2006 NBA Draft, more than a few people at Kentucky were not sad to see him leave.

"At Kentucky, we ran a system," Rondo says today, measuring his words by the syllable. "All five guys touch the ball and we pound it in to the bigs. My style is that it's better for me to get out on the break and get it to my teammates." That was what Danny Ainge saw in Rondo that prompted him to trade for his rights after the 2006 NBA Draft. "I saw an instinctiveness that you can't teach," Ainge says.

Rondo joined a Celtics team that was something of a mess. He was one of three point guards on a team that went a dismal 24-58. He was stubborn. He was impatient. He bridled somewhat at criticism from Rivers and at what he saw as his limited playing time. However, in the offseason, things happened. Ray Allen came to town. Then the Celtics traded what seemed like half their roster for Kevin Garnett. Rondo was not part of the deal.

"When the trade happened, and I was still here, that's when I knew," he says. "I was home in Louisville when we got Kevin in that seven-player trade. Danny called me and I was like, 'OK, it's my time now.'"

The championship followed that spring, and Rondo, playing with more and more confidence as the season went along, began to make his individual mark around the league. (Steve Nash, the star point guard for Phoenix, was particularly extravagant in his praise of Rondo, with whom he shares an agent.) By the beginning of last season, Rondo had established himself as a genuine NBA star, albeit still a work in progress. Then the trade rumors started again.

"I was flabbergasted," says Danny Ainge, the Celtics GM's eyes popping wide in mock shock, a look familiar to NBA referees in his playing days back in the 1980s. "I read the headlines: 'Ainge Rips Rondo.' What do you mean? All I said was that he needed to be more consistent. It was brought to my attention that other people knew that the media knew he was late to a playoff game. All I said was that those things are unacceptable. We expect

Rondo to be our point guard for a decade, but he's not ready to be anointed yet."

And the loopholes yawned wide yet again, whether in the latticework passive voice describing Rondo's tardiness last year, or in the phrase "we expect" to have him here for a decade. Absent the deal struck at the beginning of the month, Rondo's future with the Celtics could not have helped but be a point of contention as this season progressed. When negotiations on the extension initially fell apart, it meant not only that Rondo would have joined the ludicrously talented free agent field of 2010—which includes LeBron James of Cleveland and Dwyane Wade of Miami—but also that he would have had to play extraordinarily well for a team that might not have wanted to keep him if he wanted to get paid like the rest of that class. Now, even though he has his new deal, he will play for the team by playing for himself. He's stubborn that way.

He's still the future of a team with a considerable past that, as William Faulkner once said, is not even past. It's still there as Garnett rouses the crowd or Allen drains a jump shot or Pierce battles his way to the basket. And on the perimeter, eyes moving, missing nothing, Rajon Rondo looks to pick something off for himself—the ball, a moment, a career. That's what's permanent with him—motion, constant and perpetual.

His Packing the Box Score Was Great Stuff

May 10, 2010 • by Dan Shaughnessy

This was beyond stardom and fullcourt dominance. This was more than most of the guys in the rafters ever did. This was in the Cousy, Havlicek, Bird arena. Actually, it was better.

Put it this way: Four games have been played between the Celtics and Cavaliers and Rajon Rondo is enjoying a much better series than the best player in the world.

The Celtics squared the conference semifinals (the only NBA series currently worth watching) yesterday with a 97-87 victory over the stunned and overrated Cavaliers. Boston's all-galactic guard scored 29 points with an astounding 18 rebounds and 13 assists. In four games against the Cavs he is averaging 21.8 points, 8.3 rebounds, and 13 assists. And 42 minutes.

LeBron James was good for a mere 22 points on 7-for-18 shooting in Game 4. Guess the elbow was hurting again. You know how it works. When LeBron rains 38 on your head he's healthy, but when he disappears two days later (seven turnovers), he must be hurting.

Rondo, meanwhile, never sleeps. He had 27 points and 12 assists in Game 1. He had 19 assists in 45 minutes in Game 2. He was a mortal 18-point scorer when the Celtics got blown out in Game 3, but yesterday the Cavaliers felt his full fury. He was the Roadrunner, beating Cleveland baseline to baseline. Rondo was on the floor for all but 72 seconds.

Some perspective: According to a release handed out by the Celtics after the game, "Rondo's performance today was only the third time in NBA history that a player accumulated points, rebounds, and assists totals of that level in an NBA playoff game." The awkwardly worded release cited Oscar Robertson (32 points, 19 rebounds, 13 assists March 26, 1963) and Wilt Chamberlain (29 points, 36 rebounds, 13 assists April 11, 1967).

Everybody's favorite Rondo moment came late in the third quarter when he got out in front of a fast break and abused LeBron with a rock-the-cradle, behind-the-back pass to Tony Allen for a thunder dunk that broke a 70-70 tie.

"[James] is always chasing me down and he's blocked some of my layups," said Rondo. "Baby [Glen Davis] made a great pass. I knew LeBron was coming. I had to sell it like I was making a layup. He jumped, and I made the pass."

"If he would have laid it up, I would have had it," said James. "That's why he went behind the back."

Sometimes it's hard to believe Rondo is only 6 feet 1 inch. It's hard to believe he's only 24, with four years in the league. It's hard to believe he was a candidate for benching after a horrible Game 5 in the Finals against the Lakers two years ago. It's hard to remember he was in Danny Ainge's doghouse just over a year ago.

"He's a point guard that runs our team and has complete control of our team," said Celtics coach Doc Rivers. "When he won it, he was still trying to figure out how to be a point guard. Now we rely on him to win."

They rely on him in part because Paul "Big Papi" Pierce (they even share the same number) has been a no-show for most of this series. Pierce scored 9 points and had two rebounds in 31 minutes of Game 4. That made more work for Rondo.

"I feel for him at times," said Rivers. "With our foul trouble, his rest periods are taken away. What doesn't show up on the stats is his ball pressure. I thought that was the biggest difference. It allowed us to do other things. To me, that might have been the hardest thing he had to do."

What about his Bird-like box score?

"I didn't know till after the game," Rondo said. "I didn't know I had that many rebounds. I just tried to be aggressive. I just tried to help the bigs as much as possible. Everyone played great. It was a collective team effort. I had a couple of numbers, but the big thing was we got the win.

"I'm just trying to become more of a leader. We still look up to the Big Three. That's why I get so many open looks and try to capitalize on mistakes the defense makes. I'm very confident at what I do. I just have to keep maturing. The starting five has been together for three years now and we're getting a better feel for each other."

James said he would guard Rondo, if asked.

"I would love to," said the King. "It's something that maybe we should explore, because Rondo has definitely dominated the series. If the coaching staff wants me to do it, I would do it."

LeBron James wants to guard Rajon Rondo. That's what it's come to. Makes you look forward to Game 5 tomorrow night and Game 6 back at the Garden Thursday.

Celtics Put Cavs and James in Rearview Mirror

May 14, 2010 • by Julian Benbow

He sounded increasingly crazy every time he said it.

When the Celtics killed the momentum of a huge win with a staggeringly confusing loss, coach Doc Rivers said, "I like this team."

When injuries derailed a 23-5 start and forced him to patch together lineups night to night, Rivers said, "We like who we are."

When the window on an era seemed to be shutting and when the Celtics looked like they couldn't be further from a championship, sliding down to the fourth seed as the regular season ended, Rivers said, "I think we're close."

"I know it sounds crazy," Rivers said last night. "But I thought we were phenomenal in training camp. I thought we looked better in training camp than we did two years ago, quite honestly. As a team, I thought we were close, we started out great and then obviously we fell apart with injuries and all kinds of other issues, but you could see that everybody wanted to get back. It was tough the last three weeks of the season because we had to make a choice."

Rivers was more than transparent about his plan. He would bet the fate of the season on the hope that he could get the Celtics to the playoffs healthy.

"It was the only bet," Rivers said. "That was the only way we're going to be able to try to win this is by guys being healthy."

Facing the league's best team, with the challenge of stifling the league's best player, LeBron James, the Celtics were largely considered a long shot in these Eastern Conference semifinals. After overwhelming the Cavaliers in last night's 94-85 series-clinching victory in Game 6, Rivers and the Celtics looked like the smartest people in TD Garden.

"The big thing with Doc, he just kept faith," said Kendrick Perkins. "I know we ended the regular season on a bad note, but at the end of the day it starts over in the playoffs. We came together at the right time in the playoffs. All it takes is a couple of games to get your stride back and guys were locked in."

The Celtics executed early, piling pressure on James, who for 48 hours had to deal with speculation the homegrown superstar would be playing his final game for a city he gave a face to the past seven years.

The urgency was there—the first time James touched the ball, he made a beeline for the rim, flushing the ball with two hands and hanging on the rim for emphasis. The aggressiveness was there, too—James took eight of Cleveland's first 20 shots,

at times trying to sneak into the paint for easier looks. But James's jumper was still missing.

James had taken four perimeter shots through the 10-minute mark of the fourth quarter, clanging all of them. Then he pulled up from 25 feet.

Swish.

He came down again and pulled up from the same distance.

Swish.

With two shots, a Cleveland team that had to claw just to stay in the game suddenly had its first ounce of momentum.

Then Paul Pierce (13 points), who had hit a pair of third-quarter 3-pointers that were like a right-left combo to the Cavs' chest, drilled one from 25 feet with 7:55 left in the fourth, leaving Cleveland coach Mike Brown with no choice but to call a timeout.

Momentum killed.

James said during the regular season that the Celtics didn't look like a bad team, only a bored one.

"They've got a lot of veteran players," James said. "They have a lot of playoff experience and it worked for them."

Everything the Celtics did funneled through either Kevin Garnett (22 points, 12 rebounds) or Rajon Rondo (21 points, 12 assists). Garnett continued to toy with Antawn Jamison, who completely melted in the burning light of the postseason. The Celtics went up, 88-74, after Garnett threw down a dunk on a fast break. From there it was just a matter of time.

With the Orlando Magic rested and waiting, they couldn't bask in the victory, but they could reflect.

Ray Allen looked back at the trade deadline, when the uncertainty surrounding the Celtics couldn't have been higher.

"At the trade deadline, Doc addressed what was going on in the media," Allen said. "He just told us as a team, he likes this team. He likes who we are with this team. So we always as a team liked who we were. We didn't worry about, we lost this game, we lost that game. As a team we were still a very formidable team and there were a lot of teams around the league playoff-wise that were afraid of us come playoff time. Rightfully so. Cleveland, we sent them home."

In Sports History, Nothing Can Rival It

June 2, 2010 • by Bob Ryan

The Celtics and Lakers already have met more times to decide a major American sports championship than any two clubs have in any of our four major team sports, and now they are about to play for a 12th time. How could anyone not be at least a little bit engulfed in this history?

Where would Celtics history be without Selvy's (Missed) Shot, Cooz's Last Game, the Balloon Game, Henderson Steals The Ball, The Great Takedown, the Heat Game, the Great '08 Comeback, and, of course, 131-92?

Where would Lakers history be without Elgin scoring 61, West scoring 40 again and again and again, Kareem's '85 Redemption, and the "Junior, Junior Sky Hook"? Sure, the Los Angeles list is a bit shorter. The Lakers are 2-9 against the Celtics in Finals. Of course the list is shorter.

When this rivalry began, the Lakers were still in the Land of 10,000 Lakes. (Why they never changed the nickname when they headed westward in 1960 has never satisfactorily been explained.) The year was 1959, and the Minneapolis Lakers had no chance whatsoever against Bill Russell, Bob Cousy, Tom Heinsohn, Bill Sharman, Frank Ramsey, Jim Loscutoff, and the Jones Boys, all of whom, save Loscy, are in the Hall of Fame (and Loscy has his name/No. 18 retired). All the Lakers had to offer was a sensational rookie named Elgin Baylor, and, as great as he was, that wasn't enough to challenge the Celtics, who pulled off the first four-game sweep in NBA Finals history.

That mismatch aside, the rivalry we will celebrate for the 11th time encompasses three distinct eras, and it tells us a lot about how the NBA has grown and how spoiled we have all become. I mean, you don't like a 9 p.m. EDT starting time? Back in the '60s, if the game from LA was on TV at all, it would start at 8 o'clock PDT, which means 11 here. Don't like it? Don't watch.

Of course, not to watch was to miss seeing the greatest team-sport player in North American history. For the '60s belonged to Bill Russell, who was undefeated against the Lakers and 9-1 overall in championships sought and won. The Lakers had Baylor, who merely invented modern offensive basketball with his astonishing array of pumps, double-pumps, and up-and-under moves that forever changed the concept of what shooting a basketball could entail. They also had Jerry West, the Logo, who played with a ferocity, dignity, and, of course, an extraordinary skill that earned him universal respect. Good Lord, even *Johnny Most* could not bring himself to utter a negative word about the man he called "Gentleman Jerry."

With the help of such accomplices as Rudy LaRusso (dubbed "Roughhouse Rudy" by Most, obviously unimpressed with Rudy's Dartmouth pedigree), Dick Barnett, Frank Selvy, Hot Rod Hundley, Tom Hawkins, Leroy Ellis, Gail Goodrich, etc., Messrs. Baylor and West reached the Finals six times between 1962 and 1969, and six times they were turned back by the Celtics. The confrontations in 1962, 1966, and 1969 all went seven. The Lakers were in all three Game 7s, losing by 3 (OT), 2, and 2.

Seven lousy little points over 149 minutes. And there was no doubt in anyone's mind what the ultimate difference in these two teams was. He wore No. 6.

"You had to change your complete game because of Russell," lamented Fred Schaus, the losing coach in 1962, 1963, 1965, and 1966.

The truly legendary Chick Hearn broadcast all those games. "If Russell had been the Lakers center," Hearn sighed, "they would have won the ballgames the Celtics did."

THE ONE-SIDED '60S

The Lakers coulda/shoulda/woulda won in 1962, and who knows how that would have affected their psyche for the remainder of the decade? Baylor scored a then-record 61 points (still the non-OT standard) in Game 5, sending Boston back to LA, trailing, 3-2. But the Celtics won Game 6. In Game 7, the Lakers had the last shot in regulation with the score tied, but Selvy missed a left-side jumper estimated at 8 to 12 feet (no video exists), and Russell grabbed the rebound, one of his 40 for the evening, to go with a personal playoff career high of 30 points; 30 and 40 gives young fellers such as Dwight Howard something to shoot for, wouldn't you say? Anyway, the

Celtics prevailed, 110-107, to win title No. 5 in their run of 11 in 13 years.

A year later, the Celtics would win in six as Cousy limped back onto the court with a sprained ankle to steady the troops in his final game. Two years after that, the Celtics smashed the Lakers in five, which was understandable since Baylor had a knee injury that would hamper him the rest of his career, and West likewise had a bad leg. Of course, Gentleman Jerry also averaged 40.

A gallant Laker team came from 3-1 down in 1966 to tie the series, but Game 7 was in Boston and there was no way Russell was going to lose what was going to be Red Auerbach's last game. Neither team made it to the final series in 1967, but the league took a vote and decided to hold the Finals anyway. A year later, Boston defeated the Lakers for a fifth time in the decade, with John Havlicek scoring 40 points in the Game 6 clincher.

The next one really hurt.

LA had loaded up in the offseason, bringing in the inimitable Wilt Chamberlain to augment West and what was left of Baylor. The Majestic Three averaged a combined 70 points per game during the regular season, and they made the Lakers a clear favorite to win their first LA title, especially since their nemesis on the East Coast had barely qualified for the playoffs, finishing fourth in the East.

But guess who was waiting for them in the Finals? Yeah, that dastardly No. 6, plus his aged associates.

West asserted himself with 53 in Game 1, but LA won by only 2. It was indeed 2-0, LA, after the first two in the newly opened Fabulous Forum, and no team ever had won an NBA series after losing the first two games. The key was Game 4. LA led by a point, but the Celtics had the last shot. Havlicek and Larry Siegfried suggested an old Ohio State play that would involve setting a triple pick for 35-year-old Sam Jones, their best clutch shooter. He stumbled as he took Havlicek's pass, but managed to get off a shot that bounced on the rim a few times as a certain purple-clad 7-footer watched with interest.

"He was just waiting there like a vulture to gather the ball in when it fell off the rim," said Havlicek of Wilt. "But it fell in."

It all came down to a Game 7 in LA. Lakers owner Jack Kent Cooke, a flamboyant fellow, had his building ready for the expected celebration.

Havlicek somehow obtained a copy of the in-house itinerary, and he read it off to his teammates: the USC band, the balloons that would be released from the roof, the champagne, etc.

With Don Nelson making a fortuitous shot to put the Celtics ahead by a needed 3 with just over a minute to play, the Celtics won yet another title by a 108-106 score. West was distraught.

"Most years we played them, they were better than we were," he said. "But in '69, they were not better. Period.

"I don't care how many times we played it, they were not better. We were better. Period. And we didn't win. That was the toughest one."

Jerry West had scored 53, 41, 34, 40, 26, 39 and, finally, 42 (to go with 13 rebounds and 12 assists), and still had come up empty. No wonder he was so morose.

TURNING POINT IN THE '80S

Much had changed by the time the rivalry entered its second phase 15 years later. In the '60s, it was all about the basketball, specifically, the Laker frustration in being unable to defeat Bill Russell. But by 1984, the Lakers had become entrenched as a major part of the Southern California culture and had become identified as an auxiliary arm of the town's major industry, which was entertainment. The Celtics, meanwhile, entered the 1984 Finals against the Lakers as cultural ambassadors for the tried-and-true approach to the sport.

The Laker Girls pioneered the idea of mixing a little abstract sex and glamour into the NBA. The Celtics wouldn't have a dance team for another 23 years. The Lakers had a guy named Dancing Barry who sashayed down the aisle each night in the fourth quarter. The Celtics were years away from a harmless mascot called "Lucky." The Lakers warmed up to Randy Newman's "I Love LA." The Celtics stuck to an organist.

The Lakers had Magic.

The Celtics had Bird.

The Celtics had K.C. Jones, whose flamboyance was limited to singing a few songs at piano bars.

The Lakers had Pat Riley, who wore Armani suits, slicked his hair back, and introduced jargon such as "focus" and "skirmishes" and "hidden agendas."

And everyone hated everyone. Oh, it was great.

It was all different now. Boston fans regarded Laker fans as come-late, leave-early dilettantes who wouldn't know a pick-and-roll from a pick and shovel. Laker fans thought Boston fans were get-a-life geeks who cared too much about what was only, after all, a game. Laker fans wanted to be oohed and aahed en route to victory. Magic was their man. Celtics fans wanted to see someone hit the cutter in stride. No frills. Larry was their guy.

"Back in the old days," agrees the Los Angeles Times' Mark Heisler, then, as now, a first-rate observer of the NBA scene, "it was sport for sport's sake. It wasn't a test of your culture."

But that was the backdrop of the 1984 Finals, which easily could have been an LA sweep had a) Gerald Henderson not stolen a foolish James Worthy pass and scored to send Game 2 into OT (eventually won on a Scott Wedman jumper) and b) Kevin McHale, acting completely out of character, had not viciously brought down Kurt Rambis on a sneakaway in Game 4. This display of aggression emboldened the Celtics and somehow unnerved the Lakers.

From the minute that series ended with a Boston Game 7 victory, Pat Riley began plotting revenge. He was a charter Celtics-hater from way back, anyway, and now he had become obsessed with those monsters in green and white.

"On the subject of the Boston Celtics, Riley was virulent," says Heisler. Well, OK, then.

But there was still a need for a final epiphany, and it came with what became known as the "Memorial Day Massacre," a 148-114 Boston victory in Game 1 of the 1985 Finals. It took place on a Monday, and on Tuesday and Wednesday, Riley was merciless, making his team watch the tape over and over while questioning their testosterone level.

Taking all this the hardest was Kareem Abdul-Jabbar, who had been ineffective in Game 1. He came out for Game 2 energized and determined, and when the LA win was over, he had scored 30 points and grabbed 17 rebounds, which matched his high total of the previous 10 years! Ten days later, he led his team to a Game 6 victory that gave the Lakers their first-ever series win over the Celtics and earned him the Finals MVP award.

"They are not the Fakers any more," proclaimed M.L. Carr. "They are the Lakers. They are real, and have to be believed. They are the champs."

"This removes the most odious sentence in the English language," said Lakers owner Jerry Buss. "It can never be said that the Lakers have never beaten the Celtics."

But the ramifications went further.

"All Laker history dates from those two days between Games 1 and 2," maintains Heisler. "What took place then not only won them the title in 1985, but also set up the next two in '87 and '88."

The highlight of 1987 was Game 4. Leading, 2-1, the Lakers were outplayed by the Celtics for 46-plus minutes, trailing by 16 with just under 17 minutes to play, by 8 with 3:29 to go, by 6 with 1:50 left, and, finally, by 1 in the waning seconds. That's when Magic Johnson made a left-to-right perambulation across the lane before launching a 13-foot hook over both Kevin McHale and Robert Parish for the game-winning basket.

"A junior, junior skyhook," Magic called it. He could just as easily have called it a dagger in the heart of the Celtics, who would lose the series in six.

ONE MORE TIME

That closed the books on these two until 2008. This time, the high-powered Lakers, led by a virtuoso named Kobe Bryant, took on the traditional-model Celtics.

The Celtics had home-court advantage and went up, 2-0. Again, Game 4 was crucial. LA was up by 24 in the third before the Celtics made one of the greatest comebacks in their history. The Celtics won that game and pretty much established that they would not be beaten. But no one foresaw the shocking events of Game 6, when the Lakers capitulated after getting down by 20 at the half, losing by a 131-92 score that may very well serve as a motivational tool when the two resume play tomorrow night.

The dynamics haven't changed since the Bird-Magic Era. The Lakers have the glam coach, 10-time champion Phil Jackson. The Celtics have an underrated mentor in Glenn "Doc" Rivers, who seeks no undue attention, makes no inflammatory comments, and shrewdly deflects all praise toward his players.

The fan contrast hasn't changed a bit. If anything, it's only gotten bigger. Boston fans still think LA fans are frauds (with the exception of the extremely loyal and eternally cool Jack Nicholson) and Laker fans still don't understand why Boston fans care so much.

There is nothing in the NBA like it. Truthfully, there is nothing in sports like it. Red Sox and Yankees fans are essentially the same people. That is not the case here. We're talking Pluto vs. Venus.

Orlando vs. Phoenix might very well have been a nice basketball series. But the league can have that anytime. It's a lot more fun when it's the Celtics and the Lakers. Welcome to Chapter 12.

Allen Puts on Historic Shooting Display

He sets record with eight treys.

June 7, 2010 • by Bob Hohler

LOS ANGELES—The script seemed tailor-made for a stocky guy styling courtside in the designer shades. Yo, that guy, "Rocky" Stallone.

Three nights after Ray Allen sat helplessly foul-ridden on the Celtics bench, Allen last night played the avenger, rising from basketball's version of the canvas with such record-setting force that he changed the course of the championship series.

Pow. Allen all but KO'd the Lakers defense single-handedly as he struck for 32 points, including a Finals-record eight 3-pointers to power the Celtics to a series-tying 103-94 victory in Game 2 at a sold-out Staples Center.

It was a world title fight, as basketball audiences in 215 countries witnessed Allen's televised masterwork. The game was broadcast in 41 languages, and you could all but imagine the superlatives tossed Allen's way in every tongue from Togo to South Philly.

"He's a master of his art," Glen Davis said as the Celtics prepared to jet home in far better position than before Allen's remarkable performance.

Allen's eight treys, including seven in the first half, broke the record for the

NBA Finals shared by himself, Scottie Pippen, and Kenny Smith.

"Obviously, Ray was the catalyst for us," said Paul Pierce, whose diminished offense (10 points on 2-for-11 shooting) was offset by Allen's excellence.

When Allen sank a 25-footer on a pass from Davis with 3:57 to go in the third quarter for his eighth trey, he eclipsed the seven 3-pointers he sank in the championship-clinching Game 6 in 2008 against the Lakers. Pippen hit his seven June 6, 1997, for the Bulls against the Jazz, after Smith sank seven for the Rockets June 7, 1995, against the Magic.

Allen also had shared the record for six 3-pointers in a half in a championship series before he hit his seventh in the second quarter. He had shared the record with Smith and Michael Jordan, who hit his six in a magnificent performance in Game 1 of the 1992 Finals against Portland.

"I do remember that, and Mike, I'm going to tell him that his were a lot easier," Allen said. "He wasn't running off screens. He was just shooting the ball

The referee's signal tells the story: Ray Allen was on fire in Game 6 of the 2010 Finals, hitting eight 3-pointers.

and had it going. As a child, those were some of my favorite memories, being a fan of MJ and the things he did in the playoffs and the Finals. That's something that's going to stand out in my mind for the rest of my life."

Allen, who scored only 12 points as he played fewer than 28 minutes because of foul trouble in Game 1, helped to compensate not only for Pierce's meager scoring but a second straight sluggish offensive performance from Boston's bigs, particularly Kevin Garnett (6 points and four rebounds in 23:43).

"He carried us the whole way," Rajon Rondo said of Allen. "Guys were in foul trouble, and we were playing on the edge, but he helped us get through it. It was fun to watch."

Allen finished shooting 8 for 11 from 3-point range and 11 for 20 overall. He hit both his free throw attempts, added two assists, and grabbed three rebounds. In a stunning turnaround, Allen hit his first seven threes after the Celtics sank only 1 of 10 3-point attempts in Game 1.

"When he gets into one of those zones . . . I was happy," Celtics coach Doc Rivers said. "Our team could see it and you could see they were doing everything they could to find him. They got him open."

Allen toyed with three defenders: Derek Fisher, Shannon Brown, and Kobe Bryant.

"The other night was frustrating," Allen said. "Bigs created screens for me today. Rondo pushed the ball in transition, we got a lot more fast-break opportunities this time than we did in Game 1. We got stops and we were able to run, so the three ball did go in the air definitely a little more."

Allen's threes helped the Celtics open a 14-point lead in the first half before the Lakers cut the difference to 6 at the half. At one point, he seemed so pleased with making a three that he smiled heading back down court.

"I was just thinking about going back to Game 1, just having that feeling of being resilient as a team," he said. "When I got that three, it was a sense of calmness and reward that I knew I had at that moment."

Yo, Ray, how did it really feel after the game?

"Great to be able to look at it and say I did that," he said. "This is definitely the time. This is definitely our time."

Bench Gives Boston Plenty to Shout About

June 11, 2010 • by Dan Shaughnessy

Nobody puts Baby in a corner.

On the night Glen Davis was drafted three years ago, Danny Ainge spoke of Big Baby having "big upside," and we chortled and said, "Yeah, sure. Big backside, too."

Last night, Baby and his fellow subs ran the Celtics to a 96-89 victory over the Lakers in Game 4 of the NBA Finals, squaring the series at 2-2.

"I just felt like a beast," said Davis. "There's not too many times you get to be part of something so great. I just couldn't be denied."

Baby was good for 18 points and four offensive rebounds (five total) in 22 minutes. There were moments when it looked as if he had consumed every can of Red Bull in New England. He even drooled after one play.

Is that cool or gross . . . Big Baby drooling?

"When you're in the moment, you're in the moment," said Davis.

Red Auerbach basically invented the concept of keeping good players (Frank Ramsey, John Havlicek, Kevin McHale) on the bench at the start of a game. Baby and Friends—Nate Robinson, Rasheed Wallace, and Tony Allen—paid homage to the Pine Brothers of parquet past, building an 11-point fourth-quarter lead after the Celtics trailed (by as many as 8) for most of the first three quarters.

The burst from the bench saved the Celtics' season: No NBA team has recovered from a 3-1 deficit in the Finals.

So now it comes down to a best-of-three. The Celtics will close down the Garden Sunday night, and the NBA championship will be won in Los Angeles Tuesday or Thursday. I don't know about you, but I could watch these two teams play from now until August.

No Banner

Celtics' quest comes to a frustrating end in Game 7.

June 18, 2010 • by Dan Shaughnessy

LOS ANGELES—For a while it looked as if maybe they'd be smoking victory cigars in a champagne-soaked visitors' locker room at Staples Center.

But then the Celtics wilted, turned into pumpkins, and suddenly there was gold and purple confetti raining down on their heads.

The Los Angeles Lakers beat the Celtics, 83-79, in Game 7 of the NBA Finals last night, purging a few of those Green Ghosts of decades past. Series MVP Kobe Bryant scored 23 points, but made only 6 of 24 shots in a game that was utterly lacking in grace and flow.

"I told my guys after the game I couldn't be more proud of the group than any I've ever been around," said Celtics coach Doc Rivers, who hasn't decided if he wants to come back for 2011. "We're not going to be the same team next year. Guys are going to not be there, so that was tough for me."

In some ways it felt like high school graduation night. Boston's New Big Three Era is probably over. It yielded one championship and another trip to the Finals, where the fourth-seeded Celtics overcame many obstacles and almost willed themselves to an 18th championship.

"There's a lot of crying in our locker room and a lot of people who care," said Rivers. "I don't think there was a dry eye. A lot of hugs, a lot of people feeling awful. That's a good thing. That means everybody cared."

This was a game the Celtics could have won. They led the Lakers by 13 points in the second half, and led, 57-53, going into the fourth. But they came up short, figuratively and literally. They missed center Kendrick Perkins, who tore ligaments in his knee in Game 6. They went as far as they could go with Rasheed Wallace and Glen Davis, but they were outrebounded, 53-40, and the team that won the rebounding battle won every game of this grueling series.

The frustrating loss came two years to the day that this same group beat the Lakers to win banner No. 17. Those Lakers were humiliated by 39 points in Game 6, and their team bus was rocked by rowdy Celtics fans on the streets outside the Garden.

In 1985, Lakers coach Pat Riley spoke of defeating the "mythology of the Celtics," and this Laker group faced the same challenge. The 2010 Lakers had to be worried that the old-guard Celtics were somehow going to stagger ahead again, but it did not happen this time. In the end, the Lakers had the mental toughness necessary to win a close Game 7.

The tone was set early. It looked as if Joey Crawford, Danny Crawford, and Scott Foster had been sent from league headquarters with a directive to swallow their whistles. The rules were pretty simple: no blood, no foul. The zebras were letting the fellas play and this helped Boston immensely.

What hurt the Celtics was their inability to keep the Lakers away from second shots. Los Angeles worked for an astounding 10 offensive rebounds in the first quarter. Still, the Lakers couldn't penetrate Tom Thibodeau's defense (the Celtics are really going to miss this guy) and Boston led, 23-14, after one.

The Lakers burst out of the blocks with an 11-0 run to start the second, taking a 25-23 lead when Ron Artest went over a pair of Celtics for another follow-up bucket.

Paul Pierce got in the zone after that and the Celtics were able to grind their way to a 40-34 lead at intermission. Kobe had 8 points on 3-for-14 shooting at halftime. The Lakers also missed 6 of 12 free throws in the first two quarters.

A runner by Rajon Rondo made it 47-36 in the third minute of the third and forced Lakers coach Phil Jackson to call a rare timeout. At that moment, Kobe was 3 for 16 from the floor and it felt as if we were watching a silent movie at Staples. The Last Picture Show. Boston's lead peaked at 13, but we all know the Celtics blew a lot of second-half, double-digit leads in 2010.

The Lakers cut the margin to 4 at the end of three. Kobe was 5 for 20 in the first three quarters, while Ray Allen was staring at 1 for 9.

Derek Fisher tied it with a three midway through the fourth. At 5:56, Kobe made two free throws to give the Lakers their first lead since 25-23.

The Celtics couldn't convert late in the fourth and the Lakers went up by 6 with a minute and a half left. Rondo and Wallace (starting in place of Perkins) hit a couple of treys, but it was too late.

Jackson had his 11th championship (two more than Red Auerbach), Kobe finally had a Finals win over the Celtics, and we witnessed the end of ubuntu on the floor of the Staples Center in downtown Los Angeles.

Quite an Attraction in the Center Ring

August 5, 2010 • by Bob Ryan

Shaq, too?

Let the jokes begin.

Instead of a bench, the Celtics will have a couch. No, make that easy chairs and hassocks. All team meals will be Early Bird Specials. A typical player anecdote begins, "So I said to Dr. Naismith . . . "

The 2011 Boston Celtics won't be a basketball team. They will be a walking hoop museum. Among them, Shaquille O'Neal, Kevin Garnett, Ray Allen, Paul Pierce, and Jermaine O'Neal have a combined total of 71 years of service, good for 5,655 regular-season and playoff games and 200,371 minutes. They have combined for 51 All-Star Game appearances. They have 10 All-NBA third-team selections, eight second-team selections, and 12 first-team selections. If honors and plaques were all that mattered, we could book the parade right now, Miami Heat or no Miami Heat.

It goes without saying, of course, that they also lead the league in O'Neals.

But seriously, folks . . .

Danny Ainge certainly has guts and imagination. What if someone had told you at the conclusion of the 2007 season that, by the summer of 2010, among the people they'd have seen wearing a Celtics uniform would be Kevin Garnett, Ray Allen, Sam Cassell, Rasheed Wallace, Jermaine O'Neal, and now Shaquille O'Neal, and let's not forget Nate Robinson? I know I would have said something like, "Sure, and the next thing you'll tell me is that LeBron James, Dwyane Wade, and Chris Bosh will all be playing for the same team."

But how many times must I remind you that in the matter of Truth vs. Fiction, you'd always be wise to take Truth, plus the points, every time? Those two highly unlikely scenarios have indeed come to pass.

Yup, Shaq is now ours for two seasons. If the Heat didn't exist in their current form, the Celtics would be the most talked-about team in the league.

What the Celtics are getting is a 38-year-old, 7-foot-1-inch, 300-and-whatever-pound guy who still commands a great deal of attention once he is passed the basketball in the low post. That's where he operates, and don't you forget it.

Shaq never got the memo that seems to have been passed around to just about every other big man, be he domestic or foreign, during the past 20-some years, said memo informing those large fellows that it was no longer necessary to perform with one's back to the basket. Hence the onslaught of 7-foot jump shooters with zero pivot moves.

Shaq is a pleasant exception. Here is a big man—no, a BIG man—who walks, struts, flexes, and generally acts as a big man. Shaq's idea of great fun always has been to plant that large posterior into the chest of a defender, back the hapless foe in the direction of the basket as far as he could, and then dunk in the guy's face. That, plus a reasonably broad assortment of little banks and turnarounds, is how he has become the second-best percentage shooter of all-time. That's how Shaq came into the league and that's how he will leave it.

Even at his advanced age, Shaq is still an effective scorer. He averaged 12 points and 6.7 rebounds in 23 minutes a game last year for Cleveland. In the 24 games prior to Feb. 25, when he injured his thumb against the Celtics and missed the remainder of the regular season, he scored in double figures 22 times. In fact, he was coming off back-to-back 20-point games. He still knows what he's doing in that low post.

The free throws? The free throws are the free throws; there's nothing much you can do about that. You have to live with Hack-a-Shaq tactics late in games.

The downside is when the ball changes hands. Things are fine if Shaq is guarding someone close to the basket. The problem is that the NBA has become a pick-and-roll league, and it's a common belief that Shaq is the worst pick-and-roll defender there is. And that Kendrick Perkins is one of the very best. The Celtics have been built on defense the past three years, and figuring out how to factor in Shaq is something that will occupy a great deal of Lawrence Frank's time now that he is inheriting the Tom Thibodeau role.

So it's a plus-minus/risk-reward situation. There will be a large element of Shaq giveth vs. Shaq taketh away to the story, with the Celtics gambling that there will be an advantage leaning toward the giveth.

Remember, always, that so much of what transpires in team sports depends on context. By signing Shaq, the implication on the part of the Celtics is that they have the proper mix of teammates to maximize Shaq's assets while minimizing his deficiencies.

Much will depend on Shaq's attitude, naturally. It has to be humbling for him to know that not many teams were interested in his services, just as it must be humbling for him to be playing for relative chump change, i.e., the veteran's exception, in the $1.4 million range.

He went to Cleveland billed as the final piece of the puzzle (leading him to proclaim that he had come in to get "a ring for the king"), but now he comes here as sort of an insurance policy. 'Tis said you can't have too many starting pitchers, nor can you have too many "bigs," as Doc Rivers likes to say. Shaq is here to be a generic "big," albeit one with a glittering résumé.

Boston could be an ideal place for him to spend his sunset years. Surely Red Auerbach, who once upon a time provided late-career employment for the likes of Clyde Lovellette and Wayne Embry, would have approved of the idea.

Shaq should like it here. He undoubtedly will plug himself into the tradition, and he will get himself around town. The "Names and Faces" folks will be on constant alert (the folks at Symphony Hall should book him for a "Night Before Christmas" Pops reading right now).

All that aside, look at it this way: The Celtics find themselves in need of a big body. Should it be Semih Erden? Or should it be Shaquille O'Neal? If you need to think it over, then perhaps you really don't care about the subject in the first place.

Allen Felt the Connection

AFTER SETTING MARK, HE ABSORBED SCENE

February 11, 2011 • by Frank Dell'Apa

Ray Allen converted his first NBA 3-pointer as a 21-year-old member of the Milwaukee Bucks in 1996. Fifteen years and 2,560 3-pointers later, he has become the league record-holder.

Allen entered last night's game against the Los Angeles Lakers one 3-pointer behind Reggie Miller on the career list. Allen tied the record with 4:14 remaining in the opening quarter, then overtook Miller with 1:45 left in the first.

No. 2,561 happened about the way Allen had choreographed it in his mind. He ran in front of the scorer's table, just past the Red Auerbach signature on the court, took a pass from Rajon Rondo, and fired away. What happened next, Allen had not planned. In fact, Allen said, "it was such an overwhelming feeling—if I could have hid, I would have."

But Allen did the opposite, completing a sort of victory lap.

"The last thing I told Reggie when we met in the back over there [before the game]," Allen said. "I told him, 'What do I do?' I never expected anything like this situation. Do I sit there and look stupid or stand up? I don't know. He said, 'I don't know, either. Do whatever you have to do because it is your moment.' And, I said, 'It is your moment, as well.'"

In fact, Allen went directly to embrace Miller, who was working as a commentator on the TNT broadcast. Then, after a timeout was called, Allen again embraced Miller. Then there were hugs for his mother, who left her courtside seat, and his wife and children, the youngest also receiving a caress of the face and hair mussing.

"Once the timeout came, I knew I had to go over there to Reggie," Allen said. "My mom was in tears. I had to make sure to thank my family because you don't do anything without your family. Without them, I can't be who I am."

Allen had been anticipating this moment and, rather than shying away from the attention, embraced the countdown.

"I thought about how is it going to happen?" Allen said. "The second three was like slow motion for me because I had seen the whole thing develop. As I've gotten older, I could see the ball coming so slow, like somebody slo-mo'd it on TV.

"I said to myself, this is it. Rondo took the ball up, I knew what he was thinking, we've seen it a thousand times. People asked me who I thought would give me the pass and I said it's a no-brainer, I knew it would be Rondo. So, when I got the ball and let it go, it felt so good behind it. Once the ball was in the air I knew it was good. The one before felt the same but it didn't go in. It was definitely a magical moment, being in this building, the support I had coming into this moment, this situation.

"I almost felt a little embarrassed there was so much attention. Because this is a team sport. Rarely do you get that much individual support. I'll remember this for the rest of my life."

Thunderbolts

CONTRACT ISSUE AT THE CENTER OF THE DEAL

February 25, 2011 • by Gary Washburn

DENVER—For a few final moments, he was one of the guys. Kendrick Perkins walked through the tunnel at Pepsi Center yesterday morning to participate in his final function as a Celtic.

It appeared to be a normal shootaround as Perkins, Kevin Garnett, Paul Pierce, and Ray Allen walked onto the court having a passionate conversation that induced a couple of four-letter words from Garnett. It was time for business.

But Perkins, as it turns out, is no longer a part of the Celtics' business.

Team president Danny Ainge executed a stunning deal yesterday that sent Perkins—one of the team's most popular players and hardest workers—along with Nate Robinson to Oklahoma City for former Celtics draft pick Jeff Green, center Nenad

Krstic, and the Clippers' 2012 first-round pick (a selection owned by the Thunder).

The initial reaction is shock and disappointment, but Ainge has shown throughout the years that he's unafraid of a bold move. Perkins is an impending free agent, so his expiring contract was an attractive trade piece.

Perkins appeared destined for long-term security in Boston until he tore the anterior cruciate ligament in his right knee during Game 6 of the NBA Finals last year. Since then, Ainge has had to ask himself whether it would be economically sound to invest about $10 million per season in a center coming off major knee surgery.

But that's the market, and that's what Perkins was going to ask for. He watched Brendan Haywood sign a six-year, $52 million contract with the Mavericks and wondered, why not me? The Lakers' Andrew Bynum signed a four-year, $57 million extension. Joakim Noah re-signed in Chicago for five years and $60 million. And Chris Kaman signed a five-year, $52 million contract with the Clippers in 2006.

The Celtics offered Perkins four years and $22 million, but he was looking for about double that. So there was going to be an impasse in the summer, and it's apparent that Ainge chose to focus on impending free agent Glen Davis and perhaps using the team's mid-level exception—if it still exists under the new collective bargaining agreement—to attract a new big man.

But he will be hard-pressed to replace the toughness and defensive prowess of Perkins, whose exit brought exhalations of relief in Miami, Orlando, and Chicago.

Krstic can't be viewed as a replacement for Perkins. He is effective off the pick-and-roll because he is a better-than-average jump shooter. Whereas Perkins lacked a jumper and fluid post game, Krstic will open the floor because of his outside shooting. But that doesn't make the Celtics any tougher in the paint.

The Celtics players were shocked by the deal. No one on the roster expected Perkins to be uprooted so suddenly, and even some team officials and coaches were perplexed by the trade.

What Ainge did also will smooth the transition from "the Big Three" to "Rondo and the Boys." Green averaged more than 15.2 points and 5.6 rebounds as

Kendrick Perkins brought toughness, rebounding, defense—and the occasional dunk—to the Celtics.

Celtics' Green Needs Heart Surgery

He'll miss the season but may be able to resume his career.

December 18, 2011 • by Gary Washburn

TORONTO—The Celtics yesterday revealed that small forward Jeff Green will miss the season after doctors discovered an aortic aneurysm that will require surgery.

Green, 25, recently signed a one-year, $9 million contract and was expected to be one of the Celtics' key contributors. But he failed a stress test during his team physical Dec. 9, which sparked a series of examinations.

Green said at the team's media day Tuesday that he was healthy and only a case of fatigue caused the failed physical. But he received a second opinion Friday while accompanied by team president of basketball operations Danny Ainge and surgery was the final decision.

The team said Green will undergo surgery Jan. 9 at the Cleveland Clinic.

The club said Green should be able to resume his career next season, and that if his contract is voided, as expected, the Celtics would have first rights to re-sign him as a restricted free agent.

Green, who could not be reached for comment, did address his situation on Twitter shortly after the announcement.

"Thank you everyone for your thoughts and prayers . . . much appreciated love you all . . . and I'll be back soon stronger and better than ever I promise," he tweeted.

According to the Mayo Clinic website, an aortic aneurysm is an "abnormal bulge that occurs in the wall of the major blood vessel [aorta] that carries blood from your heart to your vital organs."

Per Green's wishes, Ainge and coach Doc Rivers did not speak about his condition, but Ainge did release a statement.

"While we are saddened that Jeff will not be able to play this season, the most important thing is his health, and we were fortunate to have access to an

the third option in Oklahoma City, and his hulking size enables him to play two positions. He doesn't turn 25 until August, meaning he is the second-youngest Celtic, behind Avery Bradley.

Critics have lambasted the Celtics about their advanced age and ability to remain healthy during a long playoff run. Ainge has done something about that and is banking that the Celtics can compensate for the absence of their toughest guy with a committee of bigs and an improved bench.

All we can do now is see how this plays out. The Celtics have 26 games to establish the chemistry and execution they maintained with Perkins. The veterans will have to deal with the loss of their security blanket and move forward.

amazing team of specialists to evaluate Jeff's case," he said. "The entire Celtics family supports Jeff during this difficult time in his career."

Couldn't Ask More from Rondo

May 31, 2012 • by Dan Shaughnessy

MIAMI—This was Bob Cousy going for 50 against Syracuse in 1953. It was Sam Jones promising Bill Russell he'd "take care of things" in the deciding game, then going off for 47 against the Cincinnati Royals. It was John Havlicek scoring 43 against the Lakers in the noble 1969 Finals.

Rajon Rondo did it all Wednesday night. He hit jump shots. He banked in a reverse layup. He hit a couple of desperation threes in the final seconds of overtime. He dished. He rebounded. He made 10 of 12 free throws. He even guarded LeBron James after three of his teammates fouled out.

And he never came off the floor. Rondo played all 53 minutes. Just like Hondo back in the day.

"I felt fine," Rondo said. "It was a mental grind for me individually, and for us as a team. It's the conference finals. I wanted to play every minute. I thought I didn't hurt my team by me playing every minute."

Rondo scored 44 points with 10 assists and 8 rebounds in a 115-111 Celtic loss to the Miami Heat. Just when you think he can't get any better, he comes up with the ultimate game.

"It's irrelevant," said Rondo. "We lost. It's as simple as that."

"His performance will go down in the record books," said James. "He showed tonight why he's one of the superstars in the league."

It was one of the great Celtic performances of all time. Unfortunately, it was not enough.

The Celtics now trail Miami, 0-2, as they come home to play Game 3 Friday night in the Garden. They have not recovered from an 0-2 deficit since Russell and Jones beat the Lakers in seven after losing the first two games of the Finals in '69.

These 2012 Celtics are a lot like those old-guard Celtics who patched it together with a bunch of guys on their way out the door. Those Celtics had Russell and Sam ready to retire. They had Emmette Bryant playing the point. They had one player in his athletic prime: Havlicek.

Today, Rondo is the guy who has the motor that never stops running.

He made 16 of 24 floor shots Wednesday night. The Heat played back on him and let him shoot and he made them pay. He scored 12 in the first quarter and had 22 at halftime.

In overtime, one of the key plays of the game, Rondo missed a layup on a hard, contested drive to the basket. He was hit in the face by Dwyane Wade with no call. The score was 105-105 with less than two minutes to play when the officials missed the foul. Celtics coach Doc Rivers put himself between Rondo and the officials after the non-call.

"It was obvious," said Rondo. "I can't comment on that play in particular. It's part of the game. Things didn't go our way. That was a big swing for us. I think we had the momentum. A lot of controversy out there, just didn't go our way."

Rondo at times has been a frustrating player for Rivers and general manager Danny Ainge. He's been immature, had issues with officials, and sometimes seems to leave his best game at home. Ainge tried to trade him before the start of this season and he's been scolded for sometimes saving his best games for national television.

But he is the best player on the Celtics now. It's not even close. Wednesday night, he was also better than LeBron James and Dwyane Wade. Too bad it wasn't enough.

Stunning Win for Celtics

BIG NIGHT IN MIAMI PUTS TEAM ON BRINK OF THE FINALS

June 6, 2012 • by Bob Ryan

MIAMI—First reaction: Wow!

Immediate question: How?

How did the Boston Celtics pull off their biggest win of the year? How did they come into Miami, shoot 33 percent in the first half, lose a 6-point fourth-quarter lead (68-62) to fall behind by 6 (78-72) with 6:17 remaining, and then re-group to walk off the American Airlines Arena floor with a 94-90 victory that leaves them one home victory away from a total surprise berth in the NBA Finals?

"We were just hanging in there," said coach Doc Rivers. "They jumped on us in the beginning and we just told our guys, 'Just hang in there. Don't overreact. Just hang in there.'"

The Celtics have won three games in succession after losing Games 1 and 2 in Miami last week.

But "hanging in there" against the Heat means dealing with the menacing LeBron James and the acrobatic Dwyane Wade, who combined for 57 points and 19 rebounds. Their mutual greatness is no myth.

Neither, it should be pointed out, is the greatness of Boston's proud veterans, most notably 36-year-old Kevin Garnett, who, despite laboring at times, found a way to come up with 26 points and 11 rebounds while directing the defense; and 34-year-old Paul Pierce, who was a shaky 2 for 10 in the first half and a wobbly 5 for 18 overall when he administered a vital 3-point facial to Mr. James to give Boston a desperately needed 4-point cushion (90-86) with 52.9 seconds to play.

Pierce was isolated with James deep to the left of the circle. "I kind of wanted him to drive, honestly," Rivers acknowledged. "I've been around Paul long enough. Right when he gets into the footwork, you knew he was going to shoot it. At least I did, because I've seen him enough. That's what players like Paul do. It really is. He's a big shot-maker. He always has been."

The third Oldie-But-Goodie, 36-year-old Ray Allen, had his big moment, too. Fouled on an in-bounds play with 13.8 seconds remaining and the Celtics ahead by 2 (90-88), he did the typical Ray Allen thing by swishing his free throws. Garnett mimicked him with two perfect swishes of his own at 8.8 to wrap it up.

It's perfectly clear by now that the Celtics are playing comfortably, something that cannot be said for the Heat, a team that performs under more ludicrous minute-by-minute scrutiny than any team in American professional sports.

The "How?" question remains unanswered. Perhaps it's just sports' version of a supernatural mystery.

James Foils Celtics' Hopes of Ending Series Early

June 8, 2012 • by Dan Shaughnessy

So, here we go. After 11 days, six games, and thousands of erroneous predictions and definitive statements (the Celtics are too old, the Heat always choke), we are down to one game for the right to represent the Eastern Conference in the NBA Finals.

Led by LeBron James's 45 points, the evermaligned, hateable Miami Heat stood tall and decimated the gritty Celtics Thursday night, thrashing Boston's proud Green Team, 98-79, on the parquet floor of TD Garden. Perhaps the most ridiculed great player in the history of sports, James made 19 of 26 floor shots and added 15 rebounds. It was a performance worthy of Wilt Chamberlain or Michael Jordan.

Saturday night in Miami the Celtics and Heat will play Game 7 and the winner will ride a Conestoga wagon into Oklahoma City for Game 1 of the Finals Tuesday night.

Historically, Game 7 belongs to the Celtics. They are to Game 7 what Johnny Carson was to late-night television, what Dick Clark was to New Year's Eve.

It's always fun to hop into the way-back machine and summon the memories and ghosts of Messrs. Russell, Cousy, Havlicek, and Bird, but it's impossible to predict what might happen Saturday night. Six games have taught us that we know nothing about these two teams. At the beginning of this series it looked as though the old guard of Boston had no chance against the skill and athleticism of James and his partner, Dwyane Wade. The Heat ruled in Game 1 and appeared to break the Celtics' spirit winning Game 2 in overtime.

Then the series came to Boston, and the Celtics dominated the next three games, including Tuesday night in Miami. The Heat were humiliated. From pillar to post, from coast to coast, mocking the Heat was the national pastime.

We all showed up at the Garden Thursday night anticipating another Heat stroke and the Celtics winning at home to get to the Finals for the 22d time in franchise history. I thought it would make sense if Heat boss Pat Riley fired overwhelmed coach Erik

Spoelstra and took over his team while there was still time to save the season.

Wrong. It didn't matter who coached the Heat Thursday night. James was on a mission to assert his greatness.

Mission accomplished. There were moments when this game made you think of what it must have been like the night Wilt went for 100 points in Hershey, Pa., 50 years ago.

James dominated from the jump. He made 6 of 7 shots in the first quarter, which ended with the Heat leading, 26-16. The Celtics had one assist and five turnovers in the first 12 minutes.

It didn't get any better for Boston in the second. LeBron had 30 at intermission and the Heat led, 55-42.

"I wanted to be there for my teammates from the opening tip," James said.

The Celtics never got close. And we all know that getting close is the key to beating the Heat. Miami is a classic front-runner bully. Nobody looks better than a Heat team with a big lead. The way to beat the Heat is to get them in a close game and wait for the self-immolation. The Celtics were not able to do this Thursday night. James would not allow it.

LBJ had 41 after three, and the Heat led, 74-61.

These were not dunks and/or breakaways. James scored from every spot on the floor.

"I wasn't paying too much attention [to what the Celtics were doing]," said James. "I was focused on what I had to do. I was in such a zone—doing what I had to do."

James didn't come off the floor until the clock showed 3:11 with the Heat leading, 92-70, in the fourth.

The Celtics could do nothing to stop him. Rajon Rondo had a nice game with 21 points and 10 rebounds, but captain Paul Pierce made only 4 of 18 shots and looked old and exhausted trying to guard the indomitable James.

"It was a matter of too much LeBron," admitted Celtics coach Doc Rivers. "He made every shot and set the tone. We, on the other hand, never really established what we wanted to do. We didn't play like us. Listen, it's one loss, against a great player. I think our guys should take that very personally. We're comfortable on the road, but we're going to have to play a hell of a game."

Only one Celtics team has recovered from an 0-2 series deficit: the 1969 fourth-place Celtics. Those old C's were led by Russell and Sam Jones, both ready to retire. They staggered through the regular season, then came back to beat the Chamberlain-Jerry West-Elgin Baylor Lakers. They beat LA and Father Time, winning Game 7 on the road in the Forum.

It could happen again. But the Celtics are going to have to do something about LeBron.

No Doubt End of an Era

June 10, 2012 • by Bob Ryan

MIAMI—With 28.3 seconds remaining and the Miami Heat in firm control, Doc Rivers, as usual, had the right feel for the occasion.

He took Paul Pierce, Kevin Garnett, and Ray Allen out of the game.

The Big Three era is over.

It ended in sorrow and frustration, the Celtics outplaying the Heat for the better part of 40 minutes before a certain form of reality set in. The Heat ended a run of six consecutive fourth-quarter lead changes with a devastating run of 18-4, and that was that. Miami will play the young and dynamic Oklahoma City Thunder in the Finals and the Celtics will start working on the rest of their franchise life, one that does not figure to include Allen or Garnett, although, despite all the educated speculation, nothing is written in stone.

"Honestly," said Rivers, "I just thought we had nothing left. You could see it as a coach.

"I was trying to push every button, but we were hitting the front rim, we were starting to throw the ball away, and they were beating us off the dribble. It was a group that did everything we asked of them, but we came up short."

The five-year run of the Big Three—we'll get to Rajon Rondo in a while—began officially on Oct. 6, 2007, with an 89-85 exhibition triumph over Toronto in, of all places, Rome. There were 11,118 on hand at the Palalottomatica, and we will never know just how many of them appreciated what they were seeing.

Rajon Rondo, Paul Pierce, Kevin Garnett, and Ray Allen saw their season—and their time as a quartet—come to an end against LeBron James and the Heat in 2012.

Their actual NBA debut came on Nov. 2, when they defeated Washington by a resounding score of 103-83. Garnett had 22 points and 20 rebounds. Pierce had 28. Allen had 17. John Henry, Larry Lucchino, Tim Wakefield, Jacoby Ellsbury, Manny Delcarmen, Bob Kraft, Wes Welker, Laurence Maroney, Vince Wilfork, and Junior Seau were among the luminaries who saw the era get off to a nice start.

And now it ends in American Airlines Arena, with the screaming PA announcer, the in-house disc jockey, the quite entertaining band, and all the rest of the hoopla that is there to distract the fans from the basketball, which, when played the way it was in those final eight minutes, is of the highest quality.

The Heat took this game away from the Celtics. They did it with a terrific two-way surge in which they showcased the talents of their own Big Three, led by LeBron James, who played a brilliantly mature, but understated game, finishing with 31 points and 12 rebounds while playing all but the final 28.3 seconds.

"I really thought he played a smart, aggressive game," lauded Rivers. "He let the game come to him, and he took over after that, which is what great players do."

For 3 ½ quarters, the Celtics did all any reasonable person could ask. They led after one (27-23) and they led at the half (53-46).

"I'm really proud of the way they played, especially early on," Rivers said. "They had the fight in them, and I could see they were going to play the right way."

The only real problem was three early fouls for Garnett, who picked up two offensive, the second of which could politely be called "bogus." Doc claimed it threw Kevin out of rhythm for a long stretch.

But with Brandon Bass throwing in 14 points and Rondo again orchestrating matters (10 first-half assists), the Celtics parlayed a strong, overplaying defense and good ball movement into that halftime advantage.

Rondo would finish with yet another triple-double (22-10-14). "I already thought he was in that [elite] class," Rivers said. "If he's not, now he is."

Rondo's going to be there for a while. Pierce is destined to be a Celtics lifer. But Allen and Garnett are free agents, and common sense says that suitors will be lining up from the Atlantic to the Pacific to pay one of these guys to be the missing piece of a perceived championship puzzle. If Doc had his way, everyone would be back. But he knows better than anyone else that management has broader, long-range concerns.

So, this is where it almost undoubtedly ends.

In Miami.

With honor.

Allen: Love Was Lost

July 12, 2012 • by Gary Washburn

MIAMI—Wednesday was more a neatly written, passionate goodbye letter from Ray Allen to the Celtics than the beginning of his time with the Heat.

Allen fully realized he had to say goodbye first, and he spent his introductory news conference at American Airlines Arena offering thanks for his five years in Boston, but also explaining why he was in

Ray Allen spurned the Celtics to join the Heat after the 2012 season.

Wade and Chris Bosh, and the possibility of winning another championship.

But Allen revealed that he was lured by more than courting. There was no single determining factor, just a series of what Allen perceived as slights during his final season in Boston and the free agent process.

"It was a hard decision because as much as I felt about being home in Boston, having won a championship there, I just had to look at my own personal situation and ask myself, was I really going to be able to help coming back?" he said. "Was I going to be in a situation where I was going to be a part of what was going on moving forward?"

Allen was being pushed away, or perhaps steamrolled by the Celtics' train of progress. The signing of Jason Terry, a three-year deal given to Kevin Garnett where Allen received just a two-year offer, and no real definition of his role drove him into the waiting arms of Riley.

Allen needed to be coddled as a free agent, even at 36. After being the good soldier for years, sacrificing shots, playing time, and finally his starting spot, he wanted an outpouring of gratitude from the Celtics. Like the wife who wants her longtime husband to don a suit, dust off his wingtips, and treat her as he did when they were dating, Allen wanted the Celtics to remember back to 2007, when they convinced him that leaving comfortable Seattle for the uncertainty of Boston would change his life, which it did.

Instead, Allen felt like an afterthought. Ainge said he called Allen at midnight the day free agency

South Florida in the first place. The reasons for his departure are still cloudy.

Allen looked sullen during the news conference, as if bolting for Miami was more about what Celtics president of basketball operations Danny Ainge didn't do than what the Heat did.

Heat president Pat Riley, coach Erik Spoelstra, and team executive Alonzo Mourning simply offered their customary recruiting pitch, selling Allen on everything he already knew: great weather, the opportunity to play with LeBron James, Dwyane opened, and expressed the Celtics' desire to keep him. But Allen apparently didn't get the message.

"When Kevin signed, I was excited for him, I was excited that he signed a three-year deal, and I was expecting to be somewhere along the same [length]," he said. "It was kind of like they went in another direction and started signing everybody else, and I was sitting there in a free agency period and I'm looking at Miami and they're so excited for me to come here and have an opportunity, and I didn't get that same excitement from that side of the equation."

The near trade this past season to the Grizzlies, Allen being told he was dealt for O.J. Mayo, then informed it had fallen through, also took a toll. That uncertainty was something he said he never wanted to experience again. The Celtics dangled a no-trade clause in their two-year offer, but seemingly Allen was no longer convinced.

Allen waited too long to express his disenchantment. He quietly remained professional, believing that when free agency arrived, the Celtics would reward him for his service.

"Sometimes you've got to step out and clear your path a little bit more than you would have done otherwise and just let it be known," Allen said. "But I acquiesced so much to the point where, at some point they said, 'Well, Ray will be all right, he'll figure himself out or he'll get his touches, he'll figure it out, we don't worry about him.' At some point it was to my own detriment because I didn't create enough wave of an ego to let them know you have to stand up and speak for yourself and be accounted for."

Allen's relationship with Rajon Rondo was strained to the point where he didn't mention the Celtics point guard by name Wednesday. But he maintained it wasn't the determining factor in his exit. It appeared Paul Pierce didn't exactly recruit Allen hard, either. Allen said he primarily talked with Garnett, who told him that Ainge would "step up to the plate and do whatever you need him to do."

Ainge felt he had done enough. He insisted the Celtics treated Allen fairly, and called reporters just hours into free agency to express his desire for Allen to return. Allen took Miami's offer, but on Wednesday realized the finality and magnitude of his move. But there's no going back.

"Forever, I'll always be a Celtic, no matter what," Allen said. "I've seen [Glen Davis] down here during the playoffs watching [Game 5 vs. Miami]

and I looked at him as a brother. We played against [Kendrick Perkins] during the year, it doesn't change. In my mind, it never changes. I don't care what people say about me, I'll always stay true to the city of Boston and the fans there. They've been great to me. I'll always consider that place home."

Celtics' Rivers Set to Depart

NINE-YEAR COACH TO TAKE THE REINS OF LA CLIPPERS

June 24, 2013 •
by Baxter Holmes and Gary Washburn

After nine seasons in Boston, during which he revived its storied basketball franchise and steered it to its first NBA championship in 22 years, Doc Rivers is set to leave the Celtics to become the coach of the Los Angeles Clippers.

Under the terms of the deal, Rivers would coach the talent-laden Clippers for three seasons and earn $21 million, those sources said, which is what Rivers had remaining on the five-year extension that he signed with the Celtics in 2011.

His departure accomplishes Rivers's goals of again coaching a championship-caliber team while avoiding the grind of leading one that is in the rebuilding stages. But his exit was still abrupt.

"Coach gone?????" Celtics guard Terrence Williams tweeted.

In return for allowing one of the league's top coaches out of his contract, league sources said, the Celtics would receive a 2015 first-round draft pick, a valuable asset.

Celtics All-Star center Kevin Garnett was involved in previous incarnations of proposed deals with the Clippers, but he is not involved in this one.

And the league is expected to veto subsequent player trades between the teams, as they would appear connected and thus violate league rules forbidding side deals.

However, it's unclear what the 37-year-old Garnett, who is extremely close with Rivers and is under contract with the Celtics next season, will do next—retire or return to play in Boston.

Paul Pierce and Doc Rivers had a hard time finding answers in 2013, their final year with the franchise.

With the NBA Draft looming Thursday, and the June 30 deadline for a decision on the future of Paul Pierce also fast approaching, the Celtics already had a heavy workload before them.

But now they must begin searching for a new coach.

The pool of candidates is shallow at this point in the offseason, but league sources made early suggestions such as Brian Shaw, Lawrence Frank, and Nate McMillan, among others.

"I think they do have to go young, and Danny [Ainge] is going to want to look like a genius," a league source said. "Brian Shaw is what I think they'd hire, but I don't know. Danny might go outside the box a little."

Ainge, the Celtics' president of basketball operations, and Shaw, who was drafted by the Celtics in 1988, were teammates during the 1989 season in Boston.

Rivers posted a 416-305 regular-season record as Celtics coach, the third-most wins in franchise history behind Tom Heinsohn (427) and Red Auerbach (795).

In the postseason, Rivers went 59-47, the third-most wins for a Celtics coach behind Auerbach (90) and K.C. Jones (65).

Like It or Not, It Had to Be Done

Celtics Trade Pierce, Garnett to Nets for Three 1st-Round Picks

June 28, 2013 • by Gary Washburn

Whether the Celtics' faithful were ready or not, whether they wanted to see Paul Pierce retire a Celtic, or Kevin Garnett vigorously motion to the TD Garden crowd, or see the Big Three make one more championship run, they won't.

The Big Three era is over, crashing down to rubble on a warm summer night in Boston, when president of basketball operations Danny Ainge completed the biggest deal of his tenure.

Realizing the pressure to win disappeared with the departure of coach Doc Rivers to the Los Angeles Clippers, Ainge took mere hours to go to work on a rebuilding plan, trading Pierce, Garnett, and Jason Terry to the Brooklyn Nets Thursday night for Kris Humphries, Gerald Wallace, Keith Bogans, Reggie Evans, Kris Joseph, Tornike Shengelia, and first-round picks in 2014, 2016, and 2018.

For those who wished for Ainge to move forward with younger players, that process has begun in earnest. In a matter of three days, he has obliterated any semblance of last year's team, allowing Rivers to go to Los Angeles, and then dealing Pierce and Garnett to a division rival.

Ainge surprisingly found a team willing to take a pair of aging players, and offer the Celtics the draft picks they wanted to build a foundation for the future.

It was the right move for the Celtics. There was not going to be a smooth transition to the next phase. Pierce wanted to play next season, and Garnett has two years and $23 million left on a deal he is determined to fulfill. Ainge said years ago there was no way he was going to relive the early '90s, when the original Big Three were practically carrying walkers onto the court, the Bulls and Pistons passing them by.

It was a crushing end to a glorious time. And Ainge was reminded of a couple of deals that Red Auerbach refused to consummate because of loyalty. Auerbach had a chance to trade Larry Bird back to his native Indiana for Chuck Person, Herb Williams, and Steve Stipanovich. He refused. Auerbach also could have sent Kevin McHale to Dallas for Detlef Schrempf and Sam Perkins. Again, no deal.

Ainge could have allowed Pierce and Garnett to play out their contracts and then use the cap space, or get compensation for the Big Three now and amass the same cap space.

The 2014 pick will almost certainly be late in the first round, but the ones in 2016 and 2018 could become high picks if the Nets backslide. It is not the ideal way to rebuild. That would be through free agency. But sooner rather than later, the Celtics had to do this. They had to pull the plug eventually, move forward.

Change is painful, and the Celtics will be dramatically different without Pierce, his headband, the stepback jumper, and his appealing bravado. He overcame bouts with immaturity and selfishness to become one of the great Celtics of all time.

Garnett blended into the Boston fabric perfectly, adding a toughness and attitude the Celtics had lacked for years, and played until his knee required WD-40 to quiet the creaking. It was difficult to give up on Garnett because he had something left, but with the organization convinced they had to move Pierce, and with Rivers gone, it would have been almost unfair to run a 37-year-old Garnett out there on a 40-win team.

The trade is disheartening because the Celtics may slip back to irrelevance. The national television appearances will decrease. They'll likely have Christmas Day off. That feeling of pride when the Celtics hit the road in those green uniforms will diminish.

It was a great run. Pierce, Garnett, and even Ray Allen should be applauded when they return to Boston. They brought the Celtics back to respectability. They were victorious, and harmonious for the most part. They played at a high level.

But eventually they couldn't reach as high anymore. Garnett is now a 30-minute-per-game player, Pierce was exposed by the Knicks' Iman Shumpert's lockdown defense in the playoffs and was no longer a primary option.

By trading them, Ainge avoided the mistakes Auerbach made more than 20 years ago.

And he officially kicks off a new era. We knew this day was coming, but really never hoped it would be so sudden.

8 FROM I.T. TO KYRIE

(2014-2019)

Over his 18 seasons as the Celtics' personnel boss, Danny Ainge earned the nickname "Trader Danny" for his recurring willingness to be equal parts unsentimental and bold in constructing the roster.

His fearlessness in executing major moves, particularly during the first decade of his tenure, was best encapsulated by his era-defining bookend trades that brought superstar Kevin Garnett to the Celtics before the 2008 season, and then the move that sent an aging Garnett along with Paul Pierce and other less consequential pieces to the Brooklyn Nets in the summer of 2013 for five roster-filler players, first-round picks in 2014, 2016, and 2018, and a swap of picks in 2017. That trade abruptly ended one era and set up another.

But Ainge's most surprising move was not a trade for a player. It was the inspired hiring of a 36-year-old whiz kid college coach whose youthful looks belied a relentless competitive streak and a deep understanding of the game that surpassed that of coaching peers a generation older.

When the Celtics announced in July 2013 that Brad Stevens, aforementioned whiz kid, had accepted a six-year contract to succeed Doc Rivers and to become the 17th head coach in franchise history, it was a lightning bolt out of the blue.

Stevens had earned an impeccable reputation at Butler University, where during his six seasons he led the midmajor program to consecutive Final Fours, coming mere inches on a Gordon Hayward last-second heave from beating traditional power Duke in the 2010 men's national championship game. But he was the first coach hired by the Celtics with no pro experience since Alvin "Doggie" Julian arrived from Holy Cross in 1949, and there was a common assumption that he was destined to become a legendary college coach.

When Stevens was hired, the *Globe*'s Baxter Holmes reported that a source had told him this: "He'll line it up right and leave around the time Roy Williams and Mike Krzyzewski are done at North Carolina or Duke and he'll take one of those jobs in a couple years. I bet my house on that one."

Here's hoping for the source's sake that such a bet was never made. Stevens's first team won 25 games with a makeshift roster in 2014. But with the arrival of feisty rookie first-round pick Marcus Smart, a December trade that sent Rajon Rondo to Dallas for a package including scrappy forward Jae Crowder, and one of Ainge's all-time most satisfying deals in February that brought diminutive guard Isaiah Thomas over from the Suns, the 2015 Celtics surpassed expectations, winning 40 games and reaching the first round of the playoffs before being swept by the Cavaliers.

The 2016 Celtics made another leap in Stevens's third season, winning 48 games before bowing to the Hawks in six games in the first round of the playoffs. Thomas, though just 5 feet 9 inches, emerged a genuine star and fan favorite, averaging 22.2 points while playing all 82 games, while Smart and Avery Bradley set a relentless tone on defense.

In the summer of 2016, Ainge made two consequential moves to bolster the roster, one through the draft and one via free agency, the latter a route the Celtics had rarely taken in their history. The blockbuster trade with the Nets began paying off for the Celtics when they used the No. 3 overall pick, acquired in that deal, to select University of California forward Jaylen Brown. Less than two weeks after landing the raw but intelligent and gifted Brown, the Celtics signed free agent center Al Horford to a four-year, $113 million contract. Horford, who had spent the first eight years of his career with the Atlanta Hawks, was the first premier, prime-of-career free agent ever to sign with the Celtics, who historically had trouble recruiting coveted Black players to Boston and had typically built its best teams via the draft or clever, lopsided trades.

Horford was not even the biggest name Ainge pursued that summer. The Celtics made an aggressive push to sign superstar forward Kevin Durant—an Ainge favorite since his lone season at the University of Texas—even meeting with him to make their pitch in the Hamptons, where Patriots quarterback Tom Brady was part of their contingent. Durant ultimately chose to join forces with Steph Curry on the Golden State Warriors, but he acknowledged that he had given the Celtics serious consideration.

Missing out on Durant for a second time is a what-if for sports radio or a rainy day, but the 2017 Celtics were in no need of sympathy or consolation prizes. Thomas blossomed into an electrifying offensive force, scoring 52 points in a December game against Miami, including 29 in the fourth quarter, earning him the nickname "King of the Fourth." His scoring prowess—he averaged 28.9 points per game during the regular season, third-best in the league—continued in the postseason for the 53-win,

top-seeded Celtics, who bounced the Bulls in six games in the first round.

Thomas thrived on the court despite a heavy heart. His younger sister Chyna died in a car accident the day before the playoffs began. He attended her funeral in Washington before the second-round series with the Wizards began, then returned to Boston and proceeded to put on a show that will never be forgotten by Celtics fans. In Game 1, he scored 33 points in a Celtics win, but he did not get through it unscathed, a Wizards player's inadvertent elbow knocking out one of his front teeth. Thomas spent the day off between Games 1 and 2 undergoing extensive dental surgery, then submitted a performance for the ages in the series' second game, scoring 53 points—second-most in Celtics playoff history to John Havlicek's 54 in Game 1 against the Hawks in the 1973 conference semifinals—in an overtime victory. The Celtics finished off the series with a thrilling Game 7 victory, Thomas scoring 29 points and unlikely hero Kelly Olynyk contributing 27.

Little would anyone have suspected then that Thomas was in his last meaningful days as a member of the Celtics. An aggravation of a hip injury suffered in March led to the Celtics shutting him down after two games of the Eastern Conference finals against the Cavaliers. The Celtics lost the series in five—the one win came on an Avery Bradley buzzer-beater in Game 3—and a little more than two months after that series was complete, Thomas, whose hip injury would abbreviate his prime, was dealt to the Cavaliers along with Crowder and the last of the picks acquired from the Nets for star guard Kyrie Irving.

The deal was the ultimate example of Ainge's lack of sentimentality, but the result was a loaded Celtics roster. Free agent forward Gordon Hayward—who had starred for Stevens at Butler—signed a four-year, $128 million deal with the Celtics on the Fourth of July 2017. And the epic swap with the Nets paid its biggest dividends yet. The Celtics won the first pick in the draft lottery, but Ainge, favoring a player other than consensus top pick Markelle Fultz of Washington, traded the first selection to the Sixers for the third pick and a future first-rounder. With the third pick, he selected his favorite player in the draft, Duke forward Jayson Tatum.

The new arrivals gave the Celtics one of the deepest and most talented rosters in the league. Expectations were as high as the Garden rafters.

But less than seven minutes into the Celtics' 2018 opener, they came crashing down. Hayward dislocated his left ankle and broke his tibia after an awkward landing while trying to catch an Irving lob. His season was over before it had barely begun, and while he would be an effective player again, he was never quite the same.

Still, with Tatum immediately looking like a surefire future All-Star and an engaged Irving playing spectacular offense, the Celtics ripped off 16 straight wins after losing their first two games, finishing with 55 wins and making their second straight appearance in the conference finals. Even with Irving sidelined with a knee injury, the Celtics managed to seize a 3-2 lead over LeBron James and the Cavaliers in the conference finals. But Cleveland won the final two games despite a star turn by Tatum, who scored 24 points in both Game 6 and 7 and posterized James late in the decisive game before the Cavaliers seized control.

The 2019 season was one of great expectations and even greater disappointment. Tatum and Brown continued developing into stalwarts, and Hayward returned from his injury, even scoring 35 points in a January win at Minnesota. But team chemistry was off. Hayward didn't quite mesh with the emerging Tatum and Brown, and the fickle Irving, who had told Celtics season ticket-holders that he planned on signing a long-term contract, backpedaled when asked again later in the season, saying "Ask me July 1," the first day of free agency.

Irving left the Celtics on that date, signing a $141 million deal to join forces with Durant with the Nets. But he quit on the Celtics long before, playing with infuriating lethargy during a five-game loss to the Bucks in the East semifinals. He had more talent than Isaiah Thomas. He was more accomplished. But his heart? That was minuscule by comparison.

Going Green

CELTICS NAME STEVENS, 36, HEAD COACH

July 4, 2013 • by Baxter Holmes

In a stunning and bold move to reinvigorate a rebuilding franchise, the Celtics hired one of college basketball's brightest young stars Wednesday, naming 36-year-old Brad Stevens as the 17th head coach in their storied history.

Stevens rose to prominence during Butler University's consecutive Cinderella runs to the national title game in 2010 and 2011, after which blue-blood college teams tried to lure him away from the Indianapolis-based private school that sits about 20 miles from where he grew up in suburban Zionsville.

But the Celtics shocked the basketball landscape when they announced their hiring of a college coach with no prior NBA experience as the successor for Doc Rivers. The announcement came two days after Celtics president of basketball operations Danny Ainge said the team wasn't in a rush to select a new coach.

Rivers, 51, recently left the Celtics after nine seasons to join the Los Angeles Clippers as their head coach and a front-office executive. Stevens and his family will be introduced at a news conference Friday morning.

"Brad and I share a lot of the same values," Ainge said in a statement. "Though he is young, I see Brad as a great leader who leads with impeccable character and a strong work ethic.

"His teams always play hard and execute on both ends of the court. Brad is a coach who has already enjoyed lots of success, and I look forward to working with him towards Banner 18."

In a statement on the Butler website, Stevens, who worked for the school since 2002, said, "Our family is thrilled for the opportunity given to us by the leadership of the Boston Celtics, but it is emotional to leave a place that we have called home the past 13 years."

A league source confirmed that Stevens's contract with the Celtics is for six years, the same length of time he spent as Butler's head coach, compiling a .772 winning percentage (166-49).

After playing Division 3 basketball at DePauw University, Stevens joined Butler as a coordinator of basketball operations in 2001. He was offered a full-time assistant position in 2002. He was named head coach in April 2007, replacing Todd Lickliter. Stevens signed a 12-year contract with Butler in 2010.

Around the NBA, the outside-the-box hire, one that several league sources said should have been expected under Ainge, was met with surprise and tempered expectations. College coaches long have struggled when making the leap to the professional level. An example Celtics fans will note is Rick Pitino, who posted an underwhelming 102-146 record from 1997 to 2001 as the Celtics' head coach.

Then factor in that Stevens, the youngest coach in the NBA, will be coaching a rebuilding team without two veteran stars, as Paul Pierce and Kevin Garnett—who is just five months older than Stevens—are both being traded to the Brooklyn Nets.

"It's just a tall order," a league source said.

However, several league sources said they were fans of Stevens, praising his work ethic and basketball IQ. "He's smart, innovative and dynamic," said one league executive. "It's a huge upside hire. Big kudos to Danny Ainge."

When asked what one factor would define whether Stevens is successful, a league source said, simply, "players," referencing a key difference between college and professional basketball, which is known as a player's league.

"It's no offense to him," the source added. "You swap places with him and [Miami head coach Erik] Spoelstra, I still think the Heat win 50 or 60 games next year. He has a system, but it's who's carrying out the orders?

"He ain't out-coaching nobody. That ain't happening. You've got to get your guys to play in an effective system, but he's got to get the right blends of guys or he has no shot."

Still, the unexpected hire was deemed to be a safe one for Stevens, at the very least, "because he can always return to college and get a top-five job," one league source said. Several league sources expressed doubt that Stevens would stay with the Celtics for the full duration of his contract.

"He'll line it up right and leave around the time Roy Williams and Mike Krzyzewski are done at North Carolina or Duke and he'll take one of those jobs in a couple years," a league source said. "I bet my house on that one."

Stevens is leaving Butler as that team moves from the Atlantic 10 Conference to the Big East.

Another league source who has known Stevens for more than a decade, dating to when Stevens was an assistant at Butler, said he is confident that the new Celtics coach can win.

"He's a very smart and grounded guy and he will be a great in-game decision maker," the source said. "If he can put together a strong coaching staff with NBA experience, he has a chance to be very good."

Rivers has taken several members of the Celtics' coaching staff with him to LA, so it's unclear whom Stevens will keep. Celtics assistant coach Jay Larranaga, who was thought to be in the running for the coaching job, is under contract with the Celtics next season.

Larranaga will guide the Celtics' summer league team in Orlando, which begins practicing there Thursday.

"The biggest problem he'll face will be the shorter shot clock," said the source close to Stevens. "His sets at Butler lent themselves to late shot-clock opportunities. He's going to have to come in with new offensive ideas."

The NBA shot clock is 24 seconds compared with the 35-second shot clock in the college game.

Another key for Stevens is whether the players, especially strongheaded point guard Rajon Rondo, will respect a new coach who neither played professionally nor has basketball coaching experience beyond Butler.

"You can gain that if you win," a league source said, flatly. "If you come in and lose, guys are going to start shaking their heads."

Considering that the Celtics will have nine first-round draft picks over the next five seasons, the ability to coach and develop young talent is no doubt a priority for the franchise.

"I think their spin will be, 'This is going to take time and we're going to give him time,'" a league source said. "'We're going to learn him, he's going to learn us, he'll learn the league and we'll grow together.'"

"That's all fine and good," the source added, "but if you lose 10 in a row on the road and you're getting beat by 40, what are you going to do?"

A Mission, a Method

Some rival college coaches said you had to play a perfect game to beat Brad Stevens's team. He might not have the best talent, but he maximizes what's there, others say. He has accepted the challenge of rebuilding the Celtics. His competitiveness controls him. His wife says he is on a constant quest to compete, to win. It never ends.

October 29, 2013 • by Baxter Holmes

A secret. There had to be one, some special ingredient behind a small Indianapolis private school's improbable run to consecutive NCAA championship games in 2010 and 2011.

Numbers! Yes, that was it.

"What two or three stats do you guys look at all the time?"

Former Butler assistant Matthew Graves remembered hearing that one a lot, from coaches and other sleuths.

Truth was, it all varied game to game, opponent to opponent. But that didn't slow the inquiries.

"Everybody wants to break it down into this magical stat or formula," said Graves, now the coach at the University of South Alabama.

Often overlooked was that A) Butler wasn't a nobody out of nowhere and actually had reached four NCAA Tournaments in seven years (including two Sweet Sixteens) leading up to 2010; and that B) the program's recent success could be traced back to a mid-1990s culture shift that created "The Butler Way."

The turning point came in 1995 when Butler coach Barry Collier and another coach sat down with Wisconsin coach Dick Bennett, whose teams there and at Wisconsin-Green Bay were always a handful.

"I thought there was some kind of X's-and-O's secret I could learn," said Collier, echoing what others would say years later when Brad Stevens coached Butler.

Instead, Bennett shared five Biblical-based principles that made up his philosophy: humility, passion, servanthood, thankfulness, and unity.

"'Simple' doesn't seem like the right word," said Collier. "But in some ways, I think it is. Because something is simple does not make it easy. It's hard to follow these things."

Collier applied what Bennett taught, and Butler improved, winning nearly 70 percent of its games over the next five seasons while reaching the NCAA Tournament in three of them.

Now the school's athletic director, Collier still keeps Bennett's principles on a laminated card in his pocket.

But when Todd Lickliter became Butler's coach in 2001, he wanted to put "The Butler Way" into a one-page mission statement. So, he and then-assistant Stevens spent hours in Lickliter's office, one on a yellow legal pad, the other on a computer, writing and rewriting until it was right.

Among their key influences was a book Lickliter had given Stevens, a book by Celtics legend Bill Russell: "Russell Rules: 11 Lessons on Leadership from the Twentieth Century's Greatest Winner."

Two of Russell's ideals stuck with them, one about team ego ("My ego demands—for myself—the success of my team"); and the other about the culture of the Celtics: "'Celtic Pride' is a real concept, a culture, and a practice rather than an idea. We lived it and breathed it. But we were each responsible for it. It began with a collective determination never to embarrass ourselves."

Today, on the front wall of the Butler men's basketball room is a placard that reads: "The Butler Way begins with a 'collective determination never to embarrass ourselves.' And we agree that The Butler Way is not merely a concept, but a 'culture and a practice—and we all are responsible for it.'"

The culture is the foundation.

"Everybody thinks, 'Well, there's got to be more, there's got to be something else,'" Graves said. "There's not. But try doing this every single moment, every single day, over and over and over."

Stevens kept that copy of Russell's book, filled it with notes, and was rereading it this July during his flight to Boston, where he was to be introduced as the Celtics new head coach. As he sat in the team's practice facility beneath 11 title banners that Russell helped win in his 13 years in Boston, Stevens used the word "culture" in his first public remarks.

"I think culture," he said later, "is the most important thing."

OBSESSED WITH PREPARATION

It's after 10, maybe closer to midnight, many years ago at Stevens's childhood home in Zionsville,

Ind. His father, Mark, an orthopedic surgeon, is up late again, going over medical notes. Brad asks what he's doing at this hour. Mark replies that he's studying because he's not sure what cases tomorrow will bring. He said it's important to always be as prepared as possible.

A four-tier pyramid is fixed on a whiteboard in the Butler locker room. "Results" forms its peak. "Performance" is on the second level. "Character" makes up its base. The third tier is "Preparation." And perhaps more than any other characteristic—more than toughness, execution, or defense—Stevens's Butler teams were as prepared as any in the nation.

"You knew Butler was never going to beat themselves," said Ohio State coach Thad Matta, a former Butler coach whose teams were beaten twice in three games by Stevens's teams.

As Siena coach Fran McCaffery once said, "If you're going to beat them, you almost have to play a perfect game."

Stevens did his homework early. While he coached games, a staff member often uploaded edited video clips to his laptop—clips on each of the next opponent's players, on the sets it runs the most, a couple of its most recent games, a couple of its games against teams that played a similar style to Butler. Afterward, Stevens devoured the footage, processing information at a pace his staff members called "amazing," often on late-night flights, his face illuminated by the screen's soft glow.

By noon the next day, Stevens said, he'd have in place the firm outlines of a game plan—no matter if the game was one day or one week away, because he didn't want to have a single unprepared practice.

"I wasn't going to do a day where it's fluff and I can't answer everything that I possibly can about the other team," he said. "That's how I'm wired."

He'd study analytics and dig through books—books on leadership, on how the mind works, on successful businesses and the people who ran them—for a motivational quote or passage, because just as he told his players to "win the next possession," Stevens believed it was his job to find any edge that could help win that possession.

"People always focus on the end of the game," said former Butler forward Matt Howard, "but one thing I learned more than ever there, and just something we talked about all the time, was it's not always about what happens at the end of the game. It's about what happened leading up to that."

For instance, Stevens loved to score on out-of-bounds plays. He usually had a quick-scoring play in his back pocket, but he also could draw up something based on a weakness he'd seen. Either way, out-of-bounds plays in basketball are akin to special teams in football—not many coaches truly try to capitalize in that area. But to Stevens, they are a potential edge.

"He's one of these guys, he's going to find a way to win," said Butler assistant Michael Lewis. "It doesn't matter if it's a basketball game or golfing or tennis or walking through the building to see who can get to the next room the fastest."

It might be an unorthodox plan, said former Butler assistant Micah Shrewsberry, such as having a post player defend a point guard for a play.

"Just because nobody else had done it, he wasn't afraid to try it, just because it might give us one advantage," said Shrewsberry, now a Celtics assistant.

NEED-TO-KNOW BASIS

As Lickliter had preached, Stevens and his staff spared no detail as they prepared a scouting report.

"By the end of the week, he's got so much information on his hands that he can give out bits and pieces," Shrewsberry said. "The players are like, 'Whoa, he knows everything about these guys.'"

But, as Lickliter also preached, Stevens provided the players with only what they absolutely needed to know—nothing more.

Ronald Nored, a former Butler guard now in a player development role with the Celtics, said he realized the approach wasn't common when speaking to players on other teams who received pages and pages of notes.

Lickliter said it is a talent to find only what will enable players to be successful, just as it's a talent to teach it. These are traits, he said, that separate Stevens, whose background as a former star player (in high school) and role player (in college) helps him relate to every player on his teams. But Stevens also saw himself then (and today) as more of a teacher than a coach, curious about what each player wanted beyond the game and invested in a way to help them reach that goal.

The Bulldogs realized that the information they received would make them as game-ready as possible.

"I can't remember one game where I felt less prepared than the other team," Nored said. "Not one."

The mind-set, Howard said, was to "know your player and the tendencies of other players as well."

The result was that opposing players would use screens to free themselves from the player guarding them, but the Bulldogs could switch on screens—even three times in one possession—and stay effective, as each of them knew enough about everyone to capably guard anyone. It allowed Butler's already-stifling defense to adapt while its parts still functioned as one.

"So you have to shoot a contested shot every time you shoot it," Cleveland State coach Gary Waters once said. "Every time there's any degree of penetration, there are at least two people ready to help out against you."

Stopping opponents was a priority. Howard said about 85 percent of preseason practices were devoted to defense. Players faced countless scenarios, each designed to build muscle memory through repetition so that they could react almost at will.

"We did stuff until it was clockwork," he said.

Following Stevens's axiom, "The game honors toughness," regimented practices were "extremely physical," according to Howard, who said they left him sore head to toe. However, they were short, lasting not a minute more than necessary—Nored remembers one lasting just 28 minutes—and Howard said few fouls were called. "But that's just how they wanted us to play," he said.

Opponents would tell the Bulldogs that they were the most physical team they played all season—dirty, even. But they were unassuming. Basketball analyst Jay Bilas said Butler "looks like choirboys but defends like a motorcycle gang." The idea, Stevens said, was "set the tone," "impose your will," and break the other team's spirit. Or, as Butler players said, "Make them quit."

It worked. In 2010, Butler became the first team since the shot clock was introduced in 1986 to reach the NCAA title game by holding five opponents under 60 points.

Stevens's teams had players similar to him, his ex-teammates say. They weren't the biggest, fastest, or most talented, but they were technically sound,

Entrusting the Celtics to 36-year-old coach Brad Stevens proved to be one of Danny Ainge's wisest moves.

prepared, determined, and ferocious competitors who had high basketball IQs and were team-focused. Under Stevens, such players created a whole far greater than the sum of its parts.

"The one thing that Brad has done throughout his career, as good as anybody I've ever seen," Matta said, "is he takes what he's got and he makes it the best it can be."

THE MOVE TO THE PROS

Tracy's third date with Brad is a 92-mile drive to a high school game in Anderson, Ind. She's excited, because it's good car time together. He talks about basketball the whole way. She didn't know about this side of his life until now—this passion for the game. They marry. There would be many more dates like this.

They have a lake house in Northern Indiana. She jokingly calls it his "happy place." "Every day at the lake is a little bit of heaven for him," Tracy said. It's a physical retreat from work, but his mind is never far from the job. Even there, Stevens said, "All I do is read books and articles about what's next. It never really stops."

He craves competition, in any form. One night as he and Tracy were breaking down boxes at their new home in Massachusetts, she swore that he was trying to do it faster. After a pause, he admitted that it probably was true.

"It's not just that he's competitive," Tracy said. "It's that he always wants to be competing."

The two have two Words With Friends games going at all times, she said. They also play Scrabble, though she said he leads the series, 500-2. ("It's amazing that I still play," she said.) His youth was filled with board games, and he long has been intrigued by puzzles, the challenge of making the next move.

But as he was winning 166 games in his first six years at Butler to become the sport's winningest coach ever in such a span, Stevens also turned down several offers, including some from blue-blood programs such as UCLA.

It became clear that he wouldn't leave Butler for another college.

That left only one option: the NBA.

Someone once told Stevens that the pro game differed from the college ranks in that it was more of a chess match. Naturally, that challenge long had intrigued him.

He spoke with NBA coaches at basketball clinics, watched numerous NBA games, implemented the plays, and discussed the pro game with players almost daily. His father, Mark, even recalled that Stevens once said, "I'd like coach for 10 or 15 years, then give the NBA a shot."

Then, in late June, Stevens and his wife had sold their house and were living with his mother when a voicemail dinged on his phone. It was Celtics president of basketball operations Danny Ainge. It seemed like a sign, Tracy said: "We have no home, maybe the world is telling us we should move."

The move seemed destined—for a player whose only Division 1 scholarship offer was from Larry Bird's college coach, for a college coach whose program was greatly influenced by Bill Russell, for a Hoosier to move from the state that is the cradle of the game to the state where that very game was born.

Several notable college coaches have made the leap to the pro game and stumbled, so there is skepticism. The Celtics are a team that's rebuilding, so there is doubt, though they gave Stevens a six-year contract, a sign of their patience.

He has no NBA experience, so there will be struggles, and he'll have to endure losses, which to this day, Tracy said, brings about a noticeable physical reaction in him.

"He absolutely hates to lose," she said. "He hates it with everything that he is."

Losses eat at him.

"Of all the great moments at Butler, I still remember the losses most vividly," he said. "I don't know why. I guess that's kind of what drives you."

He still will jump in shooting drills with his players and talk trash, telling them, "I'm not going to lose!"

Said Nored, "You're never going to get in the last good word with him. You might get in the last word, but it will not be the last good word."

Stevens said he handles defeat better now because coaching has granted him perspective.

"You do everything you can to control the outcome," he said, "and at the end of the day, it's not always in your control."

He said he cannot tell you his record in every season at Butler, or his record at DePauw, or in high school in Zionsville, Ind. He said he cannot remember the exact scores of the games. He said he's not sure where the strands of twine are from the sectional championship he won as a high school senior and that he cannot find all of his NCAA Tournament rings from Butler.

"I don't keep a lot of the trophy stuff," he said. "I don't pay attention to it."

What matters most, Stevens said, are the relationships forged during those years, many of which are so deep that former players will send him Father's Day cards.

"The guy, he just invests in you," said Nored. "He just wants you to be better in any way possible. That's how he is with everyone. Once you see that, he's an easy guy to root for, an easy guy to want to do things for."

Of the more than four dozen friends, family, colleagues, coaches, teachers, professors, classmates, roommates, and teammates interviewed for this series, close to three dozen recited some version of this phrase about Stevens: "You won't find anyone who has anything bad to say about him."

Said Ryan Hidinger, a close friend and high school teammate, "He's one of those people that you see and you're like, 'Nobody's that good.' But he's squeaky clean."

Added Matt Walker, a college roommate: "He's every parent's dream."

A NEVER-ENDING QUEST

In his first days with the Celtics, the front office was impressed with how hands-on Stevens was with players, how he was able to communicate information and build relationships. At media day, Ainge said he already knew he had hired the right man but he was so impressed with Stevens since then that "I'd like to give him a four-year contract extension."

During training camp, players remarked time and again on Stevens's attention to detail.

"He works on the little things first, from setting screens the right way to getting to a certain spot on the floor," said guard Keith Bogans.

Said Jeff Green, "He's very smart, very precise. He's a perfectionist."

Said Avery Bradley, "He drills it into our heads. If we go through a play halfway, he'll keep doing it—over and over again until we get it right."

Said Kris Humphries, "This is probably . . . the most detailed I've been coached."

And Brandon Bass said the biggest difference between this staff and that of former coach Doc Rivers was "more attention to detail."

Though those details are a huge part of his life, the best part of Stevens's day is when he can spend time with his two children—and especially play basketball with his 7-year-old son, Brady, who is aptly named for this part of the country (another reason Stevens seemed destined to coach in New England). They usually play in the driveway of their new home, which, of course, already has a goal set up, or at the Celtics' practice facility in Waltham. Tracy said they're quite competitive, but that Stevens internalizes it while Brady is outward, like his father at that age.

Tracy said her husband has remained the same person that she started dating in college, and he said he has no goals: "I get great satisfaction from trying to get better and trying to do the next thing as well as I can."

Nored believes that once you stop learning and you feel satisfied, "That's when you lose," and when asked if Stevens can be satisfied, Nored doesn't hesitate.

"I don't think he will be," he said. "Ever."

Tracy pondered the question for a minute and said that if he wins a championship, he'd enjoy it for a day or two, then hunt for another.

"It's a constant quest," she said. "His desire to compete and be the best is never-ending."

Years ago, when Stevens was playing high school basketball in Zionsville, his coach Dave Sollman said of all the players on the team, Stevens was the last he'd imagine becoming a coach. He was too smart, too bound for success elsewhere.

"He's going to make a lot more money in whatever he does than coaches could ever make," Sollman believed.

Friends, family, coaches, former teammates, and colleagues say he is one of the rare few who would have excelled at anything because of his intellect and drive. But growing up in the basketball-steeped culture of Indiana and coaching in Butler's Hinkle Fieldhouse, a national historic landmark that was once the largest gym in the US and was where part of "Hoosiers" was filmed, all but ruined him for anything else.

He is all-ball, a Hoosier in search of anything with a scoreboard, who no longer plays as an outlet for his ultra-competitiveness but instead channels it with laser focus into outpreparing the competition, to finding any edge hidden in the details.

A win provides the brief fix he needs and craves, and delays the dagger of defeat for one more day. Then he'll wake in the pre-dawn hours and continue that constant quest, learning everything he can, reexamining all he knows, all to improve, streamline, and perfect the process, his process, so that he can win tomorrow, too.

A Traumatic Past Hardens Celtics Rookie Smart's Resolve

September 29, 2014 • by Baxter Holmes

LANCASTER, Texas—Marcus Smart exits the silver Ford Mustang, surveys the apartment complex, and shakes his head. In the overcast morning light, with thunderstorms stretched gray across the summer sky, he tries to remember the last time he returned to this Dallas suburb and retraced his childhood steps. But he cannot remember. It has been that long.

"This is a place," says the 20-year-old Celtics rookie guard and top draft choice, "that you don't want to come back to."

Eight years ago, Marcus prayed: "Just please get me out of this."

He prayed as he sprinted through the complex's parking lot while a Bloods gang member gave chase, pulled a gun, and started firing.

He prayed as he zig-zagged between cars while seven bullets whizzed by. He prayed as he ran harder and faster than he ever will, knowing that this could be it.

"I promise," he prayed, "I'll do better."

Today, Marcus calls that moment the lowest point in a life racked by tragedy, with so many family members and friends dying from everything but old age—a toll so steep it does not seem real.

One relative dropped a loaded shotgun during a children's game of cowboys and Indians in this town many years ago. It discharged straight into the heart of another relative, who was 5.

Another relative was found shot to death one morning in a front yard in Tyler, Texas. He was 16.

A train struck one of Marcus's ex-Amateur Athletic Union teammates four years ago in rural Oklahoma. He was 17.

Then there was Todd Westbrook, Marcus's oldest half brother, who died at 33 from cancer.

The deaths came in rapid order.

"Oh, God," says Marcus's mother, Camellia, as she fights back tears. "At one point, it was like 'pop, pop, pop, pop, pop.'"

When Marcus was 3, his grandmother—Camellia's mother—died. He was close to her and attended the funeral, but after that, he told Camellia, "If I don't have to go, I don't want to."

"I used to hate seeing someone up there and it was someone you know, you care about," he says now, "and there's nothing you can do to help them."

Marcus has a guaranteed multimillion-dollar contract with the Boston Celtics, who selected him sixth overall in June's National Basketball Association draft. He has a multiyear apparel deal with Adidas, also worth more than $1 million. He has his health.

And with Celtics star point guard Rajon Rondo out 6 to 8 weeks because of a broken left hand, Smart figures to play a more prominent role, perhaps starting through the first month of the regular season.

But what he has seen makes him more grateful than most.

"I just wake up and I thank God every day," he says, "because I easily could've been in jail or six feet under."

—

Marcus stands on a sidewalk in front of a single-story, multifamily brick home on the 1500 block of North Bluegrove Road. A large magnolia tree shades the front yard.

"This is it," he says.

There is a metal gate on the door; that was not there when his family moved here from DeSoto just after Todd died, when Marcus was 9. Across the street is a notorious trio of apartment complexes—on the left and right called The Pinks; in the middle, the Meadows.

Marcus recalls the area, known as the "1500 block," as a place where Crips and Bloods gangs waged war, where drugs were rampant, where police sirens howled, where the Fourth of July was an excuse to fire off more gunshots than normal because outsiders mistook them for fireworks.

"At the time when I was here," Marcus says, "if you heard 'Lancaster, 1500 block, Meadows,' everybody said, 'Oh, you live by the Meadows. We won't come over there. We'll talk to you later.'"

—

Born three weeks prematurely at just 6 pounds, Marcus spent nearly a month in the hospital with a feeding tube as doctors ran tests to make sure he was OK. He would be fine; more than fine. When Camellia took him back for his two-month checkup, he dwarfed other children his age. By age 1, she called him huge.

"Ever since then, he's been big," she says.

But for as big and old as Marcus always appeared for his age, there came one harrowing night when his family asked him to become a man.

He was 9 years old.

His aunt sat Marcus and a cousin down on a couch and tried to talk, but could only cry. Finally, she started to say "Todd . . . "

"And I just knew what she was about to say next," Marcus says.

He burst into tears.

Marcus Smart and James Young show off their new work clothes after being selected in the first round of the 2014 NBA Draft. For Smart, reaching the league was the culmination of an often tragic journey.

"Todd is dying," the aunt told Marcus. "The doctor said he's brain-dead. His heart is still beating, but he's not there anymore, and they're ready to take him off life support."

Marcus bolted out of the house, shattering a glass door, screaming in the yard. Neighbors looked on, concerned. His cousin tackled him. "This can't be happening!" Marcus wailed.

Todd, who had become a father figure and mentor to his siblings as their mother and father worked nights, teaching his brothers how to dress (always clean, ironed clothes), speak (yes sir, no sir), shave, shake a man's hand, and more.

Todd, who would take Marcus swimming, to the gym, to get haircuts, doughnuts, ice cream, or just horse around. And when chemotherapy sapped Todd's energy, Marcus and a brother would go into Todd's room to watch the Discovery and History channels and shoot balled-up socks into a hoop-shaped wire hanger hooked on the door.

Todd, who was 15 when doctors found a tumor behind his eye following an all-district sophomore basketball season, but who went through treatment, returned as a senior, and led his team to the state semifinals.

Todd, who checked himself out of the hospital one night, played in a high school game with his left eye swollen shut, scored 30 points, and was called "The comeback kid" by newspapers.

"This can't be happening!" Marcus wailed.

The cancer spread to Todd's lungs and stomach. Marcus had learned there was no cure.

Then in late 2003, Marcus was asked what he wanted for Christmas, and he said he only wanted one more Christmas with Todd. He got his wish, and Todd gave him a gold chain with his initial "M" to hang around his neck.

Early the following year, after one family visit, Todd gave Camellia a long hug, called her the best mom in the world, and said he loved her. She said she loved him, too, thinking he would fight another day, as he had for 18 years.

Marcus saw family in the hospital waiting room, everyone in tears. He tore down the hallway into Todd's room and Camellia grabbed him.

"She's crying and I'm crying and I just see Todd's body there, lifeless," Marcus says. "It's like a mannequin."

He touched Todd's feet.

"Why is he so cold?" Marcus asked his mom.

"It's because he's not there anymore," she said.

He climbed on top of Todd's chest and started shaking him, shouting "Wake up!"

Remembering it all now, sitting in an apartment near downtown Dallas on a recent afternoon, Marcus pauses. Tears stream down his cheeks.

"I'm sorry," he says, wiping his face.

After a deep breath, he resumes his story.

"My mom grabbed me and she's holding me and she said, 'I'm sorry, there's nothing we can do for him now.'"

He kissed Todd on the forehead.

Then, as he exited the room, Marcus's other brothers, Michael, nearly twice his age, and Jeff, even older, stopped him.

"The family is all on you now," they told him. "It's time to grow up. We had our chances, and we blew it. Now it's your turn. You're the last one. You're all mom has left."

Marcus's first love was football—he played strong safety and wide receiver—but when Todd died, Marcus switched to basketball.

"What happened with him kind of intensified the game for me even more," he says. "Basketball became my love."

He is often told he shares an uncanny resemblance to Todd on the court, with his aggressive style, but Marcus says he does not understand how that is possible. He says he never had a chance to study Todd's play; a house fire destroyed Todd's game footage.

But Marcus honors Todd with his all-out effort, a trait that coaches have praised for years.

"I've always played hard," Marcus says. "That's how I was raised. But now I'm playing more with a purpose. Now I'm playing not just for myself, I'm playing for my brother, for my family. I'm going to go out there and give it all I have, because he gave it

all he had for 18 years, and he lost his battle. I don't want to lose my battle."

—

Marcus, back in Lancaster, is wearing a lime green shirt, black shorts, and sneakers. No one has recognized him—yet.

"It feels weird being here," he says. "It really does."

He is standing on the 1500 block.

"I got kicked out of these apartments plenty of times," he says.

He recalls hitting a mailman with a rock, then the mailman calling police and describing what Marcus was wearing. Marcus stripped down to his boxers, raced down to the street, turned the corner, and hid in his house.

"I didn't come out for about three days," he says.

Marcus liked throwing rocks—at people, cars, windows, anything. It was fun, a competition among friends to see who could hit the most difficult targets from the longest distances.

"It just turned into something where you're constantly doing it and you get addicted to it—the adrenaline rush," he says.

Michael had warned him not to throw stones. He said that one day he would hit the wrong person.

—

Not long after Todd's death, Camellia noticed a hole in one of Marcus's sneakers, which she found odd. Todd had taught him to keep up appearances, but with Todd gone, Marcus said, "It just wasn't as important anymore."

His new stance worried Camellia, who says, "That's when the changes started."

There is no manual for how to channel grief, and Marcus channeled his into anger, engaging in several fights per week at school.

"The smallest thing would set me off—just the way you look at me would set me off because I was so angry," he says.

He took anger management classes. They taught him exercises to calm down—take a deep breath, close your eyes, count to 10.

"I thought it was all stupid," he says. "What is counting to 10 going to do for me? I'm still going to be angry when I'm done counting."

His anger boiled over in a school fight that ended with Marcus slamming a student's head face-first into the concrete, again and again, before a teacher finally pulled him off.

"They said I almost killed him," Marcus says.

For that, he was kicked out of school and sent to the Texas Alternative Education Program, which he described as prison, with paddlings for punishment and mandatory uniforms. After serving 30 days, he got out and returned to public school, but said students looked at him like a criminal.

"So I put a wall up," he says. "I kind of established this mean personality, this person that you don't want to talk to, that you don't want to mess with."

Another way he lashed out was by throwing rocks, and late one spring evening, with a friend on a second-floor balcony in The Pinks complex, Marcus hit a man in a hooded sweatshirt from about 15 yards away, knocking him off his bike.

Marcus and his friend shared high-fives and laughs, and then looked away. When they looked back, they saw only the bike. Soon, they heard heavy footsteps running up the stairs toward them.

Marcus and his friend jumped over the balcony, sprinting to the adjacent complex. The man followed and pulled his gun. Drenched with sweat and full of fear, Marcus and his friend ducked into a nearby apartment.

"I thought my life was over," Marcus says.

But when the door opened and the man saw who Marcus was—the brother of Michael, a fellow Bloods gang member—he walked away.

The next day, on a playground, Marcus was playing basketball with Michael when the same man approached. Marcus dropped the ball and started backpedaling. Michael was not sure why.

"Your little brother was throwing rocks at me last night," the man told Michael. "He almost got hurt."

—

Marcus once found a crack cocaine rock in Michael's room. He did not know what it was, and he nearly tasted it.

"But something told me not to," Marcus says.

Michael had given up basketball and fallen into a gang life filled with drugs, guns, and violence.

Marcus saw his friends buy drugs from Michael, and he saw Michael accumulate goods that matched what his friends had reported stolen.

"How do you tell your friend, 'Oh, I think my brother stole that'?" Marcus asks. "You don't, because that's your brother."

Though just 10 at the time, Marcus tried to convince his brother to change his ways. And Michael, resorting to threats if necessary, kept the gang leaders from recruiting Marcus to the life. But Michael did not turn his own life around until after he nearly died from a cocaine overdose.

Eventually, Camellia was determined to leave Lancaster, and they moved to Flower Mound, a suburb west of Dallas. To demonstrate how different it is, Michael points to an open door in their home there on a recent afternoon.

"You couldn't leave the door open in Lancaster," he says. "If you do, you're crazy. They'll come in and steal your stuff while you're probably sitting on your couch."

In Flower Mound, Marcus reunited with a best friend, Phil Forte. They played basketball together in high school and then at Oklahoma State.

Marcus nearly turned professional after winning the Big 12's Player of the Year honors as a freshman, but he returned for one more year.

Then in February of his sophomore year, just before tip-off at Texas Tech, Marcus was told that his mother had been rushed to the hospital and that she did not want him to know.

"I was scared," he says. "It was heavy on my mind and my heart."

Camellia, whose blood pressure was acting up, watched from her hospital bed as Marcus lost his temper on court, engaging in an altercation with a fan late in the game—an altercation that began with the fan allegedly calling him a "trashy [racial expletive]," Michael says.

Said an Eastern Conference scout: "If the racist comment was true, I know for certain, me, I'm not confrontational but I would've punched the guy."

No matter the provocation, Marcus says there is no excuse for his actions, which resulted in national headlines, a three-game suspension, and revealed a side of Marcus that he had worked so hard to keep in control—his temper.

"Off the court, I'm a totally different person," he says. "I've heard people be like, 'Oh, so sweet, like a big ole teddy bear.' But I guess I still have that look on my face in a game. I guess I still have a vibe where it's intimidating."

His fire should fit in fine in Boston. After all, from Red Auerbach punching out an opposing owner to Larry Bird mixing it up with Dr. J, to Rajon Rondo bumping a ref, fire is in the Celtics' DNA.

"I guess that's why they have all those banners up there," Marcus says.

—

Marcus has done better, as he promised God on that night when he ran and prayed for his life, a night that marked both his lowest point and a turning point.

"When you experience things like that at a young age, it does change you," he says. "It humbles you in a way that you would never imagine."

But more than anything, he has been humbled by the loss of a father figure, a brother, Todd.

"I could've easily let the passing of my brother control how I live my life," he says. "But I was determined not to let him die in vain and to make a negative into a positive. I thank God every day because now I'm here, not only living out my dream but his dream, too."

On the night he was drafted, Marcus wore a bespoke blue suit jacket with several images stitched into the lining—an Oklahoma State logo, a map of Texas, an "M" for Marcus, and a copy of the tattoo that graces his arms, an RIP for Todd.

—

Before he climbs into the Mustang, leaves Lancaster, and heads to a workout, Marcus pulls up to a single-story, three-bedroom brick home on Princeton Drive where his family lived before leaving Lancaster for good. He was in sixth or seventh grade then. He and his brother still got in trouble over at the 1500 block, which was a walk or a bike ride away.

As he stands in the road, a man exits the house, short and upbeat with a country accent.

They make small talk, and the man asks Marcus what he hopes to achieve in the NBA.

"Just to have a long career," he says. "That's it."

It is a simple answer, but there are layers there.

He is playing for something he values in a way few others ever will, something that is fleeting, something that ran out too soon for those he loved.

He is playing for time, as much as possible, for him, for them.

Celtics Trade 9-Year Fixture Rondo

REBUILDING MOVE SENDS CAPTAIN TO DALLAS FOR 3 PLAYERS, 2 PICKS

December 19, 2014 • by Julian Benbow

Trade rumors have followed Rajon Rondo for as long as he's been in the NBA. They followed him during the Big Three era and in the rebuilding years that followed.

On Thursday, the rumors became reality. The Celtics completed a trade that will send Rondo and little-used forward Dwight Powell to the Dallas Mavericks for budding center Brandan Wright, veteran point guard Jameer Nelson, swingman Jae Crowder, and future first- and second-round picks.

The trade, confirmed by the Celtics and Mavericks, ends Rondo's nine years with the Celtics, a stretch that includes the 2008 NBA championship. It leaves the Celtics clearly positioning themselves for the long-term future with a hefty collection of draft picks. The immediate future, however, will continue to feature a team that will struggle to break .500.

As much as he was the perfect complement to Ray Allen, Kevin Garnett, and Paul Pierce, Rondo was almost never a full partner. With the Big Three long gone, the Celtics attempted to build their team around Rondo, naming him captain in January.

But the 28-year-old Rondo remained an enigmatic leader, and his statistics declined in some key areas this season. His free-throw shooting percentage is a career-low .333 and his scoring average dipped to 8.3 points per game, his lowest since his rookie season of 2007, when he averaged 6.4.

In his first full season since tearing his ACL in 2013, Rondo is leading the league in assists, averaging 10.8. He also is averaging a career-high 7.5 rebounds. He has put up three triple-doubles in the first 22 games.

Rondo was a four-time All-Star with the Celtics. He led the NBA in assists average three times (2012, 2013, 2014) and led the league in steals in 2010. He hasn't played more than 68 games in a season since 2010.

The Seattle SuperSonics tried prying Rondo from Ainge in exchange for Ray Allen. The Timberwolves also were interested. Knowing he had a player who saw the floor the way few other players could, Ainge wouldn't part with Rondo.

Even with Rondo emerging as an invaluable piece of the Celtics' championship run in 2008, the trade talks lingered. There were rumors of deals to Phoenix, Memphis, and Detroit.

There was a deal that would have sent him to New Orleans for his nemesis, Chris Paul. There was a three-way deal that would have sent him to Indiana.

None of them ever materialized.

One pursuer finally caught up to him Thursday evening, when the Mavericks, starving for a point guard to direct a team with legitimate championship hopes, pulled the trigger on the multiplayer trade.

Just a night earlier, Rondo reiterated the stance he had taken since the offseason—that he wanted to remain in Boston.

"How many times you want me to say it?" Rondo said. "We discussed it on media day. My thoughts and my opinions as far as the organization hasn't changed."

Big Move Picking up This Little Player

February 20, 2015 • by Gary Washburn

SACRAMENTO—Celtics president of basketball operations Danny Ainge proved Thursday that there is indeed substance to his flirtation. He had Isaiah Thomas beaming after a midnight phone call last July 1, the first day of free agency, even though

the Celtics had no salary cap space to afford the high-scoring guard.

Ainge planted a seed with Thomas, who acknowledged he was gushing about the rich history of the Celtics even though he knew he was headed elsewhere. He eventually signed a four-year, $27 million contract with the Suns, who acquired him in a sign-and-trade with the Sacramento Kings.

Eight months later, Thomas will don green as Ainge capitalized on buddy Ryan McDonough's desire to break up his backcourt in a trade for the expiring contract of Marcus Thornton and a 2016 first-round pick that was originally the Cleveland Cavaliers'.

Thomas will become a fan favorite in Boston because of his diminutive size, his ability to score on any defender, and his fiery style. At 5 feet, 9 inches, Thomas was the 60th and final pick of the 2011 draft, and that Mr. Irrelevant status served as more motivation.

When Thomas scored 51 points in a Washington state semifinal game for Curtis High School, college scouts said he was too small to play Division 1 in college. When he flourished at the University of Washington, NBA scouts doubted his scoring against bigger guards.

Thomas has averaged 27.3 points per 100 possessions in his career and is considered a volume scorer. In his previous locations—Sacramento and Phoenix—he was required to play mostly point guard or was in a crowded backcourt.

His responsibility in Boston will be to score and play occasional point guard, with Tacoma buddy Avery Bradley or defensive-minded Marcus Smart as his partner.

Ainge reiterated over the past couple of months that he did not want to take any contracts back for trades that lasted beyond this season, but he also didn't know then that Thomas would be available. The Celtics need his fire and brashness. They need a gunslinger off the bench who intimidates defenses with the ability to score in bunches.

Thomas is exactly the type of player the Celtics need for their quest for respectability. He just turned 26, so he has enough experience to serve as a leader and enough hunger to push his teammates.

"Honestly, yeah, I got a big belief in my skills," Thomas told the Globe in November. "I've always thought the things I did in high school I could do in college, and the things I did in college I could do in the NBA. That's just the confidence I've got in myself."

The Celtics haven't possessed a pure scorer off the bench—other than Thornton—since Eddie House. And Thomas's contract is team-friendly, just in case Ainge is encouraged to make other moves in the future.

But as of now, the Celtics have found a player who is looking for a permanent residence. And Boston emerged on his radar the moment Ainge placed that midnight phone call.

Bradley said he has known Thomas since their youth basketball days in Tacoma.

"He's just a good player," Bradley said. "He never surprised me. I knew if he got a chance, he'd be good."

Thomas is the first veteran player Ainge has acquired that is considered part of the team's future, and all he had to relinquish was a low first-round pick and Thornton, who was unlikely to return next season. So, score this trade a win for the Celtics.

They got the type of player they were looking for. In a league that covets scoring and those players who can take defenders off the dribble and get to the free throw line, the Celtics got one in a pint-sized package. But don't let the lack of height serve as a detractor; Thomas has the ability to be a real contributor over the next several seasons, despite his critics.

"They even said things about Michael Jordan, about Kobe Bryant," Thomas said in November. "So they're always going to say something, so you just have to go out there and work hard. When I am out there I'm trying to make the right play. I'm fine with [the criticism]. I just have to be the best I can be. That's all."

Playing for Keeps

CELTICS TAKE BROWN THIRD

June 24, 2016 • by Adam Himmelsbach

NEW YORK—For months, as the Celtics pushed through a successful 48-win season and continued their gradual ascension, so much of the focus remained on their future. They had collected an almost embarrassing amount of assets, and, finally, they would be in position to use them. They would be in position to strike.

In the weeks leading up to Thursday night's NBA Draft here at Barclays Center, the Celtics made no secret of their intentions of being active in the trade market. They had eight picks and no desire to use all of them.

And unlike last year, when their overtures to trade up and draft Justise Winslow were rebuffed, they had a valuable chip in this draft, the third overall pick.

But for Celtics fans, this night ended without noticeable sizzle. Boston did not complete a seismic trade, instead using the No. 3 pick on California freshman Jaylen Brown, an athletic and versatile player who has great potential.

"There have been a lot of talks for the last few months," Celtics president of basketball operations Danny Ainge said. "There were a lot of good players at 3 . . . You need another team that's going to agree to do a deal with you."

The Celtics used their other two first-round picks—Nos. 16 and 23 overall—on French forward Guerschon Yabusele and Croatian big man Ante Zizic. It is likely that both players will ultimately remain overseas as the Celtics navigate a crowded roster.

Early in the night, it had seemed that the Celtics would be in position to trade the No. 3 overall pick. The team fielded numerous calls, with apparent momentum building around teams seeking to trade up to draft Providence point guard Kris Dunn.

There were also reports that the Celtics were engaged in discussions about Bulls All-Star forward Jimmy Butler. But according to one league source, the trade discussions never truly gathered steam.

"Not realistic deals," the source said.

When Celtics co-owner Wyc Grousbeck addressed fans during the first round of the draft at the TD Garden watch party, he was booed, and he jokingly cupped his ear at the reaction. When Yabusele was chosen, there were boos from some Celtics fans at Barclays Center, too, and one teenage fan pulled a sliced-open basketball over his face in frustration.

Nevertheless, the Celtics are eager to move forward with this group and are particularly excited about the potential of Brown, who could become a cornerstone of this draft.

The Celtics selected Jaylen Brown (right) with the No. 3 pick in the 2017 NBA Draft. A year later, Jayson Tatum followed.

"Everybody unanimously really liked Brown," Ainge said. "He showed to us he's a much better shooter than [reported] . . . We feel like Jaylen is not a finished product by any stretch."

When Brown was 9 months old he started walking, and he started carrying a basketball soon after. He would carry it around the house and around the yard and even to day care.

"The day care would call me and say that he can't take that to school," Brown's mother, Mechalle, said late Thursday night. "I said, 'Please, I'm begging you, I've got to go to work. Can you please just let him have the basketball?' And they did. That was his security blanket for years."

Mechalle Brown said that her son always dreamed of reaching the NBA someday, and on Thursday, they sat together at a table at the front of Barclays Center and waited to see the dream become a reality.

When commissioner Adam Silver stepped to the podium to announce the Celtics' No. 3 overall pick, Brown had not been notified that it would be him.

"We only knew," Mechalle said, smiling, "when they said 'Jaylen Brown.'"

The 6-foot-7-inch Brown, who averaged 14.6 points and 5.4 rebounds for the Bears last season, will give the Celtics an explosive, powerful front-court player capable of defending multiple positions.

He was called back to Boston for a second workout last Monday, and he believed the Celtics had great interest in him.

"I'm happy to be a part of the family," Brown said. "I know Boston has a lot of history, a lot of tradition, and I want to add to that. I know it's a playoff team, so I love playoff basketball, and I can't wait to win.

"[The] NBA is a faster pace, faster tempo, so it's a lot of transition, and I feel like that's where I excel, that's where I thrive. However, I do have to get a lot better. Decision-making has to get a lot better."

Celtics Go Big, Land Horford

LANDMARK DAY FOR TEAM, CITY

July 3, 2016 • by Gary Washburn

The addition of Al Horford helps the franchise erase the stigma of being unable to attract a major free agent.

It's been more than 30 years since the Celtics faithful can recall a day like this, when a premium free agent, a multi-time All-Star, willfully chose to join Boston in his prime years.

The surrealism of Saturday for the Celtics cannot be understated. It began with Horford informing teams that he was down to the Celtics and Wizards, each offering a four-year, maximum contract at an estimated $113 million.

It kicked into Venom GT gear when Patriots quarterback, four-time Super Bowl champion, Deflategate defendant, and all-around man of Boston Tom Brady was spotted in the Hamptons as the Celtics were about to meet with Kevin Durant in their attempt to recruit the former MVP.

As the Celtics contingent that included Brady, president of basketball operations Danny Ainge, owners Steve Pagliuca and Wyc Grousbeck, guard Isaiah Thomas, and forward Jae Crowder concluded their meeting with Durant, Horford chose to accept the Celtics' offer.

He becomes the first major free agent in generations to sign with the Celtics. Boston has carried a rather stale reputation for being a city that is difficult to play in for players of color. But while the Red Sox, Patriots, and even the Bruins have been able to attract African-American players, the Celtics struggled mightily in luring high-caliber free agents of color.

It had little to do with the city and more to do with the perception. But a funny thing occurred during the Celtics' first-round playoff series with the Atlanta Hawks this spring. The fans who hang out hours before the game around the tunnel to the visiting locker room began recruiting Horford after workouts, telling him how they would love to see him in green.

While they catcalled Dennis Schroder and booed every other Hawk, the fans slyly kept their remarks to a minimum with Horford, knowing he would be a free agent target.

The signing indicates that the Celtics no longer have a stigma when it comes to major free agents. That had become apparent over the last few years, but Horford agreeing to a deal—not just considering—shows that the city and team are capable of being a destination for players in their prime.

Horford was taken one pick after Durant in the 2007 draft. Horford is 30 and missed parts of two seasons with torn pectoral muscles, but he was reliable, steady, and vastly improved offensively during nine seasons with the Hawks.

He is not going to amass monster games, but in NBA circles his value was unquestioned to the Hawks. He was great in the community, a sparkling teammate, and he cared enough about his game to improve his shooting over the years after it was a major weakness when he left the University of Florida.

Ainge had saved his assets, scraped up resources and salary cap space to make legitimate offers to players such as Horford. With the shocking contracts being agreed upon over the past 48 hours, he knew it would take a maximum contract to attract Horford. The $113 million deal over four years is of market value. The Celtics did not get cheated.

The ownership group has sought to bring high-caliber players to Boston voluntarily, without having to sacrifice assets. There was major disappointment on draft night when the Celtics did not spin a big trade for a player such as Jimmy Butler, but that would have likely required giving up two first-round draft picks and veterans.

It would have been a heavy price.

Ainge managed the team's salary cap—helped greatly by the $20 million increase this summer with the influx of television money—in order to chase big-time free agents with cash in hand and a roster ready to take the next step.

It also helped greatly that players such as Thomas (age 27) and Jae Crowder (who turns 26 on Wednesday) signed off on Boston as a comfortable city for which to play. These millennials like Boston, and Thomas acknowledged he had conversations with Horford over the past few days after Horford expressed interest in the Celtics experience.

Saturday was a landmark day for the Celtics, an organization that carried the tag of being unable to attract a major free agent like a scarlet letter. It was an embarrassing tag, even though no one in the organization had anything to do with the city's perception and sometimes soiled racial history.

But the acquisition of Kevin Garnett nine years ago—has it been that long?—began an ascension for the reputation of this city and the Celtics. The Celtics were closing in on bringing these types of players here, but instead of making foolish trades that would have damaged the team's long-term future, Ainge waited—sometimes impatiently—to make the astute move that would improve the organization immediately and secure assets for the future.

It was a landmark day for Ainge, the Celtics, and the city.

One-Man Show

THOMAS SCORES 52 POINTS—29 IN FOURTH—TO CARRY CELTICS

December 31, 2016 • by Adam Himmelsbach

About a half-hour after the Celtics' 117-114 win over the Heat on Friday, Miami center Hassan Whiteside walked slowly down a hallway in the bowels of TD Garden and passed the Celtics' locker room just as Isaiah Thomas was walking out with his two children.

Whiteside was hit in the right eye during the game, and now he was squinting and his eye was red. Thomas's 4-year-old son, Jaiden, noticed Whiteside's eye.

"What happened to you?" he asked.

Whiteside smiled.

"Your dad killed us out there," he said. "That's what happened."

And that is exactly what happened. Thomas added his finest work to an ever-growing portfolio, erupting for a career-high 52 points, 29 of which came during a daring and enchanting fourth quarter. The All-Star made 15 of 26 shots, 9 of 13 3-pointers, and all 13 of his free throws.

"It's remarkable," Celtics coach Brad Stevens said. "I mean, I don't know what else to say."

Thomas's scoring total is the fourth-highest in franchise history, and he becomes the first Celtic to reach the 50-point mark since Paul Pierce scored 50 in Boston's double-overtime loss to the Cavaliers on Feb. 15, 2006. Thomas also set a TD Garden scoring record and a franchise record for points in one quarter.

His fourth-quarter total was 2 points shy of the NBA record for that period, which Wilt Chamberlain set during his historic 100-point game in 1962.

"That fourth quarter, it just felt like I was out there by myself," Thomas said, "like I was in the gym working on my game and throwing up everything and it was just going in. It was a special feeling."

After the Heat took an 89-84 fourth-quarter lead, Thomas drained five 3-pointers over a stretch of just 3 minutes, 30 seconds, the last one giving the Celtics a 101-93 advantage.

Thomas's mother, Tina Baldtrip, is visiting from Tacoma, Wash., and Thomas could see her in the stands pleading for him to go for 50. He looked back at her to indicate he was trying, as only a son can.

Amid the frenzy, though, the Celtics had to find a way to beat the lowly Heat.

Miami charged back and tied the score at 104 on a Wayne Ellington layup. But that is where their hopes were dashed, because the Celtics had Thomas and the Heat did not.

The All-Star hit a layup and a pair of foul shots to put the Celtics back in front, and then with 37.2 seconds left he provided the dagger, drilling his sixth 3-pointer of the quarter, a deep offering from the left arc, making it 111-106. He later added two free throws to ice the game, and he was serenaded by chants of "MVP."

"You dream of that as a kid," Thomas said of the chants. "To have it happen playing in the Garden for the Celtics, it doesn't get any bigger than that."

Ubers, Gyms, and Jumpers: A Night on the Road with Isaiah Thomas

February 19, 2017 • by Adam Himmelsbach

DALLAS—It is nearing 8 p.m. on a Sunday and the Celtics have been at the posh Hotel Crescent Court in Dallas for just a few hours. This is their fourth city in five days, and they have a rare chance to recover before they face the Mavericks the next night.

Coach Brad Stevens walks through the marble-floored lobby with a stack of papers, heading some-place quiet to scribble fresh thoughts about his surging team. A few players enter the hotel carrying food in takeout boxes and go back to their rooms. Then Isaiah Thomas steps from an elevator and walks slowly toward the entrance as the hotel's trendy music thumps in the background. He has just woken from a nap.

The 5-foot-9-inch point guard is wearing sneakers and Celtics shorts, and a hooded sweatshirt covers his long-sleeved practice warm-up. Even though it is late, even though it has been a taxing road trip that has spanned four time zones, even though there is a game tomorrow, he is going to a gym—just like he does the night before almost every Celtics road game.

This routine and, more importantly, this drive have helped Thomas blossom from the last pick in the 2011 NBA Draft into a two-time All-Star who is now chasing a league scoring title. These workouts are not the sole reason he has reached this point, but they are examples that show how it became possible.

"Some people can wake up and be really good without working," Thomas says. "Some people are that special. And I was blessed with ability, but without the work I wouldn't be close to where I am today."

Thomas is always joined at the night sessions by a devoted cadre of team staffers. The group in Dallas includes assistant coaches Jerome Allen, Kenny Graves, and Brandon Bailey, and video coordinators Alex Barlow and Matt Reynolds.

Thomas prefers to shoot at NBA arenas, but other events at the venues can complicate those plans. In this case, the comedian Jeff Dunham is performing at the American Airlines Center. So Bailey found an open court at nearby Southern Methodist University.

When an Uber car arrives it is clear there is not enough room for everyone. Allen, the 44-year-old former University of Pennsylvania coach, offers to take a taxi by himself.

"Man, why are you always trying to do different stuff?" Thomas says, smiling, before pulling out his phone to request another Uber.

There is some confusion about the destination, because instead of entering the gym address Thomas simply typed "SMU" into the app, and the university has a sprawling, 234-acre campus. So Allen just asks the driver to follow the first car. It has all turned into a bit of a production.

"They should have had me just call Mark," Thomas says, smiling, referring to Mavericks owner Mark Cuban.

"Yo, stop it, man," Allen says, shaking his head.

"He would have just let me in their arena. Should have called Mark Cuban."

UP TO SPEED

When Thomas attended the University of Washington, he learned quickly that there was a required speed. If players walked during water breaks, coach Lorenzo Romar would instantly move on to the next drill.

But the grind did not bother Thomas. He had seen his father press through so many graveyard shifts as a parts inspector for Boeing. He had seen his mother work several jobs at a time, including draining days as a hospice nurse. If he was told to run to get some water, he would run to get some water.

He maintained this intensity during his rookie season with the Kings five years ago. When others went half-speed, he sprinted. When others were still at home, he arrived early.

A Sacramento coach even called the Washington staff and asked how to get Thomas to ease up, because he was making teammates look bad. The Huskies coaches called Thomas and told him to keep going.

Thomas, who is from Tacoma, Wash., had once heard stories about former Seattle SuperSonics star Ray Allen arriving for games hours early to maintain a shooting routine. Thomas's close friend Jason Terry, who is now in his 18th NBA season, had shared similar advice.

So on game days, Thomas took taxis to arenas with assistant coach Bobby Jackson four hours before tipoff. Since he spent the first two months of his rookie year on the bench, these sessions were his games. He would shoot, then play Jackson one-on-one, and then run every stair in the arena's lower bowl, at home and on the road.

"I was like, 'This kid is gonna destroy everybody,'" Jackson says. "He didn't believe in taking days off. He believed in working his ass off."

Even though Thomas is now a star who averages 29.9 points per game, is threatening Larry Bird's franchise record for scoring average in a season, and is often serenaded with "MVP" chants at TD Garden, he still arrives at arenas earlier than the rest. He is joined by the usual group of Celtics staffers, as well as ballboys.

The shooting sessions are short and purposeful and efficient, and everyone who takes part must be just as focused as Thomas. Strength coach Bryan Doo created a rule that if the ball bounces twice on a rebound, everyone has to complete a full-court sprint. The road ballboys are made aware of this policy before they begin.

"And then," Thomas says, "they figure out if they want to stay or not."

Sometimes, Thomas will fire the ball off the backboard as a joke, just to keep everyone on their toes.

"But the way he's been shooting this year," Bailey says, "there aren't a lot of misses."

A NIGHT AT THE GYM

An SMU basketball staffer is waiting in the parking lot on this breezy night as the Celtics contingent arrives at Moody Coliseum, the university's 7,000-seat arena. As they walk into the complex, they pass children practicing in an auxiliary gym.

The kids are being instructed by Mo Williams, the 34-year-old NBA free agent who won a championship with the Cavaliers last season and now runs a basketball academy here. When Williams sees Thomas, he smiles and greets him.

"Hold up," Williams tells the children. "Everybody come here. Do y'all know who this is?"

They know. Williams tells them how many points Thomas has scored on him, and they nod.

"Listen, this is what hard work did, right here," Williams says strongly, pointing at Thomas. "He ain't too far apart from you in height. So don't let nobody tell you what you can't do, or who you can't be."

The children are starstruck. Then Williams tells them to get back on the baseline to run a sprint, and they sigh.

Just a few hours earlier in the main arena, SMU upset nationally ranked Cincinnati, with former president George W. Bush among those in attendance. Maintenance workers are still in the aisles cleaning up snack wrappers and soda cups, but otherwise the space is quiet, just as Thomas prefers.

He starts by taking 20 midrange jump shots from five spots on the court. Most go in without touching the rim. While Graves, Bailey, Barlow, and Reynolds stand under the hoop to rebound, Allen is closer to Thomas, offering instruction.

The coach had a lengthy pro career in the NBA and in Europe, and he joined the Celtics' staff in the summer of 2015. He likes to joke that Thomas did not even speak to him during his first month in Boston. After Thomas met Allen he Googled him, and his credentials checked out. They now have a trust rooted in loyalty and friendly jabs.

Allen looks for Thomas's flaws, even though it can be a challenge to find them. He recently noticed that Thomas was shooting 3-pointers higher than normal because defenders were so close. If Thomas is being forced to alter his shot, it usually means he is in position to blow past his opponent, which is the preferred option.

"I'm appreciative that he trusts me to not necessarily tell him what he wants to hear, but what he needs to hear," Allen says. "Him spending these late nights in a gym just shows a level of dedication and professionalism that most people on the periphery wouldn't really expect."

Of course, Allen is also here for the ribbing. He asks Thomas when he is finally going to get a haircut, and Thomas says he will wait until he is in Boston, because he doesn't cut his own hair like Allen does.

Thomas asks how many people attend games at the cozy Moody Coliseum, and Allen says 5,000, just like when Thomas was at Washington. Thomas isn't thrown off by the sarcasm.

"When I was at UW," he says, "we were 10,000 strong."

Thomas then needles Allen about Penn, the Ivy League school where he played and later coached.

"The students bring books to the games, huh?" Thomas says. "They study at games?"

Amid the banter, one shot after another is splashing through the net. A few children from the other gym have slithered into the arena now, and they're sitting quietly in front-row seats and taking pictures with their smartphones. When one claps after a made shot, the others scold him in fear of being kicked out. But Thomas just smiles.

He once played for an AAU team with the son of former Sonics standout Nate McMillan, and he was in awe whenever McMillan visited practice. He knows these boys are probably feeling something similar.

He has broken a sweat as he moves behind the 3-point line, where he must make 10 of 13 shots from each location before advancing. Thomas, whose current field goal, 3-point, and free throw percentages are all at career highs, has to start over in just two of the five spots. Then he concludes the session with free throws before signing autographs and taking pictures with the boys in the front-row seats.

"That's what it's all about," he says later. "I was once in their shoes, and for them to all know who I am, even in Dallas, is still crazy to me. That's everything."

About an hour after arriving, it is time to go. Thomas requests another Uber, but when he goes outside it is not there. Sometimes there are small hiccups like this. One night this season when the group went to the Jordan Brand gym in New York, they wandered around an alley unable to locate an entrance. But Thomas always finds his way to the basket.

During the ride back to the hotel, Allen is in the front seat trying to persuade the driver to root for Boston against the Mavericks. The woman has no idea one of the best basketball players in the world is in the back.

Thomas is on the phone with his wife, Kayla, who tells him their 5-year-old son, Jaiden, is upset. On a flight home to Boston earlier, he noticed a girl on the plane and began winking at her. After the flight he tried to find the girl, but then she was gone and now he is sad.

Kayla puts Jaiden on the phone so he can talk to his father about his bad day.

"Next time, just talk to her on the plane," Thomas says.

Sometimes, he explains to his young son, you've just got to take your shot.

The car pulls up to the hotel just after 9 p.m. In the morning, the Celtics will hold a shootaround. Then that afternoon Thomas will be back on the court shooting by himself, sticking with his routine, working to become great, or perhaps just greater. He scores 29 points in the win over the Mavericks, and the fact that the performance is met with a shrug shows how far he has come.

"Look at the draft picks that went before him," says Jackson, the former Sacramento assistant. "If you make it to the NBA and relax, nine times out of 10 you're not going to be successful. But hard work is going to outdo talent, and that's what Isaiah has continually shown. He's one of those guys that deserves everything he gets."

Isaiah Thomas, who scored 53 points, acknowledges the crowd in the closing moments of Game 2 of the 2017 Eastern Conference semifinals versus the Wizards.

Gap Integrity

THOMAS DELIVERS AN OTHERWORLDLY PERFORMANCE

May 3, 2017 • by Chad Finn

At some point this postseason, the Celtics will realize that there are no extra points awarded for degree of difficulty. Maybe they'll even figure it out before it's too late, when there are no more games to be played and no more comebacks left to make.

But one can't totally blame them for making it so tough on themselves.

If they made it easy, none of us would get to savor the fun of watching Isaiah Thomas bail them out.

In a season in which the 5-foot-9-inch guard provided consistent brilliance (not to mention nearly 30 points per game) to the Celtics, he delivered a tour de force even by his usual standards Tuesday night at TD Garden.

Thomas scored 53 points—including 20 in the fourth quarter and 9 more in overtime—to out-duel the Wizards' John Wall (40 points) and lead the Celtics to a multi-comeback 129-119 overtime victory and a 2-0 lead in the Eastern Conference semifinal series.

"Two great players played well," said Wizards coach Scott Brooks, who apparently dabbles in understatement.

But in the end, the stage was Thomas's. He is the definition of resilient, and not entirely in ways having to do with basketball. This enjoyable Celtics playoff run has been accompanied by unimaginable sadness.

Thomas's 22-year-old sister Chyna was killed in a car accident April 15. Her funeral was this past Saturday in Tacoma, Wash., and Thomas has somehow been navigating a relentless itinerary with staggering poise.

Thomas scored 25 points in the first-round-series clinching win over the Bulls Friday, flew to Tacoma and delivered a eulogy Saturday, arrived back in Boston for Game 1 of the Wizards series Sunday, got a tooth knocked out, and still scored 33 points in a Celtics win. He spent Monday getting significant dental work done.

"He was not feeling good and was having a tough day," said Celtics coach Brad Stevens. "I thought he was really going to have to gut this one out. He not only guts it out, he ends up with 50."

Well actually, 53, coach. That's remarkable enough. But for Thomas, it cannot be easy to play on. And yet he finds a way to play beyond our imagination. Tuesday night, however, surpassed all other previous performances, and not just because of basketball.

It would have been Chyna's 23rd birthday.

When asked on TNT's broadcast immediately following the game how he conjured up such an effort, Thomas replied, "My sister. Everything I do is for her and she's watching over me."

The Celtics began this one stuck in the same early malaise that plagued them in the opener. Against the Wizards Sunday, the Celtics spotted the Wizards a ridiculous 16-0 lead before receiving the alert that the game had indeed begun and eventually accelerating to a 123-111 win. The resilience was admirable, but it can be frustrating that the Celtics so often require it, at least until Thomas inevitably seizes the moment.

Tuesday night, the Celtics started slightly better, but it would hardly qualify as starting well—this time, they had totaled 8 points rather than zero when the Wizards hit the 16 mark on a dunk by '80s movie villain Marcin Gortat exactly halfway through the first quarter.

The feisty and fast Wizards continued to score at a rate Paul Westhead would love, building leads of 23-14 and 35-23 before wrapping up the first quarter with a 42-29 advantage on a Jason Smith 3-pointer with 1.3 seconds left.

Tuesday night the climb took longer, but lo and behold, the Celtics seized their first lead, 59-58, on an Al Horford 3-pointer with 2 minutes and 11 seconds left in the first quarter.

The Wizards bolted out on a 14-3 run to start the third quarter, taking an 81-67 lead slightly more than seven minutes into the second half. But again, the Celtics dipped into that reservoir of resilience, and by the end of the quarter trailed just 89-84 despite Wall's 12 points in the frame.

Then, Thomas seized the stage, as he has so often done in the fourth quarter this season. He scored 20 points on a variety of drives, pull-ups, and free throws. He drove and banked a shot—plus drew a foul and hit the free throw—to tie it at 99-99 with 7:36 left.

After the Wizards built a 110-104 lead, Thomas hit a 3 at 2:30 to cut the margin to 3, then found Terry Rozier for a tying 3-pointer. Thomas's jumper with 47 seconds left put the Celtics up, 112-111, and he later hit a pair of free throws to tie it at 114-114, forcing overtime.

His domination carried over to overtime, and when his drive through the heart of the Wizards defense made it 122-117, chants of M-V-P, M-V-P broke out in the Garden. In the NBA, this is the year of Russell Westbrook and James Harden in terms of individual performances. But watching Thomas seize the stage Tuesday—and knowing all that he is enduring—the least we can do is hear the crowd's argument on his behalf.

Olynyk an Unconventional Hero

May 16, 2017 • by Gary Washburn

On Monday, Kelly Olynyk grew from a dude into a man.

That is not an insult. It's accurate. For four years Olynyk has been trying to find his place in this physical NBA. Inasmuch as he wanted to be that classic finesse stretch four, the Celtics needed more. They needed Olynyk to play center duties.

So there he was setting awkward screens, posting up with his rather graceless footwork and battling opposing big men for rebounds, and the results at times were ghastly.

At the same time, the coaching staff pleaded with Olynyk to keep his confidence. His defense has improved. He is no longer a lost cause at center, and he is capable of knocking down those open shots.

Isaiah Thomas and Kelly Olynyk embrace after the Celtics' Game 7 victory over the Wizards.

When many Celtics faithful wondered why Olynyk remained in a Game 7 at such a critical time, he was busy making the biggest plays of his basketball career. His fourth quarter will be remembered for decades. He'll likely never have to buy a Molson in this town for the rest of his life.

In a game that cemented the Celtics return to basketball prominence, Olynyk was at the center of Boston's game-winning surge. He scored 14 fourth-quarter points in a span of 7 minutes 3 seconds as the Celtics rallied and held on to beat the Washington Wizards, 115-105, at TD Garden.

The Celtics now face the Cleveland Cavaliers in the Eastern Conference finals beginning Wednesday in Boston. But they could not look forward without looking back at Olynyk's impact on this pressure-packed game.

Olynyk combined for 47 points through the first six games of this series, including 4 in Game 6. But in a display of his rather unconventional skill set, Olynyk plodded his way to the basket for layups, gave a simple flick of the wrists for 3-pointers, and then added a 19-footer as the Celtics fought back a furious Washington charge after taking a 94-81 lead.

The Celtics needed offense from an unexpected source. They needed someone to relieve pressure from Isaiah Thomas, who scored 29 points on 9-for-21 shooting. The Wizards made him labor for his points save a couple of 3-pointers that helped the Celtics come back late in the third quarter.

Al Horford had his moments. Jae Crowder didn't make much of an impact. So it was up to Olynyk to become that second scorer in the fourth quarter.

He finished with 26 points, his most since a Jan. 13 win at Atlanta, catapulting the Celtics to their first conference finals in five years.

"It was unbelievable," Olynyk said of the Game 7 atmosphere. "Especially to do it in front of our fans and the city of Boston. It was unbelievable to be in there and feel that energy, that enthusiasm, the passion 20,000 people had and just thrive off that."

Celtics Will Trade Top Pick to 76ers

BOSTON TO RECEIVE NO. 3 CHOICE AND A FUTURE FIRST-ROUND SELECTION

June 18, 2017 • by Adam Himmelsbach

One month ago, as four Ping-Pong balls bounced in the Celtics' favor at the draft lottery and dropped the No. 1 overall pick in their lap, Boston's already bright future became even brighter.

The team would have a chance to select the top prospect in the draft, presumably Washington point guard Markelle Fultz, or perhaps use the pick as a chip to lure a star. But it turns out they will be in position to do something in between.

According to a league source, the Celtics have agreed upon a deal in which they will send the No. 1 pick to the 76ers. The trade is expected to be finalized on Monday. The source said that the Celtics will receive the No. 3 overall pick in this year's draft as well as a future first-round pick from the 76ers. That choice will come in either 2018 or 2019, based on protections that have been put on the pick. While the specifics of those protections were unclear, a source said the belief was that they would actually protect the value of the pick for both teams. The 76ers have four first-round picks in the next two drafts.

The Celtics have long maintained that they believe there are four elite prospects in this draft, and a league source said the team came to the decision that the gap between Fultz and the others

The Celtics selected Jayson Tatum as the No. 3 pick in the 2018 Draft. But he never wore No. 11 for the Celtics, switching to No. 0 before the start of his rookie season.

was not massive. Also, Boston already has an overflowing backcourt that is highlighted by two-time All-Star Isaiah Thomas. Still, it was long believed that Fultz, who is considered the top prospect in this draft class, would end up with the Celtics.

The guard spent two days in Boston meeting with the team this month, and the Celtics had publicly made it clear that their preference was to keep the pick rather than trade it in a deal for a star veteran. Now they are still in position to make a high pick, and they have added to their overflowing war chest of assets in the process.

Forward Thinking

CELTICS SELECT DUKE'S TATUM WITH THIRD PICK

June 23, 2017 • by Adam Himmelsbach

NEW YORK—Jayson Tatum knocked on his father's hotel room door at about 9 a.m. on Thursday morning and just wanted to talk about the big day that was ahead.

The former Duke forward wondered how he should shake commissioner Adam Silver's hand when his name was called in the first round of the NBA Draft. He wondered if he should hug his mother

or his father first. He wondered if he might cry. He told his father it was certainly a possibility.

"You can cry all you want," Justin Tatum told his son. "It's your day. You worked for this day for 19 years."

On Thursday night, Markelle Fultz and Lonzo Ball were selected with the first two picks of the draft. Tatum said he did not know the Celtics had chosen him third until ESPN's cameras swarmed to his table in the Barclays Center green room. And then it hit him. He was a Boston Celtic, just as he and his family had hoped.

"It feels great just finally knowing where I'm going and having someplace to call home," Tatum said, standing in a quiet hallway in the bowels of the arena wearing his crisp new Celtics hat. "And I'm glad it's Boston."

Tatum averaged 16.8 points, 7.3 rebounds, and 2.1 assists during his freshman season at Duke last year. He is a dynamic scorer whose versatility at both ends of the floor should be an asset in coach Brad Stevens's system.

"He's a really skilled player, really talented scorer," Stevens said. "Great kid, great work ethic. We're excited to have him aboard. We think Jayson can play a variety of positions with a variety of guys. I think that, in this kind of position-less league, those guys are really valuable."

The Celtics won the No. 1 overall pick at last month's draft lottery and for weeks it was widely believed they would select Washington point guard Fultz.

But on Saturday, Celtics president of basketball operations Danny Ainge shook up the NBA landscape by agreeing to trade the No. 1 pick to the 76ers in exchange for the No. 3 overall choice this year as well as a future first-round selection.

When news of that deal broke, Duke coach Mike Krzyzewski called Tatum and told him that the Celtics wanted to have him in for a workout. Krzyzewski got to know Stevens when he was at Butler, including when their teams met in the 2010 national title game. And he raved about Stevens to Tatum.

The forward said he felt ill on Monday, but he completed a workout with the Celtics anyway.

"He never changed his expression," Stevens said. "[He] went at a high tempo, but when he missed a shot, he never showed anything but resolve to make the next one."

Later that day, Ainge hinted that he felt there was a good chance the player the team drafted at No. 3 was also the player it would have taken at No. 1.

Justin Tatum said that after hearing Krzyzewski's endorsement, and after his son spent part of a day in Boston, the family's preference became clear. They wanted him to become a Celtic.

"Jayson is a learner," Justin Tatum said. "He absorbs the game like a sponge. Brad is somebody that's going to challenge him every game, every practice. So I think being under his tutelage is just going to make Jayson a much better player. You're going to see his skill level come to life."

Tatum said he is eager to join a Celtics team that reached the Eastern Conference finals last season, and he was excited to get started.

"It's great I think that I get to learn that much more, especially from a veteran team that knows what it takes to get there," he said. "I can't wait to go learn from Coach Stevens and Isaiah Thomas and just everybody on their roster."

Celtics Land Star: Hayward

July 5, 2017 • by Adam Himmelsbach

SALT LAKE CITY—When Brad Stevens was an assistant coach at Butler University, he began recruiting a scrawny tennis player from nearby Brownsburg (Ind.) High School named Gordon Hayward.

Stevens told Hayward he could see him becoming an NBA player someday, but he probably never envisioned that he would coach him there.

After a wild day filled with conflicting reports and speculation about his future, Hayward announced Tuesday night that he had agreed to a deal with the Celtics. According to a league source, it is a four-year, $128 million maximum contract, with a player option in the final season.

The All-Star forward's signing gives Boston the biggest prize in this free agent class and immediately positions the team more comfortably among the league's elite.

Shortly after winning 53 games and securing the No. 1 seed in the Eastern Conference, the Celtics could now challenge LeBron James and the Cavaliers in the playoffs.

The 6-foot-7-inch Hayward, who averaged 21.9 points and 5.4 rebounds for the Jazz last season, gives the Celtics a versatile, dynamic scorer who should take some of the burden off of the team's other All-Star, Isaiah Thomas.

In the 2,000-word essay posted on The Players' Tribune, Hayward spoke glowingly about his time in Utah, where he had played ever since being drafted by the Jazz in 2010. That was the same year Hayward, Stevens, and Butler lost in the NCAA title game against Duke, when Hayward's last-second, half-court heave caromed off the rim.

Hayward was just a sophomore then, and he faced the difficult decision of whether to leave for the NBA or return to Butler, where the Bulldogs would have been in position to chase another title.

"It was such a tough decision," Hayward wrote in The Players' Tribune. "But there was one person who I knew I could talk to about it from every angle, who I knew would give me the smartest and most honest perspective available: Coach Stevens."

Hayward went on to the NBA, and Stevens was hired by the Celtics three years later.

"And again, Coach Stevens and I found ourselves at a crossroads together," Hayward said. "And again, he was the person I knew I could count on the most. And now I've decided to sign with the Boston Celtics."

Hayward said he was drawn to the winning sports culture in Boston, as well as the rich history of the Celtics. He also said that the "amazing" potential he saw on Boston's current roster was a plus. And then he turned the focus back to his former mentor.

"And that unfinished business we had together, back in 2010, when I left Butler for the NBA," Hayward said. "As far as I'm concerned, all of these years later, we still have it: And that's to win a championship."

Hayward had spent this past weekend visiting with his potential suitors—the Heat, Celtics, and Jazz—and all indications were that July 4 would bring some clarity. Instead, it turned into a frenzied day filled with conflicting reports, frustrated representatives, and team executives left waiting by their cellphones.

Just after 2 p.m., ESPN reported that Hayward had agreed to a deal with the Celtics. One league source said by phone moments later that Boston had been extremely confident that it would sign Hayward, but that it was unclear whether a deal had been finalized. Then another league source said that Hayward had indeed pledged to become a Celtic.

Soon afterward, however, there was a sudden shift.

Multiple reports and sources suggested that Hayward had yet to notify the teams involved in his courtship. Hayward's agent, Mark Bartelstein, said in a telephone interview that he was in the process of meeting with Hayward and helping him finalize his choice when the news broke that an agreement had been reached. Bartelstein was agitated by the leak, and he said it was inaccurate.

"He hasn't made a final decision yet," he said.

When asked if the final word would, in fact, be announced Tuesday, Bartelstein said: "That was the goal, but now we've got to kind of regroup here a bit."

League sources said the Celtics remained in contact with Hayward's representatives, but that they were waiting for a final word just like everyone else. When afternoon turned to evening, all sides mostly went silent, stirring rampant speculation about what the holdup might be.

Then Hayward's announcement was posted and there finally was clarity.

GREEN MACHINE

ALL REVVED UP TO SEE WHAT THIS NEW ENGINE CAN DO

September 2, 2017 • by Christopher L. Gasper

Green suede sneakers and genuine joy, that was what Kyrie Irving was wearing as he reintroduced himself to the basketball world as a Boston Celtic on Friday at TD Garden. His footwear and his excitement told the Celtics that Irving is as invested in them as they are in him.

The Celtics parted with a lot of their precious assets, including favorite son Isaiah Thomas, to get Irving. It was a bold move, just as bold as Irving deciding he no longer wanted to be LeBron James's running mate in Cleveland and demanding to be traded. Irving and the Celtics have risked their reputations to be together. Their relationship has to work because they're going to be judged on whether it ends up being worth it.

Irving, who was introduced alongside premium free agent acquisition Gordon Hayward, is unique on and off the court. He is going to be scrutinized here for his style of play and his speech. Kyrie is as much Kant as Curry. He is the philosophical point guard. That's not always going to play well with the cynical sports-talk radio crowd.

But the only transcendentalism the Celtics are interested in is their belief that the 25-year-old Irving is the elusive transcendent player that can catapult them to legitimate championship contention. That's why they tolerated Cleveland's posturing and IT injury parsing, parting with a 2020 second-round pick Wednesday to close the anfractuous deal and make Irving the new Celtics centerpiece.

"Well, it's very rare to be able to get a transcendent 25-year-old player in the NBA, a No. 1 pick in the draft," said Celtics co-owner Steve Pagliuca. "[Celtics coach] Brad [Stevens] will tell you he's maybe the best ballhandler he has ever seen—that's saying a lot in the NBA—maybe him and Steph Curry. So, when you have a chance to do that you have to do that."

The Celtics introduced Kyrie Irving (11) and Gordon Hayward (20) together on September 1, 2017. From left, Wyc Grousbeck, Irving, Hayward, and Danny Ainge.

The Irving-Celtics marriage has to work because both sides sacrificed too much for it not to. The Celtics cashed in a portion of their enviable chips—Thomas, Jae Crowder, Ante Zizic, and a vaunted 2018 Brooklyn first-round pick—and traded with their biggest rival to bet on Irving.

Count me among those who believe Irving is worth it.

Kyrie left a situation in Cleveland where he was playing with the best player on the planet, won a championship, and had been to three straight NBA Finals to strike out on his own. He has a tough act to follow in Thomas, who gave his heart, his soul, and a tooth to the Celtics.

"Getting an opportunity to be a part of such an illustrious organization such as the Boston Celtics when you have the unique opportunity of being a part of an organization like this and they do everything possible in terms of putting themselves out there to make such a great thing happen you're just appreciative," said Irving. "I'm grateful. I can't wait to get on the floor and to maximize my potential . . . I feel like in doing that Boston came right at the exact time, and it was meant to be that way. I trust in that, and I'm glad to be here."

The Celtics are trusting that Irving hasn't reached his peak, that a player who shot 47.3 percent from the field last season, 40.1 percent from 3-point range, and 90.5 percent from the free throw line while averaging a career-high 25.2 points per game still has his best basketball ahead of him.

The Celtics tilled a team that was the top seed in the East last year to replant their roster. There are only four players from last year's team who remain—Al Horford, Marcus Smart, Jaylen Brown, and Terry Rozier. That's a lot of turnover. It transforms the Celtics from gritty overachievers to an All-Star-laden team with expectations as high as the Garden rafters.

Stevens sounded chary about the process of blending the talent and egos of Irving, Hayward, and nine other new faces. He understands the weight of the expectations playing for an organization that only hangs banners for NBA championships in a city that has been one big trophy room the last 15 years.

There's going to be a lot of pressure on the upgraded Green to live up to the hype, especially Irving and Hayward.

"We're all in this together," said Irving, who will don No. 11 for the Celtics. "We understand that a lot of the responsibility of growing this team and making this team go will predominantly at times be on us, but at the same time we're empowering our teammates and elevating them because this will get very real. We'll be tested in a number of ways. I can't wait. The fact that everyone is trying to put all this pressure on this team we just put together and we're just incorporating ourselves into is step one."

Just like on the court, Irving always seems to have an answer. Irving is going to have to adapt his game. There will be fewer one-on-one forays. It doesn't matter if Irving believes the Earth is flat, as long as he follows Stevens's widely endorsed round-ball beliefs.

Irving already has a championship ring and one of the biggest shots in NBA Finals history on his resume. But Boston is now his legacy place.

Both the Celtics and Irving got what they wanted, each other. Now, they have to prove it was worth it.

A Dream Season Changed in an Instant

HAYWARD INJURY IN HIS FIRST GAME SHOCKS CELTICS

October 18, 2017 • by Dan Shaughnessy

CLEVELAND—Gruesome. Grotesque. Painful to watch.

The Celtics' $128 million free agent acquisition, Gordon Hayward, broke his left ankle in the sixth minute of his first game with the team Tuesday night at Quicken Loans Arena.

Hayward crashed to the floor 5:15 into the season, in what turned out to be a 102-99 Celtics loss to the Cleveland Cavaliers. While his teammates battled back from an 18-point deficit, Hayward was wheeled out of the arena, bound for the Celtics team charter, and New England Baptist Hospital in Boston. Hayward's parents were with him on the flight.

"I really feel for him," said Celtics coach Brad Stevens, who coached Hayward at Butler when the Bulldogs went to the NCAA Final Four in 2011.

The night was supposed to be all about Kyrie Irving's return to Cleveland after the offseason point guard swap that sent popular Isaiah Thomas to the Cavaliers, but Hayward's bad break will be the lasting takeaway for Celtics fans everywhere.

Midway through the first quarter, Hayward, guarded by former Celtic Jae Crowder, leaped to convert a long alley-oop from Irving. As the ball approached Hayward's hands, LeBron James came from under the basket to help Crowder. Tangled in arms and legs, unable to catch the ball that was tipped by James, Hayward crash-landed in the wine-red paint under the basket near the Cavaliers bench. As he sat up, Hayward's left foot was bent in an unnatural manner.

In an instant, it was clear to everyone that Hayward was badly hurt. You didn't have to be a doctor to see that the man had a broken leg. After the game, Stevens said Hayward had a fracture-ankle dislocation.

Players looked away, fans looked away, as Hayward sat on the floor after the crash. He was clearly in pain, but remarkably composed considering what had just happened. His left foot was absurdly askew. Folks in the TNT studios were reluctant to show the replay. They were reluctant to even show Hayward sitting on the floor. It was that bad. It was vividly reminiscent of a "Monday Night Football" game in 1985 when Redskins quarterback Joe Theismann had his leg broken by Giants linebacker Lawrence Taylor. Paul George's gruesome broken leg during the 2014 US Olympic tryouts also comes to mind.

Players from both the Celtics and Cavaliers put their hands to their heads and wandered around the floor. A team of doctors and trainers quickly surrounded Hayward under the basket. They placed his left leg in a black compression cast and put him on a stretcher. One by one, players came over to console the Celtics forward. Dwyane Wade. Tristan Thompson. LeBron James. At the other end of the floor, Celtics players locked arms and hung their heads in a huddle.

Cleveland fans stood and applauded politely, *humanely*, as Hayward was wheeled from the court.

This was bad and unlucky for Hayward and the Celtics. A Jimmy Chitwood "Hoosiers" type, Hayward was a much-coveted free agent who delighted Boston by agreeing to a four-year contract in July. It was the beginning of a super Celtics summer which had Irving coming to Boston in the celebrated swap for Thomas.

The Celtics were going places and their season opener was much-anticipated.

There was considerable emotion around the high-profile trade of Irving and Thomas. (Thomas said he would never again speak with Danny Ainge; Ainge on Tuesday told WEEI, "I don't know what we owe him.")

Irving's reception in Cleveland was supposed to be the big story of the night. Predictably, he was booed with gusto when he was introduced as the first Celtics starter.

Then came Hayward's ugly spill and folks paid little attention to the game for the rest of the half. The Cavs ran over the shell-shocked Celtics and took a 54-38 lead at intermission. Rookie Jayson Tatum was 0 for 5 and had 2 points in the first half. It looked as if the Cavs would have their revenge and win their opener against Kyrie (who picked up a technical foul in the second half).

The Celtics rallied behind Irving (22 points, 10 assists), Jaylen Brown (25 points), and Tatum (12 in the second half), and led by 3 late in the game. But LeBron (29 points, 16 rebounds, 9 assists) was too much. As usual.

But nobody in Boston cared too much about this game after the sixth minute of the first quarter. The story changed. The Celtics' season changed. And the atmosphere on Causeway is going to be a lot different than we expected when the Celtics open at home Wednesday night against Milwaukee.

The Greening of Jayson Tatum

The Celtics rookie has known since he was 3 exactly what he would be. Inspired by his mother's struggles to get by, he would be a superstar with the means to change her life and his. He has done that, and his rise has just begun.

April 22, 2018 • by Adam Himmelsbach

Jayson Tatum's love of basketball was evident at an early age. "He was going around dunking everything," his mother said. "I had to get him onto a team."

Brandy Cole tried to shield her only child from the struggles that filled their small brick home on the west side of St. Louis, but it was not easy.

Sometimes young Jayson Tatum would find that the gas had been cut off because of unpaid bills, so his mother would turn on the clothes dryer for heat, or warm water on a stovetop for baths. On cold nights, she would plug in a small space heater in her bedroom and hold her son close.

When the electricity went out in the evening, she sometimes turned on her car's headlights so Jayson could at least play on an illuminated basketball court.

"When he was young, it was hard to explain," she said. "You just have to make hard decisions. Like, if they're talking about cutting off the gas, but it's summer, you just figure out how you can get it back on before winter."

The most humbling moments came when food was scarce. Brandy, who had Jayson when she was a freshman in college, sometimes baby-sat for a neighbor and received dinners in return. Jayson would knock on the door when it was time to eat, and the family would usually give him a frozen chicken pot pie to bring home. His mother would tell him to eat the filling and leave just the crust for her.

"My mom tried to not let me see how much we were struggling, but I noticed it," Tatum said. "I think that's what made me work harder. I saw how hard she was working, and I just wanted a better life for both of us."

As Tatum completed this thought last month, he sat on an elegant lounge chair in the lobby of the five-star Hotel Grand America in Salt Lake City. The NBA rookie was in the midst of a road trip with the Boston Celtics, and his better life had arrived.

The Celtics are paying him $5.4 million this season, and the 6-foot-8-inch forward has already emerged as one of the league's most scintillating young talents. When he was a child, he looked forward to nights when his mother had saved enough money for a pizza from Imo's, a St. Louis chain. Now, he is the company's spokesman.

The Celtics are reluctant to heap praise on a 20-year-old, but within the organization, there is measured optimism that he could turn into the franchise's next superstar. Tatum is not overwhelmed by that possibility, though, because he has been charging toward it from the start.

"Not too many people know what they want to do at 3," he said, "and then go do it."

A BASKETBALL MIND

Justin Tatum was 16 years old when he noticed a girl working at a candy store in a St. Louis mall. The two started flirting and then started dating, and when they were freshmen at separate colleges in the city, they had a baby named Jayson.

The boy's love for basketball was instantly obvious. His father played for St. Louis University, and as a toddler, Jayson would scurry onto the court at halftime and find the nearest ball. At home, everything became a hoop—trash cans, laundry baskets, the grocery bags that his grandparents held for him to aim at.

"He was going around dunking everything," his mother said. "I had to get him onto a team."

When Jayson was 3, he joined a YMCA league for 5-year-olds. As he sprouted, other parents thought he was too old for whatever league he was in, and Brandy would sigh and present a birth certificate that showed he was actually too young.

Tatum viewed the game through a unique prism. When his teachers were preoccupied, he'd sit in class and study YouTube clips of the game's greats. Then he would go home, drag a hoop onto the street, place two bricks on its base, and try to master the moves himself. When he played basketball video games, he even tried to set screens and draw up plays.

"He just kept training his mind," Justin Tatum said.

Jayson was excellent at everything except losing. Youth-league defeats crushed him to the point that teammates would go to his house afterward to check on him.

"They'd come over just to give him a hug," said Tatum's grandmother, Rose Mary Johnson, who lived nearby. "They knew he was going to cry after he lost. He'd be as red as a beet."

When Tatum was 8, his father returned from a brief, injury-plagued pro basketball career in Holland to focus on training his son. Justin Tatum worked as a substitute teacher and eventually became the varsity basketball coach at Soldan High. Jayson

Tatum holds his son Deuce after practice in April 2018.

started practicing with that team when he was just 9 years old.

"By the time he was 12," Justin Tatum says, "he was giving my players problems."

'I FELT LIKE I'D FAILED HIM'

Brandy spent eight years pushing toward an undergraduate degree at Missouri-St. Louis. She would later earn a law degree and an MBA, too. (Celtics assistant general manager Mike Zarren said that during his time with the team, no player's parent had ever had such specific, detailed questions about their son's contract as Brandy did last summer.)

When Tatum was a child, Brandy would bring him to her college classes during the day, and then have a friend or family member watch him while she worked at a Cingular Wireless store at night. She picked up shifts no one wanted, because it was easier to collect commission sales that way.

Brandy and Justin had a complicated, off-and-on relationship. Justin consistently sent money, and saw or spoke to his son almost every day, but there were still financial challenges. The utilities at Brandy's home were routinely cut off. The refrigerator was not always stocked. One day, Brandy found an eviction notice taped to the front door.

"That was the hardest," she said. "Like, how am I going to tell Jayson he can't have his house anymore? I felt like I'd failed him."

Jayson didn't understand, but he knew from his mother's tears that it wasn't good. A family friend ultimately helped pay off part of the mortgage, and Brandy kept the home. But she would not let these setbacks derail Jayson's goals.

"There were times when, yeah, maybe I shouldn't have paid for him to travel with this team or go to this tournament," she said. "There were times if I hadn't done that, we would have had the electricity on. But I knew that's what he wanted, and I knew he was special."

Brandy had played volleyball at University City High in St. Louis, where she was coached by Besta Beal, whose son, Bradley, would become an NBA All-Star. Brandy sometimes baby-sat Bradley, and the two families became close.

When Jayson was in seventh grade at Chaminade Prep and Beal was a senior, they trained together after school, and Beal would drive Tatum home when they finished. Beal's trainer, Drew Hanlen, refused for two years to start working with Tatum, because he was simply too young. Finally, when Tatum was a high school freshman and Beal was preparing for his rookie year with the Washington Wizards, Beal made one more pitch.

"You could just see Jayson could be a Magic Johnson-type player, or a scorer like Kevin Durant," Beal said. "So I told Drew, 'You've got to trust me on this one. Jayson is special.'"

DRAWING A CROWD

Beal brought Tatum to a workout with Hanlen, and the youngster nearly passed out after 20 minutes. But he came back the next day, and the next. Hanlen crafted an arsenal for Tatum by plucking other stars' powers: Kobe Bryant's fadeaway jumper and jab step, Paul George's floater, Kawhi Leonard's defense.

"Piece by piece, we built his game," Hanlen said. "I noticed Jayson doesn't practice things until he gets them right. He practices until he can't get them wrong."

Every month or so, Hanlen would send a text message to Celtics director of scouting Dave Lewin, telling him that he was training the future No. 1 overall pick. Lewin told Hanlen the Celtics liked

Tatum, but there was no way for any of them to envision what would come.

By his junior year at Chaminade, Tatum had become a superstar. He had a key to the gym and would arrive by himself for 6 a.m. workouts. His games were moved to college arenas to accommodate the swelling crowds, and fans lined up hours in advance. There was even a ticket resale market.

"Didn't matter if it was rain or snow," said Tatum's best friend, Brandon Dunlap. "People were outside with lawn chairs and Starbucks, bundled up and trying to get in."

Tatum's other grandmother, Kristie Jursch, used to arrive four hours before tipoff with a pile of long silk scarves that she would use as space savers for family. It was quite a production.

Despite the fuss made over him, Tatum was not cocky or brash. His classmates found him quite shy, but it could be dangerous for opponents to be lulled by his demeanor.

"Jayson comes across as introverted," said his former coach at Chaminade, Frank Bennett. "But the minute that boy walks between those lines, he's trying to take your heart out."

Five years after Beal was named Gatorade National Player of the Year, Tatum received the same honor at the same school. St. Louis improbably had become the epicenter of high school basketball.

"I was always chasing Brad," Tatum said. "And he always told me to be better than him and break his records. He said he didn't have anybody like that to encourage him or look up to, so he wanted to give that to me."

NO. 1 OBSESSION

In April 2015, just a few days after Duke won a national title, coach Mike Krzyzewski was scheduled to fly to St. Louis to meet with Tatum and his family on a recruiting visit. But massive storms were pushing through the area, and the pilot of Krzyzewski's private jet was hesitant about the trip. Tatum's mother urged them to reschedule.

"I was like, 'I cannot have Coach K dying on his visit to see us,'" she said.

But Krzyzewski wanted Tatum, who was just a junior, to know how important he was to Duke's plans, so he came anyway. By the end of the visit, as Krzyzewski played with Tatum's 90-pound boxer,

Lenox, Tatum was sold. He told Krzyzewski he would become a Blue Devil, and the coach started to cry.

"Jayson was so polished," Krzyzewski said. "The game came so easily to him, and we saw right away what he had a chance to become."

On Oct. 25, 2016, Tatum sprained his foot during Duke's pro day, an annual showcase held for NBA scouts and executives. He missed the season's first eight games and was rusty when he returned. After bad outings, he would go back to his dorm and inspect every online NBA mock draft he could find.

"I was consumed with getting picked first," Tatum said. "If my name dropped, or I wasn't where I thought I should be, I'd honestly be depressed."

NBA decision-makers were never really alarmed, however. They saw Tatum's length and athleticism and poetic jump shot. On Dec. 6, Celtics coach Brad Stevens was in Orlando for a game against the Magic when he and his wife, Tracy, watched on television as Duke played Florida.

"I don't know what this draft looks like," Stevens told his wife, "but if we have one of the top picks and we end up with him, we're going to be in pretty good shape."

SHIPPING UP TO BOSTON?

Last June, Tatum held individual draft workouts in Los Angeles for the Celtics, 76ers, and Suns, who had the first, third, and fourth picks, respectively. He went into the Boston session thinking it was pointless.

"It seemed like a waste of time, because everybody kept saying they were going to pick Markelle [Fultz] first," he said. "I did good in the workout, but I don't think I was engaged."

Despite his lack of interest, Tatum put on a show for Boston's brass, splashing one 3-pointer after another. The Celtics generally do not care much about shooting displays that don't involve defenders, but they had been watching Tatum for years, and they were smitten.

Tatum said that after his workout for Philadelphia, the 76ers told him they intended to select him with the third pick. He flew to Phoenix anyway to meet with the Suns, and he was enchanted by the warm weather and easygoing lifestyle. Maybe Phoenix was where he belonged, he thought.

But while he was there, Krzyzewski called.

"I just talked to Brad Stevens," Krzyzewski told him. "I think they might trade their pick. I think you should go to Boston for a workout."

Tatum was exhausted from the process. He didn't want to fly to Boston for a second workout for a trade that might not even happen. But the Celtics were moving quickly.

"Danny [Ainge] and I were talking many times a day about how to approach the Philly trade negotiations," said Zarren, the assistant general manager. "And when it became clear during that time that we were taking Jayson No. 1 anyway, it made the trade discussions much easier."

While Tatum was still in Phoenix, he received a call from his agent, Jeff Wechsler. The Celtics were going to trade the No. 1 overall pick to the 76ers for the No. 3 choice and a future first-round choice. Tatum had to visit Boston.

The Celtics did not need to see him fire up more 3-pointers. They wanted him to meet Stevens, who had missed the Los Angeles workout because the Celtics season was still going.

Tatum was battling a severe sinus infection, and the cross-country flight made him feel worse. He went from Logan Airport to Stevens's home in Wellesley for dinner. Tracy Stevens cooked steak and chicken, but Tatum had no appetite. He told them he was full, but the truth was that he felt awful.

"If I'd eaten something, I would've thrown up at the table," he said. "I thought I might pass out while Brad was talking to me."

As Tatum sat at dinner, one part of this draft process still had him baffled. He asked Stevens why anybody would ever trade away the No. 1 overall pick.

"He just said to me, 'We feel like the guy we want we can still get at No. 3,'" Tatum said. "But he didn't say it was me."

A NEW BOND

In his rookie season, Tatum quickly blossomed, averaging 13.9 points and 5 rebounds while making 43.4 percent of his 3-pointers. He helped guide Boston to 55 wins despite injuries to stars Gordon Hayward and Kyrie Irving, and he will almost certainly be named to the league's all-rookie team.

But his goals remain considerably grander. It still irks him that he was not the No. 1 overall draft pick.

And it irks him that he probably will not be named Rookie of the Year.

"I don't think he's comfortable," said Wechsler, his agent. "I think he's purposely uncomfortable, because he has a passion to be great."

Tatum has a son of his own now, Jayson Jr., who was born in December. Tatum's mother and Jayson Jr.'s mother have mostly taken care of the baby through the grind of the NBA season, but Tatum is eager for his first summer with his little boy. Last week he took him to a baby gym class and to swim lessons, and he is already looking forward to the day he can bring him on a basketball court, too.

For Tatum, despite odds that should have suggested otherwise, the NBA had always been more of an expectation than a dream. Ever since he was in fourth grade, he and his mother had talked about someday living together in whatever city he played in. Now, they both have units in an apartment complex in Waltham, with Tatum living in a second-floor unit and his mother residing two levels above. But Tatum spends most days upstairs anyway.

"His kitchen is spotless," Brandy says with a chuckle, "because he's never used it."

When the Celtics return home from road trips late at night, there is usually a home-cooked meal waiting for Tatum, regardless of the hour. He and his mother talk about the game, and sometimes they talk about how far they have come since living in the small brick house on the west side of St. Louis.

"When he was younger, he'd tell me what the other players were going to do if basketball didn't work out," Brandy says. "Then he'd tell me he didn't have a Plan B, and didn't want one. So I'd say, 'All right, let's make this happen then. Let's get it.'"

Just Too Green

Celtics' wondrous, improbable run ends in a barrage of missed shots.

May 28, 2018 • by Dan Shaughnessy

In the end, the young Celtics looked . . . young. They got tight. They couldn't put the staggering Cavaliers to bed. They couldn't stop the indomitable LeBron James. And then they collapsed altogether.

"We just had one of those nights," Celtic coach Brad Stevens said after the Celts dropped an 87-79 Game 7 to the Cleveland Cavaliers at TD Garden on Sunday. " . . . the pain is part of the path."

Ooooh. The pain.

We are not supposed to be disappointed. This was a "house money" series. The Celtics never expected to get this far after they lost Gordon Hayward and Kyrie Irving during the regular season. But then they advanced to the conference finals. And then they took 2-0 and 3-2 series leads and looked significantly better than the Cavs. Finally, most painfully, they took a 12-point lead in Game 7 on their own court.

So, yes, we are disappointed. It was there. It was winnable. This was a chance to make it to the NBA Finals a year ahead of the plan. It was the best possible audition for this young team. And they blew it. They shot 34 percent on their home court. They scored 13 points in the third quarter and 36 in the second half. After taking a 72-71 lead with 6:04 left, they went 5 ½ minutes without a basket. Everything unraveled in a hail of missed shots and lost opportunities.

And the ever-annoying and dominating LeBron James was there to capitalize on the Celtics' youth and inexperience. All of New England watched helplessly while LeBron scored 35 with 15 rebounds and 9 assists in the full 48 minutes.

In what may someday go down as the greatest achievement in what looks like the greatest career in NBA history, King James is carrying this over-the-hill gang into the NBA Finals. It will be LeBron's fourth straight Finals with the Cavs, his eighth straight overall. He's the only non-Celtic to turn that trick.

"It's ridiculous," said Stevens. "And he does it at this level and with the pressure, with the scrutiny—doesn't matter. It's just unbelievable."

The Celtics are the ones that are always supposed to win Game 7. If Reggie Jackson is Mr. October and Joe DiMaggio was Mr. Coffee, then the Boston Celtics are Mr. Game 7. Sunday's Garden showdown was the 32nd Game 7 in Boston's franchise history. The Celtics came into the night with a 23-8 record in Game 7s, including a 20-4 mark on the fabled parquet floor. But now they are 23-9 and 20-5.

It didn't feel like this was going to be a loss in the first half. With the Garden crowd in strong, earsplitting voice, shaking the tracks of the rail station below, the young Celtics raced to a 12-point second-quarter lead. But it should have been bigger.

"I thought the biggest moment of the game was when we couldn't extend the lead in the second quarter," said Stevens. "We were in really good shape and we just couldn't extend the lead."

Adding insult to injury, the Celtics were beaten not only by LeBron, but by Jeff Green, who was a total bust in Boston after Danny Ainge blew up Boston's 2011 team with the Kendrick Perkins trade. Green started in place of All-Star forward Kevin Love, who went into the league's concussion protocol after a head-to-head collision with Jayson Tatum in Game 6. Nicknamed "Gandhi" (Mr. Passive-Resistance), during his years in Boston, Green went off for 19 points.

Boston's guards, Jaylen Brown, Terry Rozier, and Marcus Smart, combined to shoot 3 for 26 from beyond the arc.

This was a wonderful Celtic season. The notion that this Green edition—playing without its two best players—could make it to the NBA Finals was akin to watching the no-name Patriots of 2002 winning their first Super Bowl in New Orleans. We all toyed with that notion in our heads after the Celtics took an early lead in this series.

And now it is all gone.

It is not supposed to be disappointing.

But it is. The Celtics should be the team going to the Finals.

main story lines heading into this much-anticipated Celtics season.

With Celtics legend Paul Pierce watching from the bench, Irving stood near midcourt with a microphone and said: "If you guys will have me back, I plan on re-signing here next year."

The estimated crowd of 3,000 gave him a standing ovation and he began hugging teammates.

Irving will become a free agent July 1 and can agree to a maximum extension of five years and approximately $188 million. Now he is officially the centerpiece of the Celtics' quest to win championships, leading a core group of Gordon Hayward, Jaylen Brown, and Jayson Tatum.

The five-time All-Star point guard hinted at his intentions at the Under-30 Summit Tuesday at Emerson College.

"To be in a position to even be considered a franchise free agent is pretty awesome," he said. "At this point in my career, it's not so much about the money, it's not so much about the extracurricular things, it's like OK, where am I happy? Where am I most comfortable? Who's going to give me that [atmosphere] where I would love to grow as a human being?

"You think, 'What about a new location?' and it's just like I want to be comfortable and what's better than being in Boston? This year has felt much different because of the environment that has been created for me and by me, and going to the new practice facility. There's nothing like playing at TD Garden.

"I didn't say that to appease you guys, I actually love Boston."

Irving says he's staying a Celtic

October 5, 2018 • by Gary Washburn

Kyrie Irving spent his Thursday evening settling any debate about his NBA future, announcing to fans at the Celtics season ticket-holders event that he plans on re-signing a maximum contract with Boston next summer.

Irving, 26, who has an opt-out clause in the five-year deal he signed with the Cleveland Cavaliers in 2014, can be a free agent in July. His intentions for next season and his future had been one of the

Irving on Plans for Free Agency: 'Ask Me July 1'

February 2, 2019 • by Adam Himmelsbach

NEW YORK—Kyrie Irving walked slowly across the Madison Square Garden floor before the Celtics' morning shootaround Friday and headed toward the courtside seat where his sneakers had been placed for him.

Before he sat down, he picked up a large mat with a Knicks logo on it and moved it out of the way. Maybe the juxtaposition was a sign, or maybe

Irving just wanted to move a mat out of the way. During this suddenly tumultuous week, the search for clues about the All-Star point guard's future has been endless.

Irving sat there as reporters inched closer, waiting to ask him to provide some clarity about his situation that once seemed quite clear.

"What's going on?" Irving said.

That was his way of saying he was ready to talk, ready to get this interview over with. The reporters stepped closer. After Irving said that the sore hip that sidelined him for two games was fine and that he was ready for Friday's game, he was asked about recent rumors that he was considering signing with a team other than the Celtics this summer, which would be a shift from a proclamation he made in the fall.

Irving could have just said he's not talking about free agency. He could have said nothing has changed. He could have told everyone to ignore the rumors about what Anthony Davis's trade demand or the Knicks' free agency push had to do with him. But he didn't really do any of that.

"Well, at the end of the day, I'm going to do what I feel is best for my career," he said. "And that's just where it stands.

"My focus this season is winning a championship with the Boston Celtics. Obviously, we had goals coming into this season, and the primary goal is to win a championship. So that's where my focus is."

He was then asked whether his plan to re-sign with Boston had shifted.

"Ask me July 1," he said.

That, of course, is the start of free agency. It was not the answer Celtics fans were hoping to hear.

Irving then held court for a 5-minute-20-second session that took several twists and turns and ended only when a Celtics media relations executive signaled that it was over.

If you closed your eyes and plucked three random sentences from the interview, you could have come upon three different messages. Sometimes Irving sounded like he is leaving. Sometimes he sounded like he is staying. Sometimes he sounded like he is just sick of all this—the media, the speculation, the intrusiveness. All of it.

"Obviously, things this season haven't gone as I planned," he said. "And that's part of being on a team where you're still trying to figure things out. So I'm always going to be mature about that, professional, come to do my job every single day, and really just see what happens."

JOHN HAVLICEK
1940-2019

A SUPERSTAR FOREVER ON THE BALL

April 26, 2019 • by John Powers

John Havlicek, the understated superstar who transformed an off-the-bench role into a Hall of Fame career and became the all-time leading scorer with the Boston Celtics, died on Thursday in Jupiter, Fla. He was 79.

Every one of Mr. Havlicek's 16 seasons was spent in a Celtics uniform, 13 of them as an all-star. Throughout, he set league records for games played (1,270) and consecutive 1,000-point seasons (all 16), as he played across Celtic dynasties. He was known for his huge lungs and an epic work ethic, constantly hustling the floor quarter after quarter and honing his skills long beyond when other basketball players hit the point of retirement.

"Havlicek stole the ball" is still one of the great rallying cries in sports history, shouted by announcer Johnny Most and quietly repeated by countless numbers of aspiring players in pickup games across the region for years after.

Mr. Havlicek suffered from Parkinson's disease. His death was confirmed by the Celtics.

"John Havlicek is one of the most accomplished players in Boston Celtics history, and the face of many of the franchise's signature moments," the Celtics said in a statement. "John was kind and considerate, humble and gracious. He was a champion in every sense, and as we join his family, friends, and fans in mourning his loss, we are thankful for all the joy and inspiration he brought to us."

Fellow Hall of Famer Bill Russell, who played alongside Mr. Havlicek for seven years before handing over the captaincy to him, simply said, "He is the best all-around player I ever saw."

Mr. Havlicek's eight championship rings were third behind Russell's 11 and Sam Jones's 10.

"If I hadn't separated my shoulder [in 1973], we definitely would have won that year," he reckoned. "And if we had hung on to [Paul] Silas and Westy [Paul Westphal], we might have squeezed out another one."

While Mr. Havlicek averaged more than 20 points per game as a swingman, despite dunking approximately once a decade, he was best known for a defensive play that saved the 1965 season and sent the Celtics to their eighth title.

With Boston clinging to a 1-point lead over Philadelphia with five seconds to play in the seventh game of the Eastern Conference finals at the old Boston Garden, the 76ers were inbounding the ball with a chance to win the game.

Most's radio call remains the most famous in franchise history: "[Hal] Greer putting the ball in play. He gets it out deep and Havlicek steals it! Over to Sam Jones! Havlicek stole the ball! It's all over!"

Although Mr. Havlicek, who was guarding Chet Walker, had his back to Greer, he had an innate sense of when the ball might be in the air.

"I knew he had five seconds to inbound, so I started counting to myself—1,001, 1,002, 1,003," Mr. Havlicek recalled. "Usually something has happened by then. So by 1,003 and a half, I started to peek a little more."

Mr. Havlicek's meticulous approach to basketball was mirrored in the precision of his daily life.

"His clothes are all hanging half an inch apart in the closet at home," said his wife, Beth, whose husband folded his socks over a dressing-room hanger and combed his hair at halftime. "Everything from the medicine cabinet to the dresser drawers to the garage is kept that way. John was probably born like that."

MULTISPORT STAR

John Joseph Havlicek, whose father emigrated from Czechoslovakia, was born in a coal-and-steel town in eastern Ohio and lived in a house above his

John Havlicek in his younger Celtic days, when he broke in as a sixth man before becoming one of the NBA's all-time greats.

parents' grocery store. His grandfather and uncles worked in the mines. Although he was frequently unwell as a child ("Crying and sickness were my trademarks"), Mr. Havlicek grew into an exceptional multisport athlete.

At Ohio State, where football coach Woody Hayes unsuccessfully recruited him for quarterback, Mr. Havlicek played first base for the baseball team and was a sophomore starter on the Buckeye basketball varsity that won its only national championship in 1960.

Two years later, the Celtics picked him seventh overall in the NBA Draft and hoped that he wouldn't opt for pro football, as the NFL's Cleveland Browns had chosen Mr. Havlicek in the seventh round of that draft even though he hadn't played since high school.

After Mr. Havlicek was the last receiver cut in Browns training camp, he turned up in Boston and ate his first meal at the Hayes-Bickford cafeteria across from the Garden.

"Look what the hell we got here," marveled coach Red Auerbach while watching Mr. Havlicek in perpetual motion during the team's first practice.

Since the Celtics were coming off their fourth straight title season and were loaded with established stars such as Bob Cousy, Tom Heinsohn, Jones, and Russell, their crew-cut rookie immediately was cast as a substitute.

"I came into a great situation where I had all the veterans around me," observed Mr. Havlicek, who was nicknamed "Hondo" for his resemblance to John Wayne in the 1953 film. "And through the process of osmosis, I guess, I became one of the people they could rely on."

Mr. Havlicek's versatility at guard and forward made him a natural sixth man, a role created for teammate Frank Ramsey, who retired after the following season.

"I think people emphasize too much who's starting," observed Mr. Havlicek, who relished the assignment. "Emphasis should be on minutes played."

Mr. Havlicek, who averaged nearly 37 minutes per game during his career, had extraordinary stamina, helped by lungs so large they had to be X-rayed separately. He took particular pride in his durability and reliability; he missed only 33 of 1,303 regular-season games and fouled out only 21 times.

"There should be a giant key sticking out of his back," Russell once cracked. "You just wind him up and click-click-click, you put him out there for 48 minutes."

Mr. Havlicek had no problem being on the floor for the full regulation and beyond.

"I'm ready to go 48 all the time," he said. "I get to rest on free throws and timeouts."

Defending Mr. Havlicek, who was continually on the move, was an exhausting assignment.

"A roadrunner taking you through every ditch, every irrigation canal, barbed-wire fence, and cattle guard," observed Los Angeles Lakers general manager Pete Newell, whose University of California team lost its title to Ohio State in the 1960 final.

"You've had a trip over the plains when you're playing him for a night."

Mr. Havlicek's capacity to go the distance game after game was especially valued during the Celtics' rebuilding period at the beginning of the '70s following the retirement of Russell and Jones when he became what Auerbach called "the guts of the team."

"I became the old man in one year because of the retirements," Mr. Havlicek observed.

By then he'd assumed he would be nearing the end of his career.

"To be truthful, I never thought I'd last more than eight or nine years," Mr. Havlicek said. "When I broke in, that was about the limit."

Yet at 30 he was the cornerstone of the team, leading the league in minutes.

"He's the complete player . . . the whole thing," said Heinsohn, who played alongside Mr. Havlicek for three seasons and coached him for nine. "He stands alone."

After turning down a million-dollar offer to jump to the rival American Basketball Association in 1969, Mr. Havlicek made it clear he expected to be compensated as the team's main man. "Now it's my turn," he said. "For years, the top contracts went to others on the team, and I could understand. I've met all the standards the Celtics use to reward players."

FINDING A WAY

What set Mr. Havlicek apart from his teammates and rivals was his obsessive attention to detail—the toiletries in his locker were arranged in descending order of height.

"I'm a man of routine and discipline," he said. "My whole life has been thought out."

But when it came to finding ways to play despite disabling injuries in the playoffs, Mr. Havlicek was craftily creative. After separating his right shoulder in the third game of the 1973 Eastern Conference finals against the New York Knicks, he strapped it in a sling and shot with his left hand for the remainder of the series.

After tearing the plantar fascia in his left foot at the beginning of the 1976 playoffs, Mr. Havlicek iced it down for six times as long as advised ("two Hondo handfuls"), missed only three games, and played 58 minutes of the epic triple-overtime victory over the Phoenix Suns at the Garden that set up Boston's 13th title.

"I don't think you should mind a little pain if you're paid to play," he said.

In 1977, when fluid on his left knee inhibited his shooting, Mr. Havlicek simply invented an impromptu repertoire.

"Left-hand hook, right-hand hook, jumping one-legged tip-in," he said. "Off-footed, half-legged jump shot . . . "

Although his exceptional conditioning could have enabled him to play for several more years, Mr. Havlicek decided to retire at 38 at the end of the 1978 season, in which he played all 82 games. He wore a tuxedo to his finale against Buffalo at the Garden ("You should wear special clothes on special occasions") and played 41 minutes, scoring 29 points.

"I'm going to remember most the people in the stands," said Mr. Havlicek, whose number 17 was retired the following October. "And the flags hanging above me."

Had he played for two more seasons, Mr. Havlicek would have been teammates with Larry Bird, with whom he once engaged in a one-on-one duel after Bird bragged that he would have dominated Havlicek had he played against him.

"I said, 'Fine, let's go right now,'" Mr. Havlicek said. "I made a swipe for the ball, but in doing so I hit him in a very tender spot. He went down and stayed down for a good two minutes. I said, 'That's it. You lose. You aren't tough enough to have played in my day.'"

Mr. Havlicek could have spent his retirement fishing, which had been a lifetime avocation. For more than three decades, he sponsored a celebrity fishing tournament on Martha's Vineyard to benefit the Genesis Foundation for Children.

Since he had deferred much of his salary and invested early in Wendy's restaurants, his financial circumstances were secure.

"I don't have to work if I don't want to," he said.

Mr. Havlicek had no interest in coaching or in being a conventional businessman.

"When I retired, I didn't want to be in a situation of working 9 to 5," he said.

Instead, Mr. Havlicek became a corporate speaker for several firms, including Xerox, whose Japanese competitors he likened to the Lakers. During his playing days, the Celtics were 5-0 in NBA Finals against Los Angeles.

"The guy is the ambassador of our sport," longtime Laker rival Jerry West said. "John always gave his best every night and had time for everybody—teammates, fans, the press. He is simply the ideal everybody expects an athlete to be."

Mr. Havlicek leaves his wife, Beth, and children Jill and Chris.

STILL IN GOOD VOICE

Gorman, 71, has called Celtics games for 38 years.

May 2, 2019 • by Adam Himmelsbach

With another Celtics broadcast complete, Mike Gorman removes his headset, puts on his coat, and heads into the chilly winter night. The fans still trickling out of TD Garden do not know him personally, but plenty call out to him by name and treat him as an old friend anyway, which is exactly how he has tried to connect while serving as the team's play-by-play announcer for 38 years.

After a short walk, Gorman is home. It's a much easier commute to the Garden than he once had, when he lived in upper Manhattan and would drive four hours each way on game days, snowstorms and bottlenecks be damned.

Now, he just goes a couple of blocks, tells his doorman how the Celtics played, and takes an elevator to his penthouse apartment that has pleasant views of the Garden and the glowing Zakim Bridge.

Inside, there are signs of the life Gorman will lead whenever he retires. The Xbox console for soccer video games. The two computer monitors that he uses to day-trade stocks. The Gibson hanging on a wall, one of his five guitars that were mostly purchased while covering games in Memphis ("I've gotten pretty good, but my wife is better").

Gorman prefers not to look back at his career, because when you're 71, that's usually a way to acknowledge a looming end, and he is not there yet. But he has stories he has never told publicly before, from a tragedy in the Navy that still haunts him, to the time he nearly fought Tommy Heinsohn, to how a few home runs in a beer-league softball game put

Mike Gorman, circa 2010.

His Brunswick, Maine, squadron deployed for 6-8 months at a time to places such as Spain, Portugal, and Bermuda. They would soar above the Atlantic in four-engine turboprops, mostly patrolling for Russian submarines lurking below.

The missions were for reconnaissance, not combat. When the Russians realized they'd been spotted, they would surface, and the US planes would drop care packages filled with cola, snacks, and Playboy magazines, mostly to show they were not there for trouble.

"You'd see the Russians standing on the deck of their sub waving and holding a centerfold in the air," Gorman said. "It was all kind of a charade."

Gorman became one of his squadron's most trusted aviators. On June 3, 1972, he was scheduled to fly a routine mission off the coast of Spain when he was summoned to handle office paperwork instead. The plane took off from Naval Station Rota in dense fog without him, and about an hour later, it crashed into the side of a 2,700-foot mountain, killing all 14 men on board.

Gorman was devastated to lose friends, and wracked with guilt because he was not in the air to help them find safe skies. He returned to the US and went to 14 funerals over the course of a week. He never flew again, and about a year after the accident he retired from the service.

He still has an interest in aviation and checks in with the pilots before Celtics charters, usually to tell sideline reporter Abby Chin what kind of turbulence to expect. But he has never truly left that fateful day behind.

"I don't really like to talk about it," he said. "It's just not something you ever forget."

After leaving the Navy, Gorman moved back in with his parents in Dorchester, grew his hair out, and did not know what to do next.

A friend in the service used to talk about working in television and radio, and it sounded magical.

him on the path to becoming the voice of one of the most famous sports franchises ever.

So after a phone call with his wife and a video chat with his daughter, he shakes some potato chips into a porcelain bowl, pours a beer into a glass, and begins a different kind of play-by-play.

FATAL CRASH, LASTING MEMORY

The son of an office secretary and an insurance agent, Gorman was the youngest of three growing up in a single-family home with a small yard in Dorchester. He was an altar boy at St. Brendan Parish and he hawked copies of the Boston American newspaper, usually ending up sitting on a curb poring over NBA box scores.

Gorman loved basketball but did not have much money, so when the Celtics played, he would climb a fire escape outside the old Garden and bang on a door at the balcony level. If an usher opened it, Gorman would scamper back down to the street. If it was anyone else, he would slither inside.

He became a standout guard at Boston Latin School and hoped to someday become a teacher and a coach. But after graduating from Boston State College in 1969, he was drafted into the Navy, enrolling in officer school and becoming an aviator.

So one morning Gorman drove to WBZ's radio studios, charmed a fellow veteran at the security gate, and talked his way into the office of longtime sportscaster Gil Santos.

WBZ did not have an opening, but Santos told Gorman that WNBH, a small station in New Bedford, did. Santos made a phone call, lied about Gorman's radio experience, and secured him an interview that day. The station was essentially a rundown house with some antennas attached.

"Do you know how to play softball?" the station manager asked Gorman.

The company team had a game that night against a rival, and it needed help. Gorman hit a couple of home runs, and WNBH won the game. Over beers later, he accepted a job that paid $150 a week to rotate tapes that played elevator music on the company's FM station.

COURTING IN THE BIG EAST

Gorman expressed interest in sports broadcasting but was told it would be feasible only if he sold the advertisements, too. So he contacted local businesses and peddled $15 ads that would be read during the high school games he was calling. The station even offered an unethical package deal: If a business owner had a child in the game, Gorman would embellish their performance at no extra cost.

He then became a news reporter at WPRO radio in Providence before being hired as a sportscaster at WPRI television. That station broadcast some Providence College basketball games, and the timing was perfect, because PC athletic director Dave Gavitt was forming a new basketball conference called the Big East, and he needed voices.

Gorman and former Seton Hall coach Bill Raftery became the lead tandem for ESPN's Big Monday games, and stars such as Patrick Ewing, Pearl Washington, and Chris Mullin turned the league into a sensation.

Before one game, the 7-foot-1-inch Ewing barreled over Gorman in the locker room tunnel, then stood over him and used an expletive to tell him to stay out of his way. Gorman was rattled, but also loved the intensity of it all. (Now when he sees Ewing, who is Georgetown's coach, he jokingly uses an expletive to tell Ewing to stay out of his way.)

Gorman met his future wife, Teri, when she was working as the television stage manager for a Villanova-Boston College matchup. On one of their first dates, Gorman took her to a Syracuse-Georgetown game at the Carrier Dome. He was still working on the romance part.

Teri started to produce Big East telecasts, and the couple would edit features in their living room, or rush to the hotel bar after road games to see their highlights. They were married in 1988 and together raised Gorman's infant daughter from a brief previous marriage, Kristen.

When Gorman called games, his wife would put on the telecast in Kristen's bedroom, and she'd fall asleep to the gentle cadence of her father's play-by-play. When he was home to read her bedtime stories, she'd often interrupt and ask him to use his TV voice instead.

(Kristen went on to work at Gorman's side as a stage manager on Celtics broadcasts for a few years. At one game, a fan came down from the stands and asked her out. He's now her husband.)

MIKE AND TOMMY

Tommy Heinsohn, the Celtics legend who is in the Basketball Hall of Fame as a player and coach, was the team's lone broadcaster until Prism Broadcasting wanted to add a play-by-play man in 1981. Heinsohn had called a few college games with Gorman and believed they would be a good team.

Before their first Celtics game, Gorman stood in the booth in the Boston Garden's upper reaches holding a pad filled with color-coded stats and facts. The 6-foot-7-inch Heinsohn glared at him.

"What is this [expletive]?" he asked, before tossing the pad over the ledge. "We're going to talk about what we see in front of us."

Their chemistry was unmistakable. Heinsohn was the boisterous, emotional franchise legend who crushed referees on air when things went sour. Gorman was the steady, soothing presence who could make viewers feel like everything would always be fine, even when it was not.

During a game in Orlando many years ago, one of the monitors on the broadcast table started smoking and caught fire. As crew members and Heinsohn quickly tried to smother it, Gorman kept speaking to New England, calm as a nap.

"Mike's our fail-safe," said NBC Sports Boston's longtime game producer, Paul Lucey. "I might be jumping up and down in the production truck going crazy about something, but you'd never know there's an issue when Mike's on the air."

Heinsohn likes to joke that he and Gorman have had just one argument over their 38 years, and that it has not ended yet.

But there actually was one that required mediation. About 20 years ago, the two were at a pregame production meeting in an Orlando restaurant when Heinsohn suggested that anyone could do Gorman's job. A shouting match ensued, and the two had to be separated.

"It wasn't good," Gorman says. "It wasn't pretty."

That afternoon, Gorman strode past Heinsohn to get on the team bus, still fuming but prepared to do the broadcast anyway. Then Heinsohn grabbed Gorman and wrapped him in a bear hug. They called the game and have pretty much been fine ever since.

"When we do a game," the 84-year-old Heinsohn says now, "I feel like we're friends watching together with popcorn and a beer."

In 2012, former Celtics forward Brian Scalabrine began filling in for Heinsohn and now does the road broadcasts. Scalabrine is energetic, loud, and sometimes over-the-top. For many play-by-play announcers who have had one teammate for so long, it could have been a jarring transition.

But Gorman's adjustment was seamless, and he and Scalabrine, 41, now have a chemistry of their own. Gorman educates Scalabrine on broadcasting and banter—"What does penultimate mean?" Scalabrine asked on air after Gorman used the word in a recent broadcast—and the knowledgeable Scalabrine gives Gorman a different view of the NBA.

'BASKETBALL COMFORT FOOD'

On game days, Gorman usually has a one-hour workout and a half-hour nap, and he spends another hour scanning the detailed notes that stat guru Dick Lipe emails to him every day.

Gorman does not like to jam a broadcast with this information—Heinsohn warned him about that years ago—but he likes to have an extensive menu to choose from when something fits.

Many broadcasters fill games with noisy calls and nonstop dialogue, but Gorman has never been tempted to alter his understated approach. The fans can see what is transpiring, so they don't always need to be told about it.

"Mike tells me that the third man in the booth, our audience, is our silent partner," Scalabrine said. "And we've got to give him the proper amount of space and respect."

After Gorman started with the Celtics, he wanted to create a signature call. The team's legendary radio announcer, Johnny Most, used to follow big shots by saying, "Bang!" Gorman came up with "Got it!" He ran it by Most, who gave an approving nod. It remains Gorman's trademark line today. "Takes it, makes it," is another favorite. But Gorman does not overwhelm a broadcast with catchphrases or hot takes.

"Instead of screaming all game long, he just calls the game," said ABC's lead NBA announcer, Mike Breen, a longtime friend. "And then when that voice goes up you know, 'Uh oh, I'm seeing something special.'"

Added Celtics co-owner Steve Pagliuca: "Mike's kind of like a home-cooked meal. He's basketball comfort food."

When Teri got a job helping found the WNBA in the mid 1990s, the couple bought an apartment on 85th Street in Manhattan. Gorman commuted on game days, usually making it home just before 3 a.m. Once he made it back just in time to wake up his wife and daughter to walk to the Hudson River and see a meteor shower, but the trips were usually less romantic than that.

The family eventually moved out of the city and bought a house on a private lake in South Salem, N.Y. Motorboats are not allowed on the water, and when the trees are covered in leaves, the place is almost invisible, just as Gorman likes it. He fishes and kayaks and is looking forward to living there year-round again someday.

DIMMING THE LIGHTS

While the end of his career is not here, Gorman knows it is within sight. He skipped a pair of road trips this year and may do that more frequently. He is under contract for two more seasons, and NBCSB holds an option for a third year.

"He's obviously earned the right to call his shots how he wants this to finish up," Lucey said. "He's in charge of that. He's still very, very popular with the bosses at NBC."

Gorman hopes to witness one more Celtics championship, mostly so he can see coach Brad

Stevens win his first. Teri remembers when the couple was on a duck boat in the 2008 championship parade and they rolled past a group of children proudly yelling "Dorchester! Dorchester!" to Gorman.

"That was just a visceral moment for me," Teri says. "It was like, 'Wow, they really appreciate him here.'"

Sometimes Gorman thinks about the various points when his career could have veered in a different direction.

He thought CBS might offer him a national college basketball job after he called a game for the network in the 1970s, but an executive approached him afterward just to say he'd done great reading a promo for the network's hit show, "Murder, She Wrote." He was contacted about the New York Mets play-by-play job in the mid '80s, but he never pursued it.

But Gorman has no regrets. For 38 years and counting, he has chronicled the team he used to sneak in through fire escapes to see. He has covered championships won by Larry Bird and Paul Pierce. He has become a Boston institution. Someone recently told him that any Celtics fan under 50 really only knows what it's like to watch a game with his voice as the soundtrack.

"I'm flattered by that," Gorman said. "But at the same time, I wonder if maybe it'll be time for somebody else's voice soon."

Walker, Celtics Reach 4-Year, $141m Deal

July 1, 2019 • by Adam Himmelsbach

The Celtics' frustrating season was followed by a rough start to the summer. They were unable to acquire Anthony Davis, and then they received word that former All-Stars Kyrie Irving and Al Horford intended to sign elsewhere.

It was enough to make the franchise wobble and even ponder whether it was time to pivot to a full youth movement. But on Sunday, the Celtics struck back.

The team agreed to a four-year, $141 million max contract with Kemba Walker, the Hornets' three-time All-Star point guard, a league source confirmed.

"When you think of the Celtics, you think of championships and winning," Walker said during an appearance on ESPN's "SportsCenter" on Sunday night. "And that's what I'm about. I'm about competing for championships and winning . . . I just felt like Boston was the best fit for me to try and accomplish those kinds of goals."

Walker will likely technically come to Boston via a trade. A league source confirmed Terry Rozier has agreed to a three-year, $58 million deal with Charlotte and that the two will ultimately switch sides via a sign-and-trade.

The Hornets are over the cap and unable to sign Rozier to a deal this size outright. The Celtics agreed to the sign-and-trade to keep other options open, according to a league source. Boston could potentially turn it into a three-team, sign-and-trade involving Horford or Irving, who agreed to deals with the 76ers and Nets, respectively, on Sunday, in order to free the $9.2 million mid-level exception that they could use on other players. But even if that does not happen, a source said, Boston will receive compensation in some form from Charlotte.

Late Sunday night, ESPN reported Horford had agreed to a four-year, $109 million contract with the 76ers, giving a major boost to one of the Celtics' top rivals after it lost Jimmy Butler to the Heat. Irving's departure to sign with the Nets, where he will team up with Kevin Durant, was more expected.

For the Celtics, though, the most important development on this busy day was that Walker is bound for Boston.

Last season, he averaged 25.6 points, 5.9 assists, and 4.4 rebounds per game for Charlotte and he received third-team All-NBA recognition.

9

TATUM, BROWN, AND THE QUEST FOR BANNER 18

(2020-2023)

n their pursuit of the franchise's 18th NBA championship, the Celtics were akin to a compelling film—one laden with plot twists both expected and stunning—whose conclusion had yet to be written.

It featured two A-list stars in Jayson Tatum and Jaylen Brown, who matured into their roles, and a supporting cast around them—on the court, bench, and front office—that evolved in the quest to find complementary personnel that also provided just the right chemistry.

They came so close to capturing the perfect final scene in June 2022. Those Celtics had undergone a seismic shake-up at the end of the 2021 season, after the Brooklyn Nets wiped out the disconnected Celtics in the first round, Boston defector Kyrie Irving stomping on the leprechaun logo on the Garden parquet as the final exclamation point after the Game 5 clincher.

The afternoon after the season ended, the Celtics announced that Danny Ainge was retiring after 18 seasons as the franchise's chief basketball executive, while Brad Stevens would vacate the bench after eight seasons and three trips to the conference finals as Celtics coach and move into Ainge's role. (Ainge's retirement did not last long. He joined the Utah Jazz as alternate governor and CEO in December 2022.)

Stevens immediately proved a swift decision-maker, reacquiring versatile big man Al Horford from the Oklahoma City Thunder in exchange for declining guard Kemba Walker, then hiring Nets assistant Ime Udoka as his successor before June was complete. Success came slowly at first as players adjusted to Udoka's defense-first ethos. The Celtics won just 18 of their first 39 games, but went on a tear in February, winning 33 of their final 43, finishing second in the Eastern Conference, and embracing a ferocious defensive intensity that resulted in Marcus Smart becoming the first guard

‹ Jaylen Brown and Jayson Tatum, the dynamic duo of the Celtics' current era.

since Seattle's Gary Payton in 1996 to be named NBA Defensive Player of the Year. Along the way, Stevens pulled off another bold move, acquiring understated but excellent guard Derrick White from the Spurs in February 2022.

The playoffs were filled with thrills. Tatum, who was named first-team All-NBA for the first time (he would earn the honor again the following season), set the tone in the opener of the first-round series against the Nets, when his spinning layup off a Marcus Smart feed gave the Celtics' a buzzer-beating 115-114 win. The Celtics would avenge the previous season's franchise-altering loss to the Nets with a first-round sweep, then oust Giannis Antetokounmpo and the defending champion Bucks in the second round, with Tatum scoring 46 points on the road in a must-win Game 6 and reserve forward Grant Williams knocking down seven 3-pointers in Game 7.

The Celtics survived the relentless Miami Heat in seven games in the conference finals, advancing to the NBA Finals for the first time since 2010. Awaiting them: Steph Curry and the three-time champion Warriors. Initially, the Celtics looked ready for the moment, winning Games 1 and 3, and leading through three quarters in Game 4. But Curry, who finished with 43 points, rallied the Warriors to victory in the fourth quarter, and the Celtics—plagued by too-frequent turnovers by Tatum and Brown— would not win another game, falling in six.

The trip to the Finals was both a learning experience and genuine progress. The Celtics had reached the conference finals—losing in six games to the Heat—in the COVID-19-abbreviated 2020 season, when the league convened 22 teams to a "bubble" at Disney World Orlando to play out the postseason amid the pandemic. Gordon Hayward, never quite the same after his devastating ankle and leg injury but still a versatile offensive contributor, departed for the Charlotte Hornets after the 2020 season. The following season had its high points—Tatum tied Larry Bird's franchise single-game scoring record with 60 points against the Spurs in late April—but the Celtics went just 36-36 in the regular season before the dismantling by Irving, Kevin Durant, and the Nets in the first round.

Even with the unfulfilling finish, the joyride to the Finals in 2022 seemed to have the Tatum/Brown Celtics, who also featured supporting talent such as Smart, Horford, White, and springy center Robert

Williams, positioned to be championship contenders for the near future. But less than a week before training camp was set to begin in September 2022, Udoka was suspended for the entirety of the upcoming season for a violation of team policies, reported to be an inappropriate relationship with a female team employee. Thirty-four-year-old assistant coach Joe Mazzulla was named interim coach. His head coaching experience had consisted of two seasons at Division 2 Fairmont State, and his place in the pecking order on Udoka's staff was such that he sat in the second row behind the bench during games.

There were occasionally perilous turns on Mazzulla's learning curve. But the Celtics, with its core bolstered by the offseason acquisition of guard Malcolm Brogdon, got off to a dazzling start offensively. Mazzulla, an intense Stevens disciple, had the interim label removed in mid-February, and the Celtics finished with 57 regular-season wins, six more than they had the season previous under Udoka.

The Celtics eliminated the Hawks in six games in the first round, and Tatum's 51-point effort in Game 7—following late heroics in Game 6—boosted the Celtics past the Sixers in the second round. But the season ended a round earlier and with far less optimism than it had the previous season. The Celtics fell behind 3-0 to the seventh-seeded Heat, won the next three games—with Derrick White's did-that-just-happen? put-back with 0.1 seconds left winning Game 6. The quest to become the first NBA team ever to win a series after falling behind 3-0 came to a crashing halt in Game 7 when Tatum rolled an ankle on the game's first possession, rendering him ineffective. Brown committed eight turnovers in the 19-point loss.

In the offseason, Stevens made his most significant—and surprising—alterations to the roster yet. While Tatum and Brown—who signed a $304 million extension in July 2023—remained, Stevens sent the popular if polarizing Smart to the Memphis Grizzlies in a stunning three-way trade in June that brought gifted if oft-injured Wizards big man Kristaps Porzingis to the Celtics. An even bigger stunner occurred shortly before camp for the 2024 season opened, when the Celtics acquired five-time All-Defense selection Jrue Holiday from the Blazers, days after the Bucks had swapped him in a deal for longtime Blazers star Damian Lillard. The price was Robert Williams, Brogdon, and a pair of draft picks, a move that left the Celtics enviably deep in high-end talent, but with questionable depth beyond their top-six players. They were built for the playoffs, when benches get shorter . . . and perhaps even built to hang Banner 18.

Meet Jaylen Brown's Quarantine Trainer: His 78-Year-Old Grandfather

May 19, 2020 • by Adam Himmelsbach

As COVID-19 began to roar across the country in March, Celtics forward Jaylen Brown immediately thought of his grandfather, Willie Brown, who lives alone in Atlanta. He knew he just had to get him to Boston.

But Willie was reluctant to leave what he viewed as his safe haven, even though it probably was not as safe as he thought. So Jaylen did not tell him he wanted him to flee because of a virus. He told him that he wanted him in Boston because he needed his help. He needed a trainer, and he couldn't think of anyone better than his grandfather.

"And he's been joyful about it," Jaylen said by phone. "I feel like it keeps him going."

Willie Brown, who turns 79 in August, did a tour in Vietnam with the Marines in 1963. Afterward, he worked as a truck driver, but really just used that job as an entryway to his true love: boxing. He dreamed of becoming a professional fighter but worried he could not make it a living. So as he crisscrossed the Midwest and the East Coast driving his truck, he offered his services as a sparring partner wherever he went.

Over time, he said, he developed a reputation as a reliable opponent for big boxers training for big fights. He said he sparred against Muhammad Ali, Joe Frazier, and Sonny Liston, among others.

"I always knew where the gym was," he said. "At that time, it didn't take that much to find out who is who, so I kept running from city to city. Once in the '70s I sparred with Joe Frazier in Philadelphia, and he hit me with a left hook down below, and it kept me on the floor of my hotel room for three days."

Willie's son, Marselles, became a professional heavyweight, compiling a 33-18-1 record that included fights with former champions Tommy Morrison and Trevor Berbick. Marselles's son became the biggest star in the family and was drafted by the Celtics with the third overall pick of the 2016 NBA Draft.

With gyms and basketball courts across the country shuttered because of the coronavirus, NBA players have been forced to find creative ways to train. And that's where Jaylen's grandfather has come in since being in Boston with Jaylen and his mother, Mechalle, and brother Quenton.

"We said we needed him to help me train and get back ready for the season, so he could feel comfortable sticking around here," Jaylen said. "But on the other side of that, he's like, 'OK, we're going to train then.' We've been training hard and a lot. On one hand, it's great that he's comfortable being here, but on the other he's making me work my [butt] off."

Willie took the assignment quite seriously from the start. Each morning he would bang at Jaylen's bedroom door at 7:30 a.m. and tell him it was time to work. As the days passed, he became more lenient with start times, but not with the training sessions.

He'll hold up boxing pads as Jaylen pounds them with his gloves. He'll have Jaylen jump rope, or carry 5-pound weights as he sprints up and down the street in front of his home. They do resistance-band, bodyweight, and core exercises. Jaylen thinks he's in the best shape of his life.

"He has me doing a lot of things I've never done before," Jaylen said. "It's the old way of training. Everything he does is kind of a throwback, but it's good. He's never been stagnant, and I got that from him."

Willie, or Paw-paw as Jaylen calls him, has been quite impressed with the progress of his student.

"It's beautiful," Willie said. "I can't believe it myself. He works like a pro. It's in his blood, you understand that? He does amazing things."

Willie is not simply barking orders at Jaylen from afar. He jumps into the workouts when he can, with Jaylen flipping the script and serving as his motivator and biggest fan. Willie said with a chuckle that Jaylen thinks he's the faster of the two, but once his left leg feels a bit better, he'd like to show him that he's not.

"It's been a wonderful way for them to help each other and have their bond grow, and I think

[Willie] has been immensely happy," said Mechalle. "Anybody getting older, they love just being involved and engaged.

"I'm glad Jaylen wanted to do this and wanted him to be a part of it. And to see the smile on his face when he's helping him, that's priceless. We didn't want this quarantine, but sometimes things pull you together."

GETTING HEATED

Sounds as if they are imploding?

September 18, 2020 • by Gary Washburn

ORLANDO—So is this what implosion looks like in person? Screaming in the locker room by multiple parties. Items, sounding like chairs, being thrown, a voice that sounded like Brad Stevens screaming for his players to calm down. A shirtless Marcus Smart walking to the bathroom telling his teammates, "Y'all on that [expletive]!"

That is what happened on Thursday night after the Celtics' second consecutive disheartening loss to the Miami Heat in the Eastern Conference finals. Again, the Celtics raced to a big lead, then blew it because they forgot how to play solid, fundamental basketball against a zone defense. They came back to take the lead again, only to watch Jimmy Butler and his buddies take their lunch money again in the waning minutes.

The result was a 106-101 loss, and the Celtics trail, two games to none, to a team that's better connected, more cohesive, and quite honestly doesn't believe the Celtics can beat them.

Facing that reality, the Celtics' locker room imploded after the game. The used-to-be-close Celtics were screaming at each other. How come they can't score against the zone? Why did so-and-so take that bad shot? Why was Butler allowed to get two critical steals on hustle plays, while the Celtics watched as Butler created two layups?

After the locker-room fracas, which lasted about 20 minutes, the Celtics were of few words. They're embarrassed. The Heat are laughing in their faces. Whatever the Celtics have, the Heat have a counter. Go ahead and take a 17-point lead, we'll come back and beat you anyway.

Last year's Celtics team gave up after falling behind to the Milwaukee Bucks, with Kyrie Irving headed out the door before the decisive Game 5. This year was supposed to be different. The Celtics were supposed to be as connected as they have been in years, but that's not the case, obviously.

They are angry and players are pointing fingers at each other, or at least they were. They came out of the meeting rather calm, brushing it off as normal following a loss. But this wasn't normal.

Jaylen Brown was the only Celtic to acknowledge the postgame argument was out of the ordinary. And he supported Smart. Can fences be mended in the next 48 hours? Was this actually a positive that a team that has been pretty cordial finally has decided it is tired of being outplayed and outhustled on the biggest stage?

"Just a lot of emotions flying around, obviously we feel like we could have, should have won, and we didn't," Brown said. "I think that's why we love Marcus. He plays with passion. He's full of fire. That's what I love about him the most. He has that desire and that will and we need him to continue to have that.

"There's ups and downs with families all the time, but we embrace each other for who we are. And for who Marcus is, I love him for it."

But the Celtics can't possibly act like everything is cool. They're halfway from being swept, and no NBA team has ever come back from a 0-3 deficit.

The Celtics will meet Friday, look at film, and try to figure out a response. But perhaps some feelings need to be repaired and egos healed after Game 2.

The Celtics are a demoralized bunch, having hearts taken by a team that is just waiting for their mistakes and lack of focus.

So Smart and others had a right to be angry, embarrassed, and defeated. The question now is how are they going to respond on Saturday? Great teams come back from adversity.

What are the Celtics? Are they just the frontrunners some around the league believe they are?

Heinsohn Loved Celtics, Not Officials

November 11, 2020 • by Chad Finn

It's not just that Celtics history cannot be told without Tommy Heinsohn, who collected eight championships as a player, two as a coach, and witnessed the rest as a broadcaster.

It's that Celtics history—especially the last four decades—cannot be told without hearing his gravelly, boisterous voice telling it.

"Well, Mike [Gorman] put it best," Heinsohn told me in 2016. "There's a generation—it's an old generation, my friend, but it's a generation!—that remembers me best as a player. There's a generation that remembers me best as a coach. There's a generation that thinks of me as a broadcaster. And kids, they think I'm Shrek. I'll tell you what, I'll take all of it."

Heinsohn, who died Monday at 86 years old, was inducted into the Basketball Hall of Fame as both a player and coach. But to generations of Celtics fans, he was best known as the color analyst alongside Mike Gorman for 39 years on the team's regional television broadcasts.

Heinsohn was informed, opinionated, quick to laugh, and intolerant of slow-paced offenses and any referee with a functioning whistle.

He was such an essential part of the fabric of the Celtics viewing experience, even with a reduced role in recent years as he battled health problems, that the sad news of his death brought at least a few fleeting smiles when some of his more famous comments and catchphrases flickered to mind.

He made hustling, limited forward Walter McCarty a cult hero among the fan base in the late 1990s with his unabashed, "I love Waltah!" proclamations. He awarded "Tommy Points" for players who went above and beyond the call of duty on a given play. (Waltah, of course, is presumably high atop that all-time leaderboard.)

He'd unapologetically dive headfirst into hyperbole when a marginal player would make a magical play, which is how Heinsohn—simply Tommy to Celtics fans—came to do such things as compare an obviously limited backup center named Greg

Stiemsma's knack for shot blocking to that of the unparalleled Bill Russell or vow that Dee Brown could be the next Isiah Thomas as a point guard.

Heinsohn's disdain for officials, surely a lingering effect from his coaching days, was amusing and, until mellower recent seasons, obsessive. I always was convinced he waited until officials were passing Heinsohn's courtside perch at the scorer's table before he unleashed his most biting criticisms of their work.

So many of the most familiar Heinsohn phrases—"You've gotta be kidding me!" . . . "They didn't touch him!" . . . "Oh, brother!" . . . "This is getting ridiculous!" . . . "You call that a hard foul?"—came from that running dialogue with the officials.

Occasionally, his passion for the Celtics and his sense that they were being wronged led him to work blue. During the 1997 season-opening win against the champion Chicago Bulls—both the debut and high point of the Rick Pitino era—an incensed Heinsohn bellowed, "That's [expletive]!" after a Celtic was called for a questionable foul on Michael Jordan.

Sometimes, the officials let him know they were listening, most memorably at the conclusion of a Celtics loss to the Phoenix Suns in December 2002. After Celtics star Paul Pierce chipped two teeth when struck by a Suns player without drawing a foul call, Heinsohn unleashed his ire on official Kenny Mauer, punctuating it at game's end with this zinger: "This Kenny Mauer should go home to his wife, because nobody here loves him!"

Mauer, walking by the scorer's table to pick up his jacket, looked at Heinsohn, smiled, and said, "Merry Christmas." That did not put Heinsohn in the holiday spirit.

Heinsohn's preoccupation with officials was such a part of his style that the Celtics acknowledged it in a statement about his death on Tuesday. But it was also a significant part of his appeal to viewers, his visceral reactions and pleas that the Celtics were getting robbed so relatable to fans that viewed sports through a similar prism.

"Tommy doesn't really do color," Gorman told the Globe once a few years ago. "In his heart, he's still coaching the Celtics and he always will be. It doesn't matter who the coach is, and it's no disrespect to the coach. This always will be Tommy's team. Tommy will be coaching this team till he takes

Tommy Heinsohn did it all for the Celtics—player, coach, and broadcaster. Here, he teaches young fans during the WBZ Basketball Clinic in the North End in October 1970.

When Gorman stopped coloring his hair before the 2001 season, surprising viewers when his dyed black hair turned white, Heinsohn asked him if he had joined the witness protection program.

But Heinsohn did call Celtics games before that fortuitous pairing. In 1966, he debuted as the color analyst on playoff games alongside Don Gillis on Ch. 7. He continued to call Celtics games—including a couple of years as the play-by-play voice with Red Auerbach on color—until taking the Celtics coaching job in 1970.

He returned to broadcasting in the late '70s, and rose to be the analyst on CBS's No. 1 team alongside Dick Stockton for four years in the mid-'80s, right in the heart of the Celtics-Lakers heyday. He also dabbled in play-by-play on Celtics road games from 1990-99, with Bob Cousy on color. (He worked with Gorman on just the home games then.)

In his national days, Heinsohn did his best to temper his affection for the Celtics, once telling me that he tried to analyze teams as if he were scouting them when he did national broadcasts, but most fans knew the roots of his allegiances.

"What keeps me going [is] watching them grow as players and people," said Heinsohn in 2016. "And when you get that close to them and you've been around so long, you necessarily get a rooting interest. Yeah, I let that show as a broadcaster. I've been accused!"

Heinsohn began cutting back his travel schedule in 2007, and in recent years had called just home games. He called just a handful of games this past season as he battled health problems, and while current analyst Brian Scalabrine is a popular figure, the void left by Heinsohn was palpable.

As the Celtics advanced in the bubble to the Eastern Conference finals, it was impossible not to wonder what Heinsohn thought and what he would say about a team he adored and knew inside and out.

his final breath. If it was possible to still be playing for this team, he would be."

Gorman understood Heinsohn well, having learned what he was all about during their first Celtics broadcast together during the 1981 season, Larry Bird's second year in the league. (They had called Providence College games together previously, so they knew each other's work.)

"Tommy claims I make this story up, but I remember this very clearly," Gorman once told the Globe. "The very first game I ever did with Tommy, I remember coming in and having just voluminous notes. A spotting chart made out with all sorts of numbers and histories and anecdotes and everything I could find out about every player on it.

"And I remember Tommy looking at it and going, 'What's that?' I said, 'Those are my notes, the stuff I'm going to use during the game.' And he reached out and picked it up and turned it over on the table and said, 'We're not gonna need that.'

"And that has kind of been our style ever since."

Gorman and Heinsohn would go on to be the longest continuous on-air broadcast pairing of any professional sports team, most recently on NBC Sports Boston (they first called games on a regional network called Prism, and it went through various incarnations through the years). Their rapport was extraordinary. One humorous moment:

That was perhaps the most remarkable feature about him as a broadcaster. While he'd occasionally gripe about the effort of current players on defense—and every old coach does that—he remained informed and engaged. He liked to talk about back in his day, sure, but he appreciated the modern NBA more than any octogenarian in the world.

Just not the referees. That always remained consistent. Tommy Points were meant for Waltah, but they were never meant for them.

He's Making His Points to Doubters

May 1, 2021 • by Gary Washburn

Friday was a byproduct of those sweltering St. Louis summers, when young Jayson Tatum, nothing but arms, legs and a baby face, was being pushed so much by his father, Justin, there were times he just wanted to quit.

The other side of Tatum wanted to prove to his old man how good of a player he was. There remains inside Tatum—despite his two All-Star appearances, despite his ascension into an elite player, despite being considered the next great Celtic—a side that seeks to quiet doubters, that still seeks full acceptance.

Perhaps it's that desire that pushes him to improve, that gives him the confidence or bravado to take the ball in clutch moments and score on whoever is guarding him.

Tatum was at his absolute best Friday at TD Garden, when the Celtics played one of their worst halves of the season and then followed it with one of their best. Tatum tied Larry Bird for the franchise record with 60 points, carrying his teammates when they were listless in the first half and then catapulting them when they joined him to rally from a 32-point deficit.

The Celtics beat the Spurs, 143-140, in overtime because of Tatum's relentlessness. He didn't attempt a series of wild shots or contested 3-pointers. He attacked the rim. He shot over overmatched defenders in the midrange. He got to the free throw line and, oh yeah, he mixed in the occasional 3-ball.

It was a brilliant performance, a testament to Tatum's true offensive talent. He is 23 but it seems as if he's been the face of this franchise for 10 years. He has his share of critics, especially during this trying Celtics season, but Friday was a reminder that the Celtics have an untouchable player; the type of star who can eventually lead teams to championships.

"That boy," teammate Jaylen Brown said, "is destined for greatness."

His growth has been swift but also bumpy at times. He has dealt with the aftereffects of COVID-19, which have taken a physical toll on his endurance. He believes he doesn't get enough respect from officials. So a few weeks ago, Tatum decided to snatch that respect by attacking the basket and drawing fouls.

Tatum has all the tools to be an all-time great Celtics' scorer. He's long, athletic and can shoot from long range. He's crafty with his drives and he has a nice touch at the rim.

On Friday, his full arsenal was on display and the most impressive aspect was the Celtics needed every one of his points. After the game, Tatum's teammates splashed him with water in celebration and he took a photo holding up the number "60" on a white sheet of paper, similar to Wilt Chamberlain's 100-point game 59 years ago.

"It was a special night," he said. "Playing with guys you enjoy being around who are genuinely happy for your success."

After the game he also called Justin, who offered his congratulations and expressed great pride in his son. Tatum admitted that Justin's harsh coaching style during his youth strained their relationship. The game wasn't fun, and only in the past few years have they truly become a father-son in which dad only offers encouragement and support.

"Everybody knows how close I've been with my mom and she's my biggest fan," Tatum said. "My dad was the one who introduced me to basketball but his tactics were extreme sometimes and he for sure pushed me when I was younger and we had some rocky times because of how hard he pushed me."

Tatum said he's driven by his own personal expectations. He has heard his share of criticism, even from former Celtic Kendrick Perkins, who said he lacked leadership during the team's difficult times. Tatum's demeanor doesn't necessarily allow him to be that vocal leader. He instead leads by example and on nights such as Friday, nearly literally carrying his team on his shoulders to prosperity.

"I have the utmost and highest expectations for myself and where I'm trying to get to and where I want to be when it's all said and done," he said. "I know I'm young and I know I have a super-long way to go, but I'm determined to get there."

Shamrock Shakeup

A Weird, Abrupt Ending for Danny Ainge, a Daunting New Challenge for Brad Stevens with Celtics

June 3, 2021 • by Dan Shaughnessy

It happened overnight.

Literally.

The soft and annoying Boston Celtics of 2021 were eliminated from the playoffs Tuesday evening in Brooklyn, a 123-109 noncompetitive whimper at the end of one of the most disappointing local sports seasons of all time.

And then, after a meeting back in Boston Wednesday morning, the team issued a press release at 11:01 a.m. announcing that Danny Ainge was retiring and coach Brad Stevens would be leaving the bench and moving into Ainge's position as president of basketball operations.

Just like that. After 18 seasons running the Celtics, Ainge was done. And after eight seasons coaching the Celtics, Stevens was done.

Nobody got fired. Ainge was allowed to step down ("It's completely his decision," said Celtics owner Wyc Grousbeck) and Stevens—who is signed through 2026 at big dollars—"voluntarily" left the bench to take over for Ainge. Flanked by owners Grousbeck and Steve Pagliuca, Ainge and Stevens appeared at a noon press conference at the Celtics' practice facility in Brighton.

"Today's not a great day," said Ainge. "I wish we would have finished the year on a better note, but I feel like there's so much hope looking forward. I'm excited for Brad. I feel like he was born for this . . . This is a great day for the Celtics. This is actually a big step forward."

Wow. These are indeed interesting times on Causeway Street.

So now the Celtics are searching for a new coach, somebody who will be able to get through to Jayson Tatum, Jaylen Brown, Marcus Smart, game-management Kemba Walker, and the raft of Boston players who believe they are better than they are.

Good luck to the next coach of this team. Clearly, it's not enough to be a master of game-planning and hoop strategy. An NBA coach today has to be a therapist, accommodator, motivator, psychologist, mind reader, and mentor. It helps if he's an ex-NBA player. A guy like Doc Rivers comes to mind. Guys like Kendrick Perkins and Chauncey Billups come to mind. If the Celtics really wanted to think outside the box, they could consider Duke women's coach Kara Lawson, a former Celtics assistant coach.

Stevens never had a chance with this crew. He was saddled with Gordon Hayward, who got hurt in his first game and never indicated that he wanted to be here. He was burdened for two years with Kyrie Irving, who could never be pleased, no matter how much the Celtics tried to accommodate him. While he was here, Kyrie lied and pouted and poisoned the minds of other young Celtics players. Then he left Boston and built his Super Team in Brooklyn.

Tuesday at Barclays Center, Kyrie's "new" team killed off what was left of what Ainge and Stevens were trying to build in Boston. When it was over, Kyrie hugged all the Celtics—Michael Corleone style—and his young admirers in Celtics uniforms hugged him back.

In the end, the 2021 Celtics players loved Kyrie more than they loved the Celtics. Certainly they loved Kyrie more than Stevens, Ainge, or Celtics fans. It was wildly disrespectful. Changes had to be made.

So now we have change. Ainge is gone. And we are going to find out if Stevens can be an NBA team-builder. Stevens's first job is to find a head coach.

Call me a dope, but I feel Stevens's skills are misused in the front office of an NBA franchise. Brad Stevens is a coach—best employed as a college coach. He's a sculptor of young basketball souls. We saw the best of him in his years at Butler. He's only 44 years old and now he's taking his talents to the swampland of NBA player procurement. I wish I felt better about him as a pro basketball boss.

"I understand and am looking forward to this new challenge and great responsibility," said Stevens. "We're driven to compete for championships . . . This morning is a hard day and I know that there's a lot of work ahead . . . I really have enjoyed coaching, but this is the new challenge and this is what we need to do to hopefully be even better."

Stevens coached the Celtics for eight seasons. He took them to the conference finals in three of the four seasons leading into the 2021 disaster. He drew up great plays after timeouts. He never said anything bad about any of his players. But he didn't seem to have the gravitas needed to coach young NBA stars who come to the league after a decade of getting their butts kissed by AAU programs.

Poor Brad Stevens. NBA coaching was too much for the man. Now he's on the midnight train to salary-cap hell, mid-level exceptions, and a league with a culture of superstars who want to relocate, poach friends from other teams, and create an instant super-power—rather than build something with the teams that draft them.

This goes down as a weird, abrupt ending for the 62-year-old Ainge, who first came to the Celtics when Red Auerbach made him Boston's second-round draft pick while Ainge was playing infield for the Toronto Blue Jays in the spring of 1981.

Ainge played eight seasons for the Celtics, starting alongside Hall of Famers Larry Bird, Robert Parish, Kevin McHale, and Dennis Johnson, winning two championships and appearing in four NBA Finals with Boston. Red traded Ainge to Sacramento in 1989, but Ainge came back to become Auerbach's ultimate successor in 2003, three years before Red's death.

Ainge has a great eye for basketball talent. He drafted and cultivated Rajon Rondo. He acquired Kevin Garnett and Ray Allen to join Paul Pierce for the 2008 championship season. In 2013, he fleeced Brooklyn, dealing the aging Pierce and Garnett for a raft of draft picks.

It was Ainge who hired Rivers as head coach. It was Ainge who hired Stevens from Butler. It was Ainge who drafted Brown and Tatum. It was Ainge who went out and got Hayward. And Al Horford. And Kyrie Irving. And Walker.

None of it worked out after 2008. Ainge never got another ring. Stevens never got to the Finals.

Now Ainge is gone (time to put his No. 44 in the rafters). And Stevens is about to find out that running the Celtics from the front office might be an even tougher job than trying to coach these guys.

QUICK FIRST STEP

STEVENS SHIPS WALKER, PICK TO THUNDER

June 19, 2021 • by Adam Himmelsbach

About a half-hour after the Celtics' season ended with a Game 5 playoff loss to the Nets June 1, point guard Kemba Walker sat down for a Zoom interview in the bowels of the Barclays Center and briefly rehashed a frustrating year.

He had missed that game and the previous one because of a bone bruise on his left knee, and that stubborn knee would end up defining his tenure in Boston.

Walker was asked about changes he anticipated in the offseason.

"I have no idea," he said. "Like I said, just need time to reflect. It's just so soon."

But on Friday, Walker's two-year stint in Boston came to a sudden end.

In his first major move as the team's president of basketball operations, Brad Stevens agreed to trade Walker, the No. 16 pick in next month's draft, and a 2025 second-round pick to the Oklahoma City Thunder for former Celtics forward Al Horford, center Moses Brown, and a 2023 second-round choice.

Walker has two years and $73 million remaining on his four-year deal, and his departure will create future financial flexibility for the Celtics. They will remain over the salary cap, but in the short term, it will increase the likelihood that they can re-sign free agent wing Evan Fournier now that the tax burden will not be as steep.

Horford has $53 million left on the four-year deal he signed with the 76ers two seasons ago, and his salary for the 2023 season is partially guaranteed.

Walker averaged 19.3 points, 4.9 assists, and 4.0 rebounds this season. His contract was widely viewed around the league as an albatross, and it was clear the Celtics would need to entice a team with some extra draft compensation in any deal involving Walker.

While Kyrie Irving's departure in 2019 was a setback for the Celtics, Horford's decision to opt out of the final year of his deal so he could sign with the 76ers was considerably more stunning. When Horford signed a four-year, $113 million contract with Boston in 2017, it was considered a substantial coup, as it accelerated what once looked as if it would be a lengthy rebuild. Horford led the Celtics to consecutive conference finals appearances before they lost to the Bucks in the 2019 semifinals.

Celtics to Name Udoka as Coach

June 24, 2021 • by Adam Himmelsbach

Since being promoted to replace Danny Ainge as the Celtics' president of basketball operations three weeks ago, Brad Stevens has worked feverishly to find his replacement as head coach. He eventually whittled a long list of candidates to a select few, and then one began to emerge.

League sources said that Stevens had numerous conversations with Brooklyn Nets assistant coach Ime Udoka. On Sunday, sources said, a Celtics contingent that included Stevens, team owners Wyc Grousbeck and Steve Pagliuca, and vice president of player development Allison Feaster conducted the final interview with Udoka in New York.

Udoka, a longtime NBA assistant, impressed the Celtics with his knowledge of the game, his attention to detail, and his passion to win. And on Wednesday, league sources said, he was hired as the Celtics' next head coach.

The hiring has not been officially announced yet, so the Celtics declined to comment, but a news conference is expected on Monday.

According to one source, Udoka was intrigued by the opportunity to work for Stevens, who developed a reputation as one of the game's brightest minds during his eight-year run as Celtics coach, in part because Stevens would understand Udoka's role as well as anyone. Also, Udoka was excited about the chance to guide a roster that included two young All-Stars in Jayson Tatum and Jaylen Brown.

Brown, Tatum, and Marcus Smart played for Team USA in the 2019 FIBA World Cup, when Udoka was an assistant coach for the team. Sources said Celtics players, particularly Tatum and Brown, were consulted about this hire, and they were pleased with the decision.

As the Celtics contacted people around the NBA to learn more about Udoka, the reviews were consistently glowing. He is known for his work ethic, and the Celtics are hopeful that as a former player he will be able to relate to this young team. One source said that during Udoka's previous stops as an assistant, he would often go out to dinner with players to find out more about them.

Udoka, 43, spent seven years as an assistant coach under Gregg Popovich in San Antonio before joining the 76ers staff in the 2020 season in place of Monty Williams, who left to coach the Suns. This year, Udoka was hired as an assistant under Brooklyn coach Steve Nash. A league source said this pedigree, particularly the extensive experience working with Popovich, was viewed as a major benefit.

Udoka grew up in Oregon and attended high school in Portland. He played college basketball at the University of San Francisco before transferring to Portland State. He went undrafted in 2000 and played independent basketball before joining the NBDL—now known as the G League—in its second season.

He went on to play for the Lakers, Knicks, Trail Blazers, and Spurs over parts of seven seasons, averaging 5.2 points per game. He spent his last four years with San Antonio and parlayed that into a role on the team's coaching staff.

In 2019, Udoka interviewed for the Cavaliers head coaching job, but that ultimately went to former Michigan coach John Beilein.

Now Udoka is getting his chance.

It Was All for One, Which Is the Opposite of Two-Headed Opponent

April 18, 2022 • by Christopher L. Gasper

The fateful final points from Jayson Tatum's tally of 31 that brought TD Garden to basketball Babel were symbolic of the path the Celtics must take in this series. The Celtics have to rely on five hoops heartbeats beating in unison to shine brighter than the Brooklyn Nets' two offensive supernovas.

That's the formula. That's how the Celtics win this best-of-seven first-round series. That's why the Celtics walked off the parquet on Sunday with a Game 1 victory by the skin of their teeth, prevailing, 115-114, on a last-second basket that was both a work of art and teamwork.

All five Celtics touched the ball on the decisive possession, starting with Al Horford snagging the rebound of a Kevin Durant long miss—one of many on this evening—with 12.2 seconds left and ending with Marcus Smart finding Tatum for the buzzer-beater. It was apropos and instructive. A loss dodged and a lesson hopefully learned for the Celtics as they opened their pursuit of Banner No. 18 in both agonizing and exciting fashion against a familiar foe and a familiar object of enmity, Kyrie Irving.

Leave the hero ball to Irving and Durant. The Celtics are going to win this series on the strength of their cohesion, balance, and chemistry at both ends. They are the better T-E-A-M. A gloved fist trumps two raised index fingers—or in Irving's case the middle digit he liberally flashed to the Celtics faithful.

"For us that's kind of been a microcosm of our season. Guys moving the ball, playing unselfish," said coach Ime Udoka. "Jaylen [Brown] could've forced the shot on [Goran] Dragic. He saw three guys on him. He kicked it to Marcus. He could've faked a shot with two guys flying at him. He pump-faked it and saw Jayson cutting. That's where we've really improved at. It kind of all came together on the last possession."

The final sequence is worthy of review. Horford got his 15th rebound. Down 1, Udoka elected not to call a timeout.

The ball bounded from Horford to Derrick White, to Brown, to Smart, who up-faked and drew two Nets (Bruce Brown and Nic Claxton). Smart passed it to a cutting Tatum, who spun around Irving.

Game over, crisis averted.

"I've always been told that you have more time than you realize you have," said Smart, one of four Celtics starters with 20 or more points. "I was about to throw it to Al off the dribble, but I saw JT cut at the last minute. We just wanted to get the easiest shot we can."

Fourth Quarter May Be the Stuff of Legends

May 10, 2022 • by Dan Shaughnessy

MILWAUKEE—If the Celtics go on to win Flag 18—years from now, when tall tales are told—this might be the night folks talk about the most. This might be like Dave Roberts stealing second base, or Adam Vinatieri drilling the ice ball through the uprights in the last game played at Foxboro Stadium.

The Celtics beat the world champion Milwaukee Bucks, 116-108, at Fiserv Forum Monday night to square their conference semifinal series, 2-2. Game 5 is Wednesday at the Garden. Game 6 is Friday back in Brewtown. Game 7 (probably necessary) will be Sunday on Causeway Street. Bring your popcorn.

This was a night the Celts could have folded their green tent and slinked home down, 3-1. They didn't have Robert Williams (knee irritation). They trailed by double digits in the second half. Everybody seemed to be in foul trouble when they started the fourth and superstar Jayson Tatum was still in a shooting slump. Only six Boston players managed to score on this crucial night, and at times it seemed all of Boston was ready to give up and try to make ourselves feel better by complaining about officiating.

Then something happened. Everything happened. Al Horford happened—in Joe Hardy, Damn Yankees, Faustian bargain fashion. "Don't-Call-Me-Average" Al dunked on Giannis Antetokounmpo, flexed his veteran muscle and erupted for 16 fourth-quarter points, making 6 of 6 shots and virtually stomping on the Bucks logo. Horford finished with 30 points and eight rebounds.

"We love Al," said Marcus Smart. "He's the best veteran we've ever had. He understands what he brings to this game and what he brings to this team."

Remember how some of us chuckled when Brad Stevens reacquired Horford in the offseason? It's that same feeling we had when Chaim Bloom went out and got JBJ back last winter.

No one's laughing now.

Horford was provoked when Giannis dunked on him, then said something early in the third with

Al Horford lets the Bucks' Giannis Antetokounmpo know he messed with the wrong guy during Game 4 of the 2022 Eastern Conference semifinals.

the Bucks leading by 6. The Greek Freak picked up a technical for his trouble and Horford appeared especially annoyed.

"This is where the Bucks [expletive] up," tweeted Anna Horford, Al's sister. "I know that look. He was pissed."

"I didn't make out what he said," humble Horford acknowledged after the game. "But the way he looked at me didn't sit well with me. That got me going. At that point, something switched with me."

In the already famous fourth, Horford postered Giannis with a dunk to tie the game, 80-80. Big Al drew a well-deserved technical for his antics, but nobody cared. Momentum had shifted and the Celtics were running downhill to victory.

"It was a big play, obviously," Horford said. "Emotional for our group. A lot of emotions at that point."

Horford's fourth-quarter wingman was the afore-mentioned Tatum (6 for 18 going into the quarter), who finally got comfortable after 3¾ games in the series. In the fourth quarter of Game 4, Tatum woke

up and poured beer on the heads of the Deer that made Milwaukee famous.

Boston made an astounding 16 of 19 floor shots (4 of 5 from international waters) in the fourth quar-ter, outscoring the staggering Bucks, 43-28.

The champs were reduced to the proverbial Deer in the headlights. The Bucks looked old. Giannis (34 points on 14-of-32 shooting) looked tired.

Not sure there has ever been anything like this. Probably not in the Russell-Cousy days. Maybe once or twice in the Larry-Kevin-Chief days. Certainly not in the KG-Pierce-Allen days. Red Auerbach must have been loving it from his perch highest above courtside.

Playing for their playoff lives, the Celtics gut-ted the Bucks. It was a quarter of almost perfect basketball, something we haven't seen maybe since Larry and Co. played a near perfect game against the Hawks in the playoff spring of 1986.

See you Wednesday.

The Celtic Revolution will be televised.

Signature Moment Came at Perfect Time

May 14, 2022 • by Gary Washburn

MILWAUKEE—Maybe Jayson Tatum knew something the Celtics faithful just couldn't imagine because there was a reason for his unwavering confidence after the Game 5 collapse. It appeared as he relished the opportunity to play his best game as a Celtic, to shine in the biggest moment with the season on the brink.

It had been a tough 48 hours since the Celtics wasted a 14-point fourth-quarter lead Wednesday. Nightmares conjured a total Game 6 collapse, a 40-point loss with the Celtics completely imploding and ruining what has been a renaissance season.

Tatum quickly erased those dreary visions by not only scoring 18 first-half points to give the Celtics a double-digit lead but also carrying his team and preventing another Milwaukee rally in the fourth with brilliant shot-making.

In the biggest game of his career, Tatum delivered his best performance, saving the Celtics season with 46 points, 16 in the final period, to lift Boston to a 108-95 win Friday at Fiserv Forum.

Not only did the win extend the season and force a Game 7 at TD Garden Sunday, it cemented Tatum's status as one of the league's elite players and rising superstars.

It was Tatum who was strangely upbeat Wednesday after one of the worst losses of his career. He still oozed confidence, still talked with that swagger and bravado as if the series was far from over.

"That was in the back of our mind, Game 5, and that's something that we talked about," Tatum said. "The eagerness, we were upbeat, we weren't defeated knowing we still had an opportunity to save our season and coming in here and get a win. We believed that. We truly did. We believed in each other and it showed tonight."

Boston took the lead with 3-point shooting Friday. It won the game with 2-point shots. In 42 minutes, 43 seconds, Tatum made 17 of his 32 shots, including seven 3-pointers, along with 9 rebounds and 4 assists. He matched the great Giannis Antetokounmpo basket for basket, burning the overwhelmed Bucks defense with his array of shots.

The Celtics desperately needed this Tatum. They needed a player who couldn't allow his team to lose, who wanted to atone for his responsibility in that Game 5 meltdown. The Milwaukee Bucks have championship mettle, making them difficult to put away, even Friday when they sliced an 18-point deficit to 4 with 7 minutes, 48 seconds left.

Tatum responded with 10 consecutive points to increase the lead to 8 with less than six minutes left. Celtics coach Ime Udoka then called an after-the-timeout play for Jaylen Brown, who helped by draining a three for an 11-point lead.

That still wasn't enough. When the Bucks appeared sagging and nearly done, Tatum ended the suspense with an acrobatic layup and free throw, and then another pair of free throws to close out his night and the Bucks.

"That's why he gets paid the big bucks, that's it right there, for moments like that," guard Marcus Smart said. "He came in and took that game over in the fourth. He went into another mode right there. We seen it in his eyes. He was aggressive. He was coming and telling us, 'Give me the ball,' and we give him the ball. We put the ball in his hands and let him create for us."

There have been moments throughout his career where Tatum has been brilliant, breathtaking because of the combination of his size, skill set and prowess, but never has there been a better time, a bigger time for him to show those attributes. The Bucks, one of the better defensive teams in the NBA who have frustrated Tatum at times in this series, including 4-for-19 shooting in Game 3, couldn't guard him.

Tatum did what the greats before him—Kobe, LeBron, Jordan—have done, elevate their games when the team needs it the most. Tatum has never hidden his desire to become one of the all-time great players. He spent quality time with many of the NBA All-Time 75 players at All-Star weekend and soaked up stories, knowledge and encouragement.

He responded with the best stretch of basketball in his young career, turning into a more consistently dominant player offensively. Since that poor Game 3, Tatum is averaging 36.6 points on 40-for-85 (47 percent) shooting. And it wasn't that he had a subpar Game 5, he did not impose his will down the stretch.

After scoring 46 points on the road in Game 6 of the 2022 Eastern Conference semifinals, Jayson Tatum and the Celtics won Game 7 in front of the appreciative TD Garden faithful.

That wasn't the case Friday, when he was the best player on the floor, even with two-time MVP Giannis Antetokounmpo single-handedly keeping the Bucks close with 44 points and 20 rebounds. Tatum was that good and now Celtics faithful know the reason he was so optimistic after Game 5.

He wasn't going to let the Celtics leave Milwaukee without atonement.

Williams's Game in Focus: 3 and D

May 16, 2022 • by Christopher L. Gasper

Based on body type, Grant Williams might seem like an unlikely dead-eye shooter. In another era of NBA basketball, there's no way an oak-tree-thick

bruiser would be asked to conduct his business 22- to 23-feet, 9-inches from the basket. But in today's NBA, Williams inhabits the arc.

The 3-point line was Grant's Arc on Sunday in Game 7 of the Eastern Conference semifinals at TD Garden. Three by three the Celtics, led by seven from Williams, used the arc to sail to a 109-81 victory over the Milwaukee Bucks and an Eastern Conference finals date with the Miami Heat.

One of the most coveted species in the NBA is the 3-and-D player who can lock up opponents defensively and stretch the floor offensively. Williams, who shot just 29 percent from three during his college career at Tennessee and attempted 103, has evolved into a primo 3-and-D guy.

Fueled by Williams's career-high 27 points, the Celtics gave 3-and-D another definition, as in three-point deluge-and-done for Giannis Antetokounmpo and the defending NBA champions. The Celtics shot the Bucks into oblivion, connecting on 22 of 55 threes

(40 percent). Williams led the Celtics in scoring for the first time in his career with a 7-for-18 3-point outing that couldn't have come at a more opportune time.

"Grant played great tonight. He took more shots than anybody on the team. I think that's a first . . . I told him don't get used to that," said Tatum, who shot 5 of 9 from three on his way to 23 points, 6 rebounds, and 8 assists.

"But, obviously, tonight we needed it. He came up big. He played amazing. In the playoffs, you need that. You need guys . . . to be a star in their role. Grant won us a playoff game tonight, a Game 7."

The stocky forward's sharpshooting wasn't a fluke. He knocked down 41.1 percent of his threes during the regular season. In Game 2, Williams notched his previous career-high of 21 points, connecting on six threes in nine attempts.

Game 7 was his unanticipated encore. He had struggled lately, losing his shot and crunch-time minutes.

Following Game 2, Williams shot 2 of 14 from three and scored 20 points, including two total in Games 5 and 6.

He had a justifiable excuse as a primary defender of Antetokounmpo, akin to trying to hold back the ocean at high tide. Williams picked the perfect time to rediscover his range.

"I've worked on my shot enough to be able to knock those down and be confident enough to shoot it," said Williams. "I think my teammates know if I get 18 of them I'm going to make 40 percent of them at least."

Successful launches run in Williams's family. His mother is an electrical engineer for NASA. Orbiting the 3-point arc is how Williams helped engineer the Celtics' fourth trip to the Eastern Conference finals since 2017, setting a Game 7 record for 3-point attempts. He eclipsed the mark of a more famous shooter who calls Charlotte, N.C., home, Steph Curry. The power forward also tied Curry's record for Game 7 makes, also held by Marcus Morris.

"He came through for us. We call him Grant Curry now," said Jaylen Brown.

FINALS STEP

CELTICS WIN WIRE-TO-WIRE, BY A WHISKER

May 30, 2022 • by Dan Shaughnessy

Remember all the parades between 2002 and 2019 . . . back in the good old days before COVID-19?

The Celtics earned a ticket to the 2022 NBA Finals with a thrilling, smashmouth, 100-96, Game 7 victory over the top-seeded Miami Heat on the road in FTX Arena Sunday night. Boston led the entire game and staved off a furious late-game comeback by Jimmy Butler and the Heat.

This means that after three, predominantly pandemic-plagued years, confetti could rain on Boylston Street next month for the first time since Tom Brady beat the Rams to win a Super Bowl in February 2019.

Playing in the image of franchise forefathers Bill Russell, K.C. Jones, and Dennis Johnson, the Celtics were the best defensive team in the NBA this year and now-ready-for-prime-time stars Jayson Tatum (26 points), Jaylen Brown (24), and Marcus Smart (24) are finally going to the Finals.

Marcus Smart, Jayson Tatum, and Jaylen Brown celebrate after their tight victory over the Heat in Game 7 of the 2022 Eastern Conference Finals. The win sent the Celtics to the NBA Finals for the first time since 2010.

Cedric Maxwell was on stage to present the Bob Cousy trophy (Eastern Conference champs) to de facto team captain, Al Horford, and the Larry Bird hardware (Eastern Conference finals MVP) to Tatum.

This new generation of Celtic stars has a chance to extend our local sports High Renaissance (12 championships in the new millennium), which started with 24-year-old Brady upsetting the St. Louis Rams in New Orleans in February of '02.

It wasn't easy. Playing their 100th game of the season, the Celtics led by 17 early in the second quarter and by 13 with 3:25 left before an 11-0 Miami late-game run.

How close did the Celts come to losing? Really close. With 18 seconds left and his team trailing by two, the indomitable Jimmy Butler (35 points in the full 48 minutes) rebounded a Smart miss, raced down the court and elected to take a pull-up 3-pointer over the outstretched arm of Horford. It would have given the Heat their first lead of the night.

It clanged off the front rim.

"When he shot that, I was like, 'Oh, man, what the hell?'" said Brown. " . . . Sometimes we like doing it the hard way . . . We've been responding all year to adversity. Today was the biggest test. We got it done."

"We finally got over the hump," added Smart.

"We can't ever quite close the door," said rookie coach Ime Udoka. "We have to grind it out."

The Celtics play the vaunted Golden State Warriors (stars Steph Curry, Klay Thompson and Draymond Green have won three titles and been in six Finals since 2015) in Game 1 of the Finals Thursday at the Chase Center in Mission Bay.

Boston is an underdog against the Warriors, but the Celts have been the best team in the NBA since late January (40-13) and their defining win in Miami makes them 7-2 on the road in this year's playoffs. They haven't lost two straight games since March.

Playing great defense ("defense is our identity" —Udoka) and crushing the Heat in transition, the Celtics burst to a 15-point lead (24-9) in the first eight minutes and led, 32-17, after one. No team in NBA history has lost a Game 7 after leading by at least 15 after one.

It was a perfect start for Boston, the polar opposite of everything we saw in Game 6. Tatum and Brown scored at will, Horford (who has never played in the NBA Finals) blocked Max Strus at the rim, Grant Williams came off the bench for 7 quick points, and the Celtics took the crowd out of the game. Boston scored 13 fast-break points in 12 minutes.

It was reminiscent of Game 4, when the Celtics led, 29-11, after one. It had many of us asking, "What are we doing here? Why was it necessary to play seven games to establish the better team in this series?"

Boston's first-half lead peaked at 17 (34-17), but Miami cut the margin to 6 at intermission.

The Heat trimmed it to 4 early in the third, but Tatum and Smart quickly pushed it back to 14 and the Celtics settled for an 82-75 lead after three.

Miami fell behind by 12 in the fourth as the Celtics tightened the screws defensively, forcing the Heat to miss nine straight shots. A three by Tatum made it, 93-81, with six minutes left.

Then came the late-game chaos. And Butler's pull-up three. A clean look.

"As it was leaving his hand, I thought for sure it was going down," said Spoelstra.

The shot did not go down.

So now the Celtics are going to the Finals with a new generation of stars. And just like in the days of Russell, Cousy, Havlicek, Cowens, Bird, Pierce, and Garnett, the Green Team from Causeway Street gives Boston a chance for a championship.

BACK IN FOURTH

It was everything a Finals game should be and more.

June 3, 2022 • by Dan Shaughnessy

This one took your breath away.

The Celtics trailed the estimable Warriors by 15 points late in the third quarter, only to roar back in the fourth on the strength of their NBA-best defense and the shooting of veterans Al Horford (26 points) and Derrick White (21 off the bench).

When it was over, the Celtics were 120-108 winners in Game 1 of the NBA Finals at San Francisco Thursday night and dreams of a championship feel very real.

"It wasn't our best game, but we continue to fight and find ways to win," said humble Horford, a 15-year veteran who had not played in a Finals game and turned 36 Friday.

Most everything was stacked against the Celts. The Warriors were 9-0 at home in these playoffs, and had a full week of rest while the Celtics were staggering through their seven-game rock fight with Miami. The Warriors have been in the Finals in six of the last eight Junes, winning three championships. Steph Curry lit up the night with 21 first-quarter points.

All of that meant nothing when the Celtics went into lockdown defense mode and rode the shooting of Horford and White to a 40-16 fourth-quarter advantage.

Instant history. No team in NBA Finals lore ever beat another team by 24 points in the fourth quarter. And the Celtics did this to the worthy Warriors . . . on the road.

Breathless.

"We hadn't played our best in the first half," said Boston's rookie coach Ime Udoka. "We knew we were in good shape. We relied on the defense and the offensive rebounds in the fourth quarter. That's who we've been all year. Tough. Grinders. We always know we can rely on our defense . . . We locked down when we needed to."

"They [Celtics] were on their [Warriors] ass like diapers on a baby," former Celtic champion Kendrick Perkins said on NBC Sports Boston's postgame show.

It was the first Finals game played at the three-year-old Chase Center. In the early years of this Warrior Dynasty, the Dubs played all their home games at the ancient, gray, concrete palace formerly known as the Oakland-Alameda County Coliseum. It was a gym Larry Bird never particularly liked and also served as the rookie home of young Robert Parish in 1976. If you want a good look at the old Coliseum, find a way to watch "Inside Moves" with David Morse and John Savage. Parish and his good pal Clifford Ray make cameos in the 1980 film.

The Warriors came into the night with five players owning Finals experience, a grand total of 123 games played by Messrs. Curry, Draymond Green, Klay Thompson and Co. The 2022 Celtics do not have a single player who'd ever played a game in the Finals before Thursday.

Robert Williams III jumped center against Kevon Looney. The last time the Celtics and Warriors met in the NBA Finals, it was Bill Russell vs. Wilt Chamberlain in the middle.

Curry drained six threes in the first, which ended with the Dubs leading, 32-28. The pace was far too fast for Udoka's liking as the Warriors led by as many as 7, but somehow the Celtics kept pace and kept it close. Curry made 7 of 9, far too many of them clean looks from downtown. He was the first player to score 21 in a Finals quarter since Michael Jordan did it in 1993. Curry was on an 84-point pace. It was delightful, scintillating basketball—no officials getting in the way early.

The Warriors ran to a 10-point lead in the second, but the Celtics responded with a 14-2 run, and led by 2 at the half. The teams combined to make 20 threes in the first half, a Finals record.

The Dubs dialed up their defense in the third, continuing to frustrate Jayson Tatum (3-for-17 shooting, 12 points) and getting big baskets from the likes of Otto Porter, Andrew Wiggins, and ancient Andre Iguodala.

Down 12 starting the fourth, the Celtics cut the hearts out of the champions with a 40-point quarter . . . with Tatum doing nothing. Horford made all four of his shots in the fourth, scoring 11. Brown shot 4 of 6 and scored 10. Curry was a feeble 2 for 6 in the fourth as the game got away.

Boston never goes away easily and folks in San Francisco have to be nervous after this one.

"We'll be fine," said veteran champion Green. "We pretty much dominated the game for the first 41, 42 minutes, so we'll be fine . . . "

Swell.

Just give us three, four, five or six more games just like this, please.

ULTIMATE WARRIORS

CELTICS BOW OUT IN GAME 6

June 17, 2022 • by Adam Himmelsbach

As the large black stage was rolled on the court and the Warriors slid their crisp, white NBA champions hats on their heads, Jayson Tatum and Jaylen Brown stood near their bench and watched, seemingly unsure what to do next.

Everything about this experience has been new for these Celtics stars, and this moment was no different.

Eventually, Tatum began wading through the families and photographers and started seeking out Warriors players to congratulate. Brown did the same before walking down through a tunnel toward his locker room with a towel draped over his head.

As Golden State's trophy presentation began moments later, many fans in green stayed at their seats to record video of the moment. Sure, they were probably crushed by the 103-90 Game 6 loss in these NBA Finals, but it's also not every day one gets to witness greatness. And these Warriors, with four titles in the last eight years, certainly qualify.

They are also everything the Celtics hope to become, and for six long, grueling games, Boston got an up-close and sometimes painful view of it all. It was a lesson in real time.

"It don't stop hurting," center Robert Williams said. "It never stops hurting until we're back in this position again."

Until then, they'll just be left with memories of a night they would probably like to forget. As players completed interviews in a quiet room in the bowels of TD Garden, the cigar smoke from the Warriors' celebration wafted in.

When Tatum finished his session and started to leave the arena, he passed several members of the Warriors traveling party who were soaked in beer and champagne, and smelled like it. Dell Curry, the former NBA sharpshooter who is also the father of Stephen, perhaps the greatest NBA sharpshooter of all time, was at the end of that group.

"Where are the Coronas at?!" he yelled to no one in particular.

There was no such joy in the Celtics' locker room after the loss. Players said it was both quiet and emotional. But the frustration about the missed opportunity seemed to quickly be tinged with appreciation for how far this team has come, and optimism about the future.

"Nobody even had us being here, let alone in the playoffs," guard Marcus Smart said. "It definitely is tough. But it's definitely one of those things we've been through hell to get here, and you take that. You know what I'm saying? We've got to use that."

In January, this team was in 11th place in the Eastern Conference and under .500. A run such as this one seemed unfathomable then.

And in the playoffs, Boston certainly tempted fate. It survived two elimination games in the semifinals against the Bucks, then went on the road to win a Game 7 in the conference finals against the Heat. But this Golden State team left no room for flaws. Instead, it pounced on them.

"What I said to the group is there are levels," Celtics coach Ime Udoka said, "and you can see the difference in Golden State."

It seems like months ago that Boston held 1-0 and then 2-1 leads in this series, flipping from slight underdogs to favorites who had ripped home court advantage away from these mighty Warriors. Boston had not lost consecutive games in these playoffs, and as long as it continued that trend, it would win the franchise's first championship since 2008.

Instead, the Celtics closed the season by losing three games in a row for the first time since December, a darker time in a year that had eventually become quite bright.

"Tough day for Boston," said Brown, who had 34 points. "Tough day for the Celtics. But, I don't know what to say."

Tatum appeared particularly gloomy afterward. This season the 24-year-old forward emerged as an MVP candidate, and these playoffs were viewed as his chance to truly ascend to superstardom.

Although he did help guide Boston to the brink of a title, this postseason was not his best work. Turnovers, missed shots, and complaints to officials sometimes outnumbered more enjoyable moments. He was 6 for 18 with five turnovers Thursday.

Tatum vowed to do more and come back better. Udoka acknowledged that this series was "a rough one" for Tatum, but he said he would learn from what it was like to have defenses build entire plans to stop him.

"It's just continuing to grow and understand you're going to see this the rest of your career," Udoka said. "This is just a start."

Curry, of course, has been operating under such a spotlight for years, and he continues to be unbothered by any of the hindrances and distractions and challenges that follow. The 34-year-old guard capped a masterful Finals performance with 34 points, 7 rebounds, and 7 assists en route to becoming one of the easiest choices for MVP ever.

There were fleeting moments Thursday when it seemed that this Celtics season would last for a few more days, with a Game 7 in San Francisco, where any fluky moment could make a Celtics championship possible.

Boston surged to a 14-2 lead, and the fans began to believe. But the Warriors punched back quickly and seized control with a silencing 21-0 run. Golden State led by as many as 22 points midway through the third period before Boston responded with one final surge.

A 3-pointer by Brown with 5:34 left in the fourth pulled Boston within eight, 86-78. But a 3-pointer by Andrew Wiggins, who blanketed Tatum throughout this series, was followed by a steal by Klay Thompson that led to a Draymond Green layup. The fact that this game was clinched by a turnover was fitting for the Celtics, because those miscues were their undoing this postseason. They had 23 of them in this game.

"Every possession is purposeful," Williams said. "It seemed the other locker room realized that; we didn't. They had a meaning to everything they were doing."

About two hours after the game ended, after Curry had finished yet another interview about yet another title, he walked down a corridor wearing his white hat and carrying the championship and MVP trophies. Down another long hallway, near the empty Celtics locker room, there was just silence.

Bill Russell: 1934-2022

THE POWERFUL CENTER OF A DYNASTY

His legacy on the court mirrored role as civil rights leader.

August 1, 2022 • by John Powers

Bill Russell, the legendary Celtics center who was the cornerstone of basketball's greatest dynasty and an exemplar of racial harmony and progress, died Sunday at age 88, his family announced on Twitter.

His wife, Jeannine, was at his side, according to the announcement, which did not say where Mr. Russell died or disclose a cause.

"To be the greatest champion in your sport, to revolutionize the way the game is played, and to be a societal leader all at once seems unthinkable, but that is who Bill Russell was," the Celtics said in a statement. "Bill was a champion unlike any other in the history of team sports—an 11-time NBA champion, including winning eight consecutive titles, a five-time MVP, an Olympic gold medalist, and the NBA's first Black head coach."

Mr. Russell, who played for two national championship varsities at the University of San Francisco and who captained the US team that won the Olympic gold medal at the 1956 Games, was Boston's imposing man in the middle for an unsurpassed string of National Basketball Association titles that made the Celtics the league's most feared and admired club. "The Yankees won 26 championships," Mr. Russell once observed. "What did it take them, 100 years?"

The Celtics claimed 11 titles between 1957 and 1969, and their championship constant was the goateed Mr. Russell, the gap-toothed, cackling "eagle with a beard" whose flair for invention and intimidation was unmatched. "Russ revolutionized basketball and he was the man who made us go," said Bob Cousy, the team's Hall of Fame playmaker. "Without him, we wouldn't have won a championship."

Only Montreal Canadiens forward Henri Richard won as many for a franchise in a North American league as did Mr. Russell, who was basketball's first Black superstar and the first in any sport in Boston, as well as a five-time Most Valuable Player and 12-time All-Star and the Celtics' player-coach for his final three seasons.

"As tall as Bill Russell stood, his legacy rises far higher—both as a player and as a person," former president Barack Obama tweeted. "Perhaps more than anyone else, Bill knew what it took to win and what it took to lead. On the court, he was the greatest champion in basketball history. Off of it, he was a civil rights trailblazer—marching with Dr. King and standing with Muhammad Ali. For decades, Bill endured insults and vandalism, but never let it stop him from speaking up for what's right. I learned so

Celtics player/coach Bill Russell, March 17, 1968.

much from the way he played, the way he coached, and the way he lived his life."

His front-and-center prominence made him both an icon and an irritant in a city that was unaccustomed to a visible and vocal Black man and that was less than welcoming to the centerpiece of its most successful sports team. His home in suburban Reading was vandalized by intruders who destroyed his trophies, painted racial slurs on the walls, and defecated in the beds.

Mr. Russell arrived in Boston, which he once called "a flea market of racism," at a time when the city still was a collection of tribal white neighborhoods whose residents were suspicious of outsiders. "I had never been in a city more involved with

finding new ways to dismiss, ignore, or look down on other people," Mr. Russell wrote in "Second Wind," whose subtitle was "The Memoirs of an Opinionated Man."

Decades later Cousy wrote Mr. Russell a letter saying that he should have been more supportive to his teammate during that time. "It was my responsibility to reach out to you and hopefully share the pain that you had during that period," Cousy acknowledged.

Mr. Russell, whose parents had been harassed in Louisiana, was sensitive to racist treatment. "The white cops in Oakland stopped me on the streets all the time, grilled me and routinely called me [n-word]," he reminisced. His Black teammates of the University of San Francisco were turned away at an Oklahoma City hotel, and, when Mr. Russell toured with his fellow NBA All-Stars in 1958, the Black players were refused rooms in North Carolina.

"It stood out, a wall which understanding cannot penetrate," Mr. Russell wrote in "Go Up For Glory." "You are a Negro. You are less. It covers every area. A living, smarting, hurting, smelly, greasy substance which covered you."

Yet Mr. Russell, who was in the prime of his career during the civil rights movement of the '60s, was a role model for Blacks who appreciated both his athletic prowess and his unabashed candor on social issues at a time when outspoken Black men often were considered "uppity" or ungrateful.

"It was the perfect time for his kind of man, a man who would step out, not be afraid to say what he thought, what he believed in, and to also provide some direction for a lot of people, not only in the sports world," said teammate Tom Sanders, who later coached the Celtics.

Mr. Russell, who believed that "my citizenship isn't a gift, it's a birthright," refused to accept second-class status when he was out of uniform. "A man without integrity, belief, or self-respect is not a man," he said. "And a man who won't express his convictions has no convictions."

Despite the city's racial friction, its basketball team during Mr. Russell's tenure was a model of progress. The Celtics, which in 1950 had been the first club to draft a Black player, also was the first to start five Black players in the '60s and, in Mr. Russell, to have a Black coach.

"I never thought I'd live to see the day when the water would run off a white man onto a Black man and the water would run off a Black man onto a white man," Mr. Russell's grandfather Jake, a former farmer and drayman, marveled when he observed Sam Jones and John Havlicek showering next to each other in the Celtics dressing room.

William Felton Russell, who was born in West Monroe, La., on Feb. 12, 1934, was a son of the segregated South who moved with his family to California when he was 8 and who lived in public housing. He was a skinny and ungainly athlete who was cut from his junior high team and had to share a uniform as the last player picked for the junior varsity squad at McClymonds High School in West Oakland. "I was an easily forgettable high school player," he observed.

Despite his extraordinary leaping ability ("I could kick the net and touch the top of the backboard") and his knack for rebounding, no college except San Francisco across the Bay offered him a scholarship. But Russell and K.C. Jones, his future Olympic and Celtics teammate, led the Dons to the 1955 and 1956 NCAA titles, winning 60 straight games along the way.

Celtics coach Red Auerbach, whose club had never made an NBA final, saw in Mr. Russell the missing piece to a championship team. "I had scorers, guys who could put the ball in the hole, but you can't win without the ball," he said. "I needed a guy to get me the ball."

So Auerbach traded All-Star center Ed Macauley and the rights to draftee Cliff Hagan to St. Louis for the second overall pick in the 1956 draft, even though Mr. Russell's Olympic duties would make him unavailable for the season's first two months.

When he returned from Melbourne with his gold medal and joined the Celtics as their only Black player, Mr. Russell, who immediately established his own air rights inside the league's arenas, redefined both his position and the sport. "I introduced the vertical game to basketball," he said.

Mr. Russell, who stood precisely 6 feet, 9 and 13/16ths inches, was an aquiline and angular raptor who unnerved opponents even when they couldn't see him. "He came out of nowhere," Johnny Most, the Celtics legendary radio announcer, would shout after Mr. Russell had swatted away a rival's shot.

His gift for defending and rebounding allowed his green-clad colleagues to run and gun at the other end of the floor. "The guy was incredible," said Havlicek. "No one won in this town like he did. And make no mistake, it was all because of him. We all knew that."

So did Auerbach, who understood that Mr. Russell, whose competitive tension made him vomit before games, needed no external motivation. If the coach wanted to criticize him, he did it by osmosis, by yelling at Tom Heinsohn, his designated whipping boy. "He'd say, 'Tommy, you gotta do this. Tommy, you gotta do that—and that goes for you, too, Russell,'" recalled Heinsohn, who succeeded Mr. Russell as coach.

Mr. Russell's professionalism, passion, and pride—Heinsohn said that he had "a neurotic need to win"—were such that Auerbach was comfortable letting him follow his own path. "Any time he found me drifting, he found a way to call me back," Mr. Russell said. "Not order me back, but call me back. He always let me know that more than anybody else, he knew what I was doing. I really loved working with him. It was almost like we were soulmates."

When Auerbach retired after the 1966 season, he named Mr. Russell as his successor. "Do them white boys really have to do what William tells them to do?" his grandfather asked his father. Mr. Russell still was their teammate, still their alpha and omega on the parquet, an underappreciated offensive weapon who scored more than 14,500 points during his career. "Every play we ran started with Russell and ran through Russell," said Havlicek. "He called them when he was the player-coach. That's what a lot of people don't understand."

Mr. Russell served in that dual role for three years and two more championships, capped by the 1969 upset of the Lakers in the seventh game in Los

Angeles. It was Mr. Russell's final duel with friend and archrival Wilt Chamberlain whom he'd bested in five of their six playoff series, twice for the title. "People say it was the greatest individual rivalry they've ever seen," observed Mr. Russell, "and I agree with that."

So Mr. Russell was disappointed and disturbed that Chamberlain took himself out of the game with the championship in the balance. "I thought to myself, 'This is my last game. Make me earn it. Come on out here,'" Mr. Russell later wrote.

By then, after 13 seasons, he was ready to move on after having collected more bejeweled rings than he could wear. "Here I am a grown man, 35 years old, running around seminude in front of thousands of people in Baltimore, playing a game and yelling about killing people," Mr. Russell mused after giving a rare fight talk during a timeout.

His teammates had dreaded his retirement, even while they knew that it was inevitable. "Year after year, we would ask him to continue," Sanders said. "Don't leave, we'd say. Our playoff shares will dwindle. Please don't do that to us."

When Mr. Russell decided to call it a career, he took his captain aside at the Garden. "Cousy passed me the torch," he told Havlicek. "I'm going to be leaving, so I'm passing it to you."

Mr. Russell also wanted to pass on his signature No. 6, which he had worn in college and at the Olympics, even though the Celtics wanted to hoist it to the rafters. "I didn't like the idea at all," Mr. Russell wrote. "I figured I'd retired myself, and my number could do whatever it wanted." When Auerbach persisted, Mr. Russell agreed to a private ceremony in 1972 with only his coach and teammates present.

Three years later he also refused to attend his enshrinement ceremony for the Hall of Fame in Springfield. "I don't respect it as an institution," Mr. Russell wrote later. "Its standards are not high enough. It's too political, too self-serving."

Mr. Russell's standards and those of his Celtics teams were lofty, which he realized during his stint as coach of the Seattle SuperSonics from 1973-77 when he was appalled by his players' obsession with their salaries (his highest was $100,000 a year, $1 more than Chamberlain's) and their short-changing of teammates on playoff shares. That

pecuniary attitude would have been unthinkable on Mr. Russell's teams in Boston. "The Celtics were a family," he observed, "but it was a family bent on winning."

Whatever his feelings about the city, Mr. Russell felt a lifetime bond to the team that played in the ramshackle old barn on Causeway Street. "It wasn't Boston, it wasn't the NBA, it was the Celtics," he said. "That was the only thing that counted, the Celtic family. I couldn't imagine ever wanting to play any place else."

After spending his post-basketball days on the West Coast, Mr. Russell found opportunities to return to what was both a changed Celtics franchise and a changed city. In 1999, when he was 65, he turned up at the new Garden for the formal retiring of his number before a full house that included Chamberlain, Larry Bird, and former Lakers star center Kareem Abdul-Jabbar, who made his professional debut the season after Mr. Russell retired. "This is a once-in-a-lifetime experience," Mr. Russell said.

In 2007, Harvard made him an honorary doctor of laws alongside Bill Gates and former university president Larry Summers.

Mr. Russell's first two marriages, to Rose Swisher and Dorothy Anstett, ended in divorce. His third wife, Marilyn Nault, was 59 when she died in 2009.

In 2016, Mr. Russell married Jeannine Fiorito. In addition to his wife, he leaves two children from his first marriage, Jacob Russell and Karen Kenyatta Russell. His other son from his first marriage, William Jr., died in 2016. Mr. Russell's older brother, the playwright Charlie L. Russell, died in 2013.

In 2011 President Obama awarded Mr. Russell the Presidential Medal of Freedom, the nation's highest civilian honor. "I hope that one day in the streets of Boston, children will look up at a statue built not only to Bill Russell the player but Bill Russell the man," Obama observed.

The statue was unveiled in November 2013 on City Hall Plaza, alongside plinths recognizing the 11 championships that Mr. Russell had helped bring to Boston.

"Bill Russell raised a lot of banners," remarked then-Mayor Thomas M. Menino, "but also he broke down a lot of barriers in our city."

Cousy Recalls His Hall of Fame Teammate 'Fought the Good Fight'

Bill Russell: 1934-2022

August 1, 2022 • by Dan Shaughnessy

They had Hall of Fame players and a Hall of Fame coach, and the Celtics were champions every year, it seemed. They won eight consecutive NBA titles in Red Auerbach's last eight years as coach. They won 11 championships in 13 seasons between 1957-69.

And the one and only constant was Bill Russell. The man in the middle. The greatest winner in team sports history.

Russell died Sunday at the age of 88.

We've been losing these fabled champs with somber regularity the last four years. Frank Ramsey died in 2018. John Havlicek in 2019, Tommy Heinsohn and K.C. Jones in 2020, then seven months ago (just before New Year's), Sam Jones. Hall of Famers, one and all.

Now, Russell. The giant of giants. The greatest of the greats.

Bob Cousy, who played with all of the above and won six championships in seven seasons with Russell, was with his daughter Marie and recovering from a kidney stone when he got the news early Sunday afternoon.

"My old friend, Russ, beat me to it," said Cousy, days shy of his 94th birthday (Aug. 9) and on the receiving end of many sad calls lately. "He got there first. I got a hunch I'm going to be seeing him shortly. I don't want to be morbid, but I'm not signing up for the Marathon these days. At 88, I suppose we expect it.

"Russell goes down as the best winner ever in American team sports. That's pretty significant and that's never going to change. He fought the good fight, obviously, on the floor, but he fought the good fight off the floor, fighting racism all his life. Sticking his tongue out at the opponent. That's not easy to do.

"People give up things to take a stand, and Russell simply never cared. Jocks generally worry about their image after they've had a successful career and they're all very careful as to what they say and how they approach every issue. Most of them are very circumspect and have people that advise them. Russell just let it flow. He spoke out against racism in every form and I'm sure he's happier for that now."

Cousy was a six-year veteran and an established NBA superstar when Russell joined the Celtics after winning Olympic gold in 1956. The early '50s Celts were perennial contenders, but were not able to win a championship until Russell came on board.

They won it all in his rookie season—Cousy was league Most Valuable Player as well—and never stopped winning until he retired, when Red shocked the sports world by naming Russell the first Black head coach in major US sports history. Russell won his final two banners as player-coach in 1968 and '69, then walked away.

"In my judgment, Boston doesn't make enough of what that group accomplished in the '50s and '60s. It's something that will never be done again in American team sports. It's spectacular and singular," said Cousy. "Eleven championships in 13 years. Given what teams go through to win a Stanley Cup or a World Series or Super Bowl, they do it twice and they burn down cities and celebrate all week. We did it 11 times in 13 years and Russ is the center point of that.

"We had eight Hall of Famers and, despite what [ESPN's J.J.] Redick thinks of players from that time being firefighters or plumbers, the competition was tough. Today's jock is better, bigger, stronger. Of course they are. But whatever the skill level was in the '50s and '60s, when it was more concentrated [with fewer teams], that made it more difficult to win. Eleven out of 13, and it should have been 12 if Russ doesn't stub his toe against St. Louis in 1958. He's the cornerstone."

Cousy retired in 1963. He spent the ensuing decades wondering why the two were never particularly close, and put his thoughts into a book, "The Last Pass," with author Gary Pomerantz in 2018. Like many in Boston, Cousy last saw Russell at a memorial service for Havlicek at Trinity Church in Copley Square in 2019.

"I thought a lot about our relationship over the years. We didn't handle it. We just let it sit. We weren't buddy-buddy. We didn't go out," said Cousy.

"I'm close today with Satch [Sanders]. I maintained a relationship with Sam Jones to some degree. And with K.C. [Jones]. But Russ was not the kind of guy you got close to easily. He came to Boston with a chip on his shoulder and none of us knew how to handle it. We were intimidated by him. We were kind of frightened by him and we didn't reach out. And that book, 'The Last Pass,' was my response, 60 years later, for not reaching out. I had regrets and would have done it differently."

Cousy and 83-year-old Sanders are the last living Hall of Famers who played with Russell, during the Eisenhower administration.

"Satch always says, 'Don't look over your shoulder. You'll see them gaining on you,'" said Cousy. "So I'm more and more aware of that every time the phone rings and I get news like this. But I'm a realist. I'm ready for the big basketball court in the sky."

What a team. No doubt Red will be berating officials and Russell will be running the floor, blocking shots and sticking up for social justice.

Celtics Suspend Coach Ime Udoka for a Year

Make Joe Mazzulla Interim Coach

September 23, 2022 • by Adam Himmelsbach

Last season, the Celtics went from scuffling for a playoff spot to coming within two wins of an unlikely NBA championship under first-year coach Ime Udoka. While there was frustration about the loss in the Finals, there was also great hope, optimism, and excitement regarding the future.

But with training camp slated to begin Tuesday, the Celtics are now in turmoil. Udoka on Thursday night received a one-year suspension for violations of team policies, the Celtics announced in a statement, adding that Udoka's future with the team beyond this season will be made at a later date.

"The Boston Celtics announced today that the team has suspended Head Coach Ime Udoka for the 2023 season for violations of team policies. A decision about his future with the Celtics beyond this

season will be made at a later date. The suspension takes effect immediately," the statement said.

According to a league source, Udoka was suspended for having an improper consensual relationship with a female member of the organization. It is a jarring punishment for the 45-year-old coach, and has put a cloud over the start of this season.

Udoka and his camp released a separate statement that was not included in the Celtics' official release.

"I want to apologize to our players, fans, the entire Celtics organization, and my family for letting them down. I am sorry for putting the team in this difficult situation, and I accept the team's decision. Out of respect for everyone involved, I will have no further comment."

Celtics assistant coach Joe Mazzulla is expected to guide the team in place of Udoka, a league source said.

Udoka's suspension is a stunning development for a Celtics team that stands as the favorite to win the NBA championship. Last season Udoka took a tough, unapologetic approach as he instilled the importance of hard work, trust, and accountability. Now, the operation will roll on without him.

Mazzulla, 34, a Johnston, R.I., native, has ascended quickly through the NBA ranks. He coached at Division 2 Fairmont State before being added to the Celtics coaching staff in 2019 by then president of basketball operations Danny Ainge.

This summer, Mazzulla interviewed for the Utah Jazz's head coach position, which ultimately went to Celtics assistant Will Hardy. Mazzulla was elevated to a Celtics bench role in place of Hardy soon after.

"I've always said this is where I want to be, because being from here and working for the Celtics means a lot more to me," Mazzulla told the Globe in August. "It's close to my heart and family. I was just fortunate Brad and Ime agreed I should move up."

Udoka worked as an assistant for Spurs Hall of Fame coach Gregg Popovich for seven seasons and had one-year stops as an assistant with the 76ers and Nets before Stevens, who left his coaching post to replace Ainge as the Celtics' lead executive in May 2021, hired him to be coach.

When the Celtics had a bumpy start and were stuck in 11th place in the Eastern Conference last January, it ignited questions about whether Udoka was ready for the top post.

Then Boston roared through the rest of the season, secured the No. 2 seed in the Eastern Conference and put a scare into Stephen Curry and the Warriors in the Finals. The league-wide perception of Udoka, who finished fourth in Coach of the Year voting, quickly shifted, and the Celtics were eager to see what it would look like when he coached a full season with no learning curve. Now, the wait will go on.

Udoka Selfish, but Celtics to Blame, Too

September 23, 2022 • by Gary Washburn

It seems the Celtics and Ime Udoka are playing the game of "Who can be most egregious?"

Udoka has damaged his career, hindered the road for aspiring Black NBA head coaches and tainted a franchise with championship aspirations. He participated in a consensual but inappropriate relationship with a Celtics employee.

It isn't good practice for professional head coaches to pursue relationships with employees. It's disappointing and disheartening that a man who has preached professionalism, showing up on time, accepting criticism and using it as motivation was living afoul off the court, falling short of the expectations he had for his players.

The one-year suspension is what Udoka has earned and he deserves it. He spent nearly a decade trying to become an NBA head coach, learning from some of the game's greats, becoming a top candidate, and earning one of the most respected jobs in professional sports. And he does this? A few months after losing in the NBA Finals?

One of the most anticipated seasons in 40 years is now tainted by a coach who acted selfishly and recklessly, choosing his physical desires over maturity, restraint and mental discipline. It's inexcusable, but eventually forgivable because none of us live in the land of perfection.

The Celtics, meanwhile, are guilty of a different transgression. First, someone from the organization leaked the story to ESPN at nearly 11 p.m. on Wednesday, which was intentional. And then once the specifics surfaced, that Udoka had an inappropriate relationship with a female member of the organization, Twitter gangsters began searching the team's website for any female-sounding name and suddenly started guessing who was Udoka's partner.

The most logical choice in their warped minds was Allison Feaster, the Celtics' vice president of player development and organizational growth. Feaster is a former Harvard star, WNBA player and a stunning Black woman. The natural assumption, because we never wait for facts, was Feaster was the woman Udoka had a relationship with.

Attractive Black man and attractive Black woman have to be fooling around, and for several hours Feaster's photo was posted on social media as the culprit. It wasn't her, and the Celtics could have protected her and many other women in their organization by at least releasing a statement offering clarity.

It wouldn't have saved every woman from scrutiny but at least it would have shown leadership and a strong voice from an organization that apparently prides itself on being the most respected and pristine in professional sports. The Celtics failed Feaster, who likely spent the day avoiding any social media pages and ignoring her direct messages and mentions.

Instead, she is left hanging, like the rest of us who are seeking answers. Professional sports coaches are generally not suspended by their teams, especially for a season. Udoka is hardly the first coach to have a questionable relationship with someone in the organization. He is not the first coach to have a questionable off-court lifestyle.

Udoka released an apologetic statement, accepting blame.

The Celtics didn't cause this situation. President of basketball operations Brad Stevens made a public appearance Wednesday night at TD Garden, taking photos and chatting with fans at the ABCD Hoop Dreams. He could have backed out. He already knew his head coach was up for a major suspension. Yet, he came in good will, knowing eventually his organization was going to be swimming in chaos.

Blame Udoka for this one. He allowed his ego to consume him, causing him to make a poor decision that could affect many people. The optics are terrible. The Celtics are the main subject of sports talk shows for the wrong reasons and media day to kick off the season is Monday.

Guess how many credential requests the Celtics probably received Thursday for that event? It's going to be a circus. And the players are going to have to field questions about their coach and then have to address how they plan to adjust and remain a championship-contending team.

Suddenly this issue is a topic of discussion, in the news just like the heinous acts of Phoenix Suns owner Robert Sarver. Udoka shared the same negative NBA news cycle as Sarver. It's embarrassing for an organization that took a chance on a first-time coach and weathered a difficult beginning to his tenure. He rewarded that patience with a trip to the NBA Finals.

The Celtics believed they had their coach for the next decade, but suddenly they don't. Will Udoka ever coach the Celtics again? It's impossible to answer that. And the Celtics couldn't have possibly provided all the answers Thursday, but didn't have to wait until the 11th hour for a calming response. Their fan base deserved better.

White's Value Second to None

January 14, 2023 • by Tara Sullivan

NEW YORK—Derrick White is an excellent defensive player. But he isn't the Celtics' best defensive player. That would be his backcourt mate Marcus Smart, who happens to be the NBA's reigning Defensive Player of the Year.

White is an astonishingly good shot blocker, especially for a guard who tops out at 6 feet 4 inches. But he isn't the Celtics' best shot blocker. That would be center Robert Williams, whose wingspan and 6-10 frame routinely inhabit the nightmares of would-be shooters.

White isn't the team's best scorer, not as long as Jayson Tatum is around, and he's certainly not its loudest talker, not when coaches and teammates routinely crack jokes about how little he says at all.

But White is one of the Celtics' most important players, as much for what he represents as what he does on the court, the embodiment of so much of what is going right in a season that counted its 31st

victory against just 12 losses with a 109-98 road win over the red-hot Nets Thursday night.

The Celtics secured the win with a dominant fourth quarter, one ignited in the opening seconds by White's leaping block on a driving T.J. Warren and secured in its final minutes by his smooth corner 3-pointer, his fourth of the game and 15th point. On a back-and-forth night that didn't quite live up to the anticipated Eastern Conference playoff preview it might have been had Kevin Durant been out there for the Nets or Jaylen Brown for the Celtics, rather than both of them sidelined by injury, White made sure to do his part.

With seven rebounds, including five on the defensive end, and an overall defensive effort alongside Smart that held Kyrie Irving to 9-of-24 shooting (including 3 of 11 from 3-point range), White continues to show in his first full season since being traded to Boston last year how much he deserves to be a starter, even if his ascension to that role began as a way to offset the absence of Williams as he battled back from knee surgery.

"He plays with such a sense of joy and toughness all the time, regardless of how the game's going, regardless of how the team is doing," Celtics coach Joe Mazzulla said. "He does a great job, and he's been doing it throughout the year. You can't be a great team without that depth, and Derrick's part of that. The joy and competition he brings on both ends, guys enjoy playing with him."

And opponents can't stand playing against him, especially when he runs down a shot and swats it away the way he did against Warren. The play came at 11:21 of the fourth, with the Celtics clinging to a 2-point lead. Two baskets apiece from Payton Pritchard and Malcom Brogdon in the next 2:23 pushed the lead to 8 and forced the Nets into a timeout. Boston wouldn't lead by less than 7 the rest of the way, with White's smooth three with 1:13 left extending the lead to 11.

For a guard who isn't afraid to remind his teammates of that shot-blocking prowess—he's up to 41 on the season—his lone block Thursday couldn't have come at a better time.

"It's obviously fun," White said. "I've kind of been doing it for a while now. It was a big play. I keep trying to tell [teammates] I'm a shot blocker, so I had to try and get another one."

As shot-blocking guards go, White is "one of the very best, one of the best I've seen," according to the veteran Brogdon, who was traded to the team this year. "That's a skill, for sure, definitely a skill."

As Celtics defense goes, it's Smart's individual skill that stands out most, and his return from a brief knee injury was vital to the effort of containing Irving. But Smart is even better because he knows he has White at his side and at his back.

"It's great playing with Derrick," Smart said. "He doesn't really say too much; that's OK, because I talk more, I balance it out.

"He's fun. His ability to be able to guard, to play the defensive end, block the shots he does, especially when he seems to be beaten and just recovers, he makes my job easier because the majority of the time I'm guarding the team's best player, he comes in and is able to switch off and give me a break.

"I definitely think [we're better together] because you got to deal with me and you got to deal with him right after that, or vice versa. We constantly keep teams on their toes, make everything tough on them, at least we try to. For us two to be on the court at the same time I definitely think we give other teams headaches."

'Interim' Tag Removed for Mazzulla

February 17, 2023 • by Adam Himmelsbach

As Joe Mazzulla flew to Salt Lake City Thursday to begin preparations to coach in Sunday's NBA All-Star Game, the Celtics took a big step in solidifying their future while moving on from a difficult time in their recent past.

The team announced that Mazzulla, who was named interim coach in September following coach Ime Udoka's suspension for violations of organizational policies, had been elevated to head coach and received a contract extension, and that Udoka was no longer a member of the franchise.

"It's going to be really hard to win, and the hardest things to do would be coaching, looking behind you and looking over your shoulder," Celtics president of basketball operations Brad Stevens said

Thursday night. "It's about looking forward and if you're in a Game 7, know that everybody in the organization believes in you, and that uncertainty erases. Like, you've earned that, and so I thought that was really important."

According to league sources, Udoka had received a one-year, unpaid suspension because of an improper consensual relationship with a subordinate team employee.

The decision to permanently promote Mazzulla is hardly surprising. He has guided the Celtics to the best record in the NBA (42-17), gained the trust of his players, and put the team in position to win its first championship since 2008. And league sources stressed in recent months that Udoka's time with the team was over, despite the fact that he had been suspended rather than fired. Still, there was a belief that, primarily for legal reasons, this move would not become official until Udoka's suspension ended June 30.

But now that potential distraction has been lifted, and the Celtics will move forward. Mazzulla said he found out about his promotion Tuesday, and that the deal was finalized following Wednesday night's win over the Pistons.

"It is pretty wild," Mazzulla said. "A lot going on, but I'm just grateful. Grateful that not many people get an opportunity to experience this, especially in the manner that I am with the players that I'm able to coach and the people I'm able to work for. And it's for the Celtics. It's a dream come true, for sure."

Initially, the transition was slightly bumpy. The players respected Mazzulla, but several also were frustrated by the lack of explanation about why Udoka—who had guided the team to the brink of an NBA title last June—had been pushed aside.

When the Nets fired coach Steve Nash after a 2-5 start, Udoka reportedly was lined up to be named as his replacement, eliciting more confusion from Celtics players.

"Obviously, we wish he was here," Marcus Smart said then. "We have no control over that. I guess it was deemed that whatever happened was enough for him not to be the coach here, but I guess not enough for him [not] to be a coach anywhere else, obviously."

The Nets front office ultimately decided against hiring Udoka and gave interim coach Jacque Vaughn the permanent role. At the time, Mazzulla said he understood his players' unease about the situation and vowed to be available to discuss any concerns. But he said he would also remain focused on his task.

If there was any remaining uncertainty about his future with the team, it has now been washed away.

Making a Splash

COLD TATUM COMES ALIVE IN THE FOURTH

May 12, 2023 • by Adam Himmelsbach

PHILADELPHIA—There weren't many quiet moments on this night, but as Jayson Tatum was struggling through one of the worst offensive games of his career at the worst possible time, his teammates took every spare second they could find to help galvanize him.

They told him to keep shooting. They told him he would look like the superstar that he is before long. They told him there was still time.

But Tatum started to get worried about that last part. He kept looking up at the clock, which was at once a reminder of possibility and looming finality, and he kept assuring himself that he was not done just yet. Not on this stage. Not now.

Then, mired in a 1-for-14 start, his team trailing in Game 6 of this conference semifinal series by 2 points with a little more than four minutes left, a sudden and stunning end of a promising season becoming more visible by the moment, he arrived.

Joel Embiid, who just won the MVP award Tatum once had his eyes on, softly closed out on Tatum in the left corner, perhaps not believing his slump would end now. But Tatum hit that 3-pointer to put the Celtics in front, then added another 39 seconds later.

The Celtics never trailed again, and Tatum added two more 3-pointers for good measure, helping Boston keep its season and championship dreams alive with a 95-86 victory.

"I just kept telling myself that I believe in myself," Tatum said, "until it turned around."

Now the Celtics will return home for Game 7 on Sunday, with the winner advancing to the conference finals. It certainly seems as if this win should embolden them, and that the 76ers will be swimming

Jayson Tatum silenced the Philly crowd in Game 6 of the 2023 Eastern Conference semifinals. This shot in the fourth quarter put the Celtics ahead 87-83.

against a now impossible current. But the road team has won four of six games in this series, so there will be no space for the Celtics to ease up.

"It's not going to be easy," Celtics guard Marcus Smart said. "But we are the more experienced team in these situations, and we've got to go out there and show it."

Tatum scored 16 of his 19 points in the fourth quarter, and if Boston goes on to win the championship, his ability to spring to life just as the season was on the brink will be the indelible memory from this night.

But the truth is that in many cases the Celtics would not be able to overcome such an off night from their star who tends to be on. And the others saved the Celtics by keeping them afloat while Tatum appeared lost.

It all started with a lineup adjustment by coach Joe Mazzulla, who reinserted center Robert Williams into the starting five in place of Derrick White to give Boston another player to help slow down Embiid, gobble up rebounds, and make life difficult for Philadelphia's guards who previously hunted for gaps in the paint.

Williams had 10 points, 9 rebounds, and 2 blocks, and the Celtics outscored the 76ers by 18 points during his time on the court. Whenever his teammates were asked about his presence after the game, they smiled before saying anything, and that mostly said it all.

"I was ecstatic about it," Smart said.

Smart, the longest-tenured Celtic who symbolizes so much of what this team has become, was also at his best for most of this night. He had 22 points, 7 rebounds, and 7 assists, and he served as the calming conductor whenever things started to go awry.

The Celtics led by as many as 16 points in the first half, but fans watching at home probably did not feel very comfortable about that given this team's propensity to wobble before good times can become great.

The 76ers charged back and took a 5-point lead late in a third quarter that saw the Celtics go 1 for 7 from the 3-point line with five turnovers.

But unlike the 76ers, who are trying to reach the conference finals for the first time in 21 years, these Celtics have been in so many of these high-pressure, high-velocity moments. And that became apparent down the stretch.

The Celtics, meanwhile, continued to trust Tatum even on a night when he hadn't done a great deal to deserve it. And Tatum said it was uplifting to see that the rest of the team was able to pick him up.

"I mean, I don't want to do this [expletive] again," he said. "Hopefully, that's a one-time thing. Hopefully, I start off better. But if this is what it takes for us to win, I'll go 0-for-whatever."

Tatum (51) and Celtics KO Sixers

May 15, 2023 • by Adam Himmelsbach

Jayson Tatum sat at the dais wearing a pink collared shirt, looking relaxed and relieved and rejuvenated, and he could freely admit the truth now.

"To be honest," he said, "they had us on the ropes in Game 6 . . . They had us."

But the 76ers were unable to take advantage of Tatum's rough start and finish the Celtics in Game 6 of this conference semifinal series Thursday night. And inside the Celtics locker room, there was a powerful belief that the 76ers would never have a chance like that again. No one believed it more than Tatum heading into Game 7 Sunday.

"I think going into Game 6, I was too—it sounds crazy—I was, like, too locked in," he said. "I was too tight, just too in my own head thinking about, 'What do I need to do? How many points do I got to score?' You know, this is a big moment. And today, I was more myself."

Being himself means laughing and smiling and revving up a lively crowd. The scoring part seemed to come easily. By the time the afternoon was complete, he had erupted for an NBA Game 7-record 51 points, guiding the Celtics to an emphatic 112-88 win.

Guard Marcus Smart was asked what it's like to watch Tatum when his game is flowing so smoothly.

"It's a movie," he said. "It's a big movie. Being able to just sit back, eat your popcorn and watch."

Boston advanced to the conference finals, where it will face the Heat for the second year in a row.

Neither of these first two rounds have been easy for the Celtics, and even though the Heat have surged into the third round as the No. 8 seed, Boston knows this one will probably not be simple, either. But these tests against the Hawks and 76ers also have hardened the Celtics, and allowed them to believe in themselves more strongly than ever before.

"In the most critical moments, they don't overreact," Celtics coach Joe Mazzulla said. "They trust each other, they stay together, and they execute. To

Jayson Tatum basks in the electric and roaring crowd after scoring 51 points in Game 7 against the 76ers.

me, one word to describe the series is ownership. They took ownership."

When the 76ers flipped an early 6-point deficit into a 9-point first-quarter lead, there was some uneasiness from this eager crowd that had already watched the Celtics drop two home games in this series. But in this case, they regrouped quickly, and with the score tied at 55 pummeled Philadelphia with a 28-3 third-quarter run.

"It was beautiful to see," forward Al Horford said. "I don't know if I'll go back and watch the game, I have to move ahead. But I may go back, just to see what we did, because it was impressive."

As important as Tatum's offense was throughout the afternoon, the Celtics won this game, and this series, with defense.

Entering this round, Boston had not held an opponent below 90 points all year. The Celtics did it three times in this series, all wins, against a 76ers offense that ranked No. 3 during the regular season.

Sunday was perhaps the finest work, and it was keyed by Horford's constant, focused and pesky defense on the league's MVP, Joel Embiid.

Left to operate in single coverage for much of the game, Horford constantly forced Embiid to catch the ball far out on the perimeter. There, he'd stay low to keep Embiid from overpowering him, and keep his arms waving to keep him from getting a clean look.

"I was just out there trying to fight for my life," Horford said, "and trying to make an impact."

Embiid made 5 of 18 shots and had 15 points and four turnovers.

With the score tied at 55 early in the third, Tatum took over, pouring in four 3-pointers during his 17-point period that gave the Celtics an 88-62 lead.

When he scored his 51st point on a 3-pointer midway through the fourth, the number was flashed on the jumbotron along with a live shot of Tatum, just in case anyone had been in the beer line for too long.

This energetic crowd responded to being challenged by these Celtics in recent days, and Tatum waved both arms through the air coaxing them to be even louder. They were happy to oblige.

"Just focused on the game and having fun," Tatum said. "I think that's when I'm essentially at my best."

10-Year-Old Gets a Special Assist from Celtics Star

CHILD IN TREATMENT FOR CANCER GOES FROM TATUM FAN TO FRIEND

May 17, 2023 • by Adam Himmelsbach

On Sunday, a basketball that started the day in the TD Garden equipment room became a keepsake after Jayson Tatum erupted for 51 points using it in the Celtics' Game 7 win over the Philadelphia 76ers in their Eastern Conference semifinal. Celtics owner Wyc Grousbeck presented the ball to Tatum afterward, but the star knew it would be more meaningful to someone else.

Hanging out with Tatum during the postgame celebrations was 10-year-old Xavier Goncalves, who has undergone three surgeries to remove a cancerous tumor from his eye, 24 rounds of chemotherapy, and months of radiation treatments.

Over the last two months, Tatum and Goncalves have become friends. Tatum has invited him to games, exchanged text messages with him, and visited him at his home. So pulling Xavier into the locker-room revelry and giving him the ball after the most impressive performance of Tatum's life was an easy choice.

"I could tell he didn't really know what to do," Tatum said. "I was like, 'Man, you're in the Garden with me. You can go anywhere you want. Come on in.'"

A DIFFICULT DIAGNOSIS

Late last summer, Samantha Bowditch noticed that her son Xavier's left eyelid was drooping. Multiple doctors mostly said the problem would resolve itself, but it didn't. When Samantha could feel a small lump in the corner of the eye in early November, she brought Xavier to Boston Children's Hospital, where

they diagnosed him with rhabdomyosarcoma, a soft-tissue cancer common in children.

The tumor under Xavier's eyelid had actually grown behind his eye and into his nasal cavity. He underwent an initial surgery to remove the tumor and spent several months making weekly 30-mile commutes from his family's Raynham home to the Dana-Farber Cancer Institute for chemotherapy.

Then in February, he started daily radiation treatments at Massachusetts General Hospital and he and his mother moved into an apartment at Christopher's Haven, a home and community for young cancer patients and their families. They have been there since.

During activities at the center, Xavier often talked about how he loved Tatum and the Celtics but had never been to a game. A staff member reached out to the Celtics, who invited Xavier, his mother, and older brother, Carter, to the April 7 game against the Toronto Raptors.

Celtics vice president of marketing Nicole Federico brought the family courtside for pregame warm-ups, and Tatum walked over and handed Xavier a pair of his new signature Nike shoes.

"You've got to wear these tonight to give me some good luck," Tatum said.

Xavier wore the shoes, the Celtics won, and Xavier took them off once the game ended to keep them safe. It was a wonderful night and a nice gesture. Xavier figured it would end there.

"Some celebrities might meet someone and then forget about them," he said. "But I'm glad we were able to make a bond."

'DO YOU GET NERVOUS?'

Tatum was impressed by Xavier's strength and courage, and drawn to his shy personality, which reminded him of himself.

"He was cool, he was quiet," Tatum said. "I just felt a connection."

The family's story struck a chord with Tatum, whose 5-year-old son, Deuce, is a constant presence at Celtics games. Tatum thought about what it would be like to go through such a challenging time with his own family, and it crushed him.

"As parents, you do everything you can to provide and protect and make sure your child is safe, and things like this are uncontrollable," Tatum said. "It must be just so tough on his mom."

So a few days after the brief TD Garden meeting, Tatum texted Federico and said he wanted to visit Xavier in a less-hectic setting. He went to Christopher's Haven a little more than a week later.

Tatum and Xavier hung out in the family's apartment while Xavier peppered Tatum with questions.

Who are your favorite NBA players ever? (Michael Jordan, Kobe Bryant, LeBron James, Magic Johnson)

How do you like to spend your time with Deuce? (Swimming is the best)

What do you miss most about living a normal life? (Grocery shopping)

Tatum asked Xavier about his own challenges, about missing his friends, about waking up and walking into a hospital to receive radiation treatments.

"I asked him, like, 'Do you get nervous?'" Tatum said. "And he just said, 'Nah, because I know it's going to help me. I know I have to do this.' And his mom and everybody around him encourage him. I thought that was cool, because I'm like, '[Expletive], I get nervous before games going out in front of these people, and for you to be 10 years old and show that courage is impactful.'"

They went to the building's activity area, where Tatum grabbed rebounds for Xavier on a small basketball hoop and added his palm print—in green paint, of course—to a collection of those of patients and families on a large mural. The visit lasted nearly three hours.

'THAT WAS THE BEST DAY OF MY LIFE'

Xavier and his mother have texted Federico updates on his progress over the last month, including a video of him ringing a bell to commemorate his final radiation treatment, and Federico sent them to Tatum, who shared support and well-wishes in return.

When the Celtics' series against the 76ers was extended to a seventh game last week, Tatum wanted Xavier there.

Xavier was back near the court for warm-ups, and this time Tatum was no stranger. He hugged Bowditch and wished her a happy Mother's Day. He asked Xavier why he wasn't wearing the signed shoes he gave him last time, and Xavier explained he just couldn't risk getting them dirty.

"Yo, we're gonna win tonight," Tatum told Xavier. "After the game, do you want to come to the locker room?"

He didn't need to ask twice. Tatum took the court and poured in an NBA Game 7-record 51 points, leading the Celtics to a 112-88 win that sent them to the conference finals.

Afterward, Xavier and his mother were ushered to a tunnel near the court, where people were lined up for various greetings, but nothing nearly as private as a locker-room visit. When Tatum arrived, he told Xavier to come with him, and off they went.

Xavier walked around and high-fived the Celtics before sitting near the locker next to Tatum's. They talked about the game, and whether Xavier could keep his bare feet in ice water like Tatum was doing.

Bowditch was in the hallway outside, and as time passed she called in a few times to make sure her son wasn't overstaying his welcome. Tatum insisted that he was not.

"He was just one of the boys," Tatum said.

Xavier Goncalves was just "one of the boys" hanging out in the locker room after the Celtics advanced to the Eastern Conference finals.

GONCALVES FAMILY

Xavier played it cool in front of the Celtics, but he was bursting inside. The truth came out during the ride home.

"He was absolutely in awe," Bowditch said. "He was like, 'Mom, that was the best day of my life.'"

Tatum wants Xavier to return for another game during these playoffs, perhaps the NBA Finals, pointing out that the Celtics are 2-0 with him in attendance.

Xavier recently underwent another round of scans and is expected to receive the results soon. If the news is good, the family is hopeful that Xavier will be able to return home and just need quarterly checkups. But Xavier insists that if he needs to fight again, he will.

"Even if it's a bad MRI, I was able to go through the treatments before that," he said. "I'd just have to pretty much do what I was doing before, just try to get through my treatments."

Except this time, he would have one of the best basketball players in the world on his side.

Add One More to the Lore

DERRICK WHITE'S PUTBACK RESCUES CELTICS

May 28, 2023 • by Adam Himmelsbach

MIAMI—There were just three seconds left in Game 6 of the Eastern Conference finals, but it surely felt like an eternity to everyone at Kaseya Center.

The Heat, who had stormed back from a 10-point deficit in the final four minutes to take a 1-point lead, were hoping that time would just hurry up and run out. They were just those three seconds from becoming the second No. 8 seed ever to reach the NBA Finals. Three seconds from sending the Celtics into a long, sad summer.

The Celtics were hoping that time would stand still. They didn't believe this could be the end. They wouldn't let themselves believe it. Jaylen Brown said a few prayers to himself, but Derrick White would be the one to actually answer them.

Everyone in the arena assumed White's sideline inbounds pass would go to Jayson Tatum, including the Heat, who sent two defenders toward him. That left White all alone.

"At the end of the games like that," Celtics coach Joe Mazzulla said, "our guys talk about crashing and giving it a chance."

Once White passed the ball in to Marcus Smart at the left arc, he knew there was time for him

Celtics players and personnel, including Al Horford (42), Marcus Smart (36), and Jayson Tatum (0), react in jubilation after Derrick White's buzzer-beating putback in Game 6 of the 2023 Eastern Conference Finals.

to have his moment. He sprinted toward the rim, unmarked and unencumbered.

"Like a splash of lightning," Brown would say later.

If Smart had held the ball a moment longer, or taken a dribble, his shot would have been the only shot, but he turned and fired a 26-footer from the left arc that went all the way in before popping out. In so many scenarios, that would have been the end.

But the ball took the perfect, gentle bounce toward the left side, where White was waiting. He jumped and gently put the layup in off the glass at the buzzer.

Celtics 104, Heat 103.

A charmed season lived on.

"The group that we have is unique, the group that we have is special," Brown said, "and sometimes you need a little bit of luck to bring it home."

The Celtics are at once chasing a championship and chasing history. They are now on the verge of becoming the first team in 151 tries ever to win an NBA playoff series after trailing 3-0. Their dreams are much bigger than becoming the answer to a trivia question, of course.

And despite the flood of emotions and joy that filled their locker room late Saturday night, this series is not over yet. These two teams will meet once more, Monday night in Game 7 at TD Garden.

"There is no guarantee," Mazzulla said. "We just have to understand why we're still alive, and the mind-set doesn't shift.

"So, we just can't relax."

White's game-winner saved what would have been a disastrous end for these Celtics, whose 0-6 record in crunch-time games in this postseason appeared on the verge of adding one final, torturous chapter.

Heat star Jimmy Butler, who appeared fatigued as he trudged through his worst game of this postseason, summoned a final burst of energy and nearly pulled off the improbable.

The Celtics led, 98-88, with under four minutes left before Butler got to the free throw line on consecutive possessions. Then his 3-pointer with 2:06 left pulled the Heat within 100-96. Boston still led by 4 when Butler converted a 3-point play with 53.2 seconds left that made it 101-100.

Celtics star Jayson Tatum, who struggled through the second half after a dominant first, was blocked inside. The Heat's Duncan Robinson missed a wide-open 3-pointer that would have given his team a 2-point lead, and Miami was forced to foul Smart with 16.9 seconds left. He made one of two free throws.

In Game 7 of these conference finals last season, Butler pulled up for a 3-pointer and went for the win. He appeared to have a similar mind-set on Saturday night, as he dribbled to the right corner and let the ball fly.

The shot was off, but Butler was fouled by Al Horford with 2.1 seconds left. The play was reviewed, and the shot determined to be a 3-point attempt. But 0.9 seconds were also added to the clock, extra time that turned out to be massive.

Butler calmly buried all three foul shots to put his team in front, but the Celtics were not done. White made sure of that.

"It felt good," White said. "Everybody was asking me, 'Did you get it off?' I was like, 'Yeah, I think so.' But it was so close that you never know."

CHANGING OF THE GUARD

It was always complicated between Smart and the Celtics fan base.

June 23, 2023 • by Chad Finn

It's fitting, isn't it, that for many of us the stunning end of Marcus Smart's tenure with the Celtics is accompanied by conflicting feelings?

In his nine lively seasons with the Celtics, Smart engendered such "love and trust" to the point that it became a slogan for his many supporters. He also was referred to as "polarizing" so often that it practically became a synonym for his name.

The love part was easy. The trust part? Let's admit it, that could waver. His heart was in the right place, always. His head didn't always abide. Oh yeah, "polarizing" was the exact right word.

It was always complicated with Smart, a distinctive, caring, enigmatic player whose desperate desire to win was sometimes impeded by his exaggerated faith in his own skills. It remained complicated during the chaotic day and late night when he became an ex-Celtic.

For much of Wednesday, it seemed that Malcolm Brogdon would be the Celtics guard on the move, part of a three-team deal sending him to the Clippers and sharpshooting big man Kristaps Porzingis to Boston. But the Clippers backed off, reportedly because of injury concerns with Brogdon.

Celtics fans who went to bed at a reasonable hour Wednesday surely woke up to a cacophony of text messages with stunning news. Smart, a staple here since 2014, the bridge between the New Big 3 and the Jayson & Jaylen era, someone who cherished being a Celtic, was the guard on the move, with the Grizzlies replacing the Clippers as the third team in the deal.

And so those of us who can admire Smart's strengths but also recognize his flaws spend the morning, as we will many mornings to come, talking through those complicated feelings.

From a completely unemotional, purely basket-ball perspective—the mind-set Celtics president of basketball operations Brad Stevens had to have to pull off this deal, which also netted a pair of first-round picks—it makes obvious, undeniable sense.

Porzingis gives the Celtics a much-needed big to ease the burden on Al Horford and Robert Williams and another much-needed knock-down shooter in Joe Mazzulla's 3-pointer-heavy offense. He's a gifted, versatile scorer, better than you think defensively, and allows the pieces to fit on the roster just a little better. He's still only 27, and it wasn't that long ago that he was being referred to as a basketball unicorn. Once again, Stevens got the best player in a deal.

I believe there are two primary reasons that Stevens was willing to deal Smart now. Given the 29-year-old Smart's fearless-to-reckless style of play, it's logical to wonder how effective he will be in his 30s. It was alarming how his defensive metrics nose-dived this season, just a year after winning Defensive Player of the Year, and the eye test wasn't his friend, either. This might be the classic, Belichickian it's-better-to-trade-a-player-a-year-too-early move.

The other reason: the magnitude of Smart's per-sonality and his ownership in how the team played affected the inexperienced Mazzulla's willingness or ability to do what was best for the team. It was both charming and absurd that Smart—who was, what, the team's fourth- or fifth-best player?—seemed to be coaching the team at times.

It was probably necessary, but it also could have been perceived as an impediment to Mazzulla's progress.

Marcus Smart at Celtics practice, April 13, 2023.

The further we get away from it, the more absurd it seems that Derrick White, the Celtics' smartest player and a connector on offense, ever sacrificed minutes for any other guard on the roster. But Mazzulla was hesitant to sit Smart late in games, even on his erratic nights. Stevens ruthlessly elimi-nated the possibility of running into that issue again.

While there are further alterations to come, I like this from a basketball perspective. Trading Smart for Porzingis is probably the right thing, and I probably don't even need that "probably." Yet it feels terrible, and that makes sense too.

Smart, as colleague Adam Himmelsbach per-fectly put it, was the connective tissue between eras. His debut, a 121-105 win over Kevin Garnett and the Nets on Oct. 29, 2014, commenced Stevens's second season as coach. The first player off the bench that night (Rajon Rondo and Avery Bradley started at guard), Smart scored 10 points on 3-of-7 shooting (1 of 4 from three), and led all players in steals (4) and plus-minus (plus-20). The man was what he was from the beginning.

He was here and prominent for Isaiah Thomas's fleeting, magical "king of the fourth" era, and Gordon Hayward's seven minutes before disaster, and Kyrie Irving's heel turn, and Horford coming and going and coming back, and Jaylen and Jayson's arrivals and ascents, and five Eastern Conference finals and one lamentable loss to the Warriors in the Finals. This era has been both successful and unfulfilled, and Smart was a reason for both.

When he was at his best—whether by driving James Harden mad, or cobra-striking to steal the ball from an unsuspecting dribbler, or heck, even drilling one of those no-no-yes! 3-pointers—he was a delight to watch. He was proud to be a Celtic, and you were proud that he was one.

Smart cared about being a Celtic the way you wish all Celtics cared about being a Celtic. (It does not go unnoticed that the Celtics are going to offer Jaylen Brown $290 million or so and still have no clue whether he actually likes it here.)

Time will tell whether this ends up like the Kendrick Perkins trade (the right basketball move but one that left a huge bruise on team chemistry) or Theo Epstein's bold decision to trade Nomar Garciaparra in 2004 (the right baseball move, and one that altered history in all the right ways).

For now, we know this, another one of those fitting Marcus Smart paradoxes. He deserved to be a champion here. But for the Celtics to have a chance of it happening in their current window, this deal probably had to happen.

Marcus Smart, always a physical player, and Raptor OG Anunoby go up for a jump ball at TD Garden on November 10, 2021.

Flaws and all, I sure will miss him, won't you? It's going to be weird when he comes back with the Grizzlies, throwing lobs, shooting all-too-confident threes, hitting back-door cutters, dogging White, and yes, maybe flopping a time or two or three.

But know this: There will be nothing polarizing about his reception that night. The cheers he will receive will remind him that he's forever a Celtic, forever green, even if his jersey and perhaps his hair are a different color for now.

Jaylen Brown brings the thunder during a March 2022 game with the Timberwolves.

Celtics Sign Jaylen Brown to 5-year, $304m Extension, the Biggest in NBA History

July 27, 2023 • by Adam Himmelsbach

Flanked by Celtics co-owners Wyc Grousbeck and Steve Pagliuca, president of basketball operations Brad Stevens, and coach Joe Mazzulla, forward Jaylen Brown smiled as he signed his five-year, $304 million supermax contract extension Wednesday afternoon.

"We've got a lot of work to do," Brown said. "So, let's get started."

Brown's press conference was held at MIT's Media Lab, in front of more than 100 high school students from the Bridge Program that Brown helped form to create opportunities in science and technology for underrepresented minority communities.

He said he actually received word that his deal had been finalized while he was in a robotics session with the students earlier in the week. There was no instant celebration.

"I was learning," he said. "I was a part of the curriculum. We were doing some teaching, doing some active engaging, some workshops. So I was able to put my phone down and just get right into class with the Bridge students."

Wednesday's event, with the splashy stage, video screens and Celtics signage, was certainly a fun moment for the students, but it also symbolized how Brown hopes to have a more lasting impact in this region after making this long-term commitment to be a Celtic through the 2029 season.

"It's not just about a contract or money or playing basketball," Grousbeck said. "It's about making a difference in life, and that's what Jaylen embodies to me."

Of course, the money and the stature are not bad, either. Brown's deal is the most lucrative in NBA history. He became eligible for a super-max, which allows players to be paid up to 35 percent of the total salary cap, when he was named second-team All-NBA this past season.

Next year, this extension will almost certainly be eclipsed by bigger deals, most notably when Brown's own teammate, Jayson Tatum, becomes eligible for a super-max worth approximately $340 million over five years.

But for now, Brown has signed the biggest deal in NBA history.

And he acknowledged that new pressures will now arrive and there will be even more scrutiny on his play. But he believes he is ready to handle it all while helping guide the Celtics to their first NBA title since 2008.

"I think all of the life circumstances, the experiences I've had through this organization, experiences I've had in the community, have all prepared me greatly to be in this spot," Brown said. "I don't shy away from pressure. I know what the demand is. I know what the expectation level is. I know the work that is required. Everything about me is about work. So I look at it as another challenge to get better, another challenge to improve. I don't think nobody has seen my best yet."

By Trading for Jrue Holiday, the Celtics Loudly Pronounce They're in Win-Now Mode

October 2, 2023 • by Gary Washburn

What has been established this offseason is the Celtics' sense of urgency. They are not going to be outshone by the Milwaukee Bucks or any contender. They proved that again Sunday by pulling off a masterful deal for All-Star Jrue Holiday.

Inasmuch as president of basketball operations Brad Stevens and coach Joe Mazzulla tried convincing the faithful that Derrick White was a more-than-adequate replacement for the traded Marcus Smart, there was a better upgrade on the market and he emerged when the Bucks dealt Holiday to the Portland Trail Blazers in the Damian Lillard deal.

It wasn't as dramatic as the Celtics throwing in all their chips for this season in acquiring Holiday. Instead, the Celtics made an astute trade where they moved an unhappy Malcolm Brogdon, who had been on the trade block all summer, gifted but oft-injured center Robert Williams, and two first-round picks.

Holiday earns $36.1 million this season and has a player option for $38.6 million next season, meaning this could be a two-year commitment, unless Holiday feels he can demand more on the open market in free agency.

For now, a motivated Holiday is headed to Boston. He's one of the best two-way players in the game; a relentless defensive ball hawk, solid shooter, and floor leader. Holiday has spent years menacing the Celtics, including that pivotal steal of Smart in Game 5 of the Eastern Conference semifinals in 2022.

Holiday replaces Smart, giving the Celtics the most talented starting lineup in the NBA with Jaylen Brown, Jayson Tatum, Kristaps Porzingis, and either Al Horford or White, depending on whether Mazzulla wants to go small or big.

It also gives the Celtics a more consistent playmaker and a better 3-point shooter. Holiday averaged 39.5 percent from beyond the arc in his three seasons with the Bucks and is at 36.6 percent for his career. By comparison, Smart shot 32.3 percent in his nine seasons.

Holiday is steadier and more consistent than Smart, and he won a championship in 2021 with the Bucks. Just days before his trade to the Trail Blazers, Holiday said he wanted to remain a Buck for the rest of his career. He is now a Celtic and will be Lillard's primary defender when the Celtics and Bucks meet in the regular season—and in the playoffs.

This is a good trade, and one that had to be done. Brogdon was salty after nearly being traded to the Los Angeles Clippers in July and the fit in Boston became uncomfortable. He won Sixth Man of Year award but his defense and ability to finish at the rim slipped considerably.

When the Celtics traded Smart to the Memphis Grizzlies, it created a void at point guard and on the bench. Mazzulla and Stevens were adamant that White, and even Tatum, would assume point guard duties. The Celtics were going to need Brogdon to fill a sixth man role, while playing some at point guard.

They were fully prepared for him to be on the roster next season until Holiday became available, and suddenly he was expendable again. Brogdon wants an opportunity to start and play point guard. That wasn't going to happen in Boston.

As for Williams, it's a bittersweet goodbye, but health was always an issue for a player who was beset by a myriad of bizarre injuries. The Celtics couldn't depend on him to play 70 games, even as he entered his prime years. He was expected to report to camp completely healthy and was the team's best frontcourt asset. That's why the Celtics were able to facilitate the trade.

This is the biggest Celtics season since 2008, when they acquired Kevin Garnett and Ray Allen to join Paul Pierce with all eyes on a title. It's the same philosophy this season. Tatum and Brown are entering their primes. Porzingis is an element they've lacked during the Stevens era, while White is coming off a stellar season.

Stevens has been aggressive in his quest to retool. The loss to the Miami Heat last season was embarrassing. The bench was too thin. The point guard position was an issue. Now the Celtics are fully loaded, a team ready to win a championship. There are no excuses, and there's still enough leeway to improve the roster as the trade deadline approaches.

The Jrue Holiday acquisition is a move that perhaps the Celtics were too conservative to pull off in recent years. But the clock is ticking and the time is now. So they pulled it off.

10 RETROSPECTIVES AND ANNIVERSARIES

O
n the occasion of his 50th birthday and nearly 15 years beyond his final NBA game, Larry Bird was just fine with leaving the nostalgia to us.

Informed by Bob Ryan for a December 7, 2006, column that NBA TV planned to run 12 consecutive hours of content from his career in celebration of the milestone birthday, Bird offered a typically straightforward response when asked if he planned to tune in for any of the programming. "I don't have to see it," said Bird. "I lived it."

Well, of course. That makes so much sense, doesn't it? While fans savor watching highlights and flashbacks from a beloved athlete's heyday, it's easy to understand why an icon like Bird wouldn't have much interest in tuning in for a "This Is Your Celtics Life" rehash of his own achievements.

He lived it. How could reliving it be even a fraction as satisfying?

Larry's relative indifference revisiting his own achievements aside, there often is genuine value in looking back, in reconsidering memorable and even seismic events years and even decades after they occurred.

After all, this entire book is in essence a look back. But even within the structure of *The* Boston Globe *Story of the Celtics*, there are stories that don't fit neatly into a chronology yet must be included to tell the complete history of the basketball team and its most significant figures, and share the *Globe*'s coverage of them in full.

Eight of those stories constitute this final chapter. Some, such as Nathan Cobb's piece on Bill Russell's 1979 return to Boston, offer welcome context, perspective, and elaboration on events of the past.

Others featured in this section celebrate anniversaries ("Havlicek stole the ball!" 20 years after he saved the 1965 Eastern Conference finals . . . an appreciation of Red Auerbach's in 1999, during his 50th season with the organization) and milestone birthdays.

And still others remind us, with proper sensitivity and compassion, about those whose lives were altered by tragedy—among them Reggie Lewis's widow, Donna Harris Lewis, and Len Bias's mother, Lonise Bias—and the birthdays that never came.

The emotions in this chapter vary, but all are visceral. Some stories elicit sadness. Others, pride. All eight are beautifully, deeply told, and fearlessness is a through line among the subjects. Many provide a reminder of greatness or

‹ Larry Bird drills the winning shot late in a December 1981 matchup with the Pistons. Bird made a habit of draining game-winners during his 13 seasons with the Celtics.

a compelling history lesson to those who didn't get to witness it, or like Larry Bird, live it.

And sometimes, even ol' Larry is up for taking a quick trip in the Way Back Machine. In early 2015, as the anniversary of his team-record 60-point performance against the Atlanta Hawks—a game with all sorts of amusing extenuating circumstances—neared, I reached out to the Indiana Pacers to gauge whether Bird, their president of basketball operations at the time, might be up for talking about it.

No response came. But one April weekday, my cellphone rang, showing a call originating from Indianapolis. I picked up, expecting a Pacers PR person to tell me Larry was not available.

Instead, the voice was one I'd never heard in person before, yet as familiar as a lifelong friend from all the times I'd heard that certain distinctive twang on television.

"Chad. Larry Bird. I hear you want to talk about that Hawks game. What do you want to know?"

I didn't say it, but I sure did think it. *Oh, I don't know, how about everything?* A half hour and several filled notebook pages later, an oral history of that game, included here, was ready to be told.

When it comes to the Celtics' triumphs, and even the tragedies, too, don't we always want to know more, no matter how many years have passed?

Here's to those who have lived the best of times, and to those who have survived the worst of times, and remain willing to share their experiences with those who never stop bleeding green for the Boston Celtics.

Bill Russell . . . without Apologies

October 17, 1979 • by Nathan Cobb

"I don't care if I ever go to Boston again."

—BILL RUSSELL, 1975

The voice on the telephone, Bill Russell's voice, was perfectly even. No, he did not want to spend our time together driving through Boston, talking about the city as it unfolded in front of him. He wanted instead to find a place to sit down. A good restaurant, perhaps, if there was one in this town. What kind of restaurant? "For lunch it doesn't matter," he answered flatly.

Sixteen hours later, 45-year-old Bill Russell pulled his 6-foot-10 body from the back seat of a gold-colored, chauffeur-driven Cadillac limousine and walked into the restaurant. He was dressed in a three-piece brown tweed suit, with light brown shirt and dark brown tie. He shook hands quickly and perfunctorily, his fingers unadorned by championship rings. He slowly stroked his sparse beard, which is turning white.

Thus was he back in Boston again earlier this week, if only for fewer than 24 hours. The reason was simply business, the publicizing of "Second Wind." It is a newly published book he has compiled with Taylor Branch, who co-authored "Blind Ambition" with John Dean. Most of us will never write our memoirs once, but Russell has already done it twice: An earlier autobiography appeared in 1966. He contends that the latest one is "a different view of events" by a self-described "free-lance Black man" who is obviously still struggling to sort himself out among "the conflicts of all those people running around inside me."

While this newest piece of Russell-on-Russell is not bursting with sports anecdotes and trivia, local sportswriters may be disappointed to learn that they missed something when the famous center for the Boston Celtics told them he played in a particular playoff game with a bandaged arm because he had recently received immunization shots for a trip he was planning. In truth, his girlfriend of the time had stabbed him with a pair of scissors. But the book is mainly a nonbasketball tale, and it contains Russell's further reflections on living in Boston for 13 years. He calls the city "a racial flea market," and later he delivers an amusing if discomforting line: "If Paul Revere were riding today it would be for racism. The niggers are coming! The niggers are coming!"

As we waited to be seated for lunch, I asked Russell how he would describe Boston to an outsider. He frowned heavily, as it is said Bill Russell frequently does. "It depends on who I'm describing it to," he answered. "Under certain circumstances and for certain people, it could be a very likable place. If it was you I was describing it to, I'd say you'd like it. For you it's probably very interesting. There are a variety of things to do and see here. And with your last name there are probably unlimited opportunities." And then he laughed this extraordinarily big, gap-toothed laugh, a startling burst which I was about to discover Bill Russell also delivers a lot.

There should be no mistaking the fact that William Felton Russell probably dominated a professional team sport as has no other athlete in America. He came to the Boston Celtics in 1956, having been an easily forgettable high school basketball player who had gone on to lead the University of San Francisco to two national collegiate championships and the US Olympic team to a gold medal in Melbourne. During his 13 seasons in Boston, the last three of which player Russell worked for coach Russell, the Celtics won 11 National Basketball Assn. Championships. After 25,825 rebounds and 17,195 points, he had been selected the league's most valuable player five times. The Associated Press named him the player of the decade.

Off the court, however, Russell was not so easily defined. He claimed he was public property when he played, but was private property otherwise. He said he wanted to be respected more than he wanted to be liked. He frequently refused, often impolitely it was reported, to sign autographs. At a time when America expected its athletes, particularly its Black ones, to been seen and not heard, he took pride in being outspoken. Yet he often seemed to contradict himself. The quest for privacy, for example, was accompanied by a wardrobe of capes and Nehru jackets which hardly appeared calculated to allow him to pass unnoticed. As a result, what you heard and read about Bill Russell made you believe that there were two people playing center for the Celtics. Either that, or there was one man who was alternately intelligent, surly, proud, arrogant, funny, uncooperative, competitive, rude, uncompromising, thoughtful, diabolical, intense and boorish.

And then there were the comments on race relations in Boston. Some of these came after Russell left town for good in 1969. (Actually, he had lived mostly in Reading.) In 1973, he claimed that Boston was "probably the most rigidly segregated city in the country." The locals hooted. When he announced during the same year that while playing in Boston "I found they had a code of ethics for athletes and another for Black athletes," certain Boston sportswriters were immediately thrown into a dither. These remarks, of course, came along before busing and its harsh revelations. And they came longer before recent concessions by Mayor Kevin White and Cardinal Humberto Medeiros that, yes, Boston is indeed suffering from a festering sore of racism.

INTERLUDE I

Busboy: Excuse me, Mr. Russell? Can I have your autograph?

Russell: I don't sign autographs, young man.

Busboy: Oh, you don't?

Russell: No, but thank you for asking me.

Busboy: Well, you've been my idol for a long time . . .

Russell: I'll shake your hand then. Thank you.

Busboy (shaking hands and backing away): Thank you.

He was somewhere into his roast lamb and O'Brien potatoes, somewhere beyond his 20th cackle and we were still talking about Boston. "For me, it had very little to offer," Russell recalled. "I came here as a rather naive young man, as a professional athlete. As an extraordinary professional athlete. And I lived in a situation where I realized quite rapidly that if I were to be a major athlete in this town it would be in spite of everybody and not because of anybody. I realized my first year that the town was basically a racist town, and not very subtle about it.

"For instance, endorsements and the opportunity to make financial investments are part of the celebrity status. I had a good friend on the team when I was young, Bob Cousy. I had a tremendous amount of respect for him. I think he conducted himself as well as any man I've ever known. He used to tell me what his activities were off the court, about the money he made away from the basketball game. And about the jobs he had offered (to him) after he left. And I saw that I had none of that. I had a restaurant, yes, but I took money out of my pocket and bought it. If I got an opportunity, it was always something I had to take for myself. And one of the things about success in business is the access to opportunities.

"The thing you have to understand is that I didn't want anybody to give me something. But if I'm in a beneficial situation, I want everything that goes with that situation. In other words, if every player on the team gets four tickets, I'm not going to take three.

"People would come in and offer things to certain teammates. For example, one of the car companies came in and gave one of the players a new car for nothing. For free, OK? And then he said to some of the other guys, 'If you want one, I can get a deal on it.' OK? And this was done along racial lines. This, and job opportunities away from the court itself.

"You know, I remember when (Carl) Yastrzemski was a rookie. (For the Red Sox.) One of the writers said, 'Too bad he ain't one of us.' This is what made Boston different for me. It really went past Black and white." (The high laugh erupts here again, causing several heads in the restaurant to turn upward toward its source.) "They would be into 'Is he a Jew?' 'Is he Irish?' 'Is he Polish?' 'Is he Italian?' And it seemed that all the ethnic groups were contemptuous of each other. It wasn't just that the whites were contemptuous of the Blacks, or vice versa.

"You know, when I came to Boston as a 22-year-old I didn't know what a Jew was. But I became aware of it here, because people here make a distinction based on ethnic background, race, religion or whatever."

INTERLUDE II

A photographer came into the restaurant to take pictures for this story. He told Russell that he used to cover him during Celtics' games at Boston Garden. He seemed genuinely surprised that Russell would now permit an interview and pictures. "Years ago you wouldn't have gone for this," the photographer remarked.

"Aren't you lucky I wrote a book?" Russell replied.

Over coffee, Russell seemed anxious to point out that Boston really doesn't concern him anymore. He said he felt no vindication, only sadness, from the city's racial tensions. "Everybody now knows it's been going on for a long time," he remarked. "I hope they acknowledge that."

He explained that he still lives in Seattle, the town where he was coach and general manager of the SuperSonics basketball team during the mid-1970s. Every week he flies to Los Angeles where he spends a couple of days preparing human interest feature stories for the six o'clock news on a local television station. He can be seen on national TV pushing Buicks. He also writes a weekly column for the daily Seattle Times, his opinions ranging from the Panama Canal ("We should call it the Cleveland Canal and no one will want to have anything to do with it.") to anti-homosexual legislation. ("Some of the unkindest things people have done to each other have been in the name of religion.") He has remarried, having divorced his first wife in 1973. Two of the three children from his first marriage live with him, and prior to his second marriage he discovered that "being a single parent was the toughest thing I ever tried to do." He plays golf regularly and is a student pilot.

As we rode back to his hotel in the low-slung back seat of the limousine, Russell mentioned what he had referred to in his book as "the conflicts among all those people running around inside me." His consistency, he seemed to be suggesting, lies in his inconsistency. "You might see me today, and one particular little person will be dominating my personality," he said. "You might see me tomorrow and it's another person."

So what would he be saying about Boston tomorrow? "I'm not real upset about Boston," he said earnestly. "I don't hate Boston." Then he smiled. "I also wouldn't go out of my way to go to Cleveland!" he bellowed. And the now familiar laugh suddenly filled up the inside of the big car, washing over the two of us and over the black-capped chauffeur riding silently in the front seat.

'Havlicek Stole the Ball!'

And Johnny Most stole the show on that memorable night, 20 years ago tomorrow.

"All right. Greer's putting the ball into play . . . He gets it out deep and Havlicek steals it, over to Sam Jones!

John Havlicek and Bill Russell, Game 7 of the Eastern Conference finals on April 15, 1965.

Havlicek stole the ball! It's all over! Johnny Havlicek is being mobbed by the fans. It's all over! Johnny Havlicek stole the ball! Oh boy, what a play by Havlicek at the end of this ballgame! Johnny Havlicek stole the ball on the pass-in. Oh my. What a play by Havlicek! A spectacular series comes to an end in spectacular fashion! John Havlicek being hoisted aloft . . . He yells and waves his hands. Bill Russell wants to grab Havlicek . . . He hugs him. He squeezes John Havlicek. Havlicek saved this ballgame. Believe that! Johnny Havlicek saved this ballgame. The Celtics win it, 110 to 109. We'll be back with our wrap-up in just one minute!"

—Johnny Most, describing the end of a basketball game played at Boston Garden on April 15, 1965

April 14, 1985 • by Bob Ryan

The single most memorable incident in the rich history of the Boston Celtics took place 20 years ago tomorrow when John Havlicek, then a third-year man with a growing reputation as an accomplished all-around basketball player, saved the seventh game of the Eastern Conference final.

The Celtics were leading the Philadelphia 76ers and the despised Wilt Chamberlain by one point with four seconds remaining. Philadelphia had the ball out of bounds underneath its own basket. But the Sixers never got a chance to attempt the winning basket because John Havlicek, known in 1965 to all Celtics' fans (thanks to Johnny Most) as "Jarrin' John, the Bouncing Buckeye from Ohio State," deflected Greer's inbounds pass into the hands of teammate Sam Jones.

In so doing, Havlicek irrevocably altered his status, becoming Instant History. "Before that," contends Most, "John was just a great ballplayer. Suddenly, he became Robin Hood, or whatever. In New England, he became Paul Revere."

If so, the major reason was Johnny Most. His frenzied, but coherent, description of the vital theft was replayed incessantly the following day by WHDH radio, then the Celtics' broadcast outlet. Most's storied exuberance, his pure passion and his journalistic sense ("A spectacular series comes to an end in spectacular fashion!") meshed perfectly in the 1 minute, 7 seconds (all but the first 14 words of it emitted in that peculiar pitch that Most freaks refer to as Voice Three) he used up before going to his commercial break.

The fervor was renewed a year later when Fleetwood Records of Revere put out an album commemorating the first decade of Celtics' championships. The obvious title of the album: "Havlicek Stole the Ball!"

The Boston Celtics of 1965 were going for their seventh consecutive NBA championship. Bill Russell was very much in his prime. Fans were used to winning, and the idea of losing—especially to Philadelphia—was anathema.

The battle with Philly had been a tough one, a hold-your-serve type series highlighted by a spectacular happening at the end of regulation in Game 4. Boston was leading by two with one second showing on the Convention Hall clock. Philly had the ball out of bounds at midcourt. The ball came into Greer, who bounced it once and let it fly from approximately 35 feet away. The ball went in to send the game into overtime. Red Auerbach accused the timer of having a slow trigger finger, but the basket stood and the 76ers pulled out a 134-131 triumph in the overtime to send the teams back to Boston tied at two games apiece.

Each team won at home in Games 5 and 6, creating a climactic seventh game in Boston. With a little over a minute to play in Game 7, the Celtics led, 110-103. But two quick Philly baskets and a Celtic 24-second violation returned the ball to the 76ers, down three (110-107), with five seconds left. Chamberlain promptly stuffed one for another easy basket, and he used up only one second while doing so.

Russell was harassed by Chet Walker on the inbounds (films would reveal Walker clearly out of bounds), and Russell's pass hit the wire that at that time ran from the first balcony to the backboard. It was a turnover, and suddenly the 76ers had a chance to win the game and the series.

The Celtics had four basic worries: (1) a pass to Chamberlain, the most prolific low-post scoring machine that ever lived; (2) a quick return pass to Greer following the inbounds, as Greer was one of the great jump shooters of all time: (3) a pass to Walker, another great middle-distance shooter (and a master of drawing fouls with a superb up-fake, as well); and (4) any shot at all that would produce an assault on the offensive boards by the 7-1 Chamberlain, 6-10 Johnny Kerr or 6-9 Luke Jackson.

Johnny Most: "Dolph Schayes, who was coaching Philly, made a really smart move. He took out Larry Costello during the timeout and put in Kerr. That left K.C. (Jones) on Kerr. (Satch) Sanders on Jackson, Russell on Chamberlain, Sam on Greer and Havlicek on Walker. Now, I think John cheated to the inside toward Kerr and Chamberlain, forcing Greer to pass to Walker, who would be the only one open. John set it up, and Greer made a very, very big mistake. He threw kind of a soft lob toward Walker, and you couldn't throw a pass like that near John Havlicek."

John Havlicek: "Johnny's wrong. I never tried to influence anybody to do anything. In that situation, you want to be on your man pretty tight. As the ball was handed to Greer, I started to count, 'One thousand one, one thousand two, etc.' By three, nothing was happening. Now I'm thinking it's coming to Walker who was a pretty good shooter. Out of the corner of my eye I saw this lob pass, and I just deflected it, tipping it over to Sam Jones. I went up, but I couldn't get control of it. I saw Sam going the other way, and, fortunately, nobody was in position to foul him."

That was the easy part. Thousands of fans had rushed onto the court, and dealing with them was even harder than contending with Chamberlain (30 points, 32 rebounds). "What an ordeal," recalls Havlicek. "My jersey was ripped completely off, and I wound up with these tremendous gashes in my shoulders, from the straps being pulled off me. They even had my pants down around my knees. Then it was a matter of throwing elbows—or whatever it took—to get to the locker room."

Havlicek thought he had seen the last of his uniform. "But," he says, "something happened four years later. When Sam retired, there was a party and a lady came up to me. She had on a dress and an extra piece of cloth attached by a pin. She said to me. 'Do you know what this cloth is?' I said, 'I don't know: It looks like a piece of cloth to me.' And she said, 'This is a piece of the jersey they tore off your back in 1965.' I told her it just looked like a rag to me."

The careers of both Havlicek and Most were affected by the incident. "I was starting to make inroads," Havlicek says, "but, after that play, people realized I might be around awhile. And the record album definitely influenced the way people thought of me."

"It gave me some of the healthiest publicity I ever got in my life," says Most. "It was something to be remembered for, something to hang my hat on. It gave John and me a sense of 'foreverness' I couldn't have had otherwise . . . And it sold about 50,000 records."

Much has happened since that night two decades ago when Havlicek Stole The Ball. The NBA has gone from nine teams to 23. Celtics' ticket prices have gone from a $3 top to $20. The price of a great player has soared from $30,000 to $2 million a year.

John Havlicek, a Hall of Famer and one of the Celtics' all-time Big Four (with Russell, Cousy and Bird), is seven years retired. Johnny Most, however, is still perched "high above courtside," a living link to historic deeds of the past.

And of all those deeds, none shine brighter in the memory of Celtics' fans than the one that happened 20 years ago tomorrow, when John Havlicek ceased being a player and instead became, forevermore, a Hero.

Len Bias:
A Trail of Tears

The Celtics' No. 1 draft choice's death from a cocaine-induced heart attack 10 years ago had a tragic impact on his mentors, friends, family and followers.

June 23, 1996 • by Michael Holley

COLUMBIA, S.C.—That morning, that day, was never right. It began with four college students chasing a series of 120-second highs, using straws to draw cocaine from a mirror to their noses and, eventually,

to their hearts. They passed the broken mirror among them from 3 a.m. until 6 in a University of Maryland dormitory. A few hours later, three of them were in tears because one of them, Len Bias, was dead.

It was never quite right on June 19, 1986. Signs of that, small at first, were evident in the early morning. As the men did drugs, the temperature in the Washington area was 60 degrees, the lowest point of the day. It would climb to 86 later, but on this most abnormal day, that was still 2 degrees below normal.

Normal. What exactly was that? It was not normal to see Bias down. He was 6 feet 8 inches, possibly the best player in the '86 NBA Draft. When he stepped on the Maryland campus as a freshman in 1982, he was athletically raw, and socially polite as well as awkward. Didn't play cards. Didn't drink. Stood stoically against the wall as others let music and the dance floor control their bodies. After the Celtics drafted him June 17, his college coach, Lefty Driesell, told a local radio station, "Leonard's only vice is ice cream."

Two days later he was gone, his death creating a circle of people who may not have shared history had Bias lived. But 10 years later they are still linked to this sphere, spinning around its center, which is occupied by the Bias family and the Celtics. On its fringes are men such as Driesell; Dick Dull, the former Maryland athletic director; Bob Wade, Driesell's successor as Terrapin coach; and Brian Tribble, a friend of Bias's who was with him when he died. Several lives changed; after Bias, another young man lost his.

When Bias died, everyone was left with what-ifs. What if he had known that a cocaine user never gets a high quite like the first one? What if he had known that each use of the drug is like pumping air into an inner tube? One pump too many and . . .

He'd be a perfect Celtic, Red Auerbach thought. A couple of hours before the draft, the Celtics president received a phone call from Cleveland Cavaliers owner Gordon Gund. The Cavs had no coach, no general manager and the first pick in the entire draft. The Celtics, the defending world champions, would pick second. Gund wanted advice from a legend.

"Red, who should we take?" Gund asked.

"You've got to go with the center," Auerbach said. "It's not often that you're going to find a good center. You can build your team around him."

The Cavs agreed and to the disappointment of their fans (some of whom chanted, "Bias, Bias" before the pick), took North Carolina's Brad Daugherty. And Auerbach, just before the Celtics' turn, smiled into the WTBS cameras and told the nation his team would get its man, an All-America forward.

What if Gund had decided to reject Auerbach's advice and draft Bias? Or if Auerbach had told the Cavs to draft Bias? Then the Celtics would have had the 7-foot Daugherty to back up Kevin McHale and Robert Parish, who was 33 at the beginning of the '86 season. Daugherty is close to retiring himself, but that's after a nine-season career in which he averaged nearly 20 points and 10 rebounds.

What if?

Ten years later, in Landover Hills, Md., Boston, Harrisonburg, Va., Kearney, Neb., Baltimore and Loretto, Pa., those in the circular universe remain attached. Auerbach said the Celtics didn't lose Bias for one year, that "it was more like 10." But can this death, any death, ever be quantified? For now, the circle is unbroken, solidified by a 22-year-old athlete who allowed cocaine to creep into his blood and stop his heart.

'KEEP MOVING ON'

She paces at the front of the gym. She is sweating. Four basketball hoops hang from the corners. They are not in use. Lonise Bias, a 6-footer with a booming voice, is speaking to 100 youths at Columbia's Department of Juvenile Justice. Young children are restless, but only a few of their eyes wander from Mrs. Bias.

She says this was a calling. When the eldest of her four children died, she worked at the National Bank of Washington. She didn't have an interest in public speaking. Until 1986. Then she spoke to a few high school and college gatherings. Then her words went from regional attacks on drugs and violence to national and international commentaries. The United States, Virgin Islands, Germany. She's seen them all. "I've been everywhere," she says.

There was no use for a microphone when Bias spoke to the children last Thursday morning. Her voice rises but never falls. It holds bodies in place. She tells the children, or "babies" as she calls them, that no matter what they have done, they can improve their situations. The important thing is that they are

here, living. When she senses they are beginning to fade she screams, "Remember: You have no business getting into a car with someone you don't know. You have no business saying, 'Well I was just . . . ' when you get pulled over and the driver of your car is drunk or has drugs. Do you understand that this is a war zone? And when you're in a war zone, no one is exempt and you could be the next casualty."

It is silent.

"This time of year is always tough for me," she says after the speech. "The anniversary of Len's death, the time of the draft, it's always difficult."

And this day, this humid Thursday in the South, is difficult. June 20. Jay Bias's birthday. Jay, the second-oldest of three sons, was never the same after his brother's death. Len Bias died the day before Jay's 16th birthday. The morning pallbearers carried the body from Pilgrim AME Church in Washington, Jay nearly collapsed. The picture of him being comforted by Jesse Jackson still is chilling.

Never the same. His big brother was a guide rail. After Len was gone, whispers were that Jay was a little wild, not hanging around the right people. On Dec. 4, 1990, a family's worst fear was revisited. Jay was at a mall near the Bias home in Landover Hills. A young man thought Jay was looking at his girlfriend, and an argument ensued. Shortly after, Jay Bias was dead, murdered in the passenger's seat of a car.

"When I lost my sons, I didn't think I'd be able to go on," Lonise Bias says. "I thought, 'Oh, no one knows how I feel. No one is feeling worse than me.' But let me tell you something. No matter how bad you think your problems are, someone has worse problems. I've talked to people who have lost their entire families. Someone always has a worse problem."

And when they do, she tells them she understands. As she watched Game 6 of the NBA Finals, she felt for Michael Jordan. His body shook as he cried for his father, murdered in the summer of 1993. "There's no difference between him and me. That's what I try to tell people," she says. "I'm no stronger than anyone else. You just have to stay focused, keep moving on."

That's easier to say now than it was in '86 and '90. Then, she and James Bias briefly considered selling their home and getting away from the area that has brought them so much pain. But they've owned the house on Columbia Road for 21 years. They like it when their neighbors smile and say that just seeing them get up and go outside is inspiring.

So Lonise continues to speak. And James gardens, making the Bias yard the most attractive in the neighborhood. No, it doesn't make the hurt go away; nothing will. But it dulls it. They will always remain locked in the circle's center. And dull pain is better than what it could be. Lonise Bias is told that a few people in the circle will not or cannot talk about the death of her eldest son, who would be 33 in November.

"Well," she says after a pause, "if anybody couldn't talk about it, it should be us. We're the ones who are affected by it the most."

'HE WAS NO DRUGGIE'

Never has the NBA lottery been as fruitless as 1986. That year illustrates the accuracy of the event's name. Lottery. Your team could cull a solid player from the group of college players at the top of the first round. Or, more likely, there can be coaches and player personnel experts who scout and screen and test and evaluate. And still miss.

Maybe, you will find out later, the man you scouted cannot hit a jump shot, create his own shot, defend or, worse, play. 1986 had them all. The only teams that got what they wanted were the Cavs (who took Ron Harper at the No. 8 spot after Daugherty) and Pacers (Chuck Person, No. 4). And then there were the others.

Bias at No. 2. Chris Washburn (drug problems) at No. 3. Kenny Walker (no game) and William Bedford (drugs) at Nos. 5 and 6. Roy Tarpley (drugs) at No. 7.

Many ask why the Celtics didn't test Bias for drugs. They did.

"He was no druggie," Auerbach said. "We weren't the only ones who tested him. The Knicks and Warriors did, too. Two weeks before the draft."

That leaves two possibilities. The first is endorsed by Auerbach and the Bias family: The morning of June 19 was the first time Bias ever experimented with cocaine. That being the case, nothing would have been in his system in early June. On Thursday, Lonise Bias said she is unconvinced that her son was a cocaine "middleman" as Washington prosecutors labeled him in 1987 during the trial of Tribble, who was acquitted of supplying Bias with the fatal dose of the drug.

Then there is the option that makes men and women silent; a possibility that elicits "no comments" from those who wish the issue would go away: Bias could have been the middleman described by prosecutors. But a smart middleman. Unlike marijuana, cocaine does not linger in the body. At most, it is in the system for 72 hours. If Bias knew tests were coming, he would have stopped using the drug at least four days before then.

"I was one of the first people Len saw when he came on campus," said Eric Turner, a Maryland graduate who works at the Federal Reserve Board in Washington. "When I heard that drugs could have been involved, I kept thinking that it didn't sound like Len. I just remember the guy who didn't drink beers when we did and, at first, didn't know how to talk to girls."

Lonise Bias said the same thing and added that the trials of '87 only proved that "a lot of people had dirty laundry and were willing to throw it in a dead man's coffin."

That debate still is delicate. One that is not is Bias's impact on the Celtics. If he were half the player people expected him to be, he would have been on the edge of All-Star status. As his mother notes, he would be close to retiring time now, which would make him a wise veteran ready to help the Celtics' young players.

Ah, but that is also part of the problem. For reasons that they may not have been able to see, the Celtics had unfortunate first-round picks in three consecutive seasons. There was Bias, then Reggie Lewis, then Michael Smith. Bias and Lewis died; Smith just couldn't play.

The Celtics were relying on Bias to be one of their pillars. As Turner said, he defied their image of a "slow white team. We were all happy for Len when he got drafted, but we thought it was kind of funny he was going to play with the Celtics. You know, it was like they were The White Team."

When Bias died, the Celtics reeled, readjusted and scrambled. They still haven't caught up to where they thought they'd be. They lost the '87 Finals to the Lakers, then began to sink from a great team to a good one. They made the Eastern Conference finals in '88, losing to the Pistons, and haven't made it past the conference semis since.

"Try taking two key players from the Bulls and see what happens to them," Auerbach said. "Not

Jordan, either. Take away Pippen and Rodman. They're a much different team. Take Reggie Miller and someone else from Indiana and see what they're like."

Probably like today's Celtics, stacked with complementary players but desperately missing a star. On Wednesday, they likely will draft a forward who will help with rebounding and scoring. They had that in Bias. They also crave a shooting guard who can score 20 points per night. They had that in Lewis.

"I still say that Len is doing more in death than he ever could have in life," Lonise Bias said. "If he were playing basketball, he would be entertaining. Even in death, he is doing much more than that."

The Celtics reached out to the Biases when Len died. They gave them a No. 30 jersey that Bias would have worn. But entertaining is part of the Celtics' business. And for what they do, the loss of Bias was an immobilizer. For the Biases, the number of years cannot be counted. The Celtics? Ten years, at least.

HEADS HAD TO ROLL

"Can I ask what this is regarding?" the secretary says.

"Len Bias," she is told.

"Well, Coach Driesell won't take the call. He will not talk about that."

So it went after several unreturned calls to James Madison University in Harrisonburg, Va. Driesell is there because he was forced to resign at Maryland in 1986. He had coached the Terrapins since 1969, never leading his team to a losing season. Basketball fans loved him in College Park, Md. Oh, they liked to question his game strategy, but they had to admit the man could recruit.

Len Bias was his last great player. There was also Buck Williams, Albert King, John Lucas, Tom McMillen. Terrific collegians, good pros.

But when a death, with undertones of drug involvement, hits a national power, someone has to be held accountable. Driesell was reassigned to help with campus fundraising, his office 25 feet from that of the new coach, Bob Wade. And athletic director Dick Dull, a man who had attended Maryland as an undergraduate and law student, had his contract bought out. He is now the AD at the University of Nebraska-Kearney, a long way from Maryland and the Atlantic Coast Conference. Dull also refused phone calls in the last two weeks.

"I'm not speaking for Lefty, but I can tell you that there were a lot of coaches around here who felt for him in '86," said Leonard Wood, who recently became head coach at Bias's high school, Northwestern, in Hyattsville, Md. "When you're a coach, you're just trying to win games. You can check on your players, call your players, whatever. You still never know what they're doing. I wish I knew, but I don't know what my players are doing and I call them all the time."

Administrators did not blame Driesell for Bias's death. But they wondered if he had control of what went on with his team. If he had answered "yes," they would have asked him to at least partly explain Bias's drug use. A "no" would certainly cost him his job. He moved down the hall and let Wade take over.

Much of Wade's time at the school was spent thinking about who was on his side. He believed there was a conspiracy to bring him down. He left Maryland in 1990 after the school was cited for 18 NCAA violations and placed on probation for two seasons. Wade hasn't coached since Maryland. He is the associate director of Parks and Recreation in Baltimore.

"It was tough being there after Len Bias," he said. "I would do it again, just a lot differently."

'CAN'T KEEP LOOKING BACK'

Today, Brian Tribble is where he feared he would be in 1987. Prison. After being acquitted in '87, he was indicted on cocaine distribution charges in 1990. Prosecutors found that he and 25 others were responsible for delivering up to 22 pounds of cocaine per month in the D.C. area. He is expected to be imprisoned in Loretto, Pa., until 2000. Tribble was in the room with Bias on the morning on June 19, 1986. He doesn't want to talk about it.

"Inmate Tribble gave no reason for not wanting to speak," said Sharon Orr, public affairs director of the Loretto facility. "He just doesn't want to."

It has been 10 years. Still, the circle forces a family, an organization, coaches, an athletic director and a friend to be rapt. In a few years, the Celtics will only have footprints in that circle. But what of the others? The Biases? Tribble? Driesell?

"You can't keep looking back," Lonise Bias said. "You have to stay directed."

Even if circles are infinite.

Cooper No Draft Dodger

**With help of Auerbach and Brown,
he helped break NBA's color barrier.**

February 26, 1999 • by Peter May

The risk was enormous. The Celtics stood on the cutting edge of history 49 years ago, but also on the brink of financial ruin. They were losing money and by making history, they were about to lose even more.

But team owner Walter Brown and coach Red Auerbach were undeterred. They were determined to stock their team with the best available players and, in the second round of the 1950 NBA Draft, Brown told his fellow owners that the Celtics were going to take 6-foot-6-inch Chuck Cooper of Duquesne. Auerbach, who technically had not even been hired yet, had seen Cooper play and thought he'd be a perfect complement.

When Brown announced Cooper's selection, the other NBA owners, gathered for the draft in Chicago on April 25, were set aback. Finally, one of them said what the others were all thinking. "Walter, don't you know he's a colored boy?"

Of course, Brown did. He also didn't care.

"Walter Brown was 100 percent for it," Auerbach said. "Without his decision, it never could have happened. I couldn't have done it without him. If he could play, he was going to take him, no matter what color he was, what religion he practiced. If he could play, Walter didn't care."

The Celtics made history with the pick, becoming the first team in the NBA to draft an African-American player. The Washington Caps, emboldened by Boston's historic move, went for another African-American, Earl Lloyd, in the ninth round and the Knicks later signed Nat "Sweetwater" Clifton, then with the Harlem Globetrotters. When the 1951 NBA season opened, there were three African-Americans where there had been none before.

Last month, almost 50 years after the fact, Lloyd and Auerbach attended a panel discussion in New York on the history of African-Americans in the NBA. When it was Lloyd's turn for an opening remark, he offered the following.

"I've never said this to Red, but he needs to know this. I believed then, and I believe now, that if Red Auerbach and Walter Brown had not drafted Chuck Cooper, I truly believe, because of the times, I don't think the Washington Capitals would have drafted me," said Lloyd, who was the first African-American to play in an NBA game. "We have allowed [Cooper] to slip away much too quietly because his contribution to the league is outstanding. And anywhere I go, when they call me the first, I clarify that."

Asked about Lloyd's comments, Auerbach said, simply, "I took it as a compliment."

CROSSING THE 'TROTTERS

There was no small gamble in taking Cooper, due solely to the omnipotent presence of the Globetrotters and their owner founder, Abe Saperstein, who had a vise-hold on all the Black basketball players. The Globetrotters also represented the biggest draw in basketball—their summer tours in Europe would draw more than 100,000 to stadiums—and NBA teams would schedule them for doubleheaders, simply to get people through the turnstiles and into the arenas.

"The Trotters outdrew all the NBA teams, by far," said former Globetrotter Marc Hannibal, who runs a television and motion picture production company in Connecticut and has been working on a documentary on the subject for years. "The league was petrified of Abe. And Abe knew that. That's why he held such power over the owners."

Saperstein logically thought Cooper was his and an obvious candidate for the Globetrotters, having been named an All-American at Duquesne. Cooper even toured with the Trotters in the summer of 1950 and, in a telegram to Cooper, Saperstein said, "To me, you were, you are, and you always will be a Harlem Globetrotter." Auerbach didn't think so.

"He was too straight for them," Auerbach said. "He wasn't a clown. He was a basketball player first and some of the Globetrotters were clowns first and basketball players second."

In addition, the Celtics couldn't afford to anger Saperstein. They already were more than $400,000 in debt, according to some accounts and the league itself was a wobbly enterprise. Auerbach said later that summer he tried to sign Clifton, but the league would not allow the deal, lest it upset Saperstein. Soon thereafter, the Knicks were allowed to sign

Clifton, but only because New York owner Ned Irish finally allowed Saperstein an entree to Madison Square Garden, the one major venue the Trotters had not been able to play in.

In one of his many books, Auerbach wrote that Brown was unfazed by the likely Globetrotter boycott if he drafted Cooper.

"You coach the team and I'll worry about the money," Auerbach said Brown told him. "If I can't stay alive in this league without those clowns, I'll pack it in. We're going to make it with a winning team, or wind up broke anyway."

Once the Cooper pick was made, Saperstein crossed Boston off the Globetrotters' itinerary, not to return until after Brown died in 1964.

SOME TRYING TIMES

Auerbach says now that Cooper's transition to the NBA was relatively placid—"it was totally unlike baseball," he said—but there are stories galore of how it was anything but. Cooper had to stay in a different hotel than his teammates in places like Baltimore and St. Louis. In a game in Raleigh, N.C., there were threats that the Celtics would not be allowed to participate because they had a Black player, although the game eventually went on as scheduled. Auerbach recalled getting turned away at a train station restaurant, so he ordered sandwiches to go and everyone ate on the platform.

Bob Cousy says to this day one of the most embarrassing situations he has ever confronted was when he and Cooper decided to use the restroom at a train station, only to discover there was one for whites and one for Blacks.

"What do you say to a friend faced with that kind of stupidity and racism? I didn't know how to handle it," Cousy said.

Added former teammate Bob Brannum, "There was a lot of stuff, but Chuck handled it. He was a gentleman, not an aggressor."

However, there was a legendary brawl in February 1952, at Moline, Ill., in a game against the Milwaukee Hawks. It was ignited by a racial epithet from a Milwaukee player, spilled over to the benches and eventually to Auerbach and his Milwaukee counterpart, Doxie Moore.

"Chuck went over to Red and said, 'I'm not going to take that stuff,'" Brannum recalled. "And Red said, 'Then don't take it.' That was permission to bust him."

Teammates offered to room with him, the first being southerner Bones McKinney. Auerbach switched roommates by the month. Brannum noted teammates loved rooming with Cooper because the team would have to order room service and the players could keep their per diem, which amounted to $6.50.

Cooper died in 1984, but said in a New York Times story in 1980 that the worst part was having to deal with the segregated hotels, restaurants, and even taxicabs.

"I had good support from the Celtics," he said. "There were never any racial problems with the team. I felt a strong relationship with them all."

Added Cousy, "There was never any problem on the team. Arnold [Auerbach] handled it by not handling it, by treating everyone the same. And that's what everyone wants, to be treated like everybody else."

IMPACT BEYOND THE COURT

Lost in much of the attention about being the first African-American drafted and signed by the NBA was Cooper's brief, relatively uneventful history in the league. He's not known today for his talent or sweeping successes—"a five on a scale of 1 to 10," Cousy said. Lloyd and Clifton had much more success and are better known today.

Cooper lasted only six seasons, four with the Celtics and one each with the Hawks and the Fort Wayne Pistons. He was never regarded as a scorer or an indispensable piece of the puzzle and averaged 6.7 points a game. He was one of many Auerbach role players.

"He was a rebounder, period," Hannibal said without equivocation. "He wasn't a shooter or a scorer. He wasn't what you'd call a dynamic player."

Auerbach said he sensed that Cooper always had a greater ambition than basketball.

"His mind was set on becoming a good teacher, in social work, that kind of stuff," Auerbach said.

Cooper earned a master's degree from the University of Minnesota. He returned to his native Pittsburgh, where he had been raised as the son of a postal worker and graduated from Westinghouse High School. He worked for the city's recreation and parks commission and became an officer at the

Pittsburgh National Bank, a position he held until his death.

His athletic achievements prior to joining the Celtics have not gone unrecognized. He has been named to Duquesne's All-Time team and was inducted into the school's Hall of Fame in 1970. He also was inducted into the Pittsburgh Hall of Fame, the Western Pennsylvania Hall of Fame, and, six years before his death, was selected as one of Duquesne's 100 Most Distinguished Living Alumni. The Chuck Cooper Award is presented to Duquesne's most outstanding underclassman basketball player.

But his main contribution to basketball was one which he did not choose, but which he endured. But he saw himself not as a trailblazer, not as the NBA's Jackie Robinson, but as one of a handful of individuals, white and Black, who combined to integrate the game.

He lauded Brown, who "made it possible when no one else would." He lauded Cousy "for not having a hint of racism." And he included himself in a roundabout way that now seems almost ridiculously understated.

"I feel a sense of accomplishment in a very modest way and can't help feeling very proud," he said. "But when I was playing, I never thought about all that. I was more preoccupied with just making the team."

Red All Over

CELTICS CELEBRATE 50 YEARS OF AUERBACH'S UNIQUE LEADERSHIP

November 3, 1999 • by John Powers

He remembers when Sheboygan was in the league and Blacks weren't. He remembers when there was no 24-second clock, when Eddie Gottlieb scribbled the schedule on scraps of paper, when the playoffs ended in April and players sold insurance during the summer.

"When you get to be my age, you can't remember what you had for breakfast," Red Auerbach says. "But I could tell you stories from 50 years ago."

It has been half a century since the man with the Brooklyn accent and the argyle socks came to Causeway Street and took over a wobbly basketball team that was losing games and money at a dizzying pace.

The Celtics were a shamrock on a shirt in 1950. By 1966, Auerbach had made them into a dynasty, winning nine NBA titles in 10 years before moving to the front office, where he won another seven.

He is 82 now and still the club's vice chairman, still puffing on his trademark cigar, still the symbol of the game's most storied franchise.

"He's the Godfather of the Celtics," says John Havlicek.

A bronze statue of Auerbach has been in Quincy Market since 1985, the same year his mythical number (2) was hoisted to the rafters of Boston Garden. He was voted into the Basketball Hall of Fame more than three decades ago. And while the hat he wears now may be largely ceremonial, the Celtics without Auerbach are unimaginable.

"There was only one guy who was with one organization as long as Red has been," says Tom Heinsohn, who will emcee tonight's tribute to Auerbach at the Celtics' home opener against Washington at the FleetCenter. "That was Connie Mack with the Philadelphia Athletics—and he owned the team."

Auerbach never owned the Celtics (though he did get a 10 percent stake after Walter Brown died), but for more than a decade he *was* the Celtics. He was general manager, coach, traveling secretary, scout, marketing director—all without a contract.

Auerbach signed one with Brown ("Because I didn't know him") for $10,000 and a piece of the non-existent profits. The rest was all done on a nod and a handshake.

"There were always people in Walter's office, so we'd go in the men's room to talk," Auerbach recalls. "He'd say, 'What do you want?' I'd say, 'Am I working next year?' 'Of course you're working next year,' he'd say. 'Why, do you want a raise?' Sometimes, I'd say, 'Yeah, I do want a raise.' Other times, when we didn't make any money, I wouldn't ask for anything more."

In the early '50s, the Celtics were a fragile franchise in a dance-hall league. Seven of the NBA's 17 franchises folded before the end of the 1951 season. Only three of the remaining 10 (Boston, New York, and Philadelphia) had been around since the league began in 1946, and the Celtics had lost nearly half a million dollars in four years.

They were a basketball team in a hockey town, playing in front of nearly 10,000 empty seats at the Garden. Brown had already mortgaged his house and sold most of his Ice Capades stock to keep the team afloat. Once, when Auerbach brought two players on the road and didn't use them, Brown gave him hell.

"What am I paying 10 men for," Brown said, "if you're going to lose with eight?"

There was never enough money, and Auerbach knew that as well as anybody. If he was a one-man band, it was because he had to be. Auerbach had no assistant coach. If he missed a practice or a game ("To my knowledge, I never did"), the players would have to coach themselves.

Auerbach had no scouts. He either watched college prospects himself, usually when they played at Madison Square Garden, or took the word of a trusted confidant.

"If we had a game in Boston on Wednesday and a game in Chicago on Friday, I'd have a practice on Thursday morning then go to New York or Philadelphia and watch a doubleheader," Auerbach recalls. "Then I'd go by myself to Chicago."

On the road, Auerbach handled the hotel bills and parceled out expense money with an accountant's eye.

"If Red's cab fare to the hotel was $2.85 and yours was $3.25 because the driver took a different way, you still only got $2.85," says Heinsohn.

And if someone was missing and his squad needed a 10th man to scrimmage, Auerbach would dust off his old set shot and step in.

"He'd be out there on these spindly little legs, trying to drive to the hoop," Havlicek remembers. "People would foul him and block his shots—and he'd foul the hell out of them at the other end."

But always, the red-haired man from Brooklyn was at the center of the franchise.

"He was the only voice," says Tom Sanders, who played half a dozen years for Auerbach and ended up coaching the club. "It was Red's show. Walter Brown had given him complete control."

Brown was an arena manager who carried the bottom line in his head. He knew ice shows and rodeos, track meets and come-to-Jesus meetings. But he didn't know basketball, and he admitted it. So Brown left everything to Auerbach: drafting, signing, trading, coaching, marketing, even proselytizing.

TAKING TO THE ROAD

James Naismith had nailed his peach baskets to the wall down the road in Springfield and Holy Cross had brought the NCAA title to Worcester, but basketball in New England was still little more than an indoor diversion when Auerbach arrived.

So he took to the road like a traveling salesman, giving hoop primers to anybody who wanted one.

"I had a truck, and in the back of the truck I had a basket," Auerbach says. "We'd go to supermarkets and give a clinic in the parking lot."

Auerbach literally wrote the book on the sport: "Basketball For the Player, the Fan and the Coach." It was a simple game, he said, and building a winning team wasn't complicated. You found good players, got them in shape, taught them a basic system, and let them go to work. Auerbach just happened to do that better than anybody else in the league.

"Arnold knew how to judge talent, he knew how to acquire it, and he knew how to motivate it," says Bob Cousy, who played 13 years for Auerbach and won half a dozen championship rings.

Nobody was better at finding collegiate gems—like Bill Russell, Sam and K.C. Jones, Havlicek, Sanders—whom others had overlooked or undervalued.

Nobody was better at horse-trading to get them. Dealing Ed Macauley and a draft pick (Cliff Hagan) to St. Louis for the right to draft Russell was arguably the best move in league history.

And nobody was better at getting them to play more for pride than for money.

"Red created an atmosphere that allowed as many players as possible to do what they did best," Russell says.

Auerbach might have had complete control, but he was no dictator.

"He understood that the greatest use of power is not to use it," says Russell, who succeeded Auerbach as coach and will be on hand tonight to honor him.

Auerbach had all the natural leverage he needed. He controlled the playing time, and there was no free agency and no rival league. He had no need to play the martinet for effect.

"Some coaches have to show every day that they're in control," Auerbach says. "That's a sign of weakness in my book."

His players were superb athletes who had been to college and were playing the game for money. Why not treat them as professionals? They knew they were supposed to arrive in camp fit and ready to run. So if they were overweight, Auerbach told them, it was their fault. If they pulled a muscle, it was their fault. Threw up? Their fault.

Conditioning, fundamentals, execution, teamwork. What else was there?

"You don't want to overcomplicate it," says Cousy. "You set up the structure, but let the talent express itself. Arnold knew how to win with the least amount of wasted motion. That was the essence. He got it done without a lot of French pastry."

Seven basic plays, with options off each. Short, intense practices.

"I could do everything I needed in an hour," Auerbach says. "I tried to make the practices interesting instead of drudgery. Competitive games. The five big men against the five little men. Things like that. I didn't think they needed two hours. Because they might get tired of my voice."

MOVING UPSTAIRS

By 1965, most of the Celtics had been listening to Auerbach's nicotine-cured growl for the better part of a decade. Not that they objected to it. How could you object to an annual ritual of champions' checks, bejeweled rings, and champagne?

But Auerbach was worn down from all the years of multiple identities.

"I was burned out," he says.

So he gave his rivals a year's notice: one last chance to shove the Redhead's cigar down his throat.

And in 1966, after an eighth straight flag, Auerbach turned the coaching job over to Russell and watched, literally, from the other side of the Garden. Auerbach didn't want anyone saying that he was pulling his successor's strings from behind.

"Red never came to practice unless I asked him to," Russell says. "He said, 'You're the coach.' Because that was the way Walter Brown had been with him."

There was plenty for Auerbach to do in the front office. Brown had died in 1964, the ownership was shaky, and the core of the dynasty—Cousy, Heinsohn, Russell, Frank Ramsey, Sam and K.C. Jones—was gone or going. Lean years were on the horizon and Auerbach's role was to rebuild from behind a desk and keep the interregnum short.

It was no different from what he'd always done, finding talent and figuring inventive ways to acquire it. Auerbach had always relished finding heirlooms (like Don Nelson and Bailey Howell) at rummage sales. He enjoyed picking up merchandise for a bargain price when nobody else realized it was available.

He'd always had the blood of the Levantine merchant in him. When Auerbach went overseas on State Department tours, he haunted the marketplaces playing "Let's Make A Deal."

"He loved to go to the bazaars in Egypt and haggle," Heinsohn says. "It was a ritual with him."

Auerbach got Jo Jo White in 1969 because White was military draft bait and other clubs were reluctant to take a chance. Auerbach drafted him, then got White into a reserve unit. Almost nobody outside of Tallahassee knew who Dave Cowens was because Florida State was on probation and off TV. Auerbach did.

"We got us a hoss," Auerbach concluded, watching Cowens yank down rebounds in rookie camp.

So it went, as Auerbach supervised one Reconstruction, then another. He traded the rights to Charlie Scott for Paul Silas. He drafted Larry Bird as a junior and waited a year for him while five other clubs passed, preferring instant gratification. He dealt two draft picks to Golden State and ended up with Robert Parish and Kevin McHale. He drafted Danny Ainge when everybody else figured he'd play baseball.

A LOCAL INSTITUTION

The most important thing, more than the deals, was that Auerbach was still working on Causeway Street, decade after decade.

"Having him there told the world that the Celtics were a stable situation," says Sanders, now the NBA's vice president for player programs. "Auerbach's still in place, the Celtics are still in place, so business is still being taken care of."

The owners came and went: Jack Waldron, Marvin Kratter, Woody Erdman, Bob Schmertz, Irv Levin, John Y. Brown, Harry Mangurian. Auerbach almost went, too, in 1978 when Brown's Kentucky fried meddling drove him nuts.

"I told him one time that we needed a backup guard," Auerbach says. "He called me up the next day and said he'd gotten one. I asked him how much. He said $50,000. That's not too bad, I said. 'By the way,' he said, 'I also gave them a first-round pick.' I said, 'You did *what*?'"

Where would it end? He was afraid he would pick up the paper one day, Auerbach said, and find out he'd been traded. So when the Knicks offered him their presidency at a record salary, Auerbach decided he'd take it—until everybody from truck drivers to shuttle pilots to former players to his wife, Dot, bade him reconsider.

He had enough money, Auerbach concluded. And even though he'd been born on the other side of the Brooklyn Bridge, Auerbach couldn't imagine himself working in New York—and coming back to Boston as a visitor.

"I thought about what it would be like to come back up to play the Celtics, to watch the ballgame and look up at the flags," Auerbach said then. "And I didn't know what my reaction would be."

He had become as much a part of the city as Durgin-Park and the Ritz and Filene's Basement. Auerbach spends most of his time in Washington now. He has survived heart surgery and 100,000 stogies and enough plates of late-night Chinese food to top the Great Wall. He still plays racquetball ("With Sam Jones's son. He's my guru.") and goes to his office and plays cards at his club and keeps up with the game he helped shape.

It is a different game now, with 29 franchises and overseas offices from Paris to Taipei, with rookies making more in a season than Cousy did in a career, with salary caps and lockouts and seasons that go to the middle of June and games that end up 85-79 and have viewers reaching for the clicker.

"David Stern has got the right idea," Auerbach muses. "The best way to save the game is to clean it up so you can see some of the skills."

Tonight he comes back to Causeway Street, a living bronze statue who is still on the masthead, right below the chairman. There will be video highlights and oral history and Auerbach's image on every ticket for every home game.

For 50 years, through the best and the worst, Arnold Auerbach and the Celtics have been mentioned in the same sentence.

"Red's been the glue that's been there for everything," says Havlicek. "When he's gone, people will look at the Celtics—and think they're like anyone else."

Happy 50th, Larry!

A DAY TO CELEBRATE BIRD'S GREATNESS

December 7, 2006 • by Bob Ryan

Yes, it's true. Larry—no surname needed—turns 50 today.

"It didn't mean anything to me," he says. "But everybody's talking about it."

"It doesn't bother me at all," he maintains. "We'll see. I was looking forward to my 40s, and they turned out to be up and down."

One thing he will not be doing is paying any attention to a 12-hour celebration of his 50th birthday that commences on NBA TV at 9 a.m. and that will feature a one-on-one interview conducted by ex-teammate Bill Walton.

"I don't have to see it," Larry says. "I lived it."

Just as older Bruins fans will tell you that hockey has never been the same for them since Bobby Orr retired, so, too, do many local basketball fans assert that the game will never again have the same allure as it did when No. 33 and friends were not only winning three championships as well as losing twice in the Finals, but were doing so with a brand of basketball that often transcended the mere entertaining to creep into the realm of inspiration.

And that's not hyperbole. That's the gospel truth.

Larry doesn't think in those terms, of course. He did the playing. He didn't really care if the rest of us put what he did in a larger philosophical context because he was enjoying himself—most of the time, anyway.

"I had fun," he points out. "I can tell you right now I did smell the roses. Any time I felt good, I completely loved playing. If I felt good during the warm-up, if I had my balance, I could definitely tell you that somebody was going to get an ass-whipping. Of course, I remember it all. I remember that first game in the Garden. There were only about 10,000 or 11,000 people there and I remember the place smelled like stale beer. Probably why I liked it."

The big "if" was health. If it weren't the heels, it was the elbow. If it wasn't the elbow, it was the back. You could pretty much say his last four years were a constant struggle just to get into the lineup. It was difficult, and it was frustrating, and when it was time to quit, he had no regrets.

"I knew it was pretty much over during that Cleveland series [first round, 1992]," he says. "I could barely move during the Olympics. I made the retirement announcement, and the next day I felt great because I knew it was over."

That was one back fusion surgery ago. Larry was not going to be one of those guys flirting with a comeback.

"Playing seems like a long time ago," he says. "I can remember it all when somebody asks me, but I never dwell on it. And college? That all seems like a blur."

He had an ill-defined role with the Celtics and he coached the Pacers. He got to the Finals once, came within 20 seconds of getting there a second time, lost in yet another conference finals, and then he quit, just as he said he would. He's still amused that people didn't seem prepared to take him at his word. Hadn't he told them when he took the job it was for three years? And didn't he coach for three years? Well?

"I said I'd coach for three," he shrugs. "I coached three and I'm never coaching again."

He's a front-office guy now. His title with the Indiana Pacers is president of basketball operations, which makes him second in command to CEO/president Donnie Walsh.

He likes it just fine, but it isn't quite as fulfilling as coaching, just as coaching wasn't quite as fulfilling as playing.

"It's nothing like playing," he admits. "And you don't get the high you do as a coach. But front-office life is interesting. I guess I've really come full circle. It's enabled me to stick around the game. You still bleed these wins and losses, but you don't have your hands directly on it."

One thing his general manager and personnel experience has taught him is that nobody was ever smarter than Red Auerbach.

"What a genius," Larry marvels. "The way he found older players to bring in. The way he used his draft choices. He never wanted to give up a draft choice to get someone once a season started. He'd say, 'It looks good now, but you never know. You don't know how a season will go and you never know when you're going to need that draft choice.' The

Two birds at Celtics' Christmas party. Larry Bird and, allegedly, "Big Bird."

Knicks gave up two No. 1s to get Eddy Curry. That's exactly what I'm talking about."

He'd like to see the Pacers playing better ("I think we should have won two or three more than we have"), but life in general is pretty good. Connor Bird is 15 now, and Larry loves watching him and his team play. "A completely different player than I was," Larry submits. "He'll take one shot a game and be happy. He's the quickest guy on the team."

That's different, all right.

He's living where he wants to live, among the people he's most comfortable with, and he's just bought a piece of Indiana on which he will retire. He's got no complaints.

No, we're the ones with the issues. Larry Bird really did spoil us. He gave those of us who truly love basketball our ultimate highs, and it's downright depressing to think we've already experienced the best example of how to play this game we can ever hope to see.

If you don't get NBA TV, you'd better buddy up quickly with someone who does.

An Oral History of Larry Bird's 60-Point Game

"It was like living in a video game."

March 12, 2015 • by Chad Finn

Roaming the basketball court during his heyday, Larry Bird was a genius, an artist, a purist, a perfectionist, an ingenious passer, deadeye shooter, savvy rebounder and sly defender. Of course, that's just the abbreviated list of attributes. Ego-puncturing trash-talker definitely should have been mentioned sooner.

During the 1985 season, Bird was 28 years old and all of those powers—visceral, intangible, and virtually unprecedented and unmatched—were operating at peak levels. Bird averaged 28.7 points and 10.5 rebounds that season. He hit 42.7 percent of his 3-pointers, 52.2 percent of his field goal attempts, and 88.2 percent of his free throws.

No one in the NBA played more minutes. No one in the NBA played *better* minutes. He won his second of three straight NBA Most Valuable Player awards, receiving 73 of 78 first-place votes.

Over 30 years ago, Bird submitted one of the most memorable performances not just of that marvelous season, but his entire career—though it should be noted that he does not consider it one of his favorites.

"Fans and you guys think in terms of points, and I get that," said Bird in a recent phone conversation. "But my favorite games are the ones in which I did a lot of different things to help us win the game."

On March 12, 1985, Bird set a Celtics franchise record by scoring 60 points in a 126-115 win over the Atlanta Hawks. It broke the record held by teammate Kevin McHale, who dropped 56 on the Detroit Pistons just nine days previous.

The performance is legendary not *just* because of Larry Legend—though his career is certainly reason enough for any celebration, anniversary or

no anniversary—but this particular game was also marked by some unusual circumstances.

It was played in New Orleans, a supposed home-away-from-home for the Hawks, but in reality, a fine place for Celtics fans to take a holiday and watch their stellar team.

Bird's performance was so electrifying—he scored 32 points in slightly more than 14 minutes of court time during a second-half scoring barrage—that opposing players on the bench got swept up in the wonder of it all. The end of the Hawks bench morphed into a Larry Bird fan club.

"The way he was shooting the ball," said Hawks star Dominique Wilkins, who scored 36 points in defeat, "was like living in a video game. It couldn't be real. But it was."

This is the story, as told through more than a dozen interviews with Celtics and Hawks players and personnel, as well as select anecdotes excavated from the archives, of that memorable night in New Orleans. But to tell the full oral history of Larry Bird's 60-point game, we must begin nine days before his achievement.

'WHY NOT GO FOR 70?'

On March 3, 1985, Bird scored 30 points, collected 15 rebounds, and dished out 10 assists in a 138-129 home victory over the Detroit Pistons. On most nights, the triple-double against an increasingly despised rival would have made Bird the talk of the league. But this night belonged to another Celtics forward.

Kevin McHale, the affable, rubber-armed sixth man—who was starting only because of a knee injury to Cedric Maxwell—scored 56 points, breaking Bird's franchise record of 53 set in March 1983 against the Pacers. McHale, who played for the Celtics from 1980-93, was just coming into his prime in 1985. Like fellow front-court partners Bird and center Robert Parish—forever known as the Big Three—he would eventually be enshrined in the Basketball Hall of Fame. But this? This was the game of McHale's life.

KEVIN McHALE, Celtics forward, 1980-93: "The only time I ever scored that many points before was in a pickup game when I was 12. And then we played for almost five hours."

Larry Bird, seen here lining up a shot during the 1985 NBA playoffs, dropped a Celtics-record 60 points against the Hawks that March. But by Bird's own accounting, it wasn't even his best game that season.

BIRD: Once you realize what's happening . . . you know, you don't get there very often, where you have a chance to do something like that. When you get there, you defer even more. You get the guy the ball. That's what I tried to do with Kevin. You defer a lot when someone gets hot anyway.

McHale might have scored more than 56, but he pulled himself from the game with a couple of minutes remaining and the victory secured—a decision that offended Bird's competitive sensibilities.

BIRD: Kevin took himself out of the game. I couldn't believe that. Especially against the Pistons. We didn't get along with them anyway, so why not go for 70, you know? They didn't have anyone who could guard him a lick. When he pointed to the bench to come out, I said, "You can't come out. You gotta get even more." I couldn't believe it.

GLENN ORDWAY, Celtics radio broadcaster, 1982-95: Bird made the famous comment after the game. "He should have stayed in there.

Should have got 60." You could see it. There was this real interesting rivalry between those two guys anyway. They were really good together on the court. They were both different off the court.

DANNY AINGE, Celtics guard, 1981-89: Larry would always come to me and say, "Hey, go tell Kevin this," and Kevin would come to me and say, "Go tell Larry that." They were such great players, but sometimes they didn't know how to talk to each other and how to yell at each other. But they knew how to yell at me.

RICK CARLISLE, Celtics guard, 1984-87: Everybody on that team took grief. There was no one that was spared. That was what made that group of guys such a special group of guys. There was a mutual respect on one hand, and on the other hand, anything was fair game, to practical jokes, humor, you name it.

SCOTT WEDMAN, Celtics forward, 1982-87: When I first got traded here, Larry put me through the wringer. He was the best psych artist ever. The master. He'd always tell me I was too short to guard him, then he'd post me up, and he'd score a lot in there. Then he'd tell me he was going to do it again. He made me a much tougher player mentally. He had his own way of dealing with each individual player. He had a different relationship with every player, a sixth sense in how to deal with people, including Kevin.

ORDWAY: There was some talking, some chirping going on with Bird in those nine days. There was some playful stuff, but remember, Bird held the record that McHale broke.

BIRD: Of course after the game, they asked me about it and I had to be a smart-ass and say, "I'll break that record in no time."

WEDMAN: He congratulated Kevin, and he never said a word to any of us that I know of about breaking it again, but it did not surprise *any* of us when he went out and got it back so soon.

'I'M PASSING LARRY BIRD!'

On March 8, Bird led the Celtics to their 50th win in 64 games, a 133-122 victory over the Dallas Mavericks in which he submitted a typically masterful 32-point, 15-rebound, 9-assist performance. With three days off until their next game against the Hawks, Bird got his competitive fix by running in the sixth annual Shamrock Classic on March 10, a five-mile road race that started at the Boston Garden.

BIRD: I used to shoot the gun off to start it. It was about 3,000-4,000 people, and it kept growing and growing until they stopped it.

WEDMAN: When I didn't play much during a game, I'd get into practice a half-hour early and I'd run for about 20 minutes beforehand around the court. About a month before that road race, I came in one time and Larry was running. I was like, "What's he doing?" He just said quietly, "I need to stay in shape."

For a week or two this went on, and after a couple of weeks—he was kind of shy—he came up to me and just goes, "Buddy of mine

is having a fundraiser for such-and-such thing. You wanna run with me?"

I said, "If [Coach] K.C. [Jones] says it's OK, sure." He said Louise Boland, our fitness instructor and a marathon runner, had to pace us, and as long as no one pulls a hamstring or gets hurt, he was all right with it.

BIRD: We went out there and just ran it. Boy oh boy, my hamstrings were never tighter after that.

WEDMAN: We were obviously recognizable, being about a foot taller than the rest of the runners. So we take off, beautiful day, and there are a couple of thousand people in this race.

So we're running along—and Boston is a big sports town—and you hear, "Hey, there's Larry Bird! Hey, there's Larry Bird! Look, Larry Bird! Hey, is that Scott Wedman?" And then you start to hear, "Hey, I'm passing Larry Bird!" People were running fast and enjoying the fact that they're passing us.

BIRD: It's amazing to me when you run those races. Some people you think can't run, they run right by you. It's amazing. Kids 10 years old flying by you at the four-mile marker. You're like, "What the hell?"

WEDMAN: So the last mile, Larry's noticing this, and he says, "Nobody's passing me anymore. Let's go." And he took off. Remembering what K.C. said, I didn't try to beat him. Don't know if I could have. He did the last mile in under five minutes.

BIRD: We used to try to get it done under 34 minutes.

Bird finished the race in 33 minutes and 40 seconds.

WEDMAN: It was a *sprint*. I experienced what a heart of a champion was. I was right behind him and I felt like my legs could have burst.

BIRD: I beat Scotty, so that was good.

'IT WAS ALL CELTICS FANS'

What wasn't so good was the condition of Bird's legs as the Celtics embarked on a trip to play the Atlanta Hawks on Tuesday, March 12. But they didn't head to Atlanta. Instead, the game was played at Lakefront Arena, a 10,900-seat arena on the University of New Orleans campus.

BIRD: That race left me so sore, my hamstrings were so tight, I went over to shootaround and I didn't feel good. I couldn't get loose. But once I got running during the game, they loosened up. But going into that game, I didn't expect to do anything.

ORDWAY: This almost felt like a preseason game, had the feel of an exhibition game, because you were not playing in an NBA arena. This had none of that routine you get from covering an NBA game. It just seemed out of place. It was this dingy little arena, tiny little place. Everyone was real close to the floor. There was no upper balcony or anything. You could hear everything everywhere. The players were talking about it in the shootaround beforehand. They weren't accustomed to playing at a place that size. Ten thousand people? C'mon.

MIKE FRATELLO, Hawks coach, 1981 (interim), 1983-90: We played a dozen games there that season. The reason was a promoter down there offered Ted Turner, our owner, a hundred thousand dollars a game. And that's when Mr. Turner was trying to get TBS off the ground. That was a lot of money to infuse into the network.

JOHN STERLING, Hawks television broadcaster, 1981-89: It made for terrible travel. But it made a lot of money for the Hawks, which is what they wanted.

FRATELLO: We basically played 53 road games and 29 home games in Atlanta.

ORDWAY: It was all Celtics fans. Like a Celtics home game.

BIRD: I noticed that right away. There were usually a lot of Celtics fans in Atlanta, but this was even more. Celtics fans traveled well. It seemed like it was about 75 percent Celtics fans. That got me fired up.

FRATELLO: That happened all over the place then. When we were in Atlanta, we'd see our share of green jerseys in the stands. We were rebuilding the team then, trying to put the group together that would end up having four to five great years together—Nique, Doc [Rivers], Kevin Willis. But that year was a tough year because we knew we were in transition.

Add on top of that that the Celtics were as good as they were and had a loyal following all over the country, and that's why you saw so many people there. A chance to see the Celtics in New Orleans? That's a big deal.

GREG KITE, Celtics center, 1983-88: One of the Boston writers used to say all the time that Larry was like Elvis, and that's exactly how it was, in New Orleans and everywhere else. He was the king. Everyone wanted to see him no matter where we went.

BIRD: I didn't think that game was played well by either team. Still don't. But the fans in New Orleans sure liked it.

'THE GAME REALLY SUCKED'

Bird's performance in the first half against the Hawks didn't suggest McHale's new record was in imminent danger. Bird was not otherworldly, but merely excellent in the first half. He scored 12 points in the first quarter, entering halftime with 23. Not that he was particularly pleased with any of it, especially when Dominique Wilkins and Eddie Johnson, who combined for 72 points, helped the Hawks tie the game 69-69 early in the third quarter.

BIRD: If you watch the tape, the game really sucked. That wasn't the kind of game I like to play in. Nobody was guarding anybody, the ball wasn't moving good.

KITE: I'm watching the YouTube clips as we talk about this. A backdoor pass from DJ [Dennis Johnson]. That was a staple for them. Beautiful play.

CARLISLE: Larry was one of the most fun players ever to watch for his fertile imagination to try different stuff on the court and pull things off.

During the third quarter, Bird seized control, seemingly making every shot in his deep repertoire—the familiar fallaways, stepbacks and leaners were out in abundance. He hit a runner with eight seconds left that made one believe he may never miss again.

Perhaps he even invented one or two new moves along the way. He finished with 19 points in the quarter, including 11 in the final three minutes and 10 seconds as the Celtics took a 100-89 lead into the final quarter.

"I could feel it at the end of the third period," said DJ in the aftermath. "He made a shot—the real high one?—and I said to myself, 'Watch out. He already had 42 points and he was just getting hot.'"

ROBERT PARISH, Celtics center, 1980-94: He told us at halftime that nobody could stop him so just give him the ball and get out of the way. Then he went out and started taunting the Atlanta players on the floor, the ones on the bench, their coaches, even the referees. He was talking so much trash he was buried in it. It was one of those nights when he could have drop-kicked the ball in. I loved it.

M.L. CARR, Celtics swingman, 1979-85: I was [on the injured list and at home in Weston] watching the game on television with my wife. I was watching and watching, rooting for us to win, and all of a sudden I got thinking about the record and Larry. My wife kept falling asleep and I kept waking her up. "Sylvia, look at this one." She'd fall asleep again and I'd have to wake her up again. "Sylvia, look at this."

STERLING: In the old days, you were so much in the game. I was sitting at the table right there next to the Hawks bench. He was making shots from our microphone, one unbelievable shot after another. You know that modern term, heat-check? Larry might have invented the heat-check that night.

BIRD: We used to do that all the time. Danny did it a lot, Kevin, and me. If you get a little space, you're going to fire it up and see if it goes in. Low-percentage shots, but somehow they end up getting in the rim and going in.

Did they ever go in during the fourth quarter. Bird scored 33 points in his last 14 minutes and 13 seconds on the court, including 18 after re-entering the game with 8:41 remaining to play. Bird's final 18 points were the Celtics' final 18 points.

BIRD: I didn't even know I was scoring at that rate until I hit a couple of free throws and the PA guy said I had 51 and 52. I knew I was scoring a lot, but I didn't know I had that many. I couldn't believe it was that many. But once it got up there pretty high, I figured you might as well go ahead and try to beat McHale's record.

FRATELLO: He was feeling it that game. His teammates knew it. This was a night where they could see Larry had it going. They made sure they got the ball in his hands as often as possible. They were pretty smart that way.

BIRD: DJ came over and said, "C'mon, let's bust Kevin's record." But Kevin helped me out just like I helped him out.

The Celtics backcourt combined for 30 assists. Johnson had 17 and Ainge 13. And McHale chipped in with five.

BIRD: Danny had 13 assists? Are you sure? That must be a mistake, first of all. We were playing in New Orleans and it wasn't a real NBA arena, so you never know who they had for a stat guy. That had to be a career-high for him.

Dominique Wilkins, the soaring star of the '80s Hawks who came up on the short end of a couple of memorable shootouts with Bird, was the primary victim of Bird's offensive spree—though he did counter with 36 points of his own.

WILKINS, Hawks forward, 1982-94: Me and Larry, we had some great battles. Legendary. Legendary. He had the heart of a lion. He was a brilliant basketball player, in every aspect of the word. I could not have more respect for him.

STERLING: I coined "Dominique is Magnifique." He loved it. He was a pleasure.

CARLOS CLARK, Celtics guard, 1983-85: They always had this real competitive rivalry going. But I knew Dominique from college [Clark went to Mississippi, Wilkins to Georgia] and knew he's a very competitive guy. Sometimes those dunks of his would come down from the rafters.

ORDWAY: You notice a lot of Larry's big, huge games are against Atlanta? That's because Larry lit up every time he was going up against Dominique. Larry just tortured him because he knew Dominique could not play a lick of defense. Larry would just go right at him. Right at him. He knew he could beat him off the dribble, hit the fadeaway, make that little dribble-drive, and then back off for that wing shot. I remember him saying once he also knew that halfway through the shot process, Dominique would cheat and start to head down the floor.

GLENN "DOC" RIVERS, Hawks guard, 1983-91: He saw Dominique as this up-and-coming player and he just tortured him, mentally. He tortured all of us. He was calling shots "off the glass, who's next, where you want this one from," and he just made one after another. When he got to about the 55th point you knew it was something special.

Wilkins wasn't just victimized by Bird on the court that night. He also was the victim of a good-natured prank by teammates afterward. The late Ray Williams, a backup guard for the Celtics in 1985 who died in 2013, recalled in the days after Bird's feat that some of the Hawks had gone to a club after the game.

Cliff Levingston, a backup forward, summoned a waiter and had a bottle of champagne sent to Wilkins's table. The inscription: "Thanks. From Larry." When Wilkins, known as the "Human Highlight Film" during his prime, was honored with a 13 ½-foot tall, 18,500-pound statue outside of the Hawks' home, Philips Arena, Bird quipped, "I'm pretty sure it's not made in a defensive stance."

WILKINS: Ah, man, that was just a bust from Larry. He's a funny guy. When you're playing against one of the greatest players ever, who was gonna guard them one-on-one? There was no one guy who was gonna guard him one-on-one.

SCOTT HASTINGS, Hawks forward, 1982-88: Larry was so on fire, and there was nothing we could do. I'll bet you eight different members of our team guarded him. In fact, after the game, a bunch of us were having a beer in the French Quarter and trying to add up how many he got on each one of us. "He only got 14 on me blah-blah-blah, yeah, he got just 12 on me." We totaled it up after everybody talked and I think it came out to 32, so how it got to 60, we never solved that one.

FRATELLO: Since it's years later, I can look at it this way. I was enjoying Larry so much I felt like why should I do something to ruin this guy's rhythm? I just let him keep going. I hope Larry appreciates that I was part of him getting that record, not disturbing his rhythm at all. I'm sure he appreciates that.

HASTINGS: I feel like he had eight or 12 on me. [Randy] Wittman had 12 or 14. Nique probably had 30 at least. Doc was on him for 10 or 12, Cliff Levingston gave up some, Antoine Carr got a bunch on him, Kevin Willis. I'm not sure there was a guard or a forward in that game, not a soul that played, that didn't get burned by Larry Bird.

WILKINS: Larry was a bitch to guard one-on-one.

'GUYS ERUPTED LIKE WE WERE CELTICS FANS'

As Bird piled up the points in the fourth quarter, seemingly increasing the degree of difficulty with each made shot, a small group of Hawks players— particularly forward Cliff Levingston and guard Eddie Johnson—began reacting animatedly. Their reactions of admiration and disbelief became especially obvious when Bird drilled a twisting, bad-angle corner jumper to get to 54 points with 43 seconds left.

HASTINGS: Three or four of the guys erupted like we were Celtics fans. A couple of the guys ran off the bench. I always sat on the bench with a towel on my lap. I took the towel—I was screaming just as loud as these guys were—but I threw the towel over my face and just started screaming and hollering. It was like a precursor to those And1 videos.

Bird got his record 57th point on a free throw, which brought a very high high-five from McHale. And points 59 and 60 came after McHale pulled down an offensive rebound of a Bird miss and kicked it back out to DJ, who fed a cutting Bird for the perfect punctuation mark: a foul line jumper at the buzzer.

BIRD: I remember DJ and Quinn [Buckner] hugging me, but I just wanted to get back to the locker room. I was exhausted.

But it was a shot that had happened a few moments before—one that didn't count—that is remembered more than any of Bird's 22 made field goals that did count.

With 14 seconds left, Bird caught a pass in front of the Hawks bench, took one dribble to his left, and launched a stepback jumper with Rickey Brown draped all over him. The shot swished through the net just as Bird, nudged by Brown, falls into the lap of Hawks trainer Joe O'Toole. The shot did not count—a foul was called on the floor—but that makes it no less amazing.

As Hawks announcer John Sterling shouts "Larry Bird! Larry Bird!" while proclaiming it the greatest shooting performance he has ever seen, the players at the end of the Hawks'

bench—particularly Levingston—can't even pretend to contain themselves now. They fall all over each in giddy amazement. Only later did we find out the real reason for the reaction: Larry Bird called his shot.

RIVERS: He said "in the trainer's lap" coming down the court, which meant it was going to be a three and it was going to from deep. Then he said, "Who wants it?" Then I think Rickey Brown, I'm not sure who it was, ran out after him, he shot this high rainbow, it goes in, Rickey bumps into him and accidentally knocks him on our trainer's lap. So it was exactly what he said. It was an accident, but it was almost fate. They show a shot of our bench, Cliff Levingston and Eddie Johnson, standing up giving each other high fives. It was pretty awesome.

CLARK: I'm not sure who it was, but I could swear one of the guys on their bench tried to give Larry a high five.

RIVERS: That night was not awesome. We had to go back to the locker room, and Mike Fratello, instead of going out to eat, had a team meeting and put the film in and said, "It's one thing to be in awe. It's another thing to cheer for the other team." And he shows this back and forth, and kept rewinding the high five. It was awesome.

FRATELLO: We're trying to beat these people. We're not going to the movies to enjoy a show. This is our competitor. I didn't appreciate the way they handled it, I let them know that, and we moved on. A lesson learned. Their lesson was that they got fined.

HASTINGS: Mike was so mad I think he fined each of those guys 500 bucks. But he didn't get me. I had the towel.

WEDMAN: I understood why they did it. It was like, where is this coming from? How is this guy doing this? It might not be funny or cool if you're on the same team, but if you know the game or play the game, especially at that level, you can't help but marvel at what Larry was doing.

BIRD: I saw the replay of that a few times where those guys are over there laughing. But hell, they guarded me at one time or another that night too. So it wasn't just one guy.

HASTINGS: It's the second game I ever played in where I saw the guys on the bench become fans of the opponent. Both times Larry Bird was involved. The other time was my first NBA pro game with the Knicks.

We were playing the Celtics in an exhibition game in Portland, Maine. Larry had one of the rookies guarding him, real athletic kid, and he was getting down low in his stance and was ready to get in Larry's jock. Larry takes the ball like he's going to make a pass and fakes like he's throwing it over this guy's head, then he pulls it back.

And the kid does about a 180-degree jump-turn and takes about two steps across the lane. And Larry just sits there and looks at him with that, you know, kind of that Larry look. He's like, "Really?"

The kid tries to recover and takes a step toward him and Larry steps back, takes a shot, hits it, and says, "Too late." We're all on the bench going, "Oh my god, oh my god," and then all of a sudden I remembered, dude, I'm not in college anymore watching Larry Bird. I'm an opponent playing against him. So it happened twice.

KITE: I'd like to say Larry and I combined for 62 points, but I don't recall if I got into the game.

Kite did not score in one minute of playing time.

WEDMAN: I believe I was excited because Larry and I combined for 78 points.

Wedman scored 12 points on 6 of 9 shooting.

WEDMAN: I only had 12? Well, Larry and I had just 72 then. Dammit. That's still pretty good.

ORDWAY: The thing I remember that was absolutely hysterical was they were doing a special drawing for fans that night. The Hawks might have been using the Celtics to draw a crowd because they knew they couldn't draw that crowd. So the prize for the drawing—you had to buy tickets for it—was the Larry Bird game jersey from the game. At the end of the game, Bird was going to take his jersey off, sign it, and hand it over to a fan.

So the game ends, they're coming off the floor, and I remember the confusion at the time because suddenly the Celtics were not giving up that jersey. Not that night. They weren't giving that up. There were, like, negotiations going on.

The person was not real happy because you could tell there was no sweat on the jersey they were given. He probably figured out he had something really precious that they were trying to swap out.

FRATELLO: I've got a story. We're going back to the hotel that night after the game, my assistant coach and I went to get something to eat, we had a little place that we stopped at to talk over the game.

We do that, then head back to the hotel. We're carrying our bags, slowly walking through the door, and the doorman there that night said, "Boy, coach, that one really surprised me. I thought for sure you guys were going to beat them, and I thought for sure that Larry wasn't going to play well."

I said, "Oh, really. Why would you say that?" He says, "Because I would say that he got in a little bit late last night. He got in a little late. I didn't think he'd have the energy to do that." So that rubbed a little salt in the wound.

BIRD: I just remember having dinner with friends and getting my rest.

FRATELLO: Whatever it was, it worked for him.

BIRD: People get caught up in points, but I can't say it's in the top 20 of my favorite games. I had games where I scored just 15 or 16 points, but I played excellent basketball in my mind, I did a little bit of everything. I didn't rebound or pass much.

Sixty points is a lot, don't get me wrong. I made shots against the Hawks that game I can't recall making in any other time. It's not easy to do. But there was a game from a little earlier that season where I had a triple-double and a bunch of steals in around 30 minutes against the Jazz. That had it all. That was what I'd call a great game. If you wanna talk about that one . . .

Fond Memories Are Living On

Those who knew Lewis best will never forget humble Celtics star.

December 23, 2018 • by Gary Washburn

The gravesite at Forest Hills in Jamaica Plain is unmarked, a patch of grass sandwiched between two large tombstones. It's hardly a fitting memorial for someone held in such high esteem and so sorely missed, but it will remain that way until it's time for Reggiena Lewis to say goodbye and hello.

The 24-year-old daughter of former Celtics great Reggie Lewis never met her father, born a few months after his tragic and untimely death 25 years ago. And until she's ready to make that trip, the grave will remain as it is, without a tombstone.

"You know what that's about, my children, you think about it, I was pregnant with my daughter and my son was 11 [months] and there's been a lot from the time they were born and defending his honor and a whole lot of different things, but they really never got a chance to be a part of anything for him," his wife, Donna Harris Lewis, now 53, said in an exclusive interview with the Globe. "The reason why it's not there yet, my daughter, when she's ready, that's when we're going to do it. It's that simple. People make a big to-do and that was explained by the family and explained to everybody, but you can't fight what a lot of people say."

It doesn't seem like 2 ½ decades since Reggie Lewis collapsed on that Tuesday afternoon at Brandeis University. July 27, 1993, still stands as a day that changed the lives of those close to Reggie forever, and the day the Celtics lost their centerpiece.

Yet, what is fresh in the minds of those who loved him, coached him, played with him, and guided him is Reggie's smile, Reggie's humility, Reggie's work ethic, Reggie's generosity, Reggie's confidence, Reggie's passion. Those good feelings, those cherished memories, those 30-year-old stories, those depictions of a selfless man who was everyday people, overshadow the circumstances surrounding his death.

Reggie told Donna he was going to Brandeis for a workout. There, on the floor of the small college gym in Waltham, he collapsed and died of heart failure at age 27, ending a remarkable life far too soon and beginning an ugly debate over Lewis's health, his decision to ignore his diagnosis, and who was exactly responsible for this tragedy.

The reflections on Lewis are kind and thoughtful. Those who knew him describe a man who was fueled by a quiet confidence but never felt above the common man. Those involved in the Black community of Boston describe a man whose charitableness was never-ending, who adopted Boston as his home and offered hope and happiness with his annual Thanksgiving turkey giveaways.

And the one who was closest to him, Donna, talks of the difficulty of moving forward, the uncertainty of his health at the time of his death. She has no regrets for their actions after he collapsed on the floor during an April 29, 1993, playoff game.

"It's always yesterday for me and I think it always will be," said Harris Lewis. "Could things have been handled differently or better? Of course they could have. Everybody learned some valuable lessons. His life could have been saved. Of course you try to do all you can to save a person's life, but at the time he really didn't know or I didn't know really what was going on. You can't for many, many years say a person has a normal athlete's heart and all of a sudden, something happens. You just try to figure it out."

THE HEIR APPARENT

Lewis was the Celtics' first-round draft pick out of Northeastern University in 1987, a year after the franchise tragically lost Maryland's Len Bias to heart failure related to cocaine use just two days

Reggie Lewis (right) and Dennis Johnson chat during an October 1988 practice.

after he was drafted. Lewis flourished as a Celtic and was tabbed the heir apparent cornerstone to Larry Bird, Kevin McHale, and Robert Parish.

Lewis would eventually break into the starting lineup in his second season and the small forward earned All-Star honors in 1992 when he averaged 20.8 points and shot a career-best 50.3 percent. When Bird retired after that season, Lewis relished the added responsibility and led the team in scoring in 1993.

In Game 1 of the first-round playoff series with the Charlotte Hornets, Lewis collapsed without contact during the first quarter. Looking disoriented and confused, Lewis was helped off the floor and given a series of tests by team trainers.

He was declared healthy enough to return and did eventually, finishing with 17 points before leaving the game midway through the third quarter with dizziness. That would be Lewis's final NBA game.

A day later, the Celtics gathered a dozen heart specialists through New England Baptist Hospital, a group they tabbed the "dream team," and their diagnosis was that Lewis suffered from "focal cardiomyopathy," a disease of the heart muscle that can cause irregular heartbeats and heart failure. The condition was considered to be career-ending.

But on the night of May 2, Lewis, Harris Lewis, and his agent arranged for the Celtics player to be discharged from New England Baptist and moved to Brigham and Women's Hospital. It was there that Dr. Gilbert H. Mudge, considered a renowned cardiologist, insisted that Lewis did not have a career-threatening heart ailment and instead diagnosed him with a nonfatal condition called "neurocardiogenic syncope," which can cause a decrease in blood pressure and fainting spells because of high exertion.

Lewis was excited about the possibility of playing again and also annoyed that the Celtics not only quickly diagnosed his ailment as career-threatening but also went public with their findings quicker than Lewis wanted.

For the next several weeks, Lewis believed Mudge's diagnosis and yet also received a third opinion in California, according to Harris Lewis.

"I remember once someone wrote he was doctor fishing," Harris Lewis told the Globe. "No. Anybody who takes it seriously, a diagnosis, you get a first opinion, you get a second opinion, sometimes you get a third opinion. I kind of laugh when I see these books after he passed away about getting a second opinion, we were criticized for that. Whatever. You can't win. You do your best. As far as he knows he left here in search of what was really going on with him."

Legal battles continued after Lewis's death. It took seven years for a jury to clear Mudge of wrongdoing in the Lewis case, as he intimated that Lewis revealed to him a history of cocaine use and said he never cleared Lewis to work out on his own. Also, Lewis didn't reveal to the "dream team" a history of family heart issues, including a heart murmur of his own when he was a child.

Mudge, 73, who recently retired from Brigham and Women's Hospital, told the Globe, "It was a very complicated case. I dealt with other very complicated cases and I moved on after this complicated case and so did my career. That's all I can say."

When Lewis died, his relationship with the Celtics was damaged because he had questioned whether the franchise truly cared about his condition or took responsibility in case something more serious occurred. The franchise, led by former Big East commissioner Dave Gavitt and general manager Jan Volk, was perplexed about the situation because of its seriousness and the possibility that Lewis's career was over.

Gavitt died in 2011. Volk said he is unsure what the Celtics could have done differently, but the pain and heartbreak remains present.

"You had a young man in the prime of his life, the prime of his career, who was an elite athlete," Volk said. "One does not expect an elite athlete to be so vulnerable as he turned out to be. There's a lot of conjecture as to the nature of the illness, the nature of the malady, but whatever it was, it was inexplicable. There was no answers, there was no explanation. It happened.

"You don't think of those things in that type of respect and I don't think anybody could have predicted the ultimate tragedy there was in this case."

'A SPECIAL GUY'

Reggie Lewis was just another skinny basketball hopeful when he was introduced to coach Bob Wade in the summer of 1981 after failing to make the varsity team at Patterson High School in Baltimore. Wade watched Lewis work out and invited him to transfer to Dunbar about 5 miles west, where he would join one of the most talented high school teams ever.

The Dunbar Poets featured future NBA players David Wingate, Reggie Williams, and Tyrone "Muggsy" Bogues, as well as three other Division 1 players. Williams, Bogues, and Lewis were all taken in the first round of the 1987 NBA Draft. Lewis never started a game in high school. He served as the sixth man, a talented player who would deliver in clutch moments.

"We had some outstanding student-athletes, and he would come to every practice and give his all," Wade said. "He played in practice against Reggie Williams, Tim Dawson, he played against those guys every day in practice and he did a great job. They made him a better player and he made them better players. But when he got his opportunity, he took advantage of it."

Lewis's shining moment was when he was named MVP of the Johnstown Tournament in Pennsylvania as a senior, taking over when two of his teammates had fouled out. At 6 feet 6 inches and lean, Lewis had the ability to score from midrange and also the length and athleticism to drive to the basket.

Perhaps it was his lack of playing time that benefited Jim Calhoun and his Northeastern assistant coach Karl Fogel as they passionately recruited Lewis after seeing him at a basketball camp before his senior year. Of course, Lewis was overshadowed by his more heralded teammates, and Calhoun was aggressive in his pursuit.

"For Reggie, you could see some of those special things, the love for the game, incredible athletic talent, and as he got stronger and better, he became a force," Calhoun said. "Northeastern tried to recruit him not because of what he is but what he was going to be. I remember talking to people [about] Reggie; there's no better first step in basketball. And he was a very good defensive player. You saw that ability. You saw that then but he was very thin, I'm talking about 155 pounds.

"That quiet confidence, I never knew where it came from, I really didn't. But he had it and it was rare and once he got his opportunity. He was a unique, unique kid."

Calhoun laughs loudly when asked for his favorite Reggie Lewis story. It occurred during his freshman year at Northeastern when he pulled his coach aside and asked him, "Coach, I have a serious question I want to ask you, can you not yell at me in front of the players? But you can say anything to me when it's just the two of us."

Calhoun didn't exactly hold to that agreement, but he admired Lewis for his fortitude.

"The reason we're doing this 25 years later is because he was a special guy and everybody who was around him I'm sure is going to come up with the same type of feelings about him," Calhoun said. "He had his own quiet, humble way which made him so refreshing, which made him a beautiful person.

"In my office, whether it was at UConn or wherever, I got a big picture of him because he reminded me of the joy of the game, the joy of a kid who came up from Baltimore eastside and became a gentle, wonderful, competitive, loving father, loving friend. We all miss him."

Lewis's humility never wavered. On the day before he was drafted, he attended Donna's graduation from Northeastern, wearing the same Filene's Basement navy blue suit and tie he would wear to the Celtics draft news conference the next day.

And how did Reggie get to Boston Garden for his news conference? He took the train to North Station.

"He was a gentleman. He was transparent," Harris Lewis said. "He was a quiet person and very reserved and there's no major surprise factor. It's interesting because I see a lot of his qualities through both of my kids. He was one of the nicest people you could ever meet."

A VOID IN THE GAME

The growth of Lewis as a player offered the Celtics hope and optimism for the post-Bird era. But then Lewis died suddenly, and the Celtics were sent reeling, making just one playoff appearance over the next eight years.

"I think it's obvious to anyone who would look that this was a loss that created holes in our game, if you will, at every level," said Volk, who resigned in May 1997, replaced by Rick Pitino. "Combined with the loss of Len Bias, that right there, the two of them would have been a dynamic duo, there's no doubt about it. We can't sit there and dwell on it. We couldn't and we didn't."

Without Lewis and Bias, the Celtics were missing two All-Star talents who would have at least helped the franchise compete with the Michael Jordan Bulls and other emerging clubs in the 1990s. Instead, they were relegated to using stopgap players and trying to recapture young prospects in the draft. The Celtics wouldn't return to prominence for another 15 years.

Guard Dee Brown was forced into a more prominent role he wasn't comfortable with.

"That happened [Reggie's death] and all of a sudden I'm thrust into a franchise role and honestly I don't remember the whole 1994 year—I played in a blur the whole year because I was thinking about Reggie," Brown said. "A lot of guys got traded and through that whole process we had a lot of down years, but I was the only guy that was connected to the old Celtics and the Pitino era. So it was tough, because I knew my career could have been different. I did my best as captain to hold the franchise together, still make it respectable, be about the right things, respect the logo."

The consensus among those who loved Lewis is that they have never gotten over what happened. This wasn't supposed to happen to Reggie. He was too kind. He had too much left to accomplish. He had a son and daughter to raise, All-Star Games to play, more lives to change.

"You really haven't completely digested losing him at such a young age," Wade said. "It still weighs heavily on my heart, his passing, because he was so young and he was just reaching the mountaintop of his career. It still lingers with me, his passing."

NO REGRETS

For Harris Lewis, who still lives in the Boston area and is active in several foundations, including the National Basketball Wives Association, she reflects on her husband with pride and admiration, but no regrets.

No regrets.

"I don't have any regrets because I wasn't a medical doctor," she said. "We were trying to get the help, we were trying to seek help. I know blame has been shifted towards Reggie and towards me but we're not . . . Everybody makes mistakes but you have to own up to them. Hindsight is 20-20, Reggie passed away trying to figure out what was wrong. We all were. Even when he was playing. He was instructed to be there because he was fine. That's what he was told.

"Nothing was ever explained. He had a normal athlete's heart. That's it. He was fine. To be honest, he left here, when he passed away, he didn't fully understand the scope of what really happened. He really didn't. We all know now. But he really didn't. He was trusting and trying to figure out what's the best direction for him.

"You have to stop back on July 27, 1993, he was following the doctor's [Mudge's] instructions and trying to figure out what was going to happen. He was secured in his contract. He wasn't worried about that. A lot of people always said, 'Oh, he was worried more about basketball than his life.' And that's not true. Absolutely not true."

Harris Lewis has moved forward. Reggie Jr. is 26, Reggiena is 24. Harris Lewis still roots for the Celtics. She's active with the Reggie Lewis Center. She continues Lewis's charity work. She is a full-time ordained minister.

"Human resources is my passion, too. So someday somebody will hire me somewhere," she said. "But I'm OK. I do the best I can. Reggie and I were 11 months apart, for him to see his kids grow up, I think that would have been a joy. I remember when we used to ride in the car and I'd say when we're older, we're going to be like that, holding hands. You go through those moments and you're kind of sad, but at the same time we are where we are and you do what you can do."

EPILOGUE

So this is how the quest for the 18th championship in Celtics history ultimately became fulfilled: with complete and utter dominance, from the beginning of the season in October to the joyous and prolonged celebration in June.

The 2024 Boston Celtics—wait, that should read World Champion Boston Celtics—were the best team in the NBA at the start of the season, winning their first 20 games at TD Garden.

They were the best team in the NBA during the long and winding course of the season, when they won 64 regular season games, finished first in the Eastern Conference by 14 games, and delivered the best offensive rating in the history of the league.

And they were the best team in the league when the green and white confetti fell on the parquet floor on June 17, in the delirious moments after defeating the Dallas Mavericks in five games to win their first championship in 16 seasons.

These champions were richly talented, uncommonly selfless, and well-rounded, with matured superstars Jayson Tatum and Jaylen Brown (the conference finals and NBA Finals Most Valuable Player) leading the way, accompanied by do-it-all guards Jrue Holiday and Derrick White, big men Al Horford (a champion for the first time in his 17-year career) and Kristaps Porzingis, and a bench full of worthy role players.

This team, like the generational champions of Russell and Havlicek and Bird and Pierce, will be beloved for all time.

Adam Himmelbach's game story here expertly tells the tale of the evening the Celtics' newest title was secured.

As I write this, the Celtics are preparing for their parade on duck boats through the heart of downtown Boston.

It is the city's celebration of a true and worthy champion, a celebration of banner 18 fulfilled.

Come next season, look up to the rafters and watch it fly.

—Chad Finn, June 2024

CIGAR TIME

CELTICS LIGHT IT UP FOR RECORD 18TH NBA TITLE

June 18, 2024 • by Adam Himmelsbach

With pieces of green and white confetti dancing in the air above him, with a thirsty and joyous Garden crowd erupting all around him, Celtics coach Joe Mazzulla wrapped his hand around the microphone that had been extended in his direction and offered one final, loud message for this arena and everyone watching around the world.

"You get very few chances in life to be great . . . When you have a chance to be great, you've just got to take the bull by the horns."

Throughout this magical season, Mazzulla has avoided looking too far ahead by always keeping his team fully focused on the next day. But now, there are no more next days, because the Celtics are NBA champions for a record 18th time.

When the final buzzer sounded in Game 5 of the Finals at TD Garden on Monday night, *Boston 106, Dallas 88* glowed on the scoreboard to make it permanent and real, and the confetti poured down like a mid-winter blizzard. But this outcome was decided much earlier in that, with another dominant performance to cap this season that has been filled with so many of them.

The celebration started soon after that, and it lasted long into the night. Jaylen Brown clutched his Finals MVP trophy that he had just won and quickly acknowledged his talented teammate who just as easily could have had it in his arms.

Al Horford, an NBA champion for the first time in his 17th season, celebrates with Celtics teammates and personnel after they receive the Larry O'Brien Trophy.

"I share this with my brothers," Brown said, "and my partner in crime, Jayson Tatum."

Tatum had his turn moments later. He said that winning his first title means the world to him, and after the crowd roared, he repeated it for emphasis.

"We knew we'd need each other," Tatum said. "We all need each other."

Guard Derrick White stepped forward on the stage with a severely chipped front tooth and sheepishly smiled, revealing his battle scar from this game. But he made it clear that he did not care. He said he would lose all of his teeth if it meant winning a championship.

Al Horford, the 38-year-old who has finally won his elusive title, received perhaps the loudest roar of all when he was introduced to the crowd.

It is the Celtics' 18th championship, breaking a tie with the Lakers for the most in NBA history. But the Celtics did not just win a title on Friday. They completed one of the most dominant seasons in the history of the NBA. Their 64-win regular season was followed by a stunning 16-3 playoff record that included a 10-game winning streak. It turned out that Friday's Game 4 loss in Dallas muted the surge only temporarily, and allowed them to return home to have an even more raucous celebration.

"Man, it's been long, a lot of hard work," Horford said, "But I'm so proud to be part of this team."

Tatum had 31 points, 11 assists and 8 rebounds to lead the Celtics, and Brown added 21 points and 8 rebounds. Luka Doncic led the Mavericks with 28 points and Kyrie Irving's struggles against his former team in this building continued with a 5 for 16 shooting effort and 15 points.

The second period ended in similar fashion. Four different Celtics drilled 3-pointers over the final 1:51 of the second quarter, with the final one somehow being at once the most improbable but also expected. Payton Pritchard, who had yet to appear in the game, checked in with Doncic at the foul line with four seconds left. He has become the equivalent of the Celtics' fearless pinch-runner in these situations, but one with a jump-shot.

Doncic missed the free throw and Horford found Pritchard, who rushed to midcourt and hit a 49-footer at the buzzer, giving the Celtics a 67-46 lead and delivering a blow that the Mavericks were never really able to recover from.

"There's nothing better than representing the Celtics," Mazzulla said, "and being part of history."

CELTICS HONORS AND ACCOMPLISHMENTS

RETIRED NUMBERS

00: Robert Parish
1: Walter Brown
2: Red Auerbach
3: Dennis Johnson
5: Kevin Garnett
6: Bill Russell
10: Jo Jo White
14: Bob Cousy
15: Tom Heinsohn
16: Tom "Satch" Sanders
17: John Havlicek
18: Dave Cowens
19: Don Nelson
21: Bill Sharman
22: Ed Macauley
23: Frank Ramsey
24: Sam Jones
25: K.C. Jones
31: Cedric Maxwell
32: Kevin McHale
33: Larry Bird
34: Paul Pierce
35: Reggie Lewis
Loscy: Jim Loscutoff
Johnny Most

MOST VALUABLE PLAYER

Bob Cousy: 1957
Bill Russell (5): 1958, 1961, 1962, 1963, 1965
Dave Cowens: 1973
Larry Bird (3): 1984, 1985, 1986

NBA FINALS MOST VALUABLE PLAYER

1974: John Havlicek
1976: Jo Jo White
1981: Cedric Maxwell
1984: Larry Bird
1986: Larry Bird
2008: Paul Pierce
2024: Jaylen Brown
—*award originated in 1969*

ROOKIE OF THE YEAR

1957: Tom Heinsohn
1971: Dave Cowens
1980: Larry Bird

DEFENSIVE PLAYER OF THE YEAR

2008: Kevin Garnett
2022: Marcus Smart
—*award originated in 1983*

SIXTH MAN OF THE YEAR

1984: Kevin McHale
1985: Kevin McHale
1986: Bill Walton
2023: Malcolm Brogdon
—*award originated in 1983*

COACH OF THE YEAR

1965: Red Auerbach
1973: Tom Heinsohn
1980: Bill Fitch
—*award originated in 1963*

EXECUTIVE OF THE YEAR

1980: Red Auerbach
2008: Danny Ainge
2024: Brad Stevens

ALL-STAR GAME MVP

1951: Ed Macauley
1954: Bob Cousy
1955: Bill Sharman
1957: Bob Cousy
1963: Bill Russell
1973: Dave Cowens
1981: Tiny Archibald
1982: Larry Bird
2023: Jayson Tatum

BASKETBALL HALL OF FAMERS (ENTIRE CAREER AS A CELTIC)

Bob Cousy
Tom Heinsohn
Bill Russell
Sam Jones
K.C. Jones
John Havlicek
Larry Bird
Kevin McHale
Bill Sharman
Frank Ramsey
Dino Radja
Chuck Cooper

BASKETBALL HALL OF FAMERS (CAREER AS A CELTIC PLUS AT LEAST ONE OTHER TEAM)

Ed Macauley
Paul Pierce
Carl Braun
Kevin Garnett
Paul Westphal
Robert Parish
Dennis Johnson

Jo Jo White
Tiny Archibald
Bob McAdoo
Dave Bing
Bill Walton
Bob Houbregs
Pete Maravich
Clyde Lovellette
Dave Cowens
Bailey Howell
Arnie Risen
Dominique Wilkins
Artis Gilmore
Gary Payton
Ray Allen
Shaquille O'Neal
Charlie Scott
Chauncey Billups

NOTABLE CELTICS FIGURES IN THE BASKETBALL HALL OF FAME

Red Auerbach
Walter Brown
Bill Russell
Tom "Satch" Sanders
Don Nelson
John Thompson
Wayne Embry
Dave Gavitt
Rick Pitino
Don Barksdale
Bill Fitch
Alvin "Doggie" Julian
John "Honey" Russell
Bill Mokray

CURT GOWDY MEDIA AWARD WINNERS

1993: Johnny Most
2021: Mike Gorman

ACKNOWLEDGMENTS

A sportswriter cannot be a fan. The journalistic requirement of objectivity—or "no cheering in the press box"—means that any allegiances must be put aside if they have not faded altogether.

Many sportswriters will pretend such detachment is easy. I believe few of them. Most of us got into this business for one of two reasons, or a combination of both.

1. We enjoyed reading and writing way more than math.

2. We deeply, *deeply* love sports, most likely from a young age, and probably because of a familial bond.

That love of the games, and choosing the words deployed to describe them, is evident beneath each byline in this book.

That particularly applies to Bob Ryan, The Commish, whose passion for sports has been apparent in every phrase he has ever turned.

No, Bob does not cheer. But he does marvel. He once offered a thought—part workaround, all wisdom—on why he likes to see the Celtics and other Boston teams win. *It's good for everyone. It's the talk of the town. The fans are happy. Business booms. And we sports writers get to cover it all. What could be better than that?*

Through the years, I've developed my own workaround to that necessary abdication of fandom: enjoying it through the eyes of someone I love.

My daughter, Leah, is the most dedicated Celtics fan I know. Often, her savvy on social media leads to her discovering a Celtics transaction before her dad, Alleged Professional Sports Columnist, is aware of it. She now goes to college a few miles from the Celtics' practice facility. I do not believe for a second this is a coincidence.

I'll never forget the wail of "Noooooooo…not Marcus!" coming from down the hallway when beloved Marcus Smart was traded to the Memphis Grizzlies in June 2023. Like most Celtics fans, she learned to appreciate Kristaps Porzingis, the return in that deal, rather fast.

The origins of Leah's fandom came from an extremely successful ploy by her old man to introduce her to the Celtics as early as possible. When she was no more than three years old, she was fully trained to point out Larry Bird among the ten players pictured on a photo in my office of a jump ball between the Celtics and Lakers.

Her version of "pointing out Larry" these days is sending me daily Instagram clips and photos of her favorite Celtics—Derrick White, first and foremost, with the occasional Marcus Smart photo mixed in, because how can we forget Marcus?

This book is dedicated to Bob, for confirming time and again that genuine enjoyment of sports is not a weakness for a columnist, but a superpower.

And to Leah, for our bond over the green-and-white that I will never take for granted.

Thank you to those who shepherded this project and made our second *"The Boston Globe* Story of…" compilation just as fulfilling as the first: Matt Pepin, Ira Napoliello, Zander Kim, Becky Koh, Melanie Gold, and Katie Benezra.

Thank you to John and Linda Henry. Thank you to Nancy Barnes and Brian McGrory. Jeremiah Manion was vital with his research expertise and unyielding willingness to track down one more article, and maybe one more article after that, and then just one more, promise. Leanne Burden Seidel and Colby Cotter were resolute in seeking photos across the eras. Joseph Eachus saved many days with his accurate and rapid-fire typesetting.

Thank you to past and present *Globe* colleagues: Adam Himmelsbach, Gary Washburn, Scott Thurston, Jim Hoban, Gary Dzen, Ken Fratus, Dan Shaughnessy, Jackie MacMullan, Alan Miller, Craig Larson, Peter Abraham, Alex Speier, the late Nick Cafardo, Bob Hohler, Fluto Shinzawa, Greg Lee, Nicole Yang, Christopher Price, Kevin Paul Dupont, Matt Porter, Tara Sullivan, Julian Benbow, Christopher L. Gasper, Greg Lang, Jim McBride, Joe Sullivan, Katie McInerney, Ben Volin, Andrew Mahoney, Julian McWilliams, Martin Pantages, Bob Fedas, Tom Westerholm, Pete Goodwin, John Carney, Michael Vega, Rich McSweeney, Steve Richards, Sean Smith, Dave Lefort, Eric Wilbur, Steve Silva, Mike Carraggi, Mike Grossi, Hans Schulz, Chris Morris, Chris Greenberg, Khari Thompson, Khari A. Thompson, Francis Storrs, Charlie Pierce, Baxter Holmes, Shira Springer, Peter May, Hayden Bird, Conor Ryan, Conor Roche, Jon Couture, Segun Oduolowu, and Armon Lee.

Thank you to so many friends and family who have supported or inspired me during my sports writing career: Mark Dodge, Mike Dodge, David Dodge, Dennis Dodge, Charlie Finn, Erin Finn, the late Mike Pride, Dr. Yuri Pride, Steve Mistler, Dave Cummings, Ray Duckler, Sandy Smith, Dana Wormald, Matthew T. Hall, Dave D'Onofrio, CJ Lampman, Steve Buckley, Peter Gammons, Leigh Montville, Bill Simmons, Dr. Bill Simmons, Kris Poulin, Tom Poulin, James Finn, Tim Hopley, Scott Talcove, Tad Steen, Chris Castellano, John Black, Chris DeBeck, Tom Maines, David Dorion, Brian Hatch, Fern Masse, Dick Whitmore, and Milo Finn.

Thank you to Christian Megliola, the John Bagley to my Dino Radja. Thank you to Mike Gorman, Brad Stevens, Danny Ainge, and Rich Gotham for their time and insights through the years.

Thank you to Larry Bird for returning the call. And just for being Larry Bird.

Thank you to Isaiah Thomas for pouring his heart into the foreword, just as he did on the hardwood. Thank you to Jon Finkel and TJ Regan for the assists.

Most of all, thank you to my wife Jennifer, son Alex, and daughter Leah once more. Bird, McHale, and Parish were special, but you're the greatest Big 3 I'll ever know.

INDEX

Images are noted in **bold**.

PHOTO CREDITS

The Boston Globe, and special thanks to their following photographers:

The Globe: 4, 7, 11, 12, 43, 86, 97, 228, 426

Blanding, John: 169, 190, 260

Brett, Bill: 91, 167

Carey, Charles B.: 50, 407

Chin, Barry: 217, 236, 268, 286, 340, 362

Clark, Erin: 435

Connell, Paul: 44, 102

Davis, Jim: 243, 244, 275, 277, 294, 303, 309, 313, 316, 342, 358, 374, 376, 390, 392, 395, 398, 399, back cover (top)

Dean, Bob: 88

Dully, Ted: 116, 132 (top), 419

Ferrand, Ed: 15,

Goshtigian, Danny: 56, 71, 72, 80, 84, 382, back cover (bottom)

Greene, Bill: 251, 429

Greenhouse, Pat: 329

Grossfeld, Stan: 131, 147, 156, 197, 205, 262, 397

Herde, Tom: 209

Landers, Tom: 112

Lee, Carol: 368

Lee, Matthew J.: 247, 314, 319, 377

Maguire, Paul J.: 18, 30, 355

McDonald, Michele: 183

O'Brien, Frank: 27, 92, 93 (top), 108, 124, 132 (bottom), 134, 194, 255, 402

O'Connor, Bill: xii

Preston, Don: 122

Rathe, Joanne: 174, 176

Richman, Evan: 213

Rinaldi, Jessica: 349

Rizer, George: 93 (bottom)

Robinson-Chavez, Michael: 233

Runci, Joseph: 67

Tlumacki, John: 146, 148, 180, 210, 221, 261, 265, 325, 335, 346

Turner, Lane: 215

Wiggs, Jonathan: 343

Wilson, Jim: 150

Getty Images:

Focus on Sport: front cover

United Press Telephoto: 35